AF673576

INTERNATIONAL ECONOMICS

INTERNATIONAL ECONOMICS

Volume 1

K.R. Gupta

Published by

ATLANTIC

PUBLISHERS & DISTRIBUTORS (P) LTD

7/22, Ansari Road, Darya Ganj, New Delhi-110002
Phones : +91-11-40775252, 40775214, 23273880, 23275880
Fax: +91-11-23285873
Web: www.atlanticbooks.com
E-mail: orders@atlanticbooks.com

Printed & bound in India by Atlantic Print Services

Preface

The book *International Economics* has been out of print for the last three decades. In spite of great demand for the book, I could not bring out the revised edition because of my preoccupation with other books. The sixth edition of the book has been thoroughly revised and considerably enlarged. While new materials have been incorporated in almost all chapters, the major change in this edition is the addition of five new chapters, viz. (i) Theories of Foreign Trade—Adam Smith and Before Him, (ii) Nature and Significance of International Trade, (iii) Optimum Tariff, (iv) World Trade Organisation, and (v) A Note on Recent Theories of International Trade. This has made the book more up to date and complete in its coverage.

The book attempts to give a clear and straightforward treatment of the main topics. For this, it uses geometry as well as mathematics, in addition to theory, as the medium of exposition. It also attempts to make the explanations both intuitively appealing and logically convincing, using simple language and lucid style.

The book has a wide coverage and comprehensively deals with the main subjects usually covered in a standard textbook, viz. various economic theories and models like those of Ricardian Trade Theory, Heckscher-Ohlin Theory, Factor-Price Equalization

Theorem, Stolper-Samuelson Theorem, Rybczynski Theorem, gains from international trade, balance of payments, foreign exchange, tariffs, quantitative restrictions, dumping, economic integration, most favoured nation clause, international organisations such as International Bank for Reconstruction and Development (IBRD), International Monetary Fund (IMF), World Trade Organization (WTO), etc.

The book is intended to meet the requirements of the students of B.A. (Hons.), M.A. (Economics), M.Com., MBA and related courses and candidates preparing for competitive cxaminations such as IAS, IES and Provincial Civil Service examinations of the States. It will also be useful as supplementary reading for students of international relations and money and banking courses.

K.R. Gupta

Contents

Preface ..... *v*

VOLUME–1

1. Distinguishing Features of International and Interregional Trade 1
2. Theories of Foreign Trade—Adam Smith and Before Him 19
3. Nature and Significance of International Trade 40
4. Doctrine of Comparative Costs 61
5. Heckscher-Ohlin Theory of International Trade 116
6. Gains from International Trade 171
7. Dynamics of International Trade 222
8. The Balance of Payments 247
9. Theory of Foreign Exchange 348
10. Exchange Control 456
11. Trade Restrictions and Economic Development 482
12. Tariffs 547

VOLUME–2

13. Optimum Tariff 577
14. Quotas 614
15. Theory of Economic Integration 636
16. Most Favoured Nation Clause 730

17. State Trading 742

18. Dumping 762

19. Stabilisation of Primary Product Markets 784

20. Foreign Capital and Economic Development 817

21. International Bank for Reconstruction and Development 915

22. International Monetary Fund 970

23. WTO: An Overview 1030

24 A Note on Recent Theories in International Trade 1077

Distinguishing Features of International and Interregional Trade

1

INTRODUCTION

The theory of international trade deals with the transactions across the national frontiers whereas the theory of interregional trade is concerned with the transaction within the national borders. One of the most distinctive features of trade theory when compared to location theory is that in the former countries are generally considered as being dimensionless. But the understanding of international trade under many respects, such a simplifying assumption has been considered as a handicap. According to Ohlin, "International trade theory cannot be understood except in relation to and as part of the general location theory, to which the lack of mobility of goods and factors has equal relevance."

The reason being that changes in the transportability of commodities as well as in the mobility of factors between and within countries affect the location of economic activities, the distribution of labour and capital, the geography of demand and, therefore, the pattern of trade. This handicap is becoming increasingly heavy as new empirical evidence is gathered, suggesting that growing openness to international trade has a significant impact on the degree of agglomeration of economic activities within countries. First, using a cross-section of 85 countries, Ades and Glaeser (1995) showed that higher tariff barriers lead to a higher degree of urban primacy. Their findings have been confirmed and extended by Henderson (2003). Second, studying the "cohesion group" of European Union (Greece, Ireland, Portugal and Spain), Quah (1996) found that the two countries that have reached the highest rates of economic growth, Spain and Portugal, are those that have experienced the most striking rise in regional imbalances. This is consistent with the evidence reported by de la Fuente and Vives (1995) who observed that the process of economic integration within the European Union fosters international convergence across countries rather than interregional convergence across regions within countries. Indeed, about half of the divergence across European regions is due to an increased polarization within some member states. Finally, Hayward (1995) showed that the impact of European integration on the US might differ from states to state. In particular, he showed that, while some US states could thrive, others might suffer from stronger import or export competition.

The case for a separate theory of international trade rests on whether or not interregional transactions differ in nature from the international transactions. In case there is no difference between the international and interregional transactions, there will be no need for a separate theory of international trade. Let us discuss the main factors, which distinguish international trade from interregional trade and see whether or not there exists the need for a separate theory of international trade.

MOBILITY OF FACTORS OF PRODUCTION

Ricardo advocates the case for a separate theory of international trade on the ground that the factors of production are immobile between nations whereas they are free to move within the nations. Immobility of the factors of production between different nations causes differences in the remuneration of similar factors of production in different countries. In contrast, within nations, there is a tendency for the equalisation of the prices of the factors of production because the factors are free to move within nations. This distinguishes the international trade from the interregional trade. This distinction, however, has aroused much criticism. It is contended that the difference in the mobility of the factors of production within and between the countries is of degree and not of kind. Factors of production are not completely mobile between different regions of the same country. The immobility between different regions of a country might arise out of differences of language, customs, traditions, habits, inability to incur expenses of transport, provincialism, etc. On the other hand, the factors of production are not completely immobile between nations. There exists a considerable degree of mobility of the factors of production, particularly that of capital, between different countries.[1]

J.E. Cairnes answers this criticism like this:

> It is by no means necessary to the truth of the doctrine, as it has been laid down, for example by Ricardo and Mill, that there should be an absolute impossibility of moving labour and capital from country to country. What the doctrine requires is not this, but such a degree of difficulty in affecting their transfer as shall interfere substantially and generally—that is to say, over the whole range of the commodities exchanged with the action of individual competition.[2]

Cairnes' answer, however, does not establish a case for a separate theory of international trade because the required substantial degree of immobility can exist even within the regions of the same country and it might not exist between the two adjoining regions of the two different countries. Thus the case established by Cairnes is not for international trade but for trade between non-competing groups (i.e. groups within which the factors of production are substantially immobile); whether they exist within or between different countries is immaterial for the theory.

The degree of immobility, of course, is generally, greater between than within countries. This can easily be verified by the statistics of inter-country and intra-country movements of factors of production. In short, the difference between international and interregional trade on this account is only of degree and not of kind.

DIFFERENT NATIONAL POLICIES

National rules, regulations and policies relating to taxation, labour standards, health, sanitation, factory organisation, social insurance, trade unions, education, public utilities, etc. are more or less uniform for different regions of a country whereas these considerably differ in different countries. This, of course, does not mean that rules, regulations and policies relating to these matters are completely uniform in the different regions of a country. To the extent these matters fall within the jurisdiction of the local governments, the standards might differ widely in the different regions of the same country. The differences with regard to these matters are generally greater between, than within countries. Thus the difference is only of degree and not of kind.

Separate Markets

National markets are separated by differences in language, customs, usages, habits, tastes, weights and measures, terms of sale, currency units, etc. Such differences, however, may also exist in markets in different regions of the same country. The difference in markets between and within countries in these respects, again, is only of degree and not of kind.

Politically Different Units

The cohesion and solidarity is greater among people belonging to the same nation than among people belonging to different nations. The recent enhancement of the spirit of nationalism has increased the importance of this distinguishing factor. The government in each country considers the welfare of its own nationals more important than that of the people belonging to other countries. Countries, often, do not hesitate to follow policies which benefit them a little and cause considerable harm to their other trading partners. This, however, in no way implies the absence of regionalism, i.e. comparatively greater cohesion and solidarity among the people belonging to different regions of the same country. The difference, once again, is only of degree and not of kind.

Different Moneys

International transactions involve the use of different currencies while the national transactions are conducted with a single currency. This won't make much difference if all the countries are on full gold standard with permanently fixed exchange rates between the currencies of different countries. Actually, however, most of the countries are having a managed currency system. The exchange rate between the currencies of the different countries is decided by their respective governments. This makes an important distinction between the international and interregional transactions. The possibility of variations in exchange rate between different currencies increases the risks and thereby discourages the movement of the factors of production, particularly that of capital, between different countries. This adds to the differences in the remuneration of the similar factors of production in different countries. Further, the currency of each country is managed by its own Central Bank. Central Banks of different countries pursue monetary policies according to the varied needs of their countries while the monetary policy pursued by the Central Bank of a country is, generally, uniform for different regions of the country. The transfer of purchasing power from one to the other region of a country causes a hundred per cent income and price effect whereas the effect of the transfer of purchasing power between the different countries might be mitigated, or even prevented altogether, by the policies of the national Central Banks.

Trade and Exchange Controls

Generally, there exist trade and exchange controls on the movement of goods, services, and factors of production between countries but not within countries.

To conclude, the fundamental differences between international and interregional trade arise only from 'differences in monetary systems and trade and exchange controls' and the other differences are only of degree and not of kind.

A MODEL OF INTERNATIONAL AND INTERREGIONAL TRADE

In this section we are going to develop an integrated model of international and interregional trade in the wake of Ohlin (1933). In developing this model, we abstract from his space-less factor proportions model, which still represents the backbone of international trade theory. Here our focus will be on Ohlin's less popularized spatial insights on how the explicit consideration of space affects some of the main conclusions of the neoclassical paradigm of trade theory. The interest of focusing on those insights is due to the fact that in the original work their robustness is often undermined by the lack of a model dealing with both increasing returns and imperfect competition. Consequently, Ohlin's contribution is mainly identified with his space-less theory, someway paradoxically labeled "International Trade Simplified."

We made following assumptions in developing the model of international and interregional trade. Our basic framework of the model is based on Krugman's *New Economic Geography* (1991).

(a) There are two countries each made of two point regions.

(b) Countries and regions are distinguished from each other by differences in both barriers to trade and factor mobility.

(c) Goods are mobile between both countries and regions, factors move only between regions within the same country.

(d) Trade is hampered by 'transport' costs between regions and by 'trade' costs between countries.

(e) Production takes place in two sectors, a perfectly competitive sector and a monopolistically competitive one. The former employs only unskilled labour, which is immobile both between and within countries, whereas the latter employs only skilled labour, which is immobile between countries but mobile within them.

(f) Here two direct competition effects are considered–First, local prices decrease with the number of local producers, in accordance with the theory of industrial organization, and second, lower transport or trade costs lead to lower prices, as suggested by Hotelling for whom "merchants would do well, instead of organizing improvement clubs and booster associations to better the road, to make transportation as difficult as possible."

The economy consists of two countries, home country (*H*) and foreign country (*F*), each having two regions, labeled $i = 1, 2$. In order to abstract from comparative advantage, both countries have the same endowments and we denote by *L* the mass of skilled and by *A* the mass of unskilled workers in each country. Each worker works and consume in the same region. Since unskilled workers are immobile, therefore they are evenly split between regions so that each region accommodates a mass *A*/2 of them. Skilled workers are mobile within but immobile between countries and are denoted by $\lambda_r \in [0, 1]$, $r = (H, F)$, their share in region 1 of country *r*. This means that the mass of skilled workers living in country *r* is constant but that its interregional distribution is endogenous. Here one point should be noted that the relative immobility of unskilled with respect to skilled workers fits empirical observation, whereas the international immobility of all workers fits a long standing tradition in trade theory.

Production takes place in two sectors. The 'traditional' sector supplies a homogeneous good under perfect competition using unskilled labour as the only input of a constant returns technology. The unit requirement is set to one by choice of units. In the 'modern' sector monopolistically competitive firms offer a mass N of varieties of a horizontally differentiated good employing both factors under increasing returns to scale. There is a one-to-one correspondence between firms and varieties so that N is also the mass of available varieties. Specifically, the firm producing variety v incurs a fixed cost of $\phi > 0$ units of skilled labour.

All goods can be shipped across countries and regions. They are, however, subject to different shipping costs. On the one hand, all shipments of the homogeneous good are free. This makes that good the natural choice for the numeraire, which implies that in equilibrium the unskilled wage is equal to one everywhere. On the other hand, both international and interregional shipments of the differentiated varieties are costly. Specifically, international shipments face the same cost per unit shipped of $\tau > 0$ units of the numeraire regardless of the regions of origin and destination. This assumption implies that any region of a country has the same access to each region of the other country. In other words, no region offers a comparative advantage in trading on the foreign markets, thus implying that international trade involves no gate effect. By contrast, interregional shipments may face different costs-shipping one unit within country $r = H, F$ requires $t_r > 0$ units of numeraire. Henceforth we refer to the international cost τ as the trade cost and to the interregional cost t as the transport cost of country $r = H, F$. Conceptually, the difference between the two shipping costs can be explained as follows.

Since, the standard distinction between tariff and non-tariff barriers is not critical for this model; the cost τ includes all impediments to trade, such as shipping costs per se, but also tariff and non-tariff barriers to trade, different product standards, difficulty of communication, and cultural differences. Differently, t_r stands for the sole costs of shipping the differentiated product between the two regions of the same country r. Clearly our model boils down to a standard trade model when $t_H = t_F = 0$.

Each worker is endowed with one unit of labour and $q_0 > 0$ units of the numeraire. The initial endowment q_0 is supposed to be large enough for his consumption of the numeraire to be strictly positive at the market outcome. All workers have the same quadratic utility. A typical resident of region i in country r solves the following consumption problem.

$$\max_{q_{ri}(v),\, v\in[0,N]} \quad \alpha \int_0^N q_{ri}(v)dv - \frac{\beta-\gamma}{2}\int_0^N [q_{ri}(v)]^2 dv - \frac{\gamma}{2}\left[\int_0^N q_{ri}(v)dv\right]^2 + q_0$$

Subject to,

$$\int_0^N P_{ri}(v)q_{ri}(v)dv + q_0 = y_{ri} + q_0$$

where $\alpha > 0, \beta > \gamma > 0$ are parameters, $P_{ri}(v)$ is the consumer price of variety v in region i of country r and y_{ri} is the resident's income which depends on his skilled or unskilled status.

It is readily verified that solving the consumption problem yields the individual demand functions given by

$$q_{rij}(v) = a - (b + cN)P_{rij}(v) + cP_{rj}$$
$$q_{rsi}(v) = a - (b + cN)P_{rsi}(v) + cP_{si} \tag{1}$$

where

$$a = \frac{\alpha}{\beta + (N-1)\gamma}, \; b = \frac{1}{\beta + (N-1)\gamma}$$

and $c = \dfrac{\gamma}{(\beta - \gamma)[\beta + (N-1)\gamma]}$

In expression (1), $P_{rij}(v)$ is the price a firm located in region i of country r charges to consumers in region j of the same country r, whereas P_{rsi} is the price a firm located in country r charges in region i of the other country r because all firms located in this country have the same access to region i of country s. Analogously, $q_{rij}(v)$ is the output of a firm located in region i of country r demanded by a consumer in region j of the same country r, whereas $q_{rsi}(v)$ is the output of a firm located in country r demanded by a customer in region i of the other country $s = r$. Finally,

$$P_{rj} = \int_0^N P_{rj}(v)dv \tag{2}$$

is the price index (i.e. N times the average price) of varieties in region j of country r. Since demands are linear and the unskilled wage is equal to one everywhere, for notational convenience we can set $m = 0$ without loss of generality as this amounts to rescaling all firms' demands intercepts. Then, skilled labour market clearing in each region implies:

$$n_{r1} = \frac{\lambda_{rL}}{\phi} n_{r2} = \frac{(1-\lambda_r)L}{\phi} n = n_{r1} + n_{r2} = \frac{L}{\phi} N = 2n \tag{3}$$

where n_{ri} is the mass of modern firms in region i of country r. Product and labour markets are segmented and entry as well as exit are free. The first assumption means that each firm is free to set a price specific to the region and the country in which it sells its output. The second assumption means that skilled wages are determined by the zero profit condition implied by free entry and exit of firms in each region. More precisely, the equilibrium wages of the skilled are determined by a bidding process in which firms compete for workers by offering higher wages until no firm can profitably enter or exit the market. Let w_{ri} be the skilled wage rate prevailing in region i of country r.

Therefore, as firms bear all trade and transport costs, a firm located in region of country H maximizes profits given by:

$$\pi_{H1} = P_{H11}q_{H11}\left[\frac{A}{2}+\lambda_H L\right]+(P_{H12}-t_H)q_{H12}\left[\frac{A}{2}+(1-\lambda_H)L\right]+$$

$$(P_{HF1}-\tau)q_{HF1}\left[\frac{A}{2}+\lambda_F L\right]+(P_{HF2}-\tau)q_{HF2}\left[\frac{A}{2}+(1-\lambda_F)L\right]-\phi W_{H1}$$

Firms located in other regions solve symmetric maximization problems. In this model we shall focus on the case in which costs are sufficiently low for interregional and international trade to be bilateral, regardless of the firm distributions λ_H and λ_F. Assuming that both t_r and τ are sufficiently low, the profit maximizing prices are as follows:

(a) interregional prices

$$P_{rii} = \frac{a+cP_{ri}}{2b+cN} \tag{4}$$

(b) interregional prices

$$P_{rij} = P_{rjj} + \frac{t_r}{2},\ i = j \tag{5}$$

(c) international prices

$$P_{rsi} = P_{sii} + \frac{\tau}{2},\ r = s \tag{6}$$

As stated above, the profit maximizing price that country s-firms set in region i of country r does not depend on the region of country s in which the firm is located; this is because all firms in country s have the same access to each region of country r.

The price a firm sets in a region depends on the price index P_{ri} of this region, which depends itself on the prices set by all other firms. Because there is a continuum of firms, each firm is negligible and chooses its optimal price, taking aggregate market conditions must be consistent with firms' optimal pricing decisions. Hence, the (Nash) equilibrium price index P^*_{ri} must satisfy the following equilibrium condition:

$$P^*_{ri} = n_{ri}P_{rii}(P^*_{ri}) + n_{rj}P_{rji}(P^*_{ri}) + nP_{sri}(P^*_{ri}) \qquad (7)$$

Under the assumption of bilateral trade between countries and regions, the equilibrium price indices can be found by solving (7) for P^*_{ri} after using (4), (5) and (6). This yields:

$$P^*_{ri} = \frac{2an + (b + 2cn)(n_{rj}t_r + n\tau)}{2(b + cn)}, \; r = H, F \text{ and } i = 1, 2 \qquad (8)$$

Note that all these equilibrium price indices depend on the average trade costs $n_{rj}t_r + n\tau$ incurred in supplying region i of country r. as expected, the price index decreases with the mass of local firms. Substituting (8) into (4) gives the equilibrium intraregional prices.

$$P^*_{rii} = \frac{2a + c(n_{rj}t_r + n\tau)}{4(b + cn)}, \quad r = H, F \qquad (9)$$

which can then be used to recover the equilibrium interregional and international prices from (5) and (6) respectively.

The expressions of the equilibrium prices reveal the crucial difference between the chosen models. Each of these equilibrium prices decreases with the number of firms located in the corresponding regions (n_{ri}, n_{rj}, n_{si}), thus showing the existence of a true competition effect consistent with the industrial organization literature. Hence, firms weakly interact in our setting. Clearly, prices also depend positively on transport and trade costs, thus accounting for intranational and international competition. Note, finally, that country r's firm's export prices decreases as the market of country s becomes more integrated (i.e. as t decreases), showing that prices are 'strategic complements' in our model.

We are now equipped to determine the conditions on τ and t_r for trade to occur between any two regions at these equilibrium prices. Starting with interregional transport costs, it is easy to check that

$$t_r \leq t_{\text{trade}}(\tau) = \frac{2a + cn\tau}{2(b + cn)}, \qquad r = H, F \tag{10}$$

must hold for interregional trade in each country to take place, regardless of the firm distributions λ_r. Observe that a lower τ leads to a decrease in the threshold value of interregional trade costs t, for which there is interregional trade. Hence, lower trade costs in the international marketplace may lead to a break down of internal trade when the regional markets of a country are poorly integrated. This is because cheaper imported varieties will displace more expensive nationally produced ones.

As to international trade costs, it is readily verified that the condition

$$\tau \leq \tau_{\text{trade}} = \frac{2a}{2b + cn} \tag{11}$$

must hold for trade between countries to arise. The value τ_{trade} does not depend on national transport costs because international trade costs are not region-specific. We assume from now on that both conditions (10) and (11) are always satisfied. Substituting the equilibrium prices (5), (6) and (9) into the individual demands (i), the equilibrium consumption levels are given by

$$q^*_{rii} = a - (b + cN)P^*_{rii} + cP^*_{ri} = (b + cN)P^*_{rii} \tag{12}$$

for shipments within the same region. They are given by

$$q^*_{rij} = q^*_{rjj} - \frac{(b + cN)t_r}{2} \tag{13}$$

for shipments between different regions of the same country ($i = j$) and by

$$q^*_{rsi} = q^*_{sii} - \frac{(b + cN)\tau}{2} \tag{14}$$

for shipments between regions belonging to different countries ($r = s$). As discussed above, the equilibrium wages of the skilled are determined by a bidding process in which all operating profits are absorbed by the wage bill. Therefore, in equilibrium the skilled wage rate in region i of country r satisfies $\pi_{ri} = 0$. This wage is determined by a national component that depends on the distribution λ_r of firms in country r, as well as by an export component that depends on the distribution λ_s of firms in the other country. This property of separability will be of fundamental importance in the subsequent equilibrium analysis. Let us write the equilibrium wage as follows:

$$w_{ri}^* = \frac{1}{\phi}[D_r(\lambda_r) + E_r(\lambda_s)] \tag{15}$$

where by (3)

$$D_r(\lambda_r) = \left(\frac{A}{2} + \phi n_{ri}\right) P_{rii}^* q_{rii}^* + \left(\frac{A}{2} + \phi n_{rj}\right)(P_{rij}^* - t_r) q_{rij}^*$$

is revenue from domestic sales of a firm located in country r, whereas

$$E_r(\lambda_s) = \left(\frac{A}{2} + \phi n_{si}\right)(P_{rsi}^* - \tau) q_{rsi}^* + \left(\frac{A}{2} + \phi n_{sj}\right)(P_{rsj}^* - \tau) q_{rsj}^*$$

stands for its export revenue from foreign sales.

Substituting the equilibrium prices as well as the equilibrium quantities (12) – (14) into (15) finally yields

$$w_{ri}^* = \frac{1}{\phi}\left[\left(\frac{A}{2} + \phi n_{ri}\right)(P_{rii}^*)^2 + \left(\frac{A}{2} + \phi n_{rj}\right)\left(P_{rjj}^* - \frac{t_r}{2}\right)^2\right] +$$

$$\frac{1}{\phi}\left[\left(\frac{A}{2} + \phi n_{si}\right)\left(P_{rsi}^* - \frac{\tau}{2}\right)^2 + \left(\frac{A}{2} + \phi n_{sj}\right)\left(P_{rsj}^* - \frac{\tau}{2}\right)^2\right] \tag{16}$$

Interregional and International Equilibrium

We first evaluate the indirect utilities of the skilled workers in regions 1 and 2 of country $r = H, F$ at the equilibrium prices and wages. The indirect utility in region i of country r may be expressed as follows:

$$V_{ri}^* = S_{ri}^* + w_{ri}^* + q_0$$

where

$$S_{ri}^* = \frac{a^2 N}{2b} - a(n_{ri} P_{rii}^* + n_{rj} P_{rji}^* + n_s P_{sri}^*) + \frac{b + cN}{2}[n_{ri}(P_{rii}^*)^2 +$$

$$n_{rj}(P_{rji}^*)^2 + n_s (P_{sri}^*)^2] - \frac{c}{2}(n_{ri} P_{rii}^* + n_{rj} P_{rji}^* + n_s P_{sri}^*)^2 \tag{17}$$

is the individual consumer surplus evaluated at the market outcome. The indirect utility differential between the two regions of country $r = H, F$ is then defined by

$$\Delta V_r^*(\lambda_r)=V_{r1}^*(\lambda_r)-V_{r2}^*(\lambda_r) \tag{18}$$

which depends only upon the distribution λ_r in country r. This stems from the fact that, as shown by (15), the equilibrium wage w_{ri}^* prevailing in region i of country r is given by the sum of two terms, $D_r(\lambda_r)$ and $E_r(\lambda_s)$ which are respectively independent of λ_s and λ_r. As a result, $E_r(\lambda_s)$ cancels out in the indirect utility differential ΔV_r^*, which becomes a function of the distribution λ_r only. This property no longer holds once we allow for economies of density in transportation.

As spatial equilibrium is such that in each country, no skilled worker has an incentive to change location, conditional upon the fact that the product markets clear at the equilibrium prices (5), (6) and (9) and the labour markets at the equilibrium wage (16). Formally, a spatial equilibrium arises at $\lambda_r \in (0, 1)$ when $\Delta V_r^*(\lambda_r) = 0$, or at $\lambda_r = 0$ if $\Delta V_r^*(0) \leq 0$, or at $\lambda_r = 1$ if $\Delta V_r^*(1) \geq 0$. Such an equilibrium always exists because V_r^* is a continuous function of λ_r. An interior equilibrium is stable if and only if the slope of the indirect utility differential (18) is negative in a neighbourhood of the equilibrium, whereas the two agglomerated equilibrium are always stable whenever they exist.

Using expressions (5), (6) and (9), (12)-(14) and (16), some cumbersome calculations yield.

$$\Delta V_r^*(\lambda_r)=\frac{n(b+2cn)t_r}{4\phi(b+cn)^2}.\left(\lambda_r-\frac{1}{2}\right)(\in_1 t_r+\in_2+\in_3\tau) \tag{19}$$

where

$$\in_1 \equiv -(5c^2 n^2 \phi+12bcn+2c^2 nA+6b^2 \phi+2bcA)<0 \tag{20}$$

$$\in_2 \equiv 4a\phi(3b+4cn)>0 \tag{21}$$

$$\in_3 \equiv 2cn\phi(2b+3cn)>0 \tag{22}$$

are constants depending on the structural parameters of the economy.

It follows immediately from (19) that $\lambda_r = \frac{1}{2}$ is always an equilibrium within each country. Since the indirect utility differential is linear with respect to λ_r, the stability of this equilibrium depends on the sign of $\in_1 t_r + \in_2 + \in_3 \tau$. When this expression is negative, dispersion is the unique stable spatial equilibrium in country *r*, when it is positive, the dispersed equilibrium is unstable so that agglomeration of all skilled workers of country *r* is the only stable equilibrium. This implies that the economic geography of a country depends on its transport costs as well as on trade costs, but not on the transport costs of the other country. Of course, this result depends on the specific assumptions made. The first key assumption is that all firms in a country have the same access to the regional markets of the other country. However, it must be kept in mind that relaxing this assumption would bias the results in favour of the region having a better access to the foreign markets. Our second critical assumption is that international markets are segmented. Indeed, assuming that interregional markets are integrated would not affect the foregoing property. By contrast, the geography of country *r* would depend on transport costs in country *s* if the international markets were integrated, but there is little empirical evidence that this is so.

As the indirect utility differential in a country depends only upon its internal distribution of economic activities, a spatial equilibrium in the global economy consists of two independent spatial equilibria, one for each country. As argued previously, agglomeration is a spatial equilibrium in country *r* if and only if $\in_1 t_r + \in_2 + \in_3 \tau \geq 0$ which means that

$$t_r \leq \frac{\in_2 + \in_3 \tau}{-\in_1} \tag{23}$$

Or alternatively, $\tau \geq \frac{-\in_1 t_r + \in_2}{\in_3}$ (24)

yields a necessary and sufficient condition for agglomeration in country *r* to be a stable spatial equilibrium (since $\in_1$ is negative).

This leads to the result that agglomeration is a stable spatial equilibrium in country r if and only if

$$t_r \leq t^*(\tau) \equiv \frac{2\phi[2a(3b+4cn)+2cn\phi(2b+3cn)\tau]}{5c^2n^2\phi+6b\phi(b+2cn)+2cA(b+cn)}$$

Or, equivalently if and only if

$$\tau \geq \tau^*(t_r) \equiv \frac{[5c^2n^2\phi+6b\phi(b+2cn)+2cA(b+cn)]t_r-4a\phi(3b+4cn)}{2cn\phi(2b+3cn)}$$

For both the agglomerated and dispersed configurations to arise as a spatial equilibrium when transport and/or trade costs vary, it must be that $\tau^*(t_r)<\tau_{\text{trade}}$ and $t^*(\tau)<t_{\text{trade}}(\tau)$. Because $\in_2>0$, when $\tau=0$ the latter inequality holds provided that $\in_1 t_{\text{trade}}(0)+\in_2<0$. By continuity, the two configuration will then emerge as equilibria in the vicinity of $\tau=0$. Because the absolute value of $\in_1$ rises with A. $\in_1 t_{\text{trade}}(0)+\in_2<0$ holds if and only if A exceeds some threshold value that we denote A. In particular, some simple calculations show that A is larger than $3L$, hence we assume throughout that $A>\bar{A}>3L$. This reflects the idea that immobile activities represent the larger share of the economy. Note also that $t^*(\tau)$ always exceeds some threshold $T>0$ when τ is arbitrarily small, whereas $\tau^*(t_r)$ equals 0 as soon as t_r is smaller than T while being strictly positive.

The two inequalities identified in the foregoing proposition can be viewed as being dual to the extent that each yields a necessary and sufficient condition to be imposed on transport or on trade costs for agglomeration to arise in a country, each condition depending on the other parameter. Because $\in_1$ is negative, for a given τ agglomeration within country r is more likely to be a stable equilibrium when the transport costs in this country are low. Everything else being equal, more intranational competition leads domestic firms to cluster because they have a larger market, which in turn makes the penetration by the foreign firms tougher. This concurs with the main result of economic geography in which agglomeration arises when trading across places becomes less expensive. The novelty is that here the occurrence of agglomeration is lowered, namely $t^*(\tau)$ decreases as trade costs keep falling. Because $\in_3$ is positive, for a given t_r such that $\tau^*(t_r) > 0$, agglomeration within a country is more likely to be a stable equilibrium when trade costs are high. Everything else equal, domestic firms react to more international competition by relaxing international competition through dispersion. This agrees with what we know in spatial competition where the spatial distribution of consumers between countries is exogenous. In this case, liberalizing trade would foster dispersion within each country. Among other things, the above mentioned proposition shows how trade impediments may affect the economic geography of countries involved in the integration process.

As $\tau^*(t_r)$ increases with t_r, it also follows from the above proposition that the country with the lower transport costs is agglomerated for a larger range of trade costs. This results suggests that lowering transport costs inside a country involved in a process of international integration could well trigger more regional imbalance within this country, unless the global economy has reached a fairly high level of integration.

The Terms of Trade

The terms of trade of region *i* in country *r* is defined as the ratio of its export unit value index to its import unit value index. The unit value index is defined as the ratio of total value (of imports or exports) to total quantity (of imports or exports). Hence, the export unit value index of region i = 1, 2 in country $r = H, F$ evaluated at the market equilibrium, is given by

$$euv_{ri} = \frac{(A/2+\phi n_{s1})q^*_{rsi}\,P^*_{rsi} + (A/2+\phi n_{s2})q^*_{rs2}\,P^*_{rs2}}{(A/2+\phi n_{s1})q^*_{rs1} + (A/2+\phi n_{s2})q^*_{rs2}}$$

$$= \theta_{s1}\,P^*_{rs1} + \theta_{s2}\,P^*_{rs2} \qquad (25)$$

where θ_{sj} is the share of exports of region *i* of country *r* to region *j* of country *s*, with $\theta_{s1} + \theta_{s2} = 1$. Because region *i* of country *r* imports all varieties produced in country *s* at the same price P^*_{sri}, the import unit value index is simply given by

$$iuv_{ri} = P^*_{sri} \qquad (26)$$

Hence, the terms of trade of region i of country r are given by

$$\rho \equiv \frac{euv_{ri}}{iuv_{ri}} = \frac{\theta_{s1} P^*_{rs1} + \theta_{s2} P^*_{rs2}}{P^*_{sri}} \tag{27}$$

Since the general analysis with asymmetric firm distribution turns out to be too complex, we focus exclusively on the symmetric setting in which both countries are dispersed. On solving the problem we find that

$$\left.\frac{\partial \rho_{ri}}{\partial \tau}\right|_{\lambda_r = \lambda_s = \frac{1}{2}} = \frac{2cn(2b+3cn)(t_r - t_s)}{(4a + cnt_r + 6\tau cn + 4\tau b)^2} \tag{28}$$

Condition (28) shows that, when the two countries are dispersed, international integration shifts the terms of trade in favour of the more integrated country. More precisely, when $t_r < t_s$, a decrease in τ raises ρ_{r1} and ρ_{r2} but both ρ_{s1} and ρ_{s2} decrease, the two regions of the same country are equally affected. This result shows that the transport costs of the trading partners have a direct impact on the terms of trade, even when the two countries have the same size and the same spatial structure. Furthermore, we have

$$\left.\frac{\partial \rho_{ri}}{\partial t_s}\right|_{\lambda_r = \lambda_s = \frac{1}{2}} = \frac{cn}{4a + cnt_r + 6\tau cn + 4\tau b} > 0 \tag{29}$$

as well as

$$\left.\frac{\partial \rho_{ri}}{\partial t_r}\right|_{\lambda_r = \lambda_s = \frac{1}{2}} = -cn.\frac{4a + cnt_s + 6\tau cn + 4\tau b}{(4a + cnt_r + 6\tau cn + 4\tau b)^2} < 0 \tag{30}$$

Conditions (29) and (30) show that each country has an incentive to decrease its transport costs in order to twist the terms of trade in its favour. Because the terms of trade are directly linked to welfare, each country also has an incentive to twist the terms of trade in order to improve its welfare.

In short when both countries are dispersed, a decrease in international trade costs shifts the terms of trade in favour of the country with lower interregional transport costs. Moreover, if transport costs fall within one country only, its terms of trade improve; if they fall equiproportionately in both countries, the terms of trade move in favour of the country with lower initial transport costs.

NOTES

1. Sometimes the mobility of the factors of production might be greater between two adjoining regions of the two different countries than that between the two regions of the same country separated by a vast distance. This, however, is an exceptional case. The general rule remains, of course, that mobility is greater within countries than between countries.
2. J.E. Cairnes, *Some Leading Principles of Political Economy Newly Expounded* (London, 1874), p. 303.

Theories of Foreign Trade—Adam Smith and Before Him

2

INTERNATIONAL TRADE BEFORE ADAM SMITH

In this section we shall give a short look on the theories of trade before Adam Smith which consist of an examination of the mercantilist doctrines with respect to foreign trade and of the contemporary criticism thereof.

In the English economic literature prior to Adam Smith, the most pervasive and the most emphasized doctrine is the importance of having an excess of exports over imports. This doctrine and the trade regulations which it inspired, named as "commercial" or "mercantile" system, which later became, with the aid of the Germans, the now familiar "Mercantilism." Many economists assign "mercantilism" only to the period after about 1620, distinguish with varying degrees of emphasis between the "bullionist" doctrines of the earlier period and the "balance-of-trade" doctrine of the later period. The following are the grounds for distinction between the two periods:

(a) Before 1620, stress was put on the importance of a favourable balance in each transaction of each merchant, whereas in the later period the emphasis was on the aggregate or national balance of trade.

(b) Before 1620, concern about the state of individual balances was due to anxiety that the country's stock of bullion be not reduced, whereas in the later period there was anxiety that it be increased.

(c) Before 1620, the chief economic objective of trade policy was to protect the national currency against exchange depreciation, whereas after 1620 this was a minor objective.

(d) In the early period, the means advocated and employed to carry out the objectives of the prevailing trade policy were close regulation of the transactions of particular individuals in the exchange market and in coin and bullion, while in the later period the policy recommended and put into practice was to seek the objective of a greater stock of bullion indirectly by means of regulation of trade rather than directly through restrictions on exchange transactions and on the export of coin and bullion.

In the earlier period, it is true, regulation of the foreign trade and exchange transactions of the merchants had been stricter and more detailed than it subsequently became. But the outstanding changes in legislation and in administrative practice extended over a long period, and all of any importance occurred long before 1620 or did not occur until long after. The institution of the Staple, which served as an instrument of regulation of individual transactions, finally expired with the loss of Calais in 1558. The Statutes of Employment requiring foreign merchants to pay for the English commodities which they bought, in part at least, in coin or bullion had become inoperative long before the end of the sixteenth century.

The most pervasive feature of the English mercantilist literature was the doctrine that it was vitally important for England that it should have an excess of exports over imports, usually because that was for a country with no gold or silver mines, the only way to increase its stock of the precious metals. The doctrine is of early origin, and some of the mercantilists, in the earlier period when it was still customary to scatter miscellaneous tags of classical wisdom through one's discourse, succeeded in finding Latin quotations which seemed to expound it. It was clearly enough stated as far back as 1381 by Richard Leicester, a mint official, in answer to an official inquiry as to the cause of, and remedy for, the supposed drain of gold out of England. Although the concept of a national balance of trade was already common in the sixteenth century, the exact term itself seems to have first been coined in 1615 when it almost immediately passed into common usage. The first appearance in print of the phrase appears to have been in the title and text of a pamphlet by Misselden published in 1623, *The Circle of Commerce, or the Balance of Trade*. It is to be found ad nauseam in the subsequent literature.

The term "favourable balance of trade" now so common, and so commonly attributed to the mercantilists, seems first to have been used in 1767 by Sir James Steuart, although the phrase "balance in our favour" had been used by Cary in 1695, Pollexfen in 1697, and Mackworth in about 1720, and corresponding terms were used by many other writers.

There is no historical basis for the distinction which some writers have tried to make between a balance-of-individual-bargains stage and a chronologically later general balance-of-trade stage in the evolution of mercantilist doctrine. Richard Jones coined the phrase "balance-of-bargain" in order to distinguish between means and not ends, "to effect their purposes, they [i.e. the early politicians] adopted a very complicated system, which we may call the balance-of-bargain system; and which through its objects was precisely the same with that of the balance-of-trade system long subsequently established, yet sought to attain that object by very different means. An influx of bullion resulting from an excess of exports over imports was the common objective both of the earlier and of the later period. To the extent that the methods advocated or actually applied to attain this end differed, it is more accurate to say that the early bullionist regulations dealt directly with the transactions in coin and bullion and foreign exchange, whereas the later customs regulations sought the same results indirectly by regulating the commodity imports and exports. No trace is to be found in the early literature of anything even approaching a theory of the importance of the individual balances except as items in a clearly conceived national balance and it is only as inference from the character of the bullionist regulations that the prevalence of the notion that such a theory was once expounded can be explained.

The mercantilists have sometimes been charged with failure to see that the international balance does not consist only of commodity exports and imports and many suppose that the "invisible items" are a recent discovery. But most of the important writers of the seventeenth and eighteenth centuries took care to point out that allowance must be made for non-commodity items in explaining the net balance payable in bullion. Reference to an "invisible" item is to be found as far back as 1381, when both Aylesbury and Lincoln explained the drain of gold as due partly to remittances to Rome. An early writer argued that if foreign merchants were required to come to England to buy English cloth instead of being permitted to buy it abroad, their living expenses in England would be an item in England's favor. Misselden, in 1623, mentioned the profits from the fisheries, reexport trade, and freight earnings as items to be added to the commodity statistics in computing the balance. Malynes, in the same year, pointed out that interest payment on foreign loans should be included in the balance. Robinson, in 1641, included diplomatic expenditures abroad, travelers' expenses, and freight charges. Mun, writing in about the year 1630, listed almost all the items which would be included today: freight earnings, military expenditures abroad, marine insurance payments, gains from fisheries, losses at sea of outward and inward shipments of goods, Catholic remittances to Rome, travelers' expenses, gifts, and the excess over their living expenses in the country for which the balance is being computed of payments to foreigners for exchange commissions, interest, and life and commodity insurance. Child, in 1690, added absentee incomes and losses from bad debts. Hugh Chamberlain, in 1606, listed, in addition to commodity trade, the earnings of migratory labor abroad, tourist expenditures ("what foreign travelers spend here to see the country"), diplomatic and military expenditures abroad, and other items. The mercantilists were most interested in the "balance of payments" in its strict sense of a net balance of immediate obligations payable in specie, and the specie flows inward or outward resulting from the balance of payments were their primary concern. Arthur Young in 1772 used the phrase "temporal balance of remittance" to signify the immediate balance of payments. The term "balance of indebtedness" seems not to have been used until the nineteenth century. Adam Smith, however, approached it at one point, where he referred to the "state of debt and credit."

The mercantilists wanted an export surplus primarily because they wanted more bullion and because they saw that for a country without gold or silver mines a favorable balance of trade was the only means available to procure bullion. The central problem in the interpretation of the mercantilist theories is the discovery of the grounds on which their belief in the desirability of an indefinite accumulation of the precious metals was based. The most common criticism of the mercantilists is that they regarded the precious metals as the sole constituents of the wealth of the nation. Adam

Smith made this charge a central feature of his criticism of the mercantilist doctrines, and he has been accused, by modern apologists for mercantilism, of inexcusable misinterpretation of their doctrines. On behalf of the mercantilists they assert that the doctrine of the identity of wealth and bullion is so absurd as to make it incredible that able men, to whom the fable of Midas must have been familiar, should have adhered to it, and they either refer to passages in writings of the period revealing a broad concept of wealth, or else deny that the words "wealth," "riches," or "treasure" had the same meaning then which they have now. The mercantilists did not have in mind the possibility that a country may make investments abroad or may borrow from abroad, and there is no mercantilist writer who explains his desire for a favorable balance of trade as a desire that his country should export capital abroad rather than borrow abroad. If indebtedness is disregarded, the one difference between an export surplus and an import surplus is that there is a net exchange of goods for money in the first case and of money for goods in the second case. It is impossible, therefore, to understand such common mercantilist arguments as that foreign trade was the only path to national wealth, that a country can gain from foreign trade only if it results in a favorable balance payable in bullion, that an export surplus is both the proof and the measure of gain from trade, and that an import surplus is both the proof and the measure of national loss, unless they believed, momentarily at least, that all goods other than money were worthless, or were of value only as they served as means of securing money. If it be replied that the mercantilists meant by "wealth," "treasure," "riches," "gain," "loss," "poverty," "prosperity," "profit," etc. only money or absence of money, their arguments generally become merely laborious tautologies, and it becomes a mystery: (a) why they should have thought it necessary to present so earnestly and at such great length arguments reducing to the assertion that the only way for a country without gold or silver mines to get more bullion is to obtain it from abroad in return for goods, and (b) what terms they used when they were thinking of what we mean today when we speak of riches, wealth, gain, prosperity.

To most of the *moderate* mercantilists the distinction between money and wealth was clear enough, if not always at least in moments of enlightenment and when recognition of the distinction would not hamper them and might even help them to make the point at issue at the moment. Thomas More had already, in 1516, tried to destroy the current illusions about the importance of gold and silver and in his ideal commonwealth they were to be relegated to use in the hire of foreign mercenaries and in the making of vessels serving lowly and unromantic purposes indeed, in order to free the Utopians from the tendency to exaggerate their importance: "And these metals, which other nations do as grievously and sorrowfully forego, as in a manner their own lives, if they should altogether at once be taken from the Utopians, no man there would think that he had lost the worth of one farthing."

The notion that saving consisted of the piling-up of valuable goods led naturally to an identification of saved wealth or "riches" with stored-up goods of a special kind suitable for accumulation and not capable of, or destined for, current consumption. Commodities of high value and of great durability and not liable to loss of value through change of fashion would be specially suitable as the constituent items of stored-up wealth. The exaltation of saving led in turn to the attachment of superior importance to such commodities than to more perishable commodities and those destined for current consumption. The precious metals met these tests of suitability as stores of wealth better than any other commodities.

With only a few exceptions, the mercantilists either identified or failed clearly to distinguish between money, on the one hand, and capital or "stock" employed by its owner or lent out at interest, on the other. They always wrote of direct employment of capital and of loans at interest in monetary terms, and as a rule they showed no signs that they had penetrated in their analysis beneath the monetary surface. Verbally, at least, they identified money with capital; much of their argument can be explained only if they regarded money and capital as identical in fact as well as in name. This is most clearly brought out in the important doctrines of the period: that interest was paid for the use of money, that the rate of interest depended on the quantity of money, and that high interest rates were proof of the scarcity of money, doctrines which were questioned by very few writers before Hume.

All the variants of the mercantilist doctrine which rest on an identification of money with wealth, or with accumulated and stored wealth, or with loanable capital, found support for their position in a superficially plausible analogy with personal finance which with unimportant modifications recurs repeatedly in the mercantilist literature from the earliest to the latest writers, and is frequently supported by citations from classical writers. There was little contemporary criticism of this analogy, obvious though its shortcomings seem to be both as an analogy and as an interpretation of personal finance. Papillon pointed out that it was foolish for a person managing a farm to buy less than he sells in order to accumulate a stock of *money*. Barbon tried to meet it by the argument that although the "stock" of a person is finite, and therefore exhaustible, that of a country is infinite, and "what is infinite can neither receive addition by parsimony nor suffer diminution by prodigality." Mandeville conceded that frugality or "saving" was the most certain method to increase an estate, but he denied, on "make-work" grounds, that this also held true for a nation. Hume pointed out, on quantity theory of money grounds, that while an individual would be richer if he had more money, the same would not hold for a country.

In the modern literature on mercantilism, the desire of the mercantilists for more money is sometimes explained as largely due to a prevailing desire for higher prices, and the apologists find economic justification for such a desire in the circumstances which they allege then prevailed, for example, the necessity for increase in the national stock of money if the period of transition from a barter to a money economy were not to be accompanied by the evils of falling prices. But even in the literature of the early seventeenth century, barter is already referred to as a system characteristic of a primitive economy from which England had long since emerged. From early in the sixteenth century to late in the eighteenth, the general trend of English commodity prices was decidedly upward rather than downward, although the economic historians do seem to be agreed that there were intervals of some length during which prices were falling. But throughout the period the complaints of scarcity of money were unintermittent. There were very few *price* inflationists among the English mercantilists, and even the advocates of paper money did not want higher prices. Many mercantilists claimed that if their projects were adopted land values would rise, but such claims were made in order to win the support or weaken the opposition of the landed classes to their proposals. In any case, they were usually based on the argument that more money meant lower interest rates, and lower interest rates meant higher land values, or on the argument that more money meant more trade and therefore a readier sale for agricultural products, or more production and therefore greater exports, and rarely made specific reference to higher commodity prices.

Many of the mercantilists, some of whom also used the arguments already discussed, wanted more money because they regarded money, not merely as a passive medium of exchange, but as a force acting through its circulation from hand to hand as an active stimulus to trade. An increased amount of money in circulation, they believed, meant (or caused) an increased volume of trade, and since men would produce only what they could sell a quickening of trade meant an increase of production and therefore a wealthier country. Here, it should be noted, money is valued as an instrument or stimulus of trade rather than for its own sake. The writers who stressed "circulation" as the valuable service of money often shifted, however, from the concept of money circulating as a medium of exchange to money passing from the hands of a lender to those of a borrower, and rarely distinguished clearly between them. The underlying reasoning is often presented in the form of analogies, especially with the circulation of the blood, which William Harvey had discovered not long before.

The mercantilist arguments for a favorable balance of trade so far considered all rest upon the desirability of more bullion. But there was one mercantilist argument which was not dependent upon the attachment of superior economic importance to the precious metals than to other commodities of equal exchange value, namely the "employment" argument. Exports were the product of English labor whereas imports, especially if they consisted of finished products and of commodities competitive with home products, displaced English labor. The greater, the exports, and the smaller the imports, the greater, therefore, was the employment of English labor. This argument was not, as is sometimes supposed, of late seventeenth century origin. It is to be found in the very earliest mercantilist writings, and it persists without break throughout the literature of the seventeenth and eighteenth centuries. It is not even clear that it was more emphasized in the eighteenth than in the seventeenth century mercantilist literature, and it could even be argued that the sixteenth century writers stressed it most of all. Of all the mercantilist reasoning, it withstood criticism most successfully, and persisted into the nineteenth and twentieth centuries as an important element in the protectionist doctrine. The stress on employment led to an appraisal of exports not merely in terms of their value, or of their value relative to imports, but in terms of the amount of labor they represented. Exports of manufactured articles were rated more highly than exports to the same value of raw materials, because the former embodied a larger proportion of labor. The stress on employment sometimes took the form of measuring the gain from trade by the exports alone, and in a few cases the argument even went to the extreme of recommending production of goods simply to employ labor, even though the product of their labor were burnt upon their completion. In the case of a few later writers, the employment argument gave rise to a new balance-of-trade concept, in which the amounts weighed against each other were not the values respectively of the exports and the imports, but the respective amounts of labor or employment they represented, i.e. the "balance of labor" or the "balance of employment." Barbon seems to have been the first to come close to this concept. The measure of benefit from different exports is the amount of employment they had given to English labor, and, similarly, the measure of benefit from imports is the amount of employment to which they will give rise in their further manufacture. His employment test leads him at times to liberal conclusions. Imports of raw silk are more profitable than imports of gold and silver, because more hands are employed in the manufacture of the first than in working the latter. If woolen goods are exported for Westphalian bacon and then the import of the latter is prohibited, England would lose even if the consumption of English bacon increased, because woolen cloth employs more hands in its production than does bacon.

After Hume and Smith had written, mercantilism was definitely on the defensive and was wholly or largely rejected by the leading English economists. That their victory was as great as it was, was due largely, of course, to the force of their reasoning and the brilliance of their exposition, but it was due also in large part to the fact that, even before they wrote, mercantilism as a body of economic doctrine had already been disintegrating because of dissension within the ranks of its adherents and attacks by earlier critics. An important element in its collapse, especially in its monetary phases, was the development of the theory of the self-regulating mechanism of international specie distribution. The most influential formulation of this theory in England prior to the nineteenth century was by Hume. But its most important constituent elements had been stated long before Hume, and several earlier writers had brought them together much as he did.

A country with a metallic currency will automatically get the amount of bullion it needs to maintain its prices at such a level relative to the prices prevailing abroad as to maintain an even balance between its exports and imports. Should more money than this happen to come into that country, its prices would rise relatively to those of other countries; its exports, consequently, would fall, and its imports increase; the resultant adverse balance of payments would have to be met in specie; and the excess of money would thus be drained off. If, on the other hand, a country's monetary supply should happen to fall below the amount necessary to maintain equilibrium, its prices would fall relative to those abroad, exports would rise and imports fall, and the resultant favorable balance of payments would bring in an amount of specie from abroad sufficient to restore equilibrium. In dealing with the factors determining the exchange rates, Locke was much more penetrating. He explains the exchange rate between two countries as due to: (a) "the overbalance of the trade," which, the context shows, means the balance of payments resulting from *past* transactions; and (b) the relative plenty of money (identified with liquid capital) which affects inversely the opportunities for profitable investment of surplus funds, and therefore determines to what country they will flow. He states fairly clearly the limits beyond which exchange rates cannot move without leading to specie flows.

North, in 1691, presented a concise formulation of an automatic and self-regulating mechanism, which provides a country with the "determinate sum of specific money" required for carrying on the trade of the nation. It is not, however, the mechanism described in the modern theory, and is not, explicitly at least, an explanation of the *international* distribution of money. The mechanism which he presents consists of an automatic ebb and flow of money into and out of circulation according to the unexplained specific requirements of trade. When because of troubled conditions money is hoarded, the mints coin more bullion, whose source is not explained. When peace returns, money comes out of the hoards, the mints cease to coin bullion, and the excess of money is melted down "either to supply the home trades or for transportation abroad. Thus the buckets work alternately; when money is scarce, bullion is coined; when bullion is scarce, money is melted." He fails to relate this process either to price movements or to movements in the balance of trade.

There has been a marked tendency in recent years, more especially perhaps on the part of German economists and of economic historians, toward a more favorable appraisal of English mercantilist doctrine than has prevailed among the economic theorists of the English classical tradition. Much of this tendency can be explained away as due to participation in the interventionist, protectionist, or aggressively nationalistic sentiments of the mercantilist writers, to misconceptions of what the economic doctrines of the English mercantilists really were, or to absence of knowledge of, or interest in, the grounds for rejecting the mercantilist doctrines afforded by modern monetary and trade theory. To those apologists who defend the mercantilist doctrines on the ground either that they were not what their critics allege them to have been, or that the theoretical objections of the critics can be successfully refuted, the foregoing presentation of the mercantilist reasoning must suffice as an answer.

The modern apologies for mercantilism, however, are also supported by several arguments which do not clash directly with the propositions of modern trade and monetary theory, and these arguments are entitled to more respectful treatment. The economic historians, for instance, seem to derive from their valid doctrine, that if sufficient information were available the prevalence in any period of particular theories could be *explained* in the light of the circumstances then prevailing, the curious corollary that they can also be *justified* by appeal to these special circumstances. There are some obvious obstacles to acceptance of this point of view. It would lead to the conclusion that no age, except apparently the present one, is capable of serious doctrinal error. It overlooks the fact that one of the historical circumstances which has been undergoing an evolution has been the capacity for economic analysis. More specifically, to be involved successfully in defense of mercantilist doctrine it needs to be supported by demonstration that the typical behavior of merchants, the nature of the gains or losses from trade, the nature of the monetary processes, and the economic significance of territorial division of labor have changed sufficiently since 1550, or 1650, or 1750, to make what was sound reasoning for these earlier periods unsound for the present-day world.

It has been claimed also for the mercantilists that they were presenting short-run doctrines and proposals, whereas their later critics had only long-run considerations in mind. It must be conceded that some of the mercantilist doctrine would not be quite so absurd if appraised from the short-run point of view. But I have found no evidence that the mercantilists intended their analysis and proposals to be regarded as holding true for the short run only, and there is abundant evidence that they were ordinarily not aware of any distinction between what was desirable monetary or trade practice, to meet a temporary situation, on the one hand, and as permanent policy, on the other.

It has been argued also, in answer to the criticisms of mercantilist doctrine by economic theorists, that the primary objective of mercantilist policy was not economic prosperity but national unity and power. In dealing with this interpretation of mercantilism, it is important to distinguish between the official and the unofficial expositions of the doctrine, between the actual policies and the reasoning by which they were supported, and between Continental and English mercantilism. In each case, it is only the latter with which this essay is concerned. Government policy, no doubt, was never governed solely by economic considerations, but for the unofficial writers this was a subject for complaint rather than for approval. Even in the unofficial literature, however, political and religious considerations were mingled with the economic to a degree without parallel in modern economic literature. But in England a strong and centralized government and an aggressive national spirit had been established long before the appearance of an important mercantilist literature, and whatever may have been the situation on the Continent the primary emphasis of the English mercantilist writers was on the means by which England's wealth could be augmented. Many writers, it is true, urged in support of the measures which they advocated that they would not only contribute to England's prosperity but would also promote her prestige and power, injure her rivals, and protect her national faith against its enemies, internal and external. But the appeal to political and religious considerations seems often to have been intended to win the support of the less commercial-minded official and landed classes for the proposals of the "merchants" or businessmen, and seems only rarely to have expressed what was really the primary concern of their authors. Especially important as a safeguard against applying erroneously to the English mercantilist literature generalizations which may be true of the Continental writers, it should be borne in mind that English mercantilist doctrine was the product of merchants to an extent without parallel on the Continent. On economic matters even the landed classes in England found their ablest spokesmen in merchants such as Child and North. And the merchants were typically impatient of official policy when it failed to place primary emphasis on the economic aspects of the matters with which it dealt, and especially when it appeared to subordinate economic to political or religious considerations.

Even if it be granted, however, that the principal objective of the English mercantilist writers was a great and powerful England rather than a prosperous England, it does not follow that appraisal of their reasoning on strictly economic grounds is unwarranted or irrelevant. It would be difficult to find convincing evidence that any of the prominent mercantilists regarded power and prosperity as generally conflicting and inharmonious objectives of national policy. On the contrary, it was a matter of general agreement among them that for England the only certain path to national power and glory was through promotion of trade and increase of wealth. Child's formula, which was often quoted approvingly, expresses accurately the mercantilist position: "Foreign trade produces riches, riches power, power preserves our trade and religion." After the Revolution, in fact, trade and wealth seem to have become almost an obsession of the mercantile classes, and the emphasis which they placed on the economic phases of national policy was, if anything, excessive. I suspect that the "trade wars" of the seventeenth and eighteenth centuries were such more in the imagination of the mercantile writers than in the intent of the governing classes who embarked upon them, and that just as the merchants appealed to non-economic considerations to make their proposals attractive to the landed classes, so the government appealed to the cupidity of the merchants to win their support for wars embarked upon for dynastic or political reasons. Even the official classes in England, however, were probably more trade-minded, and probably gave greater weight to economic considerations, than the corresponding classes on the Continent. Such, at least, appears to have been the opinion of eighteenth century Continental observers.

Not only is there little evidence that the mercantilist writers were prepared to sacrifice national economic to political interests, but a good deal of the mercantilist literature can be plausibly explained as special pleading for limited economic interests. The most ardent advocates in the seventeenth century of the revival or enforcement of the bullionist restrictions had a personal interest of one sort or another in these regulations. Malynes is said to have had expectations of getting a remunerative contract in connection with the currency if the office of the Royal Exchanger were revived. Milles was a customs official among whose duties would be the enforcement of any bullionist regulations. Violet had been a "searcher" and informer in connection with the regulations prohibiting the export of bullion, and his appeals for stricter enforcement were accompanied by pleas that he again be employed to discover violations of the regulations. Wheeler was secretary and Misselden an important member of the Merchant Adventurers, and their tracts were written in defense of their exchange transactions against the attacks of Milles and Malynes. The East India Company, in its charter of 1600, was granted the right to export a limited amount of bullion and in its early as in its later operations bullion constituted the bulk of its exports from England. This led to attacks on the company of which Robert Keales' *The Trades Increase* (1615) was typical. Digges, a member of the company, wrote his *Defence of Trade* (1615) as a reply to Keales, and Mun, an officer of the company, wrote his tracts and presented a "remonstrance" to the government primarily to ward off hostile measures against the company. Throughout the history of the company its officers and employees were publishing tracts in its defense which were important contributions to the literature of mercantilism. Toward the end of the seventeenth century, when attacks on the company turned mostly on its monopolistic character, its imports of East Indian silks and calicoes to the alleged injury of English industry, and its unfavorable balance of trade, Child and Papillon, officers of the company and with much of their private fortunes invested therein, wrote in its defense. Much of the mercantilist literature from 1670 on, written in opposition to the company, was the work of rival merchants who wanted to participate in the East India trade or of persons connected in some way with the domestic textile industries which were feeling the effects of East Indian competition. Tracts were written by factors in the woolen industry urging or supporting the prohibition of the export of wool and were answered by spokesmen for agricultural interests. John Houghton, Charles Smith, Arthur Young, and many others wrote in support of the bounties on the export of corn with an evident agrarian bias. The literature on taxation consisted in large part of tracts written by traders who wanted the main burden of taxation to rest on land, or by landed men who wanted it to rest on trade. There were contemporary charges that some of those who were urging the legal limitation of the rate of interest were rich merchants who had ample funds to finance their own activities and hoped that the reduction of the rate of interest by law would make it impossible for their poorer competitors to borrow the funds necessary for the conduct of their affairs. Pleas for special interests, whether open or disguised, constituted the bulk of the mercantilist literature. The disinterested patriot or philosopher played a minor part in the development of mercantilist doctrine.

The trouble with mercantilism was that it failed to address the relevant issues about foreign trade. The pertinent issues were finally raised by Adam Smith and the rest of the classical economist. In particular, the classical theory of international trade, associated with Adam Smith, David Ricardo, Robert Torrens and John Stuart Mill, is concerned with the following three important questions:

(a) Do countries benefit from international trade? Where do the gains from trade come from, and how are they divided among the trading countries?

(b) Which goods are exported, and which are imported, by each trading country? What are the fundamental laws that govern the international allocation of resources and the flow of trade?

(c) At what prices are the exported and imported goods exchanged?

These questions are basic to the theory of international trade and form the foundation for most of theories of the international trade.

THEORY OF ABSOLUTE ADVANTAGE

Absolute advantage theory was introduced by the Scottish economist Adam Smith in 1776. He believed that the wealth of a country was not necessarily determined by how much treasure they hold but by goods and services available to its people. He therefore developed a theory called absolute advantage which consists of that different countries produce some goods more efficiently than others therefore through free trade global efficiency can increase. From this theory Adam Smith questioned why citizens of a particular country should buy a particular product domestically when they can buy the goods more cheaply from abroad. Smith realized that if trade amongst countries was unrestricted, each country could specialize on the products that give them a competitive advantage, thus each country resources would shift to the more efficient industries because they would not be able to compete with other countries in the inefficient ones. Absolute advantage theory asserts that a nation benefits from manufacturing more output than others since it is in the possession of a particular resource or commodity. This particular resource can also be a certain method or knowledge that increases the production efficiency, and thus reduces the relative need to resources. It then follows that each country will benefit from specialization in those commodities in which it has an absolute advantage, exporting them and importing other commodities that it produces at a higher real cost than does another country. "Real cost", for Smith, meant the amount of labour time required to produce a commodity.

The explanation of the absolute advantage theory depends on the following assumptions:

(a) A labour theory of value—the only cost of production is the number of man hours (m/h) required per unit of output multiplied by the wage rate (w);

(b) Commodity prices are cost-determined; and

(c) Labour is completely immobile between nations.

The labour theory of value need not be so crude since it can be maintained if capital and other factors of production: (a) are an insignificant part of total production costs; or (b) have equal significance in all lines of production; or (c) are accumulated labour-value in the Marxist sense.

Smith further assumed that *w* is the same in all countries and that different country requires different m/h per unit of output. Hence, difference in production costs, therefore in commodity prices, can be explained in terms of different m/h requirements. Since the assumption of different m/h requirements is equivalent to different production functions for the same commodity in different countries, it follows that the principle of absolute advantage amounts to stating that the pattern of trade is determined by differences in factor productiveness or in production functions.

Here one point should be noted that in this explanation, once trade takes place there will result complete specialization in production—each country will specialize completely in the commodity in which it has an absolute advantage, i.e. a lower price. In other words, the production possibility frontiers will exhibit characteristics of constant opportunity costs. This was a simple explanation because international trade theories are interested in what happens when one country has an absolute advantage in all lines of production. Smith's explanation would seem to rule out trade under such circumstances. However, simple as it is, the principle of absolute advantage can explain the pattern of trade in commodities where the necessary environment or skills are lacking: if a country does not have the appropriate geographical conditions to produce rice or wheat, it will have to import them since the cost of domestic production would be prohibitive; and if a country does not possess the necessary skilled labour or sophisticated technology to produce a commodity, it will have to import it.

Mercantilists believed that one nation could benefit only at the expense of another nation and advocated a national policy of protectionism. But according to Adam Smith, all countries would benefit from free trade and championed a policy of laissez-fare, i.e. absence of government interference in economic affairs. With free trade, the resources of the world would be allocated efficiently, generating gains for each and every trading nation. Any interference with the free flow of trade would impede the efficient allocation of resources worldwide and would deny to the world community the opportunity to enjoy the potential gains from trade.

The immobility of labour between nations obviously poses a problem for the labour theory of value when labour requirements vary from one country to another. The real exchange ratio of commodities moving in international trade need not be equal to the ratio of labour time embodied in their production. Thus a different theory is needed to explain or account for international exchange ratios. Adam Smith did not concern himself with this problem. He wished merely to show that a nation benefited from trade in which it exported those commodities it could produce at lower real cost than other countries, and imported those commodities it produced at a higher real cost than other countries.

Let us consider an example to clarify the principle of absolute advantage. We consider two countries, India and Britain, endowed with homogeneous labour and producing two commodities, food and clothing. Now suppose that one day of labour can produce either two units of food or four units of clothing in India, and either one unit of food or six units of clothing in Britain. This information can be summarized in the following table.

Table 1: Examples of Absolute Advantage
(Output per unit of labour)

	India	*Britain*
Food	2	1
Clothing	4	6

From the above table we see that India is more efficient than Britain in the production of food, because with the same amount of labour India produces more food than Britain. On the other hand, Britain is more efficient than India in the production of clothing. This state of affairs can be stated as India has an absolute advantage in the production of food, and Britain has an absolute advantage in the production of clothing. In case of closed economy, one unit of food will exchange for two units of clothing in India and for six units of clothing in Britain.

Now if there exists free trade between India and Britain then the question arises is free trade between them mutually beneficial? Adam Smith would answer yes. Let India export to Britain two units of food (2F) in exchange for six units of British clothing (6C). India gains 2C, because domestically India can exchange 2F for only 4C. Similarly, Britain gains 1F, because domestically in Britain 6C can be exchange for only 1F. Thus, we see that before trade take place, food is cheap in India (where 1F = 2C) and expensive in Britain (where 1F = 6C). By the similar argument, clothing is expensive in India (where 1C = ½ F) and cheap in Britain (where 1C = 1/6 F). Now the golden rule for profitable business is to buy cheap and sell dear. Thus, businessmen would have a strong incentive to buy food in India where it is cheap and sell it in Britain where it is expensive. Similarly they would purchase clothing in Britain where it is cheap and sell it in India where it is expensive. Thus, we see an analogy between international trade and technical progress. In the same way that technical progress makes possible the production of commodities using fewer resources, international trade enables countries to obtain commodities at lower prices. The indirect acquisition of commodities through international trade is tantamount to the discovery of more efficient production techniques. For example, assuming that the terms of trade are 1F:3F, as before, we could say that trade acts like a new technique, whereby one unit of food can be transformed into three units of clothing and vice versa. Adam Smith stated this argument in terms of an analogy with the behaviour of an individual, treating the conclusion as self-evident. His famous passage can be quoted as follows.

"It is the maxim of every prudent master of a family, never to attempt to make at home what it will cost him more to make than to buy. The taylor does not attempt to make his own shoes, but buys them of the shoemaker. The shoemaker does not attempt to make his own cloths, but employs a taylor. The farmer attempts to make neither the one nor the other, but employs those different artificers. All of them find it for their interest to employ their whole industry in a way in which they have some advantage over their neighbors, and to purchase with a part of its produce...whatever else they have occasion for.

What is produce in the conduct of every private family can scarce be folly in that of a great kingdom. If a foreign country can supply us with a commodity cheaper than we ourselves can make it, better buy it of them with some part of the produce of our own industry, employed in a way in which we have some advantage....

The natural advantage which one country has over another in producing particular commodities are sometimes so great, that it is acknowledged by all the world to be in vain to struggle with them. By means of glasses, hotbeds, and hotwalls, very good grapes can be raised in Scotland, and very good wine too can be made of them at about thirty times the expense for which at least equally good can be brought from foreign countries. Would it be a reasonable law to prohibit the importation of all foreign wines, merely to encourage the making of claret and burgundy in Scotland? But if there would be manifest absurdity in turning towards any employment, thirty times more of the capital and industry of the country, than would be necessary to purchase from foreign countries, an equal quantity of the commodities wanted, there must be an absurdity.... In turning towards any such employment a thirtieth or even a three-hundredth part more of either. Whether the advantages which one country has over another, be natural or acquired, is in this respect of no consequence."

This explanation certainly suffices to account for much international trade. However the truth of the matter is that absolute advantage can explain only a small portion of world trade. As it turns out, mutually beneficial trade does not necessarily require exporters to have an absolute advantage over their foreign rivals. At the beginning of the nineteenth century David Ricardo demonstrated that mutually beneficial trade is possible when only comparative advantage exists which is a far weaker condition than absolute advantage. He considered the absolute advantage as a special case of the general principle of comparative advantage. We shall make a extensive study of comparative advantage in the next chapter.

Limitations of Absolute Advantage

There are several caveats in the above analysis of the absolute advantage theory, some of which we are going o discuss in this section.

(a) *Absence of absolute advantage*: The example discusses a situation where one country has an absolute advantage in the production of one good and the other country in the production of another good. It is frequently argued that developing countries may lack the technology to gain an absolute advantage in the production of any good, such that they cannot possibly compete on the global market and benefit from free trade (in Table 1, for example, if India needs one labour to produce two units of food. This conclusion is wrong, as analyzed in the Ricardian model of comparative advantage, since technologically disadvantaged countries can compete on the global market by paying lower wages. It turns out that absolute advantage is neither a necessary nor a sufficient condition for exporting a certain good and gain from international trade.

(b) *More factors of production*: In reality goods are produced using several factors of production simultaneously, such as capital, land, and various types of labour. Usually, goods cannot be ranked according to absolute advantage as their production in one country requires more of one input and simultaneously less of another input than in another country. These issues are analyzed in the Heckscher-Ohlin theory of international trade.

(c) *Intra-versus inter-industry trade*: The example discusses inter-industry trade, which is the exchange of one type of good for another type of good. Many countries engage in intra-industry trade, the exchange of similar type of goods. This type of trade is becoming ever more important. It can be based on market power and economies of scale, as analyzed in new trade theory.

Despite the limitations and complications discussed above, absolute advantages are important for explaining current international trade flows and differences between countries in terms of income levels and wage rates. Daniel Trefler (1995) systematically analyzes these issues by combining the Heckscher-Ohlin model with technology differences, while taking into consideration the empirically observed home country bias. This combination explains about 93 per cent of international trade flows. It also shows that technology differences are largely responsible for the deviations in income levels and wage rates among different countries. For this reason absolute advantage does retain relevance for understanding the modern world economy.

Nature and Significance of International Trade

3

THE SCOPE OF INTERNATIONAL ECONOMICS

International economics studies how a number of distinct economies interact with one another in the process of allocating scarce resources to satisfy human wants. Whereas general economic theory deals with the problems of a single closed economy, international economics focuses on the problems of two or more economies. It examines the same problems as general economic theory, but discusses them in their international setting. Parallel to the breakdown of economic theory into microeconomics and macroeconomics is the division of international economics into two major branches—(a) international trade and (b) international finance. The former is the long-run static-equilibrium theory of barter in which the short-run monetary-adjustment process is assumed completed, with money assuming its true classical role as a veil. The approach of international trade theory is basically microeconomic in nature. International finance theory is centered upon the monetary aspects of international monetary relations. Its approach is mainly macroeconomic in nature, and it deals particularly with the short-run problems of balance-of-payments disequilibrium and adjustment.

International economics is a field of study in which the basic principles of economics are used to analyze and interpret these economic exchanges between nations—all the transactions that cross the borders of the nation. These transactions include trade in goods and services, movement of labour and capital, and a variety of financial transactions in bonds, stocks, notes, deposits, and other financial assets. Although international economics originates in the separation of national markets, the trend in recent decades has been toward the lessening of that separation, toward a more closely integrated world economy. Modern developments in transportation and communication have greatly increased the degree of economic interdependence among nations.

The subject matter of international economics, then, consists of issues raised by the special problems of economic interaction between sovereign states. The subject matter of the international economics covers following seven themes.

(a) *The pattern of trade*: Attempts to explain the pattern of international trade—who sells what to whom—have been a major preoccupation of international economists. Some aspects of the pattern of trade such as climate and resources are easy to understand. It is easy to explain why India exports tea and Saudi Arabia exports oil. But on the other hand much of the pattern of trade is more subtle. Why does Japan export automobiles, while the United States export aircraft?

(b) *The gains from trade*: The most important insight in all of international economics is the idea that there are gains from trade—i.e. when countries sell goods and services to one another, this is almost always to their benefit. The range of circumstances under which international trade is beneficial is much wider than most people think. For example, many Indian businessmen fear that if China's productivity overtakes that of the India, trade with China will damage the Indian economy because none of our industries will be able to compete.

(c) *Protectionism*: The eternal battle between free trade and protection is the most important policy theme of the international economics. From the very beginning of the emergence of modern nation-states, governments of each country have worried about the effect of international competition on the prosperity of domestic industries and have tried either to shield industries from foreign competition by placing limits on imports or to help them in world of competition by subsidizing exports. One of the most import tasks of the international economics is to analyze the effects of these protectionist policies and show the advantages of free trade between the countries.

(d) *The balance of payments*: What does it mean when a country runs a trade surplus or a trade deficit? To make sense of numbers like trade deficit, it is essential to place them in the broader context of the whole of a nation's international transactions. The record of a country's transactions with the rest of the world is called the balance of payments. The main theme of international economics is to explain the balance of payments and diagnose its significance. It emerges in a variety of specific contexts such as in discussing international capital movements, in relating international transactions to national income accounting and in discussing every aspect of international monetary policy.

(e) *Exchange rate determination*: One of the key differences between international economics and other areas of economics is that countries have different currencies. It is usually possible to convert one currency into another but the relative prices of currencies may change over time. It is a new field of the international economics because for most of the past century, exchange rates have been fixed by government action rather than determined in the market place.

(f) *International policy coordination*: World economy consists of sovereign nations, each free to choose its own economic policies. But in an integrated world economy one country's economic policies affect other countries as well. Differences in goals between countries often lead to conflicts of interest. Even when countries have similar goals, they may suffer losses if they fail to coordinate their policies. A fundamental problem in international economics is how to produce an acceptable degree of harmony among the international trade and monetary policies of different countries. While coordination of international trade policies is a well-established tradition, coordination of international macroeconomic policies is a newer and more uncertain topic. Attempts at international macroeconomic coordination are occurring with growing frequency of trade in the real world.

(g) *The international capital market*: In a sophisticated economy there is an extensive capital market—a set of arrangements by which individuals and firms exchange money now for promises to pay in the future. The growing importance of international trade has been accompanied by a growth in the international capital market, which links the capital markets of the individual countries. International capital markets differ in important ways from domestic capital markets. They must cope with special regulations that many countries impose on foreign investments. As a result of international trade, huge international capital markets have arisen, most notably the remarkable London Eurodollar market, in which billions of dollars are exchanged each day without ever touching the United States.

INTERNATIONAL ECONOMICS—A SEPARATE FIELD

"Economic agents maximize their own self-interest" is the base assumption for both the international trade theory and the domestic microeconomics. But there are important differences between domestic and foreign transactions. In the same way, international finance is closely tied to domestic macroeconomics, but political borders do matter, and international finance is far more than a modest extension of domestic macroeconomics. The differences between international and domestic economics activities that make international economics a separate body of theory are as follows:

(a) In the domestic economy labour and capital are free to move among regions, which imply the existence of the national markets for labour and capital. It may be possible that the wage rates differ modestly among regions, such differences are reduced by an arbitrage process in which workers move from low to high wage locations. There exists a small difference in the return to financial capital across regions because investors have lower costs of moving funds from one location to another. As a result, domestic microeconomic analysis generally rests on the assumption that firms competing in a market pay comparable wages and borrow funds at comparable interest rates. International trade is different in this regard. Immigration laws greatly limit the arbitraging of wage rates among nations, so that wage rates differ sharply across the world. Although capital flows among nations more easily than does labour, exchange controls, additional risks, costs of information, and other factors are sufficient to maintain significant differences among interest rates in different countries. Hence, international trade theory centers on competition in markets where firms face very different costs.

(b) The movement of goods within a country is free from government-imposed barriers. Therefore, firms in one region compete against firms in another region of the country without government protection in the form of tariff or quotas. Domestic microeconomics deals with such free trade within a country. On the other hand, tariffs, quotas, and other government-imposed barriers to trade are important factors in international trade.

(c) Domestic macroeconomics normally deals with monetary and fiscal policy choices that address cyclical economic fluctuations that affect the country as a whole. With one currency used throughout the country, establishing a different monetary policy or interest rate for different regions is not possible. While there are differences across regions in the way central government spending is allocated and in the location of interest-sensitive industries, essentially fiscal and monetary policies that exist in one part of the country also prevail in other parts. On the other hand, international finance, or open economy macroeconomics, is about a very different situation. Different countries have different business cycles; the significance of strikes, droughts, or shifts in business confidence, for example, regularly differs across countries. This is because some countries may be in a recession while others enjoy periods of economic expansion; they generally choose different monetary and fiscal policies to address these circumstances. These differences in macroeconomic conditions and policies among countries have major consequences for trade flows and other international transactions.

(d) Since a country has a single currency, the supply of which is managed by the central bank operating through a commercial banking system, there are no internal exchange markets or exchange rates within a country. On the other hand, international finance involves a very different set of circumstances. There are almost as many currencies as there are countries, and the maintenance of a currency is typically viewed as a basic part of national sovereignty. International finance is concerned with exchange rates and exchange markets, and the influence of government intervention in those markets.

(e) While most of international economics represents the application of general microeconomic and macroeconomic principles to the international context, many theoretical advances were made in the field of international economics itself and only subsequently found their way into the body of general economic theory. One example is the so-called "theory of the second best". Production and general equilibrium theory, welfare economics and growth theory, and many other theories have also benefited from work in the international sphere. These contributions attest to the vitality and importance of international economics as a special branch of economics.

TRADE AND MONEY IN INTERNATIONAL ECONOMICS

We can divide the economics of the international economy into two broad sub-fields of the study—(a) international trade and (b) international money. International trade analysis focuses primarily on the real transactions in the international economy, i.e. on those transactions that involve a physical movement of goods or a tangible commitment of economic resources, whereas international monetary analysis focuses on the monetary side of the international economy, i.e. on financial transactions such as foreign purchases of Indian rupees. An example of an international trade issue is the conflict between the developed countries and India over India's subsidized exports of agricultural products; an example of an international monetary issue is the dispute over whether the foreign-exchange value of the rupees should be allowed to float freely or be stabilized by government action. But in the material world there is no simple dividing line between trade and monetary issues. Most international trade involves monetary transactions, while, many monetary events have important consequences for trade.

THE ROLE OF TRADE

It is the nature of human to cooperate in the use of their scarce resources for their own gain as well as for the benefit of the society. We can see such behaviour of the people even in the most primitive societies. The reason for such behaviour is that through such cooperation more goods are produced. The high degree of specialization that exists in our society reflects the fact that specialization increases the standard of living by making more goods and services available for consumption.

The extensive degree of specialization that exists in the societies is the cause of trade. In other word, specialization necessarily implies trade and cannot occur without it. Specialized producers use only a small part or may be none of their output for their personal consumption and exchange the surplus for the goods and services of other specialized producers. For example, a cloth maker does not, and cannot, consume only cloths; he needs, in addition, many other goods and services, such as food, shelter, entertainment, and transportation. To obtain these other goods and services, he exchanges his surplus production of cloths for the specialized outputs of farmers, auto producers, physicians, builders and the like. Such an exchange of goods and services among specialized producers is exactly what is meant by trade. The exchange of goods and services among residents of the same country is called domestic trade; and the exchange of goods and services among residents of different countries is called international trade.

In the present scenario countries cannot live isolated any more effectively than individuals can. Each country tends to specialize in the production of those commodities it can produce more cheaply than other countries, and then exchanges its surplus for the surpluses of other countries. This process brings about an international division of labour that makes it possible for all nations to consume more of all goods and services than in the absence of such specialization. A country's imports can be divided into two categories:

(a) those goods that other countries produce more cheaply than the importing country and

(b) those goods that the importing country cannot produce at all.

In the same way, the division of labour within a single closed economy increases the standard of living of all its residents, the international division of labour (specialization among nations) increases the standard of living of all countries. And just as specialization within a single closed economy necessarily implies the existence of domestic trade and cannot occur without it, international specialization necessarily implies the existence of international trade and cannot occur without it either.

Knowing the benefits of the existence and importance of the gains from trade, nations often move to liberalize international trade. There are basically two approaches to international trade liberalization—(a) the international approach and (b) the regional approach. The former involves international effort under the GATT, such as the Kennedy Round and the Tokyo Round of multilateral trade negotiations, whose purpose is to reduce tariffs and nontariffs barriers to international trade. The regional approach involves agreements among small numbers of nations whose purpose is to promote free trade among themselves while maintaining barriers to trade with the rest of the world.

THE ROLE OF INTERNATIONAL MONEY

The "great wheel", the name given to the international monetary system by Adam Smith, when turns effortlessly, international specialization produces a maximum flow of goods and services that go to satisfy human wants in every corner of the globe. In the opposite case, the international flow of goods and services is interrupted, with serious consequences to the economic welfare of nations.

The short-run significance of the money is unquestionable while in the long run money is treated as a veil. Indeed, economies, including the world economy, live only in the short run. In real world, long run is treated as an ideal that is almost never attained. International finance deals with the foreign exchange market and the balance of payments and it studies the short-run adjustment processes and the difficulties that the world economy faces in attaining international equilibrium. In addition, international finance is concerned with the economic policies that may be necessary for the achievement of international equilibrium when the automatic processes are too slow or are not working properly. The main function of the international monetary system is to enable the fundamental economic processes of production and distribution to operate as smoothly and efficiently as possible, to maximize the gains from trade by permitting the fullest use of efficient division of labour among the nations of the world.

When the short-run processes do not work smoothly, those countries suffering from serious balance-of-payments problems often attempt to solve their problems by imposing trade restrictions. But such restrictions on international trade create hindrance in the beneficial division of labour among countries and deny the world the fruits of international specialization and exchange.

BASIC GLOBAL MACRO MODEL

In this section we shall consider a simple one-country basic macroeconomic model in order to understand the nature and significance of the interdependent world economy. Here we shall consider an economy measured in current prices so that every element expresses a money flow per unit of time such that:

$$Y \equiv G + \Delta S + C + X - M \tag{1}$$

where

Y = National income

G = Government expenditure

ΔS = Change in the value of stocks

C = Private expenditure on both consumption and fixed investment

X = Exports

M = Imports

The national income identity can be expressed as a flow of funds identity by subtracting the tax yield from both sides and rearranging we get

$$G - T \equiv (Y - T - \Delta S - C) + (M - X) \tag{2}$$

Equation (2) shows that in each period of time the *ex post* public sector deficit is equal to the total of the private sector's net acquisition of financial assets plus (minus) the deficit (surplus) on the current account.

The tax yield (T) and the level of stocks (S) are functions of Y such that:

$$T = tY \tag{3}$$

and

$$S = \beta Y \tag{4}$$

where β is probably a function of interest rates. Imports are related to Y such that

$$M = mY \tag{5}$$

where m is a variable. Because the various elements are expressed in current prices, the magnitude of m will depend not only on Y but also on the price of imports relative to the prices of domestic production as well as other systematic factors and time trends. Now let us assumes the existence of equilibrium between the desired stock of financial wealth (w^*)and disposable Y such that

$$w^* = \alpha(1-t)Y \tag{6}$$

where α is partly dependent on interest rates as well as an adjustment processes given by

$$w - w_{-1} = \phi(w^* - w_{-1}) \tag{7}$$

From the above equations we can derive the steady state solution to the model:

$$Y = (G+X)/(T+M) \tag{8}$$

Equation (8) expresses a process relating income determination exclusively to fiscal stance measured by G/t and to trade performance measured by X/m.

Assuming that borrowing from abroad must normally approximate to zero, the model suggests that fiscal policy must be conducted in such a way as to guarantee that the current account also approximates to zero. Incorporating $X = M = mY$ in equation (8), it follows that a necessary and sufficient condition for achieving a zero balance of payments is that fiscal stance, measured by the term G/t, must equal trade performance, measured by X/m, since

$$Y = G/t = X/m. \tag{9}$$

This equation suggests what role has to be played by fiscal policy in order to ensure that the balance of payments is equal to zero. It also indicates that if fiscal policy is operated subject to a balance of payments constraint, Y will be uniquely determined by trade performance.

If two countries are considered, one country's imports form the other's exports, it follows that, if the current account must remain balanced, $Y_1 = \dfrac{m_2 Y_2}{m_1}$ and $Y_2 = \dfrac{m_2 Y_1}{m_2}$. This tells us that the two countries are interdependent; and nature and significance of this interdependence is determined by international trade.

THE ANALYSIS OF DEMAND IN INTERNATIONAL TRADE

In this section we shall take into account the methods by which one can depict a community's consumption preferences; its planned demand per period of time for the set of goods and services it is offered at various prices, given a certain set of market circumstances.

We have four basic microeconomic theoretical concepts which can be used to analyze a single consumer's planned consumption behaviour. They are:

(a) Marshallian demand analysis;
(b) Indifference curve analysis;
(c) Revealed preference analysis; and
(d) Commodities as attributes analysis.

When we apply above mentioned approaches for the whole community, they create some difficulties as opposed to a single consumer. However, the indifference curve and revealed preference analysis are widely used in the theory of international trade.

Indifference Curve Analysis for the Whole Community

As we have studied in microeconomic analysis, the consumption preference of a single consumer can be represented by a set of indifference curves having following properties.

(a) They slope downwards from left to right;
(b) They are convex from below indicating a diminishing marginal rate of substitution in consumption;
(c) They do not intersect; and
(d) The further to the north-east a curve lies on the indifference map, the greater is the consumer's satisfaction.

In this section we turn to find out the consumption preferences for the community as a whole and try to construct a community indifference map.

Let us consider a community of two consumers—*X* and *Y*. As in microeconomic analysis we can determine the optimization decision of both the consumers with only difference being that *Y's* indifference map will not be the same as *X's* unless they have precisely the same tastes. In an ideal market situation, *X* and *Y* are faced with the same relative prices, i.e. it is assumed that sellers will not practice price discrimination between them. Hence optimization is achieved for both X and Y, where FC and F^*C^* are parallel as shown in the Fig. 3.1.

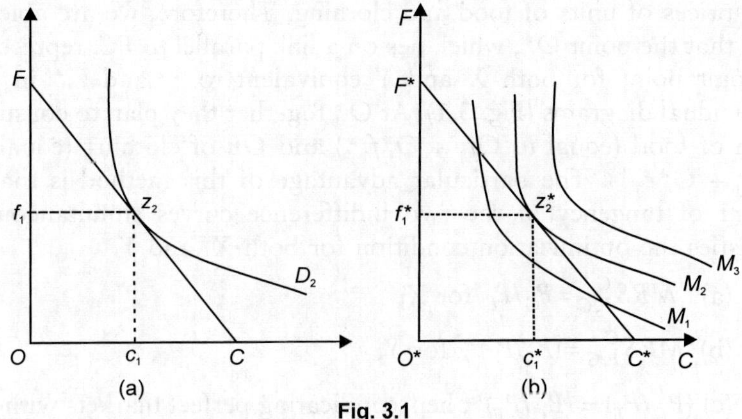

Fig. 3.1

The diagram (a) is for X and diagram (b) is for Y.

For simplicity, the above diagram is drawn on the assumption that the indifference curves for X and Y are independent of each other. Here we have considered that X has more to spend and that is why $OF > O^*F^*$ and $OC > O^*C^*$.

Now the question arises, can a single indifference curve for both X and Y be constructed? Given their total expenditure, the prices of a unit of food and clothing and their consumption preferences, it can be observed that X will choose Of_1 of food plus Oc_1 of clothing and Y will choose $O^* f_1^*$ plus $O^*c_1^*$. Hence the two together will choose $Of_1 + O^* f_1^*$ of food in addition to $Oc_1 + O^*c_1^*$ of clothing. This can be shown in Fig. 3.2 which can be drawn by combining the two section of Fig. 3.1.

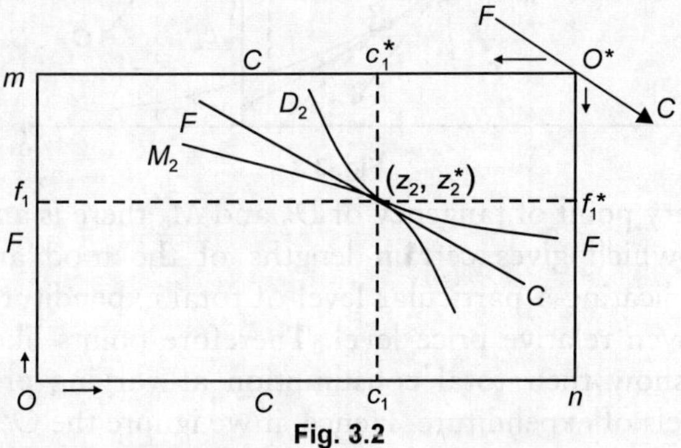

Fig. 3.2

The point O^* in relation to O shows the total of the two commodities that X and Y will choose, given their expenditures and the prices of units of food and clothing. Therefore, we are able to say that the point O^*, which lies on a line parallel to FC, represents a joint point for both X and Y equivalent to z_2 and z_2^* in the individual diagrams (Fig. 3.1). At O^* together they plan to consume Om of food (equal to $Of_1 + O^*f_1^*$) and On of clothing (equal to $Oc_1 + O^*c_1^*$). The particular advantage of this method is that a point of tangency of the two indifference curves simultaneously satisfies the optimization condition for both X and Y.

(a) $MRS^C_{F,C} = P_C/P_F$ for X;

(b) $MRS^C_{F,C} = (P_C/P_F)^*$ for Y;

(c) $(P_C/P_F) = (P_C/P_F)^*$, hence indicating perfect markets without price discrimination.

Now keeping X's axes as they are and moving the origin of $Y's$ axes around but in such a manner that the two indifference curves (D_2 and M_2) always remain at a tangent to each other as shown in Fig. 3.3.

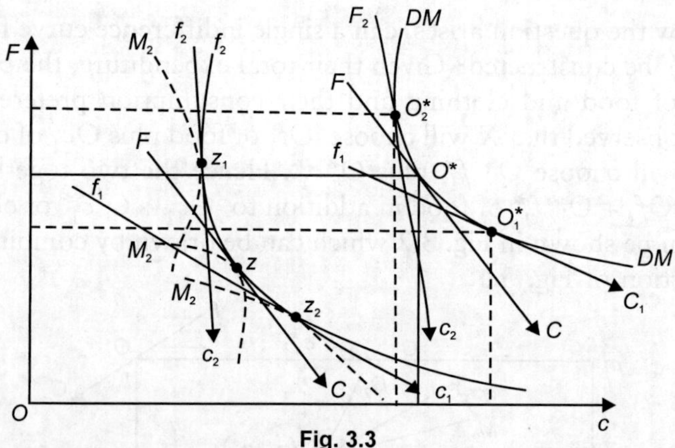

Fig. 3.3

For every point of tangency of D_2 and M_2 there is an equivalent O^* point which gives certain lengths of the food and clothing distance indicating a particular level of total expenditure by X and Y and a given relative price level. Therefore points like O^*, O_1^*, O_2^*, etc. show their total consumption at varying prices and at varying levels of expenditure. Hence, if we ignore the O^* origin, the smooth locus connecting all such points is an indifference curve for both *X* and *Y*. This process can be repeated at higher or lower levels of indifference for both *X* and *Y* by taking *X*'s D_3 and *Y*'s M_3 and then repeating the process or by taking *X*'s D_1 and *Y*'s M_1 and repeating the processes. Thus it can be seen that an indifference map for both *X* and *Y*, with similar characteristics to that of the individual consumer, can in fact be constructed as shown in Fig. 3.4.

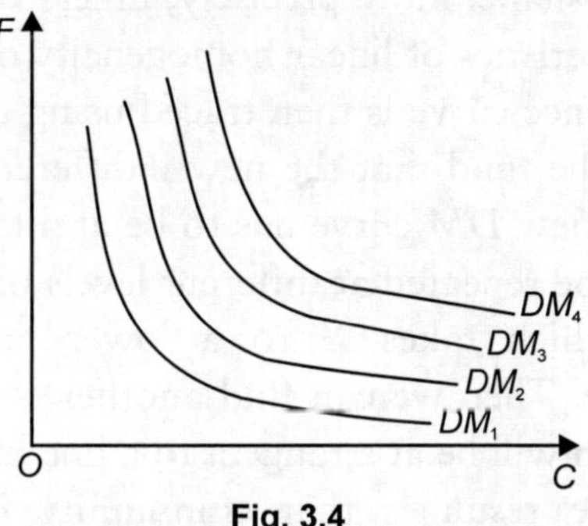

Fig. 3.4

Thus, by repeating the above procedure we can find out the indifference curves for the whole community.

However, there is one problem in finding out the community indifference curve. Consider the Fig. 3.3 where the initial point for *X* and *Y* was *z*, and assume, for the given food and clothing distances indicated by *O**, a different distribution of the total of food and clothing between *X* and *Y*. The initial situation can be given by point *z* in Fig. 3.5.

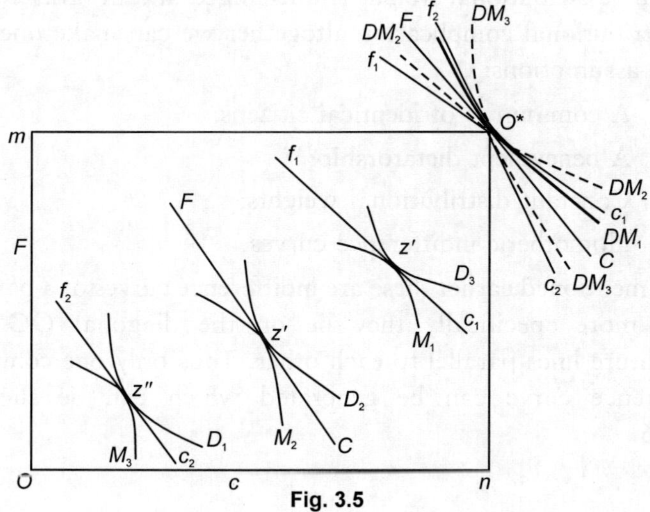

Fig. 3.5

At z', X is on a higher while Y is on a lower indifference curve but the total amount of food and clothing is exactly the same as initially. Hence, O^* is the same distance from O as before but it now lies on a different slope since the slope of the common tangent at z' will not be the same as that at z unless the indifference curves have a particular shape, more precisely, unless they are homothetic or exhibit characteristics of linear homogeneity of degree one. If the common indifference curve is then traced using the same procedure as before, it will be fund that the new indifference curve intersects the old one—the new *DM* curve has to be at a tangent to f_1c_1. This process can then be repeated at different levels of distribution. Now take point z'' which takes X to a lower and Y to a higher indifference curve. Then we can find another common indifference curve at O^* which will be at a tangent to a line parallel to f_2c_1 going through O^*. The result is that community indifference curves (CICs) will intersect when distribution changes are introduced, making them different from individual consumers' curves which can never intersect.

Here one problem is raised due to intersection is that comparisons become difficult; it is no longer possible to categorically states that one situation is better or worse than another if the distributional weights in the two situations are different. This criticism is not valid when the distributional weight is unchanged and in order to avoid the distributional complication altogether we can make one of the several assumptions:

(a) A community of identical citizens;

(b) A benevolent dictatorship;

(c) Constant distributional weights;

(d) Homothetic indifference curves.

As mentioned earlier these are indifference curves of a particular shape; more specifically they lie on the diagonal OO^* with expenditure lines parallel to each other. Thus only one community indifference curve can be generated which can be shown in Fig. 3.6.

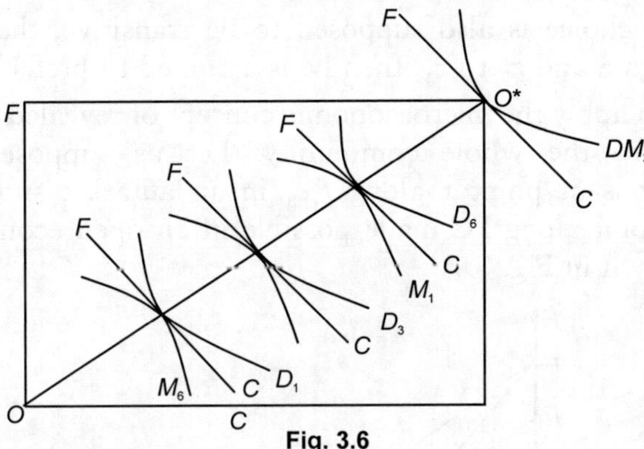

Fig. 3.6

Thus through the above mentioned assumption we can rule out intersection. The assumption actually adopted will depend on the use to be made of the CICs. Here one point should be noted that whichever assumption is chosen certain comparison will be ruled out but the whole concept of community indifference can not be rendered irrelevant.

REVEALED PREFERENCE APPROACH

To explain the behaviour of the consumer both the Marshallian theory and the indifference curve theory depend on introspective method. They derive laws about consumer's demand on the basis of how the consumer reacts psychologically to certain hypothetical changes in price and income. That is, they provide only psychological explanations of consumer's demand. An alternative theory of consumer's behaviour developed by the Paul A. Samuelson is known as revealed preference approach. This theory is not based on introspective method and psychological explanation. It seeks to enunciate things on the basis of observed market behaviourism of the consumer and it comprises of a presumption that choice reveals preference. It is also known as the behaviourstic approach because it is based on the analysis of the actual behaviour of the consumer.

Let us briefly state the basic characteristics of this hypothesis. The consumer, X, is assumed to be rational in the sense that he prefers more to less, since commodities are good. His actual choice is assumed to be consistent, that is, if in a particular situation he is observed to choose a certain combination of food and clothing, he would opt for same combination when faced with the same choice again. His choice is also supposed to be transitive, that is, if he prefers z_1 to z and z_2 to z_1, then he is assumed to prefer z_2 to z.

We can apply the microeconomic concept of revealed preference approach to the whole community. Let us suppose that the community is at point z along f_1c_1 in an autarkic situation and selects a point along FC made possible in an open economy. This can be shown in Fig. 3.7.

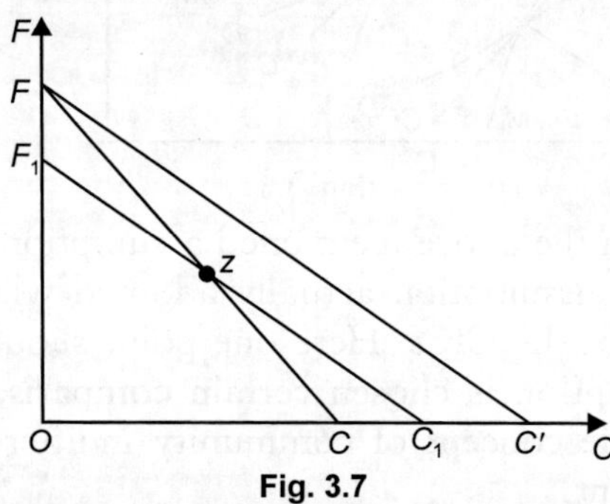

Fig. 3.7

Since *FC* includes combinations which offer the community more of both food and clothing, this implies that community must be better off. However, we cannot infer from this that every single individual is better off since the distribution of food and clothing in the open economy may be different from that in autarky; not every individual will necessarily get more of both commodities. In such circumstances the hypothesis postulates that the open economy situation is potentially better since those who gain overall can theoretically compensate those who lose and still be better off. But we can not apply this argument to a situation in which *FC* is compared with relative prices which cut this line below z. Here one point should be mentioned that no ranking is possible.

THE ANALYSIS OF SUPPLY IN INTERNATIONAL TRADE

In determining the planned supply of a commodity it is important to consider the inputs that go into its production, their quantities and prices, the available technology for combining them, etc. the relationship between factor inputs and the quantity of output can be represented by a production function (PF). This can be illustrated in Fig. 3.8.

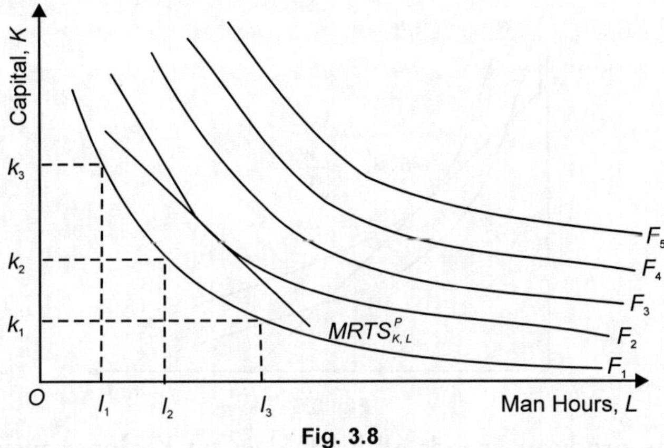

Fig. 3.8

In Fig. 3.8, on the vertical axis we measure the quantity of capital and on the horizontal the quantity of labour. The origin O is that for food. Then a *PF* for food can be represented by a set of isoquants, F_1, F_2, F_3, etc. An isoquant represents a given level of output of the product under consideration and this quantity can be produced by various combinations of capital (*K*) and labour (*L*). The slope of the isoquant gives, for infinitesimal changes, the marginal rate of technical substitution in production $MRTS^P_{K,L}$, between *K* and *L*. The isoquants are convex from the origin indicating a diminishing $MRTS^P_{K,L}$, i.e. as more *K*(*L*) is substituted for *L* (*K*), it becomes increasingly difficult to carry out further substitutions. Isoquants further away from the origin indicates a higher level of output compared with ones nearer to the origin. Thus it is the complete map of isoquants which depicts the PF for a particular commodity.

Let us assume that the hiring price of a unit of *K* can be expressed as π and the hiring price of a unit of *L* as *W*. Producers are assumed to aim for the most efficient input combination, in other words they are profit maximisers or cost minimisers. Now let us consider the Fig. 3.9.

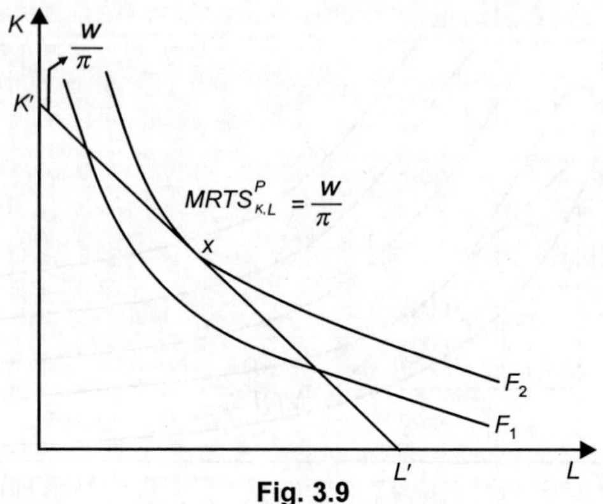

Fig. 3.9

If the producer spends all his budget on K alone, given π, the maximum he can hire is K'. Conversely, if he spends it all on L, given w, the maximum will be L'. Hence the slope of $K'L'$ measures the relative input prices (w/π). Thus the optimal choice is determined by following equality.

$$MRTS^{P}_{K,L} = \frac{w}{\pi}$$

It is possible to trace the paths generated by relative changes in the factor prices as well as the path generated by changing the size of the budget. If w falls, with π remaining constant, the budget line pivots at K' in an anti-clockwise direction; if w increases, the budget line pivots in the opposite dirction (Fig. 3.10a). Similarly, the budget line pivots at L' when π is changed with w being held constant (Fig. 3.10b). We can ten trace all possible optimal points for a given budget and a fall in w with π held constant. In short we can produce higher levels of output for a given budget when the price of one factor falls with the other remaining constant. The resulting locus is called the price expansion path (PEP); similarly for a fall in π with w held constant, the PEP is PEP′. We can also hold w and π constant and trace the path generated by the optimal input combination as the size of the budget itself is altered; this called the budget expansion path, BEP (Fig. 3.10c).

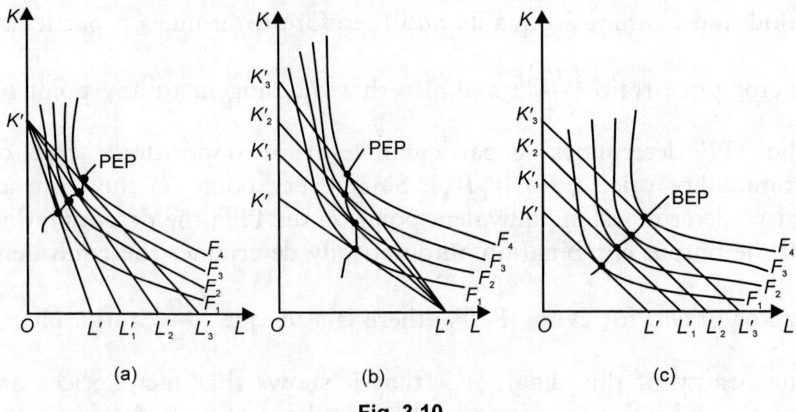

Fig. 3.10

The most convenient way of expressing how much of certain commodities a community is capable of producing given its total endowment of L and K and the use of the most efficient technological knowledge is by means of an Edgeworth-Bowley box diagram as shown in Fig. 3.11.

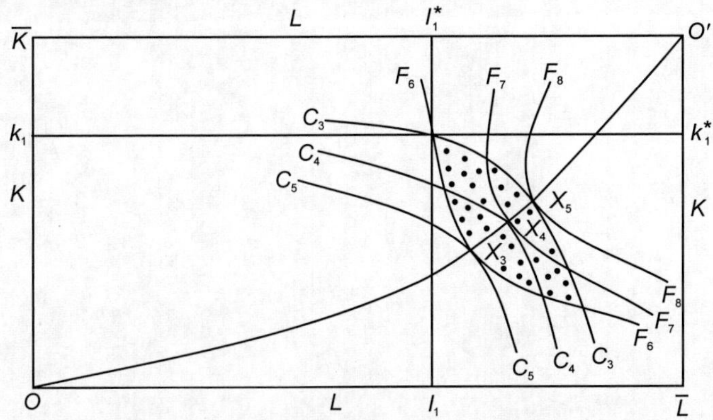

Fig. 3.11

The advantage of the box is that it defines the total endowment of K and L—the total amount of capital available is $O\overline{K}$ and of labour $O\overline{L}$.

We know from the microeconomic theory that production possibility function (PPF) is concave from the origin. Every point on the PPF is equivalent to a point on the contract curve; that every point on the contract curve is a point of common tangency of the food and clothing isoquants and therefore determines a particular factor price ratio $\left(\frac{w}{\pi}\right)$; and also that the tangent to any point on the PPF determines a particular level of opportunity cost or commodity price ratio (P_C/P_F). Since every point on the contract curve determines an equivalent point on the PPF, the determination of the output combination automatically determines the equivalent factor prices; for every (P_C/P_F) there is a unique $\left(\frac{w}{\pi}\right)$ ratio. Hence the beauty of this diagram is that it shows that facto prices are jointly and uniquely determined by the level of output. This is the simple and convenient way by which we can represent the total supply of commodities for a community as a whole.

4 Doctrine of Comparative Costs

BRIEF HISTORICAL DEVELOPMENT

In the eighteenth century, the case for free trade was based on the absolute differences in costs. It was maintained that it is in the interest of each country to import those goods in exchange for domestic goods, which either it cannot produce at home or can produce at a cost absolutely higher than that at which these can be produced abroad. According to this doctrine, under free trade, each good will be produced in the country in which its cost of production is the lowest. The doctrine of free trade advocated by Adam Smith does not go beyond this. A clue to the doctrine of comparative differences in costs can be found in the writings of certain authors even prior to Adam Smith; none of these authors, of course, states the doctrine clearly and explicitly. Statements of the doctrine before Adam Smith are more implicit than explicit. Ricardo, who is generally considered to be the first propounder of the doctrine, states the principle clearly and explicitly in his *Principles* first published in 1817. Torrens states the doctrine before Ricardo in 1815 in his *Essays on the External Corn Trade.*

> If England should have acquired such a degree of skill in manufactures, that with any given portion of her capital, she could prepare a quantity of cloth, for which the Polish cultivator would give a greater quantity of corn than she could, with the same portion of capital, raise from her own soil, then tracts of her territory, though they should be equal, nay, though they should be superior, to the lands in Poland, will be neglected; and a part of her supply of corn will be imported from the country. For, though the capital employed in cultivating at home might bring an excess of profit over the capital employed in cultivating abroad, yet, the supposition, the capital which should be employed in

manufacturing would obtain a still greater excess of profit and this greater excess of profit-would determine the direction of our industry.[1]

E. Lesser[2] and E.R.A. Seligman[3] give credit to Torrens for first propounding the doctrine. Holland refutes Seligman's attribution of credit to Torrens on the ground that Torrens does not realise the full significance of the doctrine and never applies it. The credit, generally, goes to Ricardo, mainly because it is from Ricardo and not from Torrens that later economists learnt the doctrine. In addition, Ricardo is more explicit and clear about the doctrine than Torrens.

STATEMENT OF THE DOCTRINE

The doctrine of comparative costs maintains that under free trade each country specialises in the production and export of goods in whose production it possesses a comparative advantage in terms of real costs and imports goods in exchange in whose production it has a comparative disadvantage in terms of real costs; this maximises world production from a given volume of world productive resources and benefits all the countries participating in international trade.

The classical economists express the costs in terms of labour units. They maintain that the goods are exchanged in the ratio of the labour embodied in these. Goods having equal prices contain equal amount of labour. This is true, broadly speaking, under the following assumptions:

(a) Labour is the only factor of production.

(b) All labour is uniform in quality and irksomeness.

(c) Labour is perfectly mobile.

(d) There exists free competition among labourers.

None of the above assumptions, however, is fulfilled in the actual world. There exist factors other than the labour. Of particular importance, in this connection, is the stored up labour in the form of capital goods. Labour differs widely in quality. Labour lacks mobility owing to a number of reasons. There does not exist free competition among labourers. There exist several non-competing groups of labour.

To explain the differencess in costs between different countries, the classical economists assume that the labour is completely mobile within the country and completely immobile between countries. If the labour is completely mobile within a country, different commodities will exchange in the ratio of labour embodied in these. Any divergence between the two will be eliminated automatically by the operation of demand and supply forces. Suppose, for instance, that one unit of labour can produce in India 4 apples or 12 mangoes and the ratio of exchange between apples and mangoes is 1:2. Under this ratio of exchange, more and more labour will be shifted from the production of apples towards that of mangoes because 6 apples can be obtained in exchange for the mangoes produced by a unit of labour whereas it can produce only 4 apples if employed for the production of apples. As more and more labour is shifted from the production of apples towards that of mangoes, the supply of mangoes increases and that of apples decreases. An increase in the supply of mangoes and a decrease in that of apples will raise the ratio of exchange of apples to mangoes. The shifting of labour from the production of apples towards that of mangoes will stop when the exchange ratio of apples to mangoes reaches 1:3.

The mechanism described above cannot work between two countries because of the assumption that labour is immobile between different countries. Thus, if in two countries, the ratio of exchange between two commodities is different from the ratio of labour embodied in these, there will arise profitable scope for international trade.

The differences in the costs of different countries might be absolute, comparative or equal. It is the first two kinds of differences which give rise to international trade. Let us illustrate the three kinds of differences in costs with the help of a numerical example in case of two commodities and two countries.

In the first case, country *A* has got an absolute advantage in the production of commodity *X* and country *B* in that of commodity *Y*. Both countries taken together will gain if *A* specialises in the production of *X* and imports *Y* in exchange for *X*, and *B* specialises in the production of *Y* and gets *X* in exchange for *Y*.

Case I *Absolute difference in costs*			*Case II* *Comparative difference in costs*			*Case III* *Equal difference in costs*		
Costs of production in labour units of a unit of commodity			*Costs of production in labour units of a unit of commodity*			*Costs of production in labour units of a unit of commodity*		
Country	X	Y	*Country*	X	Y	*Country*	X	Y
A	4	8	A	8	4	A	8	4
B	8	4	B	4	3	B	4	2

In the second case, country *B* can produce both the commodities at a cost lower than that of country *A* but possesses comparatively greater cost advantage in the production of *X*. Country *A* has a disadvantage in the production of both the commodities; but the disadvantage is comparatively less in the production of *Y*. Thus both countries taken together will gain if *A* specialises in the production of *X* and *B* in that of *Y*.

In the third case, *B* can produce both the commodities cheaply as compared with *A*. There will, however, arise no trade because the ratio of costs of the two commodities is the same in both the countries. Specialisation in this case will not benefit any of the two countries.

So far the presentation of the doctrine has been based on the following assumptions:

(a) There exists no money.

(b) There are only two commodities and two countries.

(c) There exist no costs of transfer.

(d) Production is subject to the law of constant returns in both the countries.

(e) Prices of different goods are determined by their real costs of production.

(f) There exists full employment of all the factors of production.

(g) There exists free competition.

Let us, now, drop the above-mentioned assumptions one by one and introduce complications in the simplest form of the theory presented above.

Introduction of Money

To begin with, we remove the first assumption that there exists no money and all trade is barter. In the actual world, goods are exchanged not for goods but for money. Importers and exporters think in terms of the prices of traded goods and not in terms of their value (i.e., ratio of exchange between different goods). When we talk in terms of money, it is the absolute differences and not the comparative differences which explain international trade. The transformation of comparative differences in labour costs into the absolute differences in money costs, however, is not very difficult. Let us illustrate the process by transforming the comparative differences in labour costs (case No. II in the earlier mentioned illustration) into the absolute differences in money costs.

	Cost of production in labour units of one unit of commodity		*Wages in Rs. per labour unit*	*Cost (or price) in Rs. per unit of commodity*	
Country	X	Y		X	Y
A	8	4	1	8	4
B	4	3	1.8	7.2	5.4

In the above table, the absolute price of commodity *Y* is lower in country *A* and that of commodity *X* in country *B*. Country *A* will, therefore, specialise in the production of *Y* and import *X* from *B* in exchange for *Y*. Country *B* will specialise in the production of *X* and import *Y* from *A* in exchange for *X*. The conclusion is the same as reached above in case of comparative differences in labour costs in case No. II of our previous illustration. In calculating the price of each commodity in the two countries, the money wage rates have been selected arbitrarily. This, however, does not affect the conclusion so long as the selected money wage rates remain between the upper and lower limits determined by the relative labour costs of production of the two commodities in the two countries. If the wage rate is Re. 1 in country *A,* the wage rate in country *B* cannot exceed Rs. 2 because the ratio of the costs of production of commodity *X* in labour units between *A* and *B* is 2:1. In case the wage rate in *B* rises above Rs. 2, the cost of production in terms of money and hence price of *X* will become higher in *B* than in *A*. Country *B* will start importing *X* instead of exporting it.

It will also continue importing *Y*. That is, it will import both the commodities and export none. This will make *B's* balance of payments unfavourable. In case both the countries are on full gold standard, gold will flow out of *B* into *A*. Prices and wages will start falling in *B* and rising in *A*. This process will continue till the ratio of money wages between *A* and *B* reaches 2:1. Similarly, it can be demonstrated that the wage rate in *B* cannot fall below Rs. 1.33 because the ratio of the costs of production of *Y* in labour units between *A* and *B* is 4:3.

The above analysis leads to the conclusion that the general level of wages will be higher in the country enjoying comparatively favourable conditions of production. Several advanced countries are levying tariffs on the import of manufactured goods from underdeveloped countries on the ground that these are the products of the sweated labour and are a great threat to the high standard of living of their labour. The fact is that the high standard of living in the advanced countries is the result of their favourable conditions of production and this in no way precludes beneficial trade with the underdeveloped countries. If the comparative cost advantage for some commodities in advanced countries arises from their superior techniques and larger stock of capital, the comparative cost advantage in less developed countries for other commodities arises from their cheap labour. If the underdeveloped countries act in the same way and argue that the cheap products from advanced countries produced with the help of a larger stock of capital and superior techniques are a threat to their standard of living, all trade will come to a cessation and both the advanced and less developed countries will lose and none will gain. Such tariffs of developed countries, therefore, are not justified.

The doctrine of comparative costs, even with its assumptions of no transport costs and constant costs of production, does not imply that each country specialises completely in the production of a single commodity in which it possesses a comparative cost advantage. One country might specialise completely before it can meet the demand of both the countries for the commodity in whose production it possesses a comparative advantage. Under such circumstances, the other country will produce a part of his commodity domestically along with the commodity in whose production it possesses a comparative advantage. This case is, particularly likely when one of the trading partners is small and the other very large, or when the commodity produced by one is very important and that produced by the other is less important in both the countries.

Introduction of More Than Two Commodities

So far we have been assuming that there are only two tradable goods. In actual practice, there is a whole range of export goods and import goods. When our earlier mentioned countries *A* and *B* exchange several goods, country *A* will enjoy a comparative advantage over country *B* in all its export goods and have a comparative disadvantage in all its import goods. Similar will be the case with country *B*. Let us suppose that the two countries trade in *l* to *z* goods in all. These are arranged below in the order of the comparative advantage of *B* over *A*:

$$\frac{l_a}{l_b} < \frac{m_a}{m_b} < \frac{n_a}{n_b} < \frac{o_a}{o_b} < \frac{p_a}{p_b} < \frac{q_a}{q_b} \ldots < \frac{z_a}{z_b}$$

l_a, m_a, n_a, o_a, p_a, q_a, ..., z_a denote the number of units of the commodities *l*, *m*, *n*, *o*, *p*, *q*, ..., *z* which can be produced with one unit of labour in *A*. Similarly, l_b, m_b, n_b, o_b, p_b, q_b, ..., z_b denote the number of units of the commodities *l*, *m*, *n*, *o*, *p*, *q*, ..., *z*, which can be produced with one unit of labour in *B*. Under free trade, *A* will specialise in the production of commodities on the right side and *B* in those on the left side of the above series; it is not possible that country *B* exports *l* and *n*, and imports *m*. The line dividing the exports and imports of each of the two countries cannot be drawn only with the data relating to comparative costs. The exact dividing line will be fixed at a point at which the balance of payments is in equilibrium. The point at which the balance of payments is in equilibrium will be determined by the reciprocal demand of the two countries for each other's products. Any deviation from this point will have a tendency to correct itself automatically. For illustration, suppose that the balance of payments of the two countries is in equilibrium if country *B* exports to country *A* commodities *l* to *p* and imports from *A* commodities *q* to *z*. If, suddenly, *B* starts importing commodity *p* (and stops its export) in addition to the previously imported commodities, its balance of payments *vis-à-vis* *A* will become unfavourable. If both the countries are on full gold standard, gold will flow from *B* to *A*. Prices and wages will rise in *A* and fall in *B*. This will encourage exports from and discourage imports into country *B*. Quite the reverse will happen in *A*. The equilibrium in the balance of payments will be restored when *B* stops importing and starts exporting *p*, and *A* does the reverse.

Introduction of More Than Two Countries

The doctrine can similarly be extended to more than two countries. Each country will export goods the costs of which are comparatively lower at home and import goods the costs of which are comparatively lower abroad. But the specific commodities which each country will export and import cannot be determined only from the data relating to the comparative costs of production in the country. Additional information about the reciprocal demand of the countries for the products of each other is required to determine the specific imports and exports of each country. Let us illustrate this with the help of a hypothetical numerical example:

Commodity	*Cost of production of one unit of commodity in labour units in*		
	India	*Pakistan*	*Myanmar*
Cloth	1	1	1
Wheat	2	3	4

In the above example, India possesses a comparative cost advantage in the production of wheat over both Pakistan and Myanmar. Myanmar has got a comparative advantage in the production of cloth over India and Pakistan. India, therefore, will specialise in the production of wheat and Myanmar in that of cloth. What about Pakistan? It has a comparative advantage in the production of wheat over Myanmar and that in the production of cloth over India. It is not possible to determine the commodity in which Pakistan will specialise till the rate of exchange between cloth and wheat is known. In order to determine the rate of exchange between cloth and wheat, we are required to know the reciprocal demand schedules of all the three countries. In equilibrium, Pakistan might share with India the export of wheat to Myanmar or share with Myanmar the export of cloth to India or trade in neither commodity. If the ratio of exchange between wheat and cloth is 1: between 2 and 3, Pakistan will specialise in the production and export of cloth along with Myanmar and import wheat from India. If the ratio is 1: between 3 and 4, Pakistan will specialise in wheat along with India and import cloth from Myanmar. If the ratio is 1:3

Pakistan will trade in neither commodity because it can produce the two commodities domestically at this ratio.

Introduction of the Costs of Transfer

So far we have been assuming that no costs are involved in transferring goods from one country to another. In fact, the transfer of goods from one country to another involves the costs of transport, insurance, etc. Introduction of transfer costs into the doctrine of comparative costs, however, is not very difficult. In the absence of transfer costs, the condition for the establishment of trade is that $\frac{X_a}{X_b} < \frac{Y_a}{Y_b}$, where X_a and Y_a denote the number of units of the commodities X and Y which one unit of labour can produce in country A, and X_b and Y_b denote the number of units of the commodities X and Y which one unit of labour can produce in country B. Introduction of transfer costs requires the fulfilment of two more conditions for the establishment of trade, viz. $\frac{X_a}{X'_b} < \frac{Y_a}{Y_b}$ and $\frac{X_a}{X'_b} < \frac{Y'_a}{Y_b}$, where X'_b denotes the number of units of commodity X which can be produced and transferred to A with one unit of labour in B and Y'_b denotes the number of units of commodity Y which can be produced and exported to B with one unit of labour in A.

Speaking in terms of money costs, the commodity will be exported or imported only if the difference between the absolute money costs of production in the two countries is more than the costs of transfer. The introduction of transfer costs decreases the extent of the division of labour between the two countries because certain commodities, the difference in whose costs of production is less than the costs of their transfer, will not be traded and each country will produce these domestically. Country A might import a commodity from country B even if its cost of production is higher as compared with that of country C if the difference between the costs of transfer from B to A and from C to A is more than the difference between the costs of production of B and C.

Variable Costs of Production

The removal of the assumption of constant production costs and the introduction of variable costs does not require substantial changes in the doctrine of comparative costs. When the production is subject to variable costs, the only modification that is needed is the use of the expression 'difference in comparative marginal costs' instead of the expression 'difference in comparative costs'. Under constant costs of production, the marginal cost is equal to the average cost and thus both the expressions become identical. The operation of the law of increasing costs decreases the scope for the division of labour between the trading countries. Suppose, for illustration, that country *A* has a comparative advantage in the production of wheat and *B* in that of cloth. With the opening of trade between the two countries, *A* starts specialising in the production of wheat and *B* in that of cloth. As *A* specialises more and more in the production of wheat and decreases the production of cloth, its cost of producing wheat goes on increasing and that of cloth goes on decreasing. On the other hand, as *B* specialises in the production of cloth and decreases the production of wheat, its cost of producing wheat goes on falling and that of cloth goes on increasing. As the process of specialisation proceeds in the two countries, the gap in their comparative costs of production goes on narrowing. Ultimately a stage might be reached at which the comparative costs become equal. At this stage, the scope for further specialisation will come to an end. Thus the specialisation will be inhibited while it would have gone further under constant costs.

In contrast, if the production is subject to the law of decreasing costs, the gap in the comparative costs, and hence the scope for trade, will go on increasing, as the specialisation proceeds. The volume of trade will be greater under decreasing costs than that under constant costs, and still greater than that under increasing costs. Under decreasing costs, scope for trade might exist even if there are no differences in the comparative marginal costs of the two countries before the establishment of trade. Once a little trade is introduced somehow or the other, it will gather momentum because the differences in comparative marginal costs go on increasing with every increase in trade.

Under constant and decreasing costs, at least, one country will specialise completely in the production of a single commodity and both may specialise completely in a single commodity if they are of almost equal size while specialisation is likely to be partial under increasing costs. It might, however, be mentioned that complete specialisation is not impossible under increasing costs. If the divergence in the comparative costs of the two countries is very wide and the costs increase very slowly with the increase in production, one or both the countries might specialise completely in the production of a single commodity before the comparative costs become equal.

It has often been contended that if a particular country possesses comparative advantage in industries subject to the law of increasing costs and a comparative disadvantage in industries subject to the law of decreasing costs, it will be disadvantageous for it to specialise in accordance with the doctrine of comparative costs. Graham illustrates the point with the help of a numerical example. Let wheat represent the industries subject to the law of increasing costs and watches those subject to the law of decreasing costs. Suppose that 40 units of wheat exchange for 40 watches in England and for 37 watches in the United States before the introduction of trade between the two countries. Thus the United States possesses a comparative advantage in the production of wheat and England in that of watches. Graham assumes for the sake of simplification that the production of both the commodities is subject to the law of constant costs in England. Further, the production of wheat is subject to the law of increasing costs and that of watches to the law of decreasing costs in the U.S. Under these conditions, it is profitable for the U.S. to shift resources from the production of watches towards that of the wheat. Let the U.S. production of watches be contracted by 37,000 units and the thus relieved resources be utilised for the production of wheat. With these additional resources, the U.S. can produce less than 40,000 units of wheat because the production of wheat is subject to the law of increasing costs. Let us suppose that it can produce 37,500 units of wheat with these additional resources. The international ratio of exchange is 40 units of wheat for 40 watches, the U.S. can obtain 37,500 watches with the additional production of wheat. With the decrease in the production of watches in the U.S. the cost of production of watches will increase because the watch industry is subject to the law of decreasing costs. Let us suppose that only 36 watches could be produced now, with the resources with which 37 watches could be produced before the first shift of resources. Shifting of resources from the production of watches towards that of wheat will continue so long as more than 36 units of wheat can be obtained in exchange for the resources of production required for the production of 36 watches. Let the U.S. production of watches be further contracted by 36,000 units and the resources relieved from the production of watches be used for the production of wheat. Let us suppose that these additional resources can produce 36,200 units of wheat. 36,200 watches can be obtained in exchange for the 36,200 units of additional wheat. The total result of specialisation is 73,700 (i.e. 37,500+36,200) watches for the resources which could produce 74,000 (i.e. 37,000+37,000) watches domestically before the establishment of trade. This means a loss of 300 watches from trade. If the above described process of specialisation continues, the loss to the U.S. from trade will go on increasing till it specialises completely in the production of wheat.

Graham reaches the above conclusion by making assumptions which do not hold in the actual world and by neglecting certain things in his analysis. He, for instance, assumes that the production of both watches and wheat is subject to the law of constant costs in England whereas the production of wheat is subject to the law of increasing costs and that of watches to the law of decreasing costs in the United States. Graham states that this assumption is made just to simplify the argument and does not affect its substance. This, of course, is not true. If we can conceive a situation in England in which the cost of production of watches falls faster than that of wheat, the international ratio of exchange might change in favour of the U.S. and thereby its loss might be converted into a gain. In fact, agriculture is not subject to the law of increasing costs and industry to that of decreasing costs at all stages of production. Law of decreasing costs might prevail in agriculture in the initial stages and the law of increasing costs will ultimately operate even in manufacturing industries. If we assume that the production of both wheat and watches is subject to the law of decreasing costs (i.e. cost of production of wheat rises and that of watches falls as resources are shifted from the production of wheat to that of watches) in England, the international ratio of exchange will move in favour of the U.S. and this might convert its loss into a gain. If the law of increasing costs starts operating in watch industry in England, after it has specialised in this industry to a certain extent, a stage might be reached where it loses its comparative advantage in this industry and further specialisation comes to an end. This stage might be reached before the United States starts losing from international trade. We can conceive several other such situations in which the United States might not lose even by specialising in industries subject to the law of increasing costs. The case examined by Graham is an exceptional one and is not very probable in the actual world.

Whole of the increase in the cost of production of wheat in the U.S. might not be owing to technological factors; a part of it might be simply pecuniary, e.g. it might be because of increase in rents as more and more land is brought under cultivation for the production of wheat. Such additional gain to domestic factors of production will have to be taken into account to arrive at the net loss arising from trade.

The conclusion reached by Graham rests on the analysis in terms of average costs. If the analysis is made in terms of marginal costs, the specialisation might stop before the U.S. starts losing. If the costs are decreasing in the watch industry because of internal economies, the situation will be incompatible with competition; the larger the size of the firm, the lower will be the cost of production; this will lead to a monopolisation of the whole industry by one firm. The relation of costs to price is different under monopoly from that under competition. In addition, the monopolist will be guided in allocating his resources by marginal and not by average costs. He will transfer no resources from the production of watches to that of wheat if he incurs a loss thereby. Even if we assume that the situation does not lead to a monopoly and the competition continues, resources will not be shifted from the production of watches to that of wheat if it involves a loss because every producer who shifts resources from watch-making to wheat-growing obtains only the marginal increment of wheat and loses the marginal output of watches, and the marginal output of watches is greater than the marginal increment of wheat.

If, however, the costs are decreasing in the watch industry because of external economies, the individual producer will not take these into account in deciding the allocation of his productive resources. The fall in the marginal cost of production of the industry if an individual produces more watches and a rise in that if he produces more wheat does not make significant difference to this individual producer. Under such circumstances, the changes in the marginal cost of industry will not regulate the production of the individual firms constituting the industry and the situation conceived in Graham's numerical example can take place.

It may be mentioned that Graham's conclusion in this case will be correct only if the external economies resulting from an increase in the size of the industry are technological and not pecuniary. If the economies are simply pecuniary, assuming that the industry employs no imported factors of production, and if it employs, their remuneration does not decrease, the fall in the cost of production of industry will be offset by a decrease in the remuneration of the local factors of production and no net national gain will accrue therefrom.

REAL COST THEORY OF VALUE

Ricardo and many of his followers state the doctrine of comparative costs in terms of labour-units and assume that the value of commodities produced within a country will be proportional to the labour-time embodied in these. This in no way implies that these economists are unaware of the existence of other factors of production. Though stating the doctrine in terms of labour units, these economists are aware of the existence of other factors of production, particularly that of capital. Different economists, of course, make different degrees of allowance for these factors, some emphasize the qualifications for these factors more and others less. To overcome this criticism, some later economists express the doctrine in terms of 'units of productive power' or similar other concepts.

The doctrine of comparative costs in terms of real costs will be valid only if it can be established that the market prices of commodities roughly correspond to their real costs of production. The concept of real costs used by the classical economists, generally, refers to the subjective costs, or 'disutilities', involved in the employment of the productive factors for the production of the commodities. Disutilities refer to the irksomeness of labour as against leisure, abstinence involved in the postponement of consumption, etc. The classical economists assume that the disutilities are proportional to the quantities of the factors of production used in the production of goods. This, however, is not true in actual practice. Firstly, the employment of different units of the same factor involves different real costs. The irksomeness involved in working for an hour differs from worker to worker. Similarly, the amount of pain involved in saving a dollar rather than spending it immediately differs from person to person. Thus the total real cost of a commodity varies according to the particular units of the factors employed in its production. Secondly, there exist some factors the utilisation of which does not involve any disutility. Utilisation of land services, for instance, involves no disutility in the form of irksomeness, abstinence, etc. Thus the land involves only opportunity cost and no real cost. There exist some factors of production which are specific, i.e. these can be used only for a particular purpose or yield so little when employed for other purposes that it is not economical to use them for these purposes. Such factors involve only real costs and no opportunity costs.

Different industries use different factors of production in different proportions. In addition, each factor of production is available in several varieties. There is no single objective measure in terms of which the real cost of the different factors can be evaluated. Evaluation will be possible only if there exists a single homogeneous factor of production.

If different wages are paid to the similar labour in different industries or different kinds of labour receiving different wages is employed in different ratios, assuming labour to be the only factor of production, the prices of commodities will be proportional to wage costs and not to labour-time costs; and the course of trade will be determined by wage costs and not by labour-time costs. Taussig has shown that if the hierarchy of labour is the same in different countries both as to rank and as to percentage differences in wages and that all industries in both the countries use labour coming from different classes of labour in the same proportion the course of trade though immediately regulated by prices or money costs will be exactly the same as if it were regulated by labour-time costs. If the differences in wages in different occupations are proportional to the differences in the attractiveness or the irksomeness, specialisation determined by money costs will be the same as if it were determined by real costs measured in terms of disutilities even if it is not in accordance with the labour-time costs. The above situation conceived by Taussig, however, relates more to the world of imagination than to the real world.

Finally, the real cost approach assumes the existence of perfect competition in the product as well as in the factor market which does not exist in the real world. Trade, in fact, is proximately determined by money costs and prices. Under imperfect competition, money costs and prices might not be equal to the real costs.

RESTATEMENT OF THE DOCTRINE IN TERMS OF OPPORTUNITY COSTS

In an attempt to avoid the criticisms labelled against the real cost theory, Haberler restates the doctrine of comparative costs in terms of the opportunity costs. The classicals need the real cost theory to express the exchange ratio between the two commodities. Haberler expresses the exchange ratio in terms of the opportunity costs. If, for instance, a particular combination of the diverse factors of production can produce, at constant costs, either 4*X* or 8*Y*, the opportunity cost of production of 1*Y* will be ½*X*; this does not involve the labour theory of value. The concept of opportunity cost can be employed however many factors of production there may be. The exchange ratio between the two commodities can be expressed in the form of a substitution curve. If the production of both the commodities is subject to the law of constant costs, the substitution curve will be a straight line of the form shown in Fig. 4.1.

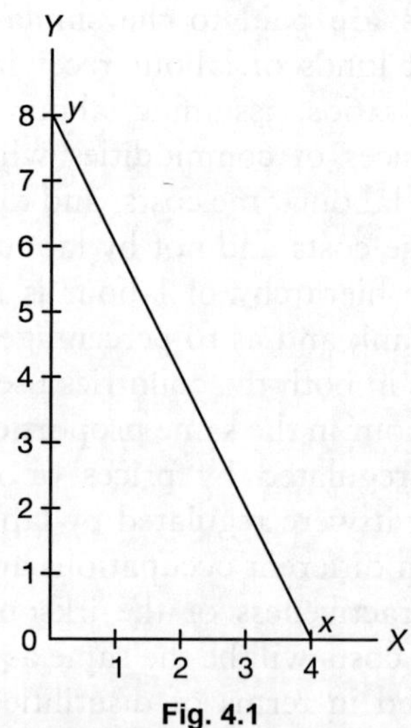

Fig. 4.1

The line *XY* shows the number of units of the commodities *X* and *Y* which can be produced with a combination of a given amount of factors of production. If we employ all the factors of production for the production of *X*, we can obtain 4*X* and no *Y*. Similarly, we can obtain 8*Y* and no *X* if all the available factors are employed for the production of *Y*. To obtain each *X*, we will have to forego two units of *Y*. Any point on the line *XY* will indicate a combination of *X* and *Y* that can be obtained with the available factors of production. If the production of both the commodities is subject to the law of increasing costs the production substitution curve will be concave towards the origin as shown in Fig. 4.2.

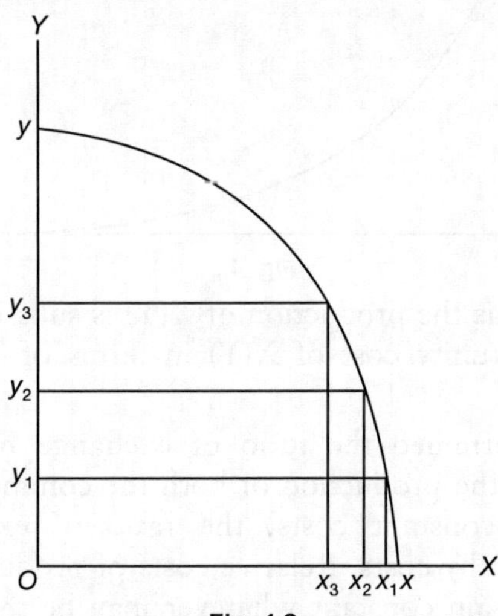

Fig. 4.2

In Fig. 4.2, we can have Ox of commodity *X* and nothing of commodity *Y*. If we want to have Oy_1 of *Y*, we will have to forego x_1x of *X*. If we want another additional unit of *Y* equivalent to y_1y_2, we will have to forego x_2x_1 of *X*. Thus as more and more of *Y* is desired, a greater and greater amount of *X* will have to be foregone for each additional unit of *Y*. In other words, as the production of *Y* is substituted for that of *X*, the opportunity cost of *Y* in terms of *X* will go on increasing. Similarly, if we start from a position of Oy of *Y* and none of *X*, as the production of *X* is substituted for that of *Y*, the opportunity cost of *X* in terms of *Y* will go on increasing.

In case the production of both the commodities is subject to the law of decreasing costs, the production substitution curve will be convex towards the origin as shown in Fig. 4.3.

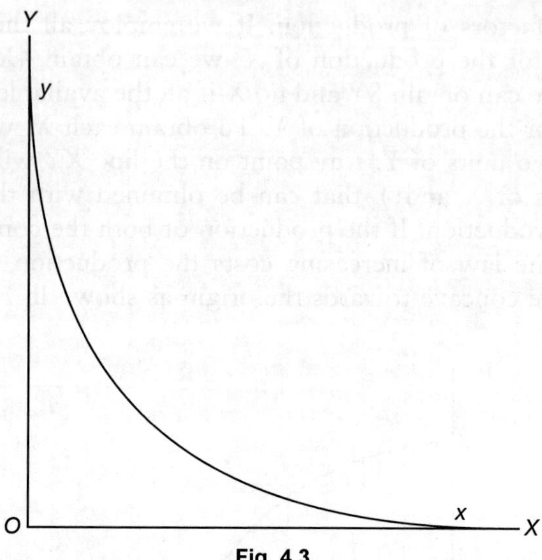

Fig. 4.3

This shows that as the production of $X(Y)$ is substituted for that of $Y(X)$, the opportunity cost of $X(Y)$ in terms of $Y(X)$ will go on decreasing.

How is determined the ratio of exchange between the two commodities? If the production of both the commodities is subject to the law of constant costs, the ratio of exchange will be determined solely by costs. Relative costs of production of the two commodities remain constant whatever may be the ratio in which the two commodities are demanded. Under variable costs, however, the relative costs of the commodities fluctuate with changes in the ratio in which these are demanded. Thus demand, along with costs, plays an active role in determining the ratio of exchange. The actual ratio of exchange will be established at the point at which the production substitution curve and the consumption indifference curve are tangential to each other. At this point the ratio of the marginal utilities from the two commodities will be equal to their marginal costs and both these will be equal to the ratio of exchange.

The existence of specific factors does not invalidate the doctrine; it only changes the form of the production substitution curve. The larger the proportion of the factors which are not specific (i.e. which can be used for the production of either commodity), the flatter will be production substitution curve and the smaller will be the changes in the relative costs caused by the changes in the ratio in which the two commodities are demanded. On the other hand, the larger the proportion of the factors which are specific to the production of either commodity, the greater will be the bulge in the production substitution curve and larger will be the movement in the relative costs caused by the changes in the ratio in which the commodities are demanded. A specimen of such a curve is shown in Fig. 4.4.

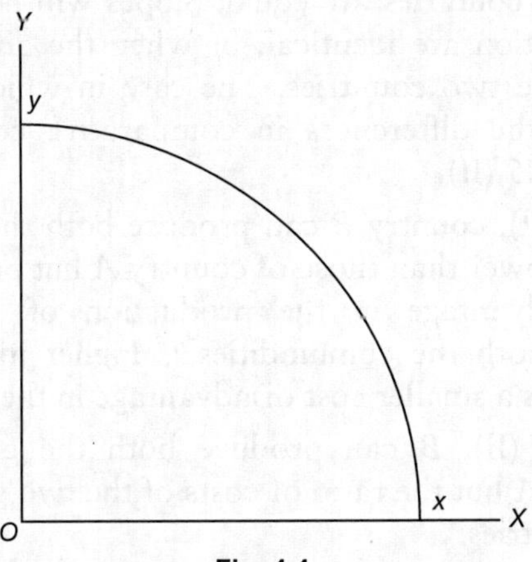

Fig. 4.4

The earlier mentioned three types of differences in costs can be shown diagrammatically (Fig. 4.5) in terms of opportunity costs, assuming that the production is subject to the law of constant costs in both, the countries, in the following manner:

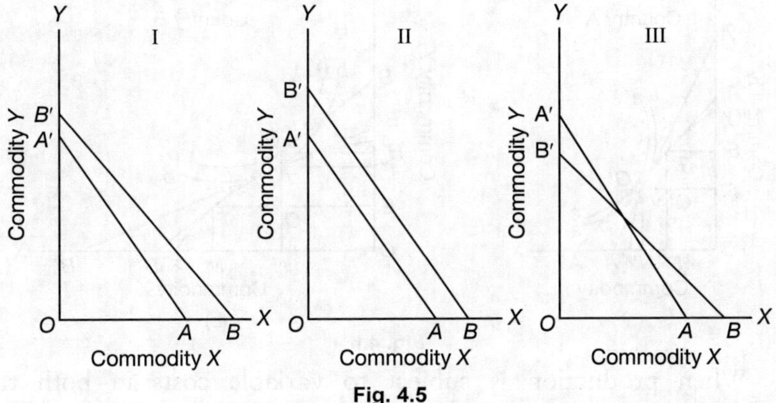

Fig. 4.5

Slopes of the lines *AA′* and *BB′* represent the relative costs of production of commodities *X* and *Y* in the countries *A* and *B* respectively. Scope for profitable trade will arise only if the production indifference lines in the two countries have different slopes as shown in Figs. 4.5 (I) and 4.5 (III). There will be no scope for international trade if the slopes of the production indifference lines in the two countries are equal. Slopes will be equal when the costs of production are identical, or when the differences in costs are equal, in the two countries. The case in which the slopes are equal because the differences in comparative costs are equal is shown in Fig. 4.5 (II).

In Fig. 4.5 (I), country *B* can produce both the commodities *X* and *Y* at costs lower than those of country *A* but possesses a greater comparative advantage in the production of *X*. The cost of production of both the commodities is higher in *A* as compared with *B* but *A* has a smaller cost disadvantage in the production of *Y*.

In Fig. 4.5 (II), *B* can produce both the goods cheaply as compared with *A* but the ratio of costs of the two goods is the same in the two countries.

In Fig. 4.5 (III), *A* possesses an absolute advantage in the production of *Y* and an absolute disadvantage in the production of *X*. *B* possesses an absolute advantage in the production of X and an absolute disadvantage in the production of *Y*.

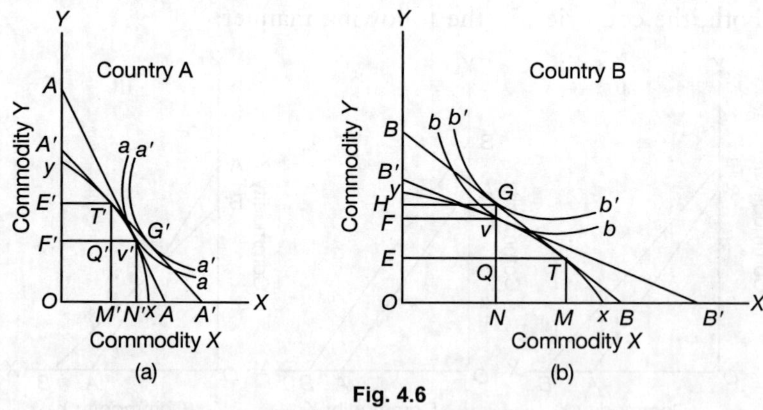

Fig. 4.6

When production is subject to variable costs in both the countries, the scope for trade is established not by differences in comparative costs but by differences in comparative marginal costs (or prices because they are equal to marginal costs under free competition). Comparative prices depend not only on the production indifference curves but also on the consumption indifference curves. Diagrammatically speaking, the relative prices are determined by the point of tangency of the consumption indifference curves and the production indifference curves.

In Fig. 4.6 comparative prices before the establishment of trade are indicated by the slope of the line *AA* in country *A* and by the slope of line *BB* in country *B*. Obviously country *A* has a comparative advantage in the production of *Y* and country *B* in that of *X*. *A* will specialise in the production of *Y* and *B* in that of *X*. As specialisation proceeds, the price of *Y* will rise and that of *X* fall in *A* and the reverse will happen in *B*. The equilibrium will be reached when the relative prices of *X* and *Y* become equal in both, the countries. Equilibrium is reached in the above diagram when *A'A'* and *B'B'* become the price line in countries *A* and *B* respectively. In equilibrium, country *A* produces an additional amount of *Y* equivalent to *F'E'* for exporting to *B* and country *B* produces an additional amount of *X* equivalent to *NM* for exporting to country *A*. Both the countries are at a higher indifference curve after the establishment of trade. In the above diagram, specialisation is partial and not complete. Country *A* still produces *OM'* instead of *ON'* and imports *Q'G'* of *X* from country *B*. Similarly, country *B* still produces *OE* instead of *OF* and imports *EH* of *Y* from country *A*. In equilibrium *A's* import of *X* must equal *B's* export of *X* and *B's* import of *Y* must equal *A's* export of *Y*.

In the following diagram, the production indifference curve *XY* is identical in both the countries. *aa'* and *bb'* are the consumption indifference curves in countries *A* and *B* respectively. Comparative prices of *X* and *Y* are indicated by the slopes of the lines *AA'* and *BB'* in countries *A* and *B* respectively. As the slopes of the lines *AA'* and *BB'* are different, there exists scope for trade. Thus the trade can arise even with identical production substitution curves in the two countries when the production is subject to the law of increasing costs.

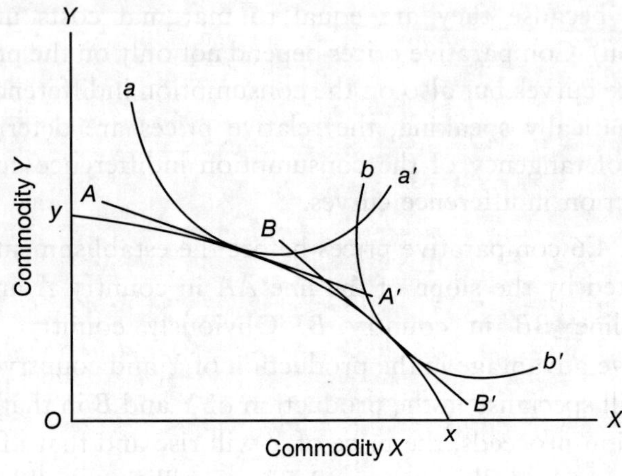

Fig. 4.7

In Fig. 4.8 country *A* has got a comparative advantage in the production of *X* and country *B* in that of *Y*.

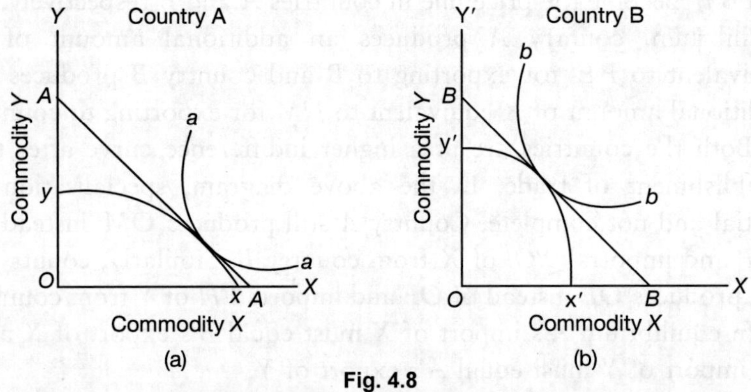

Fig. 4.8

Consumers in country *A*, however, require a substantial amount of *X* and very little of *Y*. Similarly, consumers in country *B* require a substantial amount of *Y* and very little of *X*. This raises the costs of production of *X* in *A* and that of *Y* in *B*. The differences in costs are completely offset by the differences in domestic demand and the slopes of the price lines are equal in the two countries. Since the slopes of the price lines are equal in the two countries there is no scope for trade in spite of the fact that the consumption indifference curves and the production indifference curves are widely different.

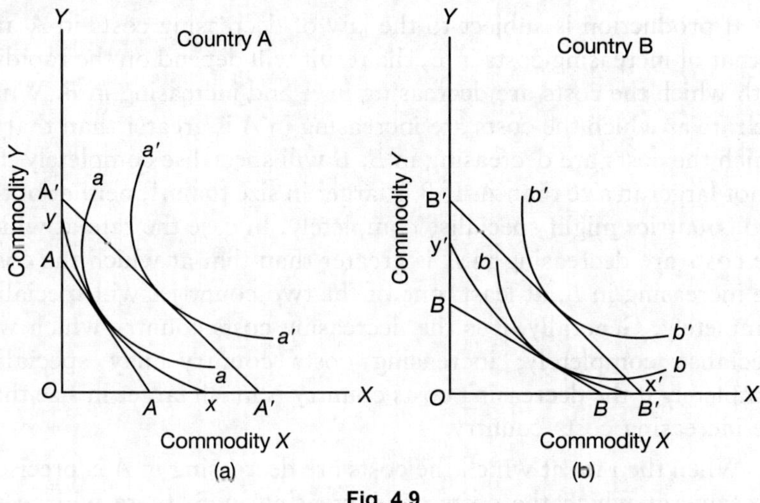

Fig. 4.9

Under decreasing costs the production substitution curves will be convex to the origin. In the above diagram, comparative prices before the establishment of trade are indicated by the slope of line *AA* in country *A* and by the slope of line *BB* in country *B*. Obviously country *A* has a comparative advantage in the production of *Y* and country *B* in that of *X*. After the introduction of trade *A* specialises completely in the production of *Y* and *B* in that of *X*. In equilibrium the slopes of the new price lines *A'A'* and *B'B'* in countries *A* and *B* respectively are equal. If specialisation is incomplete in one country because of the unequal size of the two countries, the equilibrium price line will be tangent to the production indifference curve in the larger (partially specialised) country.

If the production is subject to the law of increasing costs in country *A* and to that of constant costs in country *B*, country *B* will specialise completely if its size is smaller than or equivalent to that of country *A*. If country *B* is larger in size, neither of the two countries might specialize completely.

If production is subject to the law of decreasing costs in *A* and to that of constant costs in *B*, both the countries will specialise completely if they are not unequal in size. If the size of the two countries is unequal, the smaller will specialise completely and the larger partially.

If production is subject to the law of decreasing costs in *A* and to that of increasing costs in *B,* the result will depend on the rapidity with which the costs are decreasing in *A* and increasing in *B*. When the rate at which the costs are increasing in *A* is greater than that at which the costs are decreasing in *B, B* will specialise completely if it is not larger in size than *A*. If *B* is larger in size than *A,* neither of the two countries might specialise completely. In case the rate at which the costs are decreasing in *A* is greater than that at which the costs are increasing in *B,* at least, one of the two countries will specialise completely. Generally, it is the decreasing costs country which will specialise completely; increasing costs country may specialise completely if the decreasing costs country is much larger in size than the increasing costs country.

When the rate at which the costs are decreasing in *A* is precisely the same at which the costs are increasing in *B,* there will be no differences in comparative costs. The scope for trade will exist only if the demand conditions favour it. If the consumption indifference curves are identical in the two countries, there will be no difference in comparative costs and hence no scope for trade. If the consumption indifference curves are dissimilar, there will arise scope for profitable trade. The decreasing costs country will specialise more completely than the increasing costs country.

An Evaluation of Opportunity Cost Approach

The opportunity cost approach avoids difficulties on the cost side by creating new difficulties on the demand side. The indifference curve for an individual is drawn on the assumption that his income remains constant. A single indifference curve cannot be drawn for a community even if its total income is assumed to be constant. Any change in the distribution of the fixed total income of the community among its members will change the preference pattern of the individual members and thereby the community indifference curve. Some indifference curves representing different distributions of income might intersect each other. Application of indifference curves is based on the assumption that these do not intersect each other. If the two indifference curves intersect, it becomes impossible to decide as to which of the two is a better position. A single community indifference curve can be drawn only if we make the additional assumption that the distribution of the fixed total income of the community among its members remains unchanged. The practical value of this approach is very much restricted under the assumption of unchanged distribution of income among the members of the community because the introduction of trade is very likely to change the distribution of income. If one group of members of the community is better off and the other worse as a result of the introduction of trade, it is impossible to say unambiguously as to whether the community as a whole is better off or worse. To overcome this difficulty, Kaldor introduces the principle of compensation. If the beneficiary group can compensate (or bribe) the group which loses and still have some additional income, the new position will certainly be better than the old one.

Consumption indifference curves assume that the tastes of the consumers remain consistent over a period of time; this might not be so in actual practice.

Production indifference curves are drawn on the assumption that the factors of production are fixed in supply. This, of course, is not true. Supply of the factors of production reacts to the prices of these. Further, the earlier drawn diagrams assume that the distribution of the fixed available factors between the production of the two commodities is determined by the demand for these commodities. The distribution of the factors between the production of two commodities is determined, in fact, not only by the demand for these commodities but also by the relative preference of the factors for employment in the production of two commodities.

Production indifference curves assume that there are no external economies or diseconomies which is not true in the real world.

Production indifference curves are drawn on the assumption that there exists perfect competition in the product as well as in the factor market. In the actual world, there prevails imperfect competition and perfect competition is a very improbable exception.

The doctrine of comparative costs has two functions, viz. (i) the analytical and explanatory function; and (ii) the welfare or policy function. The first relates to causes for the emergence of trade and the second to its desirability. It is generally believed that the opportunity cost approach is better for analytical purposes and the real cost approach for welfare or policy function. Haberler doubts if the real cost approach can be much useful for welfare function if it is not suitable for analytical purposes.

> The theory cannot be useful for welfare analysis unless it also has some explanatory value. If its explanatory value is limited in the sense that, it describes only tendencies and holds only approximately (except under ideal conditions), then the same limitations apply to the welfare implications. And if it can be entirely dispensed with as an explanatory device, the same must be true, one should think, in the welfare field.[4]

In fact, neither real cost nor opportunity cost approach are completely valid. Both have their shortcomings.

RICARDIAN TRADE THEORY

Torrens (1815) and Ricardo (1817) are credited with carrying Smith's doctrine further by analyzing the case where one country has an absolute advantage in all lines of production. The assumptions of the model are as follows:

(a) There are perfect competitions in all markets. This means following conditions should be satisfied: (1) When choosing output to maximize profit each firm takes the price as given or exogenous. (2) Firms choose output to maximize profit. The rule used by perfectly competitive firms is to choose that output level which equalizes the price with the marginal cost, i.e. $P = MC$. (3) Output is homogeneous across all firms which imply that goods from different firms are perfect substitutes for all consumers. (4) Free entry and exit of firms in response to profits and in the long run economic profit is driven to zero in the industry. (5) There is perfect information, that is, all firms have the necessary information to maximize profit, to identify the positive profit and negative profit industries, etc.

(b) The world economy consists of two countries, called Home and Foreign and they differ only with respect to the production technology.

(c) Two goods are produced by both countries. We assume a barter economy. This means that there is no money used to make transactions. Instead, for trade to occur, goods must be traded for other goods. Thus we need at least two goods in the model. Let the two produced goods be coffee and sweets.

(d) Labour is the only factor of production used to produce each of the goods. The factor is homogeneous and can freely move between industries.

(e) In Ricardo's original presentation of the model he focused exclusively on the supply side. Later on John Stuart Mill introduce demand into the model. In this model we shall assume that aggregate utility can be represented by a function of the form $U = C_C\ C_S$ where C_C and C_S are the aggregate quantities of coffee and sweets consumed in the country. This function is homothetic which implies that the country consumes coffee and sweets in the same fixed proportion, at given prices, regardless of income. If two countries share the same homothetic preference, then when the countries share the same prices, as they will in fee trade, they will also consume coffee and cheese in the same proportion.

(f) The Ricardian model is a general equilibrium model. This means that it describes a complete circular flow of money in exchange for goods and services. A "general equilibrium" arises when prices of goods, services and factors are such as to equalize supply and demand in all markets simultaneously.

(g) The production functions below represent industry production, not firm production.

Production of coffee

Home country	*Foreign country*
$Q_C = \dfrac{L_C}{a_{LC}}$	$Q_C^* = \dfrac{L_C^*}{a_{LC}^*}$

Where

Q_C = Quantity of coffee produced in the Home country

L_C = Amount of labour applied to coffee production in the Home country

a_{LC} = Unit-labour requirement in coffee production in the Home country and all starred variables are defined in the same way for the Foreign country.

Production of sweets

Home country	Foreign country
$Q_S = \frac{L_S}{a_{LS}}$	$Q_S^* = \frac{L_S^*}{a_{LS}^*}$

Where

Q_S = Quantity of sweets produced in the Home country

L_S = Amount of labour applied to the production of sweets in the Home country

a_{LS} = Unit-labour requirement in the production of sweets in the Home country and all starred variables are defined in the same way for the Foreign country.

The unit-labour requirements define the technology of production in two countries.

Differences in these labour costs across countries represent differences in technology.

(h) The resource constraint in this model is a labour constraint since labour is the only factor of production.

Home country	Foreign country
$L_C + L_S = L$	$L_C^* + L_S^* = L^*$

Where L is the labour endowment in the Home country, that is, the total number of hours the work force is willing to provide. Again all starred variable refer to Foreign country.

(i) The factors of production are perfectly mobile between sectors within a country but immobile between countries. This implies that labour cannot move from one country to another in search of higher wages. But workers working in one industry can be moved to other industry without any cost incurred by the firms or the workers.

(j) There is no trade barrier, such as transportation costs or government-imposed obstacles to economic activity.

(k) In describing a model it is very essential to distinguish between exogenous and endogenous variables. Exogenous variables are those variables that are determined by processes that are not described within the model itself. When describing and solving a model, exogenous variables are taken as fixed parameters whose values are known. They are the variables over which the agents within the model have no control.

In the Ricardian model the parameters (L, a_{LC}, a_{LS}, are L^*, a^*_{LC}, a^*_{LS}) exogenous.

Endogenous variables are those variables which are determined by solving the model. Agents in the model can control or influence the endogenous variables through their actions.

In the Ricardian model the variables (L_C, L_S, Q_C, Q_S, $L^*_C, L^*_S Q^*_C, Q^*_S$) are endogenous.

(I) Technology is fixed and different countries may have different levels of technology.

We can describe the production possibility frontier (PPF) using the production functions and the labour constraint. Production functions for the home country can be written as:

$L_C = a_{LC}\, Q_C$ for coffee and

$L_S = a_{LS}\, Q_S$ for sweets.

Using the values for L_C and L_S into the labour constraint we can find the equation for the PPF as

$$a_{LC}\, Q_C + a_{LS}\, Q_S = L$$

This equation has three exogenous variables (a_{LC}, a_{LS} and L) which we assume have known values and two endogenous variables (Q_C and Q_S) whose values have to be determined. The PPF equation is a linear equation and can be rewritten as

$$Q_S = \frac{L}{a_{LS}} - \left(\frac{a_{LC}}{a_{LS}}\right) \cdot Q_C$$

The above equation of PPF can be drawn in a diagram with Q_C on the horizontal axis and Q_S on the vertical axis (Fig. 4.10).

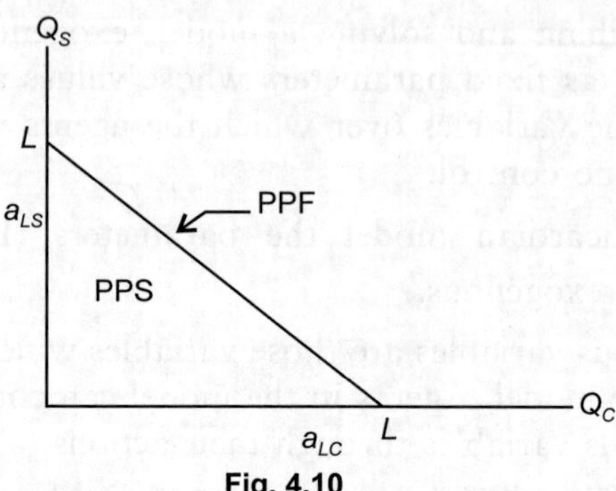

Fig. 4.10

The straight downward-sloping line is the production possibility frontier. It describes all possible quantity combinations of sweets and coffee that can be achieved by the Home country. A movement along the curve represents a transfer of labour resources out of one industry and into another such that all labour remains employed. Points inside the PPF are production possibilities but correspond to underemployment of labour resources.

The Ricardian model assumes that the coffee and sweet industries are both perfectly competitive. Among the assumptions of perfect competition is free entry and exit of firms in response to economic profit. If positive profits are being made in one industry then, because of perfect information, profit-seeking entrepreneurs will begin to open more firms in that industry. The entry of firms however, raises industry supply which forces down the product price and reduces profit for every other firm in the industry. Entry continues until economic profit is driven to zero. The same process occurs in reverse when profit is negative for firms in an industry. In this case firms will close down, one by one, as they seek more profitable opportunities elsewhere. The reduction in the number of firms reduces industry supply which raises the products market price and raises profit for all remaining firms in the industry. Exit continues until economic profit is raised to zero. This implies that if production occurs in an industry, be it is autarky or free trade, and then economic profit must be zero.

Profit of coffee industry can be written as

$$\pi_C = P_C\, Q_C - w_C\, L_C = 0$$

where

P_C = Price of coffee in (Rs./kg).

W_C = Wage paid to workers in (Rs./hr)

$P_C Q_C$ = Total industry revenue

$W_C L_C$ = Total industry cost

π_C = Profit in the coffee industry

Thus the wage in the coffee industry is given by

$$w_C = \frac{P_C Q_C}{L_C}$$

$$\text{Or, } w_C = \frac{P_C (L_C / a_{LC})}{L_C} = \frac{P_C}{a_{LC}}$$

By the same method wage in sweet industry can be given by $w_S = \dfrac{P_S}{a_{LS}}$.

Suppose that the coffee industry set a higher wage such that $w_C > w_S$. In this case all of the workers of sweet industry would want to move to the coffee industry for any wage greater than w_S. Since their productivity in coffee industry is the same as the current workers and since it does not cost anything for them to move to the other industry, the coffee industry could lower their costs and raise profit by paying a lower wage. To maximize profit they must lower their wage. Thus only equal wage rates can be sustained between two perfectly competitive producing industries in the Ricardian model.

In autarky we have, $w_C = w_S$.

Plugging in the relationship derived above yields

$$\frac{P_S}{a_{LS}} = \frac{P_C}{a_{LC}}$$

$$\text{Or, } \left(\frac{P_C}{P_S}\right)^{AUT} = \frac{a_{LC}}{a_{LS}}$$

This implies that the autarky price ratio (coffee over sweet) or terms of trade equals the opportunity cost of producing coffee.

In the autarky situation, suppose Home country has a comparative advantage in coffee production relative to the Foreign country. This implies,

$$\frac{a_{LC}}{a_{LS}} < \frac{a_{LC}^*}{a_{LS}^*}$$

Thus in turn results in

$$\left(\frac{P_C}{P_S}\right)^{AUT} < \left(\frac{P_C^*}{P_S^*}\right)^{AUT}$$

This means that the autarky price of coffee in Foreign (in terms of sweet) is greater than the autarky price of coffee in the Home country.

Similarly, by rearranging the above inequality we have

$$\left(\frac{P_S}{P_C}\right)^{AUT} > \left(\frac{P_S^*}{P_C^*}\right)^{AUT}$$

which means that the autarky price of sweet is higher in the Home (in terms of coffee) than it is in Foreign.

Now suppose barriers to trade which induced autarky are lifted and the Home country and the Foreign country are allowed to trade freely. For our simplicity we assume that there are no transportation costs to move the products across boarders. The difference in the price ratios between countries and the desire to make profit is sufficient to generate international trade. The reason for this is that the higher price of coffee in the Foreign means that coffee workers in the Home could get more sweet for their coffee in Foreign than in the Home.

Suppose one-by-one over time coffee workers begin to take advantage of the opportunity for trade and begin to sell their coffee in the Foreign market. We assume that some workers are more internationally adroit and thus move first. The motivation here is profit seeking. Workers want to get more for the goods they are selling. As the Home country coffee workers appear in the Foreign market, there is an increase in the supply of coffee. This also represents exports of coffee from the Home country to the Foreign country. The increased supply will reduce the price of coffee in the Foreign market; meaning that over time, the quantity of sweet obtained for a kg of coffee will fall. Thus P_C^*/P_S^* falls once trade is opened. Next consider Foreign sweets workers immediately after trade opens. Since the price of sweet is higher in the Home country,

Foreign sweet workers will one-by-one over time begin to sell their sweets in the Home country market. This represents exports of sweets from Foreign to Home country. The increased supply of sweets to the Home lowers its price on the Home market. Thus each kg of sweets will trade for less and less coffee. This means P_S/P_C falls which means that its reciprocal, P_C/P_S, rises. These shifts in supply will continue as long as the prices for the goods continue to differ between the two markets. Once the prices are equalized there will be no incentive to trade any additional amount. Equalized prices mean that a kg of coffee will trade for the same number of kg of sweets in both markets. The free trade prices will be those prices which equalize total supply of each good in the world with total demand for each good.

As a result of trade, the price ratio or terms of trade will lie in between the two countries autarky price ratios. In other words, the following inequality will obtain;

$$\left(\frac{P_C}{P_S}\right)^{AUT} < \left(\frac{P_C}{P_S}\right)^{FT} < \left(\frac{P_C^*}{P_S^*}\right)^{AUT}$$

Whether the free trade price ratio will be closer to the Home country autarky price ratio or Foreign country will depend on the relative demands of coffee to sweets in the two countries. These demands in turn will depend on the size of the countries. If the Home country is a much larger country, in that it has a larger workforce; it will have a larger demand for both sweets and coffee. When trade opens, the addition of Foreign country's supply and demand will have a relatively small effect on the Home country's price. Thus the free trade price ratio will be closer to the Home country's autarky price ratio.

One of the attractive features of Ricardian model is that its modeling structure allows virtually all the results obtained for the simple two-commodity and two-country case to be extended to mny countries and many commodities. For example, when the global economy consists of many commodities but only two countries, commodities can be ranked by comparative costs in a chain of decreasing relative labour costs:

$$\frac{a_{21}}{a_{11}} > \frac{a_{22}}{a_{12}} > \ldots\ldots > \frac{a_{2j}}{a_{1j}} > \ldots\ldots\ldots\ldots > \frac{a_{2n}}{a_{1n}}$$

in which a_{ij} is country i's labour requirement per unit output in sector j, $i = 1, 2, j = 1, 2, 3, ..., n$. Demand conditions determine where the chain is broke. The comparative unit costs ensure that country 1 must export all commodities to the left of the break and import all those to the right, with at most one commodity produced in common.

We can represent this theory in different ways. For example, this theory can be interpreted in terms of optimization. We consider a simple case in which the world economy consists of two countries and produces two commodities. Here, we consider the benefits from international trade in terms of an increase in the quantity of goods which can be obtained from the given amount of labour. Our optimal problem is to maximize each country's real income under constraints of the fixed labour and technology. We use P_C and P_S to denote the absolute prices of coffee and sweets. Under the assumption of free trade, perfect competition and zero-transportation cost, the Home price ratio is equal between the two countries. The exchange ratio of the two goods, P_C/P_S, is taken as given. Let C_j and S_j denote respectively country j's outputs of coffee and sweets and L_j stand for country j's fixed labour force. Country j's optimal problem is defined by

$$\max Y_j = \left(\frac{P_C}{P_S}\right) C_j + S_j$$

Subject to,

$$a_{1j}\, C_j + a_{2j}\, S_j \leq L_j, \quad C_j, S_j \geq 0, \ j = 1, 2$$

in which Y_j is country j's real national income a_{1j} and a_{2j} are respectively country j's unit costs of production of coffee and sweets. The optimal problems defined by the above expression can be easily solved graphically. It can be shown that international trade and international specialization occur as the consequence of the maximization of the real national income of each country.

An Numerical Example

The simplest way to demonstrate that countries can gain from trade in the Ricardian model is by use of a numerical example. This is how Ricardo presented his argument originally. The example demonstrates that both countries will gain from trade if they specialize in their comparative advantage goods and trade some of it for the other goods. We set up the example so that one country (Home country) has an absolute advantage in the production of both goods. Ricardo's surprising result was that a country can gain from trade even if it is technologically inferior in producing every goods. Adam Smith had explained in the Wealth of Nations that trade is advantageous to both countries, but in his example each country had an absolute advantage in one of the goods. That trade could be advantageous if each country specializes in the goods in which it has the technological edge is not surprising at all.

Suppose the exogenous variables in the two countries take the values in the following table.

Home country	$a_{LC} = 1$	$a_{LS} = 2$	$L = 24$
Foreign country	$a_{LC}^* = 6$	$a_{LS}^* = 3$	$L^* = 24$

By assumption the Home country has the absolute advantage in coffee production and sweet production since $a_{LC}(1) < a_{LC}^*(6)$ and $a_{LS}(2) < a_{LS}^*(3)$.

The Home country also has the comparative advantage in coffee production since

$$\frac{a_{LC}}{a_{LS}}\left(\frac{1}{2}\right) < \frac{a_{LC}^*}{a_{LS}^*}\left(\frac{6}{3}\right).$$

The cost of producing coffee in the Home country is ½ kg per rupees of coffee. In Foreign country, it is 2 kg per rupees. The Foreign country, however, has the comparative advantage in sweet production since,

$$\frac{a_{LS}^*}{a_{LC}^*}\left(\frac{3}{6}\right) < \frac{a_{LS}}{a_{LC}}\left(\frac{2}{1}\right)$$

The cost of producing sweet in Foreign is ½ kg of coffee per kg of sweet while in the Home country, it is 2 kg per kg.

The production possibility frontiers for both countries can be shown in Fig. 4.11.

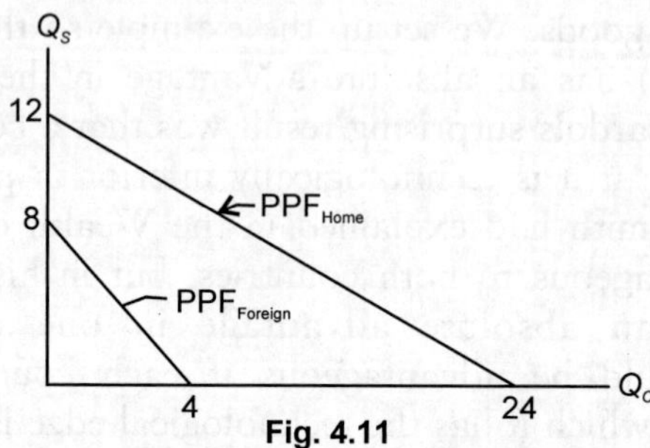

Fig. 4.11

In the above figure, PPF of Home country lies outside the PPF of the Foreign country. Since both countries are assumed to be the same size in our example, this indicates the Home country has absolute advantage in the production of both goods. The absolute value of the slope of each PPF represents the opportunity cost of coffee production. Since the PPF of Home country is flatter than Foreign's this means that the opportunity cost of coffee production is lower in the Home country and thus indicates that the Home country has comparative advantage in coffee production.

With full example of labour, production will occur at some point along the PPF. To see the effects of specialization and free trade we must compare it to a situation of no trade, or autarky. Thus we must construct an autarky equilibrium first. To determine the autarky production point requires some information about the consumer demand for the goods. Producers will produce whatever consumers demand at the prevailing prices such that supply of each goods equals demand. In autarky this means that the production and consumption point for a country are the same. For the purpose of this example we will simply make-up a plausible production/consumption point under autarky. Essentially we assume that consumer demands are such as to generate the chosen production point. The table below shows the autarky production/consumption levels for the two countries. It also shows total world production for each of the goods.

Autarky Production/Consumption

	Coffee (kg)	*Sweets (kg)*
Home Country	16	4
Foreign Country	3	2
World Total	19	6

Let us illustrate this in the following Fig. 4.12.

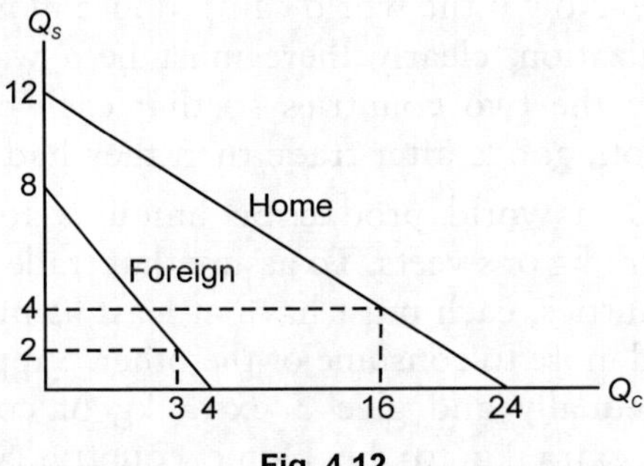

Fig. 4.12

In the above diagram we show the autarky production and consumption points for the Home country and the Foreign country. Each point lies on the interior section of the country's production possibility frontier. Ricardo argued that trade gains could arise if countries first specialize in their comparative advantage good and then trade with the other country. Specialization in our example means that the Home country produces only coffee and no sweets, while Foreign country produces only sweets and no coffee. This can be represented by the following table.

Production with Specialization in the Comparative Advantage Good

	Coffee (kg)	*Sweets (kg)*
Home Country	24	0
Foreign Country	0	8
World Trade	24	8

In the above table we see that when countries specialize in their comparative advantage good, world output of both coffee and sweets rises. The most important fact is that output increases without an increase in the quantity of labour used to produce them. In autarky it took 48 worker-hours to produce 19 kg of coffee and 6 kg of sweets. With specialization, the same 48 worker-hours produce 24 kg of coffee and 8 kg of sweets. This means that there is an increase in world productivity—more output per unit of labour.

The increase in world production efficiency does not benefit the countries unless they can trade with each other after specialization. Both production points were feasible under autarky but the countries demanded some of each good. Thus the countries will want some of each good after specialization and the only way to accomplish this is through trade. Now if the world can produce more of both goods through specialization, clearly there must be a way to divide the surplus between the two countries so that each country ends up with more of both goods after trade than they had in autarky.

The surplus in world production amounts to 5 extra kg of coffee and 2 extra kg of sweets. To assure that trade is advantageous for the two countries, each must have at least as much to consume of one good and more to consume of the other. Suppose we split the coffee surplus equally and give 3 extra kg of coffee to Foreign country and 2 extra kg to the Home country. Since the Home country consumed 16 kg of coffee and 4 kg of sweets in autarky, they would now have 18 kg of coffee and 5 kg of sweets after specialization and trade. Foreign country, which began with 3 kg of coffee and 2 kg of sweets in autarky, would now have 6 kg of coffee and 3 kg of sweets. Consumption and production after trade for the two countries is shown in the following table.

Consumption and Production after Trade

	Coffee (kg)		*Sweets (kg)*	
	Consumption	*Production*	*Consumption*	*Production*
Home Country	18	24	5	0
Foreign Country	6	0	3	8
World Total	24	24	8	8

In order for consumption of both goods to be higher in both countries trade must occur. This model assumes that countries differ in their production technologies such that one of the countries is absolutely more productive than the other in the production of each of the two goods. If these two countries specialize in their comparative advantage goods then world production rises for both goods. Increased output occurs even though there is no increase in the amount of labor input in the world, thus the example demonstrates that specialization can raise world production efficiency. Because of the increase in output it is possible to construct a terms of trade between the countries such that each country consumes more of each good with specialization and trade than was possible under autarky. Thus both countries can gain from trade. The surprising result from this example is that a country which is technologically inferior to another in the production of all goods can nevertheless benefit from trade with that country.

DOCTRINE OF COMPARATIVE COSTS AND UNDERDEVELOPED COUNTRIES

The applicability of the doctrine of comparative costs to the underdeveloped countries has been criticised on a number of grounds. The important such grounds are briefly studied below.

The doctrine of comparative costs is static in nature. It seeks to maximise the aggregate output at a particular point of time irrespective of the rate of growth. Maximisation of current output does not automatically lead to the maximum rate of growth. "Suppose that in every period 110 per cent of the GNP is consumed, would we then say that development is taking place even if in period after period the GNP is the maximum it could possibly be under the circumstances."[5] In an underdeveloped country, the acceleration of the rate of growth is more important than the maximisation of current output. Allocation of resources affects the rate of growth through its effects on the expansion of entrepreneurship, improvement in quality and increase in quantity of labour force, expansion of skills, saving habits which constitute an important factor in determining the future rate of investment, consumption pattern which is an important factor determining as to whether the consumption is simply on population maintenance or on the expansion of growth agents, rate of population growth which is an important factor determining the per capita output, etc. It may be in the interest of an underdeveloped country to invest resources in certain industries, which accelerate the rate of growth even if the same resources can produce a larger current output in some other industries without accelerating the rate of growth. Walter Galenson and Harvey Leibenstein suggest that the resources should be allocated in a manner that the per capita output potential at some future point of time is maximised. This can be achieved by allocating the resources in a manner that the marginal per capita reinvestment quotient of capital is equalised in its various alternative uses. By putting a higher value on future income than on present income, the Galenson-Leibenstein criterion errs on the other extreme. In fact, an appropriate balance is required between the present and future output. One generation should not be overstrained to provide comforts to some other generation. One way of determining the appropriate time-pattern of growth is to maximise the present value of the output stream by applying some discounting procedure.

The doctrine suffers from myopia. In determining the appropriate place for the production of a commodity, it takes into account only the current cost of production in various countries. It does not pay due consideration to the long-term costs of production. In the beginning, the cost of production of certain industrial goods might be higher in underdeveloped countries than that in developed countries. In the long run, however, given protection in the initial stages, the cost of production of these commodities may be comparatively lower in undeveloped countries because of the comparatively more favourable endowment of natural resources required for the production of these commodities. If we cast a glance on the present pattern of world trade and the endowment of natural resources in various countries, we find that the cost of production of many industrial goods is comparatively lower in developed countries not because these countries are more favourably endowed with natural resources required for the production of industrial goods but because of acquired favourable conditions, viz. a large stock of capital, superior technology, skilled labour, managerial capacity, efficient means of transportation and communication, large markets and consequent economies of production etc. In this connection the observation made by J.S. Mill is very pertinent:

> The superiority of one country over another in a branch of production often arises only from having begun it sooner. There may be no inherent advantage on one part or disadvantage on the other, but only a present superiority of acquired skill and experience.[6]

If all the facilities available to advanced countries are made available to the underdeveloped countries, they can deliver many industrial goods at a cost lower than that of developed countries because of comparatively more favourable endowment of natural resources required for the production of these goods.

The question arises, are these acquired favourable conditions such as cannot be acquired by the underdeveloped countries? The doctrine of comparative costs assumes that factor endowments are fixed and unchangeable. There is no reason, however, to assume that underdeveloped countries cannot acquire these favourable conditions if genuine efforts are made by them. It, of course, requires a fairly long period and the industries must be protected from foreign competition during the transitional period. Capital can be acquired by gradual saving and investment; public utilities can be built up; skill and organisational ability automatically develops with the development of industry; technology can be imported, adapted and further developed at home. An important reason for the lower costs of production of industrial goods in advanced countries is the larger markets available to their industries which give rise to a number of internal and external economies; economies of scale are particularly important because the production of industrial goods is subject to law of increasing returns or decreasing costs. Many underdeveloped countries have got a population bigger than that of many advanced countries and thus possess a bigger potential market. The main reason for the present small size of the market in underdeveloped countries is the lower per capita income and consequently lower per capita expenditure. As industrialisation programme proceeds, per capita income will rise and consequently market will expand. Further, for many products, a considerable portion of the market of advanced countries lies in underdeveloped countries which the latter countries can reserve for their own industries by restricting imports. Transfer of a part of the market from advanced to less developed countries will raise the cost of production in the former and lower the same in the latter countries and thus narrow the difference between the costs of production of the advanced and less developed countries. Further, the existing pattern of the endowment of factors of production is the result of past trade itself,[7] and it can be changed by further planned foreign trade.[8] A country deficient in capital and technology, for instance, can increase its stock of these through importation. From a long-term point of view, therefore, it is only the natural and unacquirable factor endowments which should be considered while determining the appropriate place for the production of a particular commodity. Thus if we take into consideration the long-term comparative advantage, we find that the present pattern of production and trade is not the optimum one and the world can obtain a higher level of production by making the countries specialise in the production and export of those commodities in which they possess a long-term comparative advantage.

An objection may be raised against specialisation according to long-term comparative advantage, that is, in a rapidly changing world it may not be advantageous to forego the benefits of specialisation according to current comparative advantage; for, before the world reaches the long-term production optimum, the comparative advantage of various countries might change owing to the discovery of new resources in certain countries or owing to changes in technology which change the raw material requirements for various products. In pursuit of this long-term optimum, the countries may go on incurring the transitional costs and losing the benefits from specialisation on the basis of current comparative advantage. This may be true in case of some commodities. On the whole, however, the advantages from specialisation on the basis of long-term comparative advantage are likely to heavily outweigh the transitional costs because the fundamental changes which alter the comparative advantage are not very rapid and so frequent.

The comparative costs theory takes into consideration only the production side; it tells us as to how the total world production can be maximised. It does not take into consideration the distribution side. In evaluating the effect of a policy on world economic welfare, its effect on the distribution of world income is no less important than on total world production. In the absence of any international agency regulating the distribution of world income, policies which maximise world income without paying any consideration to its distribution cannot be acceptable to countries whose share is adversely affected by these. Generally speaking, per capita income is higher in industry than in agriculture. If the less developed countries want to appropriate a fair share of the world income, it is very essential for them to develop domestic industry even if it decreases the total world income to some extent. They should, however, be careful that their trade restrictions do not decrease the world income to such an extent that their absolute share in it falls even if they are able to get a much higher relative share. In other words, from a purely nationalistic point of view, trade restrictions should not be carried beyond the point where the marginal increase in their absolute share is zero. From the point of view of world economic welfare, however, restrictions should stop much earlier; these should stop at the point where the increase in welfare from a less unequal distribution of world income is just equal to the decrease in welfare from a diminution in world income.

Recent developments show that the primary producing countries are not going to have very favourable terms of trade. It was held by some economists that the primary producing countries are likely to have favourable terms of trade because the production of primary goods is subject to increasing costs while that of industrial goods to decreasing costs. But the history has falsified this contention. It is believed by some people that the terms of trade are likely to move in favour of primary producing countries in the coming years because almost all the countries have started or are starting plans for industrialisation. On the one hand, industrialisation will considerably increase the supply of industrial goods, and on the other hand, it will increase the demand for primary products. If we examine the development programmes of various underdeveloped countries, however, we find that the development of agriculture is given no less importance than that of industry. Developing countries seem to have well recognised the importance of developed agriculture as a prerequisite for industrial development. There is no likelihood, therefore, of the occurrence of a raw material famine tending to improve the terms of trade of the primary producing countries. On the other hand, the terms of trade are likely to move unfavourably to the primary producing countries owing to, mainly, the following reasons.[9]

(a) Increased use of synthetic substitutes for natural raw materials, i.e. synthetic rubber, synthetic fibres, plastics, aluminium, etc.

(b) Rapid increase in domestic production of raw materials and food stuffs within the industrial countries.

(c) Recent inventions drastically decreasing the required amount of raw materials and fuel per unit of manufacturing output.

(d) Relative decline of textile industry in developed countries.

(e) Protectionist policies of developed countries.

(f) Fall in the rate of growth of population in advanced countries and the attempts for the same in underdeveloped countries.

(g) Low income elasticity of demand for primary products.

In evaluating the comparative returns from a unit of additional investment in industry and agriculture, underdeveloped countries should pay attention not to average but to marginal returns. As primary producing countries invest more and more in agriculture, the prices of agricultural products go down and thus the return is decreased on previous investment, too. The marginal return on investment in import-competing industries, therefore, is likely to be higher than on that in export industries.

The doctrine of comparative costs assumes full employment and perfect mobility of factors of production in all countries. There exists, however, vast unemployment and underemployment of manpower in developing countries. Marginal productivity of manpower in agriculture is almost zero (nay even negative in certain cases). The opportunity cost of domestic production of import-substitutes which can be produced with little capital and more manpower, therefore, is far lower than the cost of imports. The unemployed manpower can contribute something to the national dividend by producing import substitutes rather than remaining unemployed. The case against free trade in an economy suffering from unemployment was first stated in its modern form in the Addendum to the Report of the Committee on Finance and Industry presented to the British Parliament in 1931:

> The fundamental argument for unrestricted Free Trade does not apply without qualification to an economic system which is neither in equilibrium nor in sight of equilibrium. For if a country's productive resources are normally fully employed, a tariff cannot increase output, but can only divert production from one direction to another, whilst there is a general presumption that the natural direction for the employment of resources, which they can reach on their merits and without being given special advantages at the expense of others, will yield a superior national dividend. But if this condition of full employment is neither fulfilled nor likely to be fulfilled for sometime, then the position is totally different, since a tariff may bring about a net increase of production and not merely a diversion.

The nature of employment argument for protection in an underdeveloped economy, however, is different from that in an advanced country. In an advanced country, the unemployment results primarily from a shortage of effective demand. An export surplus created through restriction of imports generates additional effective demand and thus increases the volume of employment. The initial effect of an export surplus on employment is magnified in the course of time through the operation of the multiplier and accelerator principle. In contrast, the unemployment in an underdeveloped country results primarily from a shortage of resources necessary for employing labour, viz. capital, land, etc. An overall export surplus, therefore, is not enough. On the contrary, often, employment can be increased through an import surplus. Additional imports of capital equipment, for instance, make possible the employment of additional labour. Restriction of imports can increase the volume of employment only in case of commodities for which substitutes can be produced at home with the help of more unemployed labour and less other complementary factors.

The doctrine of comparative costs takes into account private costs and not social costs. Where there exists a divergence between social and private costs, socialisation on the basis of comparative costs will not maximise world economic welfare.

The doctrine of comparative costs assumes perfect competition which does not exist in the real world. In underdeveloped countries, recent emphasis on planning for rapid development has given a further blow to the freely working price mechanism. In a world of imperfect competition, prices are not equal to the marginal costs which are relevant to the doctrine of comparative costs.

If a country possesses a comparative advantage in industries subject to the law of increasing costs and a comparative disadvantage in industries subject to the law of decreasing costs, it may not be in its interest to specialise in accordance with the dictates of the doctrine of comparative costs. The underdeveloped countries are in this kind of situation. They possess a comparative advantage in agriculture, which is subject to the law of increasing costs. Cost of production will, therefore, rise with the expansion of agricultural production. They possess a comparative disadvantage in industry which is subject to the law of decreasing costs. Cost of production, therefore, will rise with the contraction of industrial production. Thus extension of specialisation in underdeveloped countries will raise the cost of production in both agriculture and industry. The increase in the cost of production in industry will further deteriorate the competitive position of underdeveloped countries in the world market for industrial products. Cumulative deterioration in the competitive position of underdeveloped countries for industrial products will handicap the exploitation of their development potentialities. Before concluding our discussion of the doctrine of comparative costs in relation to underdeveloped countries, we may mention the observation made by Singer:

> All the circumstances which (according to our economic textbooks) pu sprice mechanism out of action as an allocative force are present in underdeveloped countries: Widespread unemployment, underemployment and underutilisation of resources (the problem is how to increase total investment and total resources not primarily how to allocate them to best use), rigidities, immobilities, and non-competing groups. A considerable sector of the economy often lies outside the market mechanism altogether. Opportunities to secure external economies exist but the creation and utilisation of external economies is the very core of the process of economic development; not only are nearly all industries infants but the whole economy is an infant. The textbook exceptions to the effective operation of the price mechanism have become the rule in underdeveloped countries.[10]

RICARDIAN MODEL OF TRADE WITH MANY GOODS

In this section we shall shift our analysis from a model with only two goods to a model with a number of goods. Similar to earlier assumption, here we also consider that Home and Foreign countries have one factor of production, labour, available in quantities L and L^* in each country. However each country produces and consumes an extremely large number of goods. For each goods both Home and Foreign will have a unit labour requirement in production. Let us suppose $a(z)$ be the unit labour requirement in Home and $a^*(z)$ be the unit labour requirement in Foreign for a goods z. Then $a^*(z)/a(z)$ is the ratio of home's productivity in that goods to Foreign's. The requirement of diminishing Home country comparative advantage on the interval is represented by

$$A(z) \equiv \frac{a^*(z)}{a(z)}, \qquad A'(z) < 0$$

For generalization we consider, $A(1) > A(2) > A(3) > \ldots.$ Here we have arranged the goods in decreasing order of Home comparative advantage. The relative unit labour requirement function, $A(z)$, is also assumed to be continuous. Let $\bar{w}$ be wages measured in any common unit. Which goods will be produced in Home, and which in foreign, depends on the ratio of Home and Foreign wage rates. The cost of producing goods z in Home is $wa(z)$ and the cost of producing the same goods in foreign is $w^*a^*(z)$. The goods will therefore be cheaper to produce in Home if

$$wa(z) < w^*a^*(z)$$

Or, equivalently, $\omega \equiv w/w^* < a^*(z)/a(z)$

Or, finally, $\omega \leq A(z)$

For given ω, from equation $\omega = A(z)$, we uniquely determine

$$z^* = \phi(\omega) \tag{1}$$

Hence, for a given relative wage ω, Home and Foreign will respectively efficiently produce the rages of commodities as follows.

$$0 \leq z \leq \phi(\omega),\ \phi(\omega) \leq z \leq 1 \tag{2}$$

The relative price of a commodity z in terms of any other commodity z', when both goods are produced in Home, is equal to the ratio of home unit labour cost

$$\frac{p(z)}{p(z')} = \frac{a(z)}{a(z')},\quad 0 \leq z \leq \phi(\omega) \tag{3}$$

The relative price of a commodity z produced in Home in terms of any other commodity z'' produced in Foreign is given by

$$\frac{p(z)}{p(z'')} = \frac{\omega a(z)}{a^*(z'')}, \tag{4}$$

where $o \leq z \leq \phi(\omega)$ and $\phi(\omega) \leq z \leq 1$

Suppose that tastes in Home and Foreign countries are identical. We also consider a Cobb-Douglas demand functions that associates with commodity z a constant expenditure, $\bar{b}(z)$. Therefore, we should have,

$$b(z) = b^*(z), \tag{5}$$

And $o \leq z \leq 1$ and $\int_0^1 b(z)dz = 1$

Let Y be total income and $c(z)$ be the demand for commodity z. Then, we have

$$b(z) = \frac{p(z)c(z)}{Y} \tag{6}$$

We define the fraction of income spent on those goods in which Home has a comparative advantage as

$$\Omega(\phi) \equiv \int_0^{\phi} b(z)dz > 0 \tag{7}$$

$$\frac{d\Omega}{d\phi} = b(\phi) > 0 \quad \text{and } 1 > \Omega(\phi) \geq 0.$$

Similarly, the fraction of income spent on commodities produced by Foreign is

$$\Omega^*(\phi) \equiv 1 - \int_{\phi}^{1} b(z)dz > 0, \tag{8}$$

And $1 > \Omega^*(\phi) \geq 0$.

The total income of the domestic labour, wN, should be equal to the total expenditures of the two countries on commodities produced by Home, that is,

$$wN = \Omega(\phi)(wN + w^* N^*) \tag{9}$$

Hence, $(1-\Omega)wN = \Omega w^* N^*$, which states that imports are equal in value to exports. From this we have,

$$\omega = \frac{\Omega(z^*)N^*}{1-\Omega(z^*)N} \tag{10}$$

Equation (1) shows the behaviour of the supply side and equation (10) describes behaviour of the demand side. Equation (10) can be shown in Fig. 4.13.

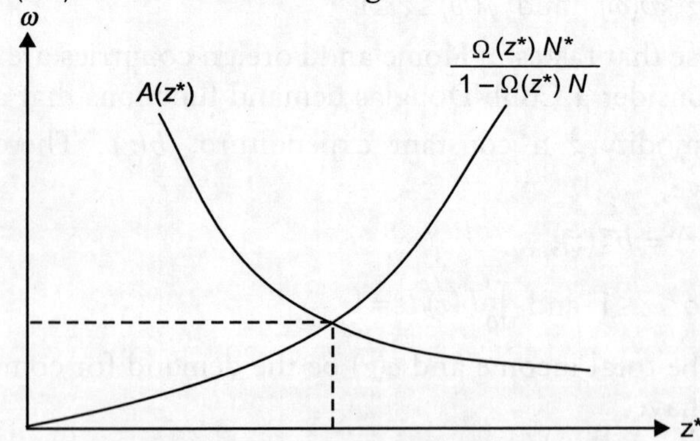

Fig. 4.13: Determination of Equilibrium.

The curve starts at zero and rises to infinity as z^* approaches unity. This equation implies that a proper level of the relative wage ratio is required to equate the demand for domestic labour to the existing supply. Equation (i) and (x) contain two variables, ω and z^*. As shown in the above figure, there is a unique solution to the equations. Once we determine the equilibrium value of z^* which is the equilibrium borderline of comparative advantage between commodities produced and exported by Home and Foreign. We determine the ranges of production of Home and Foreign as follows:

$$0 \le z \le z^* \text{ and } z^* \le z \le 1$$

The relative price structure is given by equations (iii) and (iv). From $Y = wN + w^* N^*$ and equation (vi), we determine $c(z)$. Let $\bar{N}(z)$ stands for the labour force employed for producing commodity z. Then, the output level of commodity z is equal to $\bar{a}(z)\bar{N}(z)$. From $c(z)=\bar{a}(z)\bar{N}(z)$, we determine $\bar{N}(z)$.

We can use this model to establish in a particular neat way that trade is mutually beneficial to Home and Foreign. First, we ask what the prices of goods in international trade are. In a Ricardian one-factor economy, the price of a good will simply be the labour cost of production. Since $p(z)$ is the price of good z, therefore,

(a) if the goods is produced in home then, $p(z)=wa(z)$ and
(b) if the goods is produced in foreign then, $p(z)=w^*a^*(z)$.

Now one question arises, is it more efficient for Home country to trade for its imports rather than to produce them directly?

For Home to produce one unit of goods z directly requires $a(z)$ man hours which earn an income $wa(z)$. If the goods is imported, the income from the labour that would have been used to produce one unit of goods z at Home can purchase $wa(z)/p(z)$ units of imports of z, where $p(z)=w^*a^*(z)$. It is cheaper for Home to import goods z if the labour that could produce a unit of z directly can indirectly generate more than one unit b producing instead exports to be traded, that is, if

$$wa(z)/p(z)=wa(z)/w^*a^*(z)>1$$

This is equivalent to

$$a^*(z)/a(z)=A(z)<w/w^*$$

But the pattern of specialization is determined precisely by the requirement that Home produce all goods with $A(z)<w/w^*$, while Foreign produces all goods with $A(z)<w/w^*$. Hence gains from trade are assured.

We have thus determined the equilibrium of the Ricardian economy. Now we shall examine effects of changes in some parameters on the equilibrium. Let us start with the labour endowments. An increase in N^*/N shifts the trade balance equilibrium curve given by (x) upward in proportion to the change in the relative size. We represent this change by the following Fig 4.14.

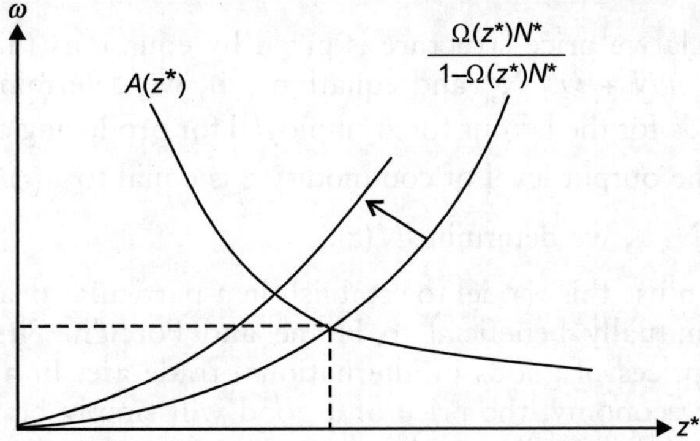

Fig. 4.14: A Rise in Labour Supply in Foreign.

From the above figure we see that the equilibrium ratio of the relative wages rise and reduces the range of commodities produced in Home. When the labour force is increased, there will initially be a labour excess in Foreign and an excess demand for labour in home. The resulting increase in Home's wages serves to eliminate the trade surplus and at the same time raise relative unit labour costs in Home. This implies a loss of comparative advantage of Home.

THE RICARDIAN THEORY OF TRADE WITH MONOPOLISTIC COMPETITION

The Chamberlinian-Ricardian model of trade with monopolistic competition was proposed by Kikuchi in 2004. Chamberlinian monopolistic competition models of trade have been extensively studied since the seminal work of Krugman (1979). Those models are very successful to explain the emergence of intra-industry trade and the industrial agglomeration. To focus on the role of increasing returns and imperfect competition, a standard model assumes the cross-country technical homogeneity-each firm in the monopolistically competitive sector incurs an identical fixed cost and a constant marginal cost. As a result, there has been little investigation of the role of technical heterogeneity among countries. However, the Ricardian comparative advantage, which plays a basic role in traditional international-trade context, is worthy of more attention. In developing this model Kikuchi made following assumptions.

(a) Cross-country technical heterogeneity in both fixed costs and marginal costs has been considered as a determinant of trade patterns.
(b) The world consists of two countries, Home and Foreign. The two countries are identical with regard to consumers' preferences but not with regard to size and production technologies.
(c) There are two sectors—the monopolistically competitive sector and the competitive sector—the former produces a large variety of differentiated products and the latter produces a homogeneous good.
(d) The homogeneous good is produced under constant returns to scale.
(e) There is only one primary factor of production – labour.

We shall start our model with the technical heterogeneity between countries. Let us consider C as the quantity index of the differentiated products, which can be specified as follows.

$$C=\left(\sum_{i=1}^{n} c_i^{\theta}+\sum_{i^*=1}^{n^*} c_{i^*}^{\theta}\right)^{1/\theta}, \quad 0<\theta<1 \qquad (1)$$

Where

$\bar{n}$ = the number of products produced in Home and Foreign,

$c_{\bar{i}}$ = the quantity of product $\bar{i}$ and

$1/(1-\theta)>0$ is the elasticity of substitution between every pair of products.

The utility function for all the consumers can be given by

$$U=\frac{C^{\varepsilon}}{\varepsilon}+Y, \quad 0<\varepsilon<1 \qquad (2)$$

where Y is the consumption level of the homogeneous goods. Now the consumer's problem can be divided into two parts.

(a) Minimizing the cost of obtaining given C yields

$$d_{\bar{i}} = \gamma \left(\frac{p_{\bar{i}}}{P} \right)^{1/(\theta-1)} . \, C, \quad i=1,\ldots, n, \; i^* = 1,\ldots, n^* \tag{3}$$

where, $p_{\bar{i}}$ is the price of good $\bar{i}$ and P is the price index given by

$$P = \left(\sum_{i=1}^{n} p_i^{\theta/(\theta-1)} + \sum_{i^*=1}^{n^*} p_{i^*}^{\theta/(\theta-1)} \right)^{(\theta-1)/\theta} \tag{4}$$

(b) The consumer's problem is to maximize the utility, dividing total income between the differentiated products in aggregate and the homogeneous good. The demand function for C is given by

$$C = P^{1/(\varepsilon-1)} \tag{5}$$

From equations (3) and (5) we have

$$d_{\bar{i}} = p_{\bar{i}}^{1/(\theta-1)} \left(\sum_{i=1}^{n} p_i^{\theta/(\theta-1)} + \sum_{i^*=1}^{n^*} p_{i^*}^{\theta/(\theta-1)} \right)^{\lambda} \tag{6}$$

where

$$\lambda \equiv \frac{\theta - \varepsilon}{(\varepsilon - 1)\theta}$$

Differentiated products are supplied by monopolistically competitive firms. Suppose $\bar{\alpha}$ and $\bar{\beta}$ represent respectively the fixed cost and constant marginal cost in Home and Foreign countries. Since the numbers of firms are assumed to be large, the elasticity of demand for each product is $1/(1-\theta)$. Therefore, each product is priced at a markup over marginal cost

$$p_{\bar{i}} = \frac{\bar{\beta}}{\theta} \tag{7}$$

Now let us consider the autarky case, that is, $n^* = 0$. Let us assume n^A firms with marginal cost β are active in Home. Using

(7) we find that the prices are the same, equaling $p_i = \beta/\theta$. Therefore we can drop index i. The profit for each firm is given by

$$\pi = (p-\beta)x - \alpha$$

$$= (1-\theta)\left(\frac{\theta}{\beta}\right)^{\theta/(1-\theta)} \left[n^A \left(\frac{\theta}{\beta}\right)^{\theta/(1-\theta} \right]^{\lambda} - \alpha \tag{8}$$

In the case of $\varepsilon > (<) \theta$, the profit rises (falls) in the number of firms. In the case of $\varepsilon > \theta$, the differentiated products would be complements rather than substitutes. To exclude this case, we require $\varepsilon < \theta$. Zero profit condition is given by

$\pi = 0$ which results in

$$n^A = \left(\frac{\beta}{\theta}\right)^{\theta/(1-\theta)} \left[\frac{\alpha}{1-\theta}\left(\frac{\beta}{\theta}\right)^{\theta/(1-\theta)} \right]^{1/\lambda} \tag{9}$$

If both countries produce differentiated products, then price of their goods are given by

$\bar{p} = \bar{\beta}/\theta$

If both countries' firms co-exist, profits must be identical for each country's firms, i.e. $\pi = \pi^* = 0$, in equilibrium. Substituting equations (6) and $\bar{p} = \bar{\beta}/\theta$ into $\pi = \pi^*$, we have

$$2(1-\theta)\theta^{\theta/(\theta-1)} \left[n\left(\frac{\beta}{\theta}\right)^{\theta/(\theta-1)} + n^* \left(\frac{\beta^*}{\theta}\right)^{\theta/(\theta-1)} \right]^{\lambda}$$

$$= \frac{\alpha - \alpha^*}{\beta^{\theta/(\theta-1)} - \beta^{*\theta/(\theta-1)}} \tag{10}$$

Inserting the right-hand side of equation (10) in the profit function we get

$$\bar{\pi} = \frac{(\alpha-\alpha^*)\bar{\beta}^{\theta/(\theta-1)}}{\beta^{\theta/(\theta-1)} - \beta^{*\theta/(\theta-1)}} - \bar{\alpha} \tag{11}$$

The equilibrium number of firms for the case in which only one country's firms exist is

$$\pi^{*T} = \left(\frac{\beta^*}{\theta}\right)^{\varepsilon\theta/(\theta-\varepsilon)} \left[\frac{(1-\theta)}{\alpha^*}\right]^{1/\lambda}, \text{ if } n=0$$

$$\pi^T = \left(\frac{\beta}{\theta}\right)^{\varepsilon\theta/(\theta-\varepsilon)} \left[\frac{(1-\theta)}{\alpha}\right]^{1/\lambda}, \text{ if } n^* = 0 \tag{12}$$

Where, T refers to the value in trading equilibrium. In free trade equilibrium with the co-existence of firms, the profit must be zero: $\pi = \pi^* = 0$. From (11), we find that this condition is satisfied only if the technology index which is defined as

$$\Omega \equiv \frac{\left(\beta/\beta^*\right)^{\theta/(1-\theta)}}{\alpha/\alpha^*}$$

is equal to unity. If $\Omega \neq 1$, one country produces only the homogeneous good and the other country produces both kinds of goods. This suggests that the co-existence of both countries' firms in the monopolistically competitive sector is very unlikely in a trading equilibrium. If $\Omega > (<) 1$, only Foreign (Home) firms produce differentiated products and Foreign (Home) is an exporter of differentiated products. Intra-industry trade occurs only when $\Omega = 1$. This implies that if the two countries are different in technologies, then intra-industry trade would not occur in the Chamberlinian-Ricardian model.

NOTES

1. Torrens, *An Essay on the External Corn Trade* (London, 1815), pp. 264-65.
2. E. Lesser, *Untersuchungen Zur Geschichte der National Okonomics,* (1881), I, pp. 82-83.
3. E.R.A. Seligman, "On Some Neglected British Economists", *Economic Journal* XIII (1903), pp. 891-97; reprinted in his *Essay in Economics* (New York, 1925), pp. 70-77.
4. G. Haberler, "Real Cost, Money Cost and Comparative Advantage", *International Social Science Bulletin* (Paris, 1951), p. 55.
5. Walter Galenson and Harvey Leibenstein, "Investment Criteria, Productivity and Economic Development", *Quarterly Journal of Economics,* 69 (August, 1955), p. 345.
6. J.S. Mill, *Principles of Political Economy* (Longmann, 1870), Vol. II, pp. 537-38.
7. J.H. Williams, "The Theory of International Trade Reconsidered" in The American Economic Association (ed) *Readings in the Theory of International Trade* (London, 1958).

8. R. Robinson, "Factor Proportions and Comparative Advantage" Part I and Part II, *Quarterly Journal of Economics* (May and August, 1956), pp. 169-93 and pp. 346-63.
9. GATT: *'International Trade, 1955* and *1956* (Geneva 1956 and 1957), pp. 6-15 and pp. 9-17 respectively.
10. H.W. Singer, commenting on Charles P. Kindleberger's paper on "The Terms of Trade and Economic Development," *The Review of Economics and Statistics, Supplement,* (February, 1959), p. 86.

Heckscher-Ohlin Theory of International Trade

5

The comparative costs doctrine of Ricardo and its later redefined versions took Smith's analysis a step further by demonstrating that international trade arises from differences in comparative costs. But they failed to explain as to why do these differences arise. This lacuna was filled up by two Swedish economists, Eli Heckscher (1919) and Bertil Ohlin (1933)[1] in their theory which was based heavily on factor-abundance. Heckscher-Ohlin Theory, thus, does not invalidate the comparative cost theory, rather supplements it and shows the cause-effect relationship with the latter. While the comparative costs theory is merely the effect, the H-O Theory gives the basic cause behind it. Before introducing the Heckscher-Ohlin theory, we develop a two-good, two-factor model.

TWO-GOOD, TWO-FACTOR MODEL

In this model we are concerned with a single country and two factors of production, labour and capital which have a fixed total supply of L and K respectively. We also assume that the economy produces two goods and follows Cobb-Douglas production function of the type:

$$Y_i = a_i\, K_i^{\alpha_i}\, L_i^{\beta_i}, \;\; i=1,2, \;\; \alpha_i, \beta_i > 0, \alpha_i + \beta_i = 1 \tag{1}$$

where K_i and L_i are respectively capital and labour inputs of sector i.

Product markets and factor markets are perfectly competitive and product prices (p_1 and p_2) are exogenously given. Capital and labour are also assumed to be freely mobile between the two sectors and immobile internationally. This assumption results in the equality of wage and rate of interest in different sectors but may vary between countries. Let w be the wage and r be the rate of interest. Profits of the two sectors are given by

$$\pi_i = p_i\, Y_i - w\, L_i - rK_i \tag{2}$$

The marginal conditions for maximizing profits are given by

$$r=\frac{\alpha_i p_i Y_i}{K_i} \quad \text{and} \quad w=\frac{\beta_i p_i Y_i}{L_i} \tag{3}$$

The resource constraints of the economy is given

$$K_1+K_2=K \text{ and } L_1+L_2=L \tag{4}$$

Equations (3) and (4) have six variables, K_i, L_i, w, and r, and six equations for given p_i, L and K. The six variables can be solved as functions of p_i, L and K. From equation (3) we have

$$\frac{\alpha_1 p_1 Y_1}{K_1}=\frac{\alpha_2 p_2 Y_2}{K_2} \text{ and } \frac{\beta_1 p_1 Y_1}{L_1}=\frac{\beta_2 p_2 Y_2}{L_2} \tag{5}$$

From these relations, we have

$$L_1 = \alpha\varepsilon L_2 \tag{6}$$

where $\alpha \equiv \dfrac{\alpha_2 \beta_1}{\alpha_1 \beta_2}$ and $\varepsilon \equiv \dfrac{K_1}{K_2}$

From (4) and (6) we can determine the labour distribution as a function of the ratio of the two sectors' capital inputs.

$$L_1=\frac{\alpha\varepsilon L}{1+\alpha\varepsilon} \text{ and } L_2=\frac{L}{1+\alpha\varepsilon} \tag{7}$$

Substituting $Y_i = a_i K_i^{\alpha_i} L_i^{\beta_i}$ into $\dfrac{\beta_1 p_1 Y_1}{L_1}=\dfrac{\beta_2 p_2 Y_2}{L_2}$ we have

$$\beta_1 p_1 a_1 = \beta_2 p_2 a_2 K_2^{\alpha_2-\alpha_1} L_2^{\beta_2-\beta_1} (\varepsilon\alpha)^{\alpha_1} \tag{8}$$

Where we also use $K_1=\varepsilon K_2$ and $L_1=\alpha\varepsilon L_2$. Here we require $\alpha_1 \neq \alpha_2$. From $\varepsilon=K_1/K_2$ and $K_1+K_2=K$, we have $K_2=K/(1+\varepsilon)$. Substituting this equation and L_2 in (7) into equation (8) we get

$$\frac{1+\alpha\,\varepsilon}{1+\varepsilon}=\alpha_0 \tag{9}$$

Where

$$\alpha_0 \equiv \left(\frac{\beta_1 p_1 a_1}{\alpha^{\alpha_1} \beta_2 p_2 a_2}\right)^{1/(\alpha_2-\alpha_1)} \cdot \frac{L}{K}$$

Solving the above equation for ε we have

$$\varepsilon=\frac{1-\alpha_0}{\alpha_0-\alpha} \tag{10}$$

If $\varepsilon > 0$, two goods are produced provided following conditions are fulfilled.

(a) $1 > \alpha_0 > \alpha$ or

(b) $1 < \alpha_0 < \alpha$

In the case of $\alpha > 1$, that is, $\alpha_2 > \alpha_1$, we should require

$$\left(\frac{\beta_1}{\beta_2}\right)^{\beta_1}\left(\frac{\alpha_1}{\alpha_2}\right)^{\alpha_1} < \frac{p_2 a_2}{p_1 a_1}\left(\frac{L}{K}\right)^{\alpha_1-\alpha_2} < \left(\frac{\beta_1}{\beta_2}\right)^{\beta_2}\left(\frac{\alpha_1}{\alpha_2}\right)^{\alpha_2} \tag{11}$$

If $\alpha_2 > \alpha_1$, the right hand side of (11) is greater than the left-hand side. Hence, under "proper" combinations of technological levels, relative prices and factor endowments, we have a unique positive solution $\varepsilon > 0$. We can similarly discuss Case (a). In the rest of this section, we require $\alpha_2 > \alpha_1$ and (11) to be held. Once we solve ε, it is simpler to solve all the other variables. From $\varepsilon = K_1/K_2$ and $K_1 + K_2 = K$, we have

$$K_1 = \frac{\varepsilon K}{1+\varepsilon}, \quad K_2 = \frac{K}{1+\varepsilon} \tag{12}$$

Equation (5) gives the labour distribution. Since we have already determined the factor endowments, it becomes easier to calculate the output levels and factor prices.

Since the production functions are neoclassical, the wage and rate of interest are determined as functions of capital intensities, K_i/L_i. From (1) and (5) we can find the capital intensities as

$$\frac{K_1}{L_1} = \left(\frac{\alpha_1 p a_1}{\alpha_2 a_2}\right)^{1/\beta_1}\left(\frac{K_2}{L_2}\right)^{\beta_2/\beta_1},$$

$$\frac{K_1}{L_1} = \left(\frac{\beta_2 a_2}{\beta_1 p a_1}\right)^{1/\alpha_1}\left(\frac{K_2}{L_2}\right)^{\alpha_2/\alpha_1} \tag{13}$$

Where $p \equiv p_1/p_2$ and we have used the fact $\alpha_i + \beta_i = 1$. Solving equation (13) we have

$$\frac{K_1}{L_1} = \omega_1 p^{\beta_0}, \frac{K_2}{L_2} = \omega_2 p^{\beta_0} \tag{14}$$

where

$$\beta_0 \equiv 1/(\beta_1 - \beta_2)$$

$$\omega_1 \equiv \left(\frac{a_1}{a_2}\right)^{\beta_0} \left(\frac{\beta_1}{\beta_2}\right)^{\beta_2 \beta_0} \left(\frac{\alpha_1}{\alpha_2}\right)^{\alpha_2 \beta_0} \quad \text{and}$$

$$\omega_2 \equiv \left(\frac{a_1}{a_2}\right)^{\beta_0} \left(\frac{\beta_1}{\beta_2}\right)^{\beta_1 \beta_0} \left(\frac{\alpha_1}{\alpha_2}\right)^{\alpha_1 \beta_0}$$

Here, we notice that the capital intensities are independent of L and K. From equation (1) and the marginal condition (3) we have

$$r = \frac{\alpha_1 a_1 p_2^{\beta_1 \beta_0}}{\omega_1^{\beta_1} p_1^{\beta_2 \beta_0}} \quad \text{and}$$

$$w = \frac{\beta_1 a_1 \omega_1^{\alpha_1} p_1^{\alpha_2 \beta_0}}{p_2^{\alpha_1 \beta_0}} \tag{15}$$

Thus we get a lemma which states that so long as two goods are produced, then each price vector (p_1, p_2) corresponds to unique factor prices (w, r). This lemma also implies that the factor endowments (L, K) do not affect factor prices (w, r). If in a two-by-two economy, with fixed product prices, the labour force or capital has no effects on its factor price, then it is known as the "Factor Price Insensitivity".

Another direct implication of our analytical results is Samuelson's factor price equalization theorem.

The Factor-Price Equalization Theorem

The factor-price equalization theorem states that when the prices of the output goods are equalized between countries, as when countries move to free trade, then the prices of the factors (capital and labour) will also be equalized between countries. This implies that free trade will equalize the wages of workers and the rents earned on capital throughout the world.

The theorem derives from the assumptions of the model, the most critical of which is the assumption that the two countries share the same production technology and that markets are perfectly competitive. In a perfectly competitive market factors are paid on the basis of the value of their marginal productivity, which in turn depends upon the output prices of the goods. Thus, when prices differ between countries, so will their marginal productivities and hence so will their wages and rents. However, once goods prices are equalized, as they are in free trade, the values of marginal products are also equalized between countries and hence the countries must also share the same wage rates and rental rates.

When trade take place, the relative price, p, is the same across the countries. As the two countries have the identical technologies, that is, α_1 and α_2 are identical across the countries, from equation (15) we find that Samuelson's theorem holds. Now one question arises that when product prices are changed, how the factor prices will be changed. Taking derivatives of equation (15) with respect to p_1 and p_2 we have

$$\frac{1}{r}\frac{dr}{dp_1}=\frac{\beta_2}{(\alpha_1-\alpha_2)p_1},$$

$$\frac{1}{w}\frac{dw}{dp_1}=-\frac{\alpha_2}{(\alpha_1-\alpha_2)p_1}$$

and $$\frac{1}{w}\frac{dw}{dp_2}=\frac{\alpha_1}{(\alpha_1-\alpha_2)p_2}, \tag{16}$$

$$\frac{1}{r}\frac{dr}{dp_2}=-\frac{\beta_1}{(\alpha_1-\alpha_2)p_2}$$

Here we have used $\beta_0=-1/(\alpha_1-\alpha_2)$. If $\alpha_2>\alpha_1$, an increase in the price of commodity 1 will increase the wage rate and reduce the rate of interest, an increase in commodity 2's price will reduce the wage rate and raise the rate of interest.

For the two industries, industry 1 is capital-intensive if

$$\frac{K_1}{L_1}>\frac{K_2}{L_2}$$

If the above inequality is reversed, then industry 1 is labour-intensive. From equation (16) we have

$$\frac{K_1}{L_1}-\frac{K_2}{L_2}=(\alpha_1-\alpha_2)\frac{\omega_2\, p^{\beta_0}}{\alpha_2\,\beta_1} \tag{17}$$

In the above expression the sign of $K_1/L_1-K_2/L_2$ is the same as that of $\alpha_1-\alpha_2$. If $\alpha_2>\alpha_1$, then industry 1 is labour intensive.

One of the important issue is related to changes in the real values, w/p_i and r/p_i, in terms of good. From (16) we have

$$\frac{d(r/p_1)}{dp_1}=\frac{\beta_1}{(\alpha_1-\alpha_2)}\frac{r}{p_1^2}<0$$

$$\frac{d(w/p_1)}{dp_1}=-\frac{\alpha_1 w}{(\alpha_1-\alpha_2)\,p_1^2}>0 \qquad (18)$$

Hence, if $\alpha_2>\alpha_1$, the real rate of interest falls and real wage rises. As the condition of $\alpha_2>\alpha_1$ implies that industry 1 is labour intensive, the price of commodity 1 rises the price of the factor that is intensively used and reduces the price of the other factor. This is the Stolper-Samuelson Theorem.

Stolper-Samuelson Theorem

This theorem states that if the price of the capital-intensive good rises (for whatever reason) then the price of capital, the factor used intensively in that industry, will rise, while the wage rate paid to labour will fall. Thus, if the price of steel were to rise, and if steel were capital-intensive, then the rental rate on capital would rise while the wage rate would fall. Similarly, if the price of the labour-intensive good were to rise then the wage rate would rise while the rental rate would fall.

This implies that when product price changes because of changes in, for example, export conditions or tariffs, there will be both gainers and losers due to the change. It means that trade has distributional consequences within the country, which make some people worse off and some better off, even though the aggregated result for the national economy is beneficial.

Now we shall examine the effect of change in the endowments. From equation (10) we have

$$\frac{1}{\varepsilon}\frac{d\varepsilon}{dL}=\frac{-(1-\alpha)\alpha_0}{(1-\alpha_0)(\alpha_0-\alpha)L}>0$$

$$\frac{1}{\varepsilon}\frac{d\varepsilon}{dK}=\frac{(1-\alpha)\alpha_0}{(1-\alpha_0)(\alpha_0-\alpha)K}<0 \qquad (19)$$

Under $\alpha_2 > \alpha_1$ and $1 < \alpha_0 < \alpha$, $\frac{d\varepsilon}{dL} > 0$ and $\frac{d\varepsilon}{dK} < 0$. Hence, an increase in either of the factor endowments reduces the ratio of capital stocks employed by industry 1 and industry 2. From equation (14), we have

$$\frac{1}{K_1}\frac{dK_1}{dL} = \frac{1}{L_1}\frac{dL_1}{dL} = \frac{1}{(1+\varepsilon)\,\varepsilon}\frac{d\varepsilon}{dL} > 0$$

$$\frac{1}{K_2}\frac{dK_2}{dL} = \frac{1}{L_2}\frac{dL_2}{dL} = -\frac{1}{(1+\varepsilon)}\frac{d\varepsilon}{dL} < 0$$

$$\frac{L_1}{L_2}\frac{d(L_1/L_2)}{dL} = \frac{1}{\varepsilon}\frac{d\varepsilon}{dL} > 0$$

$$\frac{L_1}{L_2}\frac{d(L_1/L_2)}{dK} = \frac{1}{\varepsilon}\frac{d\varepsilon}{dK} < 0$$

An increase in either of the factor endowments reduces the ratio of labour force employed by industry 1 and industry 2. From equations (12) and (14), we get.

$$\frac{1}{K_1}\frac{dK_1}{dK} = \frac{1}{L_1}\frac{dL_1}{dK} = \frac{1}{(1-\alpha_0)K} < 0$$

$$\frac{1}{K_2}\frac{dK_2}{dK} = \frac{1}{L_2}\frac{dL_2}{dK} = -\frac{1}{(1+\varepsilon)}\frac{d\varepsilon}{dK} + \frac{1}{K} > 0 \tag{20}$$

We find that changes in the endowments have no effect on the wage and the rate of interest. From equation (3), we obtain

$$\frac{1}{Y_1}\frac{dY_1}{dK} = \frac{1}{K_1}\frac{dK_1}{dK} < 0$$

$$\frac{1}{Y_2}\frac{dY_2}{dK} = \frac{1}{K_2}\frac{dK_2}{dK} > 0$$

$$\frac{1}{Y_1}\frac{dY_1}{dL} = \frac{1}{K_1}\frac{dK_1}{dL} > 0$$

$$\frac{1}{Y_2}\frac{dY_2}{dL} = \frac{1}{K_2}\frac{dK_2}{dL} < 0 \tag{21}$$

Thus we find that industry 1 is labour intensive and industry 2 is capital intensive. Equation (21) gives rise to another theorem in the trade theory, which we are going to explain in the next paragraph.

Rybczynski Theorem

This theorem states that an increase in a country's endowments of a factor (the other factor endowment remaining constant) will cause an increase in output of the good which uses that factor intensively, and a decrease in the output of the other good.

We shall use neoclassical production functions to prove this theorem. The proof of this theorem is straightforward when one assumes constant commodity prices before and after the increase in the endowment of the factor. This is because constant commodity prices imply constant factor productivities, hence constant factor prices, i.e. the factor proportions in the two industries must remain at their initial levels. Let us consider the production function of the type:

$$Y_i = (L_i, K_i) \tag{22}$$

Marginal conditions for maximizing profits are given by

$$r = p_i f_i'(k_i), \quad w = p_i [f_i(k_i) - k_i f_i'(k_i)] \tag{23}$$

Where

$$k_i \equiv \frac{K_i}{L_i}, \quad f_i(k_i) \equiv \frac{Y_i(K_i, L_i)}{L_i}$$

Now, from $p_1 f_1'(k_1) = p_2 f_2'(k_2)$, we find that k_2 can be written as a function k_1, denoted by $k_2 = \phi(k_1)$. We can show that $\phi' > 0$ using the equation

$$p_1[f_1(k_1) - k_1 f_1'(k_1)] = p_1[f_2(\phi(k_1)) - \phi(k_1) f_2'(\phi(k_1))] \tag{24}$$

The above equation has a single variable and it can be solved for k_1. Thus we find that k_2, w and r can uniquely determined as functions of k_1. Since k_1 is independent of L and K, k_2, w and r are also independent of the factor endowments. From equation (4) and the definitions of k_1, we have four equations in four variables.

$$L_1 + L_2 = L, \quad K_1 + K_2 = K, \quad \frac{K_i}{L_i} = k_i$$

The above equations can be solved as follows

$$L_1 = \frac{K - k_2 L}{k_1 - k_2}, \quad L_2 = \frac{k_1 L - K}{k_1 - k_2} \text{ and}$$

$$K_1 = \frac{(K - k_2 L) k_1}{k_1 - k_2}, \quad K_2 = \frac{(k_1 L - K) k_2}{k_1 - k_2}.$$

The economic rationale of the theorem is also straightforward. Since commodity prices are to remain constant, factor propositions have to be maintained at their initial levels. Now, the only way to guarantee full utilization of the increased endowment of *L* is obviously by explaining the labour intensive industry. However, given that the *K/L* ratio must remain constant, the expansion will require some *K*. Since the extra *K* can be acquired only from the capital intensive industry, that industry must contract. But if the capital intensive industry is to contract and still maintain its *K/L* ratio, it will release both *K* and *L* at that ratio. Hence the *K/L* ratio released will be in excess of that required in the other industry, therefore more of the newly endowed *L* can be added to the released *K* and *L* to bring the ratio to the level required in production. This process should be carried to the point where the combination of the newly endowed *L* and the released *K* and *L* give a *K/L* ratio exactly equal to that required in the production in second industry. Hence, the output of capital intensive industry must contract absolutely and the output of the second industry must expand absolutely if the assumption of constant commodity and factor prices is to be upheld.

HECKSCHER-OHLIN THEORY

The H-O Theory, also popular as "Factor-Proportions Analysis", "The General Equilibrium Theory" and "The Modern Theory of International Trade" can be explained as follows:

Assumptions

The following assumptions are made beforehand to understand the H-O Theory properly—

(a) There are only two countries.

(b) There are only two factors of production (namely capital, *K* and labour, *L*).

(c) There is perfect competition in commodity as well as in factor markets.

(d) The production functions are different for different commodities but the same for each commodity in the two countries.

(e) There are no costs of transport and insurance, tariffs, etc.

(f) There are no trade and exchange controls.

(g) Factor endowments, demand conditions and physical conditions of production are fixed in each country.

(h) Factors of production are immobile between countries but freely mobile within countries.

(i) Production functions for different commodities are such as can be distinguished by factor intensity.

(j) Both the factors of production are employed fully in each country.

Under the above mentioned assumptions, the theory can be elaborated as under—

Statement of the Theory

If country *A* possesses a larger amount of one factor of production relatively to the amount of same factor of production in country *B*, assuming that the differences in the supply of factors are not offset by differences in the demand conditions, the price of this factor will be lower in *A* as compared to that in *B*.

A will, therefore, possess a comparative cost advantage in the production of goods that employ more of the factor abundant in it. Similarly, country *B* will possess comparative cost advantage in the production of those commodities which employ more of the factor relatively abundant in *B*. Thus, both the countries will specialise in the production and export of the commodity/commodities which employ more of their relatively abundant factor and less of their relatively scarce factor.

Now the concept of relative abundance or scarcity can be interpreted in two ways, i.e. either in relation to factor prices or in factor proportions. While the first interpretation says that a country's abundant factor is its cheaper factor, the second one states that abundant in a country, is that factor which is available in more physical quantities in it. Hence, according to the first interpretation, i.e. the factor price criterion, if country *A* has relatively cheaper capital (K) and country B has relatively cheaper labour (L), it can be expressed as $\frac{PK_A}{PL_A} < \frac{PK_B}{PL_B}$ where P is price per unit. According to the second interpretation, i.e. the factor proportions criterion, if country A has a larger physical amount of K in relation to that of B and country B has a larger physical amount of L as compared to that in country A, it can be expressed as $\frac{K_A}{L_A} > \frac{K_B}{L_B}$ where K is the physical amount of capital and L is the physical amount of labour.

It becomes of utmost importance to understand that a country relatively abundant in a factor according to the factor proportions criterion might not be so according to the factor price criterion if the relative physical abundance of the factor is offset or more than that, by the differences in demand conditions to the factor price criterion if the demand conditions are such that little of this factor is employed in the production of the commodities in demand for the factor in the other country.

So, to comprehend the H-O Theory properly, we must necessarily go through the explanation of the factor price criterion and factor proportions criterion in individuality. But before that we need to be familiar with the tools that are used to explain the H-O Theory. A brief description of the tools follows—

Tools Used

(a) Isoquants. An isoquant or isoproduct curve is a curve on which various combinations of the only two factors of production being used to produce a commodity show the same output per unit of time.

Fig. 5.1 illustrates the hypothetical isoquants which show a good G being produced with the help of two factors, namely A nd B. This figure shows two different levels of G being produced (100 units and 200 units respectively) at IQ_1 and IQ_2 levels.

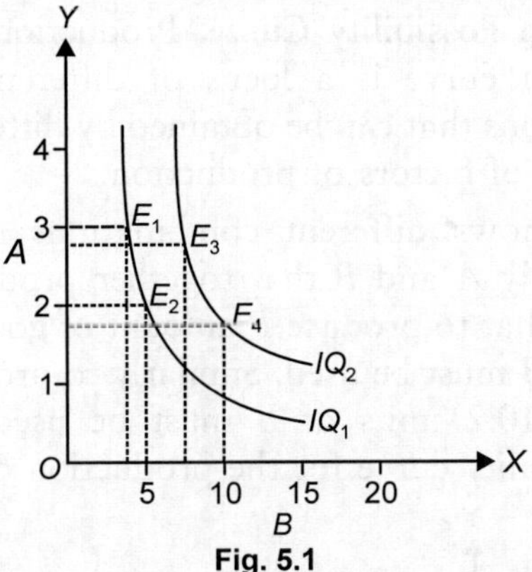

Fig. 5.1

In curve IQ_1, point E_1 shows that 100 units of G are being produced by 3 units of A and 4.7 units of B. Similarly point E_2 shows that 100 units of G are being produced by 2 units of A and 5 units of B. thus IQ_1 shows an isoquant that shows various combinations of A and B required to produce 100 units of G while IQ_2 shows the higher level (200 units) of the same good G and the various combinations (at points E_3 and E_4) of A and B needed to produce the same level of output.

(b) Isocost Curves. Also known as factor-price line, factor-cost line; price line, outlay line, constant-outlay line, etc. an isocost represents the different combinations of the only two factors of production (used by a producer to produce one commodity) If can be illustrated through Fig. 5.2 in which a commodity G is being produced at two levels of total outlays, say Rs. 50 (being represented by isocost P_1P_1) and Rs 75 (being represented by isocost P_2P_2). P_1P_1 shows different combinations of A and B so that each time, they give a sum of total of Rs 50 and the same for P_2P_2 to give a total of Rs. 75.

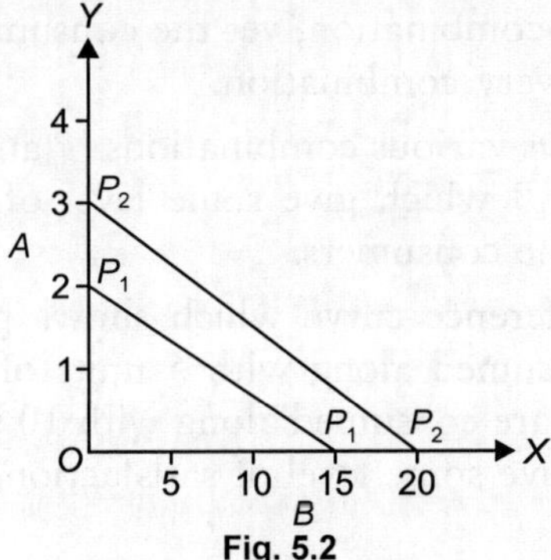

Fig. 5.2

(c) Production Possibility Curve. Production Possibility Curve or transformation curve is a locus of different amounts of the output combinations that can be obtained by different combinations of given amounts of factors of production.

Figure 5.3 shows different combinations of two factors of production, namely *A* and *B* that together produce goods *G*. The figure illustrates that to produce *P* amount of goods *G*, 4.8 units of *A* and 5 units of *B* must be used. Similarly to produce Q amount, 4 units of *A* and 10.2 units of *B* must be used. Thus *ST* is the production possibility curve for the production of goods *G*.

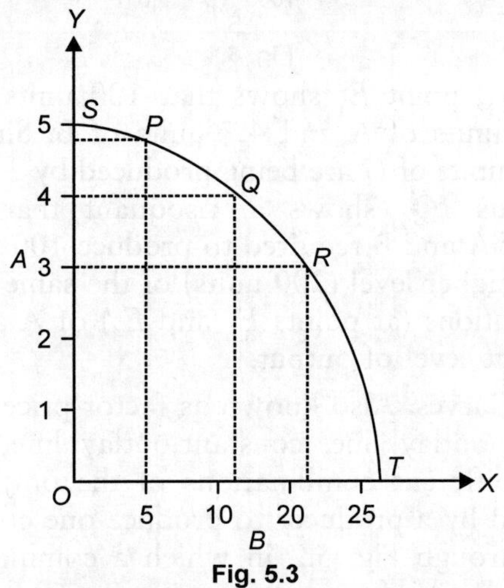

Fig. 5.3

(d) Indifference Curve. An indifference curve shows the various combinations of commodities, so arranged that a consumer is indifferent to the combinations, preferring none over another. Though the amount of different commodities being used/consumed is different in each combination, yet the consumer desires the same satisfaction from every combination.

Figure 5.4 shows various combinations (*P* and *Q*) of commodity *A* and commodity *B* which give same level of satisfaction (when used together) to the consumers.

IC is the indifference curve which shows point *P* at which 4 units of *A* are consumed along with 5 units of *B* and point *Q* at which 2 units of *A* are consumed along with 10 units of *B*. Both the points (*P* and *Q*) give some level of satisfaction to the consumer.

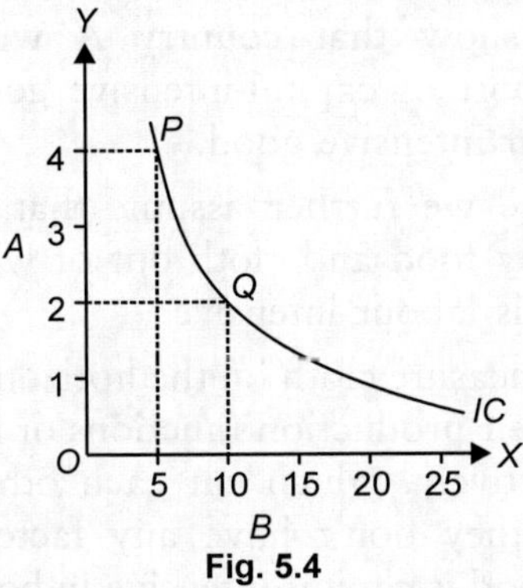

Fig. 5.4

Explanation

Coming back to the Heckscher-Ohlin Theory and reminding ourselves of factor price and factor proportions criterion, we shall first begin with the explanation of the factor price criterion.

FACTOR PRICE CRITERION

If the factor endowments and demand conditions are similar in the two countries, or if the differences in the factor endowments are exactly balanced by the corresponding differences in demand conditions, there will be no differences in the comparative costs (hence prices) of the two countries. This, however, is an exceptional case and is not very likely to occur in actual practice. Generally, wide differences in the endowment of factors of production are likely to cause differences in the relative prices of commodities in different countries. Ohlin himself defined richness in factor endowments with the help of factor prices.

To explain that H-O proposition follows if we take factor price criterion into consideration, we must go back to our assumption of country *A* and *B* where country *A* is capital (*K*) abundant and *B* is labour (*L*) abundant. To remind, the situation can be expressed as

$$\frac{PK_A}{PL_A} < \frac{PK_B}{PL_B}$$

where PK_A is the price of capital in country *A*, PL_A is the price of labour in country *A* and PK_B and PL_B are the respective prices of capital and labour in country *B*.

We will now show that country *A* will specialise in the production and export of capital-intensive good while country *B* will do so for labour intensive good.

For this purpose we further assume that there are only two commodities, namely food and cloth out of which, food is capital intensive and cloth is labour-intensive.

In Fig. 5.5, we measure cloth on the horizontal axis and food on the vertical axis. Their production functions or isoquants are shown by *ff* and *cc* respectively, which cut each other at point *E* only, which shows that they don't have any factor intensity reversal which means that food is capital-intensive in both the countries and cloth is labour-intensive in both the countries.

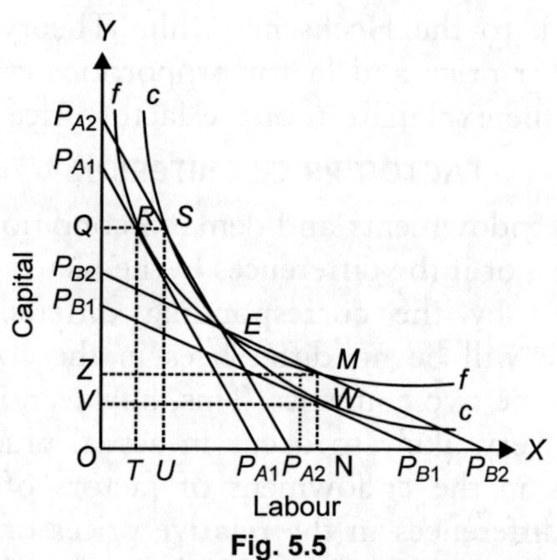

Fig. 5.5

Then we have the two price lines (or isocost curves), namely $P_{A1}P_{A1}$ and $P_{A2}P_{A2}$ respectively of country *A*, the capital surplus country, and two price lines $P_{B1}P_{B1}$ and $P_{B1}P_{B2}$ respectively of country B, the labour abundant country.

The given figure shows that to produce 1 unit of food, country A will have to employ *OQ* amount of *K* and *OT* amount of *L* and to produce 1 unit of cloth, it will have to employ *OQ* amount of *K* and *OU* amount of labour. Thus, to produce 1 unit of cloth, country *A* requires more of labour (*TU*) but equal amount of capital as well in order to produce the same amount of food. Hence, to produce food is cheaper in country *A*. In other words, country *A* has a comparative advantage in producing food than cloth. As a result, it will specialise in the production and export of food which is a capital intensive good.

Let us now take the case of country B. To produce 1 unit of cloth, it has to employ *ON* amount of labour and OV amount of capital. And to produce the same quantity of food, it has to employ *ON* amount of labour (which is equal to the labour amount needed to produce 1 unit of cloth) and *OZ* amount of capital (which is greater than the mount of capital required to produce 1 unit of food by *VZ* amount. Thus, the cost of producing cloth is lower than that of food in country B. Hence, this country will specialise in the production of cloth, which is a labour-intensive commodity.

Thus, we see that according to the factor price criterion, a country which has the availability of capital at a lower price is said to be abundant in capital and specialises in the production and export of capital intensive goods and a country having cheaper labour is said to be labour abundant and this country specialises in the production and export of labour intensive goods.

FACTOR PROPORTIONS CRITERION

At the outset of the explanation of this criterion, let us be reminded that under this definition of "abundance", physical terms are the main basis i.e. a country is said to be abundant in that factor which is present in the largest quantity in that country.

In this criterion also, we assume two countries *A* and *B*, which are abundant in capital (which us measured vertically) and labour (which is measured horizontally) respectively. Food is the capital intensive good and the situation can be expressed as:

$$\frac{K_A}{L_A} > \frac{K_B}{L_B}$$

where K_A and L_A are the total amounts of capital and labour respectively, in country *A*, and K_B and L_B are the amounts of capital and labour respectively in country *B*.

To show that country *A* being capital abundant has a bias in favour of producing capital intensive good and country B being labour abundant has a production bias in favour of labour intensive goods, we will take help of Fig. 5.6.

In this figure, we suppose that both the countries produce the goods in the same proportions along the line *OR*. In this case, country *A* will produce at E_1 (intersecting point of the production possibility curve *ff* and the isocost or the factor price ratio line P_AP_A) and country *B* will produce E_1 (intersecting point of production possibility curve cc and the isocost line P_BP_B of country *B*). The point of importance is that country *A* has both—its production possibility curve (*ff*) and isocost (P_AP_A), steeper as compared to their respective counterparts in country *B*, which as corollary to the previous explanation implies that *A* has a cheaper production of food while country *B* has a cheaper production of cloth. Hence, country *A* would tend to expand its production of food and country *B* would do so for cloth.

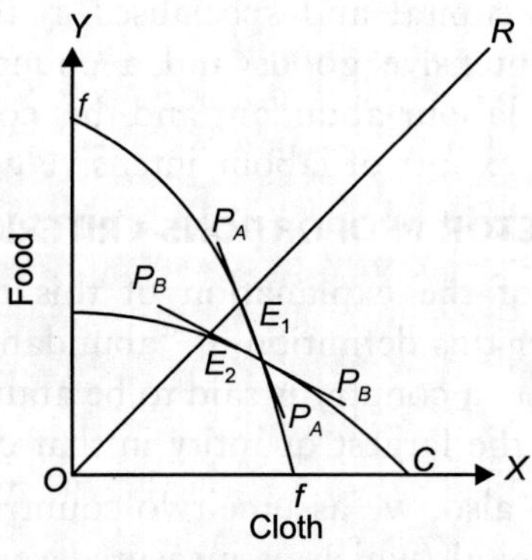

Fig. 5.6

The above explanation only shows that there is a production bias for food (capital abundant good) in country *A* and a production bias for cloth (labour abundant good) in country *B* but it does not explain whether they would specialise in the export also, of the same products. The answer to the question depends on the demand factor and there can be two conditions in that. The first condition is when the consumption and production biases are in the opposite direction. In this condition, the H-O Theory will always follow. But the second condition in which, the consumption and production biases are in the same direction, H-O Theory becomes invalid.

Let us take the first condition first, which is illustrated through Fig. 5.7. In this figure, IC_A and IC_B are assumed to be the indifferent curves of country *A* and country *B* respectively. *ff* and cc are the production possibility curves of food and cloth of country *A* and country *B* respectively. *PP* has been supposed to be the relative factor-price ratio line after trade is established between both the countries (or the common isoocost of both the countries). Hence, country *A* will consume food at point *T* (intersecting point of the IC_A and *PP*) and country *B* will consume cloth at a level of point *V* (the intersecting point of the IC_B and *PP*). Also, country *A* will produce food at point *R* (where *ff* and *PP* intersect) and country *B* will produce cloth at point *S* (intersecting point of *cc* and *PP*).

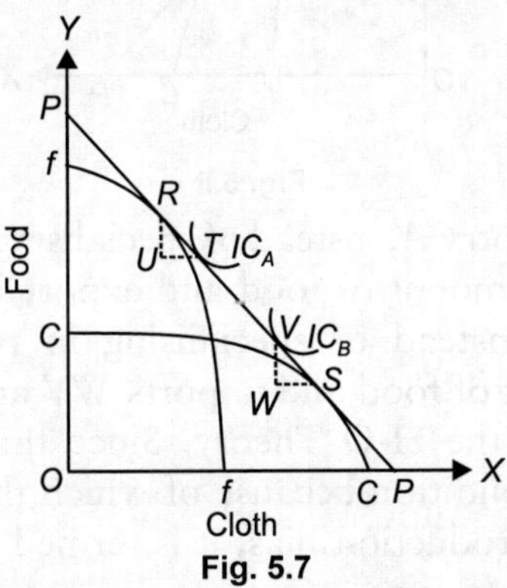

Fig. 5.7

Thus it is clear that the consumption point (*T*) of country *A* is to the right of its production point (*R*) and the consumption point (*V*) of country *B* is to the left of its production point (*S*), which means that the production bias and the consumption bias of both the countries are in opposite directions. In such a situation, country *A* will export *RU* amount of food and import *UT* amount of cloth, whereas country *B* will export *WS* amount of cloth and import *VW* amount of food.

Therefore, in this condition, the H-O proposition of a country's specialisation in production and export of the commodity which has intensive use of the abundant factor of that country, holds good. But the same is not true for the second condition in which the consumption and production biases are in the same direction.

Condition 2 can be demonstrated by Fig. 5.8, in which every assumption is same as that of Fig. 5.7 except that the IC_A curve now intersects *PP* at a point which is at the left to point *R* and IC_B curve intersects *PP* at a point that is at the right to point *S*. This implies that the consumption bias for country *A* has shifted towards the same direction in which its production bias is i.e. left and the opposite is the case for country *B*.

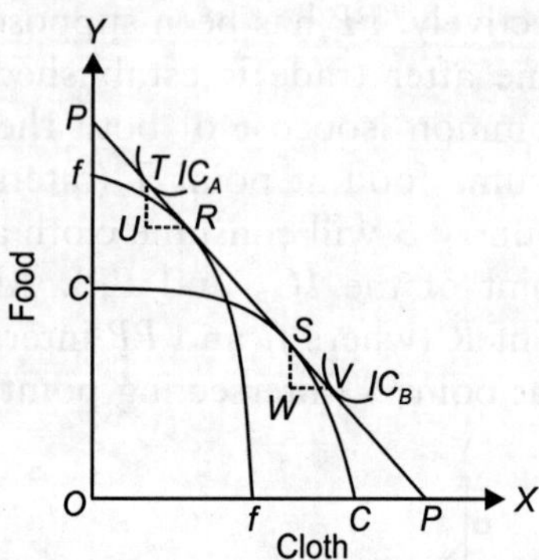

Fig. 5.8

In this case, country *A*, instead of specialising in food production, has to import *UT* amount of food and export *UR* amount of cloth while country *B*, instead of specialising in production of cloth, imports *SW* amount of food and imports *WV* amount of cloth. This is in contrast with the H-O Theory. Since this happens due to a different demand condition because of which the consumption bias more than offsets production bias, it is termed as demand reversal.

Many a people would say that there can be a third situation in which the consumption and production points of each country coincide with each other. In such a situation, each country will consume all it produces and there will be no international trade.

Eventually, to conclude the theory, it can be said that the H-O Theory states that a country will specialise in the production and export of that commodity which employs the abundant factor of that country. Factor abundance as used in H-O Theory can be explained according to the factor price criterion and factor proportions criterion. While factor price criterion gives a validity to the theory, factor proportions criterion does so only when the demand reversal doesn't take place.

HECKSCHER-OHLIN THEOREM AND THE NEOCLASSICAL TRADE THEORY

The Heckscher-Ohlin theorem implies that home country exports goods 1 and foreign country exports goods 2. In order to determine trade directions, we need mechanisms to determine prices of goods. We shall use the concept of utility function to determine prices in autarky. We can determine the directions of trade flows after we determine the prices in autarky. The utility maximizing problem can be described as follows.

$$\max C_1^{\delta_1} C_2^{\delta_2}, \; s.t \; p_1 C_1 + p_2 C_2 = y,$$

where C_i is the consumption level of good i, δ_1 and δ_2 are positive parameters, and y is the total income given by

$$y = rK + wL.$$

We also have $\delta_1 + \delta_2 = 1$. The optimal solution is given by the condition

$$p_i C_i = \delta_i y.$$

As $C_i = Y_i$, we have

$$\frac{p_1 Y_1}{p_2 Y_2} = \frac{\delta_1}{\delta_2}$$

Substituting $r = \dfrac{\alpha_i p_i Y_i}{K_i}$ into the above equation we get $k = \delta$, where we use $k = K_1/K_2$ and $\delta = \alpha_1 \delta_1 / \alpha_2 \delta_2$.

Substituting $\varepsilon = \dfrac{1-\alpha_0}{\alpha_0 - \alpha}$ into the above equation we have

$$np^{1/(\alpha_2 - \alpha_1)} = \frac{1 + \alpha \delta}{(\delta + 1)\alpha}, \tag{25}$$

where

$$n \equiv \frac{L}{K}, \quad \alpha^* \equiv \left(\frac{\beta_1 a_1}{\alpha^{\alpha_1} \beta_2 a_2} \right)^{1/(\alpha_2 - \alpha_1)}$$

Equation (25) determines the relative price in Home country. According to the assumptions that the two countries have the identical technology and preference, the values of the parameters for Foreign corresponding to α, δ and α^*. We thus have

$$np^{1/(\alpha_2 - \alpha_1)} = \tilde{n} \tilde{p}^{1/(\alpha_2 - \alpha_1)} \tag{26}$$

The assumption of $L/K > \tilde{L}/\tilde{K}$ implies $n > \tilde{n}$. Thus for $n > \tilde{n}$ and equation (26) to hold, we should have

$$p^{1/(\alpha_2 - \alpha_1)} < \tilde{p}^{\,1/(\alpha_2 - \alpha_1)}$$

Since the goods 1 is labour intensive, therefore we have $\alpha_2 > \alpha_1$. As $\alpha_2 - \alpha_1 > 0$, we have $p < \tilde{p}$, which implies $\frac{p_1}{p_2} < \frac{\tilde{p}_1}{\tilde{p}_2}$.

Hence, when the two countries are in autarky, the relative price in Home is lower than the relative price in Foreign. This implies that when the two countries start to conduct trade, goods 1 is exported to Foreign and goods 2 is imported from Foreign. Thus Heckscher-Ohlin theorem is confirmed.

The Ricardian theory can not determine the terms of trade but it can be used to determine the limits in which the terms of trade must lie. On the other hand the Heckscher-Ohlin theory provides simple and intuitive insights into the relationships between commodity prices and factor prices, factor supplies and factor rewards, and factor endowments and the pattern of production and trade. Although the Heckscher-Ohlin model was the dominant framework for analyzing trade in the 1960s, it had neither succeeded in supplanting the Ricardian model nor had been replaced by the specific-factor trade models. Each theory has been refined within its own 'scope'. As far as general ideas are concerned, the Heckscher-Ohlin theory may be considered as a special case of the neoclassical trade theory in which production technology and preferences are internationally identical.

In order to determine the terms of trade, it is necessary to build trade theory which not only takes account of the productive side but also the demand side. The neoclassical theory holds that the determinants of trade patterns are to be found simultaneously in the differences between the technologies, the factor endowments, and the tastes of different countries. Preferences accounts for the existence of international trade even if technologies and factor endowments were completely identical between countries. As an illustration of the neoclassical trade theory, we shall consider Mill and the modern analytical tool to solve the problem of trade equilibrium. Mill introduced the equation of international demand, according to which the terms of trade are determined so as to equate the value of exports and the value of imports. According to Mill, the exports and the imports between the two countries must in the aggregate pay for each other, and must therefore be exchanged for one another at such values as will be compatible with the equation of the international demand.

Now we shall use the analytical methods to prove the existence of trade equilibrium which also illustrates the difference between the Ricardian theory and the neoclassical theory. Let subscript indexes 1 and 2 represent respectively India and USA. The amount of cloth and linen produced by country i can be represented by y_{ic} and y_{il} respectively, which are non-negative. The total amount of cloth or linen produced in country i when the country is completely specified in producing cloth or linen by a_{ic} or a_{il}, the possible sets of y_{ic} and y_{il} are given by

$$\frac{y_{ic}}{a_{ic}}+\frac{y_{il}}{a_{il}}\leq 1,\ y_{ic}, y_{il}\geq 0,\ i=1,2 \tag{27}$$

From the above two equations we find that the demand for labour does not exceed the supply in each country. Let the prices of cloth and linen be represented by P_c and P_l respectively. At equilibrium country i should choose the combination of (y_{ic}, y_{il}) such that the following GDP is maximized.

$$\frac{p_c}{p_l}y_{ic}+y_{il}$$

Multiplying equation (27) by a_{ic} (i = 1, 2) and adding the two equations, we get

$$y_c+\frac{a_{1c}}{a_{1l}}y_{1l}+\frac{a_{2c}}{a_{2l}}\leq a_c$$

where

$$y_c\equiv y_{1c}+y_{2c},\ a_c\equiv a_{1c}+a_{2c}.$$

If we assume that India has the comparative advantage in linen, i.e. $a_{1c}/a_{1l}<a_{2c}/a_{2l}$, from the above inequality we get

$$\frac{y_c}{a_{1c}}+\frac{y_l}{a_{1l}}\leq\frac{a_c}{a_{1c}}, \tag{28}$$

where $y_l\equiv y_{1l}+y_{2l}$. Similarly multiplying (27) by a_{il}, we get

$$\frac{y_c}{a_{2c}}+\frac{y_l}{a_{2l}}\leq\frac{a_l}{a_{2l}},$$

where $a_l\equiv a_{il}+a_{2l}$.

Now we shall describe the demand. Let $x_c(\geq 0), x_l(\geq 0)$ and $R(\geq 0)$ represent for the demand for cloth, demand for linen, and income measured in terms of the factor of production. The problem is to maximize the following utility

$$U = x_c x_l,$$

subject to the budget constraint $p_c x_c + p_l x_l = R$. The demand functions for cloth and linen can be given by

$$x_c = \frac{R}{2p_c}, \quad x_l = \frac{R}{2p_l}$$

Since the two countries have an identical preference structure but different incomes, we have that country *i*'s demand for cloth and linen, X_{ic} and X_{il}, are given by

$$X_{ic} = \frac{R_i}{2p_c}, X_{il} = \frac{R_i}{2p_l}, \quad i = 1,2 \tag{29}$$

where R_i is country *i*'s income. Since demands for commodities cannot exceed supplies at the equilibrium of free international trade, we have

$$x_c \leq y_{1c} + y_{2c}, X_l \leq y_{1l} + y_{2l}. \tag{30}$$

where

$$X_c \equiv X_{1c} + X_{2c}, \quad X_l \equiv X_{1l} + X_{2l}.$$

Let us describe the utility function as

$U = \log X_c + \log X_l$.

Our problem is to maximize U subject to (27) and (30). The Lagrangean is given by

$$\log X_c + \log X_l + p_c(y_{1c} + y_{2c} - X_c) + p_l(y_{il} + y_{2l} - X_l) + \sum_{i=1}^{2} w_i\left(\frac{y_{ic}}{a_{ic}} + \frac{y_{il}}{a_{il}} - 1\right)$$

Thus we find that the Lagrangean has a strictly positive saddle point at which (27) and (30) are satisfied with equality at the saddle point. In fact this saddle point is an equilibrium of free international trade, with p_c/p_l, w_1/p_l and w_2/p_1 respectively satisfying the price of cloth, the price of factor of production in India and in USA. Since the world total income is equal to

$$p_c X_c + p_l X_l = w_1 + w_2,$$

we have $R_i = w_i$ $R_i = w_i$. From (29) we get X_{ic} and X_{il} which is an optimal solution of the problem that country i maximizes its utility subject to its budget constraint with the given world prices.

PUBLIC GOODS AND HECKSCHER-OHLIN THEORY OF INTERNATIONAL TRADE

As before we consider two countries Home and Foreign. Since the Foreign country is similar to Home country, we shall start with the Home country. Two goods, say 1 and 2, are produced in the economy. There are two primary factors, labour and capital, and one pure public intermediate goods. The total supplies of capital and labour, K and L, are fixed. We represent the public intermediate goods by G. For firms G is given. We consider the Cobb-Douglas type of production function of the form

$$Y_i = a_i\, G^{v_i}\, K_i^{\alpha_i}\, L_i^{\beta_i}, \tag{31}$$

where

$$i=1,2,\ \ v_i \geq 0,\ \ \alpha_i, \beta_i > 0,\ \ \alpha_i + \beta_i = 1$$

K_i and L_i are capital and labour inputs of sector i. There is perfect competition in the product market and factor markets. Also the product prices p_1 and p_2 are given exogenously. Marginal conditions for the profit maximization are given by

$$r = \frac{\alpha_i\, p_i\, Y_i}{K_i}, \qquad w = \frac{\beta_i\, p_i\, Y_i}{L_i} \tag{32}$$

For simplicity, we consider p_2=1 and express p=p_1. The production function of the public sector is given by

$$G = a_p\, K_p^{\alpha_p}\, L_p^{\beta_p} \tag{33}$$

where

$$\alpha_p, \beta_p > 0,\ \ \alpha_p + \beta_p = 0$$

K_p and L_p are respectively capital and labour inputs of the public sector and a_p is the productivity. Now suppose that the amount of public goods is fixed by the government and the public good production is financed by the income tax. The total cost of the public sector is given by rK_p + wL_p. Minimizing the total cost subject to the constraint (33), we obtain the following marginal conditions

$$\xi = \frac{\beta_p K_p}{\alpha_p N_p},$$

where $\xi \equiv w/r$. From this equation and equation (33), the optimal levels of K_p and L_p can be represented as function of r, w and G as follows

$$L_p = \frac{a_\alpha G}{\xi^{\alpha_p}}, \ K_p = a_\beta G \xi^{\beta_p}, \tag{34}$$

where

$$a_\alpha = \left(\frac{\beta_p}{\alpha_p}\right)^{\alpha_p} \frac{1}{a_p}, \quad a_\beta = \left(\frac{\alpha_p}{\beta_p}\right)^{\beta_p} \frac{1}{a_p}$$

Suppose that t be the tax rate on the total income, $Y = rK + wL$. Then we have

$$r K_p + w L_p = t(rK + wL)$$

Using this equation and (34), tax rate can be represented as a function of r, w, and G.

$$t = \frac{t_0 G \xi^{\beta_p}}{1 + n\xi} \tag{35}$$

where

$$t_0 \equiv \left[\left(\frac{\alpha_p}{\beta_p}\right)^{\beta_p} + \left(\frac{\beta_p}{\alpha_p}\right)^{\alpha_p}\right] \frac{1}{Ka_p}, \quad n \equiv \frac{L}{K}$$

Thus the tax rate can be determined as a function of the public good and the wage-rental ratio and the amount of factors employed in each sector is constrained by the endowments found in the economy. The resource constraints are given by

$$\begin{aligned} K_1 + K_2 + K_p &= K \\ L_1 + L_2 + L_p &= L \end{aligned} \tag{36}$$

The utility maximizing problem of the consumer is given by

$$\max C_1^{\varphi_1} C_2^{\varphi_2}, \qquad s.t\ p_1 C_1 + p_2 C_2 = (1-t)y,$$

where C_i is the consumption level of good i, φ_1 and φ_2 are positive parameters. For simplicity we shall consider $\varphi_1+\varphi_2=1$. Therefore the optimal solution is given by

$$p_i C_i=(1-t)\varphi_i y \tag{37}$$

For an isolated economy, we have $C_i = Y_i$. From the above equation we have

$$\frac{pY_1}{Y_2}=\frac{\varphi_1}{\varphi_2} \tag{38}$$

Substituting $r=\alpha_i p_i Y_i/K_i$ into the above equation yields $k=\varphi$, where, $k=K_1/K_2$ and $\varphi\equiv\alpha_1\varphi_1/\alpha_2\varphi_2$. From equation (32), we have

$$\frac{\alpha_1 p_1 Y_1}{K_1}=\frac{\alpha_2 p_2 Y_2}{K_2}, \quad \frac{\beta_1 p_1 Y_1}{L_1}=\frac{\beta_2 p_2 Y_2}{L_2}$$

From these relations, we have

$$L_1=\alpha L_2 \tag{39}$$

Here we have used $k=\varphi$ and $\alpha\equiv\beta_1\varphi_1/\beta_2\varphi_2$. From equation (32), we also obtain

$$\xi=\frac{\beta_1 K_1}{\alpha_1 L_1} \tag{40}$$

From equations (34) and (36) we have

$$K_1\left(1+\frac{1}{\varphi}\right)=K-a_\beta G\xi^{\beta_p}$$

$$L_1\left(1+\frac{1}{\alpha}\right)=L-\frac{a_\alpha G}{\xi^{\alpha_p}} \tag{41}$$

In the case of both goods are produced, we should have $0<K_1<K$ and $0<L_1<L$. From the above equation we see that for $\xi>0$, the conditions are satisfied if

$$\frac{K}{a_\beta G}>\xi^{\beta_p}>\frac{a_\alpha G}{L} \tag{42}$$

Equation (42) implies that the amount of public goods should not be too large for given K and L; otherwise the problem has no solution or the economy may specialize in producing a single goods.

From equations (40) and (41) we obtain

$$\vartheta(\xi) \equiv \xi + (a_{\beta} - \alpha_0\, a_{\alpha})\frac{G}{\alpha_0\, L}\xi^{\beta_p} - \frac{K}{\alpha_0\, L} = 0 \tag{43}$$

Where

$$\alpha_0 \equiv \frac{\alpha_1(1+1/\varphi)}{\beta_1(1+1/\alpha)} = \frac{\alpha_1\varphi_1 + \alpha_2\varphi_2}{\beta_1\varphi_1 + \beta_2\varphi_2}$$

The above equation contains single variable, ξ. In case of $a_{\beta} - \alpha_0\, a_{\alpha} = 0$, we have $\xi = K/\alpha_0 L$. By the definition of the parameters we have

$$a_{\beta} - \alpha_0\, a_{\alpha} = \frac{[(\alpha_p - \alpha_1)\varphi_1 + (\alpha_p - \alpha_2)\varphi_2]a_{\alpha}}{\beta_p(\beta_1\varphi_1 + \beta_2\varphi_2)} \tag{44}$$

We find that $a_{\beta} - \alpha_0\, a_{\alpha}$ may be either positive or negative. We assume that $\vartheta(\xi) = 0$ has at least one positive solution which satisfies equation (42). As

$$\vartheta' = 1 + (a_{\beta} - \alpha_0\, a_{\alpha})\frac{\beta_p\, G}{\alpha_0\, L}\xi^{-\alpha_p},$$

we find that if $a_{\beta} - \alpha_0\, a_{\alpha} > 0$, then the solution is unique. Once we find ξ, then we are able to determine all the variables as,

K_1 and L_1 by (41), L_2 by (39), K_2 by (38), L_p and K_p by (34), t by (35), Y_i by (31), C_i by (38), r and w by (32), and $p = \alpha\, \beta_2\, Y_2 / \beta_1\, Y_1$ which has been obtained using (32).

Till now we were considering the case when there is no trade between the two economies. Now we shall shift our analysis towards the situation when there is trade between the concerned countries. We assume that the two countries are identical in all aspects, except that the two countries have different levels of public goods. Our problem is to determine the direction of trade. To solve this problem, we determine the relative prices before trade liberalization. From equation (43), we have

$$\left[1+(a_\beta-\alpha_0\,a_\alpha)\frac{\beta_p\,G}{\alpha_0\,L}\xi^{-\alpha_p}\right]\frac{d\xi}{dG}=-(a_\beta-\alpha_0\,A_\alpha)\frac{\xi^{\beta_p}}{\alpha_0\,L} \tag{45}$$

If $a_\beta-\alpha_0\,a_\alpha=0$, $\frac{d\xi}{dG}=0$.

If $a_\beta-\alpha_0\,a_\alpha>0$, $\frac{d\xi}{dG}<0$.

If $a_\beta-\alpha_0\,a_\alpha<0$, from equation (33) we have

$$1+(a_\beta-\alpha_0\,a_\alpha)\frac{\beta_p\,G}{\alpha_0\,L}\xi^{-\alpha_p}=\frac{K-(a_\beta-\alpha_0\,a_\alpha)G\alpha_p\,\xi^{\beta_p}}{\alpha_0\,\xi\,L}>0$$

Hence, we have $\frac{d\xi}{dG}>0$. Here we find that $\frac{d\xi}{dG}$ is the opposite to that of $a_\beta-\alpha_0\,a_\alpha$. From (44) we find that the sign of $\frac{d\xi}{dG}$ is the same as the sign of the following term

$$\varphi\equiv(\alpha_1-\alpha_p)\varphi_1+(\alpha_2-\alpha_p)\varphi_2 \tag{46}$$

The above discussions are true for Foreign as well. As the two countries are identical (except in $\bar{G}$), we find that in the case of $\varphi>0$, if $G>(<)\tilde{G}$, then $\xi>(<)\tilde{\xi}$; and in the case of $\varphi>0$, if $G>(<)\tilde{G}$, then $\xi<(>)\tilde{\xi}$, when the two countries are in isolation.

Now we shall compare p and $\tilde{p}$. From equation (31) and (32), we have

$$p=\frac{\alpha\,\beta_2\,a_2\,G^{\mu_2}K_2^{\alpha_2}L_2^{\beta_2}}{\beta_1\,a_1\,G^{\mu_1}K_1^{\alpha_1}L_1^{\beta_1}}$$

Substituting $L_1=\alpha L_2$, and $k=\varphi$ into the above equation we have

$$p=a\,G^{\mu_2-\mu_1}\xi^{\alpha_2-\alpha_1} \tag{47}$$

Here we made the use of the equation (40) and $a\equiv\frac{\alpha_2^{\alpha_2}\,\beta_2^{\beta_2}\,a_2}{\alpha_1^{\alpha_1}\,\beta_1^{\beta_1}\,a_1}$.

Taking datives of equation (40) with respect to $\overline{G}$ we have

$$\frac{1}{p}\frac{dp}{dG}=\frac{\mu_2-\mu_1}{G}+\frac{\alpha_2-\alpha_1}{\xi}\frac{d\xi}{dG}$$

From equation (45) and the above equation we have

$$\frac{1}{p}\frac{dp}{dG}=\frac{\mu_2-\mu_1}{G}-\frac{(a_\beta-\alpha_0\,a_\alpha)(\alpha_2-\alpha_1)}{[1+(a_\beta-\alpha_0\,a_\alpha)\beta_p G\xi^{-\alpha_p}/\alpha_0 L]\xi^{\alpha_p}\alpha_0 L}$$

The magnitude of μ_i represents the degree of spillover of public input into sector i. If the public goods has no effect on the production of sector i, then $\mu_i = 0$. If the public input is effective in increasing the productivity of sector i, the parameter value is high. To determine factor intensities from $k=\varphi$ and $L_1=\alpha L_2$, we have

$$\frac{K_p}{L_1}=\frac{\alpha_1\,\beta_2\,K_2}{\alpha_2\,\beta_1\,L_1} \tag{48}$$

where we use the definitions of φ and α. Sector 1 is relatively capital (labour) intensive if $K_1/L_1>(<)K_2/L_2$. From $\alpha_i+\beta_i=1$, we find that sector 1 is relatively capital (labour) intensive if $\alpha_1>(<)\alpha_2$. We also define that the public sector is capital (labour) intensive relative to the private sectors if

$$\frac{K_p}{L_p}>(<)\frac{K_1+K_2}{L_1+L_2}=\frac{K-K_p}{L-L_p}$$

The public sector is relatively capital (labour) intensive if

$$\frac{K_p}{L_p}>(<)\frac{K}{L}$$

Using equation (34), the above inequality is equivalent to

$$\xi>(<)\frac{\beta_p\,K}{\alpha_p\,L}$$

This states that if the wage-rental ratio is higher (lower) than the ratio $\beta_p K/\alpha_p L$, then the public sector is relatively capital (labour) intensive.

Now we shall turn towards the trade pattern. First, we consider the situation when the spillover effects of the public goods are the same between the two sectors, i.e. $\mu_1 = \mu_2$. Then, by equation (47), we have

$$\frac{1}{p}\frac{dp}{dG}=\frac{(a_\beta-\alpha_0\,a_\alpha)(\alpha_1-\alpha_2)}{[1+(a_\beta-\alpha_0\,a_\alpha)\,\beta_p\,G\xi^{-\alpha_p}\,/\,\alpha_0\,L]\xi^{\alpha_p}\,\alpha_0\,L}$$

In this equation denominator is positive. Hence, the sign of $\dfrac{dp}{dG}$ is the same as that of

$$\Delta\equiv[(\alpha_p-\alpha_1)\varphi_1+(\alpha_p-\alpha_2)\varphi_2](\alpha_1-\alpha_2).$$

In the case of $\Delta>0$, if $G>\tilde{G}$, then we have $p>\tilde{p}$. Home country imports goods 1 and exports goods 2.

THE HECKSCHER-OHLIN THEORY WITH MONOPOLISTIC COMPETITION

Suppose that Home country is capital abundant, that is, $K/L>\tilde{K}/\tilde{L}$. The two industries are monopolistically competitive and produce differentiated goods under increasing returns to scale. Both industries incur identical transport cost τ (> 1) units which must be shipped from one country in order that one unit arrives in the other country. Let us define the price indices for the two industries by

$$q_i=[n_i\,p_i^{1-\sigma}+\tilde{n}_i(\tilde{p}_i\,\tau)^{1-\sigma}]^{1/(1-\alpha)},\quad i=1,2 \tag{1}$$

where $\overline{n}_i$ are the varieties of industry i produced in Home and Foreign and $\overline{p}_i$ are the prices charged for each variety. Production of each variety requires a fixed amount of α and a variable amount β of an input whose unit cost is denoted by C_i, i = 1, 2. Firms in each industry are symmetric. The total cost of a firm in industry i which produces output x_i is given by

$$TC_i=(\alpha+\beta\,x_i)C_i.$$

Let $\sigma(>0)$ stand for the constant demand elasticity products. We choose parameter values so that

$$\alpha=\frac{1}{\sigma},\quad \beta\sigma=\sigma-1$$

The price that maximizes the firms' profit is given by

$$p_i = \frac{\beta\sigma}{\sigma-1} C_i = C_i \tag{2}$$

The zero profit condition is given by

$$x = \frac{(\sigma-1)\alpha}{\beta} = 1 \tag{3}$$

The equilibrium output is the same across firms and industries. The unit cost functions, C_i, for the inputs of the two industries are given by

$$C_1 = w^{(1-\delta)\gamma} r^{(1-\delta)(1-\gamma)} q_1^{\delta}$$
$$C_2 = w^{(1-\delta)(1-\gamma)} r^{(1-\delta)\gamma} q_2^{\delta} \tag{4}$$

Where $0<\delta,\ \gamma<1$. Here, δ is the share of own industry output in total cost in the two industries.

Let K_i and L_i be the distribution of capital and labour between the two industries and

$$K_1 + K_2 = K,\quad L_1 + L_2 = L \tag{5}$$

From equation (4) and (5), we can find the shares of capital and labour in total cost as

$$wL_1 = (1-\delta)\gamma n_1 p_1$$
$$w(L-L_1) = (1-\delta)(1-\gamma) n_2 p_2$$
$$rK_1 = (1-\delta)(1-\gamma) n_1 p_1$$
$$r(K-K_1) = (1-\delta)\gamma n_2 p_2$$

From the above equation, we have

$$\frac{K_1}{L_1} = \frac{1-\gamma}{\gamma}\frac{w}{r}$$
$$\frac{K_2}{L_2} = \frac{K-K_1}{L-L_1} = \frac{\gamma}{1-\gamma}\frac{w}{r} \tag{6}$$

Now suppose that $\gamma>1/2$, which implies that industry 1 is labour intensive. Also consumers have Cobb-Douglas preferences. They spend an equal share of their income ($Y = rK + wN$) on each industry's varieties. Also consider a share δ of revenue is used to purchase its own industry varieties. Hence, total expenditure, e_i, for the two industries varieties is given by

$$e_i = \frac{rK + wN}{2} + \delta n_i p_i \tag{7}$$

Total demand for each of the two industries' varieties is given by

$$x_i = \frac{e_i q_i^{\sigma-1} + \tilde{e}_i \tau^{1-\sigma} \tilde{q}_i^{\sigma-1}}{p_i^{\sigma}} \tag{8}$$

If industry *i*'s demand is active in equilibrium then $x_i = 1$. As it is difficult to explicitly solve the model, we simulate the model with various combinations of parameters. In the following section we shall concern with the parameter values which guarantee a unique equilibrium point. It can be demonstrated that the model may have multiple equilibrium points.

Let us suppose

$$L = \tilde{K} = 0.7,\ K = \tilde{L} = 1,\ \sigma = 5,\ \gamma = 0.8 \tag{9}$$

We consider that Home is capital abundant and Foreign is labour abundant. We also consider, the share, s_2, of the capital-intensive industry's output in Home and the share, $\tilde{s}_1$, of the labour-intensive industry's output in Foreign as follows.

$$s_2 = \frac{p_2 n_2}{p_1 n_1 + p_2 n_2}, \quad \tilde{s}_1 = \frac{\tilde{p}_1 \tilde{n}_1}{\tilde{p}_1 \tilde{n}_1 + \tilde{p}_2 \tilde{n}_2}$$

Due to the symmetry of the two countries, we have $s_2 = \tilde{s}_1$ and the shares are determined as functions of τ. We solve the model for $1 \le \tau \le 2.5$ and the results are plotted in Fig. 5.9.

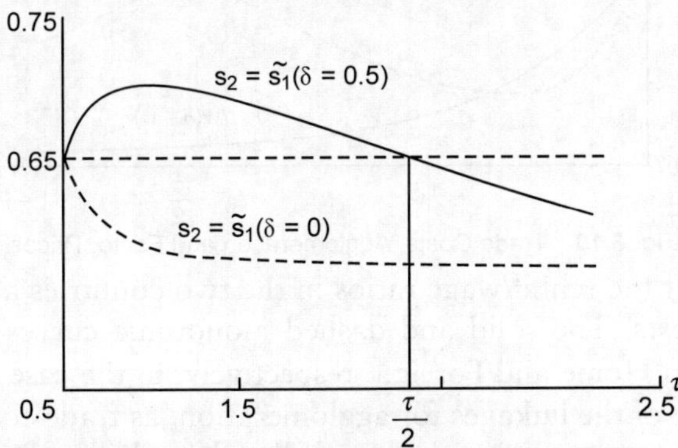

Fig. 5.9: Trade Costs, Agglomeration and Specialization.

In the absence of agglomeration economies generated by the linkages among producers (i.e., $\delta = 0$), as shown in the traditional Heckscher-Ohlin theory, trade liberalization monotonically increases specialization according to comparative advantage. In the presence of the linkages (i.e., $\delta = 0$) trade liberalization also fosters specialization according to comparative advantage. For trade costs lower than $\underline{\tau}$, i.e., $\tau \leq \underline{\tau}$, the degree of international specialization exceeds the one attained in free trade (with $\tau = 1$). We interpret that agglomeration economies exert a sort of magnification effect on the specialization based on comparative advantage. This comes from that a country specialized in its comparative advantage industry has a double advantage with respect to its partner country. The industry exploits the advantage of using intensively its abundant factor as well as the positive externalities generated by the linkages among producers in this industry. The second advantage strengthens the first advantage. The above figure shows that international specialization raises, then reaches a peak, and finally starts to decline as trade costs are increased.

The effects on the behaviour of factor prices are plotted on the following Fig. 5.10.

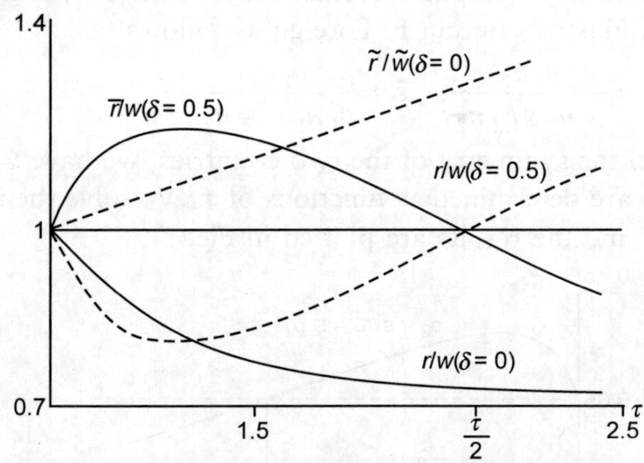

Fig. 5.10 Trade Costs, Agglomeration and Factor Prices.

We plot the rental/wage ratios in the two countries as functions of trade costs. The solid and dashed monotonic curves represents the ratios in Home and Foreign, respectively, in the case of $\delta = 0$. In the absence of the linkages for agglomeration, as trade costs fall, the factor price ratios coverage, as predicted in the traditional trade theory. As the parameters are specified such that the two goods will be produced in the absence of trade costs, we have factor price equalization in the free trade equilibrium. The solid and dashed nonmonotonic curves represent the ratios in Home and Foreign, respectively, in the case of $\delta > 0$. There are relative factor price convergence and divergence as trade costs vary. The factor price equalization is achieved at $\tau = \underline{\tau}$. From the above figure we see that, when the two similar countries become sufficiently integrated, in each country the abundant factor becomes sufficiently integrated, in each country the abundant factor becomes relatively expensive. This is due to agglomeration forces, by which specialization due to comparative advantage is strengthened and hence exacerbates the traditional Stolper-Samuelson effect.

CRITICAL EVALUATION OF THE H-O THEORY

Although the H-O Theory occupies an indispensable position in the field of International Trade and B. Ohlin even got the Nobel Prize in 1978, yet the theory is not free of criticisms.

H-O Theory has been criticised mainly on three grounds, viz., demand reversal argument, factor intensity reversal argument and Leontief Paradox. Let us go through them one by one in details.

(a) Demand Reversal. As we have already discussed this argument extensively earlier in this chapter, we will skip the description here in this segment.

(b) Factor Intensity Reversal. This argument hits one of the basic assumptions of the H-O Theory. The assumption in both the countries are the same which if simplified means that the capital intensive goods will employ exactly equal amount of capital in both the countries and the same applies for the labour intensive goods too. But in practise, there can be a situation in which the capital intensive goods can become labour intensive in another country and vice-versa. This is known as factor intensity reversal.

In such a condition, when factor-intensity reversal takes place, the two isoquants for the capital intensive good and the labour intensive goods cut each other more in Fig. 5.5. Unlike the Fig. 5.9, here both the isoquants cut each other twice i.e. at point E_1 and point E_2 respectively. As already understood, the capital abundant country A will have some amount of capital employed in producing food as well as cloth but more of labour will be required to produce cloth. It can also be said that capital-labour ratio will be higher for food which will be cheaper to produce. Thus country A will specialise in production and export of food.

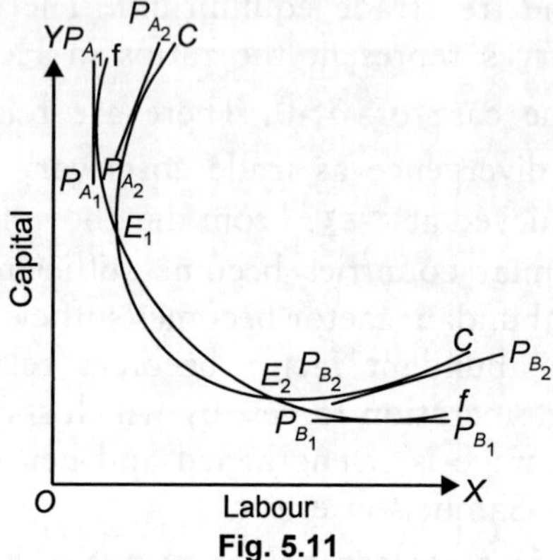

Fig. 5.11

Applying the same method of understanding to country *B*, the figure shows that this country will have a cheaper production of its labour intensive good i.e. food. Thus this country will specialise in the production and export of food which is a labour intensive goods here.

It is, hence clear from the above discussion that both the countries specialise in the production and export of the same commodity (food in the present example) which goes against the H-O Theory.

(c) Leontief Paradox. This goes against the outcome of H-O Theory which states that a capital abundant country exports capital intensive goods and imports labour intensive goods and the opposite applies to the labour abundant country.

Leontief made an extensive study on the structure of US exports and imports and found the results as contrary to H-O Theory. The study showed that though USA is a capital abundant country, its imports of capital goods exceeded the export of these goods and the exports consisting of labour goods exceeded the import of such goods. In the words of Leontief—"America's participation division of labour is.... based on its specialisation in labour intensive rather than capital intensive lines of production."[2]

The same phenomenon was reported by many more studies conducted by other economists of countries with different abundances. These studies have also refuted H-O Theory.

(d) Other. The above written criticisms were not the only points on which H-O Theory was criticised. It was Wijanholds who maintained that "the prices of the commodities are not determined by the costs of the factors of production, but the relation is quite the reverse."[3] According to him, the prices of the commodities are determined by their utility to the consumers and the prices of raw materials and labour are ultimately dependent on the prices of the final commodity. In the words of Walrus, "It is quite possible that although a certain type of labour may be scarce, wages may be at a low level for the simple reason that labour is used for the production of a commodity that is not very valuable."[4] Also, "Scarcity must always be seen in connection with the possibility of producing goods, for which consumers are prepared to pay a remunerative price. It is possible that labour in a country is scarce and at the same time wages are low because the labourers are not able (or lack initiative) to produce goods that command high prices."[5]

TRADE WITH FACTOR MOBILITY

In the previous section of this chapter we have examined traditional trade theories with factor mobility between sectors with each country but factor immobility between countries. Commodity movements are at least to some extent can be considered as a substitute for factor movements. The absence of trade impediments implies commodity price equalization and, even when factors are immobile; it is argued that there is a tendency toward factor-price equalization. In this section we shall consider trade with factor mobility, i.e. we are concerned with trade patterns with internationally mobile factor endowments. We shall consider capital and labour mobility. Here we shall prove that international capital or/and labour movement may invalidate some of the four core theorems, the factor equalization theorem, the Rybezynski theorem, the Stolper-Samuelson theorem, and the Heckscher-ohlin theorem, in the presence of international capital movement. Before we move further, we shall re-examine the 2 × 2 model, extending in two ways. Capital moves freely between countries. Also, land is considered as a production factor. The three factor model still has two immobile factor endowments, labour and land. We shall define a new variable, N, the total fixed amount of land and N_i for the amount of land used by industry i.

Now suppose that economy produces two goods using Cobb-Douglas production functions.

$$Y_i = a_i K_i^{\alpha_i} L_i^{\beta_i} N_i^{\varsigma_i}, \tag{1}$$

where

$$i=1,2, \;\; \alpha_i, \beta_i, \varsigma_i > 0, \;\; \alpha_i + \beta_i + \varsigma_i = 1$$

Let, wage, rate of interest and land rent be w, r, and R respectively. Here we assume that the rate of interest is exogenously fixed. Three prices, p_1, p_2, r are fixed exogenously and wage and land rent, w and R are determined endogenously. Thus the profits of the two sectors, π_i, can be given by

$$\pi_i = p_i Y_i - w L_i - r K_i - R N_i$$

Marginal conditions for maximizing profits are given by

$$r = \frac{\alpha_i p_i Y_i}{K_i}, \; w = \frac{\beta_i p_i Y_i}{L_i}, \;\; R = \frac{\varsigma_i p_i Y_i}{N_i} \tag{2}$$

The resource constraints are given by

$$\begin{aligned} K_1 + K_2 + K_E &= K \\ L_1 + L_2 &= L \\ N_1 + N_2 &= N \end{aligned} \tag{3}$$

where K_E is the outflow of domestic capital (negative K_E for an amount of foreign capital used in Home). The above two equations (2) and (3) contain nine variables, L_i, K_i, N_i, K_E, w and R, and nine equations for given P_i, r, K, L, and N.

From the marginal conditions in r and w, we have

$$\frac{\alpha_1 p_1 Y_1}{K_1} = \frac{\alpha_2 p_2 Y_2}{K_2}, \;\; \frac{\beta_1 p_1 Y_1}{L_1} = \frac{\beta_2 p_2 Y_2}{L_2}$$

From this equation we obtain $L_1/L_2 = \beta k$, where $\beta \equiv \alpha_2 \beta_1 / \alpha_1 \beta_2$ and $k \equiv K_1/K_2$. From $L_1/L_2 = \beta k$ and $L_1 + L_2 = L$, we solve

$$L_1 = \frac{\beta k L}{1+\beta k}, \; L_2 = \frac{L}{1+\beta k} \tag{4}$$

Similarly, from

$$\frac{\alpha_1 p_1 Y_1}{K_1} = \frac{\alpha_2 p_2 Y_2}{K_2}, \;\; \frac{\varsigma_1 p_1 Y_1}{N_1} = \frac{\varsigma_2 p_2 Y_2}{N_2}$$

We have

$$\frac{N_1}{N_2} = \varsigma k,$$

where $\varsigma \equiv \varsigma_1 \alpha_2 / \varsigma_2 \alpha_1$. From this equation and $N_1 + N_2 = N$ we have

$$N_1 = \frac{\varsigma k N}{1+\varsigma k}, \quad N_2 = \frac{N}{1+\varsigma k} \tag{5}$$

From $r = \alpha_i p_i Y_i / K_i$ and $Y_i = a_i K_i^{\alpha_i} L_i^{\beta_i} N_i^{\varsigma_i}$, we have

$$K_i = \left(\frac{\alpha_i p_i a_i L_i^{\beta_i} N_i^{\varsigma_i}}{r} \right)^{1/(1-\alpha_i)}$$

Dividing the above two equations yields

$$k = r^{\alpha} \frac{(\alpha_1 p_1 a_1 L_1^{\beta_1} N_1^{\varsigma_1})^{1/(1-\alpha_1)}}{(\alpha_2 p_2 a_2 L_2^{\beta_2} N_2^{\varsigma_2})^{1/(1-\alpha_2)}}$$

where $\alpha \equiv \dfrac{\alpha_2 - \alpha_1}{(1-\alpha_1)(1-\alpha_2)}$

Substituting equations (4) and (5) into the above equation we have

$$1 = r_0 (1+\beta k)^{r_1} (1+\varsigma k)^{r_2} \tag{6}$$

where

$$r_0 \equiv r^{\alpha} \frac{\left(\alpha_1 p_1 a_1 (\beta L)^{\beta_1} (\varsigma L)^{\varsigma_1}\right)^{1/(1-\alpha_1)}}{\left(\alpha_2 p_2 a_2 L^{\beta_2} N^{\varsigma_2}\right)^{1/(1-\alpha_2)}}$$

$$r_1 \equiv \frac{\beta_2}{1-\alpha_2} - \frac{\beta_1}{1-\alpha_1}, \quad r_2 \equiv \frac{\varsigma_2}{1-\alpha_2} - \frac{\varsigma_1}{1-\alpha_1}$$

We assume that equation (6) has a unique positive solution which implies that Home produces two goods. For a positive k, all the variables are determined by the following procedure: L_i by (4), N_i by (5), $K_E = K - K_1 - K_2$, w and R by (2) and Y_i.

From equation (2) we have

$$w = \frac{(1+\beta k) r \beta_1 K_1}{\alpha_1 \beta k L}, \quad R = \frac{(1+\varsigma k) r \varsigma_1 K_1}{\varsigma k N} \tag{7}$$

where

$$K_1 = \left(\frac{\alpha_1 p_1 a_1 \beta^{\beta_1} L^{\beta_1} \varsigma^{\varsigma_1} N^{\varsigma_1}}{r}\right)^{1/(1-\alpha_1)} \left(\frac{k}{1+\beta k}\right)^{\beta_1/(1-\alpha_1)} \left(\frac{k}{1+\varsigma k}\right)^{\varsigma_1/(1-\alpha_1)}$$

So long as two goods are produced, factor prices, (w, R), are affected by factor endowments. Here we see that the property of factor price insensitivity is not valid in general when factor mobility is allowed.

The factor price equalization theorem states that if two countries are engaged in free trade, having identical technologies but different factor endowments and if both countries produce both goods, then the factor prices (w, R) are equalized across the countries. As (w, R) are affected by the factor endowments, the factor price equalization theorem does not hold when factor mobility is allowed.

Now we shall see that when product prices are changed, how the factor prices will be changed. Taking derivatives of equation (7) with respect to p_1 and p_2 we have

$$\frac{1}{w}\frac{dw}{dp_1} = \left[1 - \frac{(\beta-\varsigma)\varsigma_1 p_0}{(1+\beta k)(1+\varsigma k)(1-\alpha_1)}\right]\frac{1}{(1-\alpha_1)p_1},$$

$$\frac{1}{R}\frac{dR}{dp_1} = \left[1 - \frac{(\varsigma-\beta)\beta_1 p_0}{(1+\beta k)(1+\varsigma k)(1-\alpha_1)}\right]\frac{1}{(1-\alpha_1)p_1},$$

$$\frac{1}{w}\frac{dw}{dp_2} = \frac{[(\beta-\varsigma)\varsigma_1 k - (1+\varsigma k)\alpha_1]p_0}{(1+\varsigma k)(1+\beta k)(1-\alpha_2)p_2 k}, \tag{8}$$

$$\frac{1}{R}\frac{dR}{dp_2} = \frac{[(\varsigma-\beta)\beta_1 k - \alpha_1(1+\beta k)]p_0}{(1+\varsigma k)(1-\alpha_2)p_2 k},$$

where

$$p_0 \equiv \frac{r_1 \beta}{1+\beta k} + \frac{r_2 \varsigma}{1+\varsigma k}$$

From its definition, we have

$$p_0 = \left(\frac{\beta_2}{1-\alpha_2} - \frac{\beta_1}{1-\alpha_1}\right)\frac{\beta}{1+\beta k} + \left(\frac{\varsigma_2}{1-\alpha_2} - \frac{\varsigma_1}{1-\alpha_1}\right)\frac{\varsigma}{1+\varsigma k}$$

Here one point should be noted that the sign of P_0 is ambiguous in general. Even if we are able determine the sign of P_0, it is still difficult to judge effects of changes in the prices on the economic equilibrium. This implies that the four core theorems may not be held in general. We shall show this assuming a special case of $\alpha_1 = \alpha_2$. It should be noted that this requirement also implies $\beta_1 + \varsigma_1 = \beta_2 + \varsigma_2$.

From equation (6) we can solve for k as a function of the prices as follows.

$$k = \frac{\bar{r}_0 - 1}{\varsigma - \bar{r}_0 \beta} \tag{9}$$

Where $\varsigma = \varsigma_1 / \varsigma_2$, $\beta = \beta_1 / \beta_2$, and

$$\bar{r}_0 \equiv \left(\frac{p_1 a_1 \beta^{\beta_1} \varsigma^{\varsigma_1}}{p_2 a_2} \right)^{1/(\beta_2 - \beta_1)} \frac{N}{L},$$

$$r_1 = -r_2 = \frac{\beta_2 - \beta_1}{1 - \alpha_1}.$$

We also make an assumption that the parameter values satisfy, $k>0$. From equation (2) we have

$$w = \frac{\beta_1 (\alpha_1 p_1 a_1)^{1/(1-\alpha_1)}}{\alpha_1 r^{\alpha_1/(1-\alpha_1)}} \left(\frac{N_1}{L_1} \right)^{\varsigma_1/(1-\alpha_1)}$$

$$R = \frac{\varsigma_1 (\alpha_1 p_1 a_1)^{1/(1-\alpha_1)}}{\alpha_1 r^{\alpha_1/(1-\alpha_1)}} \left(\frac{L_1}{N_1} \right)^{\beta_1/(1-\alpha_1)},$$

where we have used $K_1 = \left(\alpha_1 p_1 a_1 L_1^{\beta_1} N_1^{\varsigma_1} / r \right)^{1/(1-\alpha_1)}$. Substituting L_1 in (4) and N_1 in (5) and using the above equation we have

$$w = \frac{\beta_1 (\alpha_1 p_1 a_1)^{1/(1-\alpha_1)}}{\alpha_1 r^{\alpha_1/(1-\alpha_1)}} \left(\frac{p_2 a_2 \varsigma^{\alpha_2}}{p_1 a_1 \beta^{\beta_2}} \right)^{\alpha^* \varsigma_1}$$

$$R = \frac{\varsigma_1 (\alpha_1 p_1 a_1)^{1/(1-\alpha_1)}}{\alpha_1 r^{\alpha_1/(1-\alpha_1)}} \left(\frac{p_1 a_1 \beta^{\beta_2}}{p_2 a_2 \varsigma^{\alpha_2}} \right)^{\alpha^* \beta_1}, \tag{10}$$

In the above equation we have used equation (9) and

$$\alpha^* \equiv \frac{1}{(\beta_2 - \beta_1)(1-\alpha_1)}$$

From equation (10) we have following conclusions:

Factor Price Insensitivity: So long as two goods are produced under $\alpha_1 = \alpha_2$, then each price vector (p_1, p_2, r) corresponds to unique factor price (w, R). This implies that the immobile factor endowments (L, N) do not affect their prices, (w, R).

Factor Price Equalization Theorem: Let us suppose that two countries are engaged in free trade under $\alpha_1 = \alpha_2$, having identical technologies but different factor endowments. If both countries produce both goods, then the prices of the immobile factors, (w,R), are equalized across the countries.

The prices p_1, p_2, r are equal across the countries. Since the two countries have the identical technologies, that is, α_i, β_i and a_i are identical across the countries, from equation (10) we find that Samuelson's theorem holds even when we allow one factor to be freely mobile under the strict condition of $\alpha_1 = \alpha_2$. This theorem implies that trade in goods may equalize factor prices across the countries even when some production factors are immobile and some others are mobile.

Thus from equations (4) and (5), we have

$$\frac{N_1}{L_1} - \frac{N_2}{L_2} = (\varsigma_1 - \varsigma_2)\frac{(1+\beta k)(1-\alpha_1)N}{(1+\varsigma k)\beta_2 \varsigma_2 \beta L}.$$

When $\alpha_1 = \alpha_2$, sector 1 is land intensive, with a higher land-labour ratio than in sector 2 at any given factor prices, that is $N_1/N_2 > N_2/L_2$. Sector 1 being land intensive is equal to

$$\varsigma_1 - \varsigma_2 = \beta_2 - \beta_1 > 0 \tag{11}$$

We also have $\alpha^* = > 0$.

Now we shall examine the change in factor prices due to change in product prices. Taking derivatives of equation (10) with respect to p_1 and p_2 we have

$$\frac{1}{w}\frac{dw}{dp_1} = \frac{-\varsigma_2}{(\beta_2 - \beta_1)(1-\alpha_1)p_1} < 0,$$

$$\frac{1}{R}\frac{dR}{dp_1}=\frac{\beta_2}{(\beta_2-\beta_1)(1-\alpha_1)p_1}>0, \tag{12}$$

$$\frac{1}{w}\frac{dw}{dp_2}=\frac{\alpha^* \varsigma_1}{p_2}>0,\ \frac{1}{R}\frac{dR}{dp_2}=-\frac{\alpha^* \varsigma_1}{p_2}<0$$

From equation (12) we have

$$\left(\frac{p_1}{w}\right)\frac{d(w/p_1)}{dp_1}=\frac{1}{w}\frac{dw}{dp_1}-\frac{1}{p_1}<0,$$

$$\left(\frac{p_1}{R}\right)\frac{d(R/p_1)}{dp_1}=\frac{\beta_2-(\beta_2-\beta_1)(1-\alpha_1)}{(\beta_2-\beta_1)(1-\alpha_1)p_1}>0 \tag{13}$$

Stolper-Samuelson Theorem: This theorem states that an increase in the relative price of a goods will increase the real return to the factor used intensively in that goods, and reduce the real return to the other factor.

We now examine effects of changes in the endowments. From equation (8), we have

$$\frac{1}{k}\frac{dk}{dL}=\frac{(\beta-\varsigma)\bar{r}_0}{(\bar{r}_0-1)(\varsigma-\bar{r}_0\beta)L}<0,$$

$$\frac{1}{k}\frac{dk}{dN}=\frac{-(\beta-\varsigma)\bar{r}_0}{(\varsigma-\bar{r}_0\beta)(\bar{r}_0-1)L}>0, \tag{14}$$

where we have used $\beta-\varsigma=-(\beta_1+\varsigma_1)(\beta_2-\beta_1)/\beta_2\varsigma_2<0$. From equations (4), (5) and (14), we obtain the effects of change in the labour force on the factor distributions.

$$\frac{1}{L_1}\frac{dL_1}{dL}=\frac{1}{L}+\frac{1}{(1+\beta k)k}\frac{dk}{dL},$$

$$\frac{1}{L_2}\frac{dL_2}{dL}=\frac{1}{L}-\frac{\beta}{(1+\beta k)}\frac{dk}{dL}>0$$

$$\frac{1}{N_1}\frac{dN_1}{dL}=\frac{1}{(1+\varsigma k)k}\frac{dk}{dL}<0,$$

$$\frac{1}{N_2}\frac{dN_2}{dL}=\frac{-\varsigma}{1+\varsigma k}\frac{dk}{dL}>0 \tag{15}$$

From equations (4), (5) and (14) we get the effects of change in the land on the factor distributions as

$$\frac{1}{L_1}\frac{dL_1}{dN}=\frac{1}{(1+\beta k)k}\frac{dk}{dL}>0,$$

$$\frac{1}{L_2}\frac{dL_2}{dN}=-\frac{\beta}{(1+\beta k)}\frac{dk}{dN}<0,$$

$$\frac{1}{N_1}\frac{dN_1}{dN}=\frac{1}{N}+\frac{1}{(1+\varsigma k)k}\frac{dk}{dN}>0,$$

$$\frac{1}{N_2}\frac{dN_2}{dN}=\frac{1}{N}-\frac{\varsigma}{1+\varsigma k}\frac{dk}{dN}, \tag{16}$$

It should be noted that changes in the endowments have no effect on the wage and the rate of interest. From equation (2) we have

$$\frac{1}{Y_1}\frac{dY_1}{dL}=\frac{1}{N_1}\frac{dN_1}{dL}<0,$$

$$\frac{1}{Y_2}\frac{dY_2}{dL}=\frac{1}{N_2}\frac{dN_2}{dL}>0,$$

$$\frac{1}{Y_1}\frac{dY_1}{dN}=\frac{1}{L_1}\frac{dL_1}{dN}>0,$$

$$\frac{1}{Y_2}\frac{dY_2}{dN}=\frac{1}{L_2}\frac{dL_2}{dN}<0 \tag{17}$$

Here we find that industry 1 is land intensive and industry 2 is labour intensive. We have just showed that the factor price insensitivity lemma, Samuelson' factor price equalization theorem, Stolper-Samuelson theorem, and Rybezynski's theorem, are still valid when one production factor is internationally mobile. Here we shall show that the Heckscher-Ohlin theorem is also valid when one factor is internationally mobile.

Heckscher-Ohlin Theorem: According to this theorem each country will export the good that uses its abundant factor intensively.

The consumer's utility-maximizing problem is given by

$$\max C_1^{\varphi_1} C_2^{\varphi}, \ s.t.: p_1 C_1 + p_2 C_2 = y,$$

where C_i is the consumption level of good i, φ_1 and φ_2 are positive parameters, and y is the total income given by $y=rK+wL+RN$. For simplicity we assume $\varphi_1+\varphi_2=1$. The optimal solution is given by

$$p_i C_i = \varphi_1 y.$$

In case of autarky, we have $C_i = Y_i$. From $p_i C_i = \varphi_1 y$ and $C_i = Y_i$, we have

$$\frac{p_1 Y_1}{p_2 Y_2} = \frac{\varphi_1}{\varphi_2}$$

Substituting $r=\alpha_i p_i Y_i / K_i$ into the above equation we have $k=\varphi_1/\varphi_2$, where we have used $\alpha_1=\alpha_2$. Substituting equation (9) into the above equation we have

$$p^{1/\beta_2-\beta_1}\frac{N}{L}=\left[\frac{\varsigma(\varphi_1/\varphi_2)+1}{\beta(\varphi_1/\varphi_2)+1}\right]\left(\frac{a_1 \beta^{\beta_1} \varsigma^{\varsigma_1}}{a_2}\right)^{1/(\beta_1-\beta_2)} \tag{18}$$

where $p = p_1/p_2$. Equation (18) determines the relative price in the home country in autarky. According to the assumptions that the two countries have the identical technology and preference, according to equation (18) we have

$$\tilde{p}^{\,1/(\beta_2-\beta_1)}\frac{\tilde{N}}{\tilde{L}}=p^{1/(\beta_2-\beta_1)}\frac{N}{L} \tag{19}$$

when the countries are in autarky. If $N/L>\tilde{N}/\tilde{L}$, then we have $p^{1/(\beta_2-\beta_1)}<\tilde{p}^{1/(\beta_2-\beta_1)}$.

As $\beta_2>\beta_1$, we have $p<\tilde{p}$, that is $\dfrac{p_1}{p_2}<\dfrac{\tilde{p}_1}{\tilde{p}_2}$.

This implies that when the two countries are in autarky, the relative price in Home is lower than the relative price in Foreign. Hence, when the two countries start to trade, goods 1 is exported to Foreign and goods 2 is imported from Foreign. Thus, the Heckscher-Ohlin theorem is confirmed. It can be seen that in general (that is, when $\alpha_1 \neq \alpha_2$) the theorems are invalid. But when $\alpha_1=\alpha_2$, the core theorems are all held. This condition implies that the internationally mobile factor affects symmetrically the neoclassical production functions and the core theorems mainly refer to the relative properties of the two sectors, it is reasonable to expect that the core theorems hold under the requirement.

EFFECTS OF INTERNATIONAL TRADE

Heckscher-Ohlin Theory have been criticised a lot many times, yet, this is the only theory that gives the real reason behind the trade among countries. Not only does it give the reason but also tells about the effects of international trade. These effects have been told more often than not indirectly in the theory, that's why these effects are being dealt with, in separacy with the theory.

Equalisation of Commodity Prices

Under free trade, assuming perfect competition and no cost of transfer,[6] the prices of commodities will be equal in all countries. The difference in the prices of the similar commodities in any two countries cannot exceed the costs of transferring them from one to the other country. In the actual world, however, the prices of the similar commodities differ by more than the costs of transfer because of the existence of imperfect competition in international trade.

Equalisation of Factor Prices

Trade in commodities sets into operation a tendency towards the equalisation of factor prices in different countries. Will the free trade in commodities lead to partial or complete equalisation of factor prices? Ohlin states at several places that free trade in goods is not likely to bring about a complete equalisation of factor prices. His treatment of the problem, in fact, is not satisfactory. At one place, he states, "it is not worthwhile to analyse in detail why full equalisation does not occur; for when the costs of transport and other impediments to trade have been introduced into the reasoning, such an equalisation is in any case obviously impossible."[7] The question under consideration is not whether imperfect mobility of goods leads to complete factor-price equalisation, but whether perfect mobility of goods does so. At another place, he states that the localisation of industry and hence the demand for factors cannot completely adapt to the factor endowments in each region because the industrial demand is always the joint demand for several factors.[8] This, however, does not seem to be a satisfactory explanation.

Samuelson contends that the "real factor prices must be exactly the same in both countries",[9] under the following assumptions:[10]

(a) There are only two countries, each producing only two commodities.

(b) Each commodity is produced with the help of two factors and the production function of each commodity shows constant returns to scale.

(c) There operates the law of diminishing productivity i.e. if any input is increased relative to other inputs, its marginal productivity diminishes.

(d) The two commodities can be separated by their factor intensities.

(e) The two factors are identical in quality in the two countries and the technological production functions are the same in both the countries.

(f) There is perfect mobility of the commodities between the two countries. There are no tariffs or transport costs and the free trade completely equalises the price ratios of the two commodities in the two countries. There is complete immobility of factors of production between the two countries.

(g) Each country produces some amount of both the commodities with both the factors of production i.e. none of the two countries specialises completely.

Let us illustrate the process of factor-price equalisation with the help of a hypothetical example. Suppose that country *A* is relatively abundant in labour and country *B* in land. Before the establishment of trade, the price of labour will be comparatively lower and that of land higher in country *A* and reverse will be the case in country *B*. With the establishment of trade between the two countries, *A* will specialise in the commodity requiring comparatively more labour and less land (Let us say cloth) and *B* in that requiring comparatively more land and less labour (Let us say wheat). As *A* specialises in the production of cloth and diverts its resources from the production of wheat, at the ratio in which the labour and land are combined in *A* for the production of cloth before the introduction of trade, *A* will require more labour and less land than that which is being relieved from a reduction in the production of wheat. This will lead to a readjustment in the ratio in which the labour and land are employed in the two industries in order to optimise the use of the available labour and land in the two industries in *A*. In equilibrium, the ratio of the marginal productivities (and hence prices) of labour and land must be the same in the two industries and equal to the ratio of the prices of the cloth and wheat. Through a similar process, the ratio of labour to land will rise in both the industries in *B* and in equilibrium the ratio of the marginal productivities (and hence prices) of labour and land must be the same in the two industries and equal to the ratio of the prices of the cloth and wheat. After the introduction of trade, under the above mentioned assumptions, the ratio of the prices of wheat and cloth will be identical in the two countries. As the ratio of the marginal productivities (and hence the prices) of labour and capital are equal to the prices of wheat and cloth in both the countries, the ratio of the prices of wheat and cloth being identical in the two countries, the ratio of the prices of labour and capital must be identical in the two countries.

(a) Introduction of More Commodities and Countries. Introduction of a third or more commodities does not invalidate the above conclusion because what is required is that at least two commodities are produced simultaneously in both the countries. The introduction of additional commodities rather increases the chances of a complete factor-price equalisation. When there are several commodities, the chances of the existence of two commodities with widely different factor intensities are greater; the existence of such commodities makes possible a complete equalisation of factor prices even in cases in which the two countries differ widely in their factor endowments.

(b) Introduction of More Factors of Production. Commodities remaining only two, the introduction of a third factor demolishes the whole proposition. Suppose the ratio of capital to land and labour is higher in country *A* than that in country *B*. If there were no differences in the capital equipments of the two countries the marginal productivities of labour and land would have been equalised by the labour-abundant country *B* specialising in the production of cloth and the land-abundant country *A* specialising in that of wheat. With a higher ratio of capital to land and labour in *A* as compared with *B*, the marginal productivities (and hence the prices) of land and labour might be higher in *A* than those in *B*. The marginal productivity of capital, of course, will be higher in *B* than that in *A*. The prices of both the food and cloth will be the same in the two countries, the higher cost of land and labour being offset by the lower cost of capital in *A*. As the prices of the commodities have been equalised, there is no incentive for further trade and hence no further tendency towards the factor-price equalisation. Thus, when the number of factors is more than the number of commodities, the factor-prices might not be equalised completely. The proposition remains valid so long as the number of commodities is not less than the number of factors of production.

(c) **Complete Specialisation.** If specialisation is complete in one country, the marginal productivities and hence the prices of the factors might not be equalised completely between the two countries. Suppose, for instance, that country *A* is much smaller in size than country *B*; it specialises completely in the production of cloth and yet cannot produce enough to meet the whole demand of both the countries and country *B* has to devote a part of its resources to the production of cloth. Under such conditions, the marginal productivities (and hence prices) of the factors in the production of cloth might remain higher in *A* as compared with those in *B*.

(d) **Costs of Transfer.** In the actual world, the movement of goods between different countries is not free of cost. Movement of goods from one country to another involves the costs of transportation and insurance, tariffs etc. The prices of goods and hence the factor prices between the two countries might differ to the extent of the cost of movement of the good from one country to the other.

(e) **Increasing Returns to Scale.** Factor prices might not be equalised if there are increasing returns to scale. Suppose, for instance, that country *A* is endowed with double the amount of each factor of production possessed by country *B*. Further, the demand for every commodity is double in *A* of that in *B* and the production of every commodity requires the factors in the same ratio in both the countries. If there are increasing returns to scale, the marginal productivities and hence the prices of all the factors will be higher in *A* as compared with those in *B*.

(f) **Joint Demand for Factors.** The effect of the introduction of trade in commodities might be quite the reverse on the prices of some factors if these are demanded jointly with other factors.

Suppose, for instance, that country *A* is relatively scarce in a particular factor which is used in combination with other factors relatively abundant in it for the production of certain commodities. The relatively higher price of this particular factor in *A* might be offset, or even more than that, by the relatively lower prices of the other abundant factors. Introduction of trade will increase the relative scarcity of this particular factor and thereby accentuate the inequality in its relative price in the two countries.

(g) Different Technical Processes. Trade in commodities might not equalise factor prices if quite different technical processes are used in the two countries. Suppose, for instance, that country *A* is relatively abundant in labour and country *B* in capital. Further, country *A* employs more labour and less capital in the production of wheat and more capital and less labour in the production of cloth; country *B* employs the two factors for the production of wheat and cloth in quite the reverse ratios. If after the opening of trade, country *A* specialises in the production of wheat and *B* in that of cloth, the additional factors required by *A* for increasing the production of wheat will be different from those relieved in *B* from a reduction in the production of wheat which, now, it imports from *A*. Similarly, the additional factors required by *A* for increasing the production of cloth will be different from those relieved in *A* from a reduction in the production of cloth which it obtains, now, from *B* in exchange for wheat. Under such conditions, the opening of trade will not decrease the relative scarcities of the factors of production and hence the differences in their relative prices between the two countries.

(h) Differences in Production Atmosphere. The production atmosphere varies from country to country. A combination of the same amount of land, labour and capital might yield different amounts of output in different countries. The differences may be in psychological, social or physical atmosphere. Some countries, for instance, might be having better rains and climate. The propensity to work hard and honestly may be higher in one country than in others. Because of the differences in production atmosphere, the marginal productivities and hence prices of all factors might be higher in one country than in another.

(i) Possibilities of Substitution between Different Factors. Free trade in commodities might not equalise factor prices if the possibilities of substituting one factor for another differ in different industries producing traded goods. Suppose, for instance, that country *A* is relatively labour-abundant and country *B* land-abundant. Further, the production of cloth requires land and labour in a fixed ratio whatever be their prices and land and labour can be substituted for each other in the production of wheat. Rents will be higher and wages lower in country *A* than in country *B*. *A* will practice intensive farming and *B* extensive farming. As the ratio in which the factors are combined for the production of cloth is fixed, production of food will be more labour-intensive than that of cloth in country *A*, and the reverse will be the case in country *B*. The marginal productivity of land will be higher in *A* than in *B* and that of labour will be higher in *B* than in *A*. The price of food might be the same in both the countries, the higher cost of land being offset by the lower cost of labour in *A* and the higher cost of labour being offset by the lower cost of land in *B*. Thus the marginal productivities and hence the prices of land and labour might remain unequal in the production of food in the two countries in spite of the introduction of free trade in food between them.

(j) From the above analysis, it is evident that the trade in commodities alone might not bring about a complete or even a substantially complete equalisation of factor prices. Factor movements will be essential if the factor prices are to be further equalised.

(k) Movement of commodities and factors works in the same direction. Movement of commodities works towards an equalisation of factor prices and thereby reduces the incentive for factor movements. Movement of factors decreases the differences in the relative scarcity of factors between different countries and thereby diminishes the inequality in their prices which gives rise to trade in commodities. Trade in commodities alone cannot, as seen above, bring about a complete equalisation of factor prices. Movement of commodities supplemented by a movement of factors can bring about a considerable degree of equalisation in factor prices. In case trade in commodities alone can bring about an equalisation in factor prices, the possibility of factor movements works as a potential defence against any inequality in factor prices.

Similarly, movements of factors and commodities work in the same direction in bringing about an equality in the prices of the commodities. Trade in commodities equalises their prices directly while factor movements do the same indirectly by equalising the factor prices which enter into the costs and hence into the prices of the commodities.

Effect of Trade on Factor Equipment

Trade in commodities will accentuate the differences in factor equipment if the elasticity of their supply is positive. With the opening of trade, each country specialises in the industries employing more of its relatively abundant and less of its relatively scarce factors; the demand for the abundant factors rises and that for the scarce factors falls; a rise in the demand for abundant factors raises their prices and a fall in the demand for scarce factors lowers their prices; a rise in the prices of the abundant factors induces an increase in their supply and a fall in the price of scarce factors causes a decrease in their supply. Thus the net result is that the trade increases the supply of abundant factors and decreases that of scarce factors and thereby widens the differences in factor equipment of the trading countries. The widening of differences in factor equipment furthers the scope for trade of the same nature. The greater the elasticity of supply of the factors of production, the stronger will be the defence against the equalisation of factor prices in different countries. The stronger the defence against the equalisation of factor prices, the greater will be the tendency to trade and hence the total volume of trade. Generally, the longer the period permitted, the greater will be the elasticity of supply of the factors of production.

Effect of Trade on the Quality of Labour and Capital

Trade changes the quality of the people, teaches them to consume new things and to use old things in new ways. Technical knowledge is largely the result of specialisation, which trade has made possible. The character, not only of so called technical labour, but also of skilled and unskilled labour is affected.[11]

The improvements in the quality of labour and capital brought about by the specialisation cause a further tendency towards specialisation.

Acquired no less than inherited qualities which involve differences between the productive resources of various nations lead to specialisation along different lines i.e. to international trade.[12]

Thus trade creates further trade in two ways viz. (i) by accentuating differences in the factor endowments (ii) by accentuating differences in the quality of the factors of production.

Effect of Trade on the Factor Prices in Terms of Commodities

The total value of the factors of production during a given period is equivalent to the total value of the goods and services produced with the help of these factors. Opening of trade increases the efficiency of production by employing the available factors in a more economical combination. This means a greater amount of goods is produced with the same factors of production or, in other words, the value of the factors in terms of goods rises after the establishment of trade. The value of the factors of production in terms of commodities will not rise in a region which possesses factors in the ratio in which they are employed after the establishment of trade. Trade will increase the value of the factors in a region only if it affects the relative scarcity of these in it. The case in which the trade does not affect the relative scarcity of the factors is an exceptional one and is not very probable in the actual world. Generally, trade will affect the relative scarcity of the factors in a region and thereby raise their prices. Thus even if the earlier mentioned factor-price equalisation process lowers the relative value of a factor in a region, its absolute value might not fall if the fall in its relative value is offset, or more than that, by the general increased efficiency of production resulting from the use of available factors in a more economical combination.

Effect of the Movement of Factors on the Volume and Character of Trade

Movement of factors affects the volume of trade by changing.

(a) the relative scarcity and hence the prices of different factors;

(b) the size of incomes and hence the volume of demand; and

(c) the direction of demand.

Movement of factors from countries where they are relatively abundant towards those where they are relatively scarce decreases the inequalities in factor equipment and thereby the scope for trade.

Movement of factors affects the income in two ways viz., (i) by changing the total income and (ii) by changing its distribution among different regions. Optimisation of factor equipment in different countries brought about through the movement of factors will increase the total national income and thereby the volume of trade. The effect on trade is uncertain when the quantity of factors (and hence income) is decreased in one country and increased in another. Factor movements are likely to increase trade if these lead towards a reduction of inequalities in the distribution of income between different countries and decrease it in the reverse case. The trade between two countries having more or less equal incomes is very likely to be greater than that between two countries one of which has a very larger income and the other a very small one. Generally, movements are likely to be towards countries having scanty factors of production (and hence lower incomes); this will equalise the incomes and thereby increase the volume of trade. The movement of factors may be from countries having scanty factors towards those having larger quantities of factors if the production is subject to the law of decreasing costs; this will accentuate the inequalities in income and thereby decrease trade.

FUTURE OF INTERNATIONAL TRADE

Factor movements will affect the prices of factors and thereby the distribution of income within the countries, too. The effect on trade of the changes in the distribution of income within the country is very uncertain.

We saw earlier the two ways in which trade creates further trade viz. (i) by accentuating the differences in factor endowments; (ii) by accentuating the differences in the quality of factors. On the other hand, there are certain other forces which are working towards a dimunition of the inequalities in factor equipment. A substantial portion of the world trade, today, is explained by the differences in technology and capital equipment. Most of the advanced countries possess a comparative advantage in manufacturing not because of favourable endowment of natural factors but because of their superior technology and a larger amount of capital. Several less developed countries can produce many manufactured goods at a cost lower than that of the advanced countries if provided with the same technology and capital equipment. Thus the comparative cost advantage enjoyed by advanced countries is acquired rather than being natural. As time passes, the less developed countries go on acquiring technology and equipment through trade and the differences in the acquired factors of production go on decreasing. Gradually, a stage may be reached when less developed countries are in a position to produce manufactured goods domestically at competitive costs. This process may go on and some time these countries may be in a position to produce domestically even capital goods. This, of course, in no way implies that the trade will come to an end. The process described above will not stop trade but replace only that part of it which is contrary to the natural comparative advantage and is caused by the acquired comparative advantage by the trade which is in conformity with the natural comparative advantage. So long as there exist differences in the natural factor endowments, there will remain scope for trade. Even with identical factor endowments, the scope for trade can arise, as seen above, from specialisation when there exist economies of large scale production. Similarly, the differences in comparative costs caused by political, social and economic institutions will go on offering scope for trade. Actual experience shows that trade has increased with the industrialisation and the consequent rise in the income of the less developed countries. No doubt, the less developed countries start producing domestically certain manufactured goods which were being imported previously, but the rise in their incomes brought about by industrialisation arouses the demand for goods which people were not accustomed to, or could not afford to consume before. World trade statistics show that more trade is carried on among the industrialised countries than that between the industrialised and the primary producing countries or that among the primary producing countries themselves. A part of the trade between advanced countries is simply exchange between different varieties of the same commodities.

NOTES

1. Eli F. Hecksher, "The Effect of Foreign Trade on the Distribution of Income", *Ekonomisk Tidskrift*, XXI, 1991, pp. 497-512. Reprinted in American Economic Association, *Readings in the Theory of International Trade*, New York, McGraw-Hill, 1949. Bertil Ohlin, *Interregional and International Trade*, Harvard University Press, Cambridge, 1933.
2. W. Leontief, "Domestic Production and Foreign Trade: The American Capital Position Re-examined", *Proceedings of the American Philosophical Society*, 97 (Sep. 1953), and Reprinted in American Economic Association, *Readings in International Economics*, Homewood, Illinois: Richard D. Irwin, 1968), pp. 522-23.

3. H.W.J. Wijanholds, "The Theory of International Trade: A New Approach", *South African Journal of Economics* (Sep. 1953), p. 236.
4. *Ibid.*
5. *Ibid.*, p. 238.
6. Cost of transfer includes the costs of transport and insurance, tariffs, etc.
7. B. Ohlin, *Interregional and International Trade* (Cambridge, 1933), p. 115.
8. *Ibid.*, p. 38.
9. P.A. Samuelson, "International Factor-Price Equalisation", *Economic Journal* (June, 1949), p. 182.
10. *Ibid.*, pp. 181-82.
11. B. Ohlin, *Interregional and International Trade* (Cambridge, 1933), p. 125.
12. *Ibid.*, pp. 125-26.

Gains from International Trade

6

MEASUREMENT OF THE GAIN FROM TRADE

The classical economists generally follow three different methods for dealing with the question of national gains from international trade viz. (a) economy in the cost of obtaining a given national income measured with the help of the doctrine of comparative costs; (b) an increase in national income; (c) terms of trade as an index of the international distribution and the trend of gain. They often shift from one to the other measure without making a clear cut distinction between these.[1] When we are referring to a point of time, there is no difference between (a) and (b). Any specific amount of gain can be expressed either as a reduction in cost per unit of income or as an increase in income per unit of cost because the cost and price structure remains unchanged. The two may not be identical if the comparison is extended over time.

The gain from international trade might be measured by the loss that would be incurred in the absence of trade. If the domestic cost of production of imports increases due to certain reasons, the gain from an unchanged volume and composition of imports obtained in exchange for an unchanged volume and composition of exports (whose cost of production remains constant) will increase because the loss from national self-sufficiency will be greater in the changed situation. The gain from trade increases in the changed situation inspite of the fact that the national income of the country, the rate of exchange between its exports and imports and the cost of production of its exports remain the same. In a state of autarky, the national income per unit of cost would have decreased or the cost per unit of national income would have increased in the changed situation. Similarly, if the domestic cost of production of imports decreases because of technological progress or due to certain other reasons, the gain from an unchanged volume and composition of imports obtained in exchange for an unchanged volume and composition of exports (whose cost of production remains constant) will decrease because the loss from national self-sufficiency will be smaller in the changed situation. If the reduction in the cost of production of exports is equal to that in the domestic cost of production of imports, the gain from trade will remain unaffected.

It might, however, be impossible to produce domestically certain imported goods. The domestic cost of production of such goods will be infinite. This amounts to saying that the gain from international trade is infinite if there exists even a single imported commodity which cannot be produced domestically; this seems somewhat absurd. The actual loss from the denial of such commodities will be equivalent to the amount of satisfaction obtained from the consumption of these commodities minus the satisfaction from the commodities that can be produced with the resources freed from the production of goods which have got to be exported for obtaining these commodities. Thus the gain from trade will be equivalent to the difference between the domestic cost of production and the import price or the difference between the satisfaction obtained from the consumption of imported commodities minus the satisfaction from the commodities which can be produced with the resources freed from the production of goods which have got to be exported for imports obtained, whichever is less. Satisfaction being a subjective thing, it is not possible to compare, in actual practice, the satisfaction that would be obtained from the domestic consumption of exports and satisfaction that would be lost if the imports of value equivalent to that of exports were not available for consumption.

Even if it is assumed that all the imported goods can be produced domestically at a higher cost with the resources freed by the cessation of production of export goods, all goods will not be produced and consumed in the previous ratio because the pattern of production and consumption will change with the change in the costs and prices of different commodities. The actual loss from a policy of national self-sufficiency, therefore, will be smaller than that which would result if the various goods are produced and consumed in the same ratio as under international trade. The maximum gain from international trade is the reduction in income (or increase in the cost of obtaining a fixed income) that would result from an attempt to produce and consume various goods domestically in the same ratio in which these would be consumed under international trade. The minimum gain from international trade is the increase in income (or the reduction in cost of obtaining a fixed income) that would result if the goods are consumed under international trade in the same ratio in which they would be produced and consumed domestically in the absence of international trade. The actual gain from international trade is very likely to fall somewhere between the minimum and the maximum gain because the consumption pattern will adapt to each of the two situations and the goods consumed will not be identical under self-sufficiency and international trade.

The classical and neo-classical writers, generally, measure the actual gain to a country from trade at a particular time in reference to the domestic cost of production of imports but measure the trend in gain over a period of time in reference to the changes in the price ratio of exports and imports. This would not make much difference if the cost structure and the composition and character of imports and exports remain everywhere unchanged over the period under consideration. For instance, if the composition and the cost of production of the exports and imports of a country remains unchanged and the prices of its exports rise relative to those of its imports, the increase in its gain from trade can be measured by any of the above mentioned two methods without making any difference. Any increase in the gain of one party, under these conditions, will be at the cost of some other party. Changes in costs, however, create the possibilities of reciprocal increases or decreases in gain from trade. To appraise the effect of changes in the ratio between the prices of exports and imports over a period of time on the gain from trade, therefore, due consideration should be given to changes in costs in the corresponding periods. If, for instance, the increase in the prices of exports of a country is more (less) than the increase in the cost of its exports, prices of imports remaining unchanged, its gain from trade will increase (decrease). If the increase (decrease) in the prices of exports is equal to the increase (decrease) in the cost of production of exports, prices of imports remaining unchanged, the gain from trade will remain unchanged.

Changes in costs are very likely to change the composition and character of the exports and imports of a country. Changes in the composition and character of exports and imports might also be caused by changes in the ratio of exchange independent of the changes in costs. Movements of the relative prices of exports and imports might not give a correct idea of the trend of the gain from international trade even after taking into consideration the corresponding movements in costs if the composition and character of exports and imports is dissimilar during different periods.

Jevons criticises the terms of trade as an index of the gain from international trade on the ground that the terms of trade relate the utility from the marginal unit of imports with the disutility from the marginal unit of exports whereas the gain from trade is measured by the difference between the total utility from imports and the total disutility from exports.[2] We cannot obtain the total amount of gain by multiplying the gain from the marginal unit of trade with the volume of trade. It is possible that the total gain from trade may increase even with a deterioration in the terms of trade if this is accompanied by a considerable increase in the volume of trade. Assuming away the difficulties involved in applying the concept of utility to a country, the terms of trade will be equal to the ratio between the marginal utility of imports and the marginal disutility of exports; any change that occurs will alter only the terms of ratio and not the ratio itself; the marginal unit of trade yields no gain under equilibrium conditions because the marginal utility from imports equals the marginal disutility from foregoing the domestic consumption of exports. The gain from trade will be affected only if the change responsible for an alteration in the terms of trade affects any of the following:

(a) Utility function of imports, (b) disutility function of exports, (c) volume and composition of trade. An increase in the amounts of foreign goods obtained in exchange for a unit of domestic goods need not necessarily be beneficial for the country under all circumstances. Let us illustrate this point by taking a few hypothetical cases.

A country might improve its commodity term of trade by levying tariffs or quantitative restrictions on its imports. This will not be beneficial for the country if the loss to the consumers from the denial of commodities whose import has been restricted is more than the gain from the improved terms of trade. In case the country produces domestically the commodities whose import has been restricted, the loss from an increase in the opportunity cost of production of these commodities might far outweigh the gain from the exchange of the rest of the traded commodities at a slightly favourable rate of exchange. The restriction of its imports will decrease the demand for its exports because the balance of payments must balance in the long run (assuming that there are no capital or gold movements). This might cause unemployment in the export industries if the resources can not be shifted to other industries. Even if these can be shifted to some other industries, their productivity in these industries might not be as high as that in export industries.

Another way of improving the terms of trade will be the creation of an artificial inflation. The evil effects of inflation, however, might far outweigh the benefit from an improvement in the terms of trade.

If the increase in the domestic cost of production of exports is more than the improvement in the terms of trade, the gain from trade will decrease inspite of an improvement in the terms of trade. Similarly, if owing to change in tastes or due to certain other factors, the utility from imports falls by an amount larger than that of the improvement in the ratio of exchange, the gain from trade will decrease inspite of an improvement in the terms of trade.

The changes in a country's gains from trade over a period of time can be caused by changes in any of the following factors: (a) changes in the international ratio of exchange; (b) changes in the real cost of production of exports; (c) changes in the potential domestic cost of production (or the utility of imports); (d) changes in the volume of international trade; (e) changes in the composition of international trade etc. We shall not dwell any further on the first three factors because these have already been discussed above. The cost of production of exports, potential domestic cost of production of imports, and the ratio of exchange between imports and exports remaining the same, an increase in the volume of trade brought about by a change in national income, tastes, etc. will increase the gain from trade. The gain from trade vanes for different export and import commodities. The difference between the imported cost and the potential domestic cost of production varies from commodity to commodity. Total volume of trade remaining the same, if the commodities with greater difference in comparative costs are substituted for those with smaller differences in comparative costs, the gain from trade will increase and fall in the reverse case.

DISTRIBUTION OF THE GAINS FROM TRADE

Ricardo states that the cost of production theory which explains domestic values is inadequate to explain the international values because of the possibility of differences in the remuneration of the factors of production caused by the immobility of the factors of production between different countries but he does not show as to how the international values are determined or the gain from trade is distributed. James Mill, in the first edition of his *Elements of Political Economy* commits the error of attributing the whole gain to each of the trading parties.[3] This aroused a lot of criticism by his friends and his son sometime between the period 1825 to 1828. As a result of these criticisms, James Mill unsuccessfully tries to remove the error in the third edition of his *Elements*. In the third edition, he states that the gain from international trade would be distributed equally among the trading countries as a result of the competition;[4] this again is not the correct position. Pennington seems to be the first who explicitly points out in print that the comparative costs set the maximum and the minimum limits within which the terms of trade can vary and the actual terms of trade within these limits will be determined by the force of reciprocal demand.[5] The role of demand force in determining the actual terms of trade is recognised by some of the classical economists prior to Pennington among whom the names of Longfield and Torrens deserve special mention. Longfield and Torrens recognise the principle while dealing with certain other problems and do not connect it with the doctrine of comparative costs. Torrens, discussion of the problem arouses interest in J.S. Mill and leads him to publish in 1844 some essays written in 1829-30. One of these essays relates to the problems of the distribution of gains from international trade and the terms of trade.[6] Mill, later on, develops and repeats this essay in his *Principles*.[7] The credit for the doctrine, however, generally goes to J.S. Mill because it is from his *Principles* and not from the works of the earlier authors that the later economists learn the doctrine. In addition, he is the first to state the doctrine though he does not publish it first.

Mill's Theory of International Values

Country	*Cost of production in labour units of a unit of commodity*	
	X	Y
A	8	4
B	4	3

Before the introduction of trade, the rate of exchange between *X* and *Y* will be 1:2 in *A* and 3:4 in *B*. When trade starts between *A* and *B*, the former will specialise in the production of *Y* and the latter in that of *X*. *A* will be ready to give at the most 2*Y* for each *X*. If the value of 1*X* rises above 2*Y*, it will pay country *A* to produce *X* domestically instead of obtaining it from *B* in exchange for *Y*. Similarly, if the price of *X* falls below 1.33, it will pay *B* to produce *Y* at home instead of getting it from *A* in exchange for *X*. Thus the actual value of 1*X* can fluctuate between 2 and 1.33*Y*. The actual rate of exchange between the two commodities will be determined by the reciprocal demand of the two countries for each other's products. Demand has two aspects (a) the size of the amount demanded (and therefore of the amount supplied) at a given ratio of exchange; (b) the elasticity[8] of the demand in response to a change in the ratio of exchange. Both these aspects affect the ratio of exchange. The greater is the demand for *Y* in exchange for *X* in *B*, the nearer will be the ratio of exchange between X and *Y* to 1:1.33. Similarly, the greater is the demand in *A* for *X* in exchange of *Y*, the nearer will be the ratio of exchange between X and *Y* to 1:2. Other things remaining the same, the ratio will be more favourable to *A* the more elastic is its demand for X and the less elastic is *B*'s demand for *Y*. The actual ratio of exchange will be fixed at a level at which the balance of payments between the two countries is in equilibrium.

Shadwell criticises Mill's doctrine that the ratio of exchange will be fixed at the point at which the value of imports and exports is in equilibrium, on the ground that it is a mere truism and does not throw any light on the determination of the rate of exchange.[9] This criticism, of course, is not justified. As pointed out by Bastable, Mill's doctrine not only states the equilibrium but also indicates the forces which are operating to bring about the equilibrium.[10]

Mill's doctrine is based on the following assumptions: (a) there are only two commodities and two countries; (b) production of both the commodities is subject to the law of constant returns; and (c) there are no costs of transport. Graham points out that under these assumptions, barring the exceptional case when the two countries are of equal size and the two commodities of equal importance, the ratio of exchange is likely to settle nearer the ratio between the costs of production of the two commodities either in one or in the other country. If a small country, for instance, trades with a larger country, it will specialise completely in the production of a single commodity whereas the large country will specialise only partially and continue producing both the commodities. Under these conditions, the international ratio of exchange between the two commodities will be identical with the ratio between the costs of production of the two commodities in the large country and thus the small country will appropriate the whole gain arising from trade. Similar will be the case when the commodity in whose production one country has a comparative advantage is so important to the trading countries that it can completely specialise in its production. The gain from trade will be divided between the two countries only when they are approximately of the same size and produce commodities which are almost equally important and consequently each specialises completely in the production of a single commodity. Thus what is the normal case with J.S. Mill is the exceptional case with Graham under the assumptions made by Mill. Graham, however, agrees with J.S. Mill that normally the gain from trade is likely to be divided between the trading countries because of the existence of many commodities, many countries, transportation costs and the operation of the law of variable costs of production. When there exist several countries and several commodities, some commodities are very likely to be marginal in some countries; marginal in the sense that the countries are in the zone of indifference as to whether to import, or to produce domestically, or to export these commodities. Under such conditions, any change in demand can be met by appropriate adjustments in production without any significant change in the terms of trade. As seen above, the existence of transport costs and the working of the law of increasing costs decreases the chances of complete specialisation and works towards a diversification of domestic production; this increases the number of common commodities and thereby checks violent fluctuations in the terms of trade as a result of any change in demand. In addition, when the production is subject to the law of increasing costs, the cost of production and hence the exchange value of the commodities for which the demand has increased will rise and the reverse will happen to the cost of production and the exchange value of the commodities for which the demand has fallen; this will check the increase in demand for the former and the decrease in demand for the latter commodities and thereby the fluctuations in the terms of trade. Graham emphasizes the supply conditions while the classicals emphasize the demand conditions in determining the international values. Graham maintains that when the demand conditions are unimportant, the determination of international values will be similar to the determination of the domestic values i.e. international values will be determined by the relative costs of production. It may, however, be pointed out that Graham is not the first to recognise these shortcomings of J.S. Mill. Nicholson points out in 1897 with the help of a series of arithmetical illustrations that if there are only two commodities and two countries and if the relative size of the two countries is not the same, the terms of trade would be fixed at or near the comparative costs of the larger country and consequently the smaller country would obtain the whole or nearly whole of the gain arising from international trade.[11] Pennington points out in 1840 that the entrance of more commodities and more countries will prevent the ratio of exchange being fixed at a point at which the whole gain arising from trade goes to one or the other country.[12]

MARSHALL'S GENERALISATION OF THE THEORY OF INTERNATIONAL VALUES

When each country has a whole range of import goods and export goods and the dividing line between the two categories is not known before hand, it becomes difficult to express the demand and supply of each country because the goods in each category are not constant. To overcome this difficulty, Marshall expressed the export goods of a country in terms of one common unit. He expresses the German exports, for instance, in terms of 'representative bales of German Goods.' A unit of a 'bale' embodies a constant amount of German labour (of different qualities) and capital. Marshall demonstrates the determination of international values with the help of a numerical illustration. He starts by making the following five assumptions.[13]

(a) There are only two countries carrying on trade exclusively with each other i.e. these do not trade with other countries.

(b) Each country bears the costs of delivering the goods at the other's frontier and the values of the goods are reckoned on this basis. Or the conduct of the trade is divided equally between the merchants of the two countries. This supposition helps in avoiding the discussion of the costs of transport.

(c) Neither of the countries is under any obligation to make payments other than those arising from trade. This avoids the complication introduced by capital movements.

(d) Each merchant does an all-round trade. He brings back to his country the goods obtained in exchange for his exports and draws no bills against his exports. This avoids the problem of foreign exchange.

(e) The currency of each country has no value except in its own domestic economy.

Below are given the demand schedules employed by Marshall:[14]

(1) *Terms of trade Number of G-bales per* 100 *E-bales*	(2) *E's demand for G-bales [Sales of G-bales in E at the price shown in* (1)*]*	(3) *E's Supply of E-bales [Total receipts from the sale of* (2) *in E at the ratio shown in* (1)*]*	(4) *Price (in G-bales per* 100 *E-bales) at which the E-bales shown in* (3) *can be sold in G*	(5) *G's supply of G-bales in exchange for* (3)*= [Total receipts from the sale of* (3) *in G at the ratio shown in* (1)*]*
10	1,000	10,000	230	23,000
20	4,000	20,000	175	35,000
30	9,000	30,000	143	42,900
35	14,000	40,000	122	48,000
40	20,000	50,000	108	54,000
46	27,600	60,000	95	57,000
55	28,500	70,000	86	60,000
68	54,400	80,000	82½	66,000
78	70,200	90,000	78	70,000
83	83,000	1,00,000	76	76,000
86	94,600	1,10,000	74½	81,950
88½	106,200	1,20,000	73½	88,500

A portion of the demand schedule of England is shown by columns 1 to 3 and that of Germany by columns 3 to 5. The table shows the amounts of goods which countries *E* and *G* are willing to exchange at various terms of trade. The ratio of exchange between the two bales will be fixed at the point where the bales supplied and demanded by the two countries are equal. In the above table the ratio of exchange between the German and the English bales is 78:100 because the demand and supply are in equilibrium at this point. Let us represent the schedules graphically (Fig. 6.1).

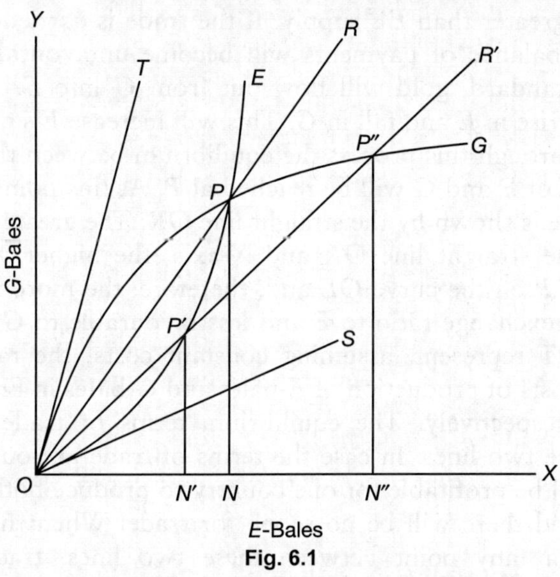

Fig. 6.1

Let *E*-bales supplied by *E* be measured along *X*-axis and the corresponding *G*-bales demanded by *E* on *Y*-axis. Curve *OE* shows the terms on which *E* is willing to trade i.e. the supply-demand curve of England. Similarly *OG* shows the terms on which *G* is willing to trade *i.e.* the supply-demand curve of Germany. The curve *E* is convex towards the *X*-axis, showing that the subsequent additional *G*-bales can be sold in *E* only for smaller and smaller additional *E*-bales. As the supply of *G*-bales and the demand for *E* bales increases, the terms of trade of *G* go on deteriorating. Similar is the case with *G*-curve. Every point at which the two curves cut each other indicates a situation in which the trade is in equilibrium. When the demand conditions are normal, the two curves cut each other only at one point and the trade will be in equilibrium at that point. In the above diagram, the equilibrium point is at *P*. At this point the demand and supply of *E* is equal to the demand and supply of *G*. The demand and supply of *E* and *G* are unequal at any point other than *P*. Let us take, for illustration, any other point *P′*. At this point *P′N′* *G*-bales can be exchanged for *ON′* *E*-bales in *E*. The exchange ratio $\frac{P'N'}{ON'}$ is indicated by the slope of the straight line *OR′* relatively to *X*-axis. At this ratio, however, *ON′* *E*-bales will be sold in *G*. This means that at this ratio, the demand of *G* for *E*-bales is greater than *E's* supply. If the trade is carried on at this ratio, *G*'s balance of payments will become unfavourable. Under full gold standard, gold will flow out from *G* into *E*. Prices and wages will rise in *E* and fall in *G*. This will increase *E*'s demand for *G*-bales. Through this process the equilibrium between the demand and supply of *E* and *G* will be reached at *P*. At this point, the ratio of exchange is shown by the straight line *OR*. The greater the angle between the straight line *OR* and *X*-axis, the higher will be the position of *P* on the curve *OE* and, therefore, the more favourable will be the exchange ratio to *E* and less favourable to *G*. The lines *OS* and *OT* represent, assuming constant costs, the ratio of the domestic costs of production of *E*-bales and *G*-baIes in England and Germany respectively. The equilibrium terms of trade must fall within these two lines. In case the terms of trade are outside these lines, it will be profitable for one country to produce both the bales at home and there will be no scope for trade. When the terms of trade are at any point between these two lines, trade will be profitable for both the countries.

Relation Between the Marshallian Curves and the Ordinary Demand and Supply Curves

The ordinary demand curve expresses the various quantities of a commodity demanded at different prices; it generally slopes downward from left to right indicating that greater quantities are demanded at lower prices. An ordinary supply curve expresses the various quantities supplied at different prices; it generally slopes upward from left to right indicating that greater amounts are supplied at higher prices. The Marshallian curve expresses the demand for one commodity in terms of the supply of another. The ordinate of the Marshallian demand curve measures not the value per unit of the commodity concerned but the total receipts from the exchange of the quantity shown on the horizontal axis. The Marshallian curve is a total revenue and total cost curve whereas the ordinary demand (or supply) curve is an average revenue (or cost) curve. The Marshallian curves by aggregating all commodities in representative bales give a complete picture of the whole international trade mechanism while the ordinary curves show the relation between the money price and individual commodities on the assumption that other things remain constant and thus show only a partial picture.

Graham criticises Mill, Marshall and their followers for grossly exaggerating the role of reciprocal demands and utterly neglecting that of comparative-cost conditions in determining the terms of trade. He contends, in contrast, that the reciprocal demands have almost no influence in determining the long-term terms of trade. Graham's criticism is invalid. As Viner points out "The terms of trade can be directly influenced by the reciprocal demands and by nothing else. The reciprocal demands in turn are ultimately determined by the cost conditions together with the basic utility functions."[15] The real error of Mill and his followers is that they exaggerate the importance of basic utility functions and neglect the cost conditions. The error arises out of their assumption of only two commodities, two countries, fixed goods in each country's categories of imports and exports and the constant costs of production. Under these assumptions cost conditions play little role in influencing the reciprocal demands and set only the upper and lower limits within which the actual ratio of exchange will be fixed by the interaction of demand schedules of the trading countries. Viner maintains that it may be true of Mill but Marshall, Edgeworth and other followers of Mill are aware of the fact that the larger the number of countries and commodities, the greater will be the influence of cost conditions on reciprocal demands and hence on terms of trade and the smaller range, assuming constant costs, within which the terms of trade will vary as a result of the changes in basic utility functions. Viner cites quotations from Marshall and Edgeworth in support of his contention.[16] Graham's error arises out of his failure to distinguish between the reciprocal demands and the basic utility functions and to see the entrance of supply conditions in reciprocal demands.

Graham also criticises Marshall's use of the concept of a representative bale in expressing the reciprocal demands. He contends that the reciprocal demand is for individual commodities and not for bales of goods; the composition of bales is not fixed and commodities remain shifting from one bale to another as a movement takes place along the demand schedules. Viner admits the imperfections of the concept but defends its use on the ground of the non-availability of superior alternatives. The use of reciprocal demand schedules for individual commodities seems to be still less satisfactory. Reciprocal demand schedules for a particular pair of individual commodities is not independent of the reciprocal demand schedules for pairs of other commodities.

> The prices of any particular export commodity and any particular import commodity are functionally related to each other, react upon each other, not directly (except to an insignificant degree) but through their membership in the price and utility and cost systems of the trading world taken as a whole.[17]

On the assumption of two countries and unchanged cost conditions, any change in the gain of one country will be at the cost of the other country. In other words, if one country gets a larger share from an unchanged total gain from international trade, the other must get a smaller one. The change in the distribution of gain will be indicated by an alteration of the ratio of exchange. When there are more than two countries, a country may import a particular commodity from several countries, all of whom supply it at the same price. The source of supply is immaterial to the amount of gain obtained by the importing country on this commodity. The respective total gains from trade between the importing country and its several suppliers, however, may vary widely. If so, the importing country will be getting a widely varying proportion of the several bilateral gains. The amount of the various bilateral gains depends upon the difference in opportunity cost structures of the importing country and those of its various suppliers. The division of these bilateral gains between the importing country and its suppliers will depend on the degree of deviation of the internal cost structures of the countries from the international ratio of exchange of the products exchanged between the importing country and its suppliers.

In a multi-country world, the gain from trade for each individual country will depend on the deviation of its internal cost structure from the international ratio of exchange established for world-traded products. Thus, the gain for each country will be determined largely by accident. No single country of a normal size can influence by its own actions the international ratio of exchange which is established by the interplay of the world demand and supply forces for various products. One way for a country to alter its gains from trade is to change its internal cost structure. The capacity of a country to alter its internal cost structure, however, is very much limited. The gain of a country from trade will expand if its internal cost ratios move away from the international ratio of exchange and contract in the reverse case. The internal cost structure of a country is determined mainly by the endowment of natural resources and the development of technology and skills in it. If the endowment of natural resources and the development of technology in a particular country is very similar to that in the world at large, its internal cost structure will be very near the international ratio of exchange and consequently it will derive little gain from international trade. If, on the other hand, the endowment of natural resources and the development of technology in the country is very different from that in the world at large, its internal cost structure will be widely different from the international ratio of exchange and hence it will considerably gain from international trade.

SPECIAL GAINS OF SMALL COUNTRIES

Small countries are likely to gain more from international trade than the large countries. A small country can specialise in the production of a single commodity without significantly affecting its exchange ratio in the world market and obtain gain on all its imports. If a large country tries to specialise in a single commodity, it will considerably increase the supply of the commodity and thereby lower its value in the world market; if the value of the export commodity falls to the level of the potential domestic cost of production of its imports, its gain from trade will disappear altogether. The international ratio of exchange is affected more by the cost structures of the large countries than by those of the small countries and therefore is nearer to the international cost structure of the former countries and further from those of the latter countries. As a country becomes larger and larger by annexing other states, its influence on the world ratio of exchange goes on increasing and the gain from trade accruing to it goes on decreasing.

Does it mean that the gain goes on disappearing as more and more countries amalgamate into a single entity? The actual fact is that as a country enlarges its size, and gain from international trade decreases, the gain from domestic exchange increases which is in no way different from the gain from foreign trade. In the limiting case if all the countries amalgamate into a world state, the gain from international trade will disappear because the international trade itself disappears. The gain from specialisation within the world state, however, remains and arises from domestic exchange because the foreign trade is converted into domestic trade with the amalgamation of the separate territories.

If a small country trades with a large country at highly favourable terms of trade, it does not imply that the large country is having unfavourable terms of trade when it is trading in the same commodities at the same ratio of exchange with other large countries. Confusion about this, often, arises from different bases of comparison. When taking the case of a small country trading with a large country, we consider its gain from a substantial portion or whole of its trade and therefore get a complete picture. In contrast while taking the case of a large country trading with a small country, we consider its gain from a very small portion of its total trade, or from a small portion of its trade in a single commodity, and get a very incomplete picture of the gain from its total trade, or the trade in a single commodity, a part of which is imported from the small country. In fact, the large country might be deriving good amount of gain from its trade with large countries dealing in identical commodities and at the same ratio of exchange as between the small and the large country. The existence of a small country in a world of large countries does not significantly affect the gains from international trade for large countries. If this small country happens to disappear suddenly, the ratio of exchange and the composition of exports and imports and hence the gains from trade for the large countries will remain almost undisturbed.

It may be mentioned that the small country does not get larger gains from trade simply because of its size. If its internal cost structure is nearer the world ratio of exchange because the endowment of its natural resources and the development of its technology is very similar to that of the world at large, it will obtain very small gain from trade. On the other hand, a large country might obtain considerable gains from international trade, if its internal cost structure is far away from the world ratio of exchange because of the marked dissimilarity of its natural resources, skills and technology from that of the world trade at large. Ultimately, the gains of a country from trade are determined by the deviation of its internal cost structure from the world ratio of exchange; the size of the country is one, though important enough, of the several factors influencing the degree of this deviation.

GAINS OF RICH COUNTRIES

Rich countries are likely to obtain smaller gains from international trade than the poor countries. While discussing above the relation between the gains from trade and the size of a country, we were referring to the economic (and not merely to the geographical) size of the country. Per capita income is an important determinant of the economic size of a country. The effect of the income on the gains from trade, therefore, is quite similar to the effect of the size of the country. It may, however, be mentioned that the higher income of a country may be either because of favourable endowment of natural resources, superior technology, etc. or because it enjoys highly favourable terms of trade with the outside world. If the higher income of the country is owing to its highly favourable terms of trade, it cannot be said that this will diminish the gains of the country from foreign trade.

The gain from trade in different commodities is very likely to vary widely. The potential cost of production of (or the utility from) a unit of different commodities imported in exchange for a unit of exports varies widely. There are certain commodities which are very important for the nationals but cannot be produced at home or can be produced at a prohibitively high opportunity cost; the gain from the import of such commodities is very large. There are other commodities which are not very important for the nationals or can be produced domestically at a slightly higher opportunity cost; the gain from the import of such commodities is not very significant.

TERMS OF TRADE

Various Concepts of Terms of Trade

Different authors use the concept of the terms of trade to mean different things. It will be better if before proceeding further, we discuss the different meanings of the concept of terms of trade. The simplest form of the concept is the commodity terms of trade, which is symbolically represented by Viner as

$$T_c = \frac{\dfrac{{}_eP_1}{{}_eP_0}}{\dfrac{{}_iP_1}{{}_iP_0}}$$

where *e* stands for export commodities, *i* for import commodities, *P* for the price index number, 0 for the initial year and 1 for the current year. T_c represents the index of foreign goods received in exchange for one physical unit of the export good.[18] A rise in the index number (T_c) will represent a favourable movement in the terms of trade. This measure, however, might not be a correct index of the trend of the gain from trade. Suppose, for instance, that the cost of production (and hence prices) of exports decreases in a country; this will deteriorate its terms of trade without affecting its gain from international trade.

To overcome this shortcoming, Viner constructs another index by multiplying the commodity terms of trade index with the reciprocal of the export commodity technical coefficients index. He calls it the single factoral terms of trade index and represents it symbolically as:

$$T_{cf} = \frac{\dfrac{{}_eP_1}{{}_eP_0} \cdot \dfrac{{}_eF_0}{{}_eF_1}}{\dfrac{{}_iP_1}{{}_iP_0}} = T_c \, \frac{{}_eF_0}{{}_eF_1}$$

where $\frac{{}_eF_0}{{}_eF_1}$ represents the reciprocal of the index of cost in terms of quantity of factors of production used per unit of exports, and T_{cf} represents the index of the physical amount of foreign goods obtained per unit of cost in terms of the quantity of factors of production.[19] This index suffers from the shortcoming that it does not take into consideration the potential domestic cost of production of imports. If the potential domestic cost of production of the imports is falling simultaneously and equally with the fall in the cost of exports, the single factoral terms of trade will show the gain from trade in a magnified form.

To remove this shortcoming, Viner constructs a third index by multiplying the single factoral terms of trade index with the reciprocal of an index of the 'disutility coefficients' of the technical coefficients of the export commodities. He calls it the real costs terms of trade index and represents it symbolically as

$$T_{cfr} = \frac{\dfrac{{}_eP_1}{{}_eP_0}}{\dfrac{{}_iP_1}{{}_iP_0}} \frac{{}_eF_0}{{}_eR_1} \frac{{}_eR_0}{{}_eR_1} = T_{cf}. \frac{{}_eR_0}{{}_eR_1}$$

where $\dfrac{{}_eR_0}{{}_eR_1}$ represents the index of amount of disutility (amount of irksomeness) per unit of the technical coefficients, and T_{efr} represents the index of the physical amount of foreign goods obtained per unit of real cost.[20] This index, again, is incomplete because it relates only the amount of foreign goods that a country can get per unit of the real cost involved in the production of exports and neglects the relative utility obtained from imports as compared with the utility lost as a result of the denial to natives of the consumption of goods which could have been produced with the resources employed for the production of exports needed to pay for imports; the evaluation of the latter relation is no less important than the former one for determining the trend of the gain from trade.

To overcome this shortcoming, Viner introduces an index of the relative utility of imports and the foregone commodities which is

$$\frac{{}_iU_1}{{}_aU_1} \Big/ \frac{{}_iU_0}{{}_aU_0}$$

where U stands for average utility and a for the commodities whose production for domestic consumption has to be foregone to relieve the resources for the production of exports.[21] Incorporating this in the real cost terms of trade index, Viner[22] gets the utility terms of trade index which is represented symbolically as

$$T_{efru} = \frac{\dfrac{{}_eP_1}{{}_cP_0}}{\dfrac{{}_iP_1}{{}_iP_0}} \cdot \frac{{}_eF_0}{{}_eF_1} \cdot \frac{{}_eR_0}{{}_eR_1} \cdot \frac{\dfrac{{}_iU_0}{{}_aU_1}}{\dfrac{{}_iU_0}{{}_aU_0}}$$

Some older writers use the index of the relative amounts of the productive resources embodied in imports exchanged for the products of the one unit of the native resources of production. Viner calls this the double factoral terms of trade and represents it symbolically as[23]

$$\left(\frac{{}_eP_1}{{}_iP_0}\bigg/\frac{{}_iP_1}{{}_iP_0}\right)\cdot\left(\frac{{}_iF_1}{{}_iF_0}\bigg/\frac{{}_eF_1}{{}_eF_0}\right)$$

Professor Robertson calls this index as the 'true' terms of trade.[24] Under the assumption of the constant returns to scale, the double factoral terms of trade become identical with the commodity terms of trade.

This index, however, may not be a correct measure of the gain from trade. If country *A* imports a commodity from country *B* at the same opportunity cost, and the number of units of the productive resources required for production of this commodity decreases in *B* because of improvements in its productive efficiency the double factoral terms of trade of *A* will deteriorate but its gain from trade remains unaffected. If the productive efficiency, of *B* decreases, other things remaining the same, *A*'s terms of trade improve though its gain from trade remains unaffected. Similarly, if the productivity is increasing very fast in *A*, its commodity terms of trade might deteriorate along with an improvement in its double factoral terms of trade.

Taussig introduces the concept of 'gross barter terms of trade'; this index relates the total physical quantity of imports to the total physical quantity of exports.[25] If the total physical quantity of imports of a country rises, that of exports remaining the same, the terms of trade of the country will improve and deteriorate in the reverse case. Taussig constructs this index to incorporate unilateral payments like tributes, immigrants' remittances etc. into the commodity or 'net barter' terms of trade. The appropriateness of incorporating unilateral payments into the terms of trade is doubtful because these arise, mainly, from factors other than the international trade; these payments remain unaffected whether or not there exists any trade. The loss or gain arising from unilateral payments should not be incorporated into the gain arising from international trade. In addition, it will treat all the exports and imports for which payment is to be made after some time or has already been made in the past as unilateral transactions.

G.S. Dorrance[26] introduces the concept of income terms of trade. He defines income terms of trade as the index of the value of exports divided by the price index for imports i.e. $\frac{{}_eP_1 \, {}_eQ_1}{{}_eP_0 \, {}_eQ_0}$[3]. The index seems to indicate better a country's capacity to import rather than the changes in its real income. To take a hypothetical example, if a country's export prices fall by 50 per cent (price of imports remaining the same) and the quantity of its exports rises by the same percentage, the terms of trade index remains unchanged but it is evident that the real income of the country has decreased.[27] Statistics show that during the periods of falling prices, quantity of many primary products exported by the underdeveloped countries increases and thus this index will not show the full deterioration in the position of these countries during a recession.

Mostly, it is the commodity terms of trade which have been employed for practical purposes. Single factoral and double factoral terms of trade have not been used because of the difficulties involved in calculating the movements in productivity. Real cost terms of trade and utility terms of trade have not been employed because of the difficulties of measuring utilities and disutilities quantitatively.

Trade Pattern and Variable Returns to Scale

Suppose that the economy produces two goods with the flowing Cobb-Douglas production functions with variable returns to scale. We assume that capital and labour, K and L are fixed.

$$Y_j = \phi_j(Y_j) K_j^{\alpha_{0j}} L_j^{\beta_{0j}}, \; j=1, 2, \alpha_{0j}, \beta_{0j} > 0, \alpha_{0j} + \beta_{0j} = 1 \qquad (1)$$

where K_j and L_j are respectively capital and labour inputs of sector j.

Variable returns to scale are measured by the functions, $\phi_j(Y_j)$. Perfect competition is assumed in the product markets and factor markets. It is also assumed that product prices, denoted by $p_1(=p)$ and $p_2(=1)$, are given exogenously. It is also assumed that labour and capital are freely mobile between the two sectors and are immobile internationally. For individual firms, $\phi_j(Y_j)$ are given. The marginal conditions are given by the following equations.

$$r = \frac{\alpha_{0j}\, p_j\, Y_j}{K_j}, \quad w = \frac{\beta_{0j}\, p_j\, F_j}{L_j} \qquad (2)$$

For simplicity we consider

$$\phi_j(Y_j)=A_{0j}\,F_j^{V_j},\quad A_{0j}>0, V_j<1$$

If $V_j = 0$, sector j exhibits constant returns to scale. If $V_j > (<)\ 0$, sector j exhibits increasing (decreasing) returns to scale. From these condition and equation (i) we have

$$Y_j = A_j\,K_j^{\alpha_j}\,L_j^{\beta_j} \tag{3}$$

where

$$A_j \equiv A_{0j}^{1/(1-V_j)},\ \alpha_j \equiv \frac{\alpha_{0j}}{1-V_j},\ \beta_j \equiv \frac{\beta_{0j}}{1-V_j}$$

It should be noted that as $\alpha_j+\beta_j \neq 1$ for $V_j \neq 0$, the production functions are not "neo-classical". The resource constraints are given as

$$K_1+K_2=K,\ L_1+L_2=L \tag{4}$$

Equations (1)-(4) contain 6 variables, L_j, K_j, w and r, and 6 equations for given p_j, L, and K. Six variables can be solved as functions of p, L and K.

From equation (3), we have

$$\frac{\alpha_{01}\,p\,Y_1}{K_1}=\frac{\alpha_{02}\,Y_2}{K_2},\quad \frac{\beta_{01}\,p\,Y_1}{L_1}=\frac{\beta_{02}\,Y_2}{L_2} \tag{5}$$

From these relations, we have

$$L_1=\alpha k L_2$$

where

$$\alpha=\frac{\alpha_{02}\,\beta_{01}}{\alpha_{01}\,\beta_{02}},\ k\equiv\frac{K_1}{K_2}$$

From $L_1 = \alpha k L_2$ and $L_1 + L_2 = L$, we determine the labour distribution as a function of the ratio of the two sectors' capital inputs as follows.

$$L_1=\frac{\alpha k L}{1+\alpha k},\ L_2=\frac{L}{1+\alpha k} \tag{6}$$

Substituting $Y_j = A_j K_j^{\alpha_j} L_j^{\beta_j}$ into $\beta_{01} p_1 Y_1 / L_1 = \beta_{02} p_2 Y_2 / L_2$ we get

$$\alpha^{\beta_1 - 1} \beta_{01} p A_1 k^{\alpha_1 + \beta_1 - 1} = \beta_{02} A_2 K_2^{\alpha_2 - \alpha_1} L_2^{\beta_2 - \beta_1} \tag{7}$$

where $K_1 = kK_2$ and $L_1 = \alpha k L_2$.

Also from $k = K_1/K_2$ and $K_1 + K_2 = K$, we have $K_2 = K/(1+k)$. Substituting $K_2 = K/(1+k)$ and L_2 in (6) into equation (7) we have

$$(1+k)^{\alpha_2 - \alpha_1} (1+\alpha k)^{\beta_2 - \beta_1} k^{\alpha_1 + \beta_1 - 1} = \alpha_0 \tag{8}$$

where we have considered

$$\alpha_0 \equiv \frac{\beta_{02} A_2 K^{\alpha_2 - \alpha_1} L^{\beta_2 - \beta_1}}{\alpha^{\beta_1 - 1} \beta_{01} p A_1}$$

Two goods are produced if $k>0$. We assume that the good prices and factor endowments are fixed at such values that equation (8) has a meaningful solution. As we are mainly interested in comparative statics analysis, this assumption is acceptable. Once we solve k, it is straightforward to solve all the other variables. From $k = K_1/K_2$ and $K_1 + K_2 = K$, we have

$$K_1 = \frac{kK}{1+k}, \quad K_2 = \frac{K}{1+K} \tag{9}$$

Equation (6) represents labour distribution. As the distributions of the factor endowments are already determined, it is straightforward to calculate the output levels and factor prices. As the production functions are not neoclassical, in general the wage and rate of interest will not be determined as functions of capital intensities, K_j/L_j. From equations (2) and (3) we have

$$r = \frac{\beta_r}{(1+k)^{\alpha_2 - 1} (1+\alpha k)^{\beta_2}}, \quad w = \frac{\beta_w}{(1+k)^{\alpha_2} (1+\alpha k)^{\beta_2 - 1}} \tag{10}$$

where we have used (6), (9) and

$$\beta_r = \alpha_{02} A_2 K^{\alpha_2 - 1} L^{\beta_2}, \quad \beta_w = \beta_{02} A_2 K^{\alpha_2} L^{\beta_2 - 1}$$

From equations (2), (10) and (9), we have

$$Y_1 = \frac{rkK}{(1+k)\alpha_{0j}\, p}, \quad Y_2 = \frac{rK}{(1+k)\alpha_{0j}} \tag{11}$$

Equations (6) and (9) gives the expression for the capital intensities as

$$\frac{K_1}{L_1}=\frac{(1+\alpha k)K}{(1+k)\alpha L},\ \frac{K_2}{L_2}=\frac{(1+\alpha k)K}{(1+k)L} \tag{12}$$

Comparative Statics Analysis

Here we shall consider the effect of changes in parameters such as relative price and capital on the trade pattern.

The impact of the relative price: Let us consider the change in p. Taking derivatives of equation (8) with respect to p gives

$$\frac{dk}{dp}=-\frac{\Delta}{p} \tag{13}$$

where

$$\Delta\equiv\left(\frac{\alpha_2-\alpha_1}{1+k}+\frac{\alpha(\beta_2-\beta_1)}{1+\alpha k}+\frac{\alpha_1+\beta_1-1}{k}\right)^{-1}.$$

From equation (11) we have

$$\frac{1}{Y_1}\frac{dY_1}{dp}=-\frac{1}{p}+\left(\frac{1}{k(1+k)}-\frac{\alpha_2-1}{1+k}-\frac{\alpha\beta_2}{1+\alpha k}\right)\frac{dk}{dp},$$

$$\frac{1}{Y_2}\frac{dY_2}{dp}=\left(\frac{\alpha_2}{1+k}+\frac{\alpha\beta_2}{1+\alpha k}\right)\frac{dk}{dp},$$

$$\frac{d(Y_1/Y_2)}{dp}=-\left(\frac{\Delta}{k}+1\right)\frac{k}{p^2}, \tag{14}$$

where we have used

$$\frac{1}{r}\frac{dr}{dp}=-\left(\frac{\alpha_2-1}{1+k}+\frac{\alpha\beta_2}{1+\alpha k}\right)\frac{dk}{dp}$$

For simplicity we require $\alpha=1$, i.e $\alpha_{01}=\alpha_{02}$. By equation (12) the two sectors have the same capital intensity. The capital input ratio is now determined by

$$(1+k)^{\theta_2-\theta_1}k^{\theta_1-1}=\hat{\alpha} \tag{15}$$

where

$$\alpha_j+\beta_j=\theta_j\equiv\frac{1}{1-V_j}>0,\quad \hat{\alpha}\equiv\frac{A_2}{p\,A_1\,K^{\alpha_{01}\theta}\,L^{\beta_{01}\theta}}>0,$$

$$\theta\equiv\theta_1-\theta_2.$$

We also have

$$\frac{dk}{dp}=-\frac{(1+k)k}{[(\theta_2-1)k+\theta_1-1]p}, \tag{16}$$

As $\theta_j-1=V_j/(1-V_j)$, we have θ_j-1 is positive (zero, negative) if sector j exhibits increasing (constant, decreasing) returns to scale. If the two sectors exhibit increasing (decreasing) returns to scale, then the capital input ratio falls (rises) as the relative price is increased (decreased). If one sector exhibits increasing returns and the other sector decreasing returns to scale, then the effects are ambiguous. Now equation (10) can be rewritten as

$$r=\frac{\beta_r}{(1+k)^{\theta_2-1}},\; w=\frac{\beta_w}{(1+k)^{\theta_2-1}} \tag{17}$$

Hence we have

$$\frac{1}{r}\frac{dr}{dp}=\frac{1}{w}\frac{dw}{dp}=\left(\frac{1-\theta_2}{1+k}\right)\frac{dk}{dp},$$

$$\frac{d(w/r)}{dp}=0 \tag{18}$$

The wage-rental ratio is not affected by changes in the relative price. The sign of dw/dp is the opposite to that of $(\theta_2-1)dk/dp$. If both sectors exhibit increasing (decreasing) returns to scale, then the wage and rate of interest rise. If one sector exhibits increasing returns and the other sector decreasing returns to scale, then the effects are ambiguous.

From equations (9) and (12) we have

$$\frac{d(w/r)}{dp}=0,$$

$$\frac{dK_1}{dp}=-\frac{dK_2}{dp}=\frac{1}{1+k}\frac{dk}{dp},$$

$$\frac{1}{L_j}\frac{dL_j}{dp}=\frac{1}{K_j}\frac{dK_j}{dp}.$$

Thus we find, if k rises (falls) as p is increased, sector 1's capital and labour inputs are increased (reduced) and sector 2's capital and labour inputs are reduced (increases).

From (12) we have

$$Y_1=\frac{\beta_r K k}{(1+k)^{\theta_2}\alpha_{0j}\,p},\ Y_2=\frac{\beta_r K}{(1+k)^{\theta_2}\alpha_{0j}},\ \frac{Y_1}{Y_2}=\frac{k}{p} \tag{19}$$

We have

$$\frac{1}{Y_1}\frac{dY_1}{dp}=-\frac{\theta_1}{[(\theta_2-1)k+\theta_1-1]p}$$

$$\frac{1}{Y_2}\frac{dY_2}{dp}=\frac{\theta_2\,k}{[(\theta_2-1)k+\theta_1-1]p}$$

$$\frac{1}{Y_1/Y_2}\frac{d(Y_1/Y_2)}{dp}=-\frac{\theta_1+\theta_2\,k}{[(\theta_2-1)k+\theta_1-1]p}.$$

If the two sectors exhibit increasing returns to scale, then if the relative price rises, the output of sector 1 and the ratio between sector 1's and sector 2's output levels are increased and sector 2's output level is increased.

The effects of change in capital: We still require α=1, that is, $\alpha_{01}=\alpha_{02}$. By equation (15) we have

$$\frac{dk}{dK}=-\frac{(1+k)\alpha_{01}\,k\theta}{[(\theta_2-1)k+\theta_1-1]K} \tag{20}$$

As

$$\theta_1-\theta_2=\frac{V_1-V_2}{(1-V_1)(1-V_2)},$$

If the two sectors exhibit increasing returns and if $V_1>(<)V_2$, then k falls (rises); if the two sectors exhibit decreasing returns and if $V_1>(<)V$, then k rises (falls). If one sector exhibits increasing returns and the other sector decreasing returns to scale, then the effects are ambiguous. From equation (17) we have

$$\frac{1}{r}\frac{dr}{dK}=\frac{\alpha_2-1}{K}-\left(\frac{\theta_2-1}{1+k}\right)\frac{dk}{dK},$$

$$\frac{1}{w}\frac{dw}{dK}=\frac{\alpha_2}{K}-\left(\frac{\theta_2-1}{1+k}\right)\frac{dk}{dK},$$

$$\frac{d(w/r)}{dK}=\frac{1}{K}>0.$$

From equations (9) and (12) we have

$$\frac{1}{K_1}\frac{dK_1}{dK}=\frac{1}{K}\frac{dK}{dK}+\frac{1}{(1+k)k}\frac{dk}{dK},$$

$$\frac{1}{K_2}\frac{dK_2}{dK}=\frac{1}{K}\frac{dK}{dK}-\frac{1}{(1+k)}\frac{dk}{dK},$$

$$\frac{1}{L_1}\frac{dK_1}{dK}=\frac{1}{(1+k)k}\frac{dk}{dK},$$

$$\frac{1}{L_2}\frac{dL_2}{dK}=-\frac{1}{(1+k)}\frac{dk}{dK}.$$

From (19), we have

$$\frac{1}{Y_1}\frac{dY_1}{dK}=\frac{\alpha_2}{K}+\frac{1+k-\theta_2 k}{(1+k)k}\frac{dk}{dK},$$

$$\frac{1}{Y_2}\frac{dF_2}{dp}=\frac{\alpha_2}{K}-\frac{\theta_2 k}{(1+k)}\frac{dk}{dK},$$

$$\frac{1}{Y_1/Y_2}\frac{d(Y_1/Y_2)}{dp}=\frac{dk}{dK}.$$

Thus we find that the existence of invariable returns to scale makes the core theorems in trade theory invalid under certain condition.

FACTORS GOVERNING THE TERMS OF TRADE OF A COUNTRY

The most important factor determining the terms of trade of the two countries is the relative intensity of their demand for each other's products. The relative intensity of demand depends upon the following main factors: (a) resourcefulness of supply, (b) population, (c) nature of goods, (d) tastes and the capacity to buy and (e) state policy. If a country *A* produces a large variety of goods, the intensity of demand of another country *B* for its goods is likely to be considerably high; on the other hand, *A*'s demand for *B*'s goods will be less intense because it can produce domestically most of the goods. The larger the population of a country, other things remaining the same, the larger is likely to be its demand for imports and the smaller the capacity to export. If a country produces goods which are consumed on a mass scale, the demand for its exports is likely to be very intense. On the other hand, if it produces goods the consumption of which is limited to a small special class of people, the demand for its exports is not likely to be very intense. Tastes determine the goods to be imported by each country and the capacity to buy determines the quantity of these goods to be bought. State policy might restrict the importation of goods which would have been imported otherwise; this will improve the country's terms of trade.

The effect of any change in the intensity of demand of any country on the terms of trade will depend on the relative elasticities of demand and supply of the two countries. If, for instance, country *A*'s demand increases for the goods of country *B* because of an increase in its population, the extent of deterioration in its terms of trade will depend on *A*'s elasticity of demand and *B*'s elasticity of supply. If *A*'s demand and *B*'s supply are inelastic, *A*'s terms of trade will deteriorate considerably. In contrast, if *A*'s demand and *B*'s supply are very elastic, the deterioration in *A's* terms of trade will be very slight.

Another factor determining the terms of trade is the relative amount of the unilateral payments to be made by the two countries to each other. The effect of unilateral payments on the terms of trade has been discussed in detail in a separate chapter and, therefore, we will not dwell on it here any further.

Most of the countries of the world, today, are on a managed currency system and the rate of exchange between the two currencies is regulated not by market forces but by the state policy. Under such conditions, the government exchange policy plays an important role in determining the terms of the trade between the two countries.

STATISTICAL PROBLEMS IN MEASURING THE TERMS OF TRADE

Problems of Index Numbers

Measurement of the terms of trade will be very simple if the country imports only one homogeneous commodity and exports a single homogeneous commodity. In actual practice, however, each country exports and imports a large number of goods and services. The existence, of several import and export goods gives rise to the formidable problem of index numbers for measuring any change in the terms of trade.

Changes in Quality

Changes in relative prices fail to be a good guide if the traded goods change in quality over time. In the past, far greater improvements have occurred in the quality of manufactured goods than in that of the primary products. If this factor is taken into account, the deterioration in the relative prices of underdeveloped countries is not so much as indicated by the indices of relative prices over the last sixty years.

Changes in Composition

Most of the goods are available in several different varieties, grades, sizes, etc. A part of the changes in the relative prices of imports and exports may be simply because of the change in the composition of imports and exports over a period of time.

Use of Unit Values

Prices of imports and exports available in official statistics are generally based on price declarations made to customs offices. Actual prices of the goods are not known till they are sold in the market, and the declarations are based on prices expected to prevail at the time of sale. Actual prices, however, might deviate, sometimes considerably, from the expected prices. In addition, there is often a tendency on the part of the traders to understate the value of the imports and exports to evade a part of an *ad valorem* tariff. Under-invoicing of imports and exports is also practised to evade exchange control regulations. Special problems arise in case of intra-company dealings. When the goods are exchanged between different branches of the same company working in different countries, the quoted prices might not be the genuine market prices because the interests of the exporters and importers do not clash. Valuation of the exports to and imports from different branches may be manipulated in a way which shifts the profits from branches in countries with higher profit taxes to the branches in countries with comparatively lower profit taxes.

Problem of Weightage

Construction of price indices of imports and exports gives rise to the problem of weightage for different commodities. All commodities cannot be given equal importance in the process of averaging the prices of different commodities. The importance of various commodities in trade changes over time and the weights representative during a particular period might not be so during another period.

Cost of Shipping Transport, Insurance, etc.

Most of the countries value imports c.i.f. (i.e. inclusive of transportation and insurance charges) and exports f.o.b. (i.e. exclusive of these charges). A major portion of the shipping and insurance business being in the hands of the developed countries, these charges are an additional burden on the foreign exchange resources of the underdeveloped countries. In contrast, the c.i.f. import prices of the developed countries include charges which are not actually paid to the underdeveloped countries. Thus a part of the rise in the prices of imports of the advanced countries might consist of a rise in the costs of transportation, insurance etc. which remains at home and is not paid to the exporting underdeveloped countries. The terms of trade index will be more realistic if it includes not only merchandise but also services. Since the terms of trade refer to price ratios and not to absolute prices, costs of transportation and insurance will not distort the picture if the movements in these costs are identical in direction and extent with the movements in the general level of prices. The United Nations Report on the *Relative Prices of Exports and Imports* states that there is no evidence that the changes in the costs of transport have been altogether disproportionate to the changes in other prices and, therefore, there is no reason to discard the statistics of the industrialised countries.[28]

Sampling

The terms of trade indices change with every change in the size of the sample. It has been found that the terms of trade indices are highly sensitive to the variations in coverage.[29]

Time-lag Between Exports and Imports

The terms of trade refer to the relative prices of the exports and imports at a particular point of time. There might, however, be a time-lag between the exports and imports. There occurs a time-lag between exports and imports whenever there is a surplus or a deficit in the balance of payments. If a country exports when the terms of trade are favourable because of lower prices of imports (prices of exports remaining the same as in the base year) and imports when the terms are favourable because of higher prices of exports (prices of imports remaining the same as in the base year), its actual terms of trade remain unchanged though the indices show an improvement in the terms of trade. The terms of trade will be a valid measure only if the exports and imports are simultaneous.

The above discussed difficulties involved in the measurement of the term of trade should not be taken to mean that the attempts at measuring the terms of trade are absolutely useless. In fact, these warn us against the indiscriminate use of the terms of trade statistics. Further, these caution us that the movements in the terms of trade should be interpreted in the light of all the relevant facts and that these should be used to indicate only the broad qualitative trends. Particular caution is needed in comparing the terms of trade ratios over a long period.

THE GAINS FROM TRADE AND THE INCOME DISTRIBUTION

The gains from trade would make a country as a whole better off, but that it need not necessarily make every citizen better off. Let us consider the following box diagram and a production possibility curve derived from this box diagram as the means of exposition.

From Fig. 6.2 we drive the Fig. 6.3 which shows a production-possibility curve *RR*.

Before trade, under autarky, the country produces and consumes at point S' on its production possibility curve. Relative commodity prices before trade are given by the line P_0P_0, tangential to the production-possibility curve at S'. The point on the contract curve in the box diagram that corresponds to S' is S. In this set up, now we assume that a possibility for trade is introduced and that the international terms of trade are given by the line P_1P_1. As goods B is relatively more expensive, the country changes its pattern of production and produces more of good B, thus moving to point T' on its production-possibility curve, where the international price line P_1P_1 is tangential to the production-possibility curve. The country can then trade along the international price line.

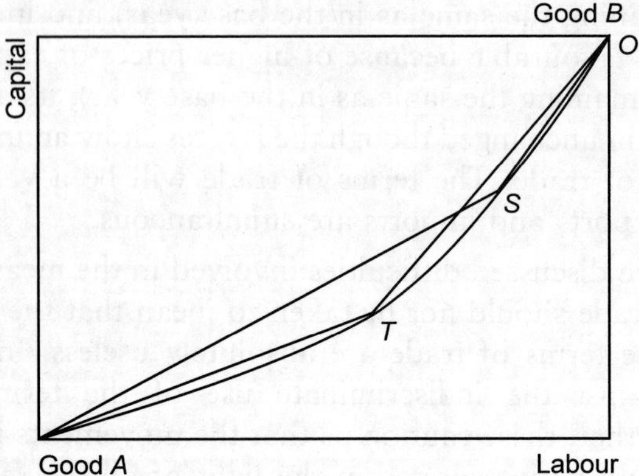

Fig. 6.2: Gains from Trade and Resource Allocation.

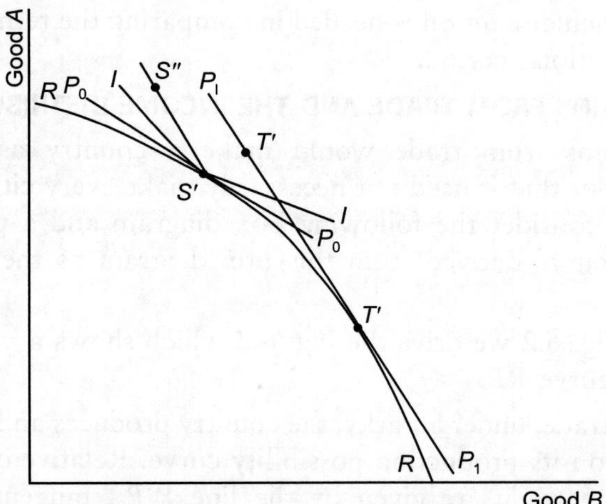

Fig. 6.3: Gains from Trade and Resource Allocation.

Now suppose that the country moves to point *T''* by trading. *T''* is obviously better than the point *S'* because it represents more of both goods. This establishes the fact that the country as a whole can be made better off by trading. But the point is, what about factor prices, and what happens with the income distribution. The movement of the production possibility curve from *S'* to *T'* have any impact on the income distribution.

The point on the contract curve in the box that corresponds to point *T'* on the production possibility curve is point *T*. Comparing the factor prices at points *S* and *T* on the contract curve, we find that at point *T* the methods of production are more labour-intensive in both industries than they are at *S*. This implies that the marginal productivities of labour are lower and those of capital higher at *T* than *S*. therefore, wages are lower and returns to capital higher at *T* than at *S*. Thus the income distribution has moved against labour and in favour of the owners of capital.

The above fact can be explained in another ways as follows. At point *T* every worker in both industries has less machinery to work with than he had at point *s* as the methods of production become more labour-intensive. This means that the marginal productivity is lower, and because the marginal productivity determines the wage, the wage is also lower. The wage times the amount of labour employed determines the income that goes to labour. As there is full employment both before and after trade, there is no change in the volume of employment. Hence the income going to labour decreases when the country goes from autarky to fee trade. Thus it follows that the ones who gain from free trade in our example the owners of capital will have to compensate the workers for their loss of income in order for us to be sure that all citizens are at least as well off at point *T″* as they were at point *S′*. Only if this is done can we say unconditionally that free trade is better than no trade. This was the point that Ricardo and the classical economists failed to see.

In the two-factor model, the factor that is used intensively in the import-competing industry will always suffer when going from autarky to free trade. Therefore, a policy of free trade will generally have to be accompanied by measures of redistribution in order to make sure that free trade will be an advantage over no trade.

Here one point arises if those who gain from free trade are not willing to compensate those who suffer? Could some degree of trade still be advantageous? The answer is 'yes'. If the capital-owners are not willing to compensate the workers, the workers could refuse to move into the other industry. Then we would have the same pattern of production after trade as before trade and the country would still be producing at point *S′* on the production-possibility curve. The country would still have the option, however, to trade according to the international terms of trade. It could trade along the price line *S′ S″* (which is parallel to P_1P_1). It would then produce at point *S′* but consume; for instance, at point *S″*. This would clearly be advantageous, as point *S″* lies to the right of the indifference curve

II, which is tangential to the production-possibility curve at S' and represents the highest level of utility obtainable under autarky. This shows that restricted trade is better than no trade. But restricted trade is potentially less advantageous than free trade.

TERMS OF TRADE AND ECONOMIC DEVELOPMENT

Fair terms of trade are very important for the development of the underdeveloped countries, particularly for the development of those in whose economy international trade plays a considerable role. An improvement in a country's terms of trade enables it to import a larger quantity of goods for the same quantity of exports or the same quantity of goods for a smaller quantity of exports. This raises the national income of the country directly. It helps the country in raising its national income indirectly too. The saving in exports for a given quantity of imports or the additional imports obtained for the same exports can be utilised for development purposes.

> The great advantage of this potential source of capital formation is that it gives rise neither to foreign debt burden nor to the various frictions that may arise from inter-governmental loans and grants.[30]

It eases the balance of payments difficulties which are very common in the developing economies. Some countries heavily depend on foreign trade even for their budgetary resources. In such countries, an unfavourable movement in the terms of trade might cause serious budgetary difficulties.

The importance of the terms of trade in influencing the national income and the resources available for development, however, should not be overemphasized. The terms of trade is only one of the several factors affecting the national income and the resources available for development.

> I am not aware of a single case in which the direction of secular trend of terms of trade seriously influenced the actual production and other development policies of an underdeveloped country. Here again cyclical instability matters much more.[31]

An improvement in the terms of trade does not accelerate development automatically. It will further development only if the additional resources thus made available are saved and invested fruitfully. If the additional resources made available by an improvement in the terms of trade are consumed and not invested by the persons to whom these accrue, the improvement in the terms of trade will fail in accelerating the rate of development of the country. Thus the improvement in the terms of trade gives rise to only a possibility of furthering the development and whether or not the possibility is transformed into a reality depends on the concerned country.

If the improvement in the terms of trade is brought about by restricting exports, the adverse effect on development resulting from a decrease in the total foreign exchange proceeds available for importing equipment, technical know-how and essential raw materials might far outweigh the favourable effect of the improvement in the terms of trade. In addition, the resources relieved from the export industries as a result of the decrease in exports are likely to be employed domestically in less productive lines. The value of import substitutes produced with resources relieved from a decrease in the production of exports might be less than even the value of exports at old prices.

If the improvement in the terms of trade is brought about by creating an artificial inflation, the adverse effect of the inflation on the development process might be much more than the favourable effect of the improvement in the terms of trade.

When the improvement in the terms of trade is due to a fall in the supply of exports caused by either natural or human factors, it will not further development if the increase in the prices is offset, or more than that, by the fall in the total quantum of exports; it might, however, be noted that it will avoid or mitigate the adverse effects on development which have occurred in the absence of an improvement in the terms of trade.

The terms of trade relate the average prices of a country's exports and imports. It does not refer to the prices of the particular groups of the commodities. In many underdeveloped countries, certain sectors of the economy are mainly in the hands of the foreign investors. A rise in the export prices of such products will benefit mainly the foreigners and not the natives of underdeveloped countries. Similarly, if the prices fall only of those imports which are required mainly by foreign investors, the improvement in the terms of trade will benefit mainly the foreigners and not the natives of the country. In such cass, the terms of trade might not be a good index of the deterioration or improvement in the position of a country.

The terms of trade might serve as a rough indicator of a change in a country's real income in the international sector if the assumptions on which the classical theory of international trade is based hold true in actual practice.[32] The classical economists assume fixed supply of factors of production, unchanged techniques of production, full employment of all the factors of production, existence of pure competition satisfying all the optimum marginal conditions. In the actual world not to talk of long run, these assumptions are not fulfilled even in the short run and, therefore, the concept of the terms of trade is unsuitable for analysing the changes in a country's real income in the international sector. A country might, for instance, expand its exports by utilising the unemployed resources of production. Under such conditions, its national income might rise even if the terms of trade move against it. Similarly, an improvement in terms of trade will not increase national income if the resources saved by exchanging a smaller quantum of exports for the same imports remain unemployed and cannot be used for the production of certain other goods because they are specific to export industries or because of certain other reasons.

The classical static model ignores the dynamic repercussions of the international sector on the domestic economy by assuming that all other things remain the same.[33] An increase in the imports of capital equipment, skill and raw materials required for development plans might deteriorate the terms of trade and thereby decrease the national income in the short run; but in the long run, it is likely to considerably further the development of the country and thereby raise its national income. Thus if the changes in other things that follow the changes in the terms of trade were not taken into account, the changes in the terms of trade will not be a reliable indicator of the changes in the country's position.

> The widely expressed view on the part of representatives of the underdeveloped countries that measures must be taken to stop the secular decline in their commodity terms of trade may well lead to disastrous policy decisions.[34]

In short, terms of trade throw little light on the change in a country's economic position. The effect of the changes in the terms of trade should be appraised in the light of other relevant effects like changes in productivity, demand, total exports and imports, employment etc.

CAUSES OF DETERIORATION IN THE TERMS OF TRADE OF THE UNDER-DEVELOPED COUNTRIES

Doubtlessly, the deterioration in the terms of trade of the primary producing countries is not because the productivity is increasing in these economies at a rate faster than that at which it is increasing in the industrial countries. If this were so, the deterioration in their terms of trade will not be serious because this involves only a sharing of the increased productivity with the industrial countries and no positive loss. On the contrary, the fact is that productivity has increased faster in the industrial countries than in the primary producing countries.

> All the evidence is that productivity has increased if anything, less fast in the production of food and raw materials, even in the industrialised countries but most certainly in the underdeveloped countries, than has productivity in the manufacturing industries of the industrialised countries. The possibility that changing price relations could merely reflect relative terms in productivity may be considered as disposed by the very fact that standards of living in industrialised countries (largely governed by productivity in manufacturing industries) have risen demonstrably faster, than standards of living in underdeveloped countries (generally governed by productivity in agriculture and primary production) over the last sixty or seventy years.[35]

After dismissing the proposition that productivity might have increased faster in the primary producing countries than in the advanced countries, Singer sets out to give his own explanation for deterioration in the terms of trade of the primary producing countries. He maintains that the fruits of technical progress can either be appropriated by the producers in the form of higher incomes or passed on to the consumers in the form of lower prices.[36] In manufacturing, the fruits of technical progress have been appropriated by the producers in the form of higher income while these have been passed on to the consumers in the form of lower prices in the case of primary products. Singer does not give any explanation as to how the fruits of technical progress have been retained by producers in manufacturing countries and those transferred to consumers in the primary producing countries A.N. McLeod states that this has happened because of the existence of a greater degree of monopolistic elements in manufacturing than in primary production.[37] Trade unions of labour are, generally, far stronger in industry than in agriculture where the labour is scattered widely. In addition, vast unemployment and the pressure of the fast increasing population decreases the bargaining strength of the labour in primary producing countries. Prebisch goes a step further and states that in advanced countries the incomes of the factors of production have increased more than the increase in their productivity while in the periphery the increase in the incomes of the factors of production has been less than the increase in their productivity.[38]

The diversified economies of the manufacturing countries are more flexible than those of the primary producing countries. When the world prices of certain products are falling, manufacturing countries shift to the production of other commodities whose prices are not falling. "This is not possible in primary producing countries because their economies are very rigid and lack adaptability. This explains why the advanced countries producing some primary products in large quantities do not suffer from a deterioration in their terms of trade when the world prices of such products decline considerably.

Vast increase in the domestic production of foodstuffs and raw materials in advanced countries has decreased their need for the import of these from the underdeveloped countries. Progress in technology has drastically decreased the required amount of raw materials (which are the main exports of the primary producing countries) per unit of manufactured output in advanced countries. Recent inventions of synthetic substitutes (such as synthetic rubber, synthetic fibres, plastics, aluminium etc.) for natural raw materials have adversely affected the demand for the exports of the primary producing industries. Instability in the export prices of the primary produce is one of the important reasons for the adoption of more and more synthetic substitutes in advanced countries. Violent fluctuations in the prices of the raw materials upset the cost calculations and thereby increase the risks of manufacturers. In addition, once the overhead costs of installing the equipment, economising raw material and producing synthetic substitutes have been incurred during periods of higher prices, the working costs of producing the substitutes might be lower than the prices of imported raw materials in normal times or even during depressions, and thus the production of substitutes might be continued.

The underdeveloped countries specialise, mainly, in the export of agricultural and mineral goods, the income elasticity of demand for which is very low. In contrast, the advanced countries specialise, mainly, in the export of industrial goods, the income elasticity of demand for which is comparatively higher. As the national income of a country rises, its proportionate expenditure on manufactures increases and that on food decreases. Thus, with the increase in world income, the demand for the exports of advanced countries increases much more than that for the exports of the primary producing countries.

Restrictions on the import of agricultural goods to safeguard the domestic agriculture in advanced countries is another important factor decreasing the demand for the exports of the agricultural countries. Particular mention might be made in this connection of the United States restrictions on the import of agricultural products. Till recently the United States was enjoying a highly favourable balance of payments and, yet, she imposed restrictions on the import of agricultural goods to prevent unemployment in her agriculture. Some advanced countries, particularly the United States, have not only restricted the import of agricultural goods to prevent unemployment in agriculture but also unfairly competed with the less developed countries by sub siding the exports of agricultural goods.[39] This has adversely affected the demand for the exports of the less developed countries.

Population is growing at a faster rate in underdeveloped countries than in advanced countries. Increase in population in the underdeveloped countries has increased the demand for imports. On the other hand, the decline in the rate of growth of population in advanced countries has inhibited the expansion of demand for the exports of the underdeveloped countries.

In the past, most of the foreign private investments were made in export industries. This tendency continues even now. The expansion of the export industries in primary producing countries has lowered the prices of their exports.

The underdeveloped countries depend much more on developed countries for their imports as well as for their exports than the vice versa.[40] In addition, these countries lack waiting power because of their meagre foreign exchange reserves and urgent need for the import of capital goods, technical know-how and essential raw materials required for the development programmes. This weakens their bargaining power *vis-a-vis* the advanced countries.

PORTFOLIO CHOICE AND TRADE IN RISKY

This section develops our theoretical analysis. Our key assumption is that investors have exponential utility, which implies constant absolute risk aversion in the face of wealth shocks. Exponential utility leads to closed-form expressions for consumption, portfolio allocations, equilibrium asset returns and the gains to trade in a setting with many agents, many assets, incomplete financial markets and heterogeneity in exposure to undiversifiable risks. We also rely on normality of asset returns and endowment shocks, but this assumption is less essential. It can be relaxed while preserving the ability to derive closed-form solutions.

Most dynamic analyses of consumption, portfolio choice and equilibrium asset pricing rely heavily on analytical or numerical approximation techniques to obtain solutions. This is especially true in the analysis of rich environments like ours that consider incomplete markets, many assets, many agents who differ in risk exposures and limited participation in financial markets by some agents. In contrast, our approach relies on exponential preference specifications to obtain exact closed-form analytical solutions that are easy to compute and easy to interpret.

Our approach, too, is an approximation. In particular, exponential utility can be interpreted as a local approximation to preferences that display constant relative risk aversion. In calibrating the theoretical model, we assume that all agents have the same degree of relative risk aversion, and we approximate the corresponding exponential utility function using a country's per capita income level at the midpoint of our sample period. We could also approximate around the expected growth path of per capita income by allowing the risk aversion parameter in the exponential utility function to vary over time. However, in view of the modest average growth rates experienced by the countries, we opt for the simpler approach that specifies absolute risk aversion to be constant over time.

Like most work on international risk sharing, we consider an endowment economy. We model the world economy as containing many countries, each of which is populated by many individuals who receive stochastic endowments of a single consumption good. We do not explicitly treat nontraded goods in the formal analysis, but the model can be interpreted to cover two special cases: perfect substitution between internationally traded and nontraded goods, or additive separability between traded and nontraded goods.

Our empirical work treats both cases. To reduce the notational burden, we assume that each country is populated by a fixed set of individuals who live forever. It is straightforward, but tedious, to consider overlapping generations of individuals with finite life spans. Since life-cycle considerations play no essential role in this study, we opt for the simpler infinite horizon formulation.

Our theoretical analysis and empirical investigation are directed to the gains from trade among countries. These gains make up only part of the benefits to domestic residents from trading risky foreign assets. In particular, trade in foreign assets can expand risk sharing opportunities within countries, whether or not the foreign assets are useful for risk sharing between countries. To evaluate the within-country consumption risk-sharing benefits of trade in foreign assets, it would be necessary to investigate the covariance between foreign asset returns and that part of individual specific income innovations that cannot be hedged using domestic financial assets.

The world economy contains H investors indexed by h and G countries indexed by g. A country is a collection of investors $h \in g$. Each person lives forever and has preferences defined over current and future consumption of a single goods. A consumption path is a random vector $C^h = (c_t^{-h})_{t=0}^{\infty}$. Our most important condition pertains to preferences over these consumption paths.

Condition (a): Agents have exponential utility given by

$$U^h(C^h) = E_t\left[\sum_{t=0}^{\infty}(\delta^h)^t(-1/A^h)\exp(-A^h C_t^h)\right]$$

where A^h is the coefficient of absolute risk aversion, and δ^h is the subjective rate of time preference.

Let $A^g = \left[(1/H^g)\sum_{h\in g}(1/A^h)\right]$ be the harmonic mean of investor's absolute risk aversion for country g, where H^g is its population size. Also let $\delta^g = \Pi_{h\in g}(\delta^h)^{A^g/(A^h H^g)}$ be the\average" subjective discount rate in country g. Here, variables with a "g" or "h" superscript refer to country and investor level quantities, respectively.

Condition (b): Individuals can freely borrow or lend at a gross one-period rate of return, R_0. This risk-free rate of return is nonstochastic, although it may vary over time.

Using the risk-free rate, define the present value operator,

$$PDV_t(\{z_s\}_{S=t}^T) = \sum_{S=t}^{T}\frac{1}{R_0^{S-t}}E_t(\tilde{z}_S) \tag{1}$$

where $E_t(\tilde{z}_S)$ denotes the expected value of $\tilde{z}_s$ conditional on information available at t. The further restriction to a constant risk-free rate embedded in (1) is easily relaxed as the cost of added notational complexity.

Individuals receive endowments of labour or other non-financial income, $\tilde{y}_t^h$, measured in units of the consumption goods. Let $\tilde{Y}_t^h = PDV\left(\{\tilde{y}_S^h\}_{S=t}^{\infty}\right)$ be the present value of non financial income, which includes labour income and proprietary business income. Each country also has marketable, securitized assets that generate stochastic income streams for their owners. Let e^g be the per capita value of these risky financial assets measured in units of the consumption good. e^g is the market value of securitized wealth, and $\tilde{Y}_t^g$ is the present value of non marketable income, discounted at the risk-free rate. Domestic output in period t equals the period t payoff to risky financial assets plus non-financial income.

There are $J + 1$ marketable asset in the world economy: J risky assets with gross one-period rates of return from $t - 1$ to t given by R_t and a riskless asset with certain return R_0. Write the $(H + J)\times 1$ vector of non marketable income present values and marketable asset returns as $\phi_t = [\tilde{Y}_t^1 - - - - - \tilde{Y}_t^H\ \tilde{R}_{1,t} - - - - - \tilde{R}_{J,t}]$. Our last main condition involves the covariance matrix of ϕ_t.

Condition (c): Financial asset returns and the present value of non-financial income have a joint normal distribution. The joint covariance matrix of asset returns and endowment present values is nonstochastic:

$$\phi_t \sim N(E(\phi_t),\ Cov(\phi_t))$$

where

$$Cov(\phi_t) = \left[\begin{array}{c|c} \Xi & \beta \\ \hline \beta' & \Sigma \end{array}\right]$$

Investor h invests in a subset J^h of the J risky assets. Specifically, he chooses a J^h dimensional portfolio of risky assets, $\omega^{h'}$, and invests $\omega_0^{h'}$ in the riskless asset. The portfolio allocations ω and ω_0 are measured in units of the consumption good. We state our propositions for the case of no further restrictions on ω so that investors can adopt unlimited long or short positions on risky assets in J_h. However, it is not difficult to treat short-sale or other restrictions on risky asset holdings. Initially, we assume that everyone in country g trades the same set of assets, J_g.

We can now specify the budget set for person h in country g as

$$B^h(R) = \left\{ \begin{array}{c} (c_t^h, \omega_t^h)_{t=0}^{\infty} \ni c_t^h + \sum_{j=0}^{J} \omega_{j,t}^h = y_t^h + \sum_{j=0}^{J} \omega_{j,t-1}^h R_{jt} \\ \omega_{j,t}^h = 0 \ if \ j \notin J^g \\ \lim_{T\to\infty} PDV\left(\left\{\sum_{j=0}^{J} \omega_{j,t}^h R_{jt}\right\}_{t=T}\right) = 0 \end{array} \right\}$$

The budget set incorporates a transversality condition, and it restricts trade by investor h to assets in J^g. We will often refer to the J-dimensional vector of expected excess returns as ER, which has representative element $E(\tilde{R}_j)-R_0$. We also refer to the multivariate Sharpe ratio, $S=\sum^{-1/2} ER$. Per capita country level security holdings are $\omega_0^g=\sum_{h\in g}\omega_0^h/H^g$ and $\omega^g=\sum_{h\in g}\omega^h/H^g$. Asset prices and returns will generally differ between autarky and free trade. We shall often use g superscripts to denote autarky outcomes in country g. We let e_A^g denote the autarky value of securitized assets in country g, and e^g be the value of those same assets at world prices under free trade.

Above discussion establishes that:

(a) Consumption is the annuity value of a broad definition of wealth. This implies that consumption innovations are linear in innovations to income and portfolio returns.

(b) We can decompose demand for risky assets into a 'risk-exploitation' component that depends on excess returns and risk aversion and a 'hedging' component that depends on the covariance between nonmarketable asset values and returns on risky financial assets.

(c) International trade is riskey assets depends on the difference between the autarky price of risk and the world price of risk. A country will go (long) short in an asset if the autarky price of risk is below (above) the world price.

(d) Gains from trade rise in the square of the difference between autarky and world prices of risk.

(e) We can decompose the gains from trade into three components: a 'hedging benefits' that measures the potential reduction in the variance of national income made possible by an asset; a 'hedging cost' that measures the change in excess returns resulting from a hedge position; and a 'risk premium benefit' that measures the gains to taking on market risk.

Our first proposition converts a complex dynamic programming problem into a simple annuitization exercise. We use a broad wealth measure called 'generalized wealth' that incorporates future non-financial income, future wealth uncertainty, future excess returns on risky assets and the difference between an investor's subjective discount rate and the risk-free interest rate.

Consumption and portfolio choice: Under conditions *a*, *b* and *c* we have

$$c_t^h = aGW_t^h$$

where the marginal propensity to consume out of generalized wealth is

$$a = 1/PDV\left(\{1\}_{S=t}^{\infty}\right) = (R_0 - 1)/R_0.$$

Generalized wealth at time *t* is given by

$$GW_t^h = \tilde{Y}_t^h + R_0\,\omega_{0,t}^h + \tilde{R}_t\,\omega^h + \frac{1}{R_0 - 1}$$

$$\left(ER'w^h + \frac{1}{aA^h}\ln R_0\,\delta^g - \frac{aA^h}{2}Var\,(GW^h)\right) \qquad (2)$$

Risky asset holdings are constant over time and given by $\omega^h = (1/aA^h)\sum^{-1}ER - \sum^{-1}\beta^h$. Thus, under our assumptions, consumption is simply the annualized value of generalized wealth. To understand portfolio choice, consider an economy with only one risky asset, asset 1. Note that only the present discounted values of future non-financial income $\tilde{Y}_t^h$ and portfolio returns $\omega_{1,t-1}^h\tilde{R}_{1,t}$ are stochastic. Thus innovations to generalized wealth and consumption depend only on innovations to $\tilde{Y}_t^h$ and $\omega_{1,t-1}^h\tilde{R}_{1,t}$.

The Euler equation for risky financial assets relates consumption innovations to asset prices. Specifically,

$$ER_{1,t} = A^h\,Cov(\tilde{c}_t^h, \tilde{R}_{1,t})$$

Using our characterization of consumption, substitute for $\tilde{c}_t^h$,

$$ER_{1,t} = aA^h\,Cov(\tilde{Y}_t^h + \omega_{1,t-1}^h\tilde{R}_{1,t}.\ \tilde{R}_{1t});$$

and solve for individual demand, $\omega_{1,t-1}^h$:

$$\omega_{1,t-1}^h = \frac{1}{aA^h}.\frac{ER_{1,t}}{Var(\tilde{R}_{1,t})} - \frac{Cov(\tilde{Y}_t^h.\tilde{R}_{1t})}{Var(\tilde{R}_{1t})} \qquad (3)$$

The first term in the right hand sight of equation (3) is the "Risk premium exploitation" and the second term is the "Hedging". It represents the portfolio choice of the consumer. All else equal, investment in a risky asset is increasing in the return ($ER_{1,t}$) and decreasing in absolute risk aversion (A^h), the marginal propensity to consume out of wealth (a) and the covariance between nonmarketable wealth and the return ($Cov(\tilde{Y}_t^h, \tilde{R}_{1,t})$). The size of the asset position is also decreasing in risk, ($Var(\tilde{R}_{1,t})$).

To analyze international trade in risky assets, we borrow a device from classical trade theory, 'the Law of Comparative Advantage'. We will show that equation (3) implies a law of comparative advantage that relates net national demand for risky financial assets to the difference between the price of risk (i.e. Sharpe ratio) in world markets and the price of risk under autarky.

First, we define autarky.

(a) Under "autarky", a country can trade the consumption good and freely engage in international borrowing and lending, but it cannot trade risky assets internationally.

Note two important things about our definition of "autarky." First, it only applies to risky assets. We assume that countries face the same riskless rate under autarky and free trade. Second, our definition of autarky does not prohibit within-country trade in risky financial assets. It will be helpful to spell out certain relationships between asset prices and returns across trade regimes. By definition, the gross return on asset j is $\tilde{R}_{j,t} = (\tilde{\pi}_{j,t} + \tilde{d}_{j,t})/\pi_{j,t-1}$, where $\tilde{d}_{j,t}$ is the payoff at t, and $\tilde{\pi}_{j,t}$ is the ex-dividend asset price at t. Under our assumptions, equilibrium implies that $\tilde{\pi}_{j,t} = PDV(\{d_{j,S}\}_{S=t+1}^{\infty}) + k$, where k is a deterministic term. Thus $\tilde{R}_{j,t} = (PDV(\{d_{j,S}\}_{S=t}^{\infty}) + k)/\pi_{j,t-1}$, and innovations to returns are given by

$$[PDV(\{d_{j,S}\}_{S=t}^{\infty}) - E_{t-1}(PDV(\{d_{j,s}\}_{S=t}^{\infty}))]/\pi_{j,t-1}$$

The numerator depends only on the dividend process and the riskless rate, both of which we assume to be invariant across trade regimes. So, asset prices and returns are related across trade regimes as follows:

$$R_{j,t-1} - E(R_{j,t-1}) = \frac{\pi^g_{j,t-1}}{\pi_{j,t-1}}(R^g_{j,t-1} - E(R^g_{j,t-1})) \quad (4)$$

Now, to illustrate the analysis, consider the case of a single risky marketable asset.

Let $\sigma_1 = Std(\tilde{R}_{1,t})$ be the standard deviation of returns on the asset at world prices (i.e. under free trade). Summing equation (3) across agents in country g, we can express national demand for the asset under free trade as a function of the world Sharpe raio:

$$\omega^g_{1,t-1} = (1/\sigma_1)\left[\frac{1}{aA^g}S_1 - \frac{Cov(\tilde{Y}^h_t.\tilde{R}_{1t})}{\sigma_1}\right] \tag{5}$$

Under autarky, aggregate demand in the same way and equate to supply to obtain

$$e^g_{A,1,t-1} = \left(1/Std(\tilde{R}^g_t)\right)\left[\frac{1}{aA^g}S^g_1 - \frac{Cov(\tilde{Y}^h_t\tilde{R}^g_{1,t})}{Std(\tilde{R}^g_{1,t})}\right].$$

Solving for the autarky Sharpe ratio,

$$S^g_1 = aA^g\left(Std(\tilde{R}^g_{1,t})e^g_{A,1,t-1} + \frac{Cov(\tilde{Y}^h_t,\tilde{R}^g_{1,t})}{Std(\tilde{R}^g_{1,t})}\right) \tag{6}$$

Equation (4) implies that we can rewrite (6) using free trade outcomes:

$$S^g_1 = aA^g\left(\sigma_1 e^g_{1,t-1} + \frac{Cov(\tilde{Y}^h_t\tilde{R}_{1,t})}{\sigma_1}\right)$$

Solving for $Cov(\tilde{Y}^h_t,\tilde{R}_{1t})/\sigma_1$ and substituting into equation (5), we have

$$\omega^g_{1,t-1} - e^g_{1,t-1} = \frac{1}{aA^g\sigma_1}(S_1 - S^g_1) \tag{7}$$

In words, the net national demand for the risky asset under free trade is proportional to the difference between the world and autarky Sharpe ratios.

Law of comparative advantage for risky assets: Under conditions a, b and c, the autarky Sharpe ratio is

$$S^g = aA^g\,Var(\tilde{R})^{-1/2}\,Cov(e^g\tilde{R} + \tilde{Y}^g\tilde{R}).$$

S^g can be calculated using world returns or autarky returns. Furthermore, the net national demand for risky assets in country g can be written as

$$\omega^g - e^g = \frac{1}{aA^g} \Sigma^{-1/2} (S - S^g) \tag{8}$$

We now introduce a welfare measure for the gains from trade in risky assets.

(b) Consider two consumption profiles C^h and $\tilde{C}^h$. Suppose investor h consumes C^h. GFT^h is the amount of the consumption good that we need to give to investor h on every date and in every state to make him as well off as he would be if he consumed $\tilde{C}^h$. That is

$$U^h(C^h + GFT^h) = U^h(\tilde{C}^h)$$

GFT stands for gains from trade. We will typically think of C^h and $\tilde{C}^h$ as consumption under more and less restrictive trade regimes, respectively.

Gains from trade in risky financial assets: Investors in country g initially trade assets x internationally and assets z domestically. Suppose that international trade in assets z is now allowed in country g. Let $\tilde{R}_{z/x} = \tilde{R}_z - E(\tilde{R}_z / \tilde{R}_x)$ be the part of returns on assets z that are orthogonal to returns on x. Under conditions a, b and c, the gains from trade are

$$GFT^g = \left(\frac{1}{R_0}\right) \cdot \frac{1}{2aA^g} \left(S_{z/x} - S^g_{z/x}\right)' \left(S_{z/x} - S^g_{z/x}\right) \tag{9}$$

And the present discounted value of the increase in consumption is

$$PDV(GFT) = \left(\frac{1}{R_0 - 1}\right) \frac{1}{2aA^g} \left(S_{z/x} - S^g_{z/x}\right)' \left(S_{z/x} - S^g_{z/x}\right) \tag{10}$$

Thus the gains from trading risky assets are increasing in the size of the difference between world and autarky Sharpe ratios, regardless of the sign. For example, when there is only one risky financial asset, the per capita benefit of international trade for country g is

$$GFT^{g}=\left(\frac{1}{R_0}\right)\frac{1}{2aA^{g}}(S_1-S_1^{g})^2$$

In a classical mean-variance setting, an investor is endowed with a lump of wealth, so that the no-trade price of risk is zero. Hence, in the classical setting the gains from trade can be calculated in terms of the observed Sharpe ratio, S, on a new asset without reference to the asset's autarky Sharpe Ratio, S^g, implicitly, $S^g = 0$ in the classical setting.

To more fully understand the gains from trade in risky assets, expand the quadratic expression $\left(S_1 - S_1^g\right)^2$ and substitute in the equation for the autarky Sharpe ratio:

$$GFT^{g}=\left(\frac{1}{R_0}\right)\left[\frac{1}{2aA^{g}}.\frac{ER_1^2}{\sigma_1^2}-ER_1\frac{\beta_1^g}{\sigma_1^2}+\frac{aA^{g}}{2}\frac{(\beta_1^g)^2}{\sigma_1^2}\right] \quad (11)$$

In equation (11), the first term in the bracket represents "risk premium benefit", the middle term represents "hedging cost" and the last term denotes "hedging benefit".

This expression additively decomposes the gains from trade into three pieces. The risk premium benefit is proportional to the square of the reciprocal of absolute risk aversion. The "hedging cost" is the change in excess returns that results from minimizing the variance of consumption. If the world Sharpe ratio on the asset and its covariance with domestic non-financial wealth are both positive, this effect reduces the gains from trade. However, if the covariance is negative, the "cost" will be negative, and this term will add to the gains from trade. The "hedging benefit" reflects the lower variance of consumption available from hedging shocks to Y^g. This term is always positive. However, the hedging benefit need not exceed the hedging cost. That is, it is not always optimal to hedge a position, even if it is possible to do so.

The gains from trade for country g can be decomposed as follows.

$$GFT^{g}=\left(\frac{1}{R_0}\right)\left[\frac{1}{2aA^{g}}ER'_{z/x}\sum_{z/x}^{-1}ER_{z/x}-ER'_{z/x}\sum_{z/x}^{-1}\beta^{g}\right.$$
$$\left.+\frac{aA^{g}}{2}\beta^{gt}\sum_{z/x}^{-1}\beta^{g}\right]$$

The first term in the bracket is "risk premium benefit", middle term is "hedging cost" and the last term is "hedging benefit".

NOTES

1. Jacob Viner, *Studies in the Theory of International Trade* (London 1955), p. 47.
2. W.S. Jevons, *The Theory of Political Economy* (1871), p. 136.
3. James Mill, *Elements of Political Economy* (London, 1821), p. 86.
4. James Mill, *Elements of Political Economy* (London, 1826), p. 122.
5. James Pennington, *A Letter to Kirkman Finlay, Esq., on the importation of foreign corn, and the value of the precious metals in different countries* (London, 1840), pp. 32-41.
6. J.S. Mill, "On the Laws of Interchange between Nations; and the Distribution of the Gains of Commerce among the Commercial World" Written in 1829-30, and reprinted as essay I of his *Essays on Some Unsettled Questions of Political Economy* (London, 1844).
7. J.S. Mill, *Principles of Political Economy* (London, 1848), Book III, Chapter XVIII.
8. It might be mentioned that Mill is not familiar with the term elasticity and uses the word 'extensibility' for it.
9. J.L. Shadwell, *A System of Political Economy* (London, 1877), p. 406.
10. Bastable, *Theory of International Trade* (London, 1903), p. 180.
11. J.S. Nicholson, *Principles of Political Economy* (London, 1897), II, p. 302.
12. *A Letter from Pennington to Kirkman Finlay Esq., 'On the importation of foreign corn'* (London, 1840), p. 41.
13. A. Marshall, *Money, Credit and Commerce* (London, 1929), p. 158.
14. *Ibid.*, p. 162.
15. Jacob Viner, *Studies in the Theory of International Trade* (London, 1955), p. 549.
16. *Ibid.*, pp. 550-51.
17. *Ibid.*, p. 555.
18. *Ibid.*, p. 558.

19. *Ibid.*, p. 559.
20. *Ibid.*, pp. 559-60.
21. *Ibid.*, p. 560.
22. *Ibid.*, p. 561.
23. *Ibid.*
24. D.A. Robertson, "The Terms of Trade", *International Social Science Bulletin* (Spring, 1951), p. 29.
25. F.W. Taussig, *International Trade* (New York, 1927), pp. 113-14.
26. G.S. Dorrance, "Income Terms of Trade", *Review of Economic Studies* (Edinburg, 1950), p. 52.
27. Robert E. Baldwin, "Secular Movements in the Terms of Trade", *American Economic Review,* Papers and Proceedings (May, 1955), pp. 264-65.
28. United Nations, *Relative Prices of Exports and Imports* (New York, 1949), pp. 132-33.
29. Hans Steakle, "Some Notes on the Terms of Trade", *International Social Science Bulletin* (Spring 1951), p. 36.
30. Ragnar Nurkse: *Problem of Capital Formation in Underdeveloped Countries* (New York, 1933), p. 98.
31. H.W. Singer commenting on Kindleberger's Paper on "Terms of Trade and Economic Development", *Review of Economic Studies* (Edinburg, 1950), p. 86.
32. Robert E. Baldwin, "Secular Movements in the Terms of Trade", Papers and Proceedings, *American Economic Review* (May, 1955), pp. 263-64.
33. *Ibid.*, p. 264.
34. *Ibid.*
35. W.H. Singer, "The Distribution of Gains Between Investing and Borrowing Countries", *American Economic Review, Paper and Proceedings* (May, 1950), pp. 477-78.
36. *Ibid.*, p. 478.
37. A.N. McLeod, 'Trade and Investment in Underdeveloped Areas: A Comment", *American Economic Review* (June, 1951), p. 411.
38. United Nations, *The Economic Development of Latin America* (New York, 1959), p. 10.
39. United Nations, *Measures for the Economic Development of Underdeveloped Countries* (New York, 1950).
40. For statistics see GATT, *International Trade,* 1956 (Geneva, 1957), p. 7.

Dynamics of International Trade

7

The classical theory of trade is static in nature. It assumes productive resources to be fixed in supply, tastes, constant technical knowledge given, and imports equal to exports with no international capital movements. The lack of dynamic element in the theory of international trade limits the insight that can be given to several important issues.[1] For instance, Myrdal has put forward a thesis that free trade has inhibited the economic growth of the underdeveloped countries resulting in an increase in inequalities in the distribution of world income.[2] This is contrary to the Heckscher-Ohlin theorem that the introduction of trade tends to equalise the prices of the factors of production. In fact, Myrdal does not challenge the logic of the static model; what he challenges is the applicability of the static model to actual problems. Johnson points out that trade may tend to equalise prices of factors of production but still the international income per capita may become more unequal if the amounts of productive factors per capita are becoming more unequal among different countries. This is very likely because the will and capacity to save differs in different countries which results in different rates of capital accumulation in developed and underdeveloped countries.[3]

If we are to study the theory of international trade in the context of economic development, we must take into consideration the effects of continual increase in productive factors, the evolution of demand conditions, technical progress and international capital movements. These changes affect international trade, and international trade, in turn, affects the process of economic development. We analyse below the effects on international trade of changes in factor supplies, technological progress and changes in pattern of demand. We shall analyse effects of capital movements later on in a separate chapter.

CHANGES IN FACTOR SUPPLIES AND INTERNATIONAL TRADE

The question of trade effects resulting from a change in factor supplies is of great importance, particularly in the context of the problems of economic development. It involves, from the world viewpoint, more efficient utilisation of available factors of production, or in other words, an overall improvement in the quality of the factors. We are concerned here with an autonomous change in factor supplies which takes place with economic growth and the effect of this on international trade.

The classical writers assumed a given quantity of productive factors already in existence and in employment. The importance of the development of new resources and productive forces referred to in their earlier writings is now being more fully realised. Ohlin was not ignorant of the interaction between trade and increase in factor supplies and that of the opposite process. He, for instance, states, "The supply of productive factors is not given once for all, nor is it variable only under the influence of circumstances which have nothing to do with trade and pricing. The supply of industrial agents may sometimes more adequately be described as the *result* of trade than as its cause."[4] But he emphasised simple one-way relation and did not elaborate the dynamic conditions of production and trade. Robinson,[5] for instance, recognises the great importance of the stimulus which international trade provides for creating new productive factors. He is of the view that the gain from the new factors is greater than the gain obtained from a rise in the marginal productivity of existing factors.

Increase in a Single Factor Rybczynski's Theorem: Rybczynski has analysed the effect of an increase in factor supply on production, consumption and terms of trade.[6] He has shown that, in case of the two-country, two-commodity and two-factor model, an autonomous increase in one factor leads to an absolute increase in production of the commodity using a considerable quantity of the increasing factor and a decline in the production of the commodity using relatively a smaller quantity of that factor. In order to absorb the increased factor at an unchanged price, it is necessary to obtain more of the other factor also. This can be obtained only by releasing the other factor from the industry in which it is used intensively, resulting in a decline in the output of that industry. To put the matter in a more precise manner, this result follows from the condition that if the ratio of product prices is to be kept constant, it is necessary that the ratio of factor prices remains constant; this, in turn, requires maintenance of the labour-capital ratio which originally existed in each industry; an unchanged factor ratio will keep relative marginal productivities of factors and hence their prices constant. But to maintain a constant factor ratio in the industry which uses the increased factor intensively, it is necessary to release the other factor by decreasing output in the industry which uses it intensively.

If there occurs an increase in the supply of labour without an increase in the quantity of capital in the country specialising in relatively labour-intensive commodity, the production effect of this will be to expand the supply of exportables and reduce the domestic supply of importables at constant prices. This type of output expansion is known as 'ultra-export-biased'. On the other hand, if the increase is in the supply of capital without an increase in the supply of labour, the production effect will be an increase in the output of capital-intensive importables and a decline in the output of labour-intensive exportables. This type of expansion in output is called 'ultra-import-biased'.

The above analysis is based on the assumption of linear, homogeneous production functions and unchanged marginal rates of substitution in production with the same terms of trade. Rybczynski has also shown that an increase in one factor necessarily leads to a deterioration in the terms of trade or a decline in the relative price of the commodity using relatively in larger quantity of the increasing factor. In case the commodity in question is an export good, the external terms of trade would deteriorate; if it is an import commodity, there would take place an improvement in the external terms of trade.

Increase in Two Factors: Rybczynski's analysis just showed that an increase in one factor, say labour, results in a decline in the prices of labour-intensive commodities relative to the prices of capital-intensive commodities. Rybczynski pointed out that the analysis could be extended to analyse the effects of changes in quantities of two factors, although he did not do that exercise himself. Some other economists have tried to analyse the effects of increase in the supplies of more than one factor.

If the absolute amount of the factors increases proportionately over a period so that the relative factor endowment remains unchanged, the production frontier would retain the same shape but would shift outward proportionately for both commodities. The effect on production, at constant prices, is the same proportionate increase in the outputs of exportable and importable goods. This type of increase in output is known as 'neutral'. In case, the increase in the supply of labour is proportionately more than in that of capital, in the relatively labour-abundant country, the supply of exportables increases in greater proportion than the supply of importables. This type of expansion in output is called 'export-biased'. In contrast, if the increase in the supply of capital is proportionately more than in that of capital, the domestic supply of importables increases in greater proportion than the supply of exportables. This type of expansion in output is known as 'import-biased'.

The Rybczynski theorem has been expanded and put into a general form by Amano[7] and Guha[8]. Let us consider a proportionate rate of increase in one factor, say labour (L), greater than in another, say capital (K). Amano shows that an absolute expansion in the output of commodity X, which uses relatively more of labour, and an absolute decline in the output of commodity Y, which uses relatively more of capital, takes place only if the ratio of the absolute increase in labour to the absolute increase in capital is less than the ratio of labour and capital used in the production of commodity X. Similarly if the increase in labour relative to an increase in capital is greater than the relative factor proportions in the initial endowment, the labour-intensive commodity X will increase proportionately more than the capital-intensive commodity Y. But if the relative increase in factors corresponds to the factor intensity of producing commodity Y, that is, relative increase in K is larger than the relative increase in L, the output of commodity X will remain unchanged while that of Y will expand. Thus the basic relationship for the relative change in outputs and hence their relative prices is the relationship of the incremental labour-capital ratio to relative factor intensities of productive processes. The output of the labour-intensive commodity will expand relative to that of the other commodity only if the incremental labour-capital ratio is greater than the labour-capital ratio used in the production process.

The above analysis is based on the assumption that the relative commodity prices remain constant. This will hold true in case of growth in a small country which faces more or less given price patterns determined by the world demand and supply forces. In the normal case of an open economy, however, the terms of trade of the country would deteriorate if the output using more of the factor growing at a relatively higher rate were exported.

If the assumption of fixed factor supplies of the traditional model is dropped, the elasticity of the supply of labour in regard to changing wage rates becomes greater or less than zero. Kemp and Jones are of the opinion that relaxation of the assumption makes possible a decline in the output of a commodity in association with an increase in its price.[9] A backward-bending offer curve is also possible so that a larger quantity of imports is demanded at a higher price associated with a deterioration in the terms of trade. In order to produce this result, the supply of labour must decline with rising wages at a faster rate than the decline in output of import goods associated with increasing prices. This is essential because to consider the opposite case, when the supply of labour increases, the rising income induces more importables demanded at the same time as the output of importables increases. The perverse results which the authors develop use an elasticity of supply less than zero and depend on income inducements to importables being greater than output effects on importables.

The possibility of factor-intensity reversal damages the rigour of the Heckscher-Ohlin theorem regarding factor proportions and trade structures. But there is another dimension. Countries with abundant labour and low wages, for instance, might possess a comparative advantage in capital-intensive industries in which the elasticity of substitution between capital and labour is low. This can happen because, technologically, a given capital intensity determines the feasible minimum size of plants independently of relative factor prices. When the plants are of large size, factor proportions can be varied depending upon factor substitutability. The possibility of factor intensity reversal damages the predictive powers of the factor proportions theory in regard to the direction of trade.

EFFECT OF TECHNOLOGICAL PROGRESS ON FACTOR SUPPLIES AND TRADE

Heckscher-Ohlin theory of international trade is based on the assumption that the techniques of production remain unchanged and are identical in the two countries. It is, however, quite possible that, in the absence of differences in factor endowments, the scope for trade may arise from differences in technology.

Technological progress leads to a change in the production function. Technological change may lead to a larger volume of output with unchanged combinations of factor inputs or increased efficiency of one input in relation to another. It may also lead to an increase in effective factor supply. Innovations, for instance, have been classified according to their effect on factor supply. Johnson, for instance, considers a labour-saving innovation as equivalent to an increase in the marginal productivity of capital and in the 'effective' supply of labour.[10] A capital-saving innovation is equivalent to an increase in the marginal productivity of labour and in the 'effective' supply of capital. A technological improvement is considered to be neutral if the factor proportions remain unchanged for the same level of output with unchanged factor prices. The same absolute combination of factors, however, would yield a larger volume of output. Neutral technological progress in all industries leads to a proportional expansion of all industries.

Considering the three different types of innovations, let us study what type of bias in production would result according to whether the innovation occurs in labour-intensive industry—say wheat industry, or capital-intensive industry—say cloth industry. In studying this, we shall concentrate on the country specialising in the production of labour-intensive commodities and analyse what will be the shift, at constant relative product prices, in the output of one commodity as a consequence of an innovation in the production of the other commodity.

Neutral Innovation

If this takes place in the labour-intensive wheat industry, the output of wheat would increase, and at the original relative factor prices, its cost of production would decline. To have the original product price ratio remain unchanged after this innovation, there must take place a shift in the factor price ratio. In this situation, there would be an incentive for factors to move from cloth industry to wheat industry where the marginal productivities and hence factor earnings are higher. As a result of this movement, the price of labour would rise and that of capital decline because capital is used less intensively in wheat industry where the innovation takes place. The relative costs of wheat and cloth are thereby changed and the original product price ratio is restored. Thus, at constant relative prices, the neutral technical progress in the exportable commodity wheat leads to an expansion in the output of wheat and a decline in the output of the importable commodity cloth. The production effect of a neutral innovation in the export industry is ultra-export-biased. On the other hand, if the neutral innovation takes place in the production of the importable commodity cloth, the production effect would be ultra-import-biased.

Labour-saving Innovation

If this occurs in the wheat industry, cost of production in this industry will decline and some of the labour would be released. As in the previous case, the decline in cost requires a shift of resources from cloth industry to the wheat industry in which the innovation occurs. As in the case of an increase in the supply of labour, the labour released by the innovation in wheat industry must be absorbed by an increase in the output of exportable commodity wheat which uses labour relatively intensively, and by a decrease in the production of importable commodity cloth. The production effect is, therefore, ultra-export-biased. Further, since in this case technical progress saves the factor which is employed relatively intensively in the production of the exportable commodity wheat, the production effect is more ultra-export-biased than in case of neutral innovation.

If, however, the labour-saving innovation occurs in the capital-intensive industry cloth, the production effect may be anywhere between the extremes of ultra-import-biased and ultra-export-biased. This range is possible because the innovation not only reduces the cost of production in cloth industry and thereby tends to increase the supply of importable commodity cloth but also releases labour from commodity cloth and thereby tends to increase the supply of exportable commodity cloth, because at constant factor prices the labour which is released from commodity cloth must be absorbed by an increase in the output of labour-intensive industry cloth. Depending upon the respective strengths of the cost-reducing and factor-saving effects which work in opposite directions, the net production effect may vary from being ultra-import-biased to being ultra-export-biased. In case the innovation is only slightly labour-saving, the production effect will be ultra-import-biased. If, however, the innovation is so strongly labour-saving that it counteracts the substitution effect of cheaper labour, the production effect will be ultra-export-biased.

Capital-saving Innovation

In case the innovation is in the capital-intensive industry cloth, by logic similar to that in case of a labour-saving innovation in industry wheat, the supply of importable commodity cloth will increase at the cost of exportable commodity wheat. The production effect will be ultra-import-biased.

In case, the capital-saving innovation occurs in the labour-intensive industry wheat, the production effect may vary from being ultra-export-biased to being ultra-import-biased, depending upon the quantity of capital released by the innovation. In this case also, the cost-reducing effect of the innovation and the factor-saving effect operate in opposite directions. Depending upon the relative strength of these two effects, the net production effect may vary from being ultra-export-biased to being ultra-import-biased.

Increase in Labour Efficiency

The production effects resulting from an increase in labour efficiency can be derived from the analysis already made in cases of an increase in labour supply or technical progress. An increase in labour efficiency is analytically equivalent to an increase in the supply of labour; it results in the same combination of inputs yielding a larger output than before, or, alternatively, it permits the production of same output with a smaller quantity of labour. This is equivalent to a shift in the production function, each iso-quant now representing a larger product. When this is simply because of greater efficiency of labour (e.g. through an improvement in skill) with no dependence on technical change or capital accumulation, the production effect of increased efficiency would be the same as that of an increase in labour supply. If (which is more likely), the increase in output per man-hour is because of neutral or labour-saving innovations, the production effect would be identical with that of technical progress.

CONSUMPTION EFFECTS OF GROWTH

We have analysed above the production effects of increase in factor supply, technical progress and increase in labour efficiency. Let us now analyse the effects of these developmental changes on the pattern of consumption.

Considering the relatively labour-abundant country, we analyse the consumption effects of an increase in real income, assuming that the relative commodity prices and the preference system remains unchanged. If the income elasticity of demand for importables as well as for exportables equals unity, the ratio in which the two types of commodities are purchased would remain unchanged. In this case, the increase in income raises the demand for importables in the same proportion as it increases the demand for exportables. Thus the consumption effect is neutral. Though neutral income effect is possible, it is not likely to be a common case. If the income elasticity of demand for importables is greater than unity and that for exportable less than unity, the ratio of importables to exportables which would be purchased at original prices is higher after the increase in income. In this case, the increase in income raises the demand for importables in greater proportion than it increases the demand for exportables. Thus the consumption effect is export-biased. But if the income elasticity of demand for importables is less than unity and that for exportables is greater than unity, the ratio of importables to exportables which would be purchased at original prices is lower after the increase in income. In this case, the increase in income raises the demand for importables in lesser proportion than it increases the demand for exportables. The consumption effect thus is import-biased. In addition to these three cases, there are two extreme cases viz. (i) ultra-export-biased when the demand for exportables declines absolutely with a rise in income and (ii) ultra-import-biased when the demand for importables declines absolutely with a rise in income.

NATURAL RESOURCES AND TRADE

Though Heckscher-Ohlin theory as well as the doctrine of comparative costs recognised the importance of natural resources in influencing comparative commodity prices, they concentrated on labour and capital. Empirical investigations made from time to time normally provided measures in terms of labour and capital. The reason for concentration on labour and capital is the great difficulties involved in measuring natural resource availability and employment. Kindleberger emphasizes that natural resources should be described in relation to a given technology. Changes in technology change the characteristics, the availability, and the value attached to natural resources.[11] Normally, the natural resource factor cannot be separated from other factors, particularly capital. However, size of land area, its fertility, the distribution of minerals and fossil fuels, and other aspects of natural resources, together with labour, capital and technology, account for differences in endowment which provide the basis for foreign trade.

Vanek has analysed the way in which resource elements enter into a country's foreign trade and the way in which the relationship may be influenced by changes in factor endowments, technology, and demand conditions.[12] Long-run development means an outward extension of the transformation curve and a consumption path, leading to higher levels of national economic welfare. The long-run relationship between production and consumption is influenced by the possibilities of foreign trade. Vanek's hypothesis is that natural resources in foreign trade show the relative abundance of this factor in the economy and the natural resource content of foreign trade changes with changes in relative abundance of natural resources. An economy with a relatively abundant supply of one factor will have a tendency to expand in order to exploit this factor. Output of the commodity using this factor more intensely will increase more than that of the other commodity and will become the exportable commodity. During the period 1870-80, land was the relatively abundant factor in the United States' economy and as such land-intensive commodities constituted the major exports. But with the growth of capital and population, natural resources tended to become relatively more scarce. As a result, there was a tendency for an increase in the export of capital-labour-intensive commodities and the United States emerged from a net exporter of resource products and a net importer of capital-labour-intensive products to a net importer of resource products and a net exporter of the capital-labour-intensive products.

The results which arise from disproportional growth in the various factors are similar to those arising from technological improvements. A faster rate of technological improvement in one industry than in another, factor endowments remaining unchanged, gives rise to more or less the same effects as those resulting from a disproportional growth in factors, technology remaining unchanged.

A MODEL ON DYNAMICS OF INTERNATIONAL TRADE WITH INNOVATION AND FIRM DYNAMICS

In this section we shall study a general equilibrium model of the decisions of firms to innovate and to engage in international trade. Here we analyze the impact of a reduction in international trade costs on firms' process and product innovative activity.

In this model we consider that each firm has a stock of some firm specific factor that determines its current profit opportunities. Examples of this firm specific factor include productivity, managerial skill, product quality, or brand name. Here we consider two forms of innovation: innovation to increase the stock of this firm specific factor in an existing firm—process innovation, and innovation to create new firms with a new initial stock of the firm specific factor—product innovation. We use the model to study the dynamic gains from trade that arise as process and product innovations respond to a decline in the costs of international trade. We show in this model that if all firms export (so the fixed costs of international trade are zero) then, in general equilibrium, a decrease in the marginal costs of international trade has no impact at all, in steady-state, on firms' process innovation decisions and hence no impact on aggregate productivity and output over and above the impact of this trade cost reduction on the volume of trade and production in a version of the model that abstracts from process innovation.

If all firms export, a reduction in the marginal costs of international trade changes the profit opportunities of all firms by the same proportion. The returns to process innovation are proportional to firm profits, so a reduction in the marginal costs of international trade also changes the returns to process innovation by the same proportion for all firms. In general equilibrium with free entry, the expected profits of starting a new firm and the cost of innovative inputs must rise by the same amount to ensure that there are zero profits to product innovation. Because the reduction in trade costs affects the opportunities of all firms proportionally, this free condition implies that the ratio of the returns to process innovation to the cost of innovative inputs remains unchanged for all firms. Hence, the equilibrium process innovation decisions are left unchanged. This result implies that when all firms export, our model has steady-state implications for the impact of changes in marginal trade costs on product innovation.

The Model

Time is assumed to be discrete and labeled $t = 0, 1, 2, \ldots$ There are two countries: home and foreign. We denote the variables pertaining to the foreign country with a star. Households in each country are endowed with L units of time. Production in each country is structured as follows.

There is a single final nontraded good that can be consumed or used in innovative activities, a continuum of differentiated intermediate goods that are produced and can be internationally traded subject to a fixed and a variable trade cost, and a nontraded intermediate good that we call the research good. This research good is produced using a combination of final output and labour, and is used to pay the costs associated with both process and product innovation, as well as the fixed costs of exporting. The productivities of the firms producing the differentiated intermediate goods are determined endogenously through equilibrium process innovation, and the measure of differentiated intermediate goods produced in each country is determined endogenously through product innovation. To simplify the presentation of the analytical results in the paper, the benchmark model abstracts from fixed operating costs (that give rise to endogenous exit), and time varying fixed export costs (to account for the extent of firm switching between exporting and non-exporting status).

Households in the home country have preferences of the form $\sum_{t=0}^{\infty} \beta^t \log(C_t)$, where C_t is the consumption of the home final goods at date t. Households in the foreign country have preferences of the same form over consumption of the foreign final goods C_t^*. Each household in the home country faces an intertemporal budget constraint of the form

$$\sum_{t=0}^{\infty} Q_t (P_t C_t - W_t L) \leq \bar{W} \tag{1}$$

where Q_t are intertemporal prices, W_t is the wage in the home country, P_t is the price of the home final good, C_t is the household's consumption, and $\bar{W}$ is the initial stock of assets held by the household. Households in the foreign country face similar budget constraints with the same intertemporal prices Q_t and wages, prices, and assets all labeled with stars. Intermediate goods are differentiated products each produced by heterogeneous firms indexed by z, which indicates their productivity. A firm in the home country with productivity index z has productivity equal to $\exp(z)^{1/(\rho-1)}$ and produces output $y_t(z)$ with labor $l_t(z)$. According to the CRS production technology

$$y_t(z)=\exp(z)^{1/(\rho-1)}\, l_t(z) \tag{2}$$

We rescale firm productivity using the exponent $1/(\rho-1)$ so that, as explained below, labour and profits are proportional to exp (z).

The output of this firm can be used in the production of the home final goods, with the quantity of this domestic absorption denoted $a_t(z)$. Alternatively, some of this output can be exported to the foreign country to be used in the production of the foreign final good.

International trade is subject to both fixed and iceberg type costs of exporting. The fixed, per-period cost of exporting in terms of the research goods is denoted by n_x. The iceberg type marginal cost of exporting is denominated in terms of the intermediate good being exported. The firm must export $Da_t^*(z)$ units of output, with $D \geq 1$, to have $a_t^*(z)$ units of output arrive in the foreign country for use in the production of the foreign final good.

Let $x_t(z) \in \{0, 1\}$ be an indicator of the export decision of home firms with productivity index z (it is 1 if the firm exports and 0 otherwise). Then, feasibility requires that

$$a_t(z)+x_t(z)Da_t^*(z)=y_t(z) \tag{3}$$

and that $x_t(z)n_x$ units of the research goods be used to pay fixed costs of exporting. A firm in the foreign country with productivity index z has the same production technology, with output denoted $y_t^*(z)$, labor $l_t^*(z)$, and domestic absorption $b_t^*(z)$. Exports to the home country, $b_t(z)$, are subject to both fixed and marginal costs and hence feasibility requires that $x_t^*(z)Db_t(z)+b_t^*(z)=y_t^*(z)$, and that $x_t^*(z)n_x$ units of the foreign research goods be used to pay the fixed costs of exporting.

The home final goods is produced from home and foreign intermediate goods with a constant returns production technology of the form

$$Y_t=\left[\int a_t(z)^{1-1/\rho}dM_t(z)+\int x_t^*(z)b_t(z)^{1-1/\rho}dM_t^*(z)\right]^{\rho/(\rho-1)} \tag{4}$$

where $M_t(z)$ is the measure of operating firms in the home country with productivity less than or equal to z, and $M_t^*(z)$ the corresponding measure in the foreign country. Production of the final goods in the foreign country is defined analogously. It will be useful below to distinguish between the total measure of operating firms given by $N_t=M_t(\infty)$, and the distribution of z across operating firms which has a cumulative distribution function given by $M_t(z)/N_t$.

The final goods in the home country is produced by competitive firms that choose output Y_t and inputs $a_t(z)$ and $b_t(x)$ subject to (4) to maximize profits taking prices P_t, $p_{at}(z)$, $p_{bt}(z)$, export decisions $x_t(z)$, $x_t^*(z)$, and measures of operating intermediate goods firms M_t and M_t^* as given. Standard arguments give that equilibrium prices must satisfy

$$P_t=\left[\int p_{at}(z)^{1-\rho}dM_t(z)+\int x_t^*(z)p_{bt}(z)^{1-\rho}dM_t^*(z)\right]^{1/(1-\rho)} \tag{5}$$

and quantities

$$\frac{a_t(z)}{Y_t}=\left(\frac{p_{at}(z)}{P_t}\right)^{-\rho} \text{ and } \frac{b_t(z)}{Y_t}=\left(\frac{p_{bt}(z)}{P_t}\right)^{-\rho} \tag{6}$$

Analogous equations hold for prices and quantities in the foreign country.

The research goods in the home country is produced with a constant returns to scale production technology F that uses X_t units of the home final goods and L_{mt} units of labor to produce Y_{mt} units of the research goods according to $Y_{mt} = F(X_t, L_{mt})$. As is standard, the equilibrium price of the home research goods, denoted by W_{mt}, is given as a function of the price of the home final goods P_t and the home wage W_t, by the unit cost function associated with the production function F. We write this cost function $W_{mt} = W_m(P_t, W_t)$. Likewise, in the foreign country we have, $Y^*_{mt} = F(X^*_t, L^*_{mt})$ and $W^*_{mt} = W_m(P^*_t, W^*_t)$.

Intermediate goods firms in each country are monopolistically competitive. A home firm with productivity $\exp(z)^{1/(\rho-1)}$ faces a static profit maximization problem of choosing labor input $l_t(z)$, prices $P_{at}(z)$, $p^*_{at}(z)$, quantities $a_t(z)$, $a^*_t(z)$, and whether or not to export $x_t(z)$ to maximize current period profits taking as given wages for workers W_t, the price of the home research goods W_{mt}, and prices and output of the final goods in both countries P_t, P^*_t, Y_t, and Y^*_t. This problem is written as

$$\pi_t(z) = \max_{y,l,p_a,p^*_a,a,a^*,x\in(0,1)} p_a a + x p^*_a a^* - W_t l - W_{mt} x n_x \tag{7}$$

Subject to (2), (3) and demand functions

$$a = \left(\frac{p_a}{P_t}\right)^{-\rho} Y_t \text{ and } a^* = \left(\frac{p^*_a}{P^*_t}\right)^{-\rho} Y^*_t \tag{8}$$

Productivity at the firm level evolves over time depending both on idiosyncratic productivity shocks hitting the firm and on the level of investment in productivity improvements undertaken within the firm. We model the evolution of firm productivity as follows. At the beginning of each period t, every existing firm has probability δ of exiting exogenously, and corresponding probability $1-\delta$ of surviving to produce. A surviving firm with current productivity $\exp(z)^{1/(\rho-1)}$, and that invests $H(z,p) = h\exp(z)c(p)$ units of the research good in improving its productivity in the current period t, has probability p of having productivity $\exp(z+s)^{1/(\rho-1)}$ and probability $1-p$ of having productivity $\exp(z-s)^{1/(\rho-1)}$ in the next period $t+1$.

We assume that $c(p)$ is increasing and convex in p, and h is a positive constant. We will also show that this form of $H(z,p)$ allows us to obtain analytical results for process innovation.

With this evolution of firm productivity, the expected discounted present value of profits for the firm satisfies the Bellman equation

$$V_t(z) = \max_{p\in[0,1]} \pi_t(z) - W_{mt} H(z,p)$$
$$+(1-\delta)\frac{Q_{t+1}}{Q_t}\left[pV_{t+1}(z+s)+(1-p)V_{t+1}(z-s)\right] \tag{9}$$

Let $p_t(z)$ denote the optimal choice of investment in improving productivity in the equation (9). We refer to $p_t(z)$ as the process innovation decision of the firm. Note that if the time period is small, our binomial productivity process approximates a geometric Brownian motion in continuous time in which the firm controls the drift of this process through investments of the research good.

New firms (or new products) are created with investments of the research good. Investment of n_e units of the research good in period t yield a new firm in period t+1 with initial productivity $\exp(z)^{1/(\rho-1)}$ drawn from a distribution over z given by G. New firms are not subject to exogenous exit in their entering period. In any period in which there is entry of new firms, free entry requires that

$$W_{mt} n_e = \frac{Q_{t+1}}{Q_t}\int V_{t+1}(z)\,dG \tag{10}$$

Let M_{et} denote the measure of new firms entering in period t that start producing in period t + 1. The analogous Bellman equation holds for the foreign firms as well. We refer to M_{et} as the product innovation decision as this is the mechanism through which new differentiated products are produced.

Feasibility requires that for the final good

$$C_t + X_t = Y_t \tag{11}$$

in the home country and the analogous constraint holds in the foreign country. The feasibility constraint on labor in the home country is given by

$$\int l_t(z)\,dM_t(z) + L_{mt} - L \tag{12}$$

and likewise in the foreign country. The feasibility constraint on the research good in the home country is

$$M_{et} n_e + \int \left[x_t(z) n_x + H(z, p_t(z)) \right] dM_t(z) = F(X_t, L_{mt}) \quad (13)$$

and likewise in the foreign country.

The evolution of $M_t(z)$ over time is determined by the exogenous probability of exit δ, the decisions of operating firms to invest in their productivity $P_t(z)$, and the measure of entering firms in period t–1, M_{et-1}. The measure of operating firms in the home country with productivity less than or equal to z', denoted by $M_{t+1}(z')$, is equal to the sum of three inflows: new firms founded in period t, firms continuing from period t that draw positive productivity shocks (and hence had productivities lower than z'+s in period t), and firms continuing from period t that draw negative productivity shocks (and hence had productivities below z'+s in period t). We write this as follows:

$$M_{t+1}(z') = G(z') M_{et} + (1-\delta) \int_{-\infty}^{z'-s} p_t(z) dM_t(z)$$

$$+ (1-\delta) \int_{-\infty}^{z'+s} (1-p_t(z)) dM_t(z) \quad (14)$$

The evolution of $M_t^*(z)$ for foreign firms is defined analogously.

We assume that the households in each country own those firms that initially exist at date 0. Thus we require that the initial assets of the households in both countries adds up to the total value of these firms

$$\bar{W} + \bar{W}^* = \int V_0(z) dM_0(z) + \int V_0^*(z) dM_0^*(z) \quad (15)$$

An equilibrium in this economy is a collection of sequences of prices and wages $\{Q_t, P_t, P_t^*, W_t, W_t^*, W_{mt}, W_{mt}^*, p_{at}(z), p_{at}^*(z), p_{bt}(z), p_{bt}^*(z)\}$ a collection of sequences of quantities $\{Y_t, Y_t^*, C_t, C_t^*, X_t, X_t^*, L_{mt}, L_{mt}^*, a_t(z), a_t^*(z), b_t(z), b_t^*(z), l_t(z), l_t^*(z)\}$ initial assets $\bar{W}$, $\bar{W}^*$, and a collection of sequences of firm value functions and profit, export, and investment decisions $\{V_t(z), V_t^*(z), V_t^0(z), V_t^{0*}(z),$

$\pi_t(z), x_t(z), x_t^*(z), p_t(z), p_t^*(z)\}$ together with measures of operating and entering firms $\{M_t(z), M_{et}, M_t^*(z), M_{et}^*\}$ such that household in each country are maximizing their utility subject to their budget constraints, intermediate goods firms in each country are maximizing within period profits, final goods firms in each country are also maximizing profits, all of the feasibility constraints are satisfied, and the measures of operating firms evolve as described above. A steady-state of our model is an equilibrium in which all of the variables are constant. In what follows, we omit time subscripts when discussing steady-states.

Characterizing equilibrium: We start with an analysis of the static profit maximization problem (7) for an operating firm in the home country. All firms choose a constant markup over marginal cost, so equilibrium prices are given by

$$p_{at}(z)=\frac{\rho}{\rho-1}\frac{W_t}{\exp(z)^{1/(\rho-1)}} \text{ and } p_{at}^*(z)=\frac{p}{p-1}\frac{DW_t}{\exp(z)^{1/(\rho-1)}} \tag{16}$$

The production employment of home firms is given by

$$l_t(z)=\left(\frac{\rho-1}{\rho W_t}\right)^{\rho}\left[(P_t)^{\rho}Y_t+x_t(z)(P_t^*)^{\rho}Y_t^*D^{1-\rho}\right]\exp(z) \tag{17}$$

Equation (17) implies that there is a simple relationship between the productivity index exp (z) and firm size measured as workers employed in production of output for domestic consumption. In contrast, there is no relationship between productivity in the model, measured as $\exp(z)^{1/(\rho-1)}$ and standard measures of labor productivity. This is because the average productivity of workers in the firm (measured as sales per worker) is given by $\rho W_t/(\rho-1)$ and hence is constant across firms. Differences in productivity across firms in the model, measured by, are manifest in measures of firm size and not in measures of labor productivity. Hence, firms' innovation decisions, $p_t(z)$, together with the stochastic shocks to firm productivity and firms' decisions to export determine the dynamics of firm size and the long run distribution of firms by size in our economy.

Home firms have variable profits $\pi_{dt}\exp(z)$ on their home sales, with

$$\pi_{dt}=\frac{(W_t)^{1-\rho}(P_t)^{\rho}Y_t}{\rho^{\rho}(\rho-1)^{1-\rho}} \tag{18}$$

and variable profits $\pi_{xt}\exp(z)$ on their foreign sales, with

$$\pi_{xt}=\frac{(W_t)^{1-\rho}(P_t^*)^{\rho}Y_t^*}{\rho^{\rho}(\rho-1)^{1-\rho}}D^{1-\rho} \tag{19}$$

Therefore, there is a cutoff firm productivity index $\bar{z}_{xt}$ such that firms with productivity index below $\bar{z}_{xt}$ do not export and those with productivity index above $\bar{z}_{xt}$ do export. Hence, we have that firms' static profits are given by

$$\pi_t(z)=\pi_{dt}\exp(z)+\max(\pi_{xt}\exp(z)-W_{mt}n_x,0) \tag{20}$$

The decision of a firm to invest research goods in improving productivity, if interior, must satisfy the first order condition

$$W_{mt}\frac{\partial}{\partial P}H(z,p)=(1-\delta)\frac{Q_{t+1}}{Q_t}[V_{t+1}(z+s)-V_{t+1}(z-s)]$$

This first order condition must satisfy the obvious inequality if the optimal choice of $p_t(z)$ is equal to either 0 or 1.

ECONOMIC DEVELOPMENT AND INTERNATIONAL TRADE

The relation between economic development and international trade has two aspects viz. (a) impact of development on trade and (b) impact of trade on development. In this section, we deal with the first aspect.

Factor proportions are of considerable importance in helping to analyse the influence of economic development on trade. Disproportional rates of growth of factors, of factor efficiency, and of technology, which lead to differential rates of economic development, cause differences in comparative costs and thus give rise to world trade. Economic development generally involves a rise in capital-labour ratio and capital deepening. In the initial stages, being relatively deficient in capital, the underdeveloped countries tend to import capital-intensive commodities and export labour-resource intensive commodities, though much of the capital for social overheads cannot be imported directly and domestic capital can be increased if imports release productive factors. After an initial increase in foreign trade caused by economic development, foreign trade tends to decline proportionately to total economic activity. Empirical studies partially confirm this tendency of a declining share of foreign trade in total economic activity, though many uncertainties and exceptions remain unexplained.[13]

We have analysed separately the production and consumption effects associated with the autonomous increase in factor supply, technical progress and increase in labour efficiency. The overall strength of the combined production and consumption effects would determine the direction and extent of the shifts in each country's offer curve and thereby the changes in the volume and composition of trade.

The overall bias in the development of the relatively labour-abundant country is neutral if the biases on both the production and consumption sides are neutral. In this case, the country's demand for importables and its supply of exports increase proportionately to the increase in total output. But since imports equal excess of consumption over the domestic production of importables, the domestic supply of importables must be a smaller fraction of total output than is consumption of imports of total consumption. Under conditions of neutral total bias, the difference between the demand for and the home supply of importables at constant prices would therefore necessarily become larger. The country's offer curve would shift indicating that at each level of the terms of trade, the demand for imports and the supply of exports is greater than before the production frontier shifted outwards. If, for the sake of simplification, we assume that no development occurs in the other country and hence its offer curve remains unchanged; in the new position of trade equilibrium, the volume of trade has increased and the commodity terms of trade have moved against the country in which growth occurs.

In case both the production effect and consumption effect are export-biased, the total effect is also export-biased. The total effect will also be export-biased if the production effect is neutral and the consumption effect is export-biased, or if the production effect is export-biased and the consumption effect is neutral. In this case, the demand for imports and the supply of exports increase more than proportionately to the growth of total output. In the new position of trade equilibrium, the volume of trade expands and the terms of trade move against the developing country. With the same rate of growth in total production, the increase in the volume of trade and the deterioration in the terms of trade are greater in this case than in the previous case when the total bias is neutral.

If the consumption effect is import-biased and the production effect is neutral or import-biased, the total effect would be import-biased or possibly ultra-import-biased, depending upon the strength of bias in production and consumption. The total effect will also be import-biased or possibly ultra-import-biased if production effect is import-biased and the consumption effect is neutral. When production is not sufficiently import-biased to more than counteract the greater absolute demand for imports, the total effect will be simply import-biased. In this case, the demand for imports and the supply of exports increases less than proportionately to total output. The absolute increase in demand for imports moves the terms of trade against the developing country. But, with the same rate of growth in total output, the deterioration in the terms of trade is less in this case than in the neutral case of an increased demand for imports proportional to output.

In case, the import bias in production is adequate to meet not only the increased absolute demand for importables resulting from expansion in output but also some of the original demand for imports, the total effect will be ultra-import-biased. There would occur a decline in the absolute demand for imports and the supply of exports. In the new position of trade equilibrium, the volume of trade is smaller than before development took place and the terms of trade move in favour of the developing country.

If the production effect is ultra-import-biased, the total effect would also be ultra-import-biased. Since the ultra-import-bias in production means that the domestic output of importables increases more than total output, there occurs an absolute decline in the demand for imports and the supply of exports.

In case, the production effect is ultra-export-biased, the total effect cannot be ultra-import-biased because there occurs an absolute decline in the domestic output of importables. Depending upon the consumption effect, the total effect may be ultra-export-biased, export-biased or import-biased. If it is ultra-export-biased, the absolute demand for imports increases by more than the total increase in national income, and the supply of exports increases more than in even the case of export-bias. In this case, the volume of trade would be larger and the deterioration in the developing country's terms of trade would be greater than in case of an overall export-bias.

Black has analysed how trade balances and terms of trade change between two countries with change in supplies of exports and demand for imports in each country caused by economic development.[14] He assumes that each country deals in four types of commodities viz. (i) exportables, (ii) importables, (iii) commodities which are produced but not exported and (iv) commodities which are consumed but not produced. This approach makes possible a separation of long-run demand and supply effects at work in a partial equilibrium model. Another assumption made is that the ratio in which the fixed total of productive effort is divided between the production of non-traded goods and exports in each country is determined by relative prices of goods. Export supply curves are based on the assumption that price levels of domestic non-traded goods are kept unchanged.

Shifts in demand and supply curves are determined by the type of development which may be export-biased or import-biased owing to consumption influences or production changes. In analysing examples of ultra-bias on both export and import sides, Black came to the conclusion that, on the one hand, home country's trade balances have a tendency to improve when the rate of growth is higher in the foreign country and when the growth of foreign demand is more export-biased. On the other hand, export-bias in the development of foreign supply worsens domestic trade balances if the domestic demand price elasticity is greater than unity.

The analysis of the impact of economic development on international trade has caused concern among some economists to the possibility of harm to the growing country. Bhagwati calls it 'immiserizing growth'.[15] For instance, if economic expansion is restricted to one country and if it leads to a substantial increase in output, it is feared that the terms of trade may worsen to such an extent that the economic gains to the country become negative. According to Bhagwati, the crucial conditions for immiserizing growth arc an inclastic offer curve by the remaining world and a decline in domestic production of importables at constant relative commodity prices.

INTERNATIONAL TRADE AND ECONOMIC DEVELOPMENT

There is a lot of controversy as to whether international trade promotes or inhibits economic development. On the one hand, there is the view that international trade is an important engine of economic growth in advanced and unindustrialised countries. On the other hand, it is held by some that international trade inhibits the economic development of the underdeveloped countries.

The basic issue can be put as a conflict between the gains from trade and the gains from growth. Meier stresses that if the production increases are in accordance with the comparative advantage, and trading takes place at the international ratio of exchange, there arises a gain or increase in real income as a result of a more efficient allocation of resources. This is equivalent to an outward shift in the country's frontier even when resources and techniques of production remain unchanged. Most of the traditional theory holds that gain from trade are equivalent to the gains from growth and one leads to the other.

The classical economists viewed the major influence of trade on domestic factor supply in the form of an increase in the capital stock. Introduction of international trade leads to a more efficient allocation of resources; this raises real income and thereby the capacity to save and invest. International trade increases the size of the market, which stimulates investment, particularly under conditions of increasing returns. Increase in the size of the market also permits economies of large-scale production and the use of the most advanced techniques of production. In short, introduction of trade enables a country to utilise its domestic factor supplies in a more efficient manner. Static gains from a more efficient utilisation of productive resources are supplemented by a greater access to technology, skills, and managerial talent, to capital equipment, and to raw materials as well as by the increase in competition. This led the classical economists to conclude that international trade is a great stimulant to economic development.

Following classicists, many advocates of the factor endowment theory believed that international trade leads to economic development, though the contrary view is growing. The Heckscher-

Ohlin theorem suggests that the factor-price changes caused by trade lead to a change in the use of productive factors. Factor reallocation, however, need not necessarily lead to a reallocation of gains from trade. As is held by the traditional trade theory, introduction of free trade enables a country to move to a higher level of consumption than before. It may, however, often be prevented from attaining a higher level of consumption because of rigid factor prices. But still the gains from trade can be obtained and economic welfare increased by a reallocation of consumption.

Reallocative activity is of great importance; it is an important characteristic distinguishing the underdeveloped country from the developed country. In an underdeveloped country characterised by factor prics rigidity, output of the import-competing commodity with greatest use of the factor subject to rigid returns will decline and thus lead to unemployment of the factor. The resultant loss in economic welfare may exceed the gain realised from consumption reallocation. This is likely to happen in underdeveloped countries characterised by a very low reallocative ability. Factor price flexibility which leads to factor reallocation, therefore, ensures realisation of some gains from international trade. In underdeveloped countries characterised by an absence of factor flexibility or a lack of reallocative ability, the introduction of trade may be to their long-run disadvantage.

Empirical Evidence: Contrary to the conclusions reached by the traditional theory of international trade, empirical evidence has been used to show that foreign trade does not lead to economic development. But it cannot be denied that in some countries, foreign trade has considerably assisted the process of economic development. In these countries, exports of industrial products as well as those of raw materials have contributed to economic development to a considerable extent. National economic policy is vitally concerned with natural resources and factor endowments, which have generally higher value in world use than in local use.

NOTES

1. M.O. Clement et al., *Theoretical Issues in International Economics* (London, 1967), pp. 8-9.
2. O. Myrdal, *An International Economy* (1956).
3. H.G. Johnson, "Review of S.B. Linder, *An Essay on Trade and Transformation*", *Economica* (February, 1964).

4. B. Ohlin, *Interregional and International Trade* (1935), p. 67.
5. R. Robinson, "Factor Proportions and Comparative Advantage", *Quarterly Journal of Economics* (Part I, May 1956 and Part II, August 1956).
6. T.N. Rybczynski, "Factor Endowment and Relative Commodity Prices", *Economica* (November 1955).
7. A. Amano, "Factor Endowment and Relative Prices: A Generalization of Rybczynski's Theorem", *Economica* (November 1963).
8. A. Guha, "Factor and Commodity Prices in an Expanding Economy", *Quarterly Journal of Economics* (February 1963).
9. M.C. Kemp and R.W. Jones, "Variable Labour Supply and the Theory of International Trade," *Journal of Political Economy* (February 1962).
10. H.G. Johnson, "Economic Expansion and International Trade", *Manchester School of Economic and Social Studies* (May 1965).
11. C.P. Kindleberger, *Foreign Trade and the National Economy* (1962).
12. Vanek, *The Natural Resource Content of United States Foreign Trade 1810-1955* (1963).
13. C.P. Kindlebeger, *Foreign Trade and the National Economy* (1962), p. 179.
14. J. Black, "Economic Expansion and International Trade: A Marshallian Approach", *Review of Economic Studies,* No. 3 (1956).
15. J. Bhagwati, "Immiserizing Growth: A Geometrical Note", *Review of Economic Studies* (June 1958).

The Balance of Payments

8

The balance of payments of a country is a systematic record of all economic transactions which have taken place during a given period of time between the residents of a country and the residents of other countries.

The above definition seems to be very clear but its terminology is not as simple as it seems to be. Hence, to get a clearer picture, let us explain the meaning underneath the words "economic transactions" and "residents" as used in the definition.

There are five basic types of economic transactions, viz.

(a) purchase or sale of goods and services with a financial quid pro quo, (one real and one financial transfer)

(b) exchange of goods and services for goods and services (two real transfers)

(c) exchange of financial items for financial items, e.g. purchase of bonds as against cash, (two financial transfers)

(d) transfer of goods and services without a quid pro quo (one real transfer)

(e) transfer of financial items without quid pro quo (one financial transfer).

A transaction will be international obviously only if it takes place between two countries or as stated in the definition between the residents of a country and the non-residents of it. The interesting concept here is that the residents of a country include not only its individuals, but also its government and enterprises (private and public, both).

Components

The balance of payments usually comprises two sections, namely: the current account and the capital account. This classification is based on the concept of economic transaction being (a) real and (b) financial.

Current account consists of real transactions. In other words current account comprises those transactions that create income for the country, while capital account consists of financial transactions. Such transactions involve only the transfer of money or claims to money. Also to be kept in mind is the fact that all the transactions showing receipt of the foreign exchange are treated as credits with the "+" (plus) sign, while transactions involving the payments of foreign exchange are treated as debits with the "–" (minus) sign.

To know about these accounts in detail, one has to go through the following discussion—

Current Account

The current account includes goods, services, and unilateral transfers. It comprises two groups, viz.

(a) The Trade Account

(b) The Invisible Account.

The trade account, which is also known as the merchandise account, has entries of the goods only, i.e. the commodities that can be felt by the touch of hand.

The invisible account consists of transfer payments made against the services imported in or exported from the country. International Monetary Fund includes the following as invisible transactions—

(a) International transportation of goods, including warehousing while in transit and other transit expenses

(b) Travel for reasons of business, education, health, international conventions or pleasure

(c) Insurance premiums and payment of claims

(d) Investment income, including interest, rents, dividends, profits

(e) Miscellaneous service items such as advertising commissions, film rental pensions, patent fees, royalties, subscriptions to periodicals and membership fees

(f) Donations, migrant remittances, legacies

(g) Contractual amortisation and depreciation of direct investment.

It should be kept in mind that the current account never includes transactions in the financial assets and liabilities.

Capital Account

The capital account includes all changes in the country's foreign financial assets and liabilities (also known as capital movements).

The capital account further comprises

(a) private capital account, which has the entries of all the corporate bodies and/or commercial banks.

(b) international institutional capital account, which shows the interactions (financial of course) with the international institutions like IMF, IBRD, IFC, etc.

(c) specie account, which comprises the import and export of gold bullion.

(d) government capital account that consists of all governmental capital transactions in the form of grants or loans, short term as well as long term.

DISEQUILIBRIUM IN THE BALANCE OF PAYMENTS

Thus, balance of payments is a system of double entry book-keeping under which total debits equal total credits. In this accounting sense, balance of payments of a country must always balance. There can be no disequilibrium in the balance of payments as a whole. But balance of payments does have disequilibrium at times. When we talk of disequilibrium, we refer not to the balance of payments as a whole but to the balance in certain categories of credits and debits in the balance of payments. A list in the increasing order of coverage is as follows:

(a) **Trade Balance:** This is the balance of exports and imports. The trade balance includes the current account only (the mercantilist view).

(b) **Balance on Good and Services:** This balance measures the net transfer of real resources between an economy and the rest of the world. Visible as well as invisible trade is considered in such balance.

(c) **Current (Account) Balance:** Obtained by adding net unilateral transfers to the balance on goods and services, and representing the transactions that give rise to changes in the economy's stock of foreign financial items, this balance is one of the most important ones.

(d) **Basic Balance:** This is also known as balance on current account and long term capital and includes, besides the items of the current account balance, the flow of long term capital, and is intended to be a rough indicator of long term trends in the balance of payments.

(e) **Overall Balance:** All that has to be added to the definition given above is the convention that the net errors and omission items are included above the line. The obvious reason is that the use and acquisition of reserves is usually known and measured with a high degree of accuracy, so that errors and omissions must pertain to items above the line.

Hence, if the adjustment process of the balance of payments is to be undertaken, one must always state clearly as to which type of balance is being considered.

Most of the mercantilists consider only the current account and determine the surplus or deficit in the balance of payments by the movement of specie. This is justified to a large extent because the movements of capital were not considerable in the mercantilist period. If the purpose of the balance of payments statistics is to indicate the strength of the currency, this measure of the disequilibrium might not be infallible. A gold producing country, for instance, might export gold in exchange for goods and services without any sign of weakness of its currency.

The importance of capital movements in the balance of payments account, though recognised by some mercantilists, is emphasised by the classicists and neo-classicists. They measure the extent of disequilibrium in the balance of payments by the movements of gold and 'induced' or 'equilibrating' capital. A distinction is drawn between 'induced' (or 'equilibrating') and autonomous capital movements. Those capital movements which occur in response to market forces (e.g. interest differentials) and are not induced by surpluses or deficits in the balance of payments are considered as 'autonomous'. In contrast, the movements influenced by the surpluses and deficits in the balance of payments and not in response to market forces are regarded as 'induced'. The classification of the actual capital movements into these two categories, however, is an extremely difficult job. The distinction lies in the underlying motive of the capital movements which is very difficult to discover. Some authors[1] label all short-term capital movements as 'induced' and all long-term capital movements as 'autonomous'. Ragnar Frisch determines the demarcation line on the basis of the liquidity of assets instead of their term.[2] Sometimes a long-term asset might be more liquid if there exists a ready market for it than the short-term asset for which there exists no market. Classification of capital movements based on the terms of liquidity of the assets is not very satisfactory. Several capital movements through short-term and liquid assets occur, in response to market forces and independent of deficits and surpluses in the balance of payments. On the other hand, long-term loans have, often, been arranged by the governments of some countries to cover a deficit in their balance of payments.

International Monetary Fund introduced the concept of 'official compensatory financing' to measure the extent of disequilibrium in the balance of payments of a country. It defines the concept as "the financing undertaken by the monetary authorities to provide exchange to cover a surplus or deficit in the rest of the balance of payment".[3] Official compensatory financing consists, mainly, of movements of monetary gold, official foreign exchange reserves, grants and loans. The concept of 'official compensatory financing' differs from the classical concept of 'movements of gold and equilibrating capital' to the extent the former concept concentrates exclusively on the official financing (i.e. the financing undertaken by the monetary authorities) and neglects the 'movement of gold and equilibrating capital, on private account. Private compensatory financing, of course, is unimportant in the present world. In almost all countries, there exists strict exchange control and the central monetary authority exercises a comprehensive control over the gold and foreign exchange resources of commercial banks and private individuals. Insofar as the foreign exchange resources of the commercial banks and private individuals are at the disposal, and under the influence, of central monetary authorities, any movement in these in response to the balance of payments position of the country will form a part of the official compensatory financing. Further, movements in the foreign exchange reserves of commercial banks and private individuals are more for profits and safety than in response to changes in the country's balance of payments position. The possibility of private compensatory financing, however, is not entirely ruled out. There may occur certain movements of foreign exchange resources on private account, uninfluenced by the central monetary authorities, which are of the nature of compensatory financing.

It is a subjective and not an objective concept. In actual practice, it is not possible to determine unambiguously as to whether a particular movement of international monetary funds is compensatory or otherwise.

The concept is circular in reasoning.

Originally the idea of the staff was to call compensatory that amount of financing that was designed to provide exchange to cover a balance of payments deficit. Now they have ended up with measuring the balance of payments deficit by the amount of financing that they choose to call compensatory.[4]

The concept is not very clear as to whether it refers to market or programme balance of payments which are two different things.[5]

Absence of official compensatory financing does not mean that the balance of payments is in equilibrium. Equality between the demand for and supply of foreign exchange may be achieved without compensatory official financing through any of these measures: (a) restriction of imports, (b) artificial stimulation of exports through subsidies and other measures, (c) depreciation of the domestic currency, (d) deflation of domestic income and prices and (e) attraction of foreign capital by raising interest rates and by offering other inducements.

Eventually, the International Monetary Fund itself discarded the concept of official compensatory financing in the *Balance of Payments Yearbook 1947-53* published in 1954. Apparently, the reason for this was the insurmountable difficulties involved in classifying the various items in the balance of payments into autonomous and compensatory ones.

The most popular definition of disequilibrium in the balance of payments in an inequality between the demand for and supply of foreign exchange. This definition immediately gives rise to a number of questions as to the (a) relevant time period, (b) rate of exchange, (c) level of income and employment, (d) extent of the openness of the economy etc. Let us briefly consider these questions one by one.

To begin with the first question, what is the period of time over which the equilibrium in the balance of payments is being considered? The relevant period may be a day, week, month, quarter, season, year, or whole or part of the business cycle. Whether the balance of payments is in equilibrium or not depends upon the length of the period under consideration. The balance of payments may be in disequilibrium over a certain length of period and in equilibrium over a different length of period.

The second question relates to the rate of exchange at which the demand for and supply of foreign exchange is being considered. Demand for and supply of foreign exchange will be different at different rates of exchange. Normally, demand will be larger and supply smaller at a higher rate of exchange and conversely at a lower rate of exchange. Determination of the appropriate rate of exchange itself is a highly controversial issue. Some authors define the appropriate rate at exchange in reference to the balance of payments, i.e. the rate at which the balance of payments is in equilibrium. This, however, begs the very question we are trying to answer. The only possible way of determining the correct rate of exchange is in reference to the purchasing power parity theory. No doubt, the theory suffers from a number of defects, discussed in a latter chapter. Yet, after making proper adjustments for these shortcomings, it can be applied to roughly estimate the proper rate of exchange.

Thirdly, the demand for and supply of foreign exchange will vary with the income and employment situation in the country (concerned) and that in the rest of the world. Any deficit in the balance of payments of a country can be removed by a deflation of domestic income. Equilibrium in the balance of payments will exist only if the equality between the demand for and supply of foreign exchange is achieved without any excessive unemployment of the national productive resources. Equilibrium in balance of payments will be compatible with the existence of excessive unemployment if it is due to factors other than international trade. Demand for the foreign exchange varies not only according to the level of income and employment but also according to the rate at which the economy is growing.

A fourth condition of equilibrium in the balance of payments is that the equality between the demand for and supply of foreign exchange should be achieved without undue restrictions on imports and undue fillip to exports. The absence of undue restrictions on imports in no way means exclusion of all tariffs and quantitative restrictions. Tariffs and quantitative restrictions are compatible with an equilibrium in the balance of payments if the motives behind these are other than correcting a disequilibrium in the balance of payments. These may exist, for instance, for protecting domestic infant industries from foreign competition, or for collecting revenue for the public treasury. Similarly, exports should not be stimulated by artificial methods (e.g. government subsidies) to equate foreign exchange earning with foreign exchange expenditure. Subsidies are not incompatible with equilibrium in the balance of payments if the motives behind these are other than correcting disequilibrium in the balance of payments. In addition to the above mentioned major conditions of an equilibrium in the balance of payments, there are several minor conditions e.g. inventories should be at a normal level, quantity of money and the rate of interest should be appropriate to the liquidity preference schedule etc.

Machlup distinguishes between three distinct concepts of the balance of payments[6] viz. (a) A Market Balance i.e. a balance of supply and demand. (b) A Programme Balance i.e. a balance of hopes and desires. (c) An Accounting Balance i.e. a balance of credits and debits. He maintains that confusion arises because, often, the three different concepts are called by the same name. A deficit in the market balance of payments is defined as the excess of effective demand for foreign exchange (in the absence of trade and exchange restrictions) over the supply (when there is no supply to support the rate of exchange) at a given rate of exchange. Deficit in the programme balance of payments is the excess of foreign exchange needed or desired for certain specific purposes over the expected supply of it. Deficit in the accounting balance of payments is the excess of foreign exchange entered on the debit side of certain accounts over the credit side of the same accounts in a necessarily balancing annual statement of international transactions. This classification is by no means exhaustive and the meaning of the deficit in the balance of payments will differ for each in-between category.

There may be several different deficits depending on a number of arbitrary definitions, assumptions, hypotheses, judgments and objectives, even after one has decided whether one speaks of a market, a programme or an accounting balance.[7]

The first two of the earlier mentioned three concepts of balance of payments are *ex ante* while the third is *ex post*. Interest in the *ex post* concept lies, mainly, in the light which it throws on the *ex ante* situation. The institution of strict trade and exchange restrictions in almost all countries has robbed the concept of market balance of most of its practical importance. The increasing intervention of state not only in foreign trade but also in other economic affairs has further decreased the importance of this concept. The concept of market balance has significance only in free and competitive economies. In planned economies, it is the concept of programme balance which is the most important.

KINDS OF DISEQUILIBRIUM IN THE BALANCE OF PAYMENTS

Disequilibrium in the balance of payments can arise owing to a large number of causes. Strictly speaking, there can be as many kinds of disequilibrium as many are its causes. Broadly speaking, however, there are three main kinds of disequilibrium in the balance of payments, viz. (i) cyclical disequilibrium, (ii) secular disequilibrium, (iii) structural disequilibrium.

Cyclical Disequilibrium

It arises from the occurrence of business cycles. History shows that growth in income and output has not been smooth along a rising trend. Growth over the long period has generally been characterised by short-term booms and depressions. Occurrence of business cycles, of course, is a necessary but not sufficient condition of cyclical disequilibrium in the balance of payments. Business cycles can cause cyclical disequilibrium in the balance of payments under any of the following conditions: (a) the intensity of booms and depressions differs in different countries, (b) timings of the various phases of cycles differ in different countries, (c) income elasticities of demand for imports differ in different countries etc. An important characteristic of the cyclical disequilibrium is that the balance of payments remains in equilibrium over the complete cycle.

Other things remaining the same, if the business cycle is more intense in country *A* than in country *B*, country *A* will suffer from a deficit during the boom phase and enjoy a surplus during the depression phase. Reverse will happen in country *B*. During the boom, income will rise more in *A* than in *B*. Consequently, rise in the imports of *A* will be larger than in those of *B*. During the depression, decline in income in *A* will be larger than in *B*. Consequently, the decline in imports of *A* will be larger than that in the imports of *B*.

Secondly, cyclical disequilibrium in the balance of payments will occur if the various phases of cycle occur at different times in different countries. Other things remaining equal, if the various phases of cycle lag in *B* as compared with *A* by one year, the rise and decline in (income and consequently in) imports of *B* during the boom and depression respectively will occur with a time-lag of one year as compared with the occurrence of the rise and fall in (income and) imports of *A*. Thus *A* will suffer from a deficit during the boom period and enjoy a surplus during the depression period. Reverse will happen in country *B*.

Thirdly, cyclical disequilibrium may arise from differences in the income elasticities of demand for imports. Other things remaining equal, if the income elasticity of demand for imports is higher in *A* than in *B*, *A* will suffer from a deficit during the boom and enjoy a surplus during the recession. Because of comparatively higher elasticity of demand for imports, the rise and fall in imports during the boom and depression respectively will be larger in *A* than in *B*.

Fourthly, cyclical disequilibrium may arise from differences in the price elasticities of demand for imports in different countries. Normally prices rise during the boom and fall during the depression. Other things remaining the same, if the price elasticity of demand for imports is higher in *A* than in *B*, *A* will enjoy a surplus during the boom and suffer a deficit during the recession. With comparatively higher price-elasticity of demand for imports, fall and rise in imports in *A* will be larger during boom and depression respectively than in *B*.

We have discussed above the important situations under which business cycles can cause a cyclical disequilibrium in the balance of payments. These, however, do not exhaust all the situations. There exist several other, though less important, situations in which business cycles may cause cyclical disequilibrium in the balance of payments, e.g. given the fluctuations in demand for exports, the differences in the elasticity of production and hence those in the magnitude of the variations in prices in different countries etc.

Secular Disequilibrium

It arises from long-run, slow-moving and deep-seated changes in an economy as it moves from one stage of growth to another. It may be caused by a large number of factors, viz. capital formation, growth of population, technological change, growth of markets, changes in resources etc. Let us consider one or two concrete cases of a secular disequilibrium in the balance of payments. In its early stages, a developing economy, if it is to develop at a sufficiently rapid rate, requires investment of a magnitude far larger than that made possible by the domestic savings. Imports tend to exceed exports. If sufficient foreign capital is not forthcoming, it may suffer from a secular deficit in its balance of payments. On the other hand, in a mature economy, savings may be far larger than those which can profitably be invested within the domestic economy. Imports tend to fall short of exports. In the absence of an outflow of capital, such an economy may enjoy a secular surplus in its balance of payments. To take another case, other things remaining equal, if the rate of growth of population is higher in country *A* than that in country *B,* country *A* will suffer from a secular deficit in its balance of payments with *B*. Other things remaining the same, an increase in population increases the need for imports and decreases the capacity to export.

Structural Disequilibrium

It arises from structural changes in the demand or supply conditions of exports and, or imports. Let us consider a few illustrations of structural disequilibrium in the balance of payments.

Structural disequilibrium may arise from a change in foreign demand for exports. If the foreign demand for Indian tea declines because of a change in tastes abroad, the resources employed in tea production will have to be shifted to the production of other commodities for which there exists a demand abroad. If India finds it difficult to affect the required shift in resources, demand for imports remaining the same, it will suffer from a structural disequilibrium in its balance of payments. A similar situation can arise from a change in fashions, change in technology, invention of cheaper synthetic substitutes etc.

Structural disequilibrium may arise from a change in supply. A crop failure may decrease the capacity to export and increase the need for imports and thus cause a structural deficit in the balance of payments. A similar situation can arise from a dislocation of production because of strikes or other political disturbances.

Structural disequilibrium may also arise from a decline in service income from abroad. Service income from abroad may decline because of bankruptcy, confiscation or nationalisation of direct investments abroad etc.

CAUSES OF DISEQUILIBRIUM

The above discussion leads to the conclusion that there are varied reasons behind the disequilibrium in the balance of payments of a country. Generally, disequilibrium in the balance of payments is the result of a number of factors operating simultaneously. Moreover, the causes of the disequilibrium differ from country to country and of the disequilibriums occurring at different times within the same country. Disequilibrium in the balance of payment account, generally owes to one or more of the following causes:

Huge development programmes going on in the developing economies is the most important cause of the disequilibrium in the balance of payments of these economies. Besides the indirect effects, rapid development affects the balance of payments adversely, mainly speaking, in two ways. Firstly, import of huge quantities of capital goods, technical know-how and essential raw materials is required to carry on the development programmes. Newly set-up industries might require continuous imports of spare parts, raw materials etc. Secondly, many goods which were previously available for export may now be consumed by the newly created domestic industries.

In addition to the above mentioned direct effects, rapid development affects the balance of payments adversely, mainly speaking, in two indirect ways i.e. through income effect and price effect. The additional expenditure on development projects results in an increase in income in the hands of the consumers. With the increase in income the demand for imports rises, too, the extent depending on the marginal propensity to import. The marginal propensity to import is, generally, high in underdeveloped countries. With the increase in income, the demand for superior goods and luxuries increases which are not available within the country. Increased incomes in the hands of the consumers affect the balance of payments not only through increased imports but also through decreased exports. Some of the goods which were being exported previously might now be consumed within the country. The expansion of home market which is profitable enough might relax the interest of the industrialists in foreign markets which have recently become highly competitive. Secondly, development at a rate higher than that allowed by the available resources, generally, results in a rise in the price level. This is particularly so in underdeveloped countries in which a high marginal propensity to consume is combined with comparatively inelastic production due to lack of excess capacity, shortage of complementary factors and other bottlenecks. In addition, because of lack of other sources, deficit financing has got to be resorted to step up the rate of economic development. A rise in the comparative price level encourages imports and discourages exports. Stimulation to imports may not be very strong in controlled economies yet the discouragement to exports works fully (unless the rise in the price of exports is counterbalanced by subsidies or other export promotion measures).

No doubt, development has also got favourable effects on the balance of payments. It affects the balance of payments favourably by increasing the capacity to export with the increase in production and by decreasing the necessity to import because many goods which were being imported previously may now be produced by the industries newly established within the country. In the preliminary stages of development, however, the unfavourable effects are more powerful than the favourable ones because the investment undertaken during a certain period increases the money incomes almost simultaneously but starts yielding real goods after the lapse of some time.

The above analysis, of course, should not be taken to mean that development is invariably accompanied by the balance of payments difficulties. In fact, whether or not economic development is followed by a deficit in the balance of payments and its magnitude depends on a number of factors, viz. magnitude and direction of investment, size of previous surplus, financing policies, the extent to which export capacity is correspondingly expanded, the degree to which increased productivity occurs in the existing industries, rapidity with which new consumable products become available from new investments, the degree to which the economy has been and can continue to be self-sufficient in foodstuffs production, the extent to which the domestic raw materials can be utilised in developing industries, the level of consumption presently prevailing, proportion of the economy devoted to producing for export, the geographic size of the country, the amount and nature of natural resources which it has available, the size, density and other factors pertaining to its population etc. If the magnitude of investment is kept within the limits permitted by the available savings and foreign exchange earnings, development will not be accompanied by balance of payments difficulties. But this amount of investment may not lead to a sufficiently high rate of development. The balance of payments difficulties arise, generally, when a country is not satisfied with the rate of development permitted by the available savings and foreign exchange earnings and tries to develop at a rate higher than this. If a considerable portion of the investment is made in export or import-substitute industries, the balance of payments difficulties may not arise. In contrast, if most of the investment is on economic and social overheads (viz. roads, railways, waterworks, education, health etc.), which directly produce no goods that can be exported or substituted for imports, there may arise balance of payments difficulties. The import content of investment differs from industry to industry. Import content of investment is much higher in heavy industries than in manufacturing industries. It is very low in small scale and cottage industries which use primarily indigenous equipment. Whether or not development is accompanied by balance of payments difficulties will considerably depend on the ratio of investment going into different industries.

If a country possesses foreign exchange reserves accumulated out of past surpluses, the development may not be accompanied by foreign exchange difficulties. The additional goods required for the development programmes may be imported by a utilisation of the accumulated reserves without involving any strain on the balance of payments. India, for instance, possessed large sterling balances at the beginning of the planned development programmes. These considerably eased the foreign exchange position for some time. Similarly, other factors mentioned above play an important role in determining as to whether or not development is accompanied by balance of payments difficulties.

The underdeveloped countries specialise, mainly, in the export of agricultural and mineral goods for which the income elasticity of demand is very low. In contrast, the advanced countries specialise, mainly, in the export of industrial goods for which the income elasticity of demand is comparatively higher. As the national income of a country rises, proportionate expenditure on manufactures increases and that on food decreases. Therefore, with the increase in world income exports of the advanced countries increase more than those of the underdeveloped countries and the latter run into deficits in their balance of payments.

The advanced countries have built up reputation for their products through several decades of export. 'Made in England' or 'Made in U.S.A.' mark on the product is considered to be a guarantee of superior quality. The developing countries have yet to establish reputation for their products. Sometimes, the importers are ignorant even about the availability of certain goods from the underdeveloped countries. An Indian trade mission to Asian countries found that many of these countries were not aware of the availability of several engineering goods from India. Governments and business firms in advanced countries are spending considerable amounts on salesmanship and publicity in foreign countries. Industrialists and governments in underdeveloped countries cannot afford to spend so much on export promotion activities; export promotion activities require expenditure mainly in foreign exchange of which these countries are already short.

Even if the underdeveloped countries can compete on price and quality basis, they find it difficult to compete on 'terms of sale' basis. Firms in advanced countries are of a relatively larger size and possess better resources. They can provide larger credit facilities which are particularly important for the poor countries. Moreover, government, semi-government and private agencies in some advanced countries are lending abroad. This diverts demand from underdeveloped countries to the lending advanced countries whose currencies become more readily available. Sometimes the loans are tied (for instance, U.S. Import-Export Bank loans). Supplies are more prompt and regular from advanced countries than from underdeveloped countries. Advanced countries can afford and generally maintain excess capacity and thus are in a better position to adjust supply to demand promptly.

Vast increase in the domestic production of foodstuffs, raw materials etc. in advanced countries has decreased their need for the import of these from underdeveloped countries. Progress in technology has drastically decreased the required amount of raw materials (which are the major exports of the underdeveloped countries) per unit of manufactured output in advanced countries. Recent invention of synthetic substitutes (such as synthetic rubber, synthetic fibres, plastics, aluminium etc.) for natural raw materials have adversely affected the exports of underdeveloped countries.

Prices of primary products are much more unstable than those of manufactures in the world market. If the fluctuations in prices arise from changes in the supply of exports, the effects on proceeds is likely to be offset to some extent by changes in the quantities exported. If the fluctuations arise, however, from changes in demand, the effect on proceeds is likely to be magnified by changes in supply. During periods of high proceeds from exports, the underdeveloped countries become accustomed to a certain level of imports for consumption or investment. Once accustomed to a certain level, it becomes difficult to curtail imports during periods of low export proceeds and thus these countries run into deficits. Greater instability in the proceeds from exports discourages investment in export industries and thereby causes a decrease in the exports of the underdeveloped countries.[8]

Instability in the export prices of primary products has more and more led to the adoption of synthetic substitutes as the fluctuations in the prices of raw materials upset the cost calculations and thereby increase the risks of the manufacturers. Moreover, once the plants have been set up to produce synthetic substitutes during periods of higher prices of natural raw materials, they may continue production even during periods of low prices; it may be uneconomical to close these plants because huge fixed costs have already been incurred and the variable cost may be lower than the import price of natural raw materials.

Population is growing at a faster rate in underdeveloped countries than in advanced countries. Increase in population increases the need for imports and decreases the capacity to export as a part of the previously exported goods might be consumed domestically by the new mouths. It might be contended that the increase in population will increase production, too. This, however, is not true in underdeveloped countries having vast unemployment and underemployment; marginal productivity of labour is almost zero (nay, even negative in some lines of production). On the other hand, the decline in the rate of growth of population in advanced countries has inhibited the expansion of their demand for the exports of the underdeveloped countries.

Import restrictions of advanced countries with a surplus balance of payments is another important factor causing disequilibrium in the balance of payments of the underdeveloped countries. Particular mention might be made of USA in this connection. Till recently the United States was having a highly favourable balance of payments; yet, it imposed restrictions on the import of agricultural goods to prevent unemployment in agriculture. "Reciprocity has been a central feature of the American trade agreements programme since 1934. The United States has made sizable reduction in its tariff duties, but only after long and hard bargaining in return for no less sizable tariff cuts by other countries."[9] The difficulties of United States in removing or reducing tariffs have been exaggerated by the vested interests. No doubt, the reduction or removal of tariffs will necessitate some structural changes in its pattern of production and might, also, cause some frictional unemployment in the short run. For instance, it might eliminate some of the uneconomical farms producing agricultural goods sheltered by tariffs and cause frictional unemployment till the labourers relieved from uneconomical farms get themselves absorbed for the production of industrial goods. These changes, however, are not very difficult because of the comparatively greater flexibility of the advanced economies. Labour is comparatively more mobile in advanced countries. These countries have better training facilities for labour. Labour relieved from agriculture can be trained for industry and absorbed there.

Employment exchange service is highly efficient. These countries have got enough capital to start new industries to absorb labour relieved from agriculture. Foreign trade plays so small a role in the economy of the United States that these changes are not likely to affect total income and employment to any considerable extent. Above all, the removal of tariffs will rectify the misallocation of resources and thereby increase aggregate production from the given productive resources.

The surplus countries have failed to invest in underdeveloped countries to the required extent. One of the reasons why underdeveloped countries did not suffer heavy deficits with United Kingdom in the nineteenth century is the considerable investment made by United Kingdom in these countries. Foreign investments will relieve not only the short term balance of payments problem but also help towards long-term solution by expecting the development of these countries.

ADJUSTMENT MECHANISM IN BALANCE OF PAYMENTS

The adjustment process is concerned with how a nation reacts to imbalance in the balance of payments and how the balance of payments returns to equilibrium. In other words, it is concerned with how differences between the demand for and supply of foreign exchange at a given price are reconciled. There are several systems of international adjustment, each related to a system for regulating the foreign exchange market. We study below the important mechanisms of international adjustment.

(a) Automatic Adjustments

(b) Adjustment policies induced by the governments

(c) Approaches to adjust the balance of payments

Automatic Adjustments

In such types of adjustments the economy works on its own to bring about an equilibrium in the balance of payments account if it is otherwise. It can be of two types, i.e.

(a) Automatic Adjustment through changes in Income and Prices

(b) Automatic Price Adjustment under Flexible Exchange Rates

Let us explain them one by one:

(a) *Automatic Adjustment through changes in Income and Prices.* In such type of adjustment any disequilibrium in balance of payments has a tendency to correct itself automatically through changes in relative prices and incomes set into operation by the disequilibrium in the balance of payments.

(b) *Automatic Price Adjustment under Flexible Exchange Rate.* Under the system of free and flexible exchange rates, any disequilibrium in the balance of payments is corrected automatically through movements in exchange rates caused by changes in the demand for and supply of foreign exchange in the foreign exchange market.

Actually the exchange rate of a currency is the price of that currency which is determined like any other commodity, by demand for and supply of it. Any deficit in a country's balance of payments is corrected automatically by depreciation in its currency. Depreciation means that the relative value of the currency has decreased (appreciation means the opposite). As contrary to it, any surplus in the balance of payment of a country is checked automatically by the appreciation in the currency of that country.

This self adjustment process is explained by Fig. 8.1 where it is assumed that there are two countries, say India and USA. Both of them have flexible exchange rates and have free trade between themselves. In this figure, II is the Indian demand curve of foreign exchange representing its demand for US imports and *UU* is the Indian supply curve of foreign exchange representing its exports to USA. The demand for and supply of the Indian foreign exchange are in equilibrium at point *S* and the rate of exchange between Indian currency (Rupee) and US currency (Dollar) is *OE* and the quantity of exchange is *OQ*.

Now suppose the Indian demand increases for the US imports, consequently the demand for Dollar will also increase in India. This implies depreciation of Rupee and appreciation of Dollar, as a result, the price of US imports in India increase. A new equilibrium is shown at point *T*, the new exchange rate is *OE*, and the incipient deficit in the balance of payments (*SV*) is eliminated.

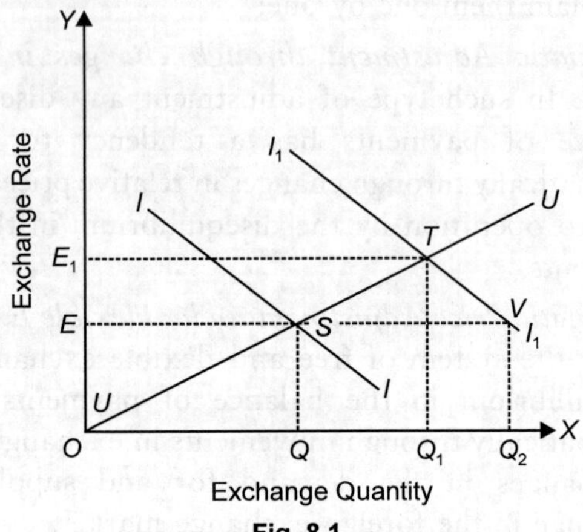

Fig. 8.1

When the exchange rate rises to OE, Indian goods become cheaper in US. Thus, as a result of changes in relative prices, the lower prices of Indian goods increase their demand in US and the demand curve again shifts to D_1. And the equilibrium moves from S to T. Meanwhile, relatively higher price of US goods reduces their demand and the movement from V to T takes place, thereby eliminating incipient deficit SV.

Hence we observe that the deficit is removed by increase in foreign exchange supplied by QQ_1 and decrease in the foreign exchange demanded by Q_2Q_1 so as to make balance of payment in equilibrium. OE_1 is the equilibrium rate of exchange with OQ_1 being the equilibrium quantity of exchange demanded and supplied.

The above analysis is based on the assumption of high relative elasticities of demand and supply for foreign exchange. But depreciation and appreciation lead to severe depressions and inflations in economies where the relative elasticities are low. Thus such automatic adjustments lead to instability and to avoid it, the governments of the countries adopt various policy measures.

Adjustment Policies Induced by the Government

Ajustment in balance of payment of a country if left in hands of market forces can lead to drastic repercussions, hence the government of a country which has its balance of payment in disequilibrium has to resort to various policy measures. To bring the balance back in equilibrium. A few of such measures are as under

(a) *Devaluation.* The foreign price of exports of a country is reduced, hence the value of its currency is brought down in terms of the foreign currency. Devaluation is same as depreciation, the only and the most important difference being the latter is automatic while the former (devaluation) is government induced. The effects are same as depreciation.

(b) *Exim substitute stimulation.* If the exports are constantly encouraged by producing better quality, better marketing, better positioning, etc. and imports are discouraged by producing more domestically, in the beginning the imports will lessen and export will increase, but in the long run, the export of even that good increases which was being imported initially because of its better production now.

(c) *Direct Controls.* Direct controls like restricting import of less desired/needed commodities, levying heavy import duties, fixing huge quotas, etc. are resorted to by the government of a country which has a deficit in the balance of equilibrium and vice-versa.

APPROACHES TO ADJUST THE BALANCE OF PAYMENTS

Apart from the above measures, there are a few approaches that help a country having a disequilibrium in its balance of payment account come back to having an equilibrium in it.

Approaches that we are going to study are (a) The Elasticity Approach (b) The Absorption Approach (c) The Monetary Approach.

Let us now go through each of them in detail.

(a) *The Elasticity Approach.* Propounded separately by Marshall and Lerner, this approach studies the conditions under which exchange rate changes restore equilibrium in balance of payments by devaluing a country's currency. The analysis is based on the following assumptions:

(i) Imports and exports have perfectly elastic supply

(ii) Product prices in home country are fixed

(iii) Income levels are fixed in the devaluing country

(iv) The supply elasticities are large

(v) Price elasticities refer to absolute values

(vi) Price elasticities of demand for exports and imports are arc elasticities

(vii) Country's current account balance equals its trade balance.

Given these assumptions, when a country devalues its currency, its export prices are reduced and import prices are increased. Devaluation thus helps in removing the deficit of the balance of payment but the extent depends on the country's price elasticities of domestic demand for imports and foreign demand for exports.

The theory states that if the condition of

$$e_x + e_m > 1$$

where e_x = demand elasticity of exports

e_m = demand elasticity of imports

is fulfilled, the devaluation improves the country's balance of payments. But there can be two more conditions, viz. $e_x + e_m = 1$, in which the devaluation casts no impact on the balance of payments and $e_x + e_m < 1$, in which devaluation has unfavourable effect on the already in-deficit balance of payment.

The whole process can be understood by the following discussion.

Devaluation though reduces the foreign price of exports and the volume of import of goods, yet by how much this volume declines, will depend on demand elasticity of imports. This in turn depends on the nature of goods imported by the devaluing country. If the imports are consumer goods, raw materials, inputs for industries, etc. the elasticity for demand of these imports will be low. In such a case, devaluation shall only worsen the already deficit balance of payment.

This theory has been empirically proved in many advanced countries. But economists normally believe that the effects of devaluation on domestic price and demand for exports and imports will take time for consumers and producers to adjust themselves to the new situation. The short run price elasticities are lower and hence do not satisfy the Marshall Lener condition. Therefore, devaluation, in the short run, has a negative impact on the balance of payment but as the time passes on, it starts improving.

The above process is illustrated in Fig. 8.2 where the vertical axis measures deficit-surplus and the horizontal axis measures time. If devaluation is made at time *T*, in the beginning, there is still a deficit which is only worsening (from pt. T to pt. S), but as the time passes by, the condition starts improving. At point T_1, the balance of payments takes an upward direction showing decrease in deficit and after a long time has passed, at point T_2, the balance of payments reaches a point after which it will be surplus. This effect is known as J-effect.

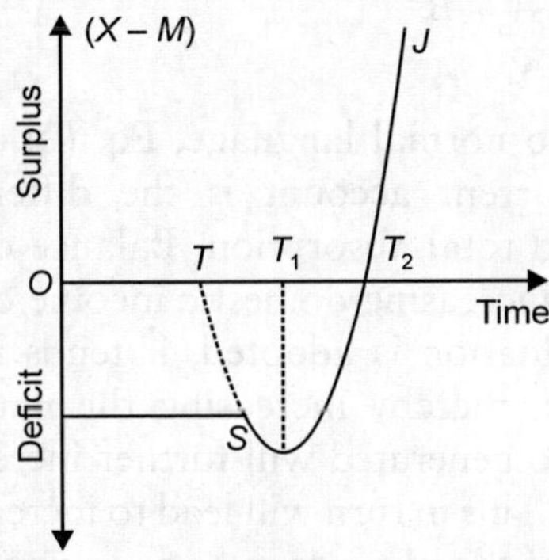

Fig. 8.2

But this whole theory becomes invalidated in a country which is on a flexible exchange rate. This is because devaluation creates excess supply of currency in the foreign exchange market which may lead to further depreciation in the currency, thereby causing depression in the economy and a situation of instability may arise.

(b) *The Absorption Approach*. This approach is based on the Keynesian theory of income. It runs through the income effect of devaluation as against the price effect to the elasticity approach. According to the theory, deficit in the balance of payments shows that the people of this country are absorbing more than what they are producing. Domestic expenditure on consumption and investment is greater than national income. Balance of payment is taken here as the difference between the national income and domestic expenditure.

The theory can be elaborated by the help of following expression.

$$Y = C + I_d + G + X - M \quad (1)$$

where Y = national income; I_d = domestic investment; C = consumption expenditure; G = autonomous government expenditure; X = exports and M = imports.

Also (i) $C + I_d + G = A$ and is also known as the total absorption

(ii) $X - M = B$ and is also known as the balance of payments.

∴ Eq (1) can also be written as

$$Y = A + B$$

or $$B = Y - A \tag{2}$$

If translated into normal language, Eq. (2) means that balance of payments on current account is the difference between the national income and total absorption. Balance of payments can be improved either by increasing domestic income or by reducing total absorption. If devaluation is adopted, it tends to increase exports and reduce imports, thereby increasing the national income. The additional income so generated will further increase the income via the multiplier effect. This in turn will lead to increase in consumption. Thus the net effect of the increase in national income on the balance of payments is the difference between the total increase in income and the induced increase in absorption, i.e.

$$\Delta B = \Delta Y - \Delta A \tag{3}$$

Here ΔA (absorption) depends on the marginal propensity to absorb, a, when there is devaluation. Devaluation also directly affects absorption through the change in income which we write as D. Thus

$$\Delta A = a\Delta\gamma + \Delta D \tag{4}$$

Substituting eq. (4) in eq. (3), we get

$$\Delta B = \Delta\gamma - a\Delta\gamma + \Delta D$$

or $$\Delta B = (1 - a)\, \Delta\gamma + \Delta D \tag{5}$$

Eq. (5) tells us that devaluation has three factors to affect the balance of payment. They are

(a) the marginal propensity to absorb

(b) change in income ($\Delta\gamma$)

(c) change in direct absorption (ΔD)

Here it may be kept in mind that "a" being the marginal propensity to absorb, "$1 - a$" (used in eq. (5) is the marginal propensity to save. All these factors are influenced by the idle as well as fully employed resources in the devaluing country.

(c) *The Monetary Approach.* This approach explains changes in the balance of payments in terms of demand for and supply of money and is an explaination of the overall balance of payments. This approach states that a balance of payments deficit is always and everywhere a monetary phenomenon.

The theory assumes that

(i) The 'law of one price' holds for identical goods sold in different countries after allowing for transport costs.

(ii) Perfect substitution exist in both the product and capital markets.

(iii) The level of output of a country is assumed exogenously.

(iv) The supply of money is a multiple of monetary base which includes domestic credit and the country's foreign exchange reserves.

(v) The demand for money is a stock demand and is a stable function of income, prices, wealth and interest rate.

(vi) All countries are fully employed.

(vii) The demand for nominal money balances is a positive function of nominal income.

Given these assumptions, according to the theory—

The demand for money (M_D) is a stable function of income (Y), prices (P) and rate of interest (I)

$$M_D = f(Y, P, I) \tag{1}$$

The money supply (M_S) is a multiple of monetary base (m) which consists of domestic money (D) and foreign exchange reserves (R). Ignoring m for simplicity's sake

$$M_S = D + R \tag{2}$$

We already know that at equilibrium, supply is equal to demand. Thus, it can be said that

$$M_D = M_S \tag{3}$$

or $$M_D = D + R \text{ (from eq. (2), } M_S = D + R) \tag{4}$$

The theory also states that a balance of payments in deficit or surplus can be represented by changes in the country's foreign exchange reserves.

$$\therefore \quad \Delta R = \Delta M_D - \Delta D \tag{5}$$

$$\Delta R = B$$

where ΔM = change in demand for money, ΔD = change in domestic money, B = balance of payments, and ΔR = changes in foreign exchange in foreign exchange reserves.

A negative B means deficit balance of payments, positive B means surplus balance of payments and when $B = O$, it means that the balance of payment is in equilibrium.

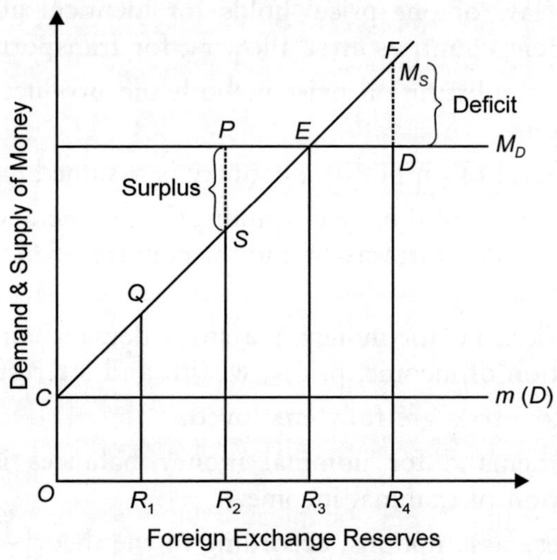

Fig. 8.3

The automatic adjustment mechanism can be explained by Fig. 8.3 and Fig. 8.4 in which the horizontal axis measures foreign exchange reserves and vertical axis in Fig. 8.3 measures demand and supply of money and that in Fig. 8.4 measures payments disequilibrium. Let us interrelate and interconnect these figures now. In Fig. 8.3 M_S is the money supply curve and M_D is the stable money demand curve. Monetary base (domestic money) D is also constant. M_S curve starts from point C because this is the domestic component of money supply. M_S and M_S curve intersect at point E which shows the equilibrium point of balance of payments. At this point, the foreign exchange reserves are OR_3. If $M_S < M_D$, balance of payments is in surplus (as in SP) and if $M_D < M_S$, balance of payments is in deficit (as in FD). In the first condition, the foreign exchange reserves will flow in the economy and the balance of payment will be in equilibrium because forex reserves will rise from OR_2 to OR_3 and in the second case they will decrease from OR_4 to

OR_3 and the outflow will take place so as to bring the balance of payment automatically in equilibrium.

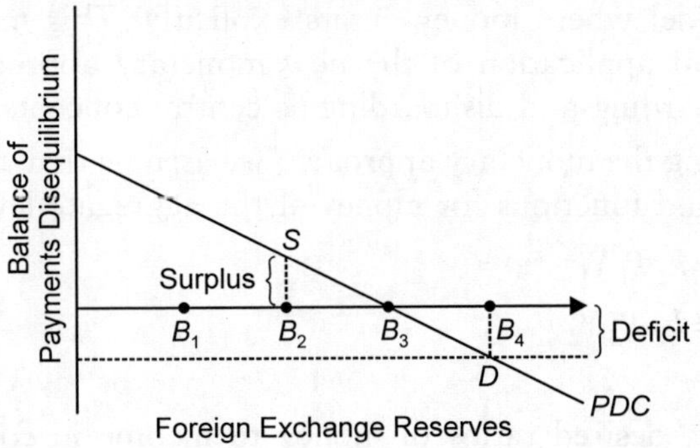

Fig. 8.4

In Fig. 8.4, under a system of floating exchange rates when $B=O$, foreign exchange reserves remain unchanged. But the deficit and surplus in the balance of payment are adjusted automatically by changes in the demand for money and exchange rate. Suppose the money supply is increased so that it becomes greater than the demand for it ($M_S > M_S$), in such a situation, there will be a balance of payment deficit. People with additional cash will start purchasing more and the prices of the domestic as well as the imports will increase. Domestic currency will depreciate and exchange rate will increase. The price rise increases the demand for money and the $M_S - M_D$ equality is established without any outflow of foreign exchange reserves. The opposite happens when $M_D > M_S$, the price fall in this case brings $M_S - M_D$ equality and thus the balance of payment is brought in equilibrium automatically.

The new monetary approach to the balance of payments is essentially an application of monetary analysis to international economics. It assumes, more specifically, that the money supply and the money demand functions are stable. The proponents of the new approach argue that extensive empirical investigations show that the demand for money is a stable function of a few variables. This also implies that the approach is policy-oriented, with a strong emphasis on monetary policy. As it is assumed that the demand for money on the part of firms and households is stable, and that their role in the money supply process also is stable, the monetary policy pursued by the central authorities becomes vital for the outcome of the balance of payments. To gain a more precise insight into the new monetary approach we will consider a one-commodity, two-country model where money enters explicitly. This model can be viewed as an application of the new monetary approach with its stress on hoarding and dishoarding as central concepts.

Following the monetary approach, we assume that there exists a stable demand functions for money at the aggregate level as:

$$L_1 = k_1 P_1 Y_1 \tag{1}$$

$$L_2 = k_2 P_2 Y_2 \tag{1a}$$

where

k_1, k_2 = desired ratios of money to income in country I and country II.

P_1, P_2 = the price levels in the two countries.

Y_1, Y_2 = national incomes expressed in real terms in the two countries.

We assume that there are no tariffs or impediments to trade, the price levels in the two countries are linked to each other by the exchange rate, *r*:

$$P_1 = P_2 r \tag{2}$$

It is also assumed that the nominal quantity of money in each country, M_1 and M_2, consists of one domestic-credit, *K*, and one international-reserve component, *R* as:

$$M_1 = K_1 + R_1 \tag{3}$$

$$M_2 = K_2 + R_2 \tag{3a}$$

We assume that K_1 and K_2 do not change. Any change in the money supply will then be caused by imports or exports of money. The money supply in each country then becomes an endogenous variable. The following relationship between changes in the money supply, reserve changes and the balance of payments can then be given as:

$$dM_1 = dR_1 = H_1 = B = -rH_2 = -rdH_2 = -rdM_2 \tag{4}$$

where

B = deficit or surplus in the balance of payments

H_1, H_2 = hoarding in the respective countries.

The nominal demand for goods in each country, D_1 and D_2, equals the total money income minus the flow demand for money H_1 and H_2 and is given as:

$$D_1 = P_1 Y_1 - H_1 \quad (5)$$

$$D_2 = P_2 Y_2 - H_2 \quad (5a)$$

The hoarding, in its turn, is proportional to the excess stock demand for money:

$$H_1 = q_1 (L_1 - M_1) \quad (6)$$

$$H_2 = q_2 (L_2 - M_2) \quad (6a)$$

Here q_1 and q_2 are rates of adjustment in the two countries. In our model when the stock demand for money is in equilibrium, then the marginal propensity to spend the income on goods is unity. In the short run, however, when the monetary stock is out of equilibrium, the marginal propensity to spend on goods is less than one.

Equation (2) states that there is a perfect commodity arbitrage in the world economy, that is, if country I's price level is constant while country II's price level increase by 20 per cent, its exchange rate will also depreciate by the same percentage. This assumption is sometimes fittingly referred to as 'the law of one price".

The important role played by money in this model is described by equations (5) and (6). The demand for and supply of money will affect all markets in the economy via the hoarding function. Stock aspects also come into play since equilibrium in the money market is essentially a stock equilibrium. The adjustment to stock equilibrium will, however, not take place immediately as shown by equation (6). There is a partial adjustment mechanism that separates the short-run impact from the long-run effects.

The income can be spent in essentially two ways: it can either be used to buy goods, or it can be used to build up the stock of money, i.e. it can be used for hoarding. The demand for money is a demand expressed in nominal terms. It is therefore intimately linked to movements in the general price level. If price go up, then the demand for money will also increase. Thus money serves a real purpose. The agents in the economy, i.e. households and firms, want their cash balances to have a real value that is constant in equilibrium. Therefore, if the price level increase, the demand for money will also increase, i.e. hoarding will take place, and if the price level decreases, dishoarding will occur. It is essential to keep this point in mind in order to understand the monetary approach to the balance of payments. The following figure shows the interrelationship between hoarding and the price level.

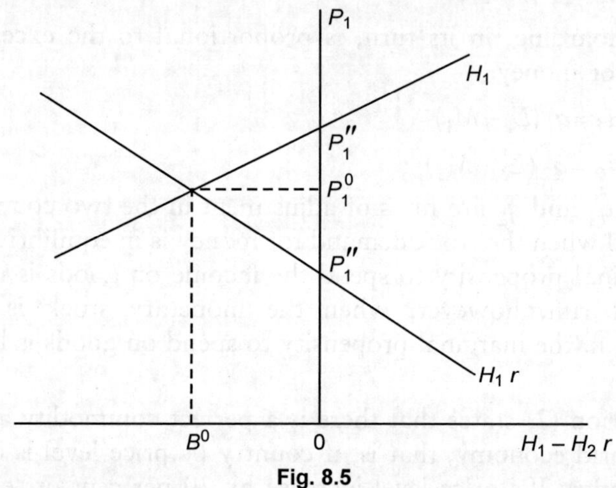

Fig. 8.5

In the above figure the horizontal axis shows the amount of hoarding taking place in the two countries and the vertical axis shows the price level in country I. Since the nominal quantity of monies is given in the two countries, hoarding in country I becomes an increasing function of the price level in that country. As the price level in the country increases, the real value of its stock of money decreases. This gives rise to an excess demand for money and an excess supply of goods. Expenditures on goods fall as the economy tries to restore the real value of its cash balances. The foreign rate of hoarding, $-H_2r$, is by the same type of reasoning a decreasing function of country I's price level, given the exchange rate.

In the above figure we see that the hoarding schedules intersect at the price level P_1^0 and at this price level the world market for goods is cleared fulfilling the condition

$$H_1 = -H_2r \qquad (7)$$

so that hoarding in one country equals dishoarding in the other country. At a higher price there would be an excess supply of goods on the world market and at a lower price there would be an excess demand. In the above figure we see that at a price which clears the world market country I will have a deficit in its balance of payments. This implies that money will transferred from country I to country II which in turn will affect the hoarding schedules. As the stock of money decreases in country I its hoarding schedule will shift downwards and as the stock of money increases in country II its schedule shift upwards. This means that they will intersect somewhere between P_1'' and P_1' on the vertical axis. This will result in a full equilibrium position where the world market for goods clears and where the balances of payments of the two countries are in equilibrium.

Now we will analyze the effect of devaluation in our one sector model. The impact of devaluation in this type of model is by the way it changes the relationship between the price levels in the two countries. Equation (2) gives a strict relationship between the price levels in the two countries. Differentiating equation (2) we get

$$\frac{dP_1}{P_1} = \frac{dP_2}{P_2} + \frac{dr}{r} \tag{8}$$

To discuss the effects of devaluation, consider the following Fig. 8.6.

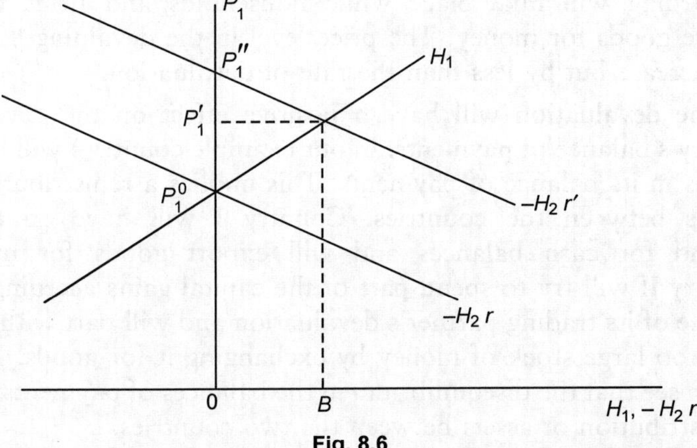

Fig. 8.6

In our analysis we consider a constant foreign price. Then the domestic price level will have to increase by the same proportion as that which the country has devalued its currency. On the other hand if we consider constant domestic price level then the foreign price level will have to decrease by the proportion by which the home country had devalued. This can be described from equation (8).

In Fig. 8.6 suppose H_1 illustrates the domestic hoarding schedule and P_1^0 domestic monetary stock equilibrium. After the devaluation the relation between the two countries' price level must change. If the domestic price level were to remain at P_1^0, the foreign price level would have to fall. This means that the foreign hoarding schedule would have to shift to the right, from $-H_2r$ to $-H_2r'$. This implies that a fall in the foreign price level creates a windfall gain for the economic agents in the foreign country. With a given stock of money the value of their real cash balance will go up. They will hoard less in nominal terms and spend more on goods. Hence at an unchanged domestic price level there will be a world excess demand for goods. This will lead to an upward pressure on goods prices, and the price level in country I will increase from P_1^0 to P_1'. Likewise the foreign price level will not fall by the full amount of the devaluation, i.e. by the proportion $\left((P_1''-P_1^0)/P_1^0\right)$, but by less than this proportion. Thus a process of hoarding will start in the devaluing country and the economic agents in the country will try to exchange goods for money. In the foreign country a process of dishoarding will take place while households and firms try to acquire goods for money. The price level in the devaluing country will increase but by less than the rate of devaluation.

The devaluation will have a positive effect on the devaluing country's balance of payments. In our example country I will have a surplus in its balance of payments. This implies a redistribution of monies between the countries. Country I will have an excess demand for cash balances and will export goods for money. Country II will try to spend part of the capital gains accruing to it because of its trading partner's devaluation and will part with some of its too large stock of money by exchanging it for goods. Hence we can see that the disequilibrium in the balances of payments cause a redistribution of assets between the two countries.

THE EFFECTS OF DEVALUATION IN THE LONG RUN

In order for equilibrium in the long run to prevail there must also be equilibria in the balance of payments and in the asset markets. The following figure shows the longrun effects of a devaluation on the supplies of money and on the price levels.

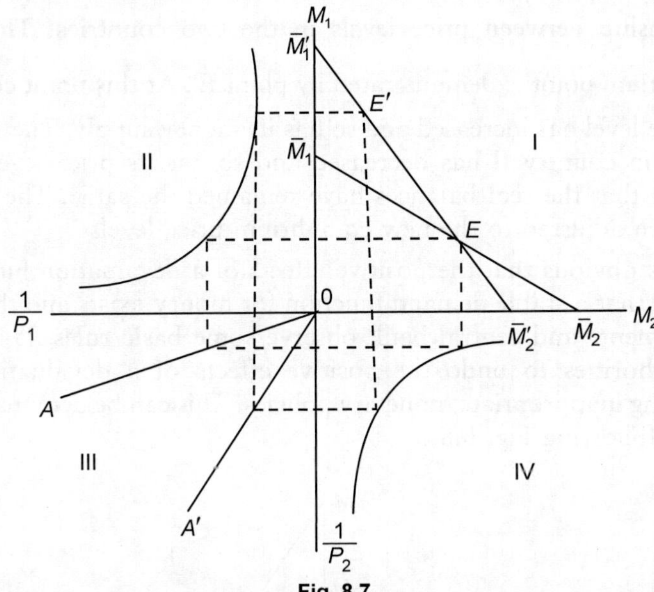

Fig. 8.7

In Fig. 8.7, quadrants II and IV show the demand for real balance in country I and country II as hyperbolae. Quadrant III shows the relationship between the price levels ($P_1 r = P_2$) at the original exchange rate as the ray OA. In quadrant I the world money supply evaluated at the initial exchange rate is given by $\bar{M}_1 \bar{M}_2$, where $\bar{M}_2 = \bar{M}_1 / r$.

The long-run equilibrium is given at point E, where the real balance held by each country is divided so that the equilibrium relationship between price levels in the two countries is satisfied. Now suppose that country I devalues. The devaluation affects both the relationship between price levels in the two countries and the world money supply. For each price level in country I, country II will now have a lower equilibrium price level. The world money supply will increase when measured in country I's currency and it will fall when measured in country II's currency. Geometrically this means that the 'budget line' relating the money supplies in the two countries will rotate around point E to the new position $\bar{M}_1' \bar{M}_2'$.

In Fig. 8.7 we find that the supplies of money which prevailed at point E before devaluation are no longer appropriate as an equilibrium position as they are not compatible with the new relationship between price levels in the two countries. The new equilibrium point is demonstrated by point E'. At this point country I's price level has increased and so has its money supply. The money supply in country II has decreased and so has its price level. The point is that the real balances have remained the same. They have just been adjusted to the new equilibrium price levels.

It is obvious that the positive effects of a devaluation hinge on the fact that a stable demand function for money exists and that the governments and central bank observe some basic rules. It is easy for authorities to undo the positive effects of a devaluation by following inappropriate monetary policies. This can be demonstrated by the following Fig. 8.8.

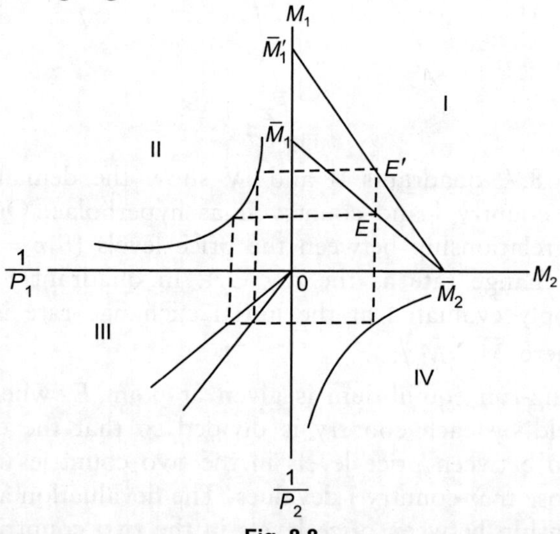

Fig. 8.8

Figure 8.8 demonstrates a case where the authorities in country I increase the money supply in proportion to devaluation. This results in a shift of the budget line in quadrant I, describing the world's monetary constraint, from $\bar{M}_2\bar{M}_1$ to $\bar{M}_2\,\bar{M}_1'$. Thus the world's money supply has remained constant in terms of country II's currency but it has increased in terms of country I's currency. There will be neither positive effects from the devaluation on country I's balance *f* payments nor any inflow of foreign currency. Hence the traditional, advantageous effects of a devaluation will be absent in the devaluing country. The restoration of an equilibrium in the balance of payments, which we may regard as the main aim of devaluation, will not come about. The end-result will only be an increase in the domestic price level proportionate to the devaluation. On the other hand the government will be able to run a transitory deficit in its budget without further worsening its balance of payments.

Thus the upshot for the balance of payments depends critically on the monetary policy accompanying a devaluation and only by keeping the money supply constant can a county be sure that a devaluation will improve its balance of payments.

BALANCE OF PAYMENTS ADJUSTMENTS

In the policy approach to open economy macroeconomics developed most extensively by Meade (1951), and extended by the important work of Mundell (1968) and Fleming (1962), it is usually assumed that the level of national income is controlled by government policy, and that maintenance of full employment (or internal balance) is the paramount objective of economic policy. In this approach, the balance of payments is a problem because maintenance of balance of payments equilibrium (or external balance) contains the use of macroeconomics policy for purposes of maintaining full employment. This problem can be satisfactorily resolved provided that governments have an adequate number of independent and effective policy instruments. More recent research on macroeconomics, for both closed and open economies, expresses far less confidence in the ability of governments to systematically affect levels of national income and consistently maintain full employment through policy manipulation. This view is reflected in the more recent research on international monetary economics where the balance of payments and the exchange rate are regarded as important in their own right, rather than as subsidiary concerns of policy management.

In much of the earlier work on international monetary economics, policy actions and economic disturbances were assumed to have essentially permanent effects on payments flows. It was recognized that the losses of foreign exchange reserves associated with official settlements deficits would imply a declining domestic money supply, unless the monetary effects of the reserve loss were sterilized by domestic credit expansion. It was also recognized that reserve losses sterilized by domestic credit expansion could not go on forever because a government would ultimately run out of reserves. However, relatively little attention was paid to the dynamic process that would operate if reserve losses (or gains) were allowed to affect the money supply, or to the long run equilibrium that would be established if this process were allowed to operate, or to the longer run consequences of changes in supplies of securities necessarily associated with policies of sterilizing reserve losses and gains.

In earlier work on exchange rate theory, the condition for equilibrium in the flow market for foreign exchange transactions (exports, imports, and capital flows) was usually regarded as the proximate determinant of exchange rate.

In some analyses, expectations of future exchange rates had an important influence on current exchange rates by affecting speculative capital flows. But, even in these analyses, expectations of future exchange rates were usually determined exogenously or by some ad hoc expectations mechanism. Recent research on the theory of exchange rates, in contrast, has focused more on the conditions for asset market equilibrium as the proximate determinant of equilibrium exchange rates, and has usually regarded expectations of future exchange rates as a critical factor affecting the conditions for equilibrium in the relevant asset markets. Moreover, by adopting the assumption of "rational expectations," many recent models of exchange rate behavior have allowed for endogenous determination of expectations of future exchange rates in a manner consistent with the structure of the economic system, and have thereby permitted explicit analysis of the role of information in forming and revising expectations critical to explaining the behavior of exchange rates.

Analogously to the characteristics of the modern theory of the balance of payments under fixed exchange rates, the modern theory of exchange rate determination has shifted the emphasis from the circular flow approach (that gained popularity with the Keynesian revolution) to considerations of portfolio choice and stock equilibrium. A consequence of this shift has been the development of the asset—market approach to the determination of exchange rates. Models which belong to the general category of the asset—market approach differ in their emphasis on the role of money and the other assets hut they all highlight the roles of expectations and of stock equilibrium. Our exposition of exchange rate theory starts with a simple exposition of the monetary approach to exchange—rate determination. In this context we highlight the roles of purchasing power parities, non-traded goods, the real exchange rate, currency substitution, as well as the interaction between real and monetary factors which determine the equilibrium exchange rate. We then present a more general framework that views the question of exchange rate determination as part of the general theory of the determination of asset prices. The broader framework highlights the unique role of expectations. The general framework is then used to characterize the interaction between the balance of payments and the equilibrium real exchange rate. This model shows that the current exchange rate depends on the entire expected future time paths of the relevant exogenous variables. The section concludes with a brief discussion of some empirical issues for exchange rate analysis.

THE MUNDELL-FLEMING MODEL

The key development in the area of balance of payments analysis in the late 1960's and early 1970's was the theoretical elaboration and empirical investigation of the dynamic mechanism of balance of payments adjustment. The essential idea of this dynamic mechanism, which dates back to Hume's discussion of the price—specie—flow-mechanism, is that changes in asset stocks (especially the money supply) associated with payments imbalances alter the instantaneous equilibrium position of the economy over time and ultimately drive it to a long run equilibrium at which the payments imbalance is eliminated. In much of the literature on balance of payments theory and open economy macroeconomics of the 1950's and 1960's, this dynamic mechanism of balance of payments adjustment was either ignored or suppressed by assuming that the domestic monetary authority sterilized the monetary effects of foreign exchange reserve gains and loses. However, at least in Mundell's (1961) description of the international disequilibrium system, this dynamic mechanism was explicitly introduced into the standard model that represented the main line of development in this earlier literature.

As illustrated in Fig. 8.9, Mundell's analysis is based on the open economy extension of the IS-LM model, frequently referred to as the Mundell-Fleming model.

In the above diagram, the positively sloped *LM* curves show combinations of national income, *y*, and the domestic nominal interest rate, I, for which the real demand for domestic money, L (*Y*, i) (where $\partial L/\partial Y > 0$ and $\partial L/\partial i < 0$), is equal to the real supply, *M*/*P*. The different *LM* curves are all drawn for the same, parametrically determined domestic price level, *p*, but for different levels of the domestic nominal money supply, *M*, with lower *LM* curves corresponding to larger domestic nominal money supplies. The negative sloped IS curve indicates the combinations of *y* and *i* for which the demand for national product is equal to national income. The demand for national product is the sum of domestic

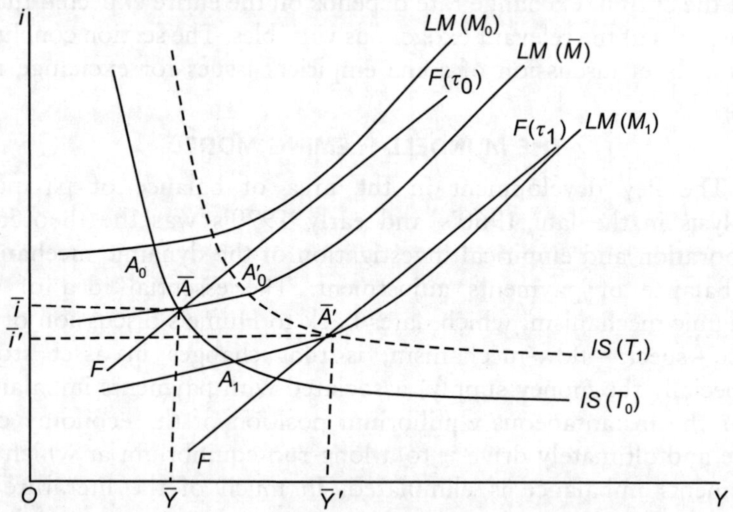

Fig. 8.9: Monetary Policy and Devaluation in the Mundell-Fleming Model with Perfect Capital Mobility.

demand for domestic product, $D(Y, i, \tau)$ (where $\partial D/\partial \bar{Y} > 0$, $\partial D/\partial i < 0$ and $\partial D/\partial \tau < 0$), plus foreign demand for domestic product, $I^*(\tau)$ (where $\partial I^*/\partial \tau < 0$); $\tau = P/S.P^*$ is the terms of trade between domestic goods and foreign goods, where P^* denotes the foreign price of foreign goods and *S* denotes the exchange rates which is defined as the price of foreign exchange in terms of domestic currency. Alternatively, the demand for national product is the sum of total domestic expenditure, $E(Y, i)$ (where $1 > \partial E/\partial Y > \partial D/\partial Y > 0$ and $\partial E/\partial i < 0$) plus the trade balance surplus. In that alternative formulation, total domestic expenditure includes expenditure on imports, $I(Y, i, \tau)=E(Y, i)-D(Y, i, \tau)$, and using this expression the trade balance surplus is, $T(Y,i,\tau)=I^*(\tau)-I(Y, i, \tau)$, where $\partial T/\partial Y<0$, $\partial T/\partial i>0$, $\partial T/\partial \tau<0$.

The positively sloped *FF* curve shows combinations of *y* and *i* for which the trade balance is zero. The terms of trade, τ, is a parameter affecting the positions of the *IS* and *FF* curves. At any moment of time, the instantaneous equilibrium position of the economy is determined by the intersection of the *IS* curve and the *LM* curve drawn for the current money supply. in particular, when the money supply is M_0 and the terms of trade is τ_0, the instantaneous equilibrium point is at A_0 in Fig. 8.9. At this instantaneous equilibrium, the trade balance is in surplus, as indicated by the fact that A_0 is above and to the left of the *FF* curve. Since the present analysis assumes an absence of private capital flows, it follows that for the government to maintain a fixed exchange rate, it must purchase foreign exchange reserves at a rate equal to the trade surplus at A_0. If the government does not sterilize the monetary effects of this reserve accumulation, the domestic nominal money supply will grow at a rate equal to the rate of accumulation of foreign exchange reserves, valued in domestic money. Growth of *M* gradually shifts the *LM* curve in Fig. 8.9 downward and to the right, moving the instantaneous equilibrium point along the IS curve away from A_0 and toward the point determined by the intersection of the *IS* and *FF* curves. When the instantaneous equilibrium point (and the *LM* curve) reach $\bar{A}$ the trade balance is zero accumulation of foreign exchange reserves ceases, and economy is in long run equilibrium. The dynamic mechanism which drives the economy from A_0 (or any other initial instantaneous equilibrium position) to long run equilibrium at $\bar{A}$ is the monetary mechanism of balance of payments adjustment. The total accumulation of foreign exchange reserve (the cumulative official settlements surplus) associated with the movement from A_0 to $\bar{A}$, valued in domestic money, is determined by the difference between the initial nominal money supply, M_0, and the long run equilibrium level of the money supply, $\bar{M}=P_0 L(\bar{Y}, \bar{i})$, where $\bar{Y}$ and $\bar{i}$ are the long run equilibrium levels of *Y* and *i* that are associated with the long run equilibrium point *A*.

Starting at the instantaneous equilibrium A_0, if the money supply were increased by a domestic credit expansion to the extent of the difference between M_0 and $\bar{M}$, the result would be an immediate shift of the *LM* curve to its long run equilibrium position and an immediate jump of national income and the domestic interest rate to their respective long run equilibrium values. As a consequence of this domestic credit expansion, therefore, the government would forego the increase in foreign exchange reserves that would otherwise occur as a consequence of the natural adjustment process of the economy in moving from A_0 to $\bar{A}$, but would gain a more immediate increase in the level of national income. Alternatively, if the government expanded domestic credit starting from a situation of long run equilibrium, it would temporarily shift the *LM* curve downward and to the right, creating an instantaneous equilibrium at a point like A_1 corresponding to the higher quantity of money, M_1. At A_1, there would be a balance of payments deficit, and the gradual adjustment of the domestic money supply implied by losses of foreign exchange reserves would ultimately drive the instantaneous equilibrium point back to $\bar{A}$. In the long run, therefore, the increase in the domestic credit component of the money supply would be fully offset by an equal loss of foreign exchange reserves, and the simulative effect of the domestic credit expansion on national income would only be temporary. If the government attempted to maintain national income at a level above its long run equilibrium level by sterilizing foreign exchange reserve losses through offsetting domestic credit expansions, it could do so for a while, but ultimately it would run out of reserves.

A devaluation from an initial equilibrium at $\bar{A}$ increases *S* and reduces τ from τ_0 to τ_1 (since in this analysis *P* and P^* are assumed to be given) shifting both the *IS* and *FF* curves to the right to $I'I'$ and $F'F'$, respectively. The new long run equilibrium is at $\bar{A}'$, with a higher long run equilibrium level of national income, $\bar{Y}'$, and a lower long run equilibrium level of the domestic interest rate, $\bar{i}'$. If at the time of this devaluation, the money supply was at the long run equilibrium level appropriate for the old exchange rate, the impact effect of the devaluation will be to move the instantaneous equilibrium point up along the *LM* curve passing through $\bar{A}$ to the intersection between this *LM* curve and the new *IS* curve as illustrated by point A_0'. The impact effect of devaluation, therefore, is to increase domestic income and the domestic interest rate and to create a balance of payments surplus. These impact effects of devaluation, however, are not the permanent, longrun effects of devaluation. Increase in the money supply resulting from payments surpluses that are the short run consequence of the devaluation drive the economy to its new long run equilibrium A_0' at which domestic income is higher and the domestic interest rate is lower than A_0' and at which the (flow) balance of payments surplus initially created by the devaluation is eliminated. With respect to the balance of payments, therefore, the long run effect of devaluation is a permanent, cumulative change in the level of reserves equal to increase in the long run equilibrium size of the nominal money supply from $\bar{M}=L(\bar{Y}, \bar{i})$ to $\bar{M}'=L(\bar{Y}', \bar{i}')$, but not a permanent surplus in the flow magnitude of the balance of payments.

When privately held financial assets are internationally mobile, this analysis of the balance of payments adjustment mechanism needs to be modified to take account of the effects of capital movements on reserve holdings and national money supplies, specifically, with perfect capital mobility, the *FF* curve indicating balance of payments equilibrium becomes a horizontal line at the level of the world interest rate, i^*, as indicated in Fig. 8.10.

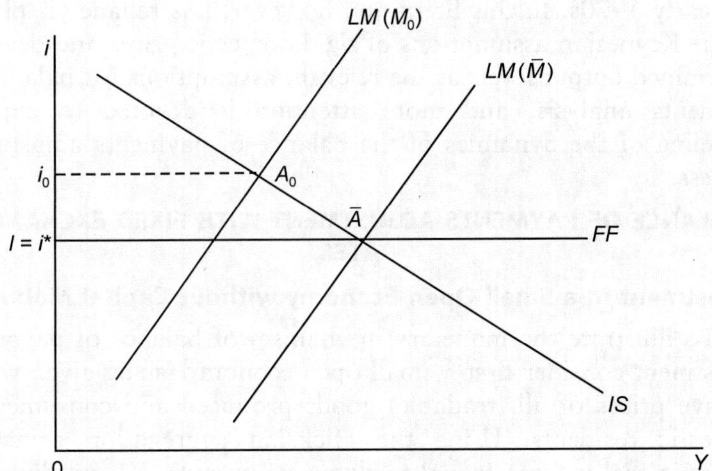

Fig. 8.10: The Mundell-Fleming Model with Perfect Capital Mobility.

In this situation an instantaneous equilibrium at a point like A_0, determined by the *IS* curve and the *LM* curve for a domestic money supply of M_0, is not sustainable as an instantaneous equilibrium because a domestic interest rate i_0 that is above the world interest rate i^* would induce a huge capital inflow. Domestic residents would sell securities to foreigners in order to increase their money balances to the level consistent with $i = i^*$. The increase in reserves implied by this capital inflow causes the *LM* curve to jump until it passes through the long run equilibrium point $\bar{A}$ determined by the intersection of the *IS* curve with the *FF* curve. Thus, with perfect capital mobility, the balance of payments adjustment process is not a gradual process in which money supply gradually adjusts to reserve gains and losses associated with trade imbalances, but rather an instantaneous adjustment process in which the level of reserves adjusts immediately in response to international capital movements.

The essential elements in this analysis of the mechanism of balance of payment adjustment, including the analysis of the cumulative effects on the balance of payments of changes in domestic credit or the exchange rate and of the consequences of international capital mobility are also central in the literature on balance of payments theory that developed during the late 1960s and early 1970s. In this literature, however, less reliance is placed on the Keynesian assumptions of rigid domestic prices and demand determined output levels as the relevant assumptions for balance of payments analysis, and more attention is devoted to explicit modeling of the dynamics of the balance of payments adjustment process.

BALANCE OF PAYMENTS ADJUSTMENT WITH FIXED EXCHANGE RATES

Adjustment in a Small Open Economy without Capital Mobility

To illustrate the monetary mechanism of balance of payments adjustment consider first a small open economy facing given world relative prices of all (tradable) goods produced and consumed by domestic residents. Using the Hicksian aggregation principle, domestic real income (equal to domestic output), Y, and domestic real expenditure, E, are measured in common units of a composite tradable good. Domestic real income is constant at the level determined by full employment of domestic resources. Domestic real expenditure depends on domestic real income, the domestic real interest rate, r, and the real value of privately held domestic assets, A/P;

$$E = E\ (Y, r, A/P), \tag{1}$$

$$\partial E/\partial Y > 0,\ \partial E/\partial r < 0,\ \partial E/\partial (A/P) > 0$$

Privately held domestic assets consists of domestic money, M, and domestic interest bearing securities, B, which are denominated in units of domestic money and have an infinitesimal maturity (like call loans);

$$A = M + B \tag{2}$$

In the absence of international mobility of capital, these assets are assumed to be non-tradable internationally. The real value of these assets depends on the domestic price level, P, which is equal to the foreign price, P^*, multiplied by the exchange rate, S:

$$P = S.P^* \tag{3}$$

The domestic money supply (under the simplifying assumption that the money multiplier is unity) is high powered money issued by the domestic central bank and is equal to the sum of the domestic money value of the foreign exchange reserves of the central bank, $S.R$, domestic securities held by the central bank, B_g and the fiat issue (the "net worth") of the central bank, J;

$$M = S.R + B_g + J \tag{4}$$

The fiat of the central bank designates a balance sheet entry which represents the "net worth" of the central bank, that is, the difference between the value of the central bank's monetary liabilities, M, and the value of its reserves and domestic security holdings, $S.R + B_g$. An increase in the domestic currency value of foreign exchange reserves due to an increase in S that is not monetized by the central bank is offset by a corresponding decline in J. Interest bearing securities and national monies are not internationally tradable. The total stock of domestic securities issued by the domestic government, $\overline{B}$, is held either by domestic residents or by the central hank

$$B + B_g = \overline{B} \tag{5}$$

Since the asset demands of domestic residents for domestic money and domestic securities must satisfy the balance sheet constraint, the condition for asset market equilibrium in this country can be expressed as the condition for money market equilibrium:

$$L(Y, i, A/P) = M/P \tag{6}$$

$$\partial L/\partial Y > 0, \ \partial L/\partial i < 0, \ 1 > \partial L/\partial (A/P) > 0$$

where $L(Y, i, A/P)$ is the real demand for domestic money, and where i denotes the domestic nominal interest rate that is equal to the real rate, r, plus the expected rate of inflation. In what follows we assume that the expected rate of inflation is zero and, therefore, we identify r with the nominal rate of interest. The condition of asset market equilibrium implicitly determines the equilibrium of the domestic interest rate so that

$$r = \tilde{r}(M/P, B/P, Y) \tag{7}$$

$$\partial \tilde{r}/\partial (M/P) < 0, \ \partial \tilde{r}/\partial (B/P) > 0, \ \partial \tilde{r}/\partial Y > 0$$

Given the interest rate (which is implicitly determined by the requirement of asset market equilibrium), the level of real domestic expenditure becomes a reduced form function of the real money supply, real private security holdings, and domestic real income:

$$E = \tilde{E}(M/P, B/P, Y) \equiv E(Y, \tilde{r}(M/P, B/P, Y), (M/P + B/P)) \tag{8}$$

An increase in M/P increases $\tilde{E}$, both, because it reduces $\tilde{r}$ and because it increases A/P. An increase in B/P has an ambiguous effect on $\tilde{E}$ because the effect on $\tilde{r}$ works in the opposite direction of the effect on A/P. An increase in Y may be presumed to increase $\tilde{E}$ provided that the direct effect, $\partial E/\partial Y$, is stronger than indirect interest rate effect, $(\partial E/\partial r).(\partial \tilde{r}/\partial Y)$. The indirect interest rate effect, however, should be sufficient to insure that $\partial \tilde{E}/\partial Y < 1$, even if $\partial E/\partial Y > 1$.

In accord with the basic equation of the absorption approach to the balance of payments, the home country's real trade balance, T, must equal the excess of domestic real income (equal to domestic output) over domestic real expenditure; that is, $T = Y - E$. Using the reduced form expenditure function, it follows that

$$T = \tilde{T}(M/P, B/P, Y) \equiv Y - \tilde{E}(M/P, B/P, Y) \tag{9}$$

An increase in M/P raises spending and worsens the real trade balance since $\partial\tilde{T}/\partial(M/P)=-\partial\tilde{E}/\partial(M/P)<0$. An increase in B/P has an ambiguous effect on the real trade balance because its influence on spending, i.e. the sign of $\partial\tilde{E}/\partial(B/P)$ is ambiguous. An increase in Y improves the real trade balance because it raises income by more than spending since $\partial\tilde{T}/\partial Y=1-\partial\tilde{E}/\partial Y$ is presumably positive.

Since, by assumption, trade imbalances cannot be financed by private capital flows or by changes in private holdings of foreign monies, they must be financed by a flow of international reserves which the domestic central bank is compelled to absorb or supply in order to maintain the fixed exchange rate. The magnitude of this reserve flow is given by

$$\dot{R}=P^*.T \tag{10}$$

where $\dot{R}$ denotes the rate of change of international reserves, i.e. $\dot{R}\equiv\dfrac{dR}{dT}$. Assuming that the central bank does not alter its domestic security holdings or fiat issue, either to sterilize the foreign exchange flow or for any other reason, the rate of change of the domestic nominal money supply, M, must equal the nominal value of the trade balance:

$$\dot{M}=P.\tilde{T}(M/P,B/P,Y) \tag{11}$$

This result captures four essential features of the monetary mechanism of balance of payments adjustment.

First, there is a natural equilibrating process through which foreign exchange reserve flows associated with trade imbalances adjust the domestic money supply to its long run equilibrium level and simultaneously bring equilibrium to the trade balance. The nature of this equilibrating process is illustrated in Fig. 8.11, where the $P.\tilde{T}(M/P,B/P,Y)$ curve shows the relationship between the rate of change of the domestic money supply and the level of the domestic money supply, given constant values of B, Y and P.

The $P.\tilde{T}(M/P,B/P,Y)$ curve is negatively sloped because an increase in M reduces the trade balance surplus or increases the trade balance deficit. The unique intersection of this curve with the M axis occurs at the long run equilibrium level of the domestic money demand, $\bar{M}(Y,B,P)$, which is determined implicitly by the requirement that

$$\tilde{T}(M/P,B/P,Y)=0 \tag{12}$$

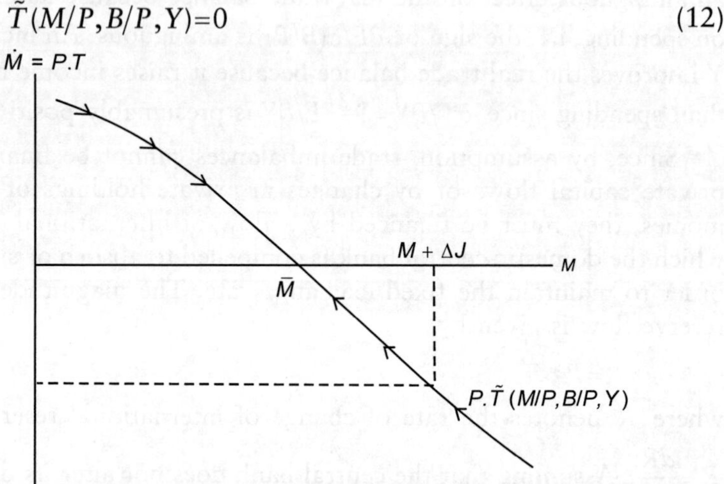

Fig. 8.11: The Dynamics of Monetary Adjustment.

When M is less than $\bar{M}(Y, B, P)$, the relatively high level of the domestic interest rate and the relatively low level of privately held domestic assets induce a level domestic real expenditure that is less than domestic real income and, correspondingly, a trade balance surplus. The reserve inflow implied by this trade surplus gradually raises the domestic money supply and ultimately drives the economy to its long run equilibrium where $M=\bar{M}(Y, B, P)$, and the trade balance is zero. The opposite process occurs if M is initially larger than $M=\bar{M}(Y,B,P)$.

Second, any change, in the supply of domestic money that is not offset by a change in the long run equilibrium level of domestic money demand leads to an equivalent change in foreign exchange reserves and to a corresponding cumulative payments surplus (or deficit). This change in reserves and cumulative payments surplus must be measured relative to the long run level of reserves and cumulative payments position that would have resulted in the absence of the initiating change in the money supply. For example, suppose that starting with a money supply of $\bar{M}$, there is an increase ΔJ in the fiat issue of the central bank. Immediately after this increase in fiat, M will exceed $\bar{M}$ by ΔJ and, as shown in

Fig. 8.11, there will be a trade deficit corresponding to the nominal value of the induced excess of domestic real expenditure over domestic real income. From the figure it is clear that the cumulative magnitude of nominal trade deficits during the process of convergence back to $\bar{M}$ must equal the initial fiat increase in the domestic money supply.

Third, any change in the long run equilibrium level of domestic money demand that is not offset by changes in the domestic assets component of the money supply ultimately leads to corresponding change in the foreign exchange reserve component of the money supply and to a corresponding cumulative payments surplus (or deficit). For example, suppose that economic growth increases domestic real income from Y_0 to Y_1, thereby increasing the long run equilibrium level of money demand from $\bar{M}_0 = \bar{M}(Y_0, B, P)$ to $\bar{M}_1 = \bar{M}(Y_1, B, P)$.

If there are no changes in the other components of the money supply, then relative to what would have happened in the absence of the increase in domestic income, there must be net inflow of foreign exchange reserves and a corresponding cumulative payments surplus equal to $\bar{M}_1 - \bar{M}_0$.

Another example is a devaluation that raises the exchange rate, S, and hence the domestic price level, $P = S.P^*$. The elasticity of the long run equilibrium level of money demand with respect to the domestic price level (and hence the exchange rate) is given by

$$\left(P/\bar{M}\right) \cdot \frac{\partial \bar{M}}{\partial P} = 1 + (B/\bar{M}).\left[\partial \tilde{T}/\partial(B/P)/\partial \tilde{T}/\partial(M/P)\right] \qquad (13)$$

If $\partial \tilde{T}/\partial(B/P) = -\partial \tilde{E}/\partial(B/P) < 0$, then a devaluation will result in a more than proportional increase in the long run equilibrium level of money demand and in a corresponding increase in foreign exchange reserves and cumulative payments surplus. If the effect of the rise in the rate of interest is sufficiently strong so as to result in $\partial \tilde{T}/\partial(B/P) > 0$, then (when the system is stable so that $\left(B/\bar{M}\right).\left[\partial \tilde{T}/\partial(B/P)/\partial \tilde{T}/\partial(M/P)\right] > -1$, a devaluation will result in a less than proportional increase in the long run equilibrium level of money demand and in a correspondingly smaller increase in foreign exchange reserves and cumulative payments surplus. The reason why the long run equilibrium level of money demand may not rise proportionately with the increase in the exchange rate (as it does in some simple monetary models of devaluation) is that the nominal stock of bonds, B, is a parameter affecting the long run equilibrium level of money balances. This non-neutrality of exchange rate changes disappears if domestic bonds are denominated in real goods rather than in domestic money, or if private residents see through the government budget constraint and regard government debt as completely and perfectly offset by expected future tax liabilities. An import tariff, in contrast to a devaluation, generally has non-neutral effects because a tariff alters relative commodity prices, in addition to affecting the general level of domestic prices, and this alteration of relative prices may influence the long run equilibrium level of real money balances.

Fourth, the factors that influence the path of convergence of the money supply toward long run equilibrium and hence the flow magnitude of payments surpluses and deficits are to a large extent distinct from the factors that influence the cumulative payments surplus or deficit that results from a change in the long run equilibrium level of money demand or in the components of the money supply other than foreign exchange reserves. For example, the speed of convergence to long run equilibrium and the magnitude of the payments flow resulting from an increase in the fiat issue of the central bank are determined by the slope of the $P.\tilde{T}$ curve in Fig. 8.11:

$$\partial\tilde{T}/\partial(M/P) = -\partial E/\partial(A/P) - (\partial E/\partial r).\left[\frac{1-(\partial L/\partial(A/P))}{\partial L/\partial r}\right] \qquad (14)$$

High responsiveness of desired spending to the real value of privately held assets and to the interest rate, and low responsiveness of money demand to these same variables all contribute to produce a high speed of convergence to long run equilibrium and hence a rapid loss of foreign exchange reserves in response to an increase in the fiat issue of the central bank. In contrast, the long-run, cumulative response of the balance of payments to an increase in the fiat issue of the central bank does not depend on any of these properties of the desired expenditure function and the money demand function, but only on the property that a change in the fiat issue does not alter the long run equilibrium level of money demand.

Extensions of the Model

The preceding analysis of the monetary mechanism of balance of payments adjustment for a small open economy employed a number of restrictive assumptions that have been the focus of much of the criticism of the monetary approach to the balance of payments. Some of the critics of the monetary approach have argued that some of its simplifying assumptions lack realism.

Among the assumptions that were singled out were (a) the reliance on some form of real balance effect, (b) the assumption that commodity and factor prices adjust instantaneously to clear commodity and factor markets and maintain full employment, (c) the assumption that central banks do not systematically offset foreign exchange reserve flows through sterilization operations, (d) the assumption that all goods are internationally traded, (e) the small country assumption that implies that the economy takes the relative prices of all goods, or at least of all traded goods, as fixed by world conditions and (f) the neglect of international capital mobility in many of the simple expositions of the monetary approach. The next section presents extensions of the simple model. It is shown that these simplifying assumptions can be relaxed without altering significantly the fundamental characteristics of the monetary approach to the balance of payments.

The Real Balance Effect: The model examined in the preceding section incorporates a "real balance effect" through the assumption that desired real spending depends positively on the real value of assets, which includes the real value of money balances. This real balance effect, however, is not necessary to deriving the critical reduced form relationship $\dot{M}=P.\tilde{T}$ of the type shown in Fig. 8.11. The essential features of the monetary mechanism of balance of payments adjustment remain unchanged even if the real balance effect is absent., in that case the reduced form effect of an increase in M on $\dot{M}$ depends exclusively on the effect of the increase in M on the rates of interest and, thereby, on desired expenditure.

Alternatively, the model of the preceding section could be modified so that the only channel through which changes in M

affect the trade balance and $\dot{M}$ is through a special form of the real balance effect known as the "hoarding function". If there are no domestic interest bearing securities (and financial capital is not internationally mobile), all saving and dissaving must take the form of accumulation and decumulation of money balances. Under these conditions, it is plausible to suppose that desired real saving, which equals the excess of domestic real income over domestic real expenditure, depends on the divergence between the long run desired level of real money balances, $\bar{L}(Y)$, and the actual level of real money balances, M/P;

$$T = Y - E = H(L(Y) - (M/P)) \tag{15}$$

where $H(\ )$ is the "hoarding function" which has the properties that $H(o) = 0$ and $H' > 0$. Since the trade surplus (or deficit) must be financed by an inflow (or outflow) of foreign exchange reserves, and since these reserve flows alter the domestic money supply in the absence of offsetting changes in other assets of the central bank, it follows that

$$\dot{M} = P.T = P.H(L(Y) - (M/P)) \tag{16}$$

The key point of this exercise is that the reduced form relationship $\dot{M} = P.H(L(Y) - (M/P))$ has the same critical properties as the reduced form relationship $\dot{M} = P.\tilde{T}(M/P, B/P, Y)$ examined in the preceding section. It follows that the specification of a hoarding function yields all of the essential features of the monetary mechanism of balance of payments adjustment discussed in the preceding section. But, neither this special form of the assumption of a real balance effect, nor any other form of that assumption is necessary to the derivation of the essential features of this adjustment mechanism.

Wage and Output Dynamics: The assumption of instantaneous adjustment of commodity and factor prices to clear all markets and maintain full employment is easily modified without altering the essential features of the monetary mechanism of balance of payments adjustment. An alternative assumption is that the domestic nominal wage rate, W, is at least temporarily fixed and that the level of employment is determined by the quantity of labor that domestic producers demand at this nominal wage rate. With this assumption about the labor market, domestic output is determined by an aggregate supply function,

$$Y = Y^S(P/W), \quad \partial Y^S/\partial(P/W) > 0 \tag{17}$$

Allowing for the endogenous determination of domestic output modifies the reduced form relationship describing the rate of change of the domestic money supply,

$$\dot{M} = P.\tilde{T}(M/P, B/P, Y^S(P/W)) \tag{18}$$

If the nominal wage rate is determined parametrically, rather than adjusted endogenously, the process of adjustment of the domestic money supply through reserve flows toward its long run equilibrium level is exactly as described in above section. Moreover, changes in the fiat issue of the central bank, in private securities holdings, or in the long run equilibrium level of money demand that do not involve changes in W or P have exactly the same long run and short run effects as shown above. A change in W, holding P constant changes Y and has exactly the same long run and short run effects as a change in Y. The only significant modification of previous results is with respect to the effects of a devaluation which raises, proportionately, the domestic price level. Previously, the long run effect of devaluation on the stock of foreign reserves reflected the typical proportional effect of a rise in the price level on the long run equilibrium level of money demand, supplemented by the effect of a reduction in the real value of privately held securities on the long run equilibrium level of money demand. Allowing for the endogenous determination of domestic output through the function Y^S (P/W) and assuming that nominal wages are given, increases the effect of devaluation in expanding the stock of foreign exchange reserves because it introduces an additional channel, an increase in domestic output, through which a devaluation increases the long run equilibrium level of money demand.

If the nominal wage rate adjusts endogenously, modifications of the above section are more substantial, but the essential features of the monetary mechanism of balance of payments adjustment remain intact. Abstracting from anticipated inflation and anticipated changes in productivity that would contribute a trend component to the rate of change of the nominal wage rate, suppose that W adjusts at a rate that is proportional to the divergence between its equilibrium value, $\bar{W}$, and its current value, W;

$$\dot{W} = \delta.(\bar{W} - W), \quad \delta > 0 \tag{19}$$

The equilibrium nominal wage rate is the value of W that would keep aggregate output at its full employment level, $\bar{Y}$; it is proportional to the domestic price level and is determined implicitly by the requirement that

$$Y^S(P / \bar{W}) = \bar{Y} \tag{20}$$

The dynamic system that jointly determines the evolution of the domestic money supply (resulting from reserve flows) and the adjustment of the domestic nominal wage rate consists of the differential equations (18) and (19). The behavior of this dynamic system (for given values of the parameters $B, P, \bar{W}, B_g$, and J) is illustrated in the phase diagram shown in Fig. 8.12.

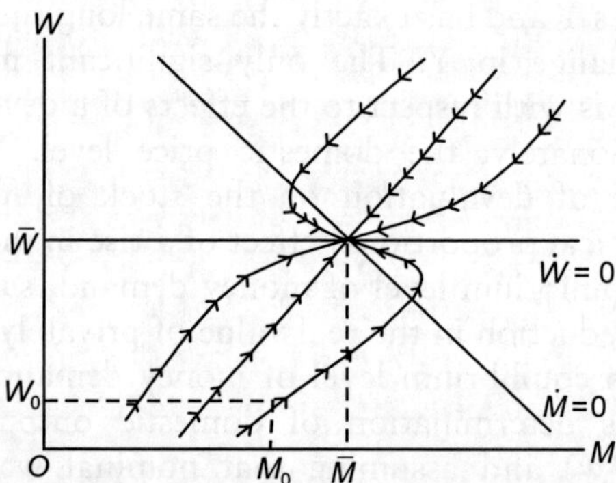

Fig. 8.12: The Dynamics of Monetary and Wage Adjustment.

The horizontal line along which $W = \bar{W}$ shows the combinations of M and W for which $\dot{W}=0$. Above this line $\dot{W}$ is negative, and below this line $\dot{W}$ is positive. The negatively sloped schedule labeled $\dot{M}=0$ shows the combinations of M and W for which $P.\tilde{T}(M/P, B/P, Y^S(P/W))=0$, for the given values of B and P. This line is negatively sloped because an increase in M which makes $\dot{M}<0$ needs to be offset by a decrease in w which makes $\dot{M}>0$ in order to keep $\dot{M}=0$. Above and to the right of the $\dot{M}=0$ line $\dot{M}$ is negative, and below and to the left of this line $\dot{M}$ is positive. The intersection of the $\dot{W}=0$ and $\dot{M}=0$ schedules occurs at the long run equilibrium point where $W=\bar{W}$, as determined by equation (20), and the nominal money supply is equal to the long run equilibrium level of money demand, $\bar{M}(\bar{Y}, B, P)$ as determined by equation (12) with $Y=\bar{Y}$.

Since the dynamic system illustrated in Fig. 8.12 is stable, for any positive speed of adjustment of the nominal wage rate, the domestic money supply will ultimately adjust to $\bar{M}$ through reserve flows associated with trade imbalances. Further, given any initial divergence of the domestic money supply from the long run equilibrium level of money demand, the cumulative payments surplus or deficit that occurs along the path of convergence to the long run equilibrium point in Fig. 8.12 must entail a cumulative gain or loss of foreign exchange reserves just sufficient to bring the domestic money supply to equality with $\bar{M}$. This conclusion also applies to any divergence between M and $\bar{M}$ that is created by a change in the non-reserve assets of the central bank or in factors that determine the long run equilibrium level of money demand. Thus, the modifications of monetary mechanism of balance of payments adjustment implied by simultaneous endogenous adjustment of the domestic nominal wage rate do not affect the stability of this mechanism or the conclusions concerning the long run, cumulative effects of disturbances to the money supply or to the long run equilibrium level of money demand. These modifications affect only the details of the behavior of the money supply and the balance of payments along the path of convergence to long run equilibrium. In particular convergence of the domestic money supply to the long run equilibrium level of money demand is always monotonic. With endogenous adjustment of the domestic nominal wage rate, however, the money supply need not converge monotonically to its long run equilibrium value. For example, if we start at the point (M_0, W_0) in Fig. 8.12, with $M_0 < \bar{M}$ and W_0 well below $\bar{W}$, the path of convergence to long run equilibrium is one along which the money supply rises above its long run equilibrium level through a series of trade surpluses and reserve inflows, and then falls back to $\bar{M}$ through a series of trade deficits and reserve out flows.

Endogenous Monetary Policy and Sterilization: Sterilization is a form of endogenous monetary policy in which a central bank offsets all or part of the changes in the money supply resulting from foreign exchange reserve flows by countervailing changes of its non-reserve assets. A simple form of sterilization policy is described by the rule

$$\dot{J}=-\phi.S.\dot{R},\ 0<\phi<1 \tag{21}$$

where the sterilization coefficient ϕ indicates the fraction of foreign exchange changes that the central bank offsets by varying its fiat issue, and where the rate of change in the domestic currency value of foreign exchange reserves, $S.\dot{R}$ is determined by the nominal trade surplus, $P.\tilde{T}(M/P, B/P, Y)$.

This form of sterilization policy does not affect the long run equilibrium level of money demand, but it does slow down the convergence of the money supply to the long run equilibrium level. Specifically, with the sterilization policy, we have

$$\dot{M}=S.\dot{R}+\dot{J}=(1-\phi).S.\dot{R}=(1-\phi).P.\tilde{T}(M/P, B/P, Y) \tag{22}$$

This slowdown in the speed of convergence to long run equilibrium comes at the expense of a greater cumulative change in foreign exchange reserves. If the initial divergence between the long run equilibrium level of money demand and the actual domestic money supply is ΔM, the cumulative change in foreign exchange reserves in the process of convergence to long run equilibrium is

$$\Delta R=(\Delta M/S)/(1-\phi) \tag{23}$$

and it is apparent that a policy of complete sterilization is not feasible. If a central bank attempts to set ϕ=1, then any small divergence between M and $\bar{M}$ will ultimately lead either to an infinite gain in foreign exchange reserves or an infinite loss of such reserves.

In addition to sterilization, it is possible to analyze other forms of endogenous monetary policy. One such policy might be directed at moderating movements in the domestic interest rate. If the only cause of interest rate fluctuations, other than variations in the domestic money supply, were changes in the long run equilibrium level of money demand, then such a monetary policy might contribute to economic stability and reduce the need for variations in foreign exchange reserves. However, if fluctuations in interest rates were caused by disturbances other than fluctuations in the long run equilibrium level of money demand, then an interest rate stabilization rule for monetary policy would probably exacerbate fluctuations in foreign exchange reserves and might destabilize the economic system.

Nontraded Goods: The assumption that a small country produces and consumes only traded goods with relative prices determined in world markets is easily modified by allowing the country to produce and consume its own nontraded goods. Equilibrium in the market for this nontraded goods requires that

$$N^d(E, Q) = N^S(Q) \tag{24}$$

$$\partial N^d/\partial E > 0,\ \partial N^d/\partial Q < 0,\ \partial N^S/\partial Q > 0$$

where N^d is demand for the nontraded goods, N^S is supply of the nontraded good, E is total real expenditure (measured in traded goods), and $Q = P_N/P_X$ is the relative price of nontraded goods (whose domestic nominal price is P_N) in terms of traded goods (whose domestic nominal price is P_X. The supply of nontraded goods, $N^S(Q)$, and the supply of traded goods, $X^S(Q)$, are determined by the point on the economy's transformation curve at which the slope of this curve, relative to the N-axis, is equal to Q. Domestic income (measured in traded goods) is given by

$$Y = Y^S(Q) = X^S(Q) + Q.N^S(Q) \tag{25}$$

$$\partial Y^S/\partial Q = N^S(Q) > 0$$

Domestic demand for traded goods, $X^d(C, Q)$, is related to domestic demand for nontraded goods through the expenditure constraint.

$$X^d(E, Q) = E - Q.N^d(E, Q); \tag{26}$$

$$\partial X^d/\partial E > 0,\ \partial X^d/\partial Q \gtrless 0$$

Desired real expenditure (measured in traded goods) depends on domestic real income (measured in traded goods), Y, on the domestic interest rate, r, and on the real value of privately held assets (measured in traded goods), $(A/P_X)=(M/P_X)+(B/P_X)$ through an expenditure function $E(Y, r, A/P_X)$. The condition of asset market equilibrium is expressed by the requirement.

$$L(Y, r, Q, A/P_X) = M/P_X \tag{27}$$
$$\partial L/\partial Y > 0,\ \partial L/\partial r < 0,\ \partial L/\partial Q > 0,\ 0 < \partial L/\partial(A/P_X) < 1$$

where L is the real demand for domestic money and M/P_x is the real supply, each measured in traded goods. The relative price of nontraded goods enters the money demand function because the general level of domestic prices, $P = P(P_X, P_N)$is a linear homogeneous function of the domestic money prices of both traded and nontraded goods.

Replacing the variable y with $Y^S(Q)$ in the real money demand function and substituting $E\ (Y^S(Q),\ r,\ A/P_X)$ for the variable E in the nontraded goods market equilibrium condition, yields equilibrium conditions for the asset market and the nontraded goods market that jointly determine the instantaneous equilibrium values of Q and r as functions of M/P_X and B/P_X;

$$Q = \hat{Q}(M/P_X, B/P_X);$$
$$\partial\hat{Q}/\partial(M/P_X) > 0,\ \partial\hat{Q}/\partial(B/P_X) \gtrless 0 \tag{28}$$

$$r = \hat{r}(M/P_X, B/P_X);\ \partial\hat{r}/\partial(M/P_X) < 0,\ \ \partial\hat{r}/\partial(B/P_X) > 0 \tag{29}$$

The domestic nominal price of traded goods is determined by the fixed exchange rate, S, and the world market price for such goods, P_X^*, through the arbitrage condition

$$P_X = S.P_X^* \tag{30}$$

Given the domestic nominal price of traded goods, the domestic nominal price of nontraded goods and the general domestic price level are determined by

$$P_N = \hat{P}_N(M, B, P_X) = P_X \cdot \hat{Q}(M/P_X, B/P_X) \tag{31}$$

$$P = \hat{P}(M, B, P_X) = P(P_X, P_X \cdot \hat{Q}(M/P_X, B/P_X)) \tag{32}$$

At an instantaneous equilibrium, the domestic supply of traded goods need not equal the domestic demand for traded goods. The excess of supply over demand is the instantaneous equilibrium value of the trade balance, measured in traded goods;

$$T = \hat{T}(M/P_X, B/P_X) = X^S(\hat{Q}) - X^d(E(Y^S(\hat{Q}), \hat{r}, A/P_X), \hat{Q})$$

$$\partial\hat{T}/\partial(M/P_X) < 0,\ \partial\hat{T}/\partial(B/P_X) < 0 \tag{33}$$

where $\hat{Q}$ and $\hat{r}$ are the functions of M/P_X and B/P_X that indicate the instantaneous equilibrium values of Q and r. Using (25) and (26) and the fact that $N^d = N^S$ at any instantaneous equilibrium, it is easily established that the trade balance at any instantaneous equilibrium is equal to the excess of domestic income over domestic expenditure, as required by the fundamental equation of the absorption approach to the balance of payments:

$$\hat{T}(M/P_X, B/P_X) = Y^S(\hat{Q}) - E(Y^S(\hat{Q}), \hat{r}, A/P_X) \quad (34)$$

Since neither monies nor securities are assumed to be internationally traded among private agents, trade imbalances occurring at any instantaneous equilibrium must be financed by a net flow of official foreign exchange reserves. Assuming no sterilization of the effects of such reserve flows on the domestic money supply, the rate of change of the domestic nominal money supply occuring at any instantaneous equilibrium is given by

$$\dot{M} = P_X . \hat{T}(M/P_X, B/P_X) \quad (35)$$

The qualitative properties of the relationship between the rate of change of the money supply and the level of the money supply embodied in (35) are exactly the same as those embodied in (18) and illustrated in Fig. 8.11. For given values of B and $P_X = S.P_X^*$ there is a unique long run equilibrium level of domestic nominal money supply, $\bar{M}$, determined by the condition

$$\hat{T}(M/P_X, B/P_X) = 0 \quad (36)$$

At which the trade balance and the rate of change of the money supply are both zero. When M is less than $\bar{M}$, there is a trade surplus and $\dot{M}$ is positive. When M is greater than $\bar{M}$, there is a trade deficit and $\dot{M}$ is negative. Thus, there is a natural dynamic process through which monetary changes resulting from reserve flows associated with trade imbalances gradually drive the economy to its long run equilibrium where the trade balance and the rate of change of the domestic money supply are both zero. Now consider the following figure.

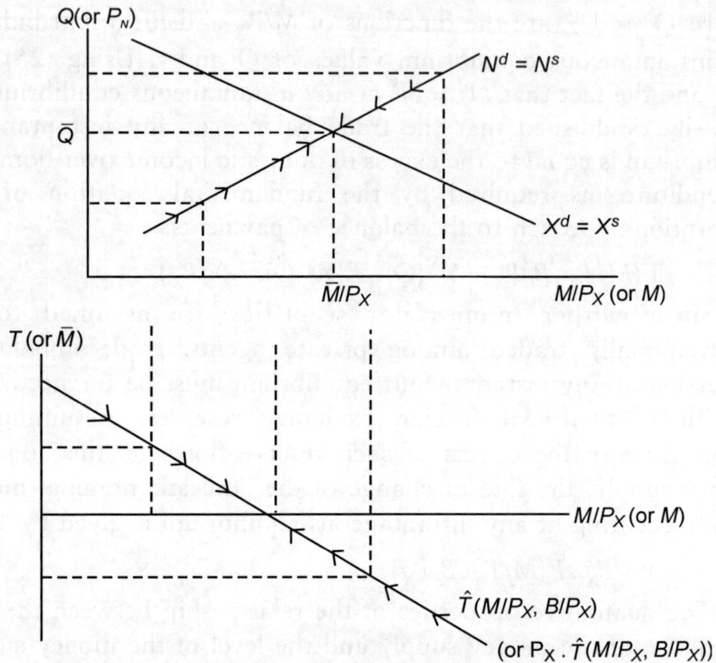

Fig. 8.13: Instantaneous Equilibrium and Dynamics with Nontraded Goods.

The positively sloped $N^d = N^S$ curve in the upper panel of Fig. 8.13 shows the relationship between $\hat{Q}$ and M/P_X for a given value of B/P_X. This curve may also be interpreted as showing the relationship between $\hat{P}_N$ and M, for given values of B and P_X. Since the market for nontraded goods must clear, the instantaneous equilibrium position of the economy must always be at the point on the $N^d = N^S$ curve, corresponding to the actual value of M/P_X.

The market for traded goods, need not clear domestically. Any excess supply of traded goods can be sold on the world market and any excess demand for traded goods can be purchased from the world market, in exchange for flows of international reserves. The trade balance surplus measures the domestic excess supply of traded goods:

$$T = X^S(\hat{Q}(M/P_X, B/P_X) - X^d(E(Y^S(\hat{Q}), \hat{r}, A/P_X), \hat{Q}) \qquad (37)$$

It is noteworthy that the function $\hat{T}(M/P_X, B/P_X, Y)$ is the same as the function $\hat{T}(M/P, B/P, Y)$ and that the trade balance can also be expressed as the difference between domestic income and domestic expenditure, i.e.

$$\hat{T}(M/P_X, B/P_X, Y^S(Q)) \equiv Y^S(Q) - \hat{E}(M/P_X, B/P_X, Y^S(Q)) \quad (38)$$

The combinations of Q and M/P_X for which $\hat{T}(M/P_X, B/P_X, Y^S(Q)) = 0$, for a given value of B/P_X, are indicated by the negatively sloped $X^d = X^S$ curve in the upper panel of Fig. 8.13. Alternatively, recognizing that P_X is fixed at $S.P_X^*$, this curve may be regarded as representing the combinations of P_N and M for which $\hat{T}(M/P_X, B/P_X, Y^S(P_N/P_X)) = 0$. In either case, above and to the right of this curve there is excess domestic demand for traded goods and a trade deficit; and below and to the left of this curve there is a trade surplus.

The intersection of the $N^d = N^S$ curve and the $X^d = X^S$ curve in the upper panel of Fig. 8.13 occurs at the point where the relative price of nontraded goods equals its long run equilibrium value $\bar{Q}$ and where the real domestic money supply is at its long run equilibrium value $\bar{M}/P_X$. Alternatively, this intersection point indicates the long run equilibrium nominal price of nontraded goods $P_N = P_X.\bar{Q}$ and the long run equilibrium level of the nominal money supply $\bar{M}$.

When the domestic money supply differs from its long run equilibrium value, the economy must be at the point in the upper panel of Fig. 8.13 along the $N^d = N^S$ curve corresponding to the actual size of the domestic money supply. At such a point, the trade balance is given by

$$T = \hat{T}(M/P_X, B/P_X) \equiv \hat{T}[M/P_X, B/P_X, Y^S(\hat{Q}(M/P_X, B/P_X))] \quad (39)$$

Corresponding to the trade balance there is a net flow of foreign exchange reserves which holding constant the other assets of the central bank, determines the rate of change of the domestic money supply;

$$\dot{M} = P_X.\hat{T}(M/P_X, B/P_X) \quad (40)$$

In the lower panel of Fig. 8.13, the curve labeled $\hat{T}(M/P_X, B/P_X)$ shows both the trade balance and the rate of change of domestic real money balances as a function of M/P_X, for a given value of B/P_X. Alternatively, if this curve is labeled as the $P_X.\hat{T}(M/P_X, B/P_X)$ curve, it shows the rate of change of the domestic nominal money supply as a function of the level of the domestic nominal money supply, for given values of B and P_X. The intersection of the $\hat{T}(M/P_X, B/P_X)$ curve with the horizontal axis occurs at the long run equilibrium level of real money balances, $\bar{M}/P_X$, where the value of $\bar{M}$ is determined implicitly by the condition

$$\hat{T}(\bar{M}/P_X, B/P_X)=0 \tag{41}$$

Comparison of the lower panel of Fig. 8.13 with Fig. 8.11 and comparison of the condition (41) with the condition (12) reveals the close analogy between the monetary mechanism of balance of payments adjustment that operates with nontraded goods and the mechanism that opetates when all goods are traded, and between the condition that determines the long run equilibrium level of money demand with nontraded goods and the condition that is relevant when all goods are traded.

The major innovations resulting from the introduction of nontraded goods are that we allow for variations in the relative price of nontradable goods and in the general domestic price level along the path of convergence to long run equilibrium. As is apparent from the upper panel of Fig. 8.13, if the domestic money supply is initially less than $\bar{M}$, the instantaneous equilibrium relative and nominal prices of nontraded goods determined by the point on the $N^d = N^S$ curve are less than their respective long run equilibrium values, $\bar{Q}$ and $P_X.\bar{Q}$. The general domestic price level, P, which is an index of the nominal prices of traded and nontraded goods will also be less than its long run equilibrium value. As the domestic money supply rises due to reserve inflows resulting from trade surpluses, the instantaneous equilibrium position of the economy moves up along the $N^d = N^S$ curve toward the long run equilibrium point, implying an increase in the relative and nominal price level as the economy converges to long run equilibrium. The opposite process occurs if the initial money supply exceeds $\bar{M}$. It follows immediately that an increase in the fiat issue of the central bank, starting from $M=\bar{M}$, would have the initial effect of raising the relative and nominal price of nontraded goods and the general domestic price level above their long run equilibrium values, and this would be followed by a period of adjustment during which the domestic money supply and these prices all returned to their respective long run equilibrium levels, Starting from an initial position of long run equilibrium, a devaluation would immediately result in an equiproportional increase in the domestic nominal price of traded goods and would increase (not necessarily proportionately) the long run equilibrium value of the domestic nominal money supply. The nominal price of nontraded goods, however, would not rise immediately in proportion with the devaluation nor will it rise to its new long run equilibrium level. The relative and nominal price of nontraded goods and the general domestic price level immediately following devaluation would all be below their new long run equilibrium values and would only gradually rise to these values as the domestic money supply rises to its new long run equilibrium level.

When we consider the effects of growth in an economy with nontraded goods, the modifications of the earlier analysis are more substantial. With only a composite traded goods, the long run, cumulative effect of growth in domestic output and income depended only on the effect of an increase in income on the demand for domestic money. With nontraded as well as traded goods, growth can affect the long run equilibrium level of money demand both through the usual effect of an increase in income and through the effect of changes in the long run equilibrium relative price of nontraded goods. For exampe, if the growth of domestic output (at constant relative prices) is biased toward traded goods, relative to the growth of domestic demand, then the long run equilibrium relative price of nontraded goods will have to rise as growth occurs. With the domestic nominal price of traded goods fixed by the exchange rate and by the given world prices of such goods, the increase in the long run equilibrium relative price of nontraded goods requires an increase in the domestic nominal price of such goods and, hence, in the general price index. This increase in the general price index enhances the effect of growth in expanding the long run demand for domestic money and, thereby, increases the cumulative payments surplus resulting from growth. The opposite holds if growth is biased towards the production of nontraded goods. It is still true, however, that the cumulative effect of growth on the balance of payments reflects the effects of growth on the long run equilibrium levels of money demand. With nontraded goods, there simply are more channels through which growth can affect the long run equilibrium level of money demand.

Large Countries: When the home country is not small relative to the rest of the world, it is necessary to modify the preceding analysis to account for the interaction between the home country and the rest of the world in determining the prices of tradable goods and the distribution of the world stock of foreign exchange reserves. To illustrate these modifications, it is useful to assume that the economic structure of the home country and the foreign country (identified with the rest of the world) is described by the model in the preceding section, with the two countries producing and consuming a common traded good, *X*, and with each country producing and consuming its own nontraded goods, *N*. Variables for foreign country are indicated by an asterisk (*).

The relative prices of nontraded goods that clear domestic markets in the two countries are given by $\hat{Q}(M/P_X, B/P_X)$ and $\hat{Q}^*(M^*/P_X^*, B^*/P_X^*)$. The trade balance surpluses for the two countries are given by $\hat{T}(M/P_X, B/P_X)$ and $\hat{T}^*(M^*/P_X^*, B^*/P_X^*)$. Nominal prices of traded goods in the two countries are linked by the fixed exchange rate through the relationship $P_X = S.P_X^*$. The condition for equilibrium in the world market for traded goods is expressed by the requirement

$$\hat{T}(M/P_X, B/P_X)+\hat{T}^*(M^*/P_X^*, B^*/P_X^*)=0 \tag{42}$$

Given the domestic and foreign nominal money supplies and the parametrically fixed values of *B*, *B** and *S*, this equilibrium condition determines the instantaneous equilibrium value of the nominal price of traded goods in the two countries, as is illustrated in Fig. 8.14.

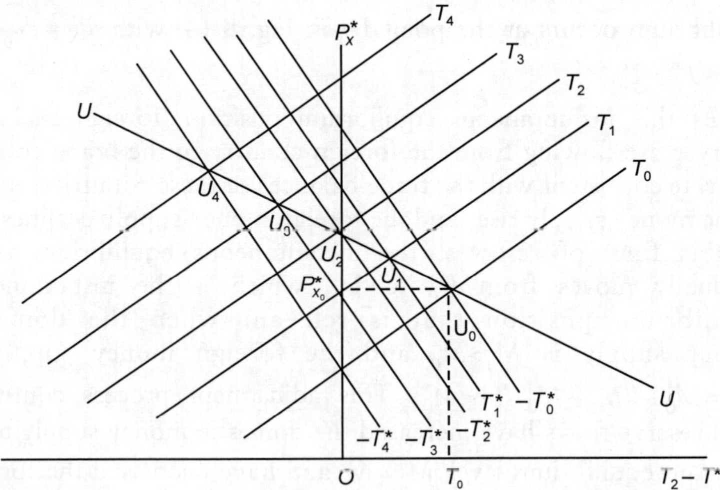

Fig. 8.14: Instantaneous Equilibrium and Dynamics in the World Market for Traded Goods.

In the above figure, P_X^* is plotted on the vertical axis and $P_X = S.P_X^*$ is assumed to vary along with the foreign nominal price. The horizontal axis measures the trade surplus of the home country, T, and the trade deficit of the foreign country, — T^*. The positively sloped curves labeled T_i show the trade surplus of the home country, $T(M_i/S.P_X^*, B/S.P_X^*)$, as a function of P_X^*, for different levels of the domestic money supply. The negatively sloped curves labeled $-T_i^*$ show the trade deficit of the foreign country, $-T^*(M_i^*/P_X^*, B^*/P_X^*)$, as a function of P_X^*, for different levels of the foreign money supply. The levels of the domestic and foreign money supplies used in constructing these curves satisfy the condition

$$\frac{M_i}{S} + M_i^* = M_W \qquad (43)$$

where M_W is the constant level of the world money supply (measured in units of foreign money). This is consistent with the assumption that the non-reserve assets of both central banks are constant and that money supply changes occur only as a consequence of redistributions of a fixed world stock of international reserves. When the distribution of this stock of reserves is such that money supplies in the two countries are M_0 and M_0^*, instantaneous equilibrium occurs at the point U_0 in Fig. 8.14, with $P_X^* = P_{X_0}^*$ and $T = -T^* = T_0$.

At this instantaneous equilibrium position, foreign exchange reserves are flowing from the foreign country to the home country at a rate consistent with the trade balances of these countries. As the home money supply rises and the foreign money supply declines due to this flow of reserves, the instantaneous equilibrium point gradually moves from U_0 to U_1, which is the instantaneous equilibrium position that is relevant when the domestic money supply is $M_1 > M_0$ and the foreign money supply is $M_1^* = M_0^* - \{(M_1 - M_0)/S\} < M_0^*$. This adjustment process continues until reserve flows have increased the domestic money supply to its long run equilibrium level $M_2 = \bar{M}$ and have decreased the foreign money supply to its long run equilibrium level $M_2^* = \bar{M}^*$. At this time the instantaneous equilibrium position is at U_2 on the $P_X{}^*$-axis, the trade balances of both countries are zero, and the world is in long run equilibrium. Similarly, if the initial distribution of international reserves is such that $M = M_4 > \bar{M}$ and $M^* = M_4^* < \bar{M}^*$, the world starts out at the instantaneous equilibrium point U_4 and gradually moves to the right along the *UU* locus, with reserves flowing out of the home country and into the foreign country, until long run equilibrium is achieved at U_2.

The behavior of the instantaneous equilibrium nominal price of traded goods (P_X^* and $P_X = S.P_X^*$) reflects a version of the "transfer problem criterion." As we move from the instantaneous equilibrium U_0 along the *UU* locus toward long run equilibrium, the nominal price of trade goods rises, as illustrated in Fig. 8.14, if and only if $|\partial\hat{T}/\partial(M/P_X)| > |\partial\hat{T}^*/\partial(M^*/P_X^*)|$; i.e. if and only if at constant nominal prices of the traded goods, the effect of an increase in the domestic real money supply on excess demand for traded goods in the home country is larger than the effect of an equivalent reduction in the foreign money supply on the excess supply of traded goods in the foreign country. If so, then at the old nominal prices of traded goods and the new distribution of the world money supply, there will be an excess world demand of traded goods, and the nominal prices of traded goods will have to rise in both countries (reducing the real values of money and bond holdings) in order to restore equilibrium to the world market for traded goods.

While the monetary mechanism of balance of payments adjustment is more complicated for the two country world than for the small country, the basic elements of this mechanism are essentially the same. Starting from a situation in which the domestic nominal money supply is below its long run equilibrium level and, correspondingly, the foreign money supply is above its long rim equilibrium level, reserve flows associated with trade imbalances gradually move the economic system to long run equilibrium by raising the domestic money supply and reducing the foreign money supply to their respective long run equilibrium levels. As in the case of the small country, the essential ingredient underlying this adjustment process is the relationship through which a deficiency in a country's money supply relative to its long run equilibrium level leads to an excess of domestic income over domestic expenditure which implies a trade surplus which brings an inflow of foreign exchange reserves and a gradual restoration of money balances to their long run equilibrium level.

In the two country world, it remains true that a given initial divergence of a country's money supply (and a corresponding divergence with the opposite sign for the other country) will ultimately lead to a cumulative payments surplus and change in reserves just equal to this initial divergence (assuming there is no change in the non-reserve assets of central banks). The long run cumulative effect of disturbances that affect money supplies and money demands, however, are somewhat different in the two country world than they are for a small country. For example, in the small country case, an increase in the fiat issue of the central bank does not alter the long run equilibrium level of domestic money demand and, hence, ultimately leads to an equal loss of foreign exchange reserves. In the large country case, an increase in the fiat issue of the home country increases the world money supply and thereby increases the long run equilibrium level of the nominal price of traded goods in both countries. This increase in the nominal price of traded goods implies an increase in the long run equilibrium level of nominal money demand in both countries, and hence a loss of foreign exchange reserves by the home country that is smaller than the increase in the fiat issue of its central bank.

Similar reasoning leads to the conclusion that a devaluation by the home country raises the long run nominal price of traded goods in that country while reducing the long run nominal price of traded goods in the foreign country. Because part of the effect of devaluation is absorbed by a decline in the foreign price level, the long run nominal demand for domestic money rises less as a consequence of devaluation than it would if the home country were small. Correspondingly, the cumulative gain in foreign exchange reserves for the home country due to devaluation is less than it would be if the country were small. Note, however, that these modifications of the small country results do not alter the basic principle that the cumulative effect of any disturbance on a country's balance of payments is equal to the effect of the disturbance on the divergence between the domestic money supply and the long run equilibrium level of domestic money demand.

When two large countries produce and consume only a single traded good, in addition to their own nontraded goods, the stability of the mechanism of balance of payments adjustment is not critically affected by the relative price elasticities of demand or of excess demand for tradable or nontradable goods. These elasticities do influence the extent of variations in the relative price of nontradables as we move along the path of convergence to long run equilibrium, and they do affect the speed of convergence to long run equilibrium. But, low price elasticities of demand do not introduce the possibility of instability in the mechanism of balance of payments adjustment. The reason for this is that the price elasticity that is critical for the stability of this mechanism is the elasticity of demand for imports of tradable into a country with respect to the relative price of tradable between the two countries. The assumption that tradable goods for the two countries are perfect substitutes implies that this elasticity is infinite, and this removes any possibility of instability.

When large countries exchange two or more tradable goods, elasticities of import demands for these countries are important for the stability of the monetary mechanism of balance of payments adjustment. In the standard two-country, two-commodity model of the pure theory of international trade, it is well known that the

Marshall-Lerner condition (the requirement that the sum of the absolute values of the import demand elasticities of the two countries be greater than one) is the necessary and sufficient condition for the existence of a unique equilibrium relative price of the two commodities. In the monetary extension of this model, in which money supplies, bond supplies and interest rates affect only the level of spending in each country but not its distribution among commodities, the Marshall-Lerner condition becomes the condition for a unique long run equilibrium in which the trade balance of each country is zero and there is no ongoing redistribution of the world money supply. If for each distribution of the world money supply, the instantaneous equilibrium position of the world economy is unique, it may be shown that the monetary mechanism of balance of payments adjustment ultimately drives the world economy to this unique long run equilibrium. Along the path of convergence to this long run equilibrium, spending differs from income by equal and opposite amounts in the two countries, implying equal and opposite trade imbalances and an ongoing redistribution of the world money supply through flows of foreign exchange reserves. The adjustment of the relative commodity price along the path of convergence to long run equilibrium is determined by application of the standard transfer problem analysis to the endogenously determined magnitude of the transfer corresponding to the trade imbalances of the two countries.

If equilibrium is not unique in the standard two-country, two-commodity trade model, long run equilibrium will not be unique in the monetary extension of this model. Corresponding to each real equilibrium, there will he a separate long run monetary equilibrium. If for each distribution of the world money supply, there is a unique instantaneous equilibrium in the monetary model, the monetary mechanism of balance of payments adjustment will still be well-defined. That is, there will be a well-defined differential equation that expresses the rate of change of the distribution of the world money supply as a function of that distribution. Moreover, it may be shown that the stable nodes of this differential equation describing the monetary mechanism of balance of payments adjustment will correspond to the real trade equilibria at which the Marshall-Lerner condition is satisfied, and that the unstable nodes of this differential equation will correspond to the real trade equilibria where the Marshall-Lerner condition is not satisfied. Thus, as suggested by many earlier writers, sufficiently large elasticities of import demand are essential for stability of the mechanism of balance of payments adjustment. While this interpretation reflects different considerations, it rationalizes some of the statements made by proponents of the elasticity approach to the balance of payments.

Capital Mobility: Two important modifications of the preceding analysis of the monetary mechanism of balance of payments adjustment are required when we allow for international mobility of privately held financial assets. First, the official settlements balance is no longer equal to trade balance but to the sum of the current account balance (which is the trade balance plus the flow of interest income that domestic residents earn on their net foreign securities holdings) and the capital account balance (which measures net sales of privately held financial assets by domestic residents to foreign residents).

Second, we must allow for the possibility of swaps of stocks of privately held assets between domestic and foreign residents that occur at an instant of time. The possibility of asset swaps does not alter the principle that the current account balance is a flow magnitude, but, it does introduce the possibility of stock unit changes in a country's international reserves resulting from private attempts to swap domestic money for financial securities.

The implications of capital mobility for the monetary mechanism of balance of payments adjustment are most easily illustrated by returning to the case of a small open economy that produces and consumes only traded goods. Our model can be modified by assuming that securities held by domestic residents, B, are perfect substitutes for securities issued in the rest of the world, and that the domestic interest rate, r, is equal to the (fixed) interest rate prevailing in the world capital market, r^*. Net foreign security holdings of domestic residents, V are the excess of domestic private security holdings over the stock of government debt that is outside of the domestic central bank,

$$V = B - (\bar{B} - B_g) \quad (44)$$

Domestic real income, Y, is equal to the full employment level of domestic output, Y, plus interest income from net foreign security holdings, $r^*.V/P$;

$$Y=\bar{Y}+r^*.V/P \tag{45}$$

The condition for asset market equilibrium, $L(Y, r^*, A/P)=M/P$, no longer determines the domestic interest rate, hut rather, the instantaneous equilibrium size of the domestic real money supply,

$$M/P=\tilde{m}(A/P, \bar{Y}, (\bar{B}-B_g)/P, r^*) \tag{46}$$

The effect of an increase in real private domestic assets on M/P,

$\partial\tilde{m}/\partial(A/P)=\partial L/\partial(A/P)+r^*(\partial L/\partial Y)[1-(\partial L/\partial(A/P))]$ is assumed to be less than one.

The excess of domestic income over domestic expenditure determines the current account balance, $\psi=Y-E$, where $E=E(Y, r, A/P)$. Setting $r = r^*$ and taking account of (44), (45) and (46), we arrive at a reduced form expression for the current account balance,

$$\psi=\tilde{\psi}(A/P, \bar{Y}, (\bar{B}-B_g)/P, r^*) \tag{47}$$

It is assumed that an increase in real private domestic assets worsens the current account balance; i.e. we assume that

$$\partial\tilde{\psi}/\partial(A/P)=-(\partial E/\partial(A/P))+r^*[1-\partial\tilde{L}/\partial(A/P)].[1-\partial E/\partial Y]<0$$

Given the domestic price level $P = S.P^*$, and holding constant the non reserve assets of the central bank, the current account balance determines the rate of change of real private asset holdings;

$$\dot{A}/P=\tilde{\psi}(A/P, \bar{Y}, (\bar{B}-B_g)/P, r^*) \tag{48}$$

This differential equation characterizes the dynamic process through which the real stock of privately held assets is adjusted to its long run equilibrium value, $\bar{A}/P$, which is determined implicitly by the condition

$$\tilde{\psi}(\tilde{A}/P, \bar{Y}, (\bar{B}-B_g)/P, r^*)=0 \tag{49}$$

This adjustment process for private assets is illustrated in the middle panel of Fig. 8.15, where the curve labeled $\tilde{\psi}(A/P, \bar{Y}, (\bar{B}-B_g)/P, r^*)$ shows the relationship between $\dot{A}/P$ and A/P.

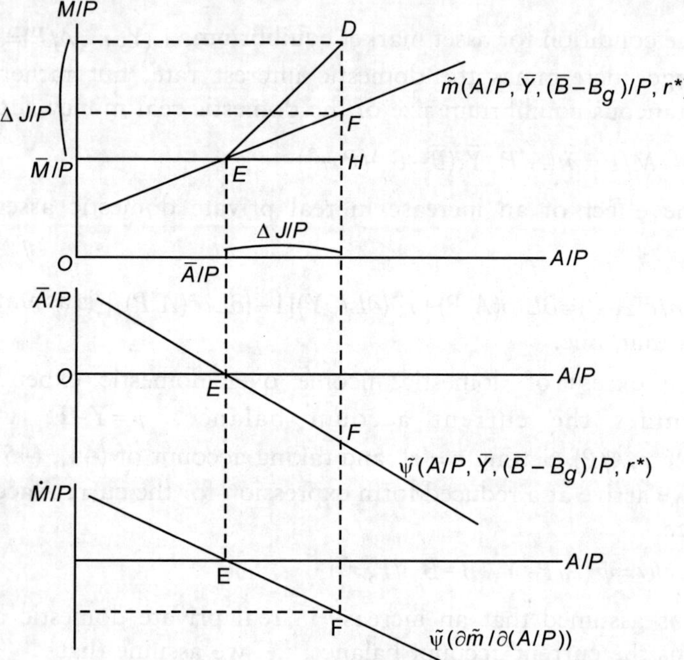

Fig. 8.15: Portfolio Balance, Assets, and Balance of Payment Adjustment with Capital Mobility.

In the top panel the curve labeled $\tilde{m}(A/P, \bar{Y}, (\bar{B}-B_g)/P, r^*)$ shows the reduced form relationship between the level of real private assets and the instantaneous equilibrium level of real money balances. Finally, in the bottom panel of Fig. 8.15, the curve labeled, $\tilde{\psi}\,(\partial\tilde{m}/\partial(A/P))$ shows the relationship between the level of real private assets and the rate of change of domestic real money balances, $\dot{M}/P$, determined by

$$\dot{M}/P = (\partial\tilde{m}/\partial(A/P).(\dot{A}/P) = (\partial\tilde{m}\,/\partial(A/P)).\tilde{\psi}(A/P, \bar{Y}, (\bar{B}-B_g)/P, r^*) \tag{50}$$

Three important principles concerning the mechanism of balance of payments adjustment when we allow for international capital mobility are reflected in Fig. 8.15.

First, the level of money balances in the economy adjusts immediately to the instantaneous equilibrium level associated with the actual level of privately held assets: that is, the economy always operates at the point on the $\tilde{m}$ curve in the top panel of Fig. 8.15 corresponding to the actual level of A/P. Achievement of such an instantaneous equilibrium position subsequent to a disturbance that creates a stock unit divergence between the demand for domestic money and the existing supply requires a stock unit change in the central bank's holdings of international reserves as private asset holders buy or sell securities in order to achieve the desired composition of their assets between money and securities.

Second, the process of adjustment of the stock of privately held assets that occurs as a counterpart of current account imbalances, as illustrated in the middle panel of Fig. 8.15, is necessarily a gradual adjustment process in which the flow or net saving determined by the excess of domestic income over domestic expenditure accumulates over time into changes in the stock of privately held assets.

Third, as illustrated in the bottom panel of Fig. 8.15, changes in the stock of privately held assets resulting from current account imbalances cause gradual changes in the instantaneous equilibrium level of money balances and corresponding flows of foreign exchange reserves which are registered as official settlements surpluses or deficits. This mechanism of monetary adjustment is similar to the monetary mechanism of balance of payments adjustment that operates in the absence of international capital mobility. In the present case however, reserve changes also occur in response to asset swaps motivated by the desire of domestic residents to adjust the actual level of money balances within their portfolio of assets to its desired level. Through reserve changes brought about by the operation of these two mechanisms, the level of the domestic money supply is ultimately adjusted to the long run equilibrium level of domestic money demand that is associated with the long run equilibrium level of privately held domestic assets and with long run equilibrium of the current account balance.

These three principles all come into operation when we consider an increase ΔJ in the fiat issue of the domestic central bank. Starting from an initial situation of long run equilibrium, domestic real assets exceed their long run equilibrium value by the amount $\Delta J/P$.

Since the entire increase $\Delta J/P$ in real privately held assets comes in the form of domestic money, the economy is tentatively at the point D in the top panel of Fig. 8.15 which lies above the $\tilde{m}$ curve as well as to the right of the long run equilibrium level of A/P. To restore the desired composition of assets individuals sell money balances and purchase securities sufficient to move the economy downward from the point D in the top panel of Fig. 8.15 to the point F that lies along the $\tilde{m}$ curve. The additional securities are purchased from foreign residents who convert the domestic money they receive from their sales of securities into foreign money, with a consequent loss of foreign exchange reserves by the domestic central bank. This immediate, stock unit loss of foreign exchange reserves accounts for the reduction in the domestic money supply implied by the jump from the point D to the point F. At the point F, the real value of private domestic assets exceeds its long run equilibrium value $\bar{A}/P$, resulting in an excess of domestic real expenditure over domestic real income and in a current account deficit, as indicated by the point F along the $\tilde{\psi}$ curve in the middle panel of Fig. 8.15.

Over time, downward adjustments in the real stock of privately held assets gradually reduce A/P to its long run equilibrium level. The gradual reductions in A/P gradually reduce the instantaneous equilibrium level of real money balances, implying, as illustrated in the bottom panel of Fig. 8.15, corresponding losses of foreign exchange reserves by the central bank. The total loss of reserves that results from this adjustment process, together with the initial swap of domestic money for foreign securities, exactly offsets the increase in the fiat issue of the central bank and restores domestic money balances to their long run equilibrium level.

The general features of this analysis extend to the effects of other types of disturbances. If the disturbance creates an incipient divergence between the actual level of money balances and their new instantaneous equilibrium level, there will be a swap of domestic money for foreign securities and a corresponding stock unit change in the central bank's holdings of international reserves. If after this asset swap the actual level of domestic privately held assets differs from the long run equilibrium level, there will be a gradual process of adjustment of asset holdings through current account imbalances toward their long run equilibrium level.

Associated with these changes in the level of assets, there will be changes in the instantaneous equilibrium level of money balances which will induce changes in the central bank's holdings of foreign exchange reserves. The total change in reseves will equal the divergence that the initiating disturbance creates between the long run equilibrium level of domestic money balances and the actual level of such balances.

The introduction of nontraded goods modifies the analysis of mechanism of balance of payments adjustment with international capital mobility in essentially the same way as it modifies the analysis of this mechanism for the case in which capital is immobile starting from a level of A/P that is below $\tilde{A}/P$, the domestic relative and nominal prices of nontradables and the general domestic price level are all below their respective long run equilibrium levels. As A/P rises due to current account surpluses, all of these prices rise toward their respective long run equilibrium levels. A modification that is in the same spirit as the introduction of nontraded goods is the introduction of a nontradable asset that domestic residents hold in addition to domestic money, and internationally tradable securities. The rate of return and the price of this nontradable asset is determined by the requirement for equilibrium in the domestic market for this asset, in much the same way that the relative price of a nontradable good is determined by the requirement for equilibrium in the domestic market for such a good.

Starting from an initial value of A/P that is less than its long run equilibrium value and assuming that asset demands are normal (in the sense that an increase in A/P increases the real demands for all assets), the instantaneous equilibrium price of the nontraded asset will be lower and the instantaneous equilibrium rate of return on this asset will be higher than their respective long run equilibrium values. As A/P rises due to current account surpluses, the price of the nontraded asset will rise, and the rate of return on the nontraded asset will fall toward their respective long run equilibrium values.

This analysis can be extended to the case of two large countries that trade a single good and exchange a single internationally mobile security.

Prices of nontraded goods and yields on nontraded assets adjust to clear domestic markets for these goods and assets in each country, conditional on the world price of the tradable good, the world yield on the mobile security, and the prevailing distribution of world wealth. Instantaneous equilibrium requires that the world price of tradable goods and the world yield on the mobile security clear the world markets for these goods and securities, conditional on the distribution of world wealth. At such an instantaneous equilibrium, one country will generally spend more than its income and the other country will spend an equal amount less than its income, implying a corresponding current account deficit and current account surplus. The country with the surplus will be increasing its share of world wealth at the expense of the country with the deficit. The redistribution of world wealth that finances the trade imbalances will be accomplished partly by a flow of privately held securities and partly by a flow of official reserves (with effects on the money supplies of the two countries). If the balance of payments adjustment process is stable, as it should be in such a world, current account imbalances between the two countries will gradually decline as the wealth of the surplus country rises and the wealth of the deficit country declines, and the world will converge to a long run equilibrium in which current account balances are zero and there is no further redistribution of world wealth.

In this type of model of the world economy, an increase in the fiat issue of the central bank of the home country results in an immediate loss of foreign exchange reserves as domestic asset owners rebalance their portfolios between money and securities. Foreign residents will accommodate this portfolio shift because the increase in the world price of traded goods and the adjustment of the world yield on internationally mobile securities induces them to swap securities for money. At the instantaneous equilibrium established immediately after the increase in the fiat issue of the home country's central bank, the wealth of home residents has risen and that of foreign residents has declined because the entire increase in the world money supply went initially to home residents while the increase in the world price level reduced the real value of the nominal assets of residents of both countries. During the process of adjustment subsequent to the establishment of this instantaneous equilibrium, the wealth of home residents will decline as they spend in excess of their income, and the wealth of foreign residents will rise as they spend less than their income. The central bank of the home country will suffer a further loss of foreign exchange reserves because the demand for money by home residents will decline along with their wealth.

In the end, however, the total loss of foreign exchange reserve by the home central bank (both from the initial asset swap and from subsequent reserve flows) will be smaller than the increase in the fiat issue of this central bank. As in the case of no private capital mobility, this is because the increase in the fiat issue of the home central bank has increased the world money supply, the long run equilibrium level of all nominal prices and, hence, the long run equilibrium level of the demand for domestic money.

An increase in the money supply of the home country brought about by an open market operation has somewhat different effects than an increase in the fiat issue of the home central bank because the open market operation affects the supplies of securities available to private asset holders. Moreover, the effects of such an open market operation depend on whether the securities purchased by the central bank are domestic nontradable securities or internationally tradable securities. Tinder standard assumptions about substitutability among assets in private portfolio demands, a purchase of domestic nontradable securities will decrease the long run equilibrium yield on such securities both absolutely and relative to the yield on internationally mobile securities; whereas an open market purchase of the internationally mobile security will have a smaller effect in reducing the long run equilibrium yield on this security and will reduce this yield relative to the yield on the domestic nontradable security. The differential effect of these two policies on the long run equilibrium world price level and on the distribution of international reserves depends on the degrees of substitution between national monies and different classes of securities. Substitution relations among assets in portfolio demands are crucial in large countries models with two or more internationally tradable securities.

We conclude the present section by only highlighting one critical feature of these models - the effects of sterilized intervention in the foreign exchange market. If the central bank of the home country intervenes in the foreign exchange market by selling foreign securities in order to prevent depreciation of the foreign exchange value of domestic money and sterilizes the monetary effect of this intervention by buying domestic securities, the overall effect of the operation will be to increase the outstanding supply of foreign securities and decrease the outstanding supply of domestic securities while holding the money supply constant. Given standard assumptions about portfolio demands for different securities, this alteration of security supplies will increase the equilibrium yield on foreign securities and decrease the equilibrium yield on domestic securities. If each country's security is a closer substitute for its money than the security of the other country, then this alternation in yields will decrease the demand for home money and increase the demand for foreign money and, thereby, tends to alleviate the monetary disequilibrium that was the cause of the drain of foreign exchange reserves.

BALANCE-OF-PAYMENTS ADJUSTMENT WITH FLEXIBLE EXCHANGE RATES

The monetary model of exchange rate determination emphasizes the role of money market equilibrium as well as the interaction between domestic and foreign commodity markets. An essential element of any monetary model is the assumption of money market equilibrium:

$$(P-P^{*})=(m-m^{*})+(l^{*}-l) \quad (1)$$

where l denotes the logarithm of the demand for domestic real balances, m denoted the logarithm of the nominal money supply, p the logarithm of the price level and where an asterisk indicates a variable pertaining to the foreign country. A second essential element in a monetary model of exchange rate determination is a link between domestic and foreign prices through some form of the purchasing power parity, the simplest form of which is expressed by

$$P=e+P^{*} \quad (2)$$

where e denotes the logarithm of the exchange rate, i.e. the price of foreign money in terms of domestic money. Using equation (2) in (1) yields

$$e=(m-m^{*})+(l^{*}-l) \quad (3)$$

which expresses the exchange rate in terms of supplies of domestic and foreign monies and demands to hold these monies. Anything that increases the supply of domestic relative to foreign money or increases the demand for foreign relative to domestic money, raises the exchange rate, (i.e. depreciates the domestic currency).

The assumption that the prices relevant for money market equilibrium are the same as those relevant for the purchasing power parities is easily relaxed by allowing the price level to be a weighted average of the prices of non tradeable goods and internationally traded goods:

$$P=\sigma P_N+(1-\sigma)P_T \quad (4)$$

$$P^*=\sigma^* P_N+(1-\sigma^*)P_T^* \quad (5)$$

where P_N and P_T denotes, respectively, the logarithm of the prices of non-tradable and tradable goods, and σ denotes the weight of non-tradable goods in the price index. If purchasing power parity holds only for tradable goods, we replace equation (2) by (6):

$$P_T=e+P_T^* \quad (6)$$

Using (4)-(6) in (1) we have

$$e=m-m^*+(l^*-l)+[\sigma(P_T-P_N)-\sigma^*(P_T^*-P_N^*)] \quad (7)$$

This equation reveals a third important factor determining the exchange rate: relative price structures in the two economies. A rise in the domestic relative price of tradable goods (a loss of competitiveness), raises the exchange rate (i.e. depreciates the domestic currency). Specification of the determinants of real money demand adds further content to the general monetary model of exchange rate determination. One such specification is given by

$$l=k+\eta Y-\alpha i \quad (8)$$

$$l^*=k^*+\eta^* Y^*-\alpha^* i^* \quad (9)$$

where y and i denote the logarithm of income and the rate of interest and where η and α denote the income elasticity and the interest (semi) elasticity of the demand for money. Substituting this specification into (7) and assuming for simplicity of exposition that $\eta=\eta^*$, $\alpha=\alpha^*$ and $\sigma=\sigma^*$ we obtain

$$e=(k^*-k)+(m-m^*)+\eta(Y^*-Y)+\alpha(i-i^*)+\sigma[(P_T-P_N)-(P_T^*-P_N^*)] \quad (10)$$

Other things constant, a rise in the level of domestic relative to foreign income, appreciates the value of domestic currency (reduces *e*) and an increase in the domestic nominal interest relative to the foreign nominal interest rate depreciates the value of domestic currency (increases *e*). The result (10) is further refined by incorporating the interest parity condition,

$$i - i^* = \pi \tag{11}$$

where π denotes the forward premium of foreign exchange (i.e. the difference between the logarithms of the forward and the spot exchange rates).

Substituting π for $(i - i^*)$ in equation (10) yields the prediction that a rise in the forward premium on foreign exchange depreciates the currency (raises *e*). This dependence of the current exchange rate on expectations concerning the future (as summarized by the forward premium) is a typical characteristic of price determination in asset markets. Thus, an expected future depreciation of the currency is reflected immediately in the current value of the currency.

In the above model we have not drawn the distinction between "the demand for domestic money" and "the domestic demand for money." Implicitly it has been assumed that domestic money is demanded only by domestic residents while foreign money is demanded only by foreign residents. Furthermore, the formulation of the demands for real cash balances (in equations 8 and 9) included the domestic interest rate in the domestic demand, and the foreign interest rate in the foreign demand; it has been implicitly assumed that the only relevant alternative for holding domestic money is domestic securities while the only relevant alternative for holding foreign money is foreign securities. In principle, however, the alternatives to holding domestic money include domestic securities, foreign securities, inventories of domestic and foreign goods as well as foreign exchange. It follows that a richer formulation of the demand for money would recognize that, as an analytical matter, the spectrum of alternative assets and rates of return that are relevant for the specification of the demand for money is rather broad, including both rates of interest, i and i^* expected domestic and foreign inflation as well as the forward premium on foreign exchange π.

Furthermore, to the extent that under flexible exchange rate system individuals might wish to diversify their currency holdings, the demand for domestic money would include a foreign component which depends on foreign income, while the demand for foreign money would include a domestic component which depends on domestic income. These characteristics reflect the phenomenon of currency substitution which is likely to arise when the exchange rate is not pegged. Under these circumstances the demand function l and l^* will be richer and, when substituted into equation (7), the predictions of the effects of parametric changes in incomes or rates of interest will depend on the relative sensitivity of the demands for domestic and foreign monies to these parametric changes, which in turn may depend on the relative degrees of substitutions among assets in portfolios. The general principles which govern the effects of parametric changes on the relative demands for money are similar to those that govern the effects of international transfers on relative demands and resemble the "transfer problem criteria".

The monetary approach that was summarized in the preceding discussion differs from the elasticity approach to exchange rate determination in that concept like exports, imports, and the like, do not appear explicitly as being fundamentally relevant for the understanding of the evolution of the exchange rate. Rather, the relevant concepts relate to three groups of variables: first are those which are determined by the monetary authorities, second are those which affect the demands for domestic and foreign monies, and third are those which affect the relative price structures. The formulation of the link between domestic and foreign prices in equation (6) assumed that purchasing power parities holds with respect to internationally traded goods. Implicitly it was assumed that there are no barriers to trade. This formulation can be easily extended so as to incorporate price differential which stem from commercial policies.

For example, when the domestic economy has tariffs on imports, equation (6) becomes

$$P_T = k + e + P_T^* \tag{12}$$

where k denotes the logarithm of one plus the proportional tariff rate.

Using equation (12) instead of (6) in the derivation of the exchange rate equation shows the negative dependence of e on k. Accordingly, the imposition of a tariff results in an appreciation of the currency. In explaining this result the monetary approach does not emphasize the effect of the tariff on the relative price of imports along the lines of the "elasticity approach" but rather, it is argued that the currency appreciates because, *ceteris paribus*, a rise in the tariff rate raises the price level, induces a rise in the demand for nominal balances and results in a rise in the relative price of nominal balances. The monetary approach also provides for a mechanism by which a tariff may result in a depreciation of the currency. If subsequent increases in tariffs result in distortions which lower real income, the reduced real income reduces the demand for money and may outweigh the effect of the rise in the price level. In that case a rise in the tariff rate may weaken the currency.

We turn now to a brief illustration of the working of the model under the assumption that capital is immobile internationally as shown in equation (10), the equilibrium exchange rate can be expressed in terms of variables pertaining to the demand and the supply of monies as well as to those which underlie the relative price structure. The equilibrium relative price structure is determined by the condition that the demands for traded and non-traded goods equal the corresponding supplies. This can be described with the help of following diagram.

Panel II of Fig. 8.16 describes the determination of the equilibrium relative price $(P_T - P) = \sigma(P_T - P_N)$ for the domestic economy that is assumed to face a given foreign price of traded goods. The *NN* and *TT* schedules describe combinations of relative prices and interest rates that maintain equilibrium in the markets for non-traded and traded goods, respectively. The *NN* schedule is positively sloped since a rise in $(P_T - P)$ creates an excess supply for non-traded goods which can be eliminated by a higher interest rate. The higher interest rate restores the equilibrium since it lowers demand. The reduction in the demand in turn is based on the assumption that aggregate spending depends negatively on the rate of interest. The *TT* schedule is negatively sloped since a rise in the relative price creates an excess supply of traded goods which can be eliminated by a fall in the rate of interest which induces a rise in spending. The equilibrium rate of interest and relative prices is designated by point Q. Panel I of Fig. 8.16 describes the condition for money market equilibrium. The horizontal axis represents the real value of cash balances as a function of the rate of interest. For subsequent use it is noted that, from equations (4)-(6), the price level that is used in the computation of real balances can be written as:

$$P = e + P^* + (P_T^* - P^*) - (P_T - P) \tag{13}$$

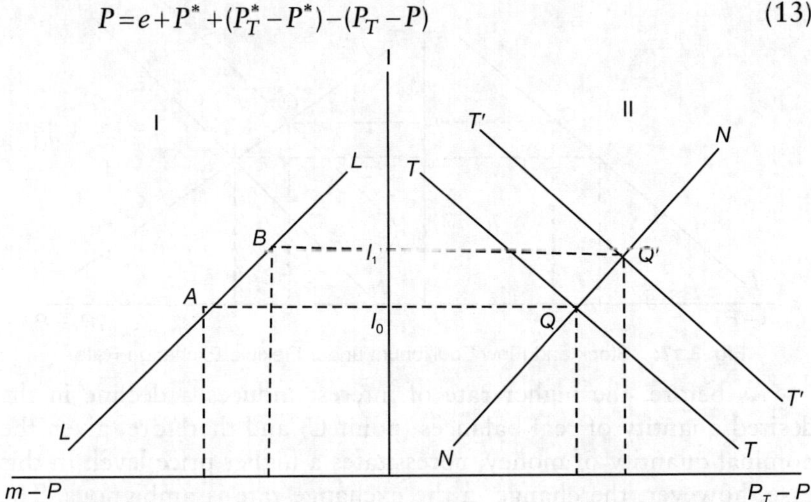

Fig. 8.16: Stock and Flow Equilibrium under Flexible Exchange Rates.

Consider a rise in spending that falls entirely on traded goods. As shown in panel II of Fig. 8.16, this induces a rightward shift of the *TT* schedule to *T′ T′* and results in a new equilibrium at point *Q′* with a higher relative price of traded goods and a higher rate of interest. The higher rate of interest in turn lowers the demand for real balances and, as shown in panel I of Fig. 8.16, results in a new equilibrium at point *B*. Inspection of equation (13) helps to ascertain the effects of the change in spending on the exchange rate. Since, given the higher interest rate, the price level must rise (so as to reduce real balances) and since the rise in $(P_T - P)$ which is induced by the decline in the nominal price of non-traded goods contributes to a fall in the price level, it follows that the exchange rate, *e*, must rise so as to more than offset the price level effect of the relative price change.

Consider now the case where the rise in spending falls entirely on non-traded goods. In this case the *NN* schedule shifts to the left as in Fig. 8.17 and the new equilibrium (point Q″) is characterized by a lower relative price of traded goods and a higher rate of interest.

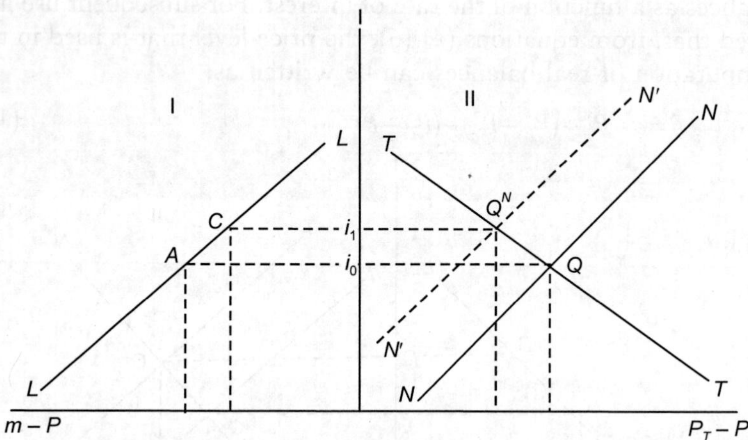

Fig. 8.17: Stock and Flow Equilibrium under Flexible Exchange Rate.

As before, the higher rate of interest induces a decline in the desired quantity of real balances (point C) and therefore, given the nominal quantity of money, necessitates a higher price level. In this case, however, the change in the exchange rate is ambiguous. The fall of the relative price lowers the price level and therefore, depending on whether this reduction in the price level exceeds or falls short of the reduction that is necessary for money market equilibrium, the exchange rate will fall or rise. We conclude by noting, that in contrast with the predictions of the "simple absorption" approach one may not conclude unambiguously that a rise in aggregate spending weakens the currency. Rather, the exchange rate effect may depend on whether the rise in spending falls on traded or non-traded goods.

The same model can be used to examine the effects of other changes like expenditure switching for which the rise in spending on one group of goods does not come at the expense of savings but rather corresponds to a decline in spending on the other group of goods. Likewise one could analyse the effects of economic expansion which originates in one of the sectors. In that case it can be shown that a rise in output originating in the traded goods sector, results in a fall in *e* (i.e. in an appreciation of the currency). On the other hand, the exchange rate effects of a rise in output originating in the non-traded sector are ambiguous. As before, this ambiguity stems from the fact that the change in the equilibrium relative prices induces a change in the price level which may exceed or fall short of the change required by money market equilibrium.

The above analysis which was intended to illustrate the working of the model was conducted under the assumption that capital was immobile internationally. Under these circumstances the balance of trade had to be balanced. The model can be extended to allow for capital mobility. In that case, flow equilibrium would require that in addition to a zero excess demand for non-traded goods, the trade balance surplus must equal the deficit on the capital account. The qualitative conclusions of the analysis remain unchanged except for the fact that the induced change in the rate of interest (and thereby the required change in the price level) would be smaller the higher the degree of capital mobility. In the extreme case, when capital is perfectly mobile, the interest rate and thus the desired level of real balances would not change. As can be seen from equation (13), in this case to maintain a constant price level, the exchange rate would have to change by the same amount as the relative price (when both are measured logarithmically).

Finally, it is noteworthy that the model satisfies the homogeneity postulate. A once and for all rise in the domestic money supply results in a once and for all rise in the exchange rate and in the nominal price of non-traded goods while leaving all real variables (like real balances, relative prices, and the rate of interest) unchanged. Likewise, a once and for all equal rise in the domestic and the foreign money raises all nominal prices while leaving all real variables and the exchange rate unchanged.

The formulation in equations (9)-(10) presumed that money market equilibrium obtains continuously. The analytical framework could be modified easily to allow for a distinction between short-run and long-run demands for money. This formulation would imply the dynamics of adjustment. Likewise, the formulation in equation (16) could be modified to allow for a gradual adjustment to purchasing power parities. While such modifications of the theoretical model do not introduce severe complexities, the implications for empirical estimates are much more involved and great care is required in the specification of the corresponding econometric model.

Further modifications of the model allow for legal restrictions on transactions in foreign currency which results in black markets, as well as for government intervention in the determination of exchange rates which results in a crawling peg. An additional modification concerns the choice of the rate of interest that is included in the demand for money. The formulation that we have used included the nominal rate of interest as an argument without drawing a distinction between the real interest rate and inflationary expectations. Likewise, the specification assumed some form of purchasing power parities. This specification can be modified so as to allow for short term price stickiness. In that case a rise in the quantity of money lowers the real rate of interest for the short-run and induces a depreciation of the currency. The discussion of currency substitution suggested the possibility that the function characterizing the demand for money includes many alternative rates of return corresponding to the many alternative assets. Again, as a theoretical matter this modification does not introduce severe complexities but the implications for empirical research may be severe since the various rates of return may be highly colinear. The degree of colinearity may be very high if the alternative rates of return are linked to each other by various parity conditions. Among such parity conditions are the interest parity-linking the forward premium on foreign exchange to the difference between domestic and foreign rates of interest, the purchasing power parity-linking domestic and foreign prices, and the Fisher relations-linking the nominal rates of interest to the real rates of interest and to inflationary expectations.

The analysis of exchange rate determination within the monetary framework did not put much explicit emphasis on the stocks of other assets. According to the monetary model changes in the stocks of alternative assets results in exchange rate changes only to the extent that they alter the various rates of return which affect the demand for money. In contrast, the portfolio balance model emphasizes the limited degree substitutability among alternative assets. According to the portfolio balance model the relative quantities of the various assets and of the rate of accumulation of these assets exert profound first order effects on the exchange rate. As an empirical matter, however, the implementation of this approach is made difficult due to limited availability of data on the various quantities of the assets that would be relevant for inclusion in the world portfolio model. Since the rate of accumulation of assets equals the current account of the balance of payments, it provides for a dynamic linkage between the current account and the exchange rate. As a result, analyses of the portfolio balance model have typically linked the exchange rate to the current account. It is relevant to note, however, that such a linkage is not specific to the portfolio balance model. Rather, it reflects the implications of the budget constraint by which the current account of the balance of payments equals the discrepancy between income and spending, and this constraint holds of course independent of the determinants of portfolio composition. Consequently, any model which allows for net savings must imply a relationship between the exchange rate and the current account.

Prior to concluding this section it might be useful to note that the monetary approach to the exchange rate does not claim that the exchange rate is "determined" only in the money or in the asset markets and that only stock rather than flow considerations are relevant for determining the equilibrium exchange rate. Obviously, general equilibrium relationships which are relevant for the determination of exchange rates include both stock and flow variables. In this respect, the money market equilibrium relationship that has been used, may be viewed as a reduced form relationship. Furthermore, the fact that the analysis of the exchange rate has been carried out in terms of the supplies and the demands for monies, does not imply that "only money matters" or that the exchange rate is determined only by the supply of domestic and foreign monies: on the contrary, in addition to the key role played by the intersectoral relative price structure, the demand for money plays a critical role and it depends on real variables like real income as well as on other real variables which underlie expectations. The rationale for concentrating on the relative supplies and demands for money is that they provide a convenient and a natural framework for organizing thoughts concerning the determinants of the relative price of monies. It is the same principle which has been used by proponents of the monetary approach to the balance of payments in justifying the use of the money demand-money supply framework for the analysis of the money account of the balance of payments under a pegged exchange rate system.

The model that was discussed in this section included anticipatory variables, like the forward premium on foreign exchange, as one of the determinants of the current exchange rate. However, this formulation has not emphasized sufficiently the critical role that expectations play in affecting the exchange rate. This unique role is best exemplified within a more general framework that views the question of exchange rate determination as part of the more general theory of the determination of asset prices.

Exchange Rates as Asset Prices: In the models of exchange rate determination examined in the preceding section, the dynamic behavior of the exchange rate is usually analyzed in terms of the response of the exchange rate to an exogenous disturbance (such as a permanent increase in the domestic money supply) and its subsequent path of convergence to its new long-run equilibrium. This general view of exchange rate determination, however, does not fully explain key empirical regularities that have been characteristic of the behavior of exchange rates during the 1970's and during earlier periods of generalized floating. As a statistical matter, the logarithm of spot exchange rates between the U.S. dollar and other major currencies (the British pound, the Deutsche mark, the French franc, the Japanese yen and the Swiss franc) is generally well described as random walks in which month-to-month and quarter-to-quarter changes are almost entirely unpredictable. Changes in spot exchange rates are generally closely correlated with contemporaneous changes in forward exchange rates (especially for large changes), indicating that movements in spot rates are closely related to movements in the market's expectation of future spot rates.

Monthly and quarterly changes in exchange rates are not, however, closely related to differentials in national inflation rates, implying that most short-run changes in nominal exchange rates correspond changes in real exchange rates (i.e. to deviations from purchasing power parities). Moreover, monthly and quarterly changes in exchange rates are not closely related to differentials in rates of monetary expansion or to current account imbalances. These facts suggest that exchange rates should be viewed as prices of durable assets determined in organized markets (like stock and commodity exchanges) in which current price reflect the market's expectation concerning present and future economic conditions relevant for determining the appropriate values of these durable assets, and in which price changes are largely unpredictable and reflect primarily new information that alters expectations concerning these present and future economic conditions. This general notion of exchange rates as "asset prices" can be represented in skeletal model in which the logarithm of the equilibrium exchange rate in period t, denoted by $e(t)$, is determined by

$$e(t)=X(t)+a.E[(e(t+1)-e(t)); t)] \tag{14}$$

where $x(t)$ represents the basic economic conditions that affect the foreign exchange market in period t, $E[(e(t+1)-e(t)); t]$ denotes the expected percentage rate of change of the exchange rate between t and $t + 1$ conditional on information available at t, and the parameter a measures the sensitivity of the current exchange rate to its expected rate of change. To close the model, it is assumed that expectations are "rational" in the sense that they are consistent with the application of (14) in all future periods (and with a suitable boundary condition). By forward iteration, it follows that the exchange rate that is expected at any $t + j$, for $j>0$, conditional on information available at t, depends on a discounted sum of expected future X's, starting at $t + j$; specifically,

$$E[e(t+j); t]=(1/(1+\alpha)).\sum_{i=0}^{\infty}(a/(1+a))^{i}.E[X(t+j+1); t] \tag{15}$$

Setting $j = 0$, we obtain the "asset price" expression for the current exchange rate as a discounted sum of present and expected future X's. Using (15), we also obtain a convenient decomposition of the change in the exchange rate, $D(e(t))\equiv e(t+1)-e(t)$, into its expected change component, $D^{e}(e(t))=E[D(e(t)); t]=E[(e(t+1)-e(t)); t]$ and its unexpected change component, $D^{U}(e(t))=e(t+1)-E[e(t+1); t]$. The expected change in the exchange rate is a discounted sum of expected future changes in the X's;

$$D^{e}(e(t))=(1/(1+a)).\sum_{i=0}^{\infty}(a/(1+a))^{i}.E[D(X(t+1)); t] \tag{16}$$

Alternatively, the expected change in the exchange rate can be expressed as proportional to the difference between the discounted sum of all expected future X's that determines $E[e(t+1); t]$ and the current X;

$$D^e(e(t)) = (1/(1+a)).[E(e(t+1); t) - X(t)] \tag{17}$$

The unexpected change in the exchange rate is a discounted sum of changes in expectations about future X's based on new information received between t and $t + 1$;

$$D^U(e(t)) = (1/(1+a)).\sum_{i=0}^{\infty}(a/(1+a)).[E(X(t+j+1); t+1);$$
$$t+1) - E(X(t+j+1); t)] \tag{18}$$

These results provide a general rationale for many of the observed regularities in the dynamic behavior of exchange rates. The expected component of monthly changes in exchange rates between major industrial countries should usually be quite small because the factor of proportionality $1/(1 + a)$ that appears in (17) is probably of the order of magnitude of 1/100, implying that only very large differences between the current X and the discounted sum of all future X's could justify a substantial expected change in the exchange rate over a period of a month. In contrast, the unexpected component of the monthly change in the exchange rate, which is necessarily unpredictable on the basis of information available at t, could be quite large. If new information received between t and $t + 1$ leads to a substantial revision, in the same direction, of expectations, we should observe changes in expectations concerning future exchange rates that are in the same direction and are of similar magnitude as the unexpected change in the spot exchange rate. This suggests a rationale for the observed relation between unexpected movements in spot and forward exchange rates, especially for large movements.

Balance of Payments Equilibrium and the Real Exchange Rate: One procedure for introducing specific economic content into the general asset price model of exchange rates is to focus on the condition of balance of payments equilibrium as the fundamental determinant of the equilibrium exchange rate, and allowing for a suitable channel through which expected changes in the exchange rate influence the balance of payments. This procedure is reminiscent of traditional flow market models of the determination of exchange rates, and is also similar to a number of more recent analyses of the interaction between the exchange rate and the current account balance. In implementing this procedure, it is convenient initially to deal with a real model of the determination of the real exchange rate, and only subsequently to introduce the monetary considerations centrally important in determining nominal exchange rates.

For a moderate size country, the real exchange rate, q, is identified with the logarithm of the relative price of domestic goods in terms of foreign goods. Domestic goods may either be exclusively non-traded goods or may be goods for which there is a less than infinitely elastic foreign demand. Consistent with either of these interpretations, it is plausible to assume that the current account surplus b, (measured in terms of imported good), is determined by

$$b=\beta.(Z-q)+r^{*}.A,\ \beta>0 \tag{19}$$

where z summarizes the exogenous real factors that affect domestic excess demand and foreign excess demand for domestic goods, β is a parameter that reflects the relative price elasticities of domestic and foreign excess demands for domestic goods, r^* is the (fixed) foreign real interest rate, and A is the net stock of foreign assets (denominated in foreign goods) held by domestic residents. Absent changes in official holdings of foreign assets, the current account surplus necessarily determines the rate of change of net private holdings of foreign assets;

$$D(A)=b=\beta.(Z-q)+r^{*}.A \tag{20}$$

The rest of the world, which is large relative to the home country, willingly absorbs changes in assets A, in exchange for foreign goods, at the fixed foreign real interest rate, r^*. Hence, the capital account deficit of the home country (measured in terms of foreign goods), denoted by c, reflects the desired rate of accumulation of net foreign assets by domestic residents. Two factors are assumed to influence the desired rate accumulation of net foreign assets: the divergence between the current "target level" of net foreign assets, $\hat{A}$ and their current actual level, A; and the expected rate of change of the real exchange rate; formally,

$$c=\mu.(\hat{A}-A)-\alpha.D^{e}(q),\ \ \mu,\alpha>0 \tag{21}$$

The effect of $D^e(q)$ on c may be thought of either as the influence of expected changes in the value of foreign assets (measured in terms of domestic goods) on desired accumulation of such assets, or as the influence of the domestic real interest rate (defined relative to a basket of both domestic and foreign goods) on desired saving. Balance of payments equilibrium requires that the current account surplus, b, is matched by the capital account deficit, c; i.e.

$$\beta.(Z-q)+r^{*}.A=\mu.(\hat{A}-A)-\alpha.D^{e}(q) \tag{22}$$

This condition, together with (xx), constitute a simultaneous system of forward looking difference equations that may be solved for the expected future time paths of the endogenous variables, q and A, conditional on the current inherited stock of net foreign assets and on the expected future time paths (based on current information) of the exogenous forcing variables, z and $\hat{A}$. In particular, the solution for the current equilibrium real exchange rate is given by

$$q(t)=\overline{q}(t)+\gamma.(A(t)-\overline{A}(t)) \tag{23}$$

where

$$\overline{q}(t)=\overline{Z}(t)+(r^{*}/\beta).\overline{A}(t)$$

$$\overline{Z}(t)=(1-\theta).\sum_{j=0}^{\infty}\theta^{j}.E[Z(t+j);t]$$

$$\overline{A}(t)=(1-\theta).\sum_{j=0}^{\infty}\theta^{j}.E[A(t+j);t]$$

$$\theta=(1/(1+\lambda)) \text{ and } \gamma=(\lambda/\beta)-(1/\alpha)>0$$

$$\lambda=(1/2).\left[\left(r^{*}+(\beta/\alpha)\right)+\sqrt{\left(r^{*}+(\beta/\alpha)\right)^{2}+4.(\mu\beta/\alpha)}\right]>[r^{*}+(\beta/\alpha)]$$

The result in (23) indicates that the current real exchange rate depends on

(a) the current estimate of the long-run equilibrium real exchange rate, $\overline{q}(t)$, that is expected to be consistent with the requirement that on average (in present and future periods), the current account is balanced (b = 0), and

(b) on the divergence between current net foreign asset holdings and the current estimate of the long-run desired level of such holdings, $\overline{A}(t)$.

The asset price property of the real exchange rate is reflected in the dependence of $\overline{q}(t)$ on a discounted sum of present and expected future z's and in the dependence of $\bar{A}(t)$ on a discounted sum of present and expected future $\hat{A}$'s. The discount rate, λ, that is applied in determining both $\bar{q}(t)$ and $\bar{A}(t)$, reflects the sensitivity of the current account surplus to the level of q and the sensitivity of the capital account deficit both to expected rate of change of q and to the divergence of net foreign assets from their target level.

It is noteworthy that the asset price expression for the real exchange rate that is embodied in (23) is consistent with a sophisticated version of the traditional flow market model of exchange rate determination. As illustrated in Fig. 18, the current real exchange rate may be thought of as being determined by the intersection of the b schedule, characterizing the flow of foreign exchange arising from current account transactions, $b=\beta.(Z-q)+r^*.A$, and the c schedule, characterizing the flow of foreign exchange arising from capital account transactions, $c=\mu.(\hat{A}-A)-\alpha(E[q(t+1);t]-q)$, where the expected future real exchange rate, $E[q(t+1);t]$, is treated as a parameter affecting the position of the c schedule.

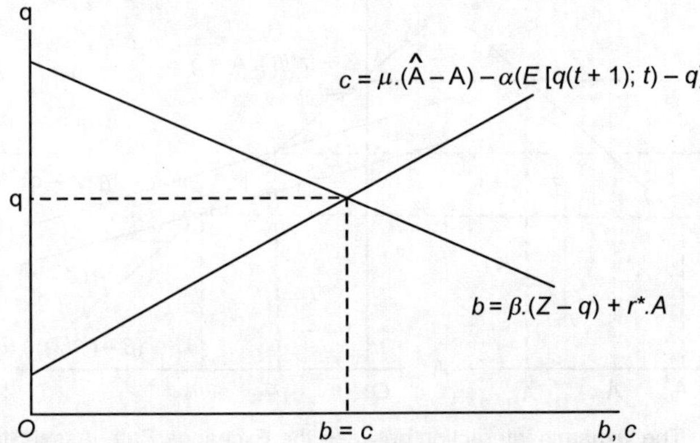

Fig. 8.18: Balance of Payments Equilibrium and the Real Exchange Rate.

The element of sophistication that transforms this traditional model into the asset pricing results expressed by (23) is the assumption that expectations concerning the future real exchange rate are consistent with the economic forces that will actually determine the future real exchange rate. The present results are also consistent with recent models of the dynamic interaction between the exchange rate and the current account which view the current exchange rate as determined by the willingness of asset holders to hold existing stocks of foreign assets, and which view the rate of change of the exchange rate as determined by rate of change of foreign assets which is equal to the current account balance.

In particular, if we assume that the exogenous factors affecting the current account (the *z*'s) and the target levels of net foreign assets (the $\hat{A}$'s) are constant, then the current real exchange rate, $q(t)$, determined by (23) becomes a function of the inherited stock of net foreign assets, as illustrated in left hand panel of Fig. 8.19.

Also, as illustrated in the right hand panel of Fig. 8.19, the current account surplus, b, is determined by this value of $q(t)$ and by the interest received on the inherited stock of net foreign assets. When $A(t)=A_0$ is less than $\bar{A}=\hat{A}$, $q(t)=q_0=\bar{q}+\gamma.(A_0-\bar{A})$ is less than $\bar{q}=Z+(r^*/\beta).\bar{A}$, and the current account surplus is

$$b_0=\beta.(Z-q_0)+(r^*/\beta).A_0=(\beta\gamma-r^*).(\bar{A}-A_0)$$
$$=(\beta-(r^*/\gamma)).(\bar{q}-q_0)>0$$

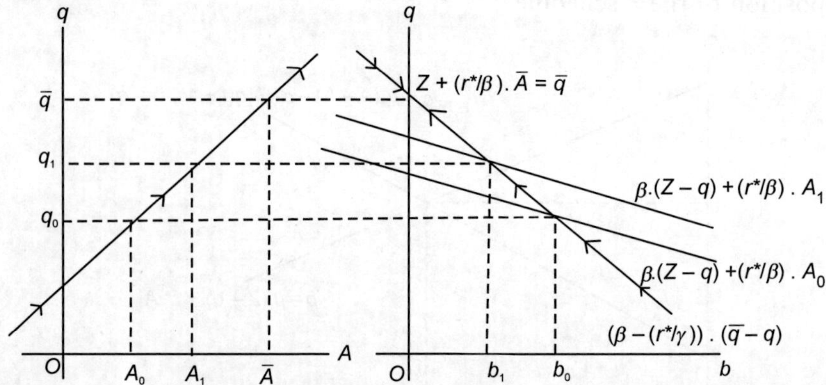

Fig. 8.19: The Dynamic Interaction between the Exchange Rate, Asset Stocks and the Current Account.

This surplus adds to the stock of net foreign assets, and the new stock, $A_1 = A_0 + b_0$, determines a new real exchange rate, q_1, where $q_1=\bar{q}+\gamma.(A_1-\bar{A})=q_0+\gamma b_0>q_0$. The new real exchange rate, together with the new stock of net foreign assets, determine a new current account surplus, b_1, where

$$b_1=\beta.(Z-q_1)+(r^*/\beta).A_1=(\beta\gamma-r^*).(\bar{A}-A_1)$$
$$=(\beta-(r^*/\gamma)).(\bar{q}-q)$$

which is still positive but is smaller than b_0. This dynamic process continues, with ever smaller current account surpluses and ever smaller increases in q, until the current account is in balance and $q=\bar{q}$.

New elements enter into the analysis of exchange rate dynamics when we consider either expected changes in the z's and the $\hat{A}$'s or changes in expectations about the future paths of these exogenous forcing variables due to new information. The general expression for the expected change in the exchange rate implied by (23) is given by

$$D^e(q(t))=(\beta\gamma-r^*).(\bar{A}(t)-A(t))+(1-\theta-\beta\theta).E[(\bar{Z}(t+1) - Z(t));t]-(\theta\gamma-(r^*/\beta)).(1-\theta).E[(\bar{A}(t+1)-\hat{A}(t));t]$$

The first term on the right hand side of (24) captures the essential element of Fig. 8.19, namely, the effect of divergences between current long-run desired level of net foreign assets and the current actual level of net foreign assets on the expected change in the real exchange rate. The second term on the right hand side of (24) represents the effect on $D^e(q(t))$ of "temporary expected disturbances to the current account" associated with differences between the expected discounted sum of all future z's, $E(\bar{Z}(t+1);t)$, and the current expected value of z. The third term on the right hand side of (24) reflects the effect of expected changes in the target level of net foreign assets, measured by $E(\bar{A}(t+1)-\hat{A}(t));t)$; on the expected change in q. The general expression for the unexpected change in the real exchange rate implied by (23) is given by

$$D^U(q(t))=\gamma.D^U(A(t))+D^U(\bar{Z}(t))-(\gamma-(r^*/\beta)).D^U(\bar{A}(t)) \qquad (25)$$

where $D^U(A(t))$ is the unexpected change in net foreign assets associated with "innovations" in the current account, $D^U(\bar{Z}(t))$ measures the effect of new information in revising expectations about future z's, and $D^U(A(t))$ indicates the effect of new information in revising expectations about future target levels of A. The new information that leads to revisions of expectations about future z's and about future target levels of wealth may come from a variety of sources, including particularly the possible effect of innovations in the current account on expectations concerning the 'future behavior of the exogenous factors affecting the current account.

Exchange Rates and Money in the General Model of Exchange Rate Determination: Models of the type examined in the preceding section are easily extended to incorporate monetary phenomena and to deal with the nominal exchange rate. Let p denote the logarithm of the domestic money price of domestic goods, p^* denote the logarithm of the foreign money price of foreign goods, and e the logarithm of the domestic money price of foreign exchange. The logarithm of the relative price of domestic goods in terms of imported goods is given by

$$q = p - (e + P^*) \qquad (26)$$

The logarithm of the general price level in the home country is given by

$$P = \sigma . p + (1 - \sigma).(e + P^*) = e + P^* + \sigma . q \qquad (27)$$

where σ is the weight of domestic goods in the domestic price index, and where P denotes the price level. The logarithm of the demand for domestic money is given by

$$m^d = K + L.P + J.e + V.q - N.i - U.D^e(e) + W.A \qquad (28)$$

where K represents all exogenous factors (such as real income) affecting the demand for domestic money, $L > 0$, $J > 0$ and $V \gtrless 0$ are the elasticities of money demand with respect to the general price level, the nominal exchange rate and the relative price of domestic goods, and $N > 0$, $U > 0$ and $W > 0$ are the semi-elasticities of money demand with respect to the domestic nominal interest rate, i, the expected rate of change of the nominal exchange rate, $D^e(e)$ and the stock of net foreign assets. The domestic nominal interest rate is determined by the interest parity condition,

$$i = i^* + D^e(e) + \rho \qquad (29)$$

where i^* is the exogenous foreign nominal interest rate and ρ is an exogenous risk premium that accounts for differences between the forward premium on foreign exchange and the expected rate of change of the nominal exchange rate.

The critical equilibrium condition for nominal variables is the requirement that the logarithm of demand for domestic money, m^d, must equal the logarithm of the supply of domestic money, m. Using equations (26)-(29), this equilibrium condition may be expressed in terms of the following "reduced form" condition for monetary equilibrium:

$$m=\kappa+\xi.e-\eta.D^{e}(e) \tag{30}$$

where $\xi=L+J>0$ and $\eta=N+U>0$, and where κ summarizes all of the factors other than e and $D^e(e)$ that influence the logarithm of demand for domestic money, i.e.

$$\kappa=K+LP^{*}-N.(i^{*}+\rho)+(V+\sigma L).q+WA \tag{31}$$

If it is assumed that paths of the real variables q and A are determined independently of the behavior of the domestic money supply, as indicated by the analysis in the preceding section, then the expected path of the nominal exchange rate may be determined from the solution of the forward looking difference equation (30). As is seen from (32) below, the expected nominal exchange rate depends on a discounted sum of expected future differences between m and κ;

$$E[e(s);t]=(1/(\xi+\eta)).\sum_{j=0}^{\infty}(\eta/(\xi+\eta))^{j}.E[(m(s+j)-\kappa(s+j));t] \tag{32}$$

Setting $s=t$, we find that (the logarithm of) the current nominal exchange rate, $e(t)=E[e(t);t]$, depends on a discounted sum of present and expected future differences between m and κ. This result represents the "asset price version" of the simple monetary model of exchange rate determination discussed in earlier section. Its advantage over this simpler model is that it indcates clearly dependence of the current exchange rate not only on current money supplies and money demands, but also on the entire expected future time paths of money supplies and money demands. In accord with the general principles of the asset price view of exchange rates, the expected rate of change of the exchange rate is a discounted sum of expected future changes in $m-\kappa$'s; and the unexpected change in the exchange rate is a discounted sum of revisions in expectations about future $m-\kappa$'s brought about by new information received between t and t+i. In general, these two components of the change in the exchange rate should reflect the stochastic process generating $m-\kappa$ and the information about this process that is available to economic agents. For example, if $m-\kappa$ is directly observable and is known to follow a random walk, then the exchange rate, e, should also follow a random walk in which all changes in e are unexpected and are proportional to the observed unexpected changes in $m - \kappa$.

Alternatively, if κ is unobservable (to private agents) and is known to follow a random walk, and if the monetary authority allows m to change to offset changes in κ and adds an uncorrelated error to changes in m, then e should still follow a random walk but, following the rules of optimal forecast, the response of e to observed changes in m should depend on the ratio of the variance of the pure error component of changes in m to the variance of changes in κ.

In (32), the influence of real factors on the expected path of the nominal exchange rate comes through their effect on the expected paths of m-the money supply variable, and κ-the money demand variable. An alternative, analytically equivalent expression for $E[e(s);t]$ brings the influence of these real factors into sharper focus;

$$E[e(s);t]= E[P(s);t]-E[P^{*}(s);t]-\sigma.E[q(s);t] \tag{333}$$

where $E[P(s),t]$ is the expectation of (the logarithm of) the general level of domestic prices, as determined by

$$E[P(s),t]=(1/(\xi+\eta)).\sum_{j=0}^{\infty}(\eta/(\xi+\eta))^{j}.E[(m(s+j)-l(s+j));t] \tag{34}$$

where l is a measure of factors affecting (the logarithm of) the demand for domestic money that is defined by

$$l=\kappa-J.P^{*}-N(i^{*}+\rho)+(V-\sigma J).q+\eta.D^{e}(P^{*})+\eta\sigma D^{e}(q)+W.A \tag{35}$$

The results (33) to (35) represent the asset price version of the extended monetary model of exchange rate determination considered before. From these results, we find that a discounted sum of present and expected future money supplies affects the nominal exchange rate by affecting the general level of all domestic prices. Movements in the nominal exchange rate that are associated with expected or unexpected changes in this discounted sum of present and future m's are consistent with the maintenance of purchasing power parity. By the same token, changes in the foreign price level, which are not associated with changes in domestic money demand or supply or in the relative price of domestic goods in terms of foreign goods, induce movements in the nominal exchange rate that are consistent with purchasing power parity.

Real economic factors influence the exchange rate through two channels: to the extent that such factors affect the discounted sum of present and future levels of demand for domestic money (measured by the US), they induce movements in the nominal exchange rate that are consistent with purchasing power parity; however, to the extent that such real factors induce movements in the relative price of domestic goods in terms of foreign goods, they require movements in the nominal exchange rate and in prices that constitute divergences from purchasing power parity. When we combine the model of the nominal exchange rate embodied in (35)-(36) with the model of the real exchange rate discussed in the preceding section, we arrive at a general model in which the exchange rate exhibits the essential properties of an "asset price", while, at the same time, the general model also incorporates the key ingredients of both monetary models that focus on conditions of flow market equilibrium, as the critical determinants of exchange rates. This already general model of exchange rate determination can be further extended by introducing phenomena associated with macroeconomic disequilibria. The two modern approaches to the modelling of such phenomena are (a) the contracting models and (b) the incomplete information models. Both share the common feature that stabilization policy (especially monetary policy) has no capacity to affect the long-run equilibrium behavior of national output, but they differ critically in their implications for the successful short-run use of stabilization policy. In the contracting models, changes in the money supply that were unanticipated at the time when existing nominal contracts were established can temporarily affect the level of national output, and the government can use its freedom to act with respect to monetary policy (while private agents are locked into existing nominal contracts) to improve the performance of national output. In contrast, in the incomplete information models, unanticipated changes in the money supply can temporarily affect national output, but stabilization policies linked to past values or variables observed by private agents have no capacity to improve the performance of national output.

The key implications of these two approaches to modeling macroeconomic disequilibrium for the behavior of national output carry over from the closed economy setting in which they were originally developed to an open economy setting. In either approach, unanticipated money supply changes temporarily affect domestic output and, in general, have some effect on foreign output; but only in the contracting approach can stabilization policy be used successfully to improve the performance on national output. In addition to these implications with respect to national outputs, models that incorporate macroeconomic disequilibrium introduce the possibility that monetary disturbances may induce short-run price and exchange rate movements that diverge from purchasing power parity. In the incomplete information approach, such divergences are simply one of the manifestations of the real effects of unanticipated monetary changes, without any policy significance. In the contracting approach, stickiness of nominal prices resulting from existing nominal contracts may necessitate "overshooting" of the nominal exchange rate in response unanticipated monetary changes and an associated temporary but persistent change in the real exchange rate. This "overshooting" response to the nominal exchange rate may provide additional leverage for monetary policy to affect the short-run behavior of national output, and may increase the usefulness of exchange rates as indicators for the conduct of stabilization policy.

The Relative Price Effect: Relative price changes produced by exchange rate movements will cause changes in a nation's trade balance that will tend to restore (or preserve) equilibrium in the balance of payments. In a country whose currency depreciates exports will tend to rise, imports to fall, thus improving the trade balance and eliminating the incipient excess demand for foreign exchange.

This conclusion depends on the assumption that the elasticities of demand and supply are sufficiently large. Specifically, it assumes that the sum of elasticities of demand and supply of foreign exchange is greater than one, satisfying the Marshall-Lerner condition. This is what we shall take to be the normal case, but we should also note what happens if this assumption does not hold. If home country's demand for imports is inelastic, higher dollar prices of imports will not deter consumers, and a higher exchange rate will

not cause much, if any, reduction in home country's imports. In the limit, if the quantity of imports remains the same, their value in pounds will remain unchanged, while the value in dollars will increase in proportion to the exchange rate change. In this case home country's demand curve for foreign exchange is vertical as shown in Fig. 8.20.

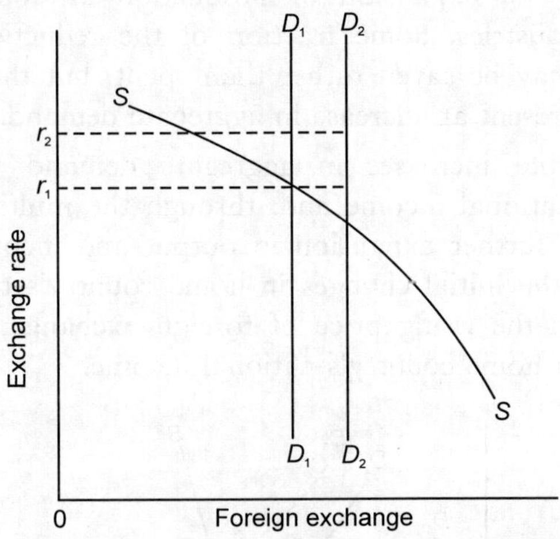

Fig. 8.20: Inelastic Demand and a Backward-bending Supply Curve for Foreign Exchange.

If foreign country's demand for imports is also inelastic, lower pound prices resulting from a dollar depreciation will not lead to an increase in the physical quantity of its imports. Consequently, fewer pounds will be supplied at the higher exchange rate, and foreign country's supply curve of pounds will be backward sloping, as shown in Fig. 8.20. Under these circumstances an increase in home country's demands for pounds, as shown by the shift from D_1D_1 to D_2D_2 in Fig. 8.20, will create an excess demand for pounds and cause the dollar price to rise. But now the rise in price does not restore equilibrium. Instead, the deficit in home country's balance of payments increases. Note that we do not have an equilibrium at the exchange rate r_2; excess demand will continue to push up the price of the pound. The foreign market is unstable.

Income Effect: Both the increase in home country's exports of goods and services and the decrease in its imports will tend to increase aggregate demand for home country's goods. The export increase is an increase in demand for the output of export industries, to which they respond by increasing production, hiring more workers, and generating increased income through payments to productive factors. In addition, when consumers decrease their purchases of imports, they will probably switch expenditures onto domestic goods whose prices are now cheaper relative to imports, thus inducing an expansion of production in domestic import competing industries. Some fraction of the reduction in import expenditure may be saved rather than spent, but the part that is spent will represent an increase in aggregate demand.

These initial increases in aggregate demand will generate increases in national income and, through the multiplier process, stimulate still further expansion in output and income. Here the point is that the initial changes in home country's trade balance, resulting from the rising price of foreign exchange, will tend to cause a rise in home country's national income.

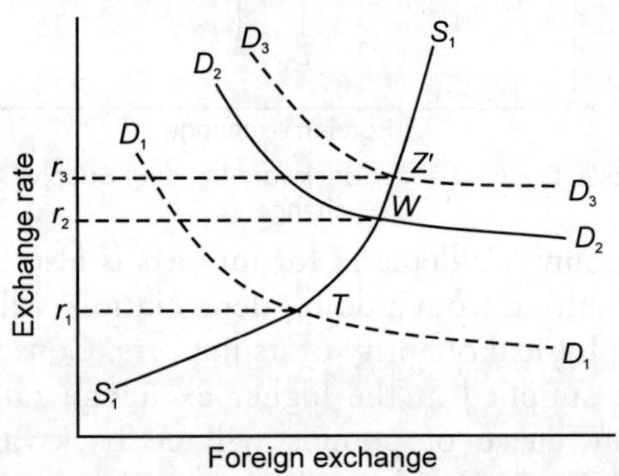

Fig. 8.21: Induced Shift in Demand for Foreign Exchange.

If this rise in national income is allowed to take place, it will in turn cause an increase in imports and thus a further increase in demand for foreign exchange. Because a nation's imports of goods and services are directly related to its national income, $M = mY$, when income increases, imports will also increase by an amount determined by the marginal propensity to import, m. It follows that the rise in imports induced by the increase in income will cause a further shift to the right in home country's demand for foreign exchange, thus upsetting the equilibrium that had apparently been reached at exchange rate r_2. The income effect tends to undo or reverse the movement toward external balance that was started by the exchange rate change. Hence, at exchange rate r_2, an incipient deficit again emerges. This situation can be represented by Fig. 8.21.

To remove the new incipient deficit, the exchange rate will now rise to r_3, producing a further price effect and induced income effect; and then another exchange rate change becomes necessary, and so. These successive "rounds" will diminish in size, and an equilibrium will eventually be reached at which both the exchange rate and national income will be stable. However, it is clear from the foregoing analysis that allowances for induced income effects will mean that a larger rise in the exchange rate must occur than would be necessary 8 if no income effect occurred. Therefore, if government policymakers wish to facilitate the process of adjustment and strengthen the tendency toward external balance with flexible exchange rates, they can take action to counteract or offset the induced rise in national income. That is, the authorities could use monetary or fiscal policy to stabilize national income, thus eliminating the induced imports that set off the second round. Then no reversal of the initial price effect would occur, and external balance would be achieved at exchange rate r_2.

The process of adjustment to other kinds of disturbances can be similarly analyzed.

NOTES

1. J.W. Angell, "Equilibrium in International Payments: The United States, 1919-1935", *Explorations in Economics* (New York, 1936), p. 14.
2. Ragnar Frisch, "On the Need for Forecasting a Multilateral Balance of Payments", *American Economic Review* (September 1947), p. 536.
3. International Monetary Fund, *Balance of Payments Year Book, 1938, 46, 47* (Washington, 1949), p. 5.
4. F. Machlup, "Three Concepts of the Balance of Payments and the so-called Dollar Shortage", *Economic Journal* (March 1950), p. 66.
5. *Ibid.*, p. 65.
6. *Ibid.*, p. 46.
7. *Ibid.*, p. 47.
8. G. Myrdal, *An International Economy* (London, 1956), pp. 21-22, 240.
9. Ragnar Nurkse, "A New Look at the Dollar Problem and the U.S. Balance of Payments", *Economia Internazionale* (February 1954), p. 52.

Theory of Foreign Exchange

9

By the words foreign exchange rate or rate of foreign exchange, we mean that rate at which the currency of one country is exchanged with that of the other. It can also be termed as the price of one currency in terms of another.

Just as other prices in the economy are determined by the interaction of buyers and sellers, exchange rates are determined by the interaction of the households, firms, and financial institutions that buy and sell foreign currencies in order to make international payments. The market in which international currency trades take place is called the foreign exchange market. The foreign exchange market performs three important functions:

(a) It transfers purchasing power from one currency to another and from one country to another.

(b) It provides credit for foreign trade.

(c) It furnishes facilities for hedging foreign exchange risks.

Out of these three functions, the first one is by far the most important. It is the fundamental cause for the existence of the foreign exchange market. The need of foreign market arises because there are as many national currencies as there are sovereign nations. The multitude of national currencies provides an extra dimension to every international economic transaction. Thus every international economic transaction requires a foreign exchange transaction, that is, the conversion of one currency into another. The primary function of the foreign exchange market is to perform this conversion of one currency into another. If a single currency were used throughout the world there would be no need for a foreign exchange market, and trade among nations would resemble trade among the various states of India. The foreign exchange market is the largest and most liquid financial market in the world, and includes trading between large banks, central banks, currency speculators, corporations, governments, and other institutions. The average daily volume in the global foreign exchange and related markets is continuously growing and was last reported to be over US$ 4 trillion in April 2007 by the Bank for International Settlement.

The foreign exchange dealers of commercial banks are constantly alert to the latest quotations in the various geographic spots of the markets. As a result, the foreign exchange market embraces all financial centers of the world. The foreign exchange market is not limited to a particular locality; rather it is an international market in which national currencies are traded. Because of its international character, the foreign exchange market is open around the clock. The economic force that keeps the various financial centers around the world united as a single market is known as arbitrage which is defined as the simultaneous purchase and sale of foreign currencies for the sake of profit. It arises either because the price of one currency in terms of another differs from one financial center to another or because the various rates of exchange are inconsistent.

Two point arbitrage (also known as spatial arbitrage) involves two currencies only. Let us suppose that the dollar exchanges for Rs. 47 in New York and for Rs. 47.20 in Mumbai. An arbitrageur can make a profit by buying dollar in New York at Rs. 47 and simultaneously selling them in Mumbai at Rs. 47.20. This kind of arbitrage tends to draw the two prices together by forcing up the price of the dollar in New York and depressing it in Mumbai. Even small discrepancies between the exchange rates quoted in various financial centers give rise to voluminous arbitrage.

Three-point arbitrage (also known as triangular arbitrage) involves three currencies. Its profitability is due to the inconsistency of the uniformly quoted rates. Let us consider three currencies: the rupee, the dollar, and the pound. All three currencies are traded in New York, London, and Mumbai. Suppose that the following prices prevail currently in all three financial centers:

£ 1 sells for either $ 2 or Rs. 80.

$ 1 sells for Rs. 47.

Since the same prices prevail in all financial centers, two-point arbitrage is no longer profitable. But the quoted prices are inconsistent; therefore an arbitrageur can make a profit as follows:

(a) Sell £ 1 for $ 2.

(b) Then sell each $ 1 for Rs. 47 to collect a total of Rs. 94.

(c) Finally, buy back the initial £ 1 for Rs. 80, and have a profit of Rs. 14.

Now we shall turn to the third function of the foreign exchange market, hedging foreign exchange risks. Ordinarily, export and import transactions involve periods of waiting, and the slightest unfavourable change in the exchange rate may involve exports and imports in losses completely unrelated to their normal business. The third function of the foreign exchange market, in addition to clearing and credit, is to provide hedging facilities to exporters and importers against possible losses due to exchange rate fluctuations. The possibility of loss because of an unfavourable change in the exchange rate is usually referred to as exchange risk. Covering an exchange risk is called hedging, and deliberately assuming an exchange risk is called speculation. Hedgers are people who dislike exchange risk insist on maintaining an exact balance between their assets and liabilities in foreign currencies. Speculators are those who think they know what the future rate of exchange will be and are willing to gamble, hold their assets in that currency which they expect to appreciate in value. A speculator with pessimistic expectations about the future price of a currency is called a bear; one with optimistic expectations, a bull. Another important form of trader speculation is what is usually referred to as leads and lags. This term refers to the adjustment that importers and exporters make in the timing of payments, the placement of orders, and the making of deliveries for the purpose of avoiding losses or making profits from an anticipated change in the rate of foreign exchange.

DETERMINATION OF EXCHANGE RATE

Rate of exchange in a free market is determined by the demand for and supply of foreign exchange or, in other words, by the supply of and demand for domestic currency because every demand for foreign exchange is identical with the supply of domestic currency and every supply of foreign exchange is identical with the demand for domestic currency.

Foreign Exchange Demand

The demand of foreign exchange can be measured as in terms of currency *A*, say Dollar for currency *B*, say Pound or (b) in terms of currency *B*, i.e. Pound for currency *A*, i.e. Dollar. Since both the ways yield to same result, we take the first way, i.e. the currency price of Dollar in terms of Pound.

The demand curve for pound is *DD* which slopes from left to right in Fig. 9.1. The shape of the demand curve depends on the elasticity of demand for imports. “If a country imports necessities and raw materials, we may expect the elasticity of demand for imports to be low and the quantity imported to be unsensitive to price changes. If, on the other hand, the country imported luxury goods and goods for which suitable substitutes exist, demand elasticities for imports might be high. Whether or not the country has a domestic import, competing industry is the second extremely imported factor. If the country has many well developed import-compelling industries, the elasticity of demand for imports most certainly is high. This is duc to the fact that if the price rises, import-competing industries will come in and take a larger share of the market and imports will fall; if the price falls, it will be the other way round.”[1]

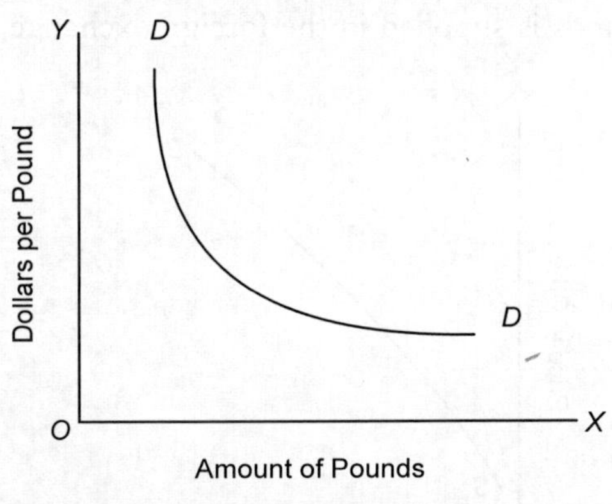

Fig. 9.1

Foreign Exchange Supply

The supply curve of foreign exchange is derived from the demand for imports. If the demand elasticity for an imported article is 1, the supply curve will be completely inelastic as *SS* in Fig. 9.2. The supply of foreign exchange shows the quantities of a currency, say, Pound, that would be supplied in the foreign exchange market at various dollar prices of pounds.

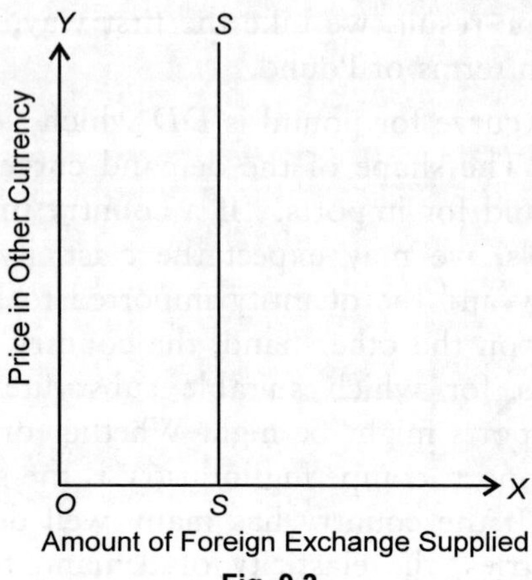

Fig. 9.2

Figure 9.3 shows one more supply curve which is upward sloping from left to right. Denoted by *SS*, this supply curve tells us that with the increase in dollar price of pounds, US goods and services turn out to be a better bargain for pound holders. As a consequence, a greater amount of pounds is supplied in the foreign exchange market.

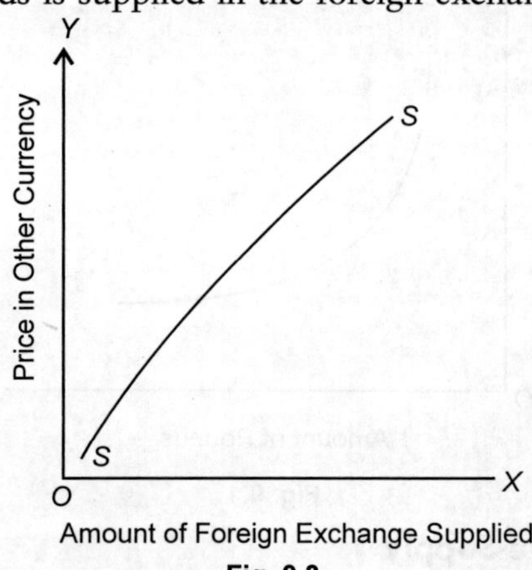

Fig. 9.3

Equilibrium

Let us now take the demand as well as the supply curve on the same figure and final out the equilibrium exchange rate.

Figure 9.4 shows how the equilibrium rate of exchange is determined when the market is left free. In panel [*A*], *SS* is the supply curve of the foreign exchange while D_1D_1, is the initial demand curve for it. Now suppose due to any reason whatsoever,

the demand for the foreign exchange increases and D_1D_1, curve shifts upwards to D_2D_2. The new equilibrium point now is E_1 in place of previous E and the new rate of foreign exchange is OR_1 instead of previous OR. This obviously lays its impacts on the supply side also and the supply now becomes S_1S_1 in panel [*B*]. Now to meet the increased demand, supply is increased to S_2S_2, thus establishing the equilibrium once again at E.

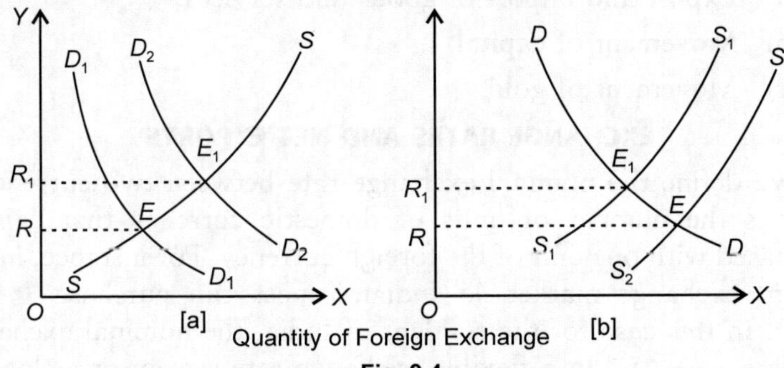

Fig. 9.4

The same process can be illustrated in Fig. 9.5 also. In this figure, the original equilibrium rate of exchange is OR and the equilibrium point E where the initial supply curve, S_1S_1 and the initial demand curve, D_1D_1 intersect. Now due to some reasons, the demand curve shifts to D_1D_1. The equilibrium is now determined at point E_1 and the rate of exchange is OR_1. To meet this increase in the foreign exchange demanded, the supply of the foreign exchange is increased, as a result of which the initial supply curve shifts to S_2S_2. The equilibrium hence determined is E_2 which brings the exchange rate level to the previous OR.

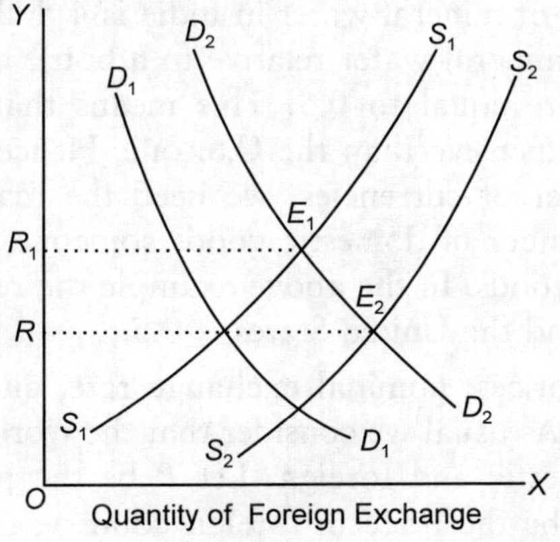

Fig. 9.5

Thus we see that if left to operate on their own, the market forces keep the rate of exchange at equilibrium level and the stability in the foreign exchange market is restored after temporary instability.

The demand for and supply of foreign exchange arise, mainly speaking, from the following transactions:

(a) Export and import of goods and services.

(b) Movement of capital.

(c) Movement of gold.

EXCHANGE RATES AND NET EXPORTS

We define the nominal exchange rate between two currencies, s_{nom}, as the number of units of domestic currency that can be purchased with one unit of the foreign currency. For instance, in the foreign exchange market 45 Indian rupees can purchase 1 U.S. dollar. In this case for the resident of India, the nominal exchange rate is $s_{nom} = 45$. In a flexible exchange rate system or a floating exchange rate system, nominal exchange rates are not officially fixed but are determined by the foreign exchange market conditions. In a fixed exchange rate system, nominal exchange rates are officially set at officially determined levels which are maintained by the commitment of nations' central banks to buy and sell their currencies at the fixed rate. Here one point should be noted that the nominal exchange rate does not tell about the purchasing power of a currency. It means that if a bottle of mineral water costs 2 dollar in U.S., it is not necessary, it will cost 90 rupees in India. Suppose for instance, one bottle of mineral water costs 180 rupees in India. That is the price of mineral water in India is 4 dollars. The price of a bottle of U.S. mineral water relative to a bottle of Indian mineral water is therefore equal to 0.5. This means that Indian mineral water is more expensive than the U.S. one. Hence, to measure the purchasing power of currencies, we need the real exchange rate, which is the number of domestic goods someone gets in exchange for one foreign goods. In the above example the real exchange rate between India and the United States is 0.5.

In general, prices, nominal exchange rate, and real exchange, are interrelated. As usual we consider that the world consists of two economies, domestic and foreign. Let P be the price in domestic country and $\tilde{P}$ be the price in foreign country, measured in their

own currencies. According to the definitions of s, s_{nom}, P and $\tilde{P}$, we have

$$s = \frac{s_{nom}\tilde{P}}{P} \tag{1}$$

A modern economy produces a large number of goods and real exchange rates are usually based on price index to measure P and $\tilde{P}$. In this case, the real exchange rate is the rate of exchange between a typical basket of goods in one economy and a typical basket of goods in the other economy. Increase in the real exchange rate over time indicates that the goods of the domestic country are becoming less expensive relative to the goods of the other country. For simplicity, we consider that real exchange rate is determined by the incomes and the real interest rates in the domestic and foreign economies. This implies that an increase in foreign income, $\tilde{Y}$, or the domestic real interest, r, tends to raise the demand for the domestic currency and thus appreciate the real exchange rate, S. An increase in domestic income, Y, or foreign real interest rate, $\tilde{r}$, tends to increase the supply of domestic currency and depreciate the real exchange rate. Let us consider a function, $s=f(Y, \tilde{Y}, r, \tilde{r})$ which shows the relation for values of output, Y, the real interest rate, r, and the price level, P.

When the nominal exchange rate, s_{nom}, rises (falls) so that a dollar buys more (less) Indian rupees, we say that the rupee has undergone a nominal depreciation (appreciation). The terms, depreciation and appreciation, are used in flexible-exchange-rates systems. In a fixed-exchange-rate system, a weakening (strengthening) of the currency is called devaluation (revaluation). Similarly, when the real exchange rate, S, rises (falls), we say that the rupee has undergone a real depreciation (appreciation). Percentage change in the real exchange rate is given by

$$\frac{\Delta s}{s} = \frac{\Delta s_{nom}}{s_{nom}} + \frac{\Delta \tilde{P}}{\tilde{P}} - \frac{\Delta P}{P}$$

As $\frac{\Delta P}{P}$ and $\frac{\Delta \tilde{P}}{\tilde{P}}$ are respectively the percentage change in the domestic and foreign prices, we can represent these in terms of domestic rate of inflation, π, and the foreign rate of inflation, $\tilde{\pi}$, and the above expression can be written as

$$\frac{\Delta s}{s} = \frac{\Delta s_{\text{nom}}}{s_{\text{nom}}} + \tilde{\pi} - \pi \quad (2)$$

This equation states that the rate of real exchange rate depreciation is equation to the rate of nominal exchange rate depreciation plus the excess of foreign inflation over domestic inflation. Let us rewrite the equation (2) as

$$\frac{\Delta s_{\text{nom}}}{s_{\text{nom}}} = \frac{\Delta s}{s} + \pi - \tilde{\pi}$$

From the above equation we find that the appreciation of the domestic currency requires a real appreciation and/or lower the domestic inflation. If we consider the concept of purchasing power parity (PPP), we find that PPP tends to hold in the long term, but over short periods it does not describe exchange rate behaviour well. In this case, the real exchange rate is 1, therefore from (1) we hav e

$$s_{\text{nom}} = \frac{P}{\tilde{P}} \quad (3)$$

Similarly from (2) we have

$$\frac{\Delta s_{\text{nom}}}{s_{\text{nom}}} = \pi - \tilde{\pi} \quad (4)$$

Now we shall consider the real exchange rate. When the real exchange rate falls, the households in the domestic country are able to obtain more foreign goods and service in exchange for a given amount of domestic production, other conditions remaining the same. Since, Net exports = exports – imports, the real exchange rate affects the country's net exports. In case of low real exchange rate, a unit of foreign goods can buy little domestic goods, domestic residents will like to buy many foreign goods and foreign residents will want to purchase relatively less domestic goods. Hence, if all the other factors which may affect an economy's export and import are kept constant, then the lower the real exchange rate is, the lower a country's net exports will be.

THE MONETARY VIEW OF EXCHANGE RATE DETERMINATION

There are many versions of monetary model of exchange rate determination all of which are outgrowths and extensions of the following three versions of the asset approach which have attained a considerable degree of popularity:

(a) The flex-price monetary approach to the exchange rate;

(b) The fix-price monetary approach to the exchange rate; and

(c) The currency substitution model.

In order to explain the variability of exchange rates, we shall move away from the flow demand/supply analysis discussed in the previous sections, to the asset approach to the exchange rate. It is argued that the exchange rate should be viewed as an asset price since it is by definition the price of one national money in terms of another. Therefore proponents of the asset approach argue that one should use tools normally used for the determination of other asset prices in analyzing the determinants of exchange rates, rather than analyzing the exchange rate in terms of flow demand and flow supplies. Also, since assets are stocks, equilibrium is defined as a situation where the stock demand for money is equal to the stock supply of money. Flows of assets across the foreign exchanges can occur, but such flows are a reflection of disequilibrium between money demand and money supply and must eventually cease. Another implication of regarding the exchange rate as an asset price is that such prices are usually regarded as being determined in efficient markets. An efficient asset market is one in which market participants exploit all profitable trading opportunities and force the current price to reflect all available information. Under certain circumstances this implies that exchange rates should behave randomly.

The Flex-Price Monetary Approach to the Exchange Rate

We consider a small country which faces an exogenously determined foreign interest rate, i^*, and price level, P^*. The home country produces a single traded good which is a perfect substitute for the foreign goods and thus purchasing power parity holds continuously and given by

$$s = p - p^* \tag{1}$$

where s, p and p^* are logarithmic values of the corresponding level terms. The central bank of the home country issues money, which is assumed to be non-traded and a bond which is a perfect substitute for a foreign bond. We further assume that asset holders can adjust their portfolios instantly after a disturbance, and thus capital is perfectly mobile, uncovered interest parity is given by

$$\tilde{s}^e = i - i^* \tag{2}$$

We also have

$$\Delta K = k(i - i^* - \tilde{s}^e) \tag{2a}$$

$$m^D - p = \alpha_1 y - \alpha_2 i \tag{3}$$

where

ΔK = capital flow

m^D = natural logarithm of money demand

p = natural logarithm of the price level

y = natural logarithm of the level of real national income

i = interest rate

α_1 = elasticity

α_2 = semi-elasticity

The money supply is assumed to be determined exogenously and money markets are in equilibrium, i.e.

$$m^D = m = m^S \tag{4}$$

The exchange rate is assumed to be perfectly flexible, therefore, ΔK must be equal to zero in this model and hence ΔM must be equal to ΔD.

From equations (3) and (4) we have

$$s = m - \alpha_1 y + \alpha_2 i \tag{5}$$

By normalizing the foreign price level to unity (and thus its logarithmic value equals zero) and substituting in (1) we have

$$s = m - \alpha_1 y + \alpha_2 i \tag{6}$$

Equation (6) gives the standard small country flex-price monetary approach reduced form. From the above equation we see that an x percent increase in the domestic money supply leads to an x percent increase in s (depreciation). An increase in income leads to an exchange rate appreciation. Similarly an increase in the domestic interest rate leads to an exchange rate depreciation and again this is in contrast to the result that an increase in the home interest rate led to an appreciation of the exchange rate. To understand the puzzling effects of y and i we shall consider that these variables affect the exchange rate via their effect on money demand. Thus an increase in income increases the transactions demand for money and with a constant nominal money supply money market equilibrium can only be maintained if the domestic price level falls and this in turn can only occur if the exchange rate changes. Thus the exchange rate appreciates in order to restore equality between real money demand and real money supply and hence the price level falls. The positive effect of the domestic rate of interest on the exchange rate reflects the effect of interest rates on money demand. We consider full employment in home country and also nominal interest rates are assumed to obey the Fisher parity relationship which is given as

$$i = r + \tilde{p}^e \tag{7}$$

where

r = real interest rate, and

$\tilde{p}^e$ = expected inflation rate.

Considering the real interest rate to be constant, equation (6) can be rewritten as

$$s = m - \alpha_1 y + \alpha_2 \tilde{p}^e \tag{8}$$

From the above equation we see that an increase in the domestic interest rate reflects an increase in expected inflation and a reduced desire to hold real money balances. Since the nominal money supply is exogenously fixed, the only way that real money balances can be altered is by an increase in the price level which is accommodated by an exchange rate depreciation. Now we shall introduce expectations in our analysis because regarding the exchange rate as an asset price means that expectations about the future course of its determinants will be important for the current determination of the exchange rate.

By substituting equation (2) in equation (6), and by normalizing the foreign interest rate to have a value of zero we have

$$s = m - \alpha_1 y + \alpha_2 \tilde{s}^e \tag{9}$$

Or, dating the variables

$$s_t = m_t - \alpha_1 y_t + \alpha_2 (s^e_{t+1} - s_t) \tag{9a}$$

where we have used $\tilde{s}^e = \tilde{p}^e$. We assume rational expectations, and thus agents know the process of exchange rate determination and its underlying stochastic structure then we have

$$s_{t+1}^e = E_t\, s_{t+1} \tag{10}$$

where E_t is the expectational operator conditioned upon the information set available at period *t*. Thus the factors that determine the expected exchange rate in the monetary model are what agents expected the money supply and income to be in the future. This can be illustrated as follows.

Equation (9a) can be rewritten as

$$s_t = \frac{1}{1+\alpha_2}[m_t - \alpha_1 y_t + \alpha_2 E_t s_{t+1}] \tag{11}$$

This equation can be used to find the expected value of the exchange rate in any future period *t* + *j* as

$$E_t s_{t+j} = \frac{1}{1+\alpha_2}[E_t (m - \alpha_1 y)_{t+j} + \alpha_2 E_t s_{t+j+1}] \tag{12}$$

By repeatedly substituting for $E_t s$ in (11) for all future time periods we get the rational expectations reduced form exchange rate equation as

$$s_t = \frac{1}{1+\alpha_2} \sum_{j=0}^{\infty} \left(\frac{\alpha_2}{1+\alpha_2} \right)^j E_t [m_{t+j} - \alpha_1 y_{t+j}] \tag{13}$$

From the above equation we find that the current exchange rate depends not just on current excess money supplies but also on expected future excess money supplies. The discounting factor, α_2, discounts expected future money growth into the current spot rate in a manner analogous to that in which revisions in expected future earnings are discounted into equity prices. The effect of current changes in the money supply on the exchange rate depends crucially on what people perceive as the stochastic structure underlying the authorities' money supply rule.

In econometrically implementing the monetary model researchers have moved from the small country model to a two country model. This seems sensible since most exchange rates studied are bilateral rates and it is difficult to think of an exchange rate in which foreign impulses are not going to be important in the determination of that exchange rate. Therefore we shall introduce foreign impulses in our analysis as follows.

Rewriting equation (6) without the normalization of p^* to be equal to unity we have

$$s = m - p^* - \alpha_1 y + \alpha_2 i \qquad (14)$$

and assuming that p^* is determined in the same way as p, we can write

$$p^* = m^* - \alpha_3 y^* + \alpha_4 i^* \qquad (15)$$

Substituting equation (15) in equation (16) we get

$$s = m - m^* - \alpha_1 y + \alpha_3 y^* + \alpha_2 i - \alpha_4 i^* \qquad (16)$$

Equation (16) is two country version of equation (6). In this equation home country variables have the same interpretation as above and foreign currency variables have the opposite effect on the exchange rate to home country variables.

The Fix-Price Monetary Approach to the Exchange Rate

This model of exchange rate consists of an economy which is small and faces an exogenously given foreign price and interest rate. The domestic money, which is held only in the home country and a foreign bond is issued by the monetary authorities. We consider perfectly mobile capital and full employment in the country. The country produces a single traded good which is assumed to be an imperfect substitute, at least in the short run, for the foreign produced good. We assume *ppp* to be hold in the long run, but in the short run deviations from *ppp* may be allowed. Long-run ppp can be described by the following equation where a bar denotes a long-run, or equilibrium, value.

$$\bar{s} = \bar{p} - \bar{p}^* \qquad (17)$$

In the flex-price monetary model the expected change in the exchange rate was shown to be continuously equal to the expected inflation differential. Since in the fix-price monetary model, *ppp* does not hold in the short run, we shall consider an alternative representation for the expected change in the exchange rate. We consider that in the short run, the exchange rate is expected to return to the equilibrium value, $\bar{s}$, by a constant proportion, ϕ, of the current gap,

$$\dot{s}^e = \phi(\bar{s} - s) \qquad (18)$$

where ϕ is a parameter, must if agents have perfect foresight be consistent with the underlying model. The monetary section of the fix-price monetary model is assumed identical to the flex-price monetary model which has been represented by equations (3) and (4) above.

Since the price level adjusts in proportion to excess demand, the demand function is assumed to have the following form:

$$d = \beta_0 + \beta_1 (s - p) + \beta_2 y - \beta_3 i \tag{19}$$

where d represents the logarithm of demand. Since $(s - p)$ term captures the effects of the real exchange rate on the trade balance and hence demand, that is, if s rises relative to p demand will be switched towards home goods. The y term reflects the effect of income on expenditure magnitudes such as consumption. The i term reflects the effect of the interest rate on domestic absorption and thus an increase in i results *ceteris paribus* in a fall in aggregate demand. The β_0 term is a shift parameter which reflects government spending. Since the output is fixed at the full employment level y, then the change in the price level is given by

$$\dot{p} = \Pi (d - y) = \Pi [\beta_0 + \beta_1 (s - p) + (\beta_2 - 1) y - \beta_3 i] \tag{20}$$

where Π is the speed of adjustment parameter.

Now consider the following figure.

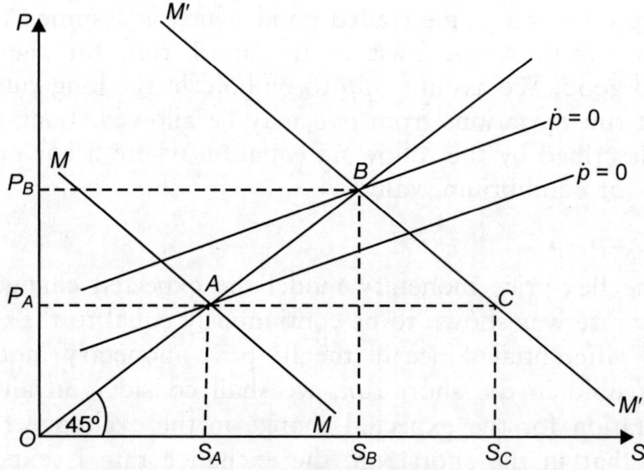

Fig. 9.6: Overshooting and the Fix-Price Model.

In the above figure *MM* line represents combinations of s and p consistent with asset market equilibrium—at all points in time the money market is assumed to clear and uncovered interest parity holds continuously. The point $\dot{p}$=0, gives the locus of s and p that are consistent with money and goods market equilibrium. Here one point should be noted that the asset markets are continuously in equilibrium whereas goods market equilibrium is only a long-run feature.

Suppose an unexpected x percent increase in the domestic money supply from the initial equilibrium at A. Since monetary homogeneity is a long-run property of this model, the exchange rate and the price level must change in proportion to the increase in the money supply and hence the new long-run equilibrium is at point B. On the other hand, in the short run prices are sticky and therefore goods market equilibrium is not immediately attained and the money market is not cleared via a price increase. Instead the money market is cleared in the short run by a fall in the domestic interest rate and hence in the short run the exchange rate changes from A to C. Here we see that the exchange rate overshoots the new long-run equilibrium exchange rate, i.e. $S_C > S_B$. This follows from the uncovered interest parity equation which implies that the home interest rate can only be below the foreign rate if market participants expect the exchange rate to appreciate and the latter can only occur if the current spot rate moves by more than the long-run exchange rate. The overshooting of the exchange rate can be given by the following equation.

$$\frac{ds}{dm}=1+1/\alpha_2 \phi \tag{21}$$

Hence the extent of any exchange rate overshooting depends upon the interest response of the demand for money and the expectations coefficient. If the interest elasticity of money demand is low, any change in the money supply will result in a relatively large change in the interest rate to restore equilibrium and therefore a relatively large change in the expected exchange rate to offset it. Here one point should be noted that the exchange rate overshooting is a result of the discrepancy of adjustment speeds in goods and asset markets; asset markets adjust instantly whereas goods markets adjust only slowly over time. This is in contrast to the flex-price monetary model where the exchange rate overshoots as a result of agents' expectations of the course of future exogenous variables.

The Hybrid Fix-flex Price Monetary Model

Inflationary expectations, a prominent feature of the flex-price monetary model, have been ignored in the fix-price monetary model. To come out of this discrepancy of the fix-price model, a hybrid model which combines the assumption of short-run price rigidity and also models agents' inflationary expectations has been provided by Frankel. The elements of both the fix and flex-price monetary approaches are considered in this model. Interest parity equation with inflationary expectations can be given by

$$\dot{s}^e = \phi(\bar{s} - s) + \dot{p}^e - \dot{p}^{e^*} \quad (22)$$

At $s = \bar{s}$, in long-run equilibrium the exchange rate is expected to change at the long-run inflation differential. The long run exchange rate is determined, as in the fixed and flex-price monetary models, by *ppp* and monetary equilibrium. In this model we consider, the foreign money market as in the empirical implementation of the flex-price monetary model. Thus we have

$$\bar{s} = \bar{m} - \bar{m}^* - \alpha_1(\bar{y} - \bar{y}^*) + \alpha_2(\dot{p}^e - \dot{p}^{e^*}) \quad (23)$$

Substituting (22) into (2) we get the short run exchange rate as

$$s - \bar{s} = \frac{-1}{\phi}[(i - \dot{p}^e) - (i^* - \dot{p}^{e^*})] \quad (24)$$

where the current exchange rate differs from its equilibrium value by a real interest differential. Let us consider a once-and-for-all increase in the money supply. Now the exchange rate must overshoot its long-run equilibrium in order to maintain interest parity. But if the money supply increase causes individuals to revise their inflationary expectations upwards, then according to equation (24), the initial exchange rate depreciation will be greater in the hybrid model. Here one question arises whether the fix price, flex-price or hybrid model provides the better description on the exchange rate.

Substituting equation (23) into (24) and assuming that current equilibrium money supplies and income levels are given by their current actual levels, we get the following equation:

$$s = m - m^* - \alpha_1(y - y^*) + \alpha_2(\dot{p}^e - \dot{p}^{e^*}) + \frac{1}{\phi}[(i - \dot{p}^e) - (i^* - \dot{p}^{e^*})] \quad (25)$$

From the above equation we see that

(a) If we consider fix-price monetary model then we expect $1/\phi$ to be negative and α_2 to be zero.

(b) In the flex-price monetary approach we expect α_2 to be positive and $1/\phi$ to be zero.

(c) And if the hybrid model is considered we expect α_2 to be positive and $1/\phi$ to be negative.

The Currency Substitution Approach to Exchange Rate

The currency substitution approach to exchange rate was first used by Girton and Roper in 1981 to describe the situations where investors hold more than one currency. In this section we shall examine the implications of currency substitution for the behaviour of exchange rates, the ability of central banks to adopt monetary targets and the implications it has for inflation.

In the flex-price and fix-price models, we have made an unrealistic assumption that monetary services are only provided by the domestic currency. But in actual practice, international companies which operate in various countries hold a variety of currencies. Thus the monetary services may be provided by other currencies and may be illustrated by the following equation:

$$s = m - \Omega - \alpha_1 y + \alpha_2 \dot{s}^e \tag{26}$$

where Ω denotes the proportion of monetary services provided by domestic money.

An increase in Ω, by increasing the demand for domestic money results in an exchange rate appreciation. We consider that the share of domestic currency depends upon the expected change in the exchange rate which in turn is dependent on expected monetary growth, $\tilde{m}^e$, and the uncertainty with which such expectations are held, denoted by the variance of monetary growth, $\tilde{m}^e$. Thus we have

$$\Omega = \beta_0 \dot{m}^e + \beta_1 \operatorname{var} \dot{m}^e; \quad \beta_0 < 0, \beta_1 < 0 \tag{27}$$

Substituting the value of Ω in equation (26) and considering $\tilde{s}^e = \tilde{m}^e$ we have

$$s = m - \alpha_1 y + (\alpha_2 - \beta_0)\dot{m}^e + \beta_1 \operatorname{var} \dot{m}^e \tag{28}$$

Since $\beta_0 < 0$, therefore $\alpha_2 - \beta_0 > 0$ in the above equation. Thus in addition to the traditional monetary effects of m and y on the exchange rate, the above equation demonstrates the effect of currency substitution on the exchange rate.

EXCHANGE RATE AND THE TERMS OF TRADE IN A TWO COUNTRY MONETARY MODEL

In this section we shall consider the monetary model of international trade developed by Ohyama in 1991. In this model we shall study an interaction of monetary and real factors affecting the terms of trade and governing the adjustment process of current account imbalances under the system of flexible rates. The following assumptions are made in this model.

(a) There are two countries: Home and Foreign.

(b) Two goods are produced in the economy: goods 1 and 2.

(c) Markets are perfectly competitive.

(d) The factor endowment and production technology of each country are fixed.

(e) The factors of production are fully employed.

(f) There is free trade between two countries with no transportation costs.

(g) Home country exports goods 1 and Foreign country exports goods 2.

(h) Moneys are held as financial assets by households of the two countries.

(i) Moneys can be exchanged freely and the exchange rate is determined through foreign exchange market.

Let a country's nominal wealth, $\bar{W}$, is a function of the exchange rate, e, defined as the price of Foreign's currency in terms of Home's currency and the current transfer of Home money, $\bar{T}_h$, and that of Foreign money, $\bar{T}_f$, as follows

$$W = V(e) + T_h + eT_f$$

$$\tilde{W} = \tilde{V}(e) + \frac{\tilde{T}_h}{e} + \tilde{T}_f \tag{1}$$

The wealth constraints of the two countries are given by

$$D_h + eD_f = W, \ \frac{\tilde{D}_e}{e} + \tilde{D}_f = \tilde{W} \tag{2}$$

where $\bar{D}_h$ and $\bar{D}_f$ are respectively the demand for Home currency and Foreign currency.

Now suppose that a country's demand for domestic money is a function of the domestic country's nominal wealth and expected rate of increase of the exchange rate entertained by the domestic residents, $\bar{\pi}$, as follows.

$$D_h = \alpha(\pi)W, \ \frac{\tilde{D}_h}{e} = \tilde{\alpha}(\tilde{\pi})\tilde{W}, \tag{3}$$

$$0 \leq \bar{\alpha}(\bar{\pi}) \leq 1, \quad \bar{\alpha}'(\bar{\pi}) < 0$$

The total demand for a country's money is equal to its total supply

$$\alpha(\pi)W + \tilde{\alpha}(\pi)e\tilde{W} = M + T_h + \tilde{T}_h,$$

$$(1-\alpha)W + (1-\tilde{\alpha})e\tilde{W} = e(\tilde{M} + T_f + \tilde{T}_f) \tag{4}$$

where $\bar{M}$ are Home's and Foreign's initial supply of money and we made the use of the following, which can be obtained from (2) and (3).

$$D_f = (1-\alpha)\frac{W}{e}, \ \ \tilde{D}_f = (1-\tilde{\alpha})\tilde{W}$$

The value of the world total wealth is equal to the value of the world total supply of money. Adding the two equations of (4) we get

$$W + e\tilde{W} = M + T_h + \tilde{T}_h + e(\tilde{M} + T_f + \tilde{T}_f) \tag{5}$$

From equations (1) and (4) we have

$$\alpha(V + T_h + eT_f) + \tilde{\alpha}(e\tilde{V} + \tilde{T}_h + e\tilde{T}_f) = M + T_h + \tilde{T}_h \tag{6}$$

Equation (6) determines the exchange rate when the other variables in the equation are given. Equation (6) is interpreted as that the exchange rate is determined to equilibrate the total demand for the foreign money with the total supply of the foreign money.

Now consider that $\bar{p}_j$ denotes the prices of good j in the domestic currency. The international price arbitrage is given by

$$p_j = e\bar{p}_j,\ j=1,\ 2$$

The relative price of goods 2 relative to goods 1 is given by

$$p = p_2/p_1 = \tilde{p}_2/\tilde{p}_1$$

The excess demand functions are assumed to be dependent on the relative price and the country's real wealth and its wealth in terms of its exportable as follows

$$E_j = E_j\left(p, \frac{W}{p_1}\right),\ \tilde{E}_j = \tilde{E}_j\left(p, \frac{\tilde{W}}{\tilde{p}_2}\right)$$

Commodity markets are at equilibrium, i.e.

$$E_j\left(p, \frac{W}{e\tilde{p}_1}\right) + \bar{E}_j\left(p, \frac{\tilde{W}}{p\tilde{p}_1}\right) = 0,\ j=1,\ 2 \tag{7}$$

Short-run equilibrium in this model is defined as the state at which both equation (6) and (7) are satisfied for fixed $\bar{T}_h, \bar{T}_f$ and $\bar{\pi}$.

Home country's current account surplus measured in the units of Foreign currency, B, is defined as

$$B = \tilde{p}_1\,\tilde{E}_1\left(p, \frac{\tilde{W}}{p\tilde{p}_1}\right) - \tilde{p}_2\,E_2\left(p, \frac{W}{p\tilde{p}_1}\right) \tag{8}$$

Each country's wealth varies over time at the rate of its current account surplus as

$$\frac{\dot{W}}{e} = -\dot{\tilde{W}} = B \tag{9}$$

The condition of the current account equilibrium is given by

$$\tilde{E}_1\left(p, \frac{\tilde{W}}{p\tilde{p}_1}\right) - p\,E_2\left(p, \frac{W}{p\tilde{p}_1}\right) = 0 \tag{10}$$

Home country's and Foreign country's wealth can be determined using equation (5) and (10) along with $\bar{M}$, e, p and $\tilde{p}_1$, $\bar{T}_h = \bar{T}_f = 0$. The world economy's long-run equilibrium is defined by equations (10), (6) and (7) for given $\bar{M}$ and $\bar{\pi} = 0$.

Determination of Exchange Rate and Price Dynamics

From equations (2) and (3), we have

$$\frac{e}{W}\frac{\partial W}{\partial e}=\frac{eD_f}{W}=1-\alpha,\quad \frac{e}{\tilde{W}}\frac{\partial \tilde{W}}{\partial e}=-\frac{e\tilde{D}_h}{\tilde{W}}=-\tilde{\alpha} \tag{11}$$

Increase in exchange rate increases the Home's nominal wealth and reduces the Foreign's nominal wealth. From equation (11) we have

$$\frac{\partial\left[\alpha(\pi)W+\tilde{\alpha}(\pi)e\tilde{W}\right]}{\partial e}=\alpha(1-\alpha)\frac{W}{e}+\tilde{\alpha}(1-\tilde{\alpha})\tilde{W}>0$$

It implies that total demand for Home money, $\alpha W+\tilde{\alpha}e\tilde{W}$, rises in e. Since, the money supply is fixed, the equilibrium exchange rate is determined at point E as shown in Fig. 8.7.

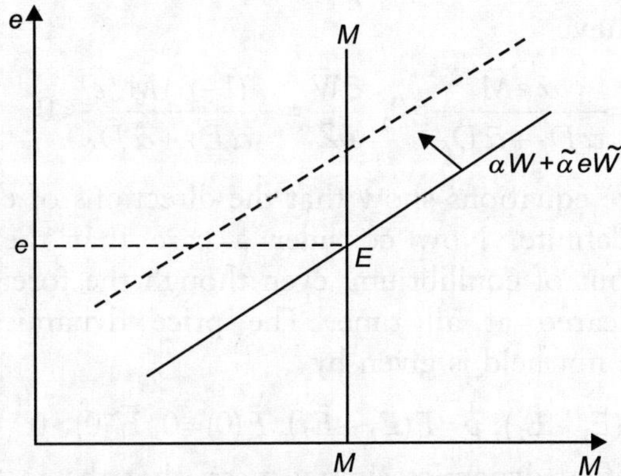

Fig. 8.7: Determination of Exchange Rate.

Suppose there is a rise in the expected rate of depreciation of Home currency. In this situation the public is motivated to sell Home money in exchange for Foreign money. This results in a left ward shift of the demand curve as shown in the above figure. In this situation the monetary authority of either country intervenes in the foreign exchange market selling Foreign money in exchange for Home money. For a fixed change rate, this operation causes the total supply of Home money to fall and the total supply of Foreign money to rise. The demand curve shifts to the left.

Now consider that a monetary transfer from Foreign to Home brings about a rise in W and a fall in $\tilde{W}$. If Home's propensity to hold Home currency, α, is greater than Foreign's propensity to hold home currency, $\tilde{\alpha}$, then the demand curve shifts to the right, resulting in the appreciation of Home currency. From equations (2) and (11), we have

$$\frac{\partial e}{\partial Z} = -\frac{(\alpha - \tilde{\alpha})e}{\alpha D_f + \tilde{\alpha}\tilde{D}_f} \tag{12}$$

where Z stands for the sum of the transfer and we use $dZ = dT_f = -d\tilde{T}_f$.

An increase in the monetary transfer from Foreign to Home results in an appreciation (depreciation) of home currency if and only if $\alpha > (<) \tilde{\alpha}$. Now we shall prove this lemma as follows.

If $\tilde{\alpha} = 0$, i.e. foreigners do not hold Home currency, then the transfer causes Home currency to appreciate. From equations (1) and (12) we have

$$\frac{\partial W}{\partial Z} = \frac{\tilde{\alpha} e \tilde{M}}{\alpha D_f + \tilde{\alpha}\tilde{D}_f} > 0, \quad \frac{\partial \tilde{W}}{\partial Z} = -\frac{(1-\alpha)M/e}{\alpha D_f + \tilde{\alpha}\tilde{D}_f} < 0$$

The above equations show that the directions of effects on the wealth are definite. Now consider a case that the commodity markets are out of equilibrium, even though the foreign exchange market is cleared at all time. The price dynamics when the equations are not held is given by

$$\dot{\tilde{p}} = \tilde{F}(E_1 + \tilde{E}_1), \ \dot{p} = F(E_2 + \tilde{E}_2), \ \bar{F}(0) = 0, \ \bar{F}'(0) > 0 \tag{13}$$

The specified dynamics simply mean that the money price of each good rises when the total demand for that good exceeds its total supply. Before stating stability conditions, we consider few assumptions.

We assume that the current account is balanced, i.e.

$$\tilde{p}_1 \tilde{E}_1 = \tilde{p}_2 E_2 > 0$$

The elasticity of a country's excess demand, $\bar{\eta}_j$, for good j with respect to the relative price is given as

$$\eta_j \equiv -\frac{p}{E_j}\frac{\partial E_j}{\partial p}, \quad \tilde{\eta}_j \equiv \frac{p}{\tilde{E}_j}\frac{\partial \tilde{E}_j}{\partial p},$$

where $\bar{\eta}_j$ may be either positive or negative.

Country's propensity to spend, $\bar{m}_j$, on good j, can be given by

$$m_1 \equiv \frac{\partial E_1}{\partial(W/p_1)}, \quad m_2 \equiv \frac{1}{p}\frac{\partial E_1}{\partial(W/p_1)},$$

$$\tilde{m}_1 \equiv p\frac{\partial \tilde{E}_1}{\partial(\tilde{W}/\tilde{p}_2)}, \quad \tilde{m}_2 \equiv \frac{\partial \tilde{E}_2}{\partial(\tilde{W}/\tilde{p}_2)}.$$

We assume that $\bar{m}_j > 0, j = 1, 2$. Now we consider

$$\varepsilon_j \equiv \eta_j + \tilde{\eta}_j, \quad \tilde{\varepsilon}_j \equiv m_j W + \tilde{m}_j e \tilde{W}.$$

By assumption, we always have $\tilde{\varepsilon}_j > 0$. The equilibrium point of (13) is locally stable if the determinant of its Jacobian matrix is positive and its trace is negative. The determinant is positive if

$$\tilde{\varepsilon}_2 \varepsilon_1 + \tilde{\varepsilon}_1 \varepsilon_2 + (m_1 \tilde{m}_2 - m_2 \tilde{m}_1)\frac{W\tilde{W}}{\tilde{p}_2 E_2} > 0 \tag{14}$$

and the trace is negative if $\tilde{\varepsilon}_j > 0$ and

$$\varepsilon_2 + \frac{\tilde{m}_2 \tilde{W}}{\tilde{p}_2 E_2} > 0 \tag{15}$$

The equilibrium point is locally stable if (14) and (15) hold near the point. To rewrite these two conditions, we define

$$E \equiv E_1 + p E_2, \quad \tilde{E} \equiv \frac{\tilde{E}_1}{p} + \tilde{E}_2.$$

$\bar{E}$ is a country's excess expenditure measured in the units of the country's exportables. Also assume that $\bar{E}$ is not affected by a change in the relative price of its importables in the neighbour of the equilibrium, or

$$\frac{\partial E}{\partial p} = 0, \quad \frac{\partial \tilde{E}}{\partial(1/p)} = 0, \tag{16}$$

where $E = \tilde{E} = 0$. From the definitions of and (16), we have

$$\eta_1 = \eta_2 - 1, \quad \tilde{\eta}_2 = \tilde{\eta}_1 - 1.$$

Under the above equations, we can rewrite conditions (14) and (15) as follows

$$\eta_m \equiv (\tilde{\varepsilon}_1 + \tilde{\varepsilon}_2)(\tilde{\eta}_1 + \eta_2 - 1) + (m_1 \tilde{m}_2 - m_2 \tilde{m}_1)\frac{W\tilde{W}}{\tilde{p}_2 E_2} > 0,$$

$$\tilde{\eta}_1 + \eta_2 - 1 + \frac{\tilde{m}_2 \tilde{W}}{\tilde{p}_2 E_2} > 0. \tag{17}$$

We conclude that the Marshall-Lerner condition

$$\eta_0 \equiv \tilde{\eta}_1 + \eta_2 - 1 > 0$$

is either sufficient or necessary for the stability of the short-run equilibrium, dependent on the sign of $m_1 \tilde{m}_2 - m_2 \tilde{m}_1$.

Exchange Rate, Terms of Trade and the Current Account

Since the effect of a monetary transfer from Foreign to Home on the commodity markets with e being fixed is still considered, therefore from equation (17) and $\tilde{p}_1 \tilde{E}_1 = \tilde{p}_2 E_2$, we have

$$\frac{1}{\tilde{p}_1}\frac{\partial \tilde{p}_1}{\partial Z} = \left[(m - \tilde{m})\eta_0 + (m_1 \tilde{m}_2 - m_2 \tilde{m}_1)\frac{\tilde{W}}{\tilde{p}_2 E_2}\right]\frac{e}{\eta_m},$$

$$\frac{1}{p}\frac{\partial p}{\partial Z} = -\frac{W + e\tilde{W}}{\tilde{p}_2 E_2 \eta_m}(m_1 \tilde{m}_2 - m_2 \tilde{m}_1), \tag{18}$$

where $\tilde{m} \equiv \tilde{m}_1 + \tilde{m}_2$. Since $\eta_m > 0$, a rise in Z will result in, an increase in Home's nominal wealth and a reduction in the Foreign's nominal wealth. If $m > (<) \tilde{m}$, the increase in Home's excess expenditure exceeds in absolute value the decrease in Foreign's excess expenditure, generating an inflationary pressure on the world price level. If $m_j = \tilde{m}_j$, $j = 1, 2$, an international monetary transfer has no impact on the price of any good. In general, prices may be either increased or decreased, depending on combinations of the parameter values.

A depreciation of Home currency generates pressure in Home and a deflationary pressure in Foreign and that Home's terms of trade is deteriorated. Suppose e varies then from equation (7) we have

$$\frac{e}{\tilde{p}_1}\frac{\partial \tilde{p}_1}{\partial e} = -\alpha + (\alpha - \tilde{\alpha})\frac{e\eta_0 \tilde{m}\tilde{W}}{\eta_m},$$

$$\frac{e}{p}\frac{\partial p}{\partial e} = -\frac{W\tilde{W}}{\tilde{p}_2 E_2 \eta_m}(\alpha - \tilde{\alpha})(m_1 \tilde{m}_2 - m_2 \tilde{m}_1) \tag{19}$$

If $\alpha = \tilde{\alpha}$, then terms of trade are not affected by a change in the exchange rate. From equation (19) we have following results:

(a) A depreciation of Home currency brings about a deterioration in Home's terms of trade iff $(\alpha - \tilde{\alpha})(m_1 \tilde{m}_2 - m_2 \tilde{m}_1) > 0$.

Home's current account balance is given by (8), which can be expressed as

$$B = -\tilde{p}_1 \left[E_1 \left(p, \frac{\tilde{W}}{p \tilde{p}_1} \right) + p E_2 \left(p, \frac{W}{p \tilde{p}_1} \right) \right]$$

Using (16) and taking total differentials of the above equation we have

$$dB = -m \left(dZ - \frac{W \, d\tilde{p}_1}{p_1} - \frac{de}{e^2} \right) \tag{20}$$

If e is fixed, then from (20) and (18), we have

$$\left. \frac{\partial B}{\partial Z} \right|_{de=0} = -\frac{m \tilde{m} \eta_0 (W + e \tilde{W})}{\eta_m}. \tag{21}$$

Since η_m is assumed to be positive, the transfer of money from Foreign to Home makes Home's current account to a deficit if the Marshall-Lerner condition, $\eta_0 > 0$, holds. Now we shall consider effects of change in e, keeping z constant.

From equation (19) and (20) we have

$$\frac{\partial B}{\partial e} = (\alpha - \tilde{\alpha}) \frac{m \tilde{m} \eta_0 (W + e \tilde{W})}{e \eta_m} \tag{22}$$

Thus the direction of the impact is not determined solely by the Marshall-Lerner condition, but also on the portfolio preference condition.

(b) Using equation (16) we find that, a depreciation of Home currency improves Home's balance of current account if $(\alpha - \tilde{\alpha}) \eta_0 > 0$

From equation (16) and $\alpha > \tilde{\alpha}$, we find that the Marshall-Lerner condition is necessary and sufficient for a depreciation of Home currency to improve Home's balance of current account.

THE PORTFOLIO BALANCE APPROACH TO THE EXCHANGE RATE DETERMINATION

This approach of exchange rate determination utilizes imperfect asset substitutability and captures stock-flow interactions. It is being applied to the determination of the exchange rate by economists since sixties. One particular feature of this approach is that wealth is included as a scale variable in the asset demand equations which is in contrast to the asset models just discussed in the above section.

To start with we consider a simple model in which domestic residents hold two non-interest bearing assets—a home asset, H, and a foreign asset, F, denominated in foreign currency and the demand for each asset depends solely on the expected change in the exchange rate. In terms of home currency, the wealth of domestic residents is given by

$$W = H + SF \tag{1}$$

Consider the Fig. 9.8.

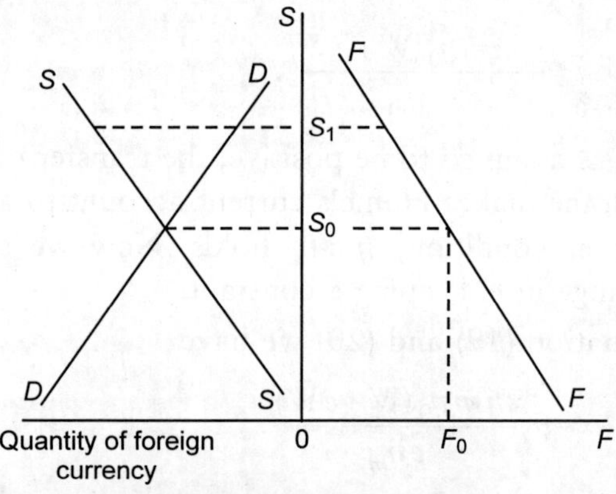

Fig. 9.8: Stock-Flow Interaction.

In the above figure FF line represents points of equilibrium for the stock of the foreign assets held by domestic residents. Thus if the foreign asset market is in equilibrium so also, with two assets, must be the home asset market. Hence FF represents overall asset market equilibrium with the stock demand for the foreign asset equal to the stock supply available to domestic residents. In the above figure, the FF schedule is drawn downward sloping because for given values of H and the expected change in the exchange rate an increase in the stock of the foreign asset requires an appreciation in the exchange rate. The left part of the above figure shows the flow demand and supply of foreign exchange underlying the current account of the balance of payments.

Both the current account and asset markets are at equilibrium at S_0 where the stock of foreign assets is F_0. If the exchange rate now moves to S_1, and if this results in a change in the terms of trade, then it is evident from the left hand side of the above figure that the current account must be in surplus, that is, domestic production exceeds domestic absorption. This current account surplus, under flexible exchange rates, will have as its counterpart a capital account deficit–the country must be accumulating foreign assets over time and thus for continuous stock market, or asset market, equilibrium to be maintained the exchange rate must be falling. This appreciating exchange rate will lead to reduced competitiveness and, if the appropriate elasticities condition holds, to a reduction in exports and an increase in imports and so a reduction of the current account surplus. This process will continue until the entire current account surplus is eliminated and the equilibrium exchange rate, S_0, is reached where both stock and flow equilibrium is achieved.

We shall consider our general model in context of two specific time periods. The impact period is one in which only asset market adjustment is considered. Asset markets are assumed to be continually equilibrated by interest rate and exchange rate movements. However in the impact period the effect of real variables and the price levels on asset stocks is ignored. The other period considered is the short run where prices and real variables are influenced by, and feedback on, asset prices. The interaction of stocks and flows in the short-run period leads eventually to a new long-run equilibrium. Thus our generalized asset market model can be described as:

$$W = M + B + SF = \int \dot{q} + \int \dot{F}(\dot{S}) \tag{2}$$

Supply = demand

$$M = m(i, i^* + \dot{s}^e)W;\ m_i < 0,\ m_{i^* + \dot{s}^e} < 0 \tag{3}$$

$$B = b(i, i^* + \dot{s}^e)W;\ b_i > 0,\ b_{i^* + \dot{s}^e} < 0 \tag{4}$$

$$SF = f(i, i^* + \dot{s}^e)W;\ f_i < 0,\ f_{i^* + \dot{s}^e} > 0 \tag{5}$$

$$m + b + f = 1 \tag{6}$$

$$S = P^T \tag{7}$$

$$Y = P^T Q^T + P^N Q^N \tag{8}$$

$$C = Y^D + \beta(w - \bar{w});\ \beta > 0 \tag{9}$$

$$Y^D = Y + i^* FS \tag{10}$$

$$P = P^{T,\alpha} P^{N,1-\alpha} \tag{11}$$

$$\dot{F} = T(S / P^N);\ T_{S/P^N} > 0 \tag{12}$$

The country described by the above equations (2 to 12) is assumed to be small and operating at full employment. This model can be explained with the help of Fig. 9.9.

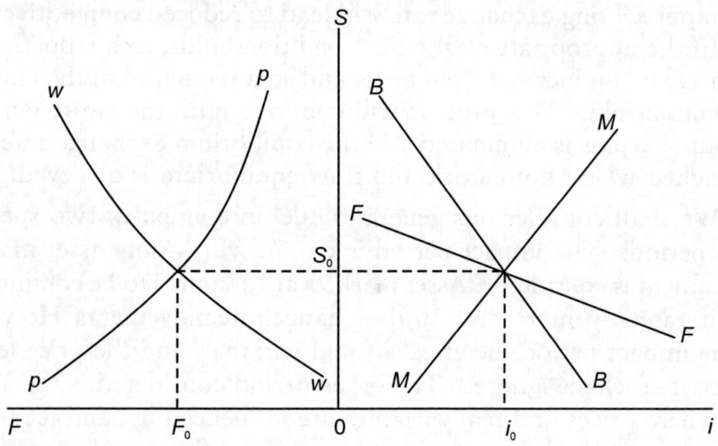

Fig. 9.9: Short and Long Run Asset Market Equilibrium.

The part *A* of the above figure shows combinations of the domestic rate of interest and the exchange rate that hold the demand for money equal to its supply which is given by *MM* schedule. The *BB* schedule describes the demand and supply of domestic bonds in equality and *FF* represents the demand and supply of foreign assets in equality. Considering money, *M*, and bonds, *B*, first, an increase in the exchange rate, *S*, from a position of equilibrium will, with the revaluation effect on wealth, lead to an increase in wealth and thus an increase in demand for both *M* and *B* to restore portfolio equilibrium. As money demanded rises- the domestic rate of interest-*i* must rise to maintain money market equilibrium. The increased demand for bonds raises their price and depresses the equilibrium rate of interest, which results in a negative sloped *BB* curve. The negative slope of the *FF* curve may be explained by a fall in *i* which increases the attractiveness of foreign assets leading to a rise in *S*. In the above figure we see that *BB* is steeper than *FF* because it is assumed that on the basis of domestic asset holders' risk preferences, domestic demand for domestic bonds is more responsive than domestic demand for foreign assets to interest rate changes. In our figure, the position S_0 and i_0 represents the equilibrium level of exchange rate and interest rate respectively. Because of the wealth constraint (equation 2), it must be that only two of the three equations 3-5 are independent. Thus, if a given change in *i* or *S* restores equilibrium in two markets then the third market must also be in equilibrium. Thus we can analyse various shocks using only two schedules.

For S_0, i_0 to be a position of long-run equilibrium the current account must equal zero and thus desired wealth must equal actual wealth. The condition of long run equilibrium can be represented by left part of the above figure, where *pp* locus represents short-run portfolio balance in *S*, *F* space and essentially the same interpretation as the *FF* schedule in right part of the above figure. The *pp* schedule shifts left-wards when the money stock is increased. Thus, for a given stock of foreign assets an increase in *M* must result in exchange rate depreciation for the maintenance of portfolio balance. The curve ww represents the locus of *S* and *F* consistent with long-run equilibrium when actual wealth equals desired wealth and it can be shown positively sloped if plausible values of trade and asset demand elasticities are chosen. Thus as *S* depreciates and with it the real exchange rate, the country's current account surplus grows and associated asset accumulation must be held in foreign bonds (*F*). An increase in domestic money supply, *M*, will shift *ww* rightwards.

THE IMPACT PERIOD AND MONETARY POLICY

(a) Suppose there is a once-and-for-all increase in money supply via through a budget deficit. Now investors will find that their portfolios have become unbalanced and will attempt to rebalance them by buying domestic bonds, *B*, and foreign bonds, *F*. With stocks of domestic and foreign bonds given in the short run, bond market equilibrium can be maintained only by a fall in interest rate and rise in exchange rate. Thus to maintain bond market equilibrium, at each exchange rate, the increased demand for bonds-domestic and foreign-reduces *ι* and pushes the *BB* curve leftwards. The increased demand for foreign bonds, with a given *i*, raises the value of *S* to maintain equilibrium in domestic holdings of foreign fixed price bonds which shifts the *FF* curve rightwards. This can be represented by Fig. 9.10.

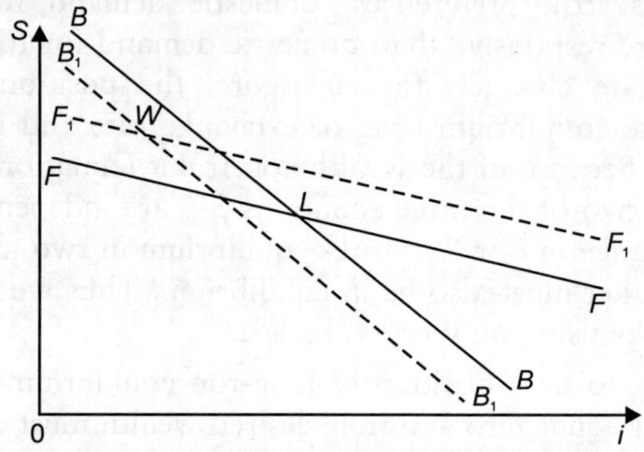

Fig. 9.10: 'Helicopter' Increase in the Money Supply.

Thus in the above figure *L* represents the initial equilibrium and *W*, post-money-supply equilibrium with a lower rate of interest and a depreciated exchange rate.

(b) Now suppose there is an increase in money supply effected by a swap of money for bonds. Consider the Fig. 9.11.

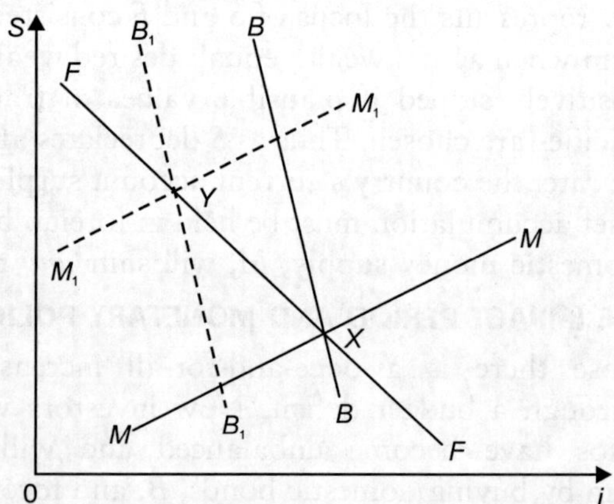

Fig. 9.11: Open Market Increase in the Money Supply.

The *FF* schedule is unchanged because at an initial equilibrium of *X* in the above figure, the open market operation leaves asset holders with an excess supply of money and excess demand for bonds. In attempting to buy bonds domestic investors will have the effect of pushing the domestic interest rate down and this in turn will lead to an increased demand for foreign bonds pushing *S* upwards. In the above figure, the *BB* and *MM* curves shift leftwards and the new equilibrium is given by the point *Y*. If the domestic interest elasticity of demand for money is less than the domestic elasticity of demand for foreign bonds, then the percentage change in the demand for foreign bonds will be greater than the percentage increase in the money stock. Thus there is a one-to-one relationship between *S* and *F*, which implies that the exchange rate change will be larger than the money supply change.

(c) Now we consider an increase in the money supply in the economy by swopping money for foreign assets held by domestic residents. This open market operation of *M* for *F* will shift *MM* leftwards since at the initial equilibrium there is an excess supply of money and the rate of interest must fall for money market equilibrium to be maintained. This can be shown in Fig. 9.12.

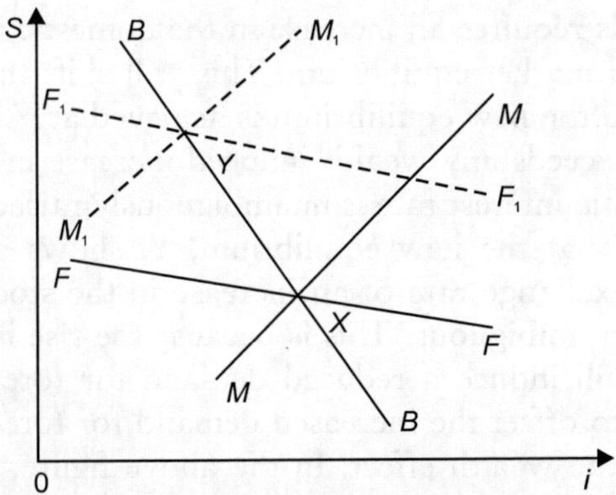

Fig. 9.12: Money for Foreign Assets.

At the initial equilibrium there will be an excess demand for the foreign asset; this will leads to rise in the exchange rate to maintain foreign asset market equilibrium. Thus the *FF* curve must shift rightwards as shown in the above figure. In the above figure *X* represents the initial equilibrium and *Y* represents the new equilibrium.

THE IMPACT PERIOD AND FISCAL POLICY

An increase in the supply of bonds increases wealth and, for a given domestic interest rate, *i*, requires an increase in the exchange rate *S*, to maintain the foreign exchange market in equilibrium as wealth holders purchase additional foreign bonds. This shifts the *FF* curve upwards to F_1F_1 as shown in Fig. 9.13.

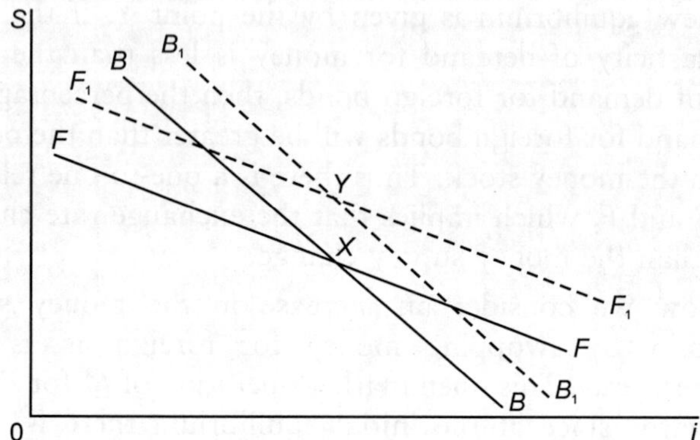

Fig. 9.13: An Increase in the Supply of Bonds.

For a given value of the exchange rate the increased supply of domestic bonds requires an increase in the domestic interest rate to maintain bond market equilibrium. This will shift the *BB* curve to rightwards and the new equilibrium is achieved at *Y*. The increased bond supply exceeds any wealth induced increase in bond demand and the domestic interest rate is unambiguously raised. In the above figure we see that the new equilibrium, *Y*, shows a higher *S* the effect on the exchange rate of an increase in the stock of domestic bonds is in fact ambiguous. This is because the rise in the domestic interest rate will induce a reduced demand for foreign assets and this will tend to offset the increased demand for foreign fixed price bonds due to the wealth effect. In the above figure, whether the *y* value of *S* will be greater or less than the *X* value depends essentially on the degree to which foreign and domestic bonds are regarded as better substitutes to domestic money. If *F* and *B* are regarded as better substitutes then the exchange rate will be lower at the new equilibrium because the shift of demand from *F* to *B* as a result of the rise in *i* will be greater the closer *F* and *B* are regarded as substitutes relative to *B* and *M*.

The Short-run Adjustment to the Steady State

In this section we shall focus on the movement from the impact period equilibrium to the new long-run steady state equilibrium following the open market purchase of domestic bonds for money.

The impact equilibrium after such a shock is represented by the right hand side of Fig. 9.14 at point Y.

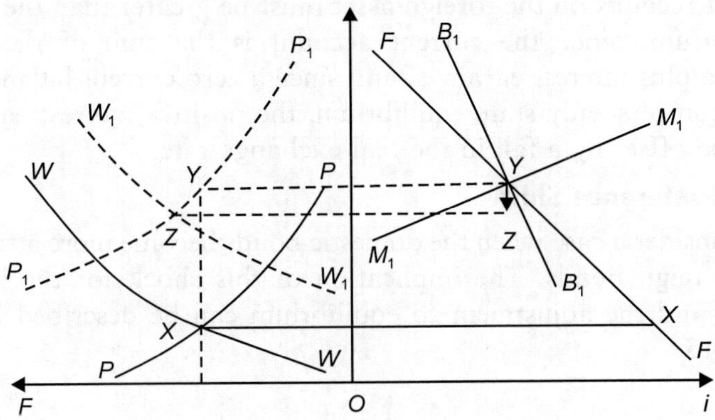

Fig. 9.14: Impact and Long Run Equilibrium.

In the left hand quadrant of the above figure, the pp curve shifts to $p_1\, p_1$. Although the valuation effect of the exchange rate will, on impact, give a rise in nominal wealth, it seems likely that moving to the short-run period this will be offset by the effect the exchange rate overshoot has on the price index and thus real wealth; actual real wealth in the short-run period will fall short of desired real wealth. Equation (9) explains this mismatch of desired and actual real wealth; the domestic residents must be saving and thus running a current account surplus during the adjustment period. Thus the desire to restore the initial value of desired wealth can only be realized by the country running a current account surplus and accumulating the foreign asset. This is possible because in the impact period relative prices have moved in favour of the traded goods sector inducing a switch in production from non-traded to traded goods and a switch in consumption from traded to non-traded goods. The current account surplus over time forces the exchange rate downwards leading to a diminution of the saving rate until equilibrium is restored on the new WW curve at point Z. In the right hand side of the above figure, the MM, BB and FF curves all shift down from Y in proportion to the accumulation of F.

If in the initial equilibrium the price of traded goods equaled the price of non-traded goods, in the new equilibrium the relative price of traded goods will have fallen. The increase in the money supply does not lead to a proportionate increase in the overall price level.

This follows since in the adjustment period the home country has been accumulating foreign assets and in the new equilibrium interest receipts on the foreign asset must be greater than the initial equilibrium. Since the current account is the sum of the trade balance plus interest earnings, and since a zero current balance is a condition of steady state equilibrium, the positive interest earnings must be offset by a fall in the real exchange rate.

Asset Preference Shift

Consider a case when the domestic bonds become more attractive than foreign bonds. The implication of this shock for the impact period and the adjustment to equilibrium can be described by the Fig. 9.15.

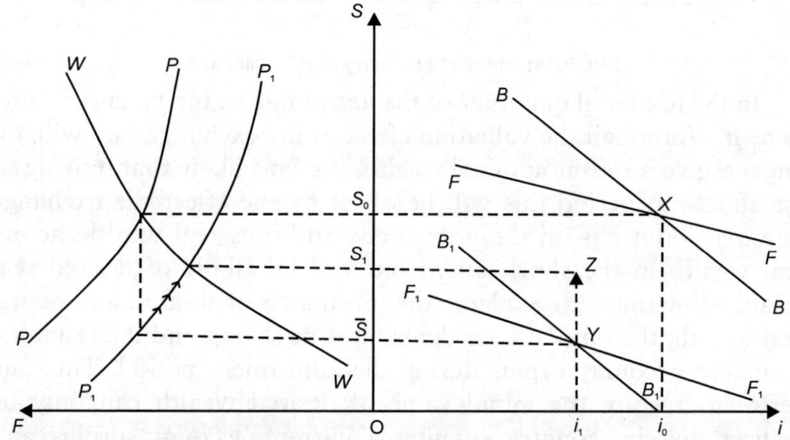

Fig. 9.15: The Impact and Long-run Effects of a Change in Preferences.

At the initial equilibrium the increased demand for domestic bonds can only be satisfied by a reduction in the rate of interest giving the leftward shift in *BB* to B_1B_1. Equally the attempt to move out of foreign bonds can, in the impact period, only be satisfied by a leftward shift of the *FF* schedule. Thus the impact effect of a change in asset preference from foreign to domestic bonds results in a reduction in the interest rate and the exchange rate—from i_0 to i_1, and from S_0 to S_1.

Moving from the impact period to the short-run adjustment period we find that private sector wealth has increased due to the fall in the price of traded goods and this, must outweigh the wealth reducing effect of the devaluation, in home currency terms, of the stock of foreign assets. Thus w must be greater than $\bar{w}$ and agents will be dissaving and using equation (ix), consumption must rise. Further, the mirror image of the dis-saving will be a current account deficit which will be induced by the initial change in relative prices. As the stock of F is reduced over time, via the current account, the rate of dissaving is reduced, whilst the initial exchange rate appreciation is gradually reversed until the new equilibrium is reached at $\bar{S}$. In contrast to the open market purchase of bonds, the new long-run equilibrium consequent upon the change in asset preferences must be one in which the relative price of traded to non-traded goods has fallen.

CROSS RATES

Cross rate is the rate of exchange between the currencies of two countries calculated from the rate of exchange of these currencies in terms of the currency of a third country prevailing in the third country. Let us take a hypothetical example to illustrate the calculation of the cross rate between the pound and the dollar. Suppose that the rate of exchange in India between dollar and rupee is 1:5 and between pound and Re. 1:15. In this example, cross rate between pound and dollar will be 1:3. Cross rate between the two currencies is said to be orderly if it is identical with the direct rate of exchanges between these two currencies. It is disorderly if it differs from the direct rate of exchange. Disorderly exchange rates can exist if the different currencies are not freely convertible. Under freely convertible currencies, any divergency between the cross rates and direct rates will be immediately eliminated by the operations of the exchange arbitragers. Institution of exchange control in almost all countries has often led to the emergence of disorderly cross rates. If the exchange rates are not orderly, the exchange rate in terms of a particular currency does not reflect the overall international position of the country. Disorderly cross rates undermine the stability of the currencies which sell at a discount in relation to hard currencies. These distort the pattern of trade and thereby result into wastage of productive resources. Distortion of world trade also increases the difficulties of restoring an equilibrium in the balance of payments and the convertibility of currencies. If the cross rate places a premium on dollar in country *A*, the traders in this country will be encouraged to buy goods from other countries and to resell these in the United States for dollars. Thus the dollars which would have accrued to other countries will go to country *A*. Before the war, disorderly cross rates were employed by Germany, Argentina, and certain other countries for underselling their competitors in the markets of third countries. These are unfair competitive practices and can lead to highly injurious economic warfare.

SPOT EXCHANGE MARKET

The spot market is the segment in which the two parties to a transaction arrange to conduct the exchange of currencies within a relatively short-term horizon. More precisely, in a spot transaction, the agreed payment date or 'value date' for debiting and crediting deposit balances is normally two business days after the transaction is arranged, although banks after trade for "next day" value. The lag allows time for banks to confirm the details of transactions and properly execute the fund transfers. Also known as "benchmark rates", "straightforward rates" or "outright rates", spot rates represent the price that a buyer expects to pay for a foreign currency in another currency. Exchange rates governing such "on-the-spot" trading are called spot exchange rates, and the deal is called a spot transaction.

Even spot exchange become effective only two days a deal is struck because in most cases it takes two days for payment instructions to be cleared through the banking system. Depending on the item being traded, spot prices can indicate market expectations of future price movements in different ways. For a security or non-perishable commodity, the spot price reflects market expectations of future price movements. In contrast, a perishable commodity does not allow the arbitrage—the cost of storage is effectively higher than the expected future price of the commodity. As a result, spot prices will reflect current supply and demand, not future price movements. Spot prices can therefore be quite volatile and move independently from forward prices.

Example: Even if we know tomatoes are cheap in July and will be expensive in January, we cannot buy them in July and take delivery in January, since they will spoil before we can take advantage of January's high prices. The July price will reflect tomato supply and demand in July. The forward price for January will reflect the market's expectations of supply and demand in January. July tomatoes are effectively a different commodity from January tomatoes.

FORWARD EXCHANGE MARKET

Normally there is no separate market, of the sort indicated by the title of this section, for forward transactions. In fact, it is one segment of the foreign exchange market as a whole, the other being the spot exchange market. In the spot exchange market, foreign exchange is bought and sold for immediate delivery against immediate payment. In the forward exchange market, in contrast to spot market, contracts are made for the delivery of foreign exchange at some specified future date at a price agreed at the time the contracts are entered into. Payment for the foreign exchange is made at the time of delivery.

Strictly speaking, forward rate is the price quoted for a currency to be delivered at some specified future date. Conventionally, however, forward exchanges are quoted not in terms of their actual price but in terms of their premium or discount over the spot rates, i.e. the difference between the rates quoted for spot and future delivery at any particular time. 'Conventionally, therefore, forward rate refers to the rate of premium or discount over the spot rate and not actual price. Some authors, however, use the terms 'forward margin', 'swap margin' or 'swap rate' for expressing the amount of premium or discount over the spot rates and use the term forward rate for the actual price quoted for a currency to be delivered at some specified future date.

The Role of Banks in the Forward Exchange Markets

Forward exchange facilities are provided mostly by banks. They charge a commission for the provision of these facilities. They normally undertake no risks in providing these facilities. There are importers who want to cover themselves against exchange risks by purchasing forward exchange. At the same time, there are exporters who want to sell forward exchange with a similar motive. The banks earn their commission simply by acting as intermediaries between the buyers and sellers of forward exchange. If a bank contracts to sell forward exchange to an importer, it at the same time undertakes to purchase forward exchange from an exporter. So long as forward purchases and sales of a bank are exactly matched, no risk is involved for it whatever may be the spot exchange rate at the time its forward contracts mature. It is, however, not necessary that the demand for and supply of forward exchange should exactly match at any point of time. If the sales of a bank exceed its purchases of forward exchange, it will be taking an uncovered position and thereby expose itself to the risks of fluctuations in exchange rates. As the bank earns its profits from the commission and does not want to indulge in speculative activities, it will try to cover its position. A number of alternatives are available to a bank which wants to cover its position. Let us take a concrete example to illustrate the main alternative available to a bank for covering its position. Suppose a bank's sale of ninety-days forward sterling exceeds its purchases of forward sterling of the same maturity. After ninety days, it will be required to deliver more sterling than that which it receives from its purchases. One way for the bank to match purchases to its sales will be to buy ninety-days sterling bills on the exchange market. These bills will mature after ninety days and provide the required sterling at the time the bank's sales of sterling fall due. An alternative will be to buy spot sterling from exporters or from banks having surplus sterling. If the bank does so, it will have to hold sterling in London for ninety days because these funds can be lent only in London; otherwise it will lose interest on these funds. Another alternative will be to buy sterling from speculators. Speculators intentionally take an open or uncovered position expecting to make profits from changes in exchange rates. In case the bank does not find it possible to buy sterling from any of these sources, it will simply refuse to sell additional forward sterling.

Determination of Forward Exchange Rates

Forward exchange rates, like spot exchange rates, are determined by the demand for and the supply of forward exchange. If the supply of forward exchange exceeds the demand for it, the forward rates will be quoted at a discount over the spot rate, i.e. forward exchange rate will be lower than the spot exchange rate. On the other hand, if the demand for forward exchange exceeds its supply, the forward rates will be quoted at a premium over the spot rate, i.e. forward rate will be higher than the spot rate. The demand for forward exchange arises, mainly from (a) imports, (b) outflow of capital, (c) arbitrage operations and (d) bullish speculation. An importer of foreign goods having to make payment after a certain period of time may contract to purchase foreign exchange in advance to avoid the risk of changes in exchange rates. Arbitragers move funds from one centre to another to earn profits out of the interest differential that may exist between the two centres. An arbitrager who transfers funds abroad to take advantage of a comparatively higher rate of interest abroad, contracts at the same time to sell forward exchange to cover himself against exchange risks. Speculators intentionally take an open or uncovered position expecting to gain from future changes in the exchange rate. If the speculators expect a rise in the exchange rate, they will have an incentive to contract for the purchase of forward exchange. Similarly, the supply of forward exchange comes, mainly from (a) exporters of merchandise, (b) exporters of capital, (c) arbitragers and (d) speculators.

Now suppose that S_t is the spot price of an asset at time t, and r is the continuously compounded rate, then the forward price must satisfy $F_{t,T} = S_t . e^{r(T-t)}$. To prove this we shall start with the negation of this statement.

(a) Let us suppose that $F_{t,T} > S_t\, e^{r(T-t)}$. Then an investor can execute the following trades at time t:

He will go to the bank and get a loan for S_t at the continuously compounded rate r and with this money he will buy one unit of stock for S_t; enter into one short forward contract costing 0. A short forward contract means that the investor owes the counterparty the stock at time T. The initial cost of trades at the initial time is to Zero.

At time T the investor can reverse the trades that were executed at time t. Specifically, the investor repays the loan to the bank. The inflow to the investor is $-S_t\, e^{r(T-t)}$. He settles the short forward contract by selling the stock for $F_{t,T}$. The cash inflow to the investor is now $F_{t,T}$ because the investor receives from the buyer. Thus the inflow of funds to the investor is $F_{t,T} - S_t\, e^{r(T-t)}$.

The sum of inflows is $F_{t,T} - S_t\, e^{r(T-t)}$, which by hypothesis, is positive. This is an arbitrage profit. Consequently, and assuming that the non-arbitrage condition holds, we have a contradiction. This is called a cash and carry arbitrage because we carry the stock until maturity.

(b) If $F_{t,T} < S_t e^{r(T-t)}$, then an investor can do the reverse of what he has done above in case (a). But if we look at the convenience yield page, we find that if there are finite stocks/ inventory, the reverse cash and carry arbitrage is not always possible. It would depend on the elasticity of demand for forward contracts and such like.

Now suppose that $FV_T(X)$ is the time value of cash flows X at the contract expiration time T. The forward price is then given by the expression:

$F_{t,T} = S_t e^{r(T-t)} - FV_T$. (All cash flows over the life of the contract)

The cash flows can be in the form of dividends from the asset, or costs of maintaining the asset. If these price relationships do not hold, there is an arbitrage opportunity for a riskless profit similar to that discussed above. One implication of this is that the presence of a forward market will force spot prices to reflect current expectations of future prices. As a result, the forward price for nonperishable commodities, securities or currency is no more a predictor of future price than the spot price is – the relationship between forward and spot prices is driven by interest rates. For perishable commodities, arbitrage does not have this. The above forward pricing formula can also be written as

$$F_{t,T} = (S_t - I_t) e^{r(T-t)}$$

where I_t is the time t value of all cash flows over the life of the contract.

Non-deliverable forward (NDF) market is an over-the-counter market and it began to trade actively in the 1990s. An NDF is a short-term, cash-settled currency forward between two counterparties. On the contract settlement date, the profit or loss is adjusted between the two counterparties based on the difference between the contracted NDF rate and the prevailing spot foreign exchange rates on an agreed notional amount.

NDF markets developed for emerging markets with capital controls, where the currencies could not be delivered offshore. Most NDFs are cash settled in US dollars. The more active banks quote NDFs from between one month to one year, although some would quote up two years upon request. The most commonly traded NDF tenors are IMM dates, but banks also offer odd-dated NDFs. NDFs are typically quoted with the USD as the reference currency, and the settlement amount is also in USD. Since an NDF is a cash-settled instrument, the notional amount is never exchanged. The only exchange of cash flows is the difference between the NDF rate and the prevailing spot market rate that is exchanged on the settlement date. Consequently, NDFs are "non-cash" products, which are off-the-balance-sheet and as the principal sums do not move, possess much lower counter-party risks. NDFs are committed short-term instruments; both counterparties are committed and are obliged to honor the deal. Nevertheless, either counterparty can cancel an existing contract by entering into another offsetting deal at the prevailing market rate.

An investor enters into a forward agreement to purchase a notional amount, N, of the base currency at the contracted forward rate, F, and would pay NF units of the quoted currency. On the fixing date, that investor would theoretically be able to sell the notional amount, N, of the base currency at the prevailing spot rate, S, earning NS units of the quoted currency. Therefore, the profit, π, on this trade in terms of the base currency, is given by:

$$\pi = \frac{NS - NF}{S} = N\left(1 - \frac{F}{S}\right)$$

NDFs can be used to create a foreign currency loan in a currency which may not be of interest to the lender. In this structure, the borrower receives (for example) a dollar sum, but repayments are fixed to a foreign currency schedule. Settlement between the borrower and the lender takes place in dollars, but fixed to the exchange rate at time of repayments. At the same time as disbursing the dollar sums to the borrower, the lender enters into a non-deliverable forward agreement with a counterparty (for example, on the Chicago market) that matches the cash flows of the synthetic foreign currency repayments schedule. Effectively, the borrower has a synthetic foreign currency loan; the lender has a (synthetic) dollar loan; and the counterparty has an NDF contract with the lender. Under certain circumstances, the rates achievable using synthetic foreign currency lending may be lower than borrowing in the foreign currency directly, implying that there is a possibility for arbitrage.

Forward Premium and Forward Discount

When dealing with foreign exchange, a situation where the spot futures exchange rate, with respect to the domestic currency, is trading at a higher spot exchange rate then it is currently. A forward premium is frequently measured as the difference between the current spot rate and the forward rate, but any expected future exchange rate will suffice. It is a reasonable assumption to make that the future spot rate will be equal to the current futures rate. According to the forward expectation's theory of exchange rates, the current spot futures rates will be the future spot rate. This theory is routed in empirical studies and is a reasonable assumption to make in the long term.

Forward discount is a foreign exchange situation where the domestic current spot exchange rate is trading at a higher level then the current domestic future spot rate for a maturity period. A forward discount is an indication by the market that the current domestic exchange rate is going to depreciate in value against another currency. A forward discount means the market expects the domestic currency to depreciate against another currency, but that is not to say that will happen. Although the forward expectation's theory of exchange rates states this is the case, the theory does not always hold.

For instance, the forward rate for a currency, say, the Indian rupee, is said to be at a premium with respect to the spot rate when Re. 1 buys more units of another currency, say, the Yen, in the forward market than in the spot market. Conversely, the forward rate for pounds is said to be at a discount with respect to the spot rate when Rs. 1 buys fewer yen in the forward market than in the spot market. For instance, when the spot rate is two yen and the three-month forward rate is 2.025 yen, we say that the rupee is at a forward premium. However, when the spot rate is two yen and the forward rate is only 1.975 yen, we say that the rupee is at a forward discount.

The forward premium or forward discount is usually expressed as a percentage deviation from the spot rate on a per annum basis (like the rate of interest). For example, when the spot rate is two yen and the three-month forward rate is 2.025 yen, the rupee is at a five percent forward premium.

$$\frac{¥\,2.025 - ¥\,2}{¥\,2} \cdot \frac{12(\text{months})}{3(\text{months})} .100 = +5(\text{premium})$$

Similarly, when the spot rate is ¥ 2 and the three-month forward rate is only ¥ 1.975, the rupee is at a 5 per cent forward discount.

$$\frac{¥\,1.975 - ¥\,2}{¥\,2} \cdot \frac{12(\text{months})}{3(\text{months})} .100 = -5(\text{discount})$$

Here one point is clear that when the rupee is at a forward premium, the yen is necessarily at forward discount. Similarly, when the rupee is at a forward discount, the yen is at a forward premium.

Thus the forward premium anomaly refers to the widespread empirical finding that the slope coefficient in the regression of the change in the logarithm of the spot exchange rate on the forward premium is invariably less than unity, and often negative. This "anomaly" implies the apparent predictability of excess returns over uncovered interest rate parity, and is conventionally viewed as evidence of a biased forward rate and/or of evidence of a time varying risk premium.

Benefits of Forward Exchange Facilities

Forward exchange operations provide an opportunity to traders to safeguard themselves against the risks arising from changes in exchange rates. Normally traders are interested in making their profits by marking up the purchase price by a certain percentage. In foreign trade, the purchase and sale price of the traders is expressed in terms of different currencies. When purchase and sale prices are expressed in terms of different currencies, changes in exchange rate may upset all the calculations of the traders. Risks from changes in exchange rates are particularly high under the system of free and fluctuating exchange rates. Such risks are not very important under pegged exchange rates and gold standard. If the traders wish to avoid these risks and to concentrate on their normal functions (i.e. trading activities), and the risks involved in these, they can contract in advance to buy or sell foreign exchange, equivalent to the amount of payment they expect to make or receive, at a guaranteed rate. Suppose, for illustration, that an Indian exporter contracts to export tea to the United Kingdom for which he will receive payment in terms of sterling after ninety days. To avoid the risk of a change in the exchange rate at the time he receives payments, he can contract with his bank in advance to sell the amount of sterling which he expects to receive after ninety days at a guaranteed exchange rate. Similarly, an importer placing an order for goods from the United Kingdom, knowing that he has to make payment in terms of sterling after ninety days, can contract with his bank in advance to buy sterling after ninety days at the guaranteed exchange rate and thus safeguard himself from the risks arising from changes in the exchange rate. Forward exchange facilities also enable foreign investors and foreign debtors to cover themselves against exchange risks. Foreign debtors can avoid exchange risks by contracting in advance to purchase the required amount of foreign exchange at a guaranteed rate at the time their payments fall due. Similarly, the holders of foreign investments and other claims can cover themselves against exchange risks by forward sales.

Limitations of Forward Exchange Facilities

Insuring against exchange risks through forward exchange deals involves a cost. If this cost is not fairly low, exporters who are ready to undertake the exchange risks in addition to trading risks will be in a position to undersell those exporters who have to pay a charge for insuring against exchange risks and may thus oust them from the export business. Similarly, importers who do not insure themselves against exchange risks can underquote those who insure against exchange risks and thus put them to great losses.

Changes in exchange rates affect not only the amount of the national currency which the exporters receive for their exports and the importers have to pay for their imports but also the prices of the exported and imported commodities in terms of the national currency. Forward exchange facilities can cover the traders against only the former type of risks (i.e. direct exchange risks). In order to avoid the risks arising from changes in the prices of commodities in terms of national currency as a result of changes in exchange rates (i.e. the indirect exchange risks), the traders will have to pay an additional charge for availing of hedging facilities available in forward commodity markets. Hedging facilities are not available for all commodities. These are available only for important commodities for which there exist forward markets. If the domestic price of the imported goods rises (falls) by the full amount of the depreciation (appreciation) of the national currency, the loss (gain) to the uninsured importers on account of depreciation (appreciation) will be fully offset by the gain (loss) from a rise (fall) in the domestic price of the imported commodity. Under such conditions, the uninsured importers will be as well of as the importers who pay to cover themselves from both the kinds of risks mentioned above, i.e. (a) the direct exchange risks and (b) the indirect exchange risks. Similar situation will arise in case of exports if the domestic price falls (rises) by the full amount of the depreciation (appreciation) of the domestic currency.

Interest Rates and Forward Rates

Differences in interest rates between different countries exert an important influence on the forward exchange rate. Let us illustrate this with the help of a concrete example. Suppose that the rate of interest is three per cent in London and two per cent in India and the spot and forward exchange rates are at par. Such a situation will offer an inducement for the transfer of funds from India to London. Those who move funds from India to London will like to cover themselves against exchange risks by buying forward rupees. The demand for forward rupees will far exceed its supply. At the same time, the spot supply of rupees will far exceed the demand for it. This will raise the forward rate and lower the spot rate of the rupee. As the funds are transferred from India to London, the discount on forward relative to spot rate will go on rising. This will diminish the profitability of, and consequently, the inducement for the transfer of additional funds from India to London. Simultaneously, there will operate another equilibrating force. Transfer of funds from India to London will tend to raise the interest rate in India and lower the same in London and thus narrow the differences in interest rates between the two countries. Diminution of the interest differential will further decrease the profitability of and hence the inducement for the transfer of funds from India to London. Ultimately, an equilibrium will be reached when the discount on forward exchange becomes equal to the interest differential and there will be no inducement for the further transfer of capital. The equilibrium may be reached either through a change in the interest differential or through a variation in the discrepancy between the spot and forward exchange rates or through a combination of the two; the last possibility is likely to be the most probable one.

Speculation and Forward Exchange

Speculators, unlike the traders, banks and arbitragers take an open or uncovered position expecting to gain from changes in exchange rates. If a speculator expects that sterling is going to depreciate in future, he will sell forward sterling at a rate slightly higher than the expected rate. In case, he expects the sterling to be strong in future, he will buy sterling at a rate slightly lower than the expected rate. In case the events go against his expectation, he suffers a loss. The activities of bear speculators can substantially depress the forward exchange rate of any currency, i.e. the exchange will be quoted at large discounts. Similarly, the activities of bull speculators can substantially raise the forward exchange rate, i.e. the exchange will be quoted at large premiums.

Speculative transactions form an important part of the forward exchange market. It is doubtful if the forward exchange markets can operate only on transactions arising from trade, capital movements and arbitrage activities.

Effect of Movements in Spot Rates on Forward Rates

Spot and forward rates act and react upon each other. Spot rates are one of the important factors which the dealers in forward exchange keep in view while quoting forward rates. Movements in spot rates, therefore, will affect forward rates. Normally, movements in spot rates will cause movements in forward rates in the same direction. Sometimes, however, the movement in spot rates may cause movements in forward rates in the reverse direction. If there is a general feeling that the spot rate has moved too far from its stable position, the forward rates may start moving in the reverse direction before the spot rate does so. On the other hand, if the general feeling is that the prevailing tendency will continue, the forward rates may move in anticipation of the movements in spot rates. The forward rates will tend to move to the level at which the spot rates are expected to be at the time the forward contracts mature.

Essential Conditions for the Existence of Forward Exchange Market

Forward exchange market can properly function only if (a) there are no unreasonable restrictions on trading in foreign exchange, speculation and interest arbitraging (i.e. international movement of funds in response to interest differentials), (b) the currency is not strongly pegged at a fixed rate of exchange, (c) the concerned currency is sufficiently important (i.e. the transactions in the currency are regular and sufficiently large in volume). The existence of exchange control may hinder the carrying out of forward contracts and thereby the working of the forward market. Some countries prohibit forward exchange dealings altogether. If the transactions in a currency are very few and fitful or if the currency is strongly pegged at a fixed rate, there will be little scope for the operation of this forward market.

FOREIGN EXCHANGE FUTURE

Foreign exchange future came into existence in 1972 at the Chicago Mercantile Exchange (CME). Some commodity traders at the CME did not have access to the inter-bank exchange markets in the early 1970s, when they believed that significant changes were about to take place in the currency market. They established the International Monetary Market (IMM) and launched trading in seven currency futures on 16 May 1972. Today the IMM is a division of CME.

A foreign exchange future is a forward contract for standardized currency amounts and selected calendar dates traded on an organized market. The currencies traded on the IMM are the Japanese yen, The German mark, the Canadian dollar, the British pound, the Swiss franc, and the Australian dollar. When one buys a future contract, one buy a promise that a specified amount of foreign currency will be delivered on a specified date in the future. A forward contract between two private parties is an alternative way to make sure that he receives the same amount of foreign currency on the date in question. But while one has no choice about fulfilling his end of a forward deal, he can sell his futures contract on an organized future exchange, realizing a profit or loss right away. Such a sale might appear advantageous, for example, if his views about the future spot exchange rate were to change. Futures are standardized and are usually traded on an exchange created for this purpose. The average contract length is roughly three months. Futures contracts are usually inclusive of any interest amounts.

Investors use these future contracts to hedge against exchange risk. If an investor will receive a cash flow denominated in a foreign currency on some future date, that investor can lock in the current exchange rate by entering into an offsetting currency futures position that expires on the date of the cash flow. For instance, a US-based investor will receive € 1,000,000 on March 1. The current exchange rate implied by the future is $ 1.5/€. He can lock in this exchange rate by selling € 1,000,000 worth of futures contracts expiring on March 1. That way, he is guaranteed an exchange rate of $ 1.5/€ regardless of exchange rate fluctuations in the meantime.

Currency futures can also be used to speculate and, by incurring a risk, attempt to profit from rising or falling exchange rates.

FOREIGN EXCHANGE SWAP

A foreign exchange swap is an over-the-counter short term interest rate derivative instrument. In emerging money markets, foreign exchange swaps are usually the first derivatives instrument to be traded, ahead of forward rate agreements and before exotics. In a swap, two parties exchange currencies for a certain length of time and agree to reverse the transaction at a later date. These are not standardized contracts and are not traded through an exchange. A foreign exchange swap consists of two legs:

(a) A spot foreign exchange transaction, and

(b) A forward foreign exchange transaction.

These two legs are executed simultaneously for the same quantity, and therefore offset each other. It is also common to trade *forward-forward,* where both transactions are for different forward dates.

The relationship between spot and forward is given by

$$F = S\left(\frac{1 + r_T.T}{1 + r_B.T}\right)$$

where

F = forward

S = spot

r_T = simple interest rate of the term currency

r_B = simple interest rate of the base currency

T = tenor calculated according to the appropriate day count conversion.

The forward points or swap points are quoted as the difference between forward and spot, $F - S$, and is expressed as the following:

$$F - S = S\left(\frac{1 + r_T.T}{1 + r_B.T} - 1\right) \approx S(r_T - r_B)T$$

where, r_T and r_B are small. Thus the absolute value of the swap points increases when the interest rate differential gets larger, and vice versa.

The most common use of foreign exchange swaps is for institutions to fund their foreign exchange balances. Once a foreign exchange transaction settles, the holder is left with a positive position in one currency, and a negative position in another. In order to collect or pay any overnight interest due on these foreign balances, at the end of every day institutions will close out any foreign balances and re-institute them for the following day. To do this they typically use *tom-next* swaps, buying (selling) a foreign amount settling tomorrow, and selling (buying) it back settling the day after. The interest collected or paid every night is referred to as the cost of carry. As currency traders know roughly how much holding a currency position will make or cost on a daily basis, specific trades are put on based on this; these are referred to as carry trades.

FOREIGN EXCHANGE OPTION

Futures or forward contracts obligate the holder to complete the transaction at maturity, unless it is sold in the meantime or offset by a contract in the opposite direction. A 90 days forward purchase of sterling, for example, could be canceled after 30 days through a sale of 60 days sterling. Otherwise the contract goes to maturity, whether or not the outcome is favourable. An option contract, in contrast, provides the opportunity to purchase or sell a fixed amount of currency or a common stock during a fixed period of time at a guaranteed price, called the strike price, but the holder of the option has the alternative of not completing the purchase or sale. A "put" gives the buyer of the contract the right to sell the asset, and a "call" provides the opportunity to buy. Because an option is a one-sided bet, an often sizable premium or price is required to purchase such a contract. In short, a foreign exchange option is a derivative where the owner has the right but not the obligation to exchange money denominated in one currency into another currency at a pre-agreed exchange rate on a specified date. The foreign exchange option market is the deepest, largest and most liquid market for options of any kind in the world. Most of the foreign exchange option volume is traded OTC (Over-the-Counter trading is to trade financial instruments such as stocks, bonds, commodities or derivatives directly between two parties) and is lightly regulated, but a fraction is traded on exchanges like the International Securities Exchange, Philadelphia Stock Exchange, or the Chicago Mercantile Exchange for options on futures contracts.

Foreign exchange options are a useful means of covering possible exchange exposure from a transaction that may not occur. If, for example, a US firm were in the midst of negotiating a contract to purchase a British firm for £2 million sterling, it might want to lock in its US dollar price but not be bound to take delivery of the sterling if the negotiations were to fail. Purchasing sterling calls totaling £2 million will protect the firm against the possibility that sterling will appreciate before the deal is completed and paid for, but will still give the firm a means of avoiding purchasing the sterling if the transaction does not occur.

Foreign exchange options can also be used to insure a pre-existing financial position against loss without giving up the possibility of a profit. If, for example, a firm owned £2 million in sterling assets and had no sterling liabilities, it would be worried about a possible future depreciation of sterling, but would profit if the currency appreciated. Purchasing £2 million in sterling puts would protect the firm against the depreciation without depriving it of the possibility of making money if sterling rose. If the firm had sterling liabilities but no sterling assets, the same insurance would be provided by purchasing sterling calls. In both cases, however, the insurance comes at the cost of the premium on the option plus brokerage commissions.

The determination of the premiums on foreign exchange options depends on both intrinsic and time value, that latter having a number of determinants. Intrinsic value is the extent to which the option is currently "in the money". If a sterling call has a strike price of \$ 1.70 and the current spot exchange rate is \$ 1.73, the intrinsic value of the option is 3 cents, and the premium must be at least that amount.

Time value results from the possibility of future exchange rate changes that could make the option worth more than its current intrinsic value. Three factors determine an option's time value—relative interest rates, expected volatility, and the length of time until the option expires. Relative interest rates determine the forward premium or discount, which in turn represents the expected change in the spot rate. If 90-day interest rates in the UK are above those prevailing in the US, sterling will be at a forward discount in the 90-day market, meaning the market expects spot sterling to depreciate during that period. This situation would reduce the time value and therefore the premium on a sterling call with a three-month maturity, because the market views it as unlikely that this option will become more profitable to exercise by the time it matures. Higher interest rates in the UK and the resulting forward discount on sterling would increase the premium on a sterling put with the same maturity, because the market is saying that option is likely to be further in the money, and therefore more worth exercising, at maturity than it is now.

The second factor in determining time value is expected volatility, which is likely to be based on volatility in the recent past. Sterling puts and calls with strike prices of $ 1.60 will be worth more if the exchange rate for sterling is expected to be quite volatile, perhaps because it has been volatile during the last year or two. If, however, sterling has not moved above $ 1.62 or below $ 1.58 during that period, and there is no reason to expect that circumstances to change, both the put and the call will be worth considerable less. Purchasing options are sometimes referred to as buying price volatility, and the premium is the cost of that purchase.

The last factor is the amount of time left until an option expires; the longer that period, the greater the opportunity for an exchange rate change that will make the option more profitable, and the higher its current premium. An option which has a year until maturity will be considerably more valuable than one which expires in three months. As maturity approaches, time value declines rapidly, there being no time value at maturity, when the premium must be the intrinsic value of the option. If a sterling call has a strike price of $ 1.60 and the spot exchange rate is $ 1.62 when the option expires, its premium must be two cents. With the same spot rate, a sterling put with the $ 1.60 strike price would have a premium of zero at maturity because it is out of the money by two cents.

Now we shall use the Garman-Kohlhagen model for the valuation of the foreign exchange options. In 1983 Garman and Kohlhagen forwarded a model to cope with the presence of two interest rates, one for each currency. Suppose that t_d is the risk-free interest rate to expiry of the domestic currency and r_f is the foreign currency risk-free interest rate, where domestic currency is the currency in which we obtain the value of the option and also it is required that both strike and current spot be quoted in terms of "units of domestic currency per unit of foreign currency". Then the domestic currency value of a call option into the foreign currency is given by

$$c = S_0 \exp(-r_f T)\mathbb{N}(d_1) - K\exp(-r_d T)\mathbb{N}(d_2)$$

The value of a put option has value

$$p = K\exp(-r_d T)\mathbb{N}(-d_2) - S_0 \exp(-r_f T)\mathbb{N}(-d_1)$$

where

$$d_1 = \frac{\ln(S_0/K) + (r_d - r_f + \sigma^2/2)T}{\sigma\sqrt{T}}$$

$$d_2 = d_1 - \sigma\sqrt{T}$$

S_0 = the current spot rate

K = the strike price

$\mathbb{N}$ = cumulative normal distribution function

r_d = domestic risk free simple interest rate

r_f = foreign risk free simple interest rate

T = time to maturity (calculated according to the appropriate day count convention)

σ = volatility of the foreign exchange rate.

Garman-Kohlhagen is the standard model used to calculate the price of an foreign exchange option, however there are a wide range of techniques in use for calculating the options risk exposure, or greeks. Although the price produced by every model will agree, the risk numbers calculated by different models can vary significantly depending on the assumptions used for the properties of the spot price movements, volatility surface and interest rate curves.

COVERED INTEREST ARBITRAGE

It is a simple currency swap in which the counterparties exchange currencies at both the spot and forward rates simultaneously. The forward swap restores currency exposures to the original position without a currency gain or loss-making this a way to adjust exposure to a narrowing or widening of interest rate differentials rather than adjusting currency exposures. Covered interest arbitrage also insures interest rate parity because this relationship prevents speculators from profiting by borrowing in a low interest rate country and simultaneously lending in a high interest rate country and hedging the currency risk. In short covered interest arbitrage is the investment strategy where an investor buys a financial instrument denominated in a foreign currency, and hedges his foreign exchange risk by selling a forward contract in the amount of the proceeds of the investment back into his basc currency. The proceeds of the investment are only known exactly if the financial instrument is risk-free and only pays interest once, on the date of the forward sale of foreign currency. Otherwise, some foreign exchange risk remains.

The theory of covered interest arbitrage was first expounded clearly by John M. Keynes (1923). It rests on the simple proposition that funds available for short-term investments, say, three months, are placed in that centre which yields the highest return. This is actually part of the normal process of maximizing earnings from investment. Keynes theory of covered interest arbitrage can be explained in the following two propositions.

(a) If the interest rate differential (that is, the domestic interest rate less the foreign interest rate) is smaller than the forward difference (discount or premium) of the foreign currency (in algebraic terms), it is possible to transfers funds from the home country to the foreign country. If the interest rate differential is higher than the forward difference of the foreign currency, it is profitable to transfer funds from the foreign country to the home country.

(b) Interest parity prevails when the forward difference (discount or premium) of the foreign currency equals the interest rate differential, that is, the domestic interest rate less the foreign interest rate. When interest parity prevails, the rate of return is equalized across countries and it is no longer profitable to transfer funds from one financial centre to another.

Suppose that

r_a = three-month interest rate in New York

r_b = three-month interest rate in London

R_s = spot rate

R_f = three-month forward rate for sterling

Now suppose that an interest arbitrageur borrows \$ R_s in New York. Three months later the person's debt will be $\$(1+r_a)R_s$. Suppose that the interest arbitrageur uses the loan proceeds (\$ R_s) to purchase £ 1 in the spot market and invests the money in London. In three months the investment will grow to £ $(1 + r_b)$. To be rid of the exchange risk, the interest arbitrageur sells £ $(1 + r_b)$ forward; thus in three months the arbitrageur will receive \$ $(1+r_b)R_f$. The interest arbitrageur will make a profit if the revenue from the action exceeds the cost; that is, if

$$\$\,(1+r_a)R_s < \$\,(1+r_b)R_f \tag{1}$$

If the above inequality is reversed, an interest arbitrageur can make a profit by transferring funds from London to New York as follows:

(a) The arbitrageur borrows £ 1 in London. After three months the debt will be equal to £ $(1 + r_b)$.

(b) To cover the exchange risk, the arbitrageur buys £ $(1 + r_b)$ forward and thus in three months will pay \$ $(1 + r_b)R_f$, which is the person's cost.

(c) The arbitrageur sells £ 1 in the spot market for \$ R_S.

(d) The arbitrageur invests \$ R_S in New York. In three months the investment will accumulate to \$ $(1 + r_a)R_S$, which is the person's revenue.

The interest arbitrageur makes a profit when

$$\$\,(1 + r_a)R_S > \$\,(1 + r_b)R_f \tag{2}$$

Interest parity prevails when the profitability in London is equal to the profitability in New York, that is, when

$$\$\,(1 + r_a)R_S = \$\,(1 + r_b)R_f \tag{3}$$

Forward difference (d) is defined as follows:

$$d = \frac{R_f - R_s}{R_s} = \frac{R_f}{R_s} - 1 \tag{4}$$

The pound sterling is at a forward premium when $d>0$ and at a forward discount when $d<0$.

From equations (1), (2) and (3) we have

$$
\begin{aligned}
1+r_a &= (1+r_b)\frac{R_f}{R_s} \\
r_a &= (1+r_b)(d+1)-1 \qquad (5)\\
&= r_b + d + r_b\, d \\
&\cong r_b + d
\end{aligned}
$$

Since $r_b\, d$ is very small, therefore it is dropped from the above expression. The above equation shows that when interest parity prevails, the currency of the low-interest country is at a forward premium. For example, when $r_a > r_b$, $d = r_a - r_b > 0$; i.e. when the interest rate is lower in London than in New York, the pound sterling is at a forward premium.

The fact that the movement of fully covered funds from one financial center to another depends not only on the interest-rate differential but also on the forward difference is of great significance to economic policy. Mainly because of the role the interest rate plays in maintaining full employment and a healthy rate of economic growth, it is important to know that the movement of arbitrage funds can be influenced through the forward market. For this reason, the forward rate becomes an important instrument of economic policy and it frees the interest rate to attend to other domestic goals.

THEORIES OF EXCHANGE RATE MEASUREMENT

Different times and cultures led different economists to come up with different theories of exchange rate determination. These theories can be named as:

(a) The Mint Parity Theory

(b) The Purchasing Power Parity Theory

(c) The Balance of Payment Theory

We shall be covering all of these one by one. To begin with, let us take the first theory.

(a) The Mint Parity Theory

This theory was used to measure the exchange rate during the days when the currency was either itself made of gold or was convertible into it at a fixed rate and the central bank of the country was ever-ready to sell and buy gold but only at a specific price. The rate at which the standard money of a country was convertible into gold was known as the mint price of gold. And the mint parity or mint par of exchange (the exchange rate's name those days) was measured by dividing one currency's mint price with the other. For example, if mint price of Pound was £ 5 per ounce and the Dollar mint price was $ 20 per ounce, the exchange rate (or mint par) between the dollar and the pound would be $20/£5 = $ 4. But this mint parity was simply meant to define the export point and the import point, also known as the upper specie point and lower specie point respectively. In practise, however, the actual exchange rate could variate very well both above and below the mint parity by the cost of shipping gold between the two countries. Here one must keep in mind that the exchange rate could be anywhere, but in between the upper and lower specie points.

The theory can be explained by the help of Fig. 9.16 which takes S_1S_2 (the supply curve) and D_1D_2 (the demand curve) intersect at point *E*. This is the point of equilibrium. Here, let us be reminded of the fact that the exchange rate can be anywhere between the upper specie point after which the supply curve will be perfectly elastic and the lower specie point at which the demand curve will be perfectly elastic. The figure takes the exchange rate to be determined at *OM*.

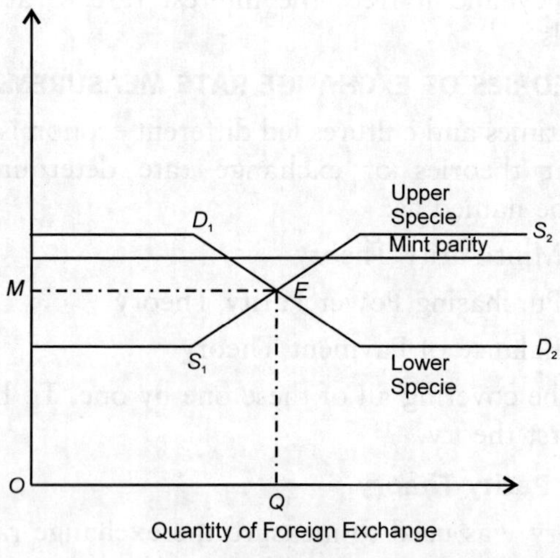

Fig. 9.16

But the above stated theory is based on certain assumptions—the price of gold is fixed by a country in terms of its currency, capital is mobile within countries, there is automatic adjustment mechanism, etc.

Criticism

The Mint Parity Theory was based on the gold standard that broke down after the great Depression. The theory could not explain the determination of exchange rates when the internal prices were not flexible. Various economists did try, but could not bring this theory to the modern times of inconvertible paper money being in vogue. Hence the theory is redundant.

(b) The Purchasing Power Parity Theory

The term 'purchasing power parity' was first introduced by the Swedish economist, Gustav Cassel. He formulated the theory to determine the correct rate of exchange between the currencies of different countries. The theory has two forms, viz. (a) Absolute and (b) Comparative. In its absolute form, it maintains that the rate of exchange will be in equilibrium when the purchasing power of money is equal in all the trading countries. The equilibrium rate of exchange will be determined by the quotient between the price levels of different countries. In its comparative form, it establishes a relationship between the changes in the purchasing power and the changes in the exchange rates. It determines the correct rate of exchange between the currencies of different countries at a point of time, given the equilibrium rate of exchange at some previous time and the price levels prevailing in different countries at both these points. Let R_0 be the correct rate of exchange between the currencies of countries a and b in the previous period. R_1, the correct rate of exchange during the current period = $R_0 \times \dfrac{P_{a1}}{P_{a0}} \times \dfrac{P_{b1}}{P_{b0}}$

where P_{a0} represents the price level in country a in the previous period, P_{a1} the price level in country a in the current period, P_{b0} the price level in country b in the previous period, and P_{b1} the price level in country b in the current period. It maintains that an increase or a decrease in the price level of one country will cause, other things remaining the same, a proportionate fall or rise in its rate of exchange.

A detailed and diagrammatic explanation of the theory follows—We know that R_1, i.e. the correct rate of exchange during current period is also known as the purchasing power parity between two countries. As in mint parity theory, this rate also has a fluctuation limit. This limit lies between the commodity export point and the commodity import point. But these limits are not as definite as in mint parity theory. Even they can fluctuate along an average point.

In Fig. 9.17, D_1D_1 and S_1S_1 are the initial demand and supply curves, respectively, for and of a foreign currency in a country. These intersect at E_1 so as to establish the initial equilibrium and the exchange rate is determined as OR_1. Now suppose the price level rises in one (domestic) country but remains constant in the other (foreign). This will make the export from the domestic country costly in the foreign land but the import from that foreign land will become cheaper. Hence the demand for foreign currency will increase in the domestic country, while the supply of the same decrease. This is depicted by the shifts in demand curve to D_2D_2 and supply curve to S_2S_2. New equilibrium will be established at E_2 and new rate of exchange will be OR_2. But this exchange rate will never become lower than OIP (lower limit) and higher than E_P (upper limit).

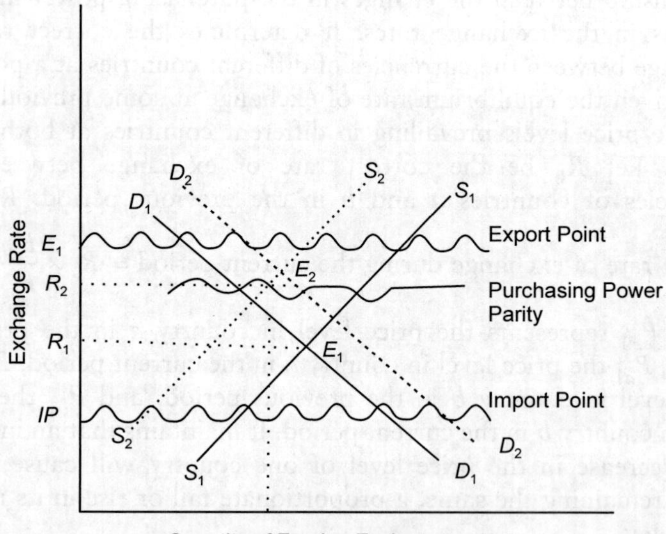

Fig. 9.17

Criticism

Though this theory gained a lot of popularity, yet it was not free of criticisms. The main problem that arises is of measuring price levels in two different countries. Index numbers also can't be calculated easily because of the base year's possibility of being different in both the countries. Moreover this theory is not applicable to those countries whose exchange rate is influenced more by capital account. Also, this theory is relevant only for bilateral exchange rate determination and fails to determine the exchange rate in the present scenario.

It has been maintained by some authors that the purchasing power parity theory is valid only when applied to internationally traded goods and does not hold when applied to the general price levels. Prices of non-traded goods remain independent of the prices in the international markets. There is no direct connection between the domestic and foreign prices of such goods and hence between the price levels and the rate of exchange. Assuming away costs of transfer, when applied only to the internationally traded goods, the theory is no more than a truism. The prices of internationally traded goods necessarily adjust themselves to changes in exchange rates. Suppose, for illustration, that the exchange rate between dollar and rupee is $ 1=Rs. 4. If commodity *A* costs 2 dollars in the United States, it will necessarily cost 8 rupees in India because the price in both the countries is governed by the world price of the commodity. If the exchange rate alters to $ 1=Rs. 5 and the price of the commodity remains unchanged in the United States, the price in India will rise to Rs. 10. Thus the relative prices between the two countries will conform to changes in the exchange rate. It will be equally true to say that the domestic prices of commodities conform to rather than determining the movements in exchange rates. Cassel maintains that the theory will not hold good if applied only to internationally traded goods. If it is assumed that the prices of all export commodities are doubled in country *B,* all other prices in country *B* and all prices in country *A* remaining unchanged, the rate of exchange will not fall by half because before the exchange rate falls by this amount, many goods whose export was not profitable at the old rate of exchange will enter the export market and the import of several previously imported goods will become unprofitable; this will check a further fall in the rate of exchange.

A distinction should be made between the sequence of events and the casual relationship. An inverse movement between the domestic price level and the foreign exchange rate need not necessarily mean that the change in the latter is caused by a change in the former. Often, the changes in the both might be caused by other factors. Sometimes, the rate of exchange may take a lead and the prices of commodities follow suit. A decline in exchange rate will raise the prices of export and import goods in terms of the domestic currency. Rise in the prices of export and import goods will raise the prices of domestic goods which can be substituted directly or indirectly for the export and import goods. The productive resources employed for the production of domestic and traded goods being more or less the same, a rise in the prices of traded goods will raise the prices of domestic goods. Thus a decline in the exchange rate will raise the general price level. It is very difficult to find out statistically as to whether the exchange rate has moved in response to changes in prices or vice versa.

The concept of a 'change in the price level' is a very vague one. Prices of all commodities never move normal. Prices of some commodities rise or fall much more than those of others. Under such conditions, no simple comparison can be made between the price movements in different countries. An average or an index number of changes in the prices of different commodities has got to be constructed in each of the different countries for making a comparison between price movements. Construction of index numbers involves a considerable element of judgement as to prices and commodities to be included, weights to be attached to each commodity, type of average to be used etc. The comparison, therefore, can only be rough and not exact.

The absolute form of the purchasing power parity theory neglects the costs of transfer of commodities. The theory will hold good only if the commodities flowed between different countries freely and without any cost. Under this assumption, it is not only the average price levels but also the prices of each and every individual commodities which will be identical in different countries if computed on the basis of the prevailing exchange rate. In actual practice, the prices of internationally traded goods may differ in two countries by the costs of transfer. The prices of internationally traded goods may differ in different countries also because of lack of information, lack of initiative, selling costs in a new market and several such other factors.

Rate of exchange between the currencies of two countries is influenced not only by the purchasing power parity but also by the reciprocal demand of the countries for each other's goods. A change in the reciprocal demand for goods brought about by a change in the tastes, fashions, incomes etc. may bring about a change in the exchange rate even if the price levels remain unchanged in both the countries. Cassel admitted the role of the reciprocal demands in determining the rate of exchange in a debate with Professor Viner but maintained that his theory was meant to apply only to the effect of monetary changes operating *ceterus paribus*.[2]

Cassel's proposition that any change in the volume of paper money will lead to a proportionate change in its internal and external value is static in nature. In a dynamic world, the change in the internal and the external value of money may be more or less than the change in its volume. If there exists excess capacity, the increase in the volume of money might lead to an increase in the supply of domestic and traded goods instead of an increase in the price level and a fall in the internal and external value of money. If the change in the volume of money affects the velocity of circulation, the effect on the price level may be more or less than the proportionate one. Expectation plays an important role in determining the internal and the external value of money. Rate of exchange, often, coincides with the expected rather than the actual purchasing power parity.

It is very difficult to find out as to when the rate of exchange is in equilibrium and, therefore, what should be the base period for calculating the correct exchange rate at any particular time with the help of the purchasing power parity formula.

The purchasing power parity is only a commodity price parity. It takes into account the demand for and the supply of foreign exchange arising only from trade in commodities. It utterly neglects the effect of long-term investments, transfer of interest and dividends, and short-term capital movements on the demand for and the supply of foreign exchange and consequently on the rate of exchange. The capital movements between the two countries may bring about a change in the exchange rate even if the price levels remain unchanged in these countries. Cassel, however, maintains that the influence of the disturbances like capital flows or tariff changes as compared with that of the comparative purchasing power of the respective currencies is not so powerful as to cause a wide divergence between the purchasing power parity and the rate of exchange between different currencies. In addition, the influence of these factors is temporary in character.

The purchasing power parity theory was first formulated to explain the movements in exchange rates that occurred during the First World War period. There developed scathing criticism of the theory in the interwar period and the theory was more or less abandoned. The most important reason for the theory being valid during the First World War period and invalid during the interwar period is that the movements in exchange rates during the First World War period were large and caused mostly by changes in prices independent of changes in the level of output and employment, changes in tastes and fashions, capital movements etc. While the movements in exchange rates in the interwar normal period were small and caused by factors other than price changes, viz. changes in the level of output and employment, changes in tastes and fashions, capital movements etc.

The above mentioned criticisms of the purchasing power parity theory in no way imply that the theory is useless. It may not be exact, yet it can serve as one of the important guides in determining the correct rate of exchange.

The Balance of Payments Theory

This theory states that under free exchange rates, the exchange rate of a country's currency depends upon its balance of payments. If the balance of payments of a country is favourable, it will increase the exchange rate and vice-versa.

This theory can be understood by going through Fig. 9.18, which shows *SS* and *DD* as the respective supply and demand curve of the foreign exchange in our country. Both of these curves intersect at *E* and the rate of exchange is determined at R_E as OR_E.

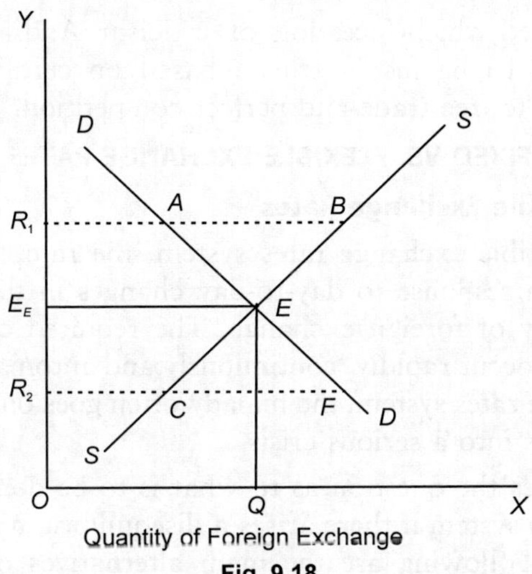

Fig. 9.18

At this rate, the quantity of foreign exchange demanded equals its supply at quantity *OQ*. At point *E* only, the balance of payments is in equilibrium. Any deviation from this point shall only bring a disequilibrium on the balance of payment. Suppose the rate of exchange goes upto OR_1. In this case, the demand for foreign exchange (R_1A) will be less than its supply (R_1B). As a consequence, the balance of payments will be favourable for our country. But this will ultimately lead in a fall in exports and rise in imports. Consequently, the demand for foreign exchange will rise and the supply will fall. Equilibrium level will be restored eventually.

Just in case, if the rate of exchange decreases from the equilibrium rate of OR_E and becomes OR_2, it will decrease the supply of foreign exchange and increase the demand for it. In such a case, balance of payments will be unfavourable to our country. But this will lead to our exports being increased and decrease in imports. Consequently, the demand for foreign exchange will decrease while the supply of it will rise. Equilibrium level will again be restored eventually.

Criticisms

The main criticisms which the theory suffers from is that the balance of payment does not wholly determine the exchange rate. Rather the case is opposite. It is the changes in exchange rate that determines the balance of payments. Price level's role also has been totally discarded which faces lots of criticism. And at the end, the theory is said to be just a truism based on certain impractical assumptions like free trade and perfect competition.

FIXED VS. FLEXIBLE EXCHANGE RATES

Case for Flexible Exchange Rates

Under flexible exchange rates system, the rate of exchange is free to vary in response to day-to-day changes in the demand for and the supply of foreign exchange. The required changes in the exchange rate occur rapidly, continuously and automatically. Under fixed exchange rates system, the malady often goes on accumulating and culminates into a serious crisis.

There arises the question as to what is to be done under fixed exchange rates system if there arises a disequilibrium in the balance of payments. Following are the main alternatives of rectifying a disequilibrium in the balance of payments under fixed exchange rates.

(a) A change in the exchange rate by government action.

(b) Deflation of domestic prices and incomes.

(c) Institution of trade and exchange restrictions.

The effect of changes in exchange rate by government action on commodity trade is very similar to that of the automatic changes in exchange rate under the flexible exchange rate system. A change in exchange rate under the flexible exchange rates system differs from the change affected by government action only to the extent the change under the former system is continuous while the same is occasional and deliberate under the latter system and the equilibrium during the transitional period is maintained either by domestic price and income changes, import restrictions or the use of monetary reserves. This difference gives rise to another important difference between the two systems, viz. their effect on the speculative transactions. When the changes in exchange rate are occasional, the variations in the balance of payments position give rise to an expectation of a change in the exchange rate. The expectation of a change in the exchange rate leads to speculative buying and selling. Sometimes a change in the exchange rate might be necessitated simply by speculative transactions on a larger scale while there would have been no such need in the absence of speculative transactions. Very little risk of loss is involved in such speculative transactions because the direction of change in the exchange rate, if it occurs, can be known beforehand from the balance of payments position of the country. The risk of loss exists only to the extent of the cost of transfer and retransfer of capital from one country to the other and the difference, if any, in the rate of interest between the two countries. In contrast, under flexible exchange rates system, the sale of domestic currency for speculative purpose immediately lowers the exchange rate and thus inflicts a penalty on speculators. Further, it is not possible for the government to know the correct rate of exchange. Government may fix it at a level either higher or lower than the appropriate one. Correct rate of exchange can be found only by trial and error by the free operation of the market forces.

The effect of depreciation on trade can also be achieved by a general lowering of the internal price level. A 20 per cent lowering of the general internal price level will have the same effect as a 20 per cent depreciation of the domestic currency. But the lowering of price level is far more difficult than the lowering of exchange rate. The lowering of the price of labour is particularly difficult in these days of strong trade unionism. The lowering of the prices may be desirable only where the prices of a few selected commodities are to be reduced. Deflation of internal incomes is a very wasteful method of correcting a disequilibrium in the balance of payments. It inflicts suffering on masses. These days, stability of internal prices, income and employment is considered to be of primary importance in all countries. No country would like to disturb the whole internal economy just for correcting a disequilibrium in the balance of payments. Under flexible exchange rates, a country can follow an independent financial policy for maintaining the internal economy in proper balance without being affected by deficits or surpluses in the balance of payments. Flexible exchange rates safeguard the internal economy against external events. Suppose, for instance, there develops a recession abroad. Under fixed exchange rates, foreign demand for exports will decline. This will transmit recession into the internal economy and also result into a decline in the country's monetary reserves. Under flexible exchange rates, the decline in foreign demand for exports will lower the exchange rate. This will stimulate exports and discourage imports. Thus the decline in monetary reserves and the transmission of recession into the internal economy will be checked. Along with this advantage, however, there is also the disadvantage that the internal events are retained within the economy and not shared by the foreign countries. A domestic deflation or inflation, for instance, will not be shared by the foreign countries. Under fixed exchange rates, domestic inflation or deflation will spread abroad and its effect on the internal economy will be moderated. Flexible exchange rates are useful for countries pursuing a full employment policy.

A third way of correcting a disequilibrium in the balance of payments is the institution of trade and exchange restrictions. Restrictions, however, have got several disadvantages. They diminish the volume of trade. Import restrictions, often, involve interference in the internal economy, e.g. rationing might be introduced to distribute the limited imports. Administration of restrictions is very arbitrary. Once restrictions have been imposed, it is very difficult to remove them because of the opposition from the vested interests which grow under protection. They direct the trade into channels other than those determined by the principle of comparative costs. They encourage corruption and bribery.

Fixed exchange rates are inconsistent with the unrestricted multilateral trade. Any disequilibrium in the balance of payments under fixed exchange rates can be met, mainly speaking, by deflation of internal prices and incomes, changes in monetary reserves, or trade and exchange restrictions. It is generally accepted that the deflation of domestic incomes and prices for rectifying a disequilibrium in the balance of payments is undesirable. The use of monetary reserves can meet only small and temporary deficits. The only alternative, that is left, is the institution of trade and exchange restrictions and discrimination in their application in case the disequilibrium is not general but only with specific countries.

It has often been contended that the flexible exchange rates create uncertainty and instability in the economic system. This discourages international trade in commodities, and the movement of the factors of production, particularly that of capital, and thereby diminishes international specialisation. This, of course, is not true. The fact is that instability is inherent in the economic conditions governing international trade. A rigid exchange rate does not remove instability. It only shifts it from exchange rate to some other elements of the economy. Let us illustrate this point by examining a few specific forms in which the argument is generally presented.

The first specific form of the argument is that the flexible exchange rates create uncertainty as to the price the importers will have to pay and the exporters will obtain for their imports and exports respectively. This problem can be overcome by the traders insuring themselves against such risks by hedging in future markets. Future markets develop rapidly under flexible exchange rates. This, of course, involves the additional cost of hedging on traders. They will have to pay the price for the services of speculators who assume risks of future changes in exchange rates. Fixed exchange rates, however, involve no less risks for the traders. The only difference is that the risks appear in certain forms other than the variations in exchange rates. For instance, the conditions that lower the exchange rate under flexible exchange rates will cause a shortage of foreign exchange under the fixed exchange rates. This will create uncertainty as to whether or not the importers will get the required amount of foreign exchange. Thus under fixed exchange rates, the uncertainty will be shifted from the price of foreign exchange that traders will have to pay to the amount of foreign exchange which the traders can obtain. If resort is taken to the deflation of domestic prices and incomes for preventing a shortage of foreign exchange, uncertainty will be created as to the domestic prices and demand. In case, the fixed exchange rates are made subject to change by government action for rectifying a disequilibrium in the balance of payments, uncertainty will be created as to the future exchange rate. The only difference is that the changes in exchange rate will be less frequent. This advantage, however, will be counterbalanced by the larger magnitude of the change. Under flexible exchange rates, the changes are small and continuous. In addition, certain measures will have to be taken to maintain the exchange rate during the periods between different changes in exchange rates. If the measure takes the form of a deflation of domestic prices and incomes, uncertainty will be created, as noticed above, about the domestic prices and demand. Another alternative for maintaining the exchange rate during the periods between different changes in exchange rate will be the use of monetary reserves. But the capacity of monetary reserves to maintain a particular exchange rate is very much limited. Further, the maintenance of monetary reserves involves a cost. The greater the capacity of the monetary reserves to maintain an exchange rate, the larger will be cost of keeping these reserves. If, on the other hand, monetary reserves are not sufficiently large, frequent changes will be necessary in the fixed exchange rate in response to changes in the balance of payments position.

A second form of the argument is that the flexible exchange rates encourage destabilising speculation. A slight fall in the exchange rate creates an expectation of a further fall among speculators and leads them to speculative selling of domestic currency. Fixed exchange rates, however, do not prevent speculation. Under fixed exchange rates combined with trade and exchange restrictions or deflation of internal prices and incomes, the speculation is shifted from exchange rates to the prices of imports and exports. As seen earlier, fixed exchange rates subject to change by government action also encourage speculation. Further, it is doubtful if speculation has, on the whole, a destabilising effect. Speculation will be destabilising only if speculators sell domestic currency when the exchange rate is going to rise and buy it when the exchange rate is going to fall. This will tantamount to saying that speculators always lose on the average which is very doubtful.

A third form of the argument is that the flexible exchange rates create instability in the internal prices. A decline in the exchange rate caused by a deficit in the balance of payments, for instance, will raise the prices of imported goods and, also, those of domestic goods which can be substituted for imported goods directly or indirectly. A rise in the prices of goods will raise the cost of living and thereby lead the labour to demand higher wages. The demand for higher wages, if accepted, will raise the cost of production and hence the prices of domestic goods still higher and thus lead to a wage-price spiral. The wage-price spiral will prevent the domestic prices from falling in relation to foreign prices which is necessary to rectify the deficit in the balance of payments and to check a further decline in the exchange rate. But a rise in the price of imported and import competing goods cannot be prevented under fixed exchange rates. The conditions which cause a decline in the exchange rate will cause a shortage of foreign exchange and thereby diminish the total amount of goods that can be imported. A shortage of imported goods will raise their prices, and can thus lead to the same kind of wage-price spiral. Similarly, fixed exchange rates subject to change by government action for correcting a deficit, in the balance of payments can cause a wage-price spiral whenever any change is made in the exchange rate. If the fixed exchange rate is maintained by a deflation of internal prices and incomes, widespread unemployment and a large decline in incomes is very likely to follow which is worse than inflation. Moreover, the danger of a wage-price spiral is more imagined than real. A wage-price spiral can occur only if the monetary authorities are ready to create substantial amounts of additional money. In case the monetary authorities are ready to do so, the wage-price spiral can develop from any situation.

Case against Flexible Exchange Rates

Under flexible exchange rates, temporary variations in exchange rate are very frequent. Variations in exchange rate change the comparative profitability of the export and import-competing industries and thereby lead to shifts of resources between these industries. To the extent, temporary variations lead to a frequent reallocation of resources, there is involved a wastage of resources. Under fixed exchange rates, small movements in the balance of payments can easily be met by using monetary reserves and thus frequent variations in exchange rate are avoided. The monetary reserves required for this purpose will not be large and hence the cost will not be very high.

Experience shows that the flexible rates cannot always be relied upon to achieve and maintain an equilibrium in the balance of payments.[3] Any considerable or continuous movement in the exchange rate is likely to generate an expectation of a further movement in the same direction. This encourages speculative movements of capital of a disequilibrating nature and thereby accentuate the problem. Speculative anticipations may, also, affect the normal transactions. A decline in exchange rate may induce traders to import larger amounts and to export less in anticipation of a further decline in the exchange rate. Importers may rush to make payments for their imports to avoid a loss from a further decline in the exchange rate. Exporters may postpone the receipt of the payments for their exports as long as possible expecting to gain from a decline in the exchange rate.

The most important objection to flexible exchange rates relates to the terms of trade. Many countries are pegging the exchange rates through trade and exchange controls at a level much higher than that which will prevail in a free market. The introduction of a free and flexible exchange rate will substantially deteriorate their terms of trade. The loss from the highly unfavourable terms of trade will be in proportionate to the gain that might result from flexible exchange rates.

Many countries, particularly the underdeveloped countries, are experiencing a serious shortage of foreign exchange. The underdeveloped countries require vast amounts of foreign exchange for importing capital goods, technical know-how and essential raw-materials. They have to institute trade and exchange controls to-ensure that only essential goods are imported and precious foreign exchange is not wasted on comfortable and luxurious goods.

> Those who advocate allowing rates to find their 'natural' level, permitting market forces to determine a rate of exchange that will be stabilised, seek to provide a simple solution for a very complex problem. There is no such thing as a 'natural' level for the rate of exchange of a currency. The proper rate will, in each case, depend upon the economic, financial and monetary policies followed by the country concerned and by other countries with whom it has important economic relationships. If the economy of a country is to adapt itself to a given exchange rate, there must be time for the producers, sellers and buyers of goods and services to respond to the new set of prices and cost relationships to which the rate gives rise. This means that in the short run changes in the exchange rate are either no test or a very poor test of basic economic inter-relationships. It also means that whether a given exchange rate is at the 'correct' level can be determined only after there has been time to observe the course of the balance of payments in response to that rate. Moreover, past experience with fluctuating rates of exchange has proved that movements in the rates are significantly affected by large speculative transfers of capital. Parenthetically it may be mentioned that generally implicit in the arguments for fluctuating rates is the assumption that some major currency will remain stable as a point against which to operate the fluctuating rate.[4]

To conclude, it will not be in the interest of many countries, especially the underdeveloped countries, to introduce flexible exchange rates. Fixed exchange rates subject to change by government action seem to be the best course. Smaller and temporary variations in the balance of payments should be met by using monetary reserves. Large and protracted deficits should be rectified with either trade and exchange restrictions, deflation of domestic prices or depreciation of exchange rate or with any combination of these methods depending upon what is more appropriate under the given circumstances.

DEVALUATION-ELASTICITIES APPROACH

Whether or not devaluation can cure a disequilibrium in the balance of payments depends upon the shape of the demand and supply curves for foreign exchange. The shape of the demand and supply curves for foreign exchange depends upon the nature of the underlying transactions. The demand for foreign currency, for instance, for paying interest on fixed-interest securities is of zero elasticity if the debt is expressed in terms of foreign currency and of unitary elasticity if the debt is expressed in terms of domestic currency and is payable in foreign currency. The shape of the demand and supply curves for foreign exchange arising out of imports and exports of goods and services depends upon and is derived from the demand for and the supply of imports and exports at home and abroad. The effect of depreciation will differ, therefore, according to the shape of the demand and supply curves for imports and exports of goods and services at home and abroad. Obviously, the volume of imports will fall and that of exports rise after the depreciation of the domestic currency. Before we discuss the effect of devaluation on the prices and value of imports and exports, we will have to decide the currency in terms of which we speak. The effect of a variation in exchange rate on the price and value of imports and exports will be different in terms of different currencies. Export and import prices after devaluation, for instance, will rise in terms of domestic currency and fall in terms of foreign currency. Under certain conditions, it is possible that the balance of payments might improve in terms of one currency and deteriorate in terms of the other. If the interest lies, mainly, in examining the effect of devaluation on the domestic income and employment, it is better to work in terms of domestic currency while working in terms of foreign currency is preferable if the interest lies, mainly, in analysing its impact on the balance of payments. Two pairs of diagrams are shown below to study the effect of devaluation in terms of foreign as well as in terms of domestic currency.

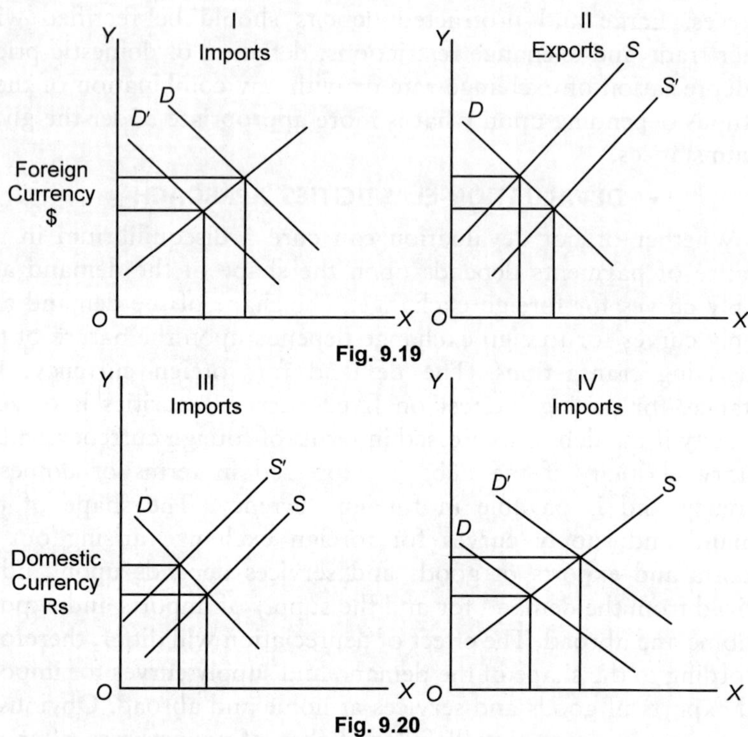

Fig. 9.19

Fig. 9.20

Figures I and II show the demand for and supply of the exports and imports with prices in terms of foreign currency; prices are expressed in terms of domestic currency in Figures III and IV. The curves *D* and *S* show the demand for and supply of foreign exchange before the devaluation of the domestic currency. These curves are identical in the two pairs of figures because it makes little difference whether the price of exports and imports is expressed in terms of one or the other currency so long as there is no change in the exchange rate.

Let us now suppose that the domestic currency depreciates in terms of foreign currency and see how it affects the price, volume and value of exports and imports in terms of domestic and foreign currency. In terms of foreign currency, the foreign supply curve of imports remain unchanged and the domestic demand curve for imports shifts from *D* to *D′*. Each point on *D* curve is vertically reduced in proportion to the depreciation of the currency. On the export side, the foreign demand curve for imports remains unchanged but the supply curve shifts down because our supply prices are lowered for the foreigners in terms of dollars in proportion to the depreciation of the domestic currency. Thus it follows that the price of imports and exports in terms of domestic currency falls (barring the exceptions when the import supply curve or the export demand curve are perfectly elastic or when the import demand curve or the export supply curve are perfectly inelastic).

The value of imports in terms of foreign currency falls (barring the exception when the demand curve is perfectly inelastic). The value of exports will remain unchanged if the elasticity of foreign demand is unity, rise if it is more than unity, and fall in case it is less than unity.

In terms of domestic currency, the demand curve for imports remains unchanged but the supply curve shifts up because the foreign goods become more expensive in terms of domestic currency after depreciation. On the export side, the supply curve remains unchanged but the demand curve shifts up. Thus it follows that the import and export prices in terms of domestic currency rise (barring certain exceptional cases when the price remains unchanged).

The value of imports depends upon the elasticity of demand. The value remains unchanged if the elasticity is unity, rises if it is more than unity and falls if it is less than unity. The value of exports will definitely go up (barring the exceptional case when the demand is perfectly inelastic).

The two tables given below summarise the effect of depreciation on the volume, prices and value of exports and imports in terms of foreign and domestic currency.

Table 1

Effect of Depreciation on

Volume		*Prices in terms of foreign currency*	*Volume in terms of foreign currency*
Exports	Rises	Fall	Rises, falls or remains unchanged depending upon whether the elasticity of foreign demand for exports is more than, less than or equal to unity.
Imports	Falls	Fall	Falls

Table 2

Effect of Depreciation on

Volume		Prices in terms of domestic currency	Value in terms of domestic currency
Exports	Rises	Rise	Rises
Imports	Falls	Rises	Rises, falls or remains unchanged depending upon whether the elasticity of domestic demand for imports is more than, less than or equal to unity.

From the earlier drawn four figures, we can derive the demand for and supply of foreign exchange from the demand and supply curves for exports and imports. In Figure I, the shape of demand curve for dollars in terms of home currency is determined by the shapes of *D* and *S* curves. The demand for dollars corresponding to a given rate of exchange is represented by the area of the rectangle under the intersection of demand and supply curves for imports. The greater will be the elasticity of demand for dollars, the larger is the shrinkage in this area upon a given appreciation of the dollars as represented by a downward shift of the *D* curve. Given the *S* curve, the elasticity of demand for dollars will be greater, the greater is the elasticity of *D* curve. If for instance, the elasticity of demand is infinite (i.e. demand curve is horizontal), the price of imports will fall by the full amount of the depreciation, and the value of imports (demand for dollars) will be reduced considerably. If, on the other hand, the elasticity of demand is zero (vertical straight line), the price and consequently the value of imports will remain unchanged or, in other words, the demand for dollars will be completely inelastic.

Let us now examine the influence of the elasticity of the S curve on the elasticity of demand for dollars, assuming a given *D* curve. It depends upon the elasticity of the *D* curve. If the elasticity of *D* curve is unity, the elasticity of demand for dollars will be unity whatever may be the elasticity of *S* curve. If the elasticity of *D* curve is greater than unity, the elasticity of demand for dollars will be greater, the greater is the elasticity of the *S* curve. If the elasticity of

D curve is less than unity, the elasticity of demand for dollars will be greater, the smaller is the elasticity of the *S* curve. Algebraically the relationship can be written as follows:

$$\eta_\$ = \eta_m \frac{\varepsilon_m + 1}{\eta_m + \varepsilon_m} = \frac{\varepsilon_m + 1}{\frac{\varepsilon_m}{\eta_m} + 1}$$

where η and ε stand for demand and supply elasticities respectively. Subscripts *m* and \$ denote that the elasticities relate to the demand or supply of imports and dollars respectively.

The rules formulated above can easily be derived from the above formula. It also follows that if $\varepsilon_m = \infty$, $\eta_\$ = \eta_m$. This is so because $\frac{\varepsilon_m + 1}{\varepsilon_m + \eta_m}$ tends to unity as ε_m approaches infinity.

Thus supply curve of dollars can be derived from Figure II. The supply of dollars corresponding to a given rate of exchange is represented by the area of the rectangle under the intersection of demand and supply curves of exports. As the dollar appreciates in terms of Rs. the *S* curve shifts down. The dollar value of exports will increase upon a depreciation of rupee (i.e. the supply curve of dollars will be positively inclined) if the elasticity of foreign demand for our exports is greater than unity. The value of exports will fall upon a depreciation of rupee (i.e. supply curve of dollars will be negatively inclined) if the elasticity of foreign demand of our exports is less than unity. The numerical value of the elasticity of supply of dollars (whether negative or positive) will be greater, the greater is the elasticity of the *S* curve. If the elasticity of the *D* curve is unity, the elasticity of the supply curve of dollars will be zero, i.e. it will be a vertical straight line whatever may be the elasticity of the *S* curve. Algebraically the relationship can be written as follows:

$$\varepsilon_\$ = \varepsilon_x \frac{\eta_x - 1}{\eta_x + \varepsilon_x} = \frac{\eta_x - 1}{\frac{\eta_x}{\varepsilon_x} + 1}$$

where η and ε stand for demand and supply elasticities respectively. Subscripts *x* and \$ denote that the elasticities relate to the demand and supply of exports and dollars respectively.

Similar rules can be derived for the demand and supply curves of the home currency from Fig. 9.20 (III) and 9.20 (IV). These can be expressed algebraically as

$$\varepsilon_{Rs.} = \varepsilon_m \frac{1-\eta_m}{\eta_m+\varepsilon_m} \text{ and } \eta_{Rs.} = \eta_x \frac{\varepsilon_x+1}{\varepsilon_x+\eta_x}$$

where subscript Rs. denotes that the elasticities relate to the demand and supply of Rs. Other scripts and subscripts remain as before. From the second formula, it follows that if $\varepsilon_x = \infty$, $\eta_{Rs.} = \eta_x$ because $\frac{\varepsilon_a+1}{\varepsilon_x+\eta_x}$ becomes unity as ε_x approaches infinity.

There exists a relationship between the elasticities of demand and supply for dollars and rupees because the demand for dollars constitutes the supply of Rs. and the supply of Rs. constitutes the demand for dollars. Algebraically the relationship is $\eta_{Rs.} + \varepsilon_\$ = 1$ and $\varepsilon_{Rs.} + \eta_\$ = 1$. This can be easily verified by inserting $\eta_\$$ etc. in the expressions stated above.

We can now derive the general condition for an improvement in balance of payments upon a devaluation. The general condition is that $\eta_\$ > \varepsilon_\$$. Substituting the expression $\eta_{Rs.} + \varepsilon_\$ = 1$ in the above condition, we obtain $\eta_\$ > 1 - \eta_{Rs.}$ or $\eta_\$ + \eta_{Rs.} > 1$.

Substituting the elasticities of demand and supply of exports and imports for the elasticities of demand and supply of currencies in $\eta_\$ > \varepsilon_\$$ from the earlier given equations, we can obtain the generalised condition for an effective devaluation in terms of the elasticities of demand and supply of exports and imports which is as follows:

$$\eta_m \frac{\varepsilon_m+1}{\eta_m+\varepsilon_m} - \varepsilon_x \frac{\eta_x-1}{\eta_b+\varepsilon_x} > 0 \text{ or } \frac{\eta_m\eta_x(1+\varepsilon_m+\varepsilon_x)+\varepsilon_m\varepsilon_x(\eta_m+\eta_x-1)}{(\eta_m+\varepsilon_m)(\eta_x+\varepsilon_x)}$$

The above formula for an improvement in the balance of payments in case of devaluation is based on the assumption that the demand for and supply of foreign currency resulting from imports and exports are equal. This formula, therefore, will have to be modified in case there exists a disequilibrium in the balance of payments at the time of devaluation. The required modification can easily be understood if we formulate the condition for an effective devaluation in terms of the slopes of the demand and supply curves. The condition is that the supply curve must be steeper than the demand curve.

It is obvious from the diagram below that the above condition can be applied without change to the case where the exports and imports are unequal. The formula will have to be modified if it is to be expressed in terms of elasticities. Slopes, however, can easily be expressed in terms of elasticities. Let D' be the slope of the demand curve and S' the slope of the supply curve. The $D' = \eta_{\$} \dfrac{M}{P}$ and $S' = \varepsilon_{\$} \dfrac{X}{P}$, where both exports ($X$) and imports ($M$) are in dollars. The condition $D'>S'$ becomes $\eta_{\$}.M>\varepsilon_{\$}.X$. If supply of \$ is translated into a demand for Rs. the condition becomes $\eta_{\$} \dfrac{M}{X} + \eta_{Rs.} > 1$. In case X becomes equal to M, the expression is reduced to the original formula. Similarly, it can be shown that the condition for an effective devaluation in terms of domestic currency is $\eta_{\$} + \eta_{Rs.} \dfrac{X}{M} > 1$. The significance of the modification is that the larger the initial disequilibrium in the balance of payments, the greater are the chances of the success of devaluation in removing the disequilibrium. In actual practice, countries resorting to a depreciation, generally, suffer from a disequilibrium in their balance of payments and hence the curative effect of the devaluation will be more than that indicated by the unmodified formula.

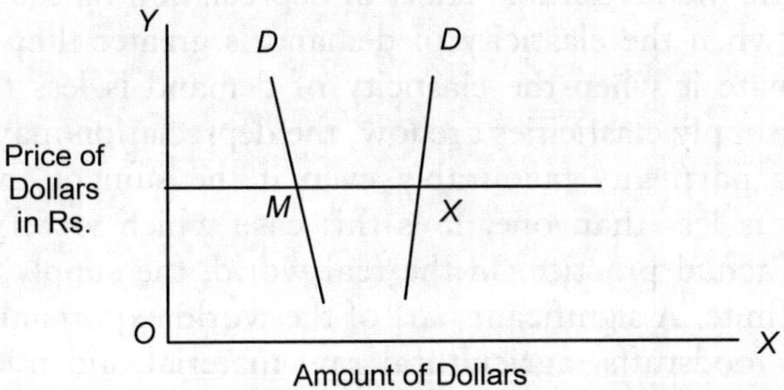

Fig. 9.21

AN APPRAISAL OF LERNER'S CONDITION

Lerner expressed the condition for an effective devaluation in terms of the elasticities of demand for imports and exports. The condition is that the sum of the elasticities of home demand for imports and the foreign demand for exports must be greater than unity.

The Lerner condition is sufficient but not necessary. Devaluation will be effective if the Lerner condition is fulfilled. Devaluation, however, may not always be ineffective if the Lerner condition is not met; it can still be effective if supply elasticities are sufficiently small. The Lerner condition becomes sufficient as well as necessary in the limiting case in which the elasticities of supply are infinite. The flaw in the Lerner condition is that it concentrates only on the elasticities of demand for exports and imports. The general condition mentioned earlier takes into account the elasticities of demand for as well as those of supply of exports and imports. The magnitude of the supply elasticities exerts no influence if the demand elasticities are zero or unity. Barring these exceptional cases, the supply elasticities play an important role in determining the effect of depreciation on the balance of payments. If the elasticity of demand for exports (imports) is greater than unity, the supply of foreign exchange from exports (the demand for foreign exchange for imports) will be more elastic, the greater is the elasticity of supply of exports (imports). On the other hand, if the elasticity of demand for exports (imports) is less than unity, the supply of foreign exchange from exports (the demand for foreign exchange for imports) will be more elastic, the smaller is the, elasticity of supply of exports (imports). Thus the assumption of infinite supply elasticities will overestimate the favourable effect of depreciation on the balance of payments when the elasticity of demand is greater than unity and underestimate it when the elasticity of demand is less than unity. When the supply elasticities are low, the depreciation may affect the balance of payments favourably even if the sum of the demand elasticities is less than one. It is this case which is very likely to prevail in actual practice. In the real world, the supply elasticities are not infinite. A significant part of the world exports and imports consist of foodstuffs, agricultural raw material and minerals, the supply elasticity of which is admittedly very low. Regarding manufactured goods, the technological conditions make possible a sufficiently elastic supply. But most of these commodities are sold under monopolistic conditions. This reduces the elasticity of supply. The monopolistic sellers will not be willing to reduce price if the demand is not sufficiently elastic. If the depreciation lowers the prices of exports in terms of foreign currency, the monopolistic exporters will raise these in terms of domestic currency. Thus in cases of low elasticity of demand, it is the selling price and not the output which will be adjusted to the changed exchange rate. Or in other words, the elasticity of supply will be lower in cases of low elasticity of demand.[5]

If neither the demand nor the supply curve for exports is infinitely elastic, the foreign price of exports will fall by less than the full percentage of the devaluation, and the local price will rise by the rest of that percentage. The result will be an incentive for foreigners to purchase more of these goods and for exports to make greater efforts to sell them. In all these cases, however, higher elasticities of demand for both imports and exports increase the desired impact of the devaluation on the balance of trade. If the elasticities of demand for exports and imports are extremely low, a devaluation can worsen the trade balance rather than improve it. If prices are always fixed in exporters' currencies, which means that both elasticities of supply are infinite, the condition for the desired response of the trade account to the exchange rate is relatively simple – the two elasticities of demand (for imports and exports) must sum to more than one, that is, average more than 0.5. if they sum to exactly one, the trade account does not change when a devaluation occurs. The perverse trade account response to the exchange rate occurs only if they sum to less than one. This is the Marshall-Lerner condition.

To develop the mathematical formulation of the Marshall-Lerner condition, we assume that the supply-of-exports schedules of both home (India) and foreign (Britain) countries are infinitely elastic, that is horizontal. The implication of this assumption is that both the rupees price of home product exportables ($\bar{p}_I$) and the pound price of exportables of foreign ($\bar{P}_B^*$) are fixed. Here note that bar (–) indicates that the price is fixed and asterisk (*) indicates that the price is expressed in pounds. A price without an asterisk is in rupees. We have following equations.

$$\bar{p}_I = s\, p_a^* \tag{1}$$

$$p_B = s\, \bar{p}_B^* \tag{2}$$

where s is the rate of exchange (rupees per pound).

The supply of pounds $S(s)$ is equal to Britain's expenditure on imports (or India's export revenue), i.e.

$$S(s) = p_I^* M_B(p_I^*) = (\bar{p}_I/s) M_B(\bar{p}_I/s) \tag{3}$$

where $M_B(p_I^*)$ is Britain's demand for imports of home country exportables. The dem and for pounds, $D(s)$, is equal to India's expenditure on imports, i.e.

$$D(s) = \bar{p}_B^* M_I(p_B) = \bar{p}_B^* M_I(\bar{s}p_B^*) \tag{4}$$

where $M_I(P_B)$ is India's demand for imports of British exportables. India's balance of trade (T) is equal to the excess supply of pounds, that is,

$$T = S(s) - D(s) = (\bar{p}_I/s) M_B(\bar{p}_I/s) - \bar{p}_B^* M_I(s\bar{p}_B^*) \tag{5}$$

Hence the equilibrium in the foreign exchange market coincides with balance-of-trade equilibrium, i.e. $S(s) = D(s)$ means that $T=0$.

Stability in the foreign exchange market requires that the excess supply of pounds be a positive function of s in the vicinity of equilibrium, i.e. stability requires

$$\frac{dT}{ds} > 0 \tag{6}$$

when $T=0$. The inequality (6) means that a devaluation of the rupees improves India's balance of trade.

Differentiating equation (5) with respect to s and using ($S=D$) we get

$$\frac{dT}{ds} = -\frac{\bar{p}_I}{s^2} M_B + \frac{\bar{p}_I}{s} \frac{dM_B}{dp_I^*} \frac{(-\bar{p}_I)}{s^2} - \bar{p}_B^* \frac{dM_I}{dp_B} p_B^* = \frac{S}{s}[-1 - e_{mI} - e_{mB}] \tag{7}$$

where,

$e_{mI} = (dM_I/dp_B)(p_B/M_I)$ = India's elasticity of demand for imports,

$e_{mB} = (dM_B/dp_I^*)(p_I^*/M_B)$ = Britain's elasticity of demand for imports.

When the bracketed expression on the right-hand side of the equation (7) is positive, inequality (6) is satisfied. Therefore, the necessary condition for the stability in the foreign exchange market as well as successful devaluation requires that

$$(-1-e_{mI}-e_{mB})>0$$

Or $$e_{mI}+e_{mB}<-1 \quad (8)$$

Inequality (8) is the Marshall-Lerner condition.

Since the supply schedule for foreign exchange is normally backward bending, equilibrium in the foreign exchange market need not be unique. This can be shown in Fig. 9.22.

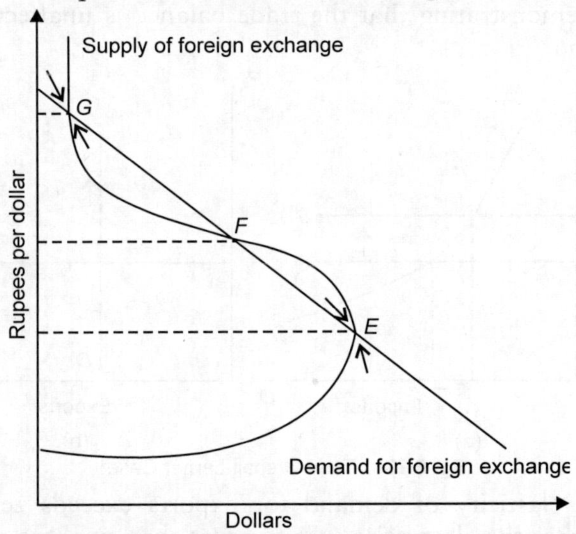

Fig. 9.22: Multiple Equilibria in the Foreign Exchange Market.

The above figure illustrates the case of three equilibrium, *E*, *F*, and *G*. Thus the foreign exchange market can be in equilibrium at any of the three above mentioned points. The multiplicity of equilibria in the foreign exchange market gives rise to several problems. First, some of the equilibria are necessarily unstable. Usually each unstable equilibrium is bounded by two stable equilibria. Secondly, from the point of view of social desirability, each country may choose different equilibrium point. For example, India may prefer point *G* to *E*, while Britain may prefer point *E* to *G*. This situation may lead to conflicting policies between countries, with deleterious effects.

The effects of a devaluation on the trade balance can be shown by the Fig. 9.23.

Prices are in local currency. Thus the devaluation causes a vertical shift in the foreign functions. A case in which the elasticities sum to exactly one is presented first. Since the foreign demand for exports is vertical, its shift upward means that it slides along itself, that is, that there is no change. Since the elasticity, of demand for imports is one, the vertical shift of the supply function means that total expenditures on imports are the same before and after the devaluation, the decline in import volume being just offset by the price increase. Neither export revenues nor import expenditures change, demonstrating that the trade balance is unaffected by the devaluation.

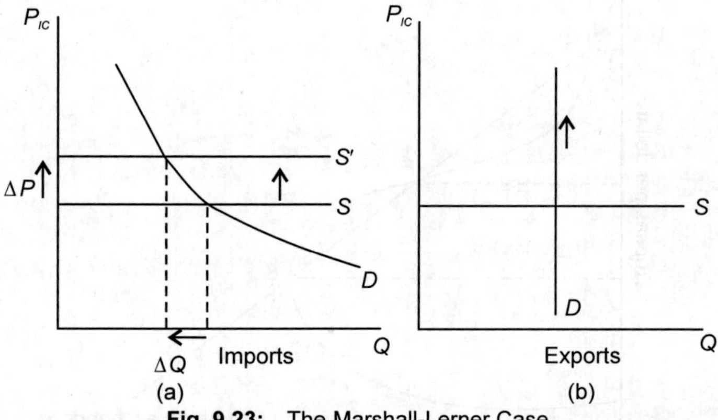

Fig. 9.23: The Marshall-Lerner Case.

If the elasticity of demand for exports exceeds zero, which indicates that the elasticities sum to more than one, the results can be shown by the Fig. 9.24.

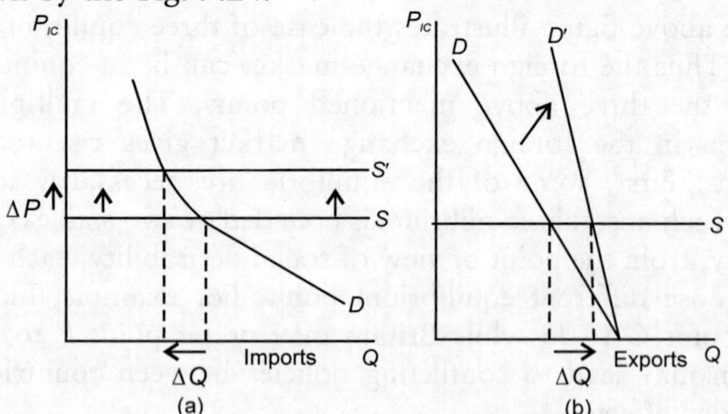

Fig. 9.24: The Marshall-Lerner Case where a Devaluation Succeeds.

Import expenditures remain unchanged, but export receipts have clearly increased. Thus the trade balance improves by the amount of the export revenue growth. The Marshall-Lerner condition is met, and a devaluation has its intended effect. But if the elasticities sum to less than one, the outcome is quite different and can be shown in Fig. 9.25.

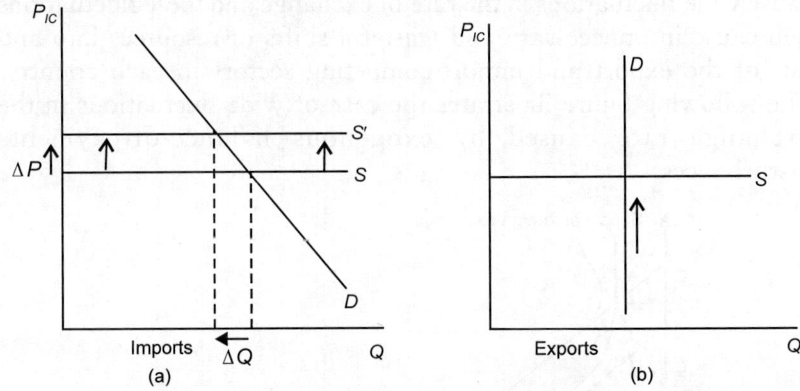

Fig. 9.25: The Marshall-Lerner Case Where a Devaluation Fails.

In the above figure the vertical foreign demand for the home country's products means that export revenues do not change, and the fact that the domestic elasticity of demand for imports is less than one means that total expenditure rises. The decline in the volume of imports is insufficient to offset the price increase, so the local currency cost of imports increases. The trade account worsens by the amount of the import expenditure growth. Thus in this case, the trade account deteriorates.

The assumption of infinitely elastic supply functions is unrealistic, but it makes possible the simple version of the Marshall-Lerner condition. If the elasticities of supply are less than infinite, the Marshall-Lerner condition becomes far more complicated. It remains true, that the higher the demand elasticities, the better the prospects that a devaluation will improve the trade balance. If these elasticities sum to more than one, the prospects that the devaluation will produce the desired change in the trade account are quite good.

Consider the exchange-rate fluctuations caused by shifts in exports and imports. Suppose that the rate of exchange increases marginally. If the speculators interpret this small increase to mean that the rate of exchange will increase further, they will start buying pounds in the hope of selling them later at a higher price. This will result in the rise in the rate of exchange to further and if it increases beyond the unstable point, the rate will certainly continue to climb. When the rate stabilizes, the speculators will sell their pounds and make a profit. In so doing, the speculators will cause the rate of exchange to fall. This self-fulfilling, profitable speculation will cause wide fluctuations in the rate of exchange and these fluctuations will cause in unnecessary and wasteful shifts of resources into and out of the export and import-competing sectors in each country. The following figure illustrates the case of wide fluctuations in the exchange rate caused by exogenous balance-of-payments disturbances.

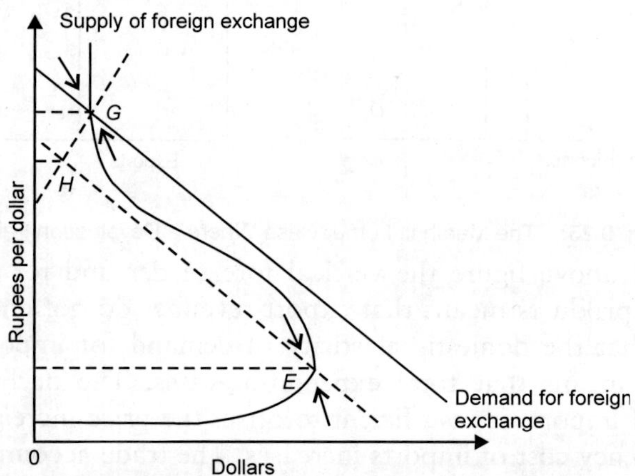

Fig. 9.26: Exchange-rate Fluctuations Caused by Shifts in Exports and Imports.

In the above figure, equilibrium occurs initially at *G*, where the solid schedules intersect. This equilibrium is unique and stable. Suppose there is recession in India which will result in a fall in imports. Due to this the demand schedule for pounds shifts to the left, as shown by the dashed line through *E*. Equilibrium moves to *E*, which is also unique and stable. If the supply schedule were upward sloping and very elastic, as shown by dashed line *HG*, the pound would have depreciated only slightly.

Following a devaluation (or depreciation) of the domestic currency, the balance of trade typically worsens for several months before it eventually improves. The effect of the time required to find new sources, and of such contracts, is to produce what is widely known as the J-curve effect. This phenomenon is known as the

J-curve, because the trade balance traces a J-shaped curve through time, as shown by the following figure.

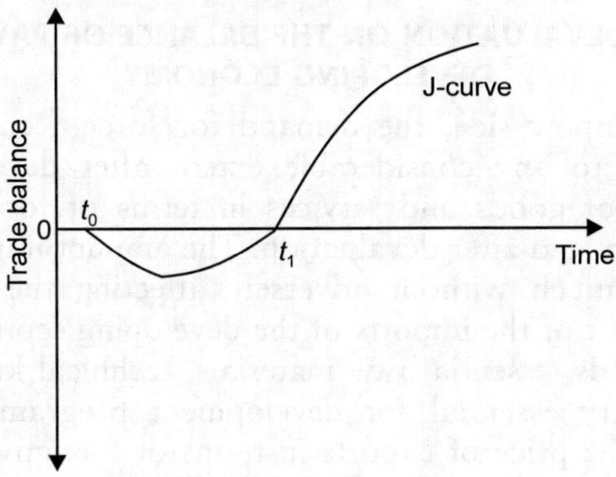

Fig. 9.27: The J-curve.

The time lag involved in the balance-of-trade improvement of devaluation varies considerably from country to country. After a devaluation, the trade balance follows a pattern that resembles a "J"; i.e. it declines slightly for a brief period and then rises sharply. The period of worsening trade results may be six months or a year, but the trade account does respond in the intended manner if sufficient time is allowed to pass. Hence countries need enough foreign exchange reserves at the time of a devaluation to finance continuing trade deficits for that period. In the above figure, devaluation occurs at time t_0 but has no immediate effect on the volumes of exports and imports. Because exports are invoiced in the exporter's currency, the export revenue (in foreign exchange) falls, while the expenditure on imports (in foreign exchange) remains the same. Thus the balance of trade deteriorates. By time t_1 the initial balance-of-trade deterioration is totally reversed. The positive effects of devaluation occur after t_1.

A flexible exchange rate can overshoot its long-run value under the J-curve effect. Consider a depreciation in the domestic currency because of an autonomous increase in the demand for foreign exchange. If the balance of payment of trade worsens in the short run, the excess demand for foreign exchange will get bigger, not smaller; thus the domestic currency may continue to depreciate beyond its long-run equilibrium value, causing an unnecessary and wasteful reallocation of resources. Borrowing from the IMF is arranged to provide the foreign exchange needed to cover the period before the trade balance can be expected to improve.

IMPACT OF DEVALUATION ON THE BALANCE OF PAYMENTS IN A DEVELOPING ECONOMY

On the import side, the demand for foreign currency is not likely to fall to any considerable extent after devaluation. The supply price of goods and services in terms of foreign currency remains unchanged after devaluation. The amount imported cannot be curtailed much without adversely affecting the development process as most of the imports of the developing economies consist of capital goods, essential raw materials, technical know-how etc. which are very essential for development programmes. On the export side, the price of exports in terms of foreign currency falls after devaluation. The value of exports will depend on the elasticity of foreign demand. Total value of exports will increase if the elasticity of foreign demand is more than unity, remain constant if it is unity, and fall if it is less than unity. What is the actual elasticity of foreign demand for the exports of an underdeveloped country? It is generally believed that the foreign demand for the exports of at underdeveloped country is comparatively inelastic as most of the exports of the primary producing countries consist of foodstuffs, minerals, agricultural raw material etc. the demand for which is comparatively inelastic. But when there are many sources of supply, the demand from one individual source is, generally, elastic even if the demand from all sources taken together is inelastic; any individual country can encroach on the market of other underdeveloped countries by lowering its rate of exchange. Thus the demand for most of the exports of an underdeveloped country is elastic enough. It is comparatively inelastic only for those commodities which are the monopoly of a particular country and for which there are no competing sources. Even when the demand for exports is elastic, the value of exports will increase only if the supply can be increased. It is here that most of the underdeveloped countries fail to realise the benefit of increased demand for exports. The supply of exports from underdeveloped countries is comparatively inelastic because of a lack of excess capacity, non-availability of complementary factors and other bottlenecks. The value of exports therefore, is not likely to increase; on the other hand, it might fall if the domestic prices of exports do not rise to counteract the fall in foreign prices caused by devaluation.

In terms of domestic currency, the prices of imports will rise after devaluation. Because the demand for imports, as discussed earlier, is almost inelastic, the value of imports is likely to rise almost in proportion to the depreciation of domestic currency. On the export side, the prices of exports in terms of domestic currency remain constant. Foreign demand is likely to increase after devaluation as the goods of the devaluing country become cheaper in terms of foreign currency after the devaluation. Value of exports, however, is not likely to increase significantly, as discussed earlier, because of the limited capacity to export. Devaluation in a developing economy, thus, is likely to increase the value of the imports considerably while that of exports only insignificantly. It can be concluded, therefore, that the effect of devaluation on the balance of payments is very likely to be adverse.

ASSUMPTIONS OF THE ELASTICITIES APPROACH

The elasticities approach assumes the existence of perfect competition. This assumption had some relevance before the thirties when the exchange and trade controls were unimportant and the commodity markets were substantially competitive. Recently, the trade and exchange controls have increased tremendously. The recent emergence of planning in most of the countries has given a further blow to free trade. Imports and exports are determined by the government keeping in view the needs of the plan rather than being determined by the comparative prices. The imports consist of two kinds of goods, viz. consumption goods and investment goods. The latter category of goods is particularly less responsive to the changes in prices. Development programmes of the country and technological requirements play a more important role than the prices in determining the amount of investment goods to be imported. Further, devaluation may do the trick if competition is only on price basis. In the actual world, competition is more important on the basis of selling costs, quality of products, terms of sale (viz. availability of credit, regular supply, prompt delivery etc.) than on the price basis.

The elasticities approach is static in nature and assumes away all dynamic changes resulting from anticipated changes in the exchange rate. The institution of restrictions on the speculative movements of merchandise and capital has considerably reduced the importance of dynamic changes. But the speculative activities within the framework of trade and exchange controls cannot be omitted without any injury to the analysis.

It concentrates on the current account and neglects capital movements caused by a variation in the exchange rate which form an integral part of the balance of payments mechanism. Strict control over the inflow of funds in almost all countries has decreased the significance of this factor in recent years.

It assumes away any change in the commodity composition. A variation in the exchange rate is very likely to change the composition of trade by changing the prices of various commodities. Devaluation lowers the prices of exports in terms of the foreign currency; this may make possible the export of certain additional goods which could not be exported before because of a comparative price disadvantage. Similarly, devaluation raises the prices of imports in terms of the domestic currency; this may discourage the importation of certain goods whose importation was profitable before devaluation. This factor is particularly important for industrial countries with a highly diversified production and consequently a large number of potential traded goods. This factor is not very important for agricultural countries specialising in the export of a few goods and unable to substitute easily and to any large extent home produced goods for imports.

The effect of depreciation was analysed above with the help of two demand and supply diagrams, one for exports and the other for imports. All imports as well as exports were aggregated or averaged into a single curve. The demand and supply curves were constructed for a 'representative bale' of imports and exports. In fact, a separate diagram should be drawn for each export and import commodity. Aggregation and averaging of different export and import commodities leads to errors and biases in the calculation of elasticities.

The elasticities approach assumes all variables other than prices to be constant. Neglect of changes in other variables particularly in income, has aroused much criticism in the recent literature. Depreciation affects income not only by changing the volume of exports and imports but also through changes in the terms of trade. The income effect of depreciation may not be substantial in the beginning but it gathers momentum, as the "multiplier mechanism" becomes operative. The total income effect of depreciation may be considerably strong to weaken or reinforce the price effect. Income effect will not be very important in the following situations: (a) the level of employment in the depreciating country is so high that an increase in exports cannot raise the total income; (b) even if there exist some unemployed resources, these cannot be utilised to raise income because of a lack of complementary factors or because of other bottlenecks; (c) the elasticities of demand and supply are such that exports are not increased to any significant extent; (d) the exports constitute an unimportant part of the total national income; (e) the country is pursuing an income stabilising policy through monetary and fiscal measures; (f) the marginal propensity to import is equal to the sum of the marginal propensity to export and marginal propensity to substitute home produced goods for the imports.

It assumes that the prices of all traded goods remain unchanged in the exporting as well as in the importing country. This, however, is not true in actual practice. Depreciation is very likely to affect the domestic prices of exports and the foreign prices of imports. If the export industries use a substantial amount of imported goods, the costs and hence prices of exports will rise in terms of domestic currency with the rise in the prices of imports. Depreciation affects the volume of demand and output of the imports and exports and thereby their prices in the country of origin. This assumption will be true in the exceptional cases in which the elasticity of supply is infinite or the elasticity of demand is zero or unity.

MEASUREMENT OF THE ELASTICITY OF THE SUPPLY OF AND DEMAND FOR EXPORTS AND IMPORTS

To evaluate the effect of depreciation on the balance of payments, we are required to know the magnitude of the elasticity of demand for and supply of exports and imports. The estimates of the elasticity of supply are so far very scanty. Several estimates have been made of the elasticity of demand for imports and exports. Most of these estimates are disappointingly low and lead to the conclusion that depreciation is an ineffective remedy for a disequilibrium in the balance of payments. These estimates, however, are generally unreliable and suffer from a downward bias because of several factors discussed below:

Firstly, it is doubtful if the true elasticity of demand can be measured from the available data. The only available data for measuring the elasticity of demand is the historical record of the prices and quantities. If a curve is fitted to this historical data relating to prices and quantities, it will not represent a demand curve. This historical price-quantity data shows not only a demand relation but also a supply relation between the prices and quantities. If the demand and supply depended exclusively on price, the various points on the curve obtained by fitting the historical price-quantity data will indicate nothing but the points of intersection of the demand and supply curves whose shapes are not known actually. The curve obtained by fitting the prices-quantity data will represent a demand curve only if (a) the amounts demanded depended solely on price and (b) the amounts supplied depended exclusively on variables other than the price. Similarly, the curve will represent a supply curve if (a) the amounts supplied depended solely on price and (b) the amounts demanded depended exclusively on factors other than the price. If both the demand and supply depended on variables other than the price, the curve will represent neither a demand curve nor a supply curve.

Secondly, most of the estimates of price elasticity of demand relate not to a single commodity but to an aggregate of a large number of heterogeneous commodities. "The concept of a demand for a bundle of commodities of changing composition is very slippery and the concept of the elasticity of that demand becomes well nigh unmanageable."[6] The methods employed for constructing the aggregative demand curve have been very rough. Usually, it has been constructed from the historical data relating to the total exports (imports) and the average export (import) price. The aggregating process involves many errors and biases. It is a generally admitted fact that price changes are larger for commodities the demand for which is comparatively inelastic, e.g. foodstuffs, raw materials etc. This means that most of the price changes in the price indices of aggregate exports (or imports) are for commodities with inelastic demand. This gives a downward bias to the aggregative elasticity of demand. A more refined way of calculating the aggregative elasticity of demand would be to calculate the elasticity of demand for each individual commodity and thereafter to calculate the aggregative elasticity of demand by attaching a suitable weight to the elasticity of demand for each individual commodity. This method, however, would involve a very large amount of labour and is not very practical.

Thirdly, the available statistics of prices and quantities generally contain errors of observation. When a curve is fitted to this data by the least square method, the estimated demand elasticity is likely to be biased in the downward direction. The errors of observation may be in the data relating either to quantities or to prices or to both quantities and prices. If the errors are only in quantity variable and not in price variable, the observational points will be scattered in a horizontal direction in the form of a parallelogram about the line representing true points as shown in the diagram given below. In this case, the curve fitted by the least square method will be unbiased. In contrast, if the errors are only in quantity variable and not in price variable, the observational points will be scattered in a vertical direction in the form of a parallelogram about the line *DD* representing the true points. In this case, the curve *D'D'* fitted by the least square method will be steeper than the true demand curve *DD* and, therefore, the elasticity of demand will be biased in the downward direction as shown in the Figure given below:

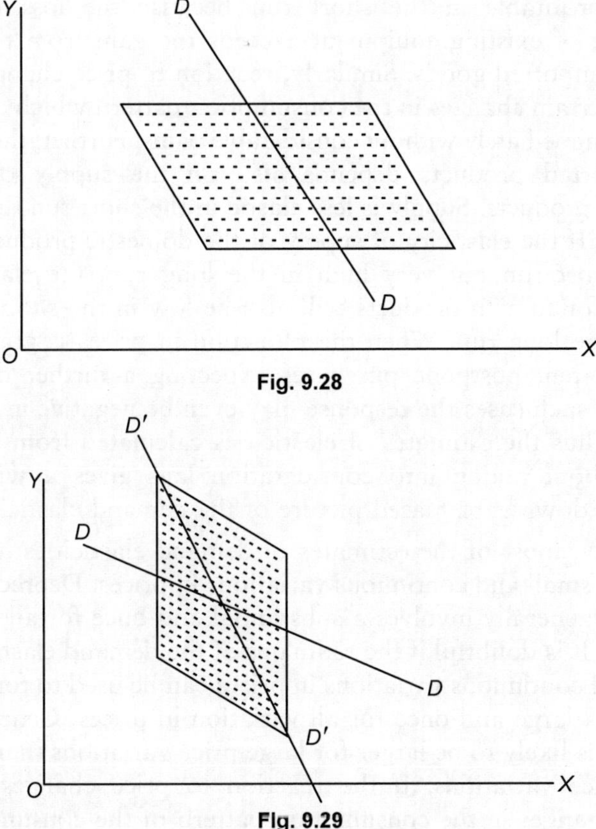

Fig. 9.28

Fig. 9.29

The likelihood of a downward bias is particularly large because the errors of observation in international trade statistics are generally, larger in prices than in quantities.[7]

Fourthly, most of the estimates of the elasticity of demand for imports and exports have been made from figures relating to the annual price indices and the annual averages of the volumes of imports and exports. The response to the changed prices is not immediate. It occurs after the lapse of a certain period of time. No doubt, certain types of effects will take place within a period of several months and thus the picture won't be much distorted if annual figures are used. But there are certain other effects which occur after a longer period. The long run elasticities are greater than the short run elasticities. The use of foreign cheaper producers' goods might require some technological adjustments which might not be profitable in the short run because the loss from the scrapping of existing equipment exceeds the gain from the use of cheaper imported goods. Similarly, reaction to price changes might require certain changes in the consumption pattern which cannot be affected immediately without considerable pains. Further, the demand for imported products depends also on the supply of similar domestic products. Supply is less elastic in the short run than in the long run. If the elasticity of supply of the domestic products is low in the short run but very high in the long run, the elasticity of demand for foreign products will also be low in the short run and high in the long run. When the reduction in prices is gradual, the buyers, often, postpone purchases expecting a further decline in prices. In such cases the response may even be negative in the short period. Thus the estimates of elasticities calculated from historical data without taking into consideration lags gives a wrong and generally downward biased picture of the demand elasticities.

Fifthly, most of the estimates of demand elasticities have been made for small and continuous variations in prices. Depreciation, in contrast, generally involves a substantial and once for all variation in prices. It is doubtful if the estimates of the demand elasticities for small and continuous variations in prices can be used to forecast the effect of a large and once for all variation in prices. Generally, the response is likely to be larger for large price variations than that for small price variations. If the reaction to price changes requires certain changes in the consumption pattern of the consumers, they may not like to undergo the pains involved in a change in the consumption pattern of small changes in prices while they would have been willing to undergo these for larger variations in prices. Similarly, if the use of cheaper producers' goods requires certain technological adjustments, it may not be profitable to make these for small variations in prices. Thus the estimates of the demand elasticities for small variations in prices are very likely to be biased, in the downward direction.

Sixthly, even if it is assumed that perfectly correct calculations of demand elasticities can be made, there arises the question as to how far the past estimates can be relevant to future periods with entirely different level of income, distribution of income, level of prices etc.

INCOME EFFECT OF DEVALUATION

So far we were examining the price effect of devaluation. Devaluation also affects the balance of payments by causing changes in income. Income effect might not be considerable in the beginning but it gathers momentum as the "multiplier and accelerator mechanism" becomes operative. Devaluation causes favourable as well as unfavourable effects on the national income of the devaluing country and, also, on that of the outside world having trade relations with it. If devaluation causes unfavourable terms of trade, the national income of the devaluing country will fall and that of the outside world rise. Devaluation increases the demand for exports by lowering their prices in terms of foreign currency. It will lead to an increase in the national income of the devaluing country if the production is sufficiently elastic. Devaluation might discourage investment by raising the cost of imported equipment and raw materials. Similarly, the consumption of certain goods which requires imported complementary goods might be discouraged.

The increase in the demand for exports caused by devaluation, however, is not likely to raise the national income considerably in underdeveloped countries because of lack of excess capacity, nonavailability of complementary factors and other bottlenecks. In several underdeveloped countries, the rational income is not likely to be affected considerably because the exports form an unimportant part of the national income. Moreover, the stabilisation policies pursued by various developing economies might counteract or dampen the effect of variations in exports, domestic consumption and investment on national income caused by devaluation.

DEVALUATION AND THE TERMS OF TRADE

Whether devaluation results in an improvement or a deterioration in the terms of trade depends upon the elasticities of demand for and supply of imports and exports. The terms of trade of the devaluing country will improve if the product of the demand elasticities for its imports and exports is greater than that of the elasticities for supply of imports and exports and deteriorate in the reverse case. The condition for an improvement in the terms of trade upon depreciation can be stated algebraically as follows: $\eta_m \eta_x > \varepsilon_m \varepsilon_x$. The condition for a deterioration is that $\varepsilon_m \varepsilon_x > \eta_m \eta_x$.

According to Robinson, the terms of trade of the devaluing country are likely to deteriorate as most of the countries specialise in the export of a few commodities, the foreign demand for which is relatively inelastic, while they import a large number of commodities from several different countries and hence the supply of their imports is relatively elastic, "...any one country plays a more dominant role in the world supply of those goods which it exports than it plays in the world market for those goods which it imports."[8] The situation imagined by Robinson is particularly relevant to the underdeveloped countries. Their imports consist of a large number of producer and consumer goods. But their exports consist of only a few major commodities.

> ...rice has recently accounted for about 80 per cent of the value of exports from Myanmar. Ninety per cent of exports from Pakistan have consisted of jute, cotton, tea, wool, hides and skins. Exports from the Federation of Malaya consisted almost exclusively of rubber and tin. Over 80 per cent of Philippine exports are covered by sugar, copper and vegetable oils and abaca, tea, rubber, copra and oil form about 90 per cent of the entire exports of Sri Lanka while Thailand's rice, rubber and tin exports account for 81 per cent of total exports.[9]

The likelihood of an unfavourable movement in the terms of trade as a result of devaluation is more due to imperfect competition and institutional factors than due to the particular elasticities of demand for and supply of the exports and imports. The existence of imperfect competition will require considerable cuts in prices if the exports are to be increased to any considerable extent. In addition, the exporters can afford and will be ready to make cuts in prices out of devaluation profits. Many differentiated products are sold at list prices at home and abroad. Prices of such products will fall in terms of foreign currency by the full amount of the depreciation of domestic currency. On the import side, the foreign exporters enjoy no devaluation profits out of which they might be induced to make price cuts. It is not possible to give price concessions only to the devaluing country, as it will arouse demands for similar concessions from other countries, too; if these demands are not acceded to, it might lead to commodity arbitration. Moreover, it is doubtful if the foreign producers can increase exports by making price cuts because of the existence of strict exchange and trade restrictions in almost all countries: it might lead even to a fall in total proceeds from exports.

DEVALUATION—ABSORPTION APPROACH

The basic identity from national accounting in an open economy is $Y = C+I+(X–M)$. The basic idea of the absorption approach is to rearrange this identity so as to highlight the trade balance and then to treat the equation as if it were derived from behavioural phenomena. Thus, after rearrangement:

$$(X-M) = Y-(C+I) \tag{1}$$

For the sake of simplification, the terms can be combined giving

$$B = Y-A \tag{2}$$

where B stands for trade balance, $(X–M)$, Y for income (output), and A for absorption $(C+I)$, all for the current period. To the extent A falls short of Y, hoarding (H) will have taken place. The identity can, therefore, be put as

$$C = Y-A = H \tag{3}$$

Since devaluation analysis is concerned with changes in the trade balance, we may conveniently express this identity as

$$\Delta B = \Delta Y - \Delta A = \Delta H \tag{4}$$

where Δ stands, as usual, for ‘changes in’. It is from this identity that the absorption approach derives the condition for effective devaluation. The trade balance would improve after devaluation—ΔB would be greater than zero—only if the current income increases relative to current absorption, or in other words, only if there occurs an increase in hoarding. Thus the condition for effective devaluation is that $\Delta Y > \Delta A$ (paying due consideration to the signs of the terms) so that ΔH is positive.

The effect of devaluation upon income will show in ΔY. The effect of change in income upon absorption, and the direct effect of devaluation upon absorption will both show in ΔA. Thus devaluation affects absorption in two ways. Firstly, since the decisions to consume and invest depend upon the level of real income, an increase in income generally leads to an increase in intentions to absorb. Secondly, devaluation may affect absorption in ways other than through changes in real income. In other words, there will be an income induced change in A and a non-income-induced, or directly affected change in A. The income-induced change in absorption may be expressed by $\alpha\Delta Y$ where α is the "marginal propensity to absorb income" (which is the sum of the marginal propensities to consume and to invest). The direct effect of the devaluation upon absorption may be expressed by βA. Making use of the new symbols, the effect of devaluation upon trade balance may be expressed in terms of the following "absorption equation":

$$\Delta B = \Delta Y - \alpha\Delta Y - \beta A = \Delta H \tag{5}$$

By combining the income effects of devaluation into one expression, we may re-write the above equation as:

$$\Delta B = (1 - \alpha)\Delta Y - \beta A = \Delta H \tag{6}$$

In this equation, the term $(1 - \alpha)$ represents the marginal propensity not-to-absorb income or the marginal propensity to hoard.

Whether or not devaluation improves the trade balance depends upon the relative values of ΔY, α and βA. If devaluation leads to an increase in income so that ΔY is positive, the balance of trade will improve if α is less than unity and βA is negative, or if βA is positive, it is less than $(1 - \alpha)\ \Delta Y$. The larger will be the improvement in the balance of trade as a consequence of devaluation, the larger is ΔY, the smaller is α, and the smaller is βA. Since absorption includes both consumption and investment expenditures, α is very likely to be greater than one. If α is greater than one with devaluation leading to an increase in income, the trade balance can improve only if βA is negative and relatively large.

Alexander,[10] the formulator of the absorption approach to devaluation, states that his analysis holds in real terms as well as in money terms but his actual analysis runs in terms of real income, real absorption and real trade balance.

Taking clue from the last equation, Alexander divides the effects of devaluation into two parts: (a) the effects upon and via income, $(1 - \alpha)\Delta Y$, (b) direct effects upon absorption—βA. He recognises the following effects:

Effects upon and via Income $[(1 - \alpha)\Delta Y]$	*Direct Effects on Absorption*
Idle-resource effect	Cash-balance effect
Terms-of-trade-effect	Income-redistribution effect
	Money-illusion effect
	Three other direct absorption effects

Idle-resource Effort: If unemployed resources are available in the devaluing country, devaluation would lead to an increase in income as a result of increase in exports and the induced stimulation of domestic demand through the familiar multiplier relationship.

Terms-of-trade Effort: Alexander believes that devaluation will deteriorate the terms of trade of the devaluing country because "a country's exports are usually more specialised than its imports". He divides the terms of trade effects of devaluation on the balance of trade into an initial effect through price changes and a secondary effect through income-induced changes in absorption. The initial effect is generally an equal and simultaneous reduction of the trade balance and of real national income. The secondary effect will depend on the marginal propensity to absorb income. The income-induced changes in absorption may either reinforce or weaken the initial terms of trade effect on the balance of trade, or may turn it in the opposite direction.

Direct Effects on Absorption

Effects of devaluation upon the balance of trade which are not related to changes in income but only to changes in the absorption of a given income are called 'direct effects on absorption'.

Cash balance Effect: Devaluation raises the domestic prices of imports and exports; this tends to raise the prices of import-substitutes, of potential exports, and of intermediate goods required for their production. Thus devaluation causes a general rise in the price level. If the monetary authorities do not create more money, and if the households and firms desire to maintain cash holdings of a certain real value, with a rise in the price level, they must accumulate more cash. They may attempt to do this by buying less and by selling assets and securities. Buying less means a reduction in their real expenditure relative to their real incomes. Selling assets and securities will lead to a decline in their prices, or which is the same thing, to a rise in interest rates; this in turn will have the effect of curtailing real consumption and investment in relation to real income.

Income-distribution Effect: The rise in the price level resulting from devaluation may also reduce aggregate spending from a given income by redistributing it from groups with higher to groups with lower marginal propensities to spend.

Money Illusion: The money illusion may contribute to the effectiveness of devaluation if it leads the people to pay more consideration to money prices than to money incomes. If at higher prices people decide to buy and consume less in spite of the fact that their money income has increased in proportion to the rise in the price level, the balance of trade will be affected favourably. But the effect would be quite the reverse if annual savings ate calculated in money terms and fail to rise in proportion to money incomes and prices.

Other Direct Absorption Effects: Alexander mentions three other effects of devaluation upon absorption and thus upon the trade balance. In the first place, expectation of a rise in prices following devaluation may lead to increased absorption causing adverse effects on trade balance. Secondly, investment which requires foreign equipment, to be imported at increased domestic prices after devaluation, may become less attractive. Thirdly, generalising the principle involved in the second effect to all kinds of imports, when domestic prices of certain goods rise after devaluation, the domestic purchasers may reduce their expenditure on these goods and buy nothing instead.

Critical Appraisal of Absorption Approach

For absorption approach to be of practical value, we must be able to make reliable quantitative estimates of marginal propensity to spend, which is the sum of marginal propensities to consume and invest, and the direct effects upon absorption. It has been difficult enough to make a reliable estimate of the marginal propensity to consume. The difficulty becomes more serious when we add to this the need to quantify the marginal propensity to invest and the direct effects upon absorption. There is also the question of impact of a change in exchange rate on output itself. Does devaluation cause an increase or decrease in output and by how much? Seen in this light, the absorption approach loses some of its attractions as a policy tool.

Comparing the 'price elasticities' and 'spending propensities' approaches, Machlup states, "From the point of view of stability over time it is hard to say which of the parameters are less reliable as indicators of the effects of devaluation on the trade balance—the price elasticities or the spending propensities. From the point of view of changeability in the very process the outcome of which they help determine, the spending propensities are probably less reliable than the price elasticities. And from the point of view of malleability through public policy, one probably should regard the price elasticities as the tougher factors to deal with, and the spending propensities more subject to the influence of (monetary and fiscal) policy—which means that in the last analysis not given propensities but chosen policies will determine the outcome."[11]

Alexander's original presentation of the absorption approach was criticised by Machlup for repressing price elasticities which were implicit in his model. "At some points elasticities work behind the scene. For example, whether there can be an idle-resources effect of devaluation depends on whether the production and sale of export goods can be expanded, hence, on elasticities of domestic supply and foreign demand; but this is not explicitly said. At other points the elasticities are clearly visible on the stage. For example, whether a direct devaluation-effect upon absorption will result in a transfer of resources or in unemployment depends on 'how the economy responds to price incentives', or on 'the substitutability of domestic goods for imports in consumption, and of resources as between the production of domestic goods and exports'. At one point at least the role of price elasticities is dominant: in the terms-of-trade effect. For it is impossible to come to any conclusion concerning the effects of devaluation upon the terms of trade except on the basis of an examination of the relevant elasticities of supply and demand."[12]

Alexander's original presentation of the absorption approach also assumed that the rest of the world passively adjusted to devaluation and balance of trade conditions in the devaluing country. In fact a change in one country's trade balance must be reflected by a corresponding change in the trade balance of the rest of the world in the opposite direction. It is not understandable how this change is imposed on the rest of the world irrespective of the magnitudes of their spending propensities etc.

Most of the analysis of the absorption model is in real terms. Alexander discusses a real absorption function, real income, and derives a real trade balance, stating that the basic relationship would hold in money terms as well. Criticising this, Machlup states: "The supposed equivalence between relationships in money and in real terms is sometimes troublesome, occasionally even meaningless. Alexander intends to 'deal only with real quantities, not with money values'. But what is 'real' trade balance? When a country has to pay increased prices for its imports and buys a slightly reduced physical quantity of imports, what is the meaning of an improved 'real' trade balance if at the same time the balance in money terms has deteriorated? Or should, perhaps, a trade balance in terms of money be translated into one in real terms by deflating the contracted foreign claims or debts by a price index? To treat exports and imports as 'real quantities' makes sense; but can the difference between the two be meaningfully treated as a real (physical) quantity? Can what is essentially an increase or decrease in foreign claims or debts be regarded as anything but a money value, however deflated."[13]

SYNTHESIS OF ELASTICITIES AND ABSORPTION APPROACHES

As a result of the above criticisms of the simple absorption approach to devaluation, Alexander recast his analysis of the devaluation mechanism, expressing it in money terms and giving elasticities an important place in his model, while retaining the basic conception of the absorption analysis.[14] In the new model the change in trade balance depends on the net result of superimposed relative price effects and income-absorption effects. The initial impact of devaluation on the trade balance depends upon the traditional, constant money income supply and demand elasticities. Since the extent of this initial impact depends in part on foreign demand and supply elasticities, as well as on purely domestic elasticities, a passive adjustment abroad is no longer implicitly assumed. In case the relevant elasticities are such that devaluation improves the trade balance, income would rise in the devaluing country and decline in the non-devaluing country. The income changes in turn generate a variety of income effects whose result, as shown through the absorption approach, is a tendency to reverse the initial improvement in the trade balance of the devaluing country. The extent to which the initial elasticities effect of devaluation on trade balance remains depends on the relative strength in each of the two countries of the impact of the additional money, income on money hoarding on the one hand, and on imports and exports on the other. The effects of these propensities in both countries are embraced by a sequential multiplier analysis so that conditions in the non-devaluing country actively contribute to the determination of the devaluing country's ultimate trade balance.

The stability condition continues to be that there must be some hoarding out of the increase in income. If either country's marginal propensity to hoard is zero, the value of the corresponding trade balance marginal propensity and the result of the initial elasticities computation would be immaterial and devaluation will not lead to an improvement in the trade balance. On the other hand, if both trade balance marginal propensities are zero and the marginal propensities to hoard are positive, the ultimate trade balance of devaluation would entirely depend on the supply and demand elasticities computation. Normally, the larger are the hoarding propensities relative to the trade balance propensities, the smaller would be the improvement in the trade balance as a result of devaluation, given the values of the various elasticities. When there exist substantial unemployed resources, devaluation is more likely to improve the trade balance than when resources are fully employed. When unemployed resources exist, the trade balance marginal propensity is likely to be smaller and the marginal propensity to hoard larger than when resources are fully employed; the tendency for the initial trade balance resulting from devaluation to be offset is weaker when there exists unemployment.

DISADVANTAGES OF DEVALUATION

Devaluation increases the burden of debts if expressed in foreign currencies. Most of the developing countries have borrowed extensively from advanced countries and international financial institutions. The burden of their debts will increase after devaluation because most of the debts are expressed in terms of foreign currencies. On the other hand, the value of their credits with foreign countries will decrease as most of these are in terms of domestic currencies.

Devaluation in one country might lead to a devaluation by other competing countries. This will counteract the effect of devaluation to a considerable extent. The effect of devaluation will be weakened, also, if the countries which are the important sources of the supply of raw materials for the export industries of the devaluing country refuse to follow suit. This will raise the price of imported raw materials and hence of export goods. The workers might demand higher wages to offset the higher cost of imported foodstuffs and other goods. The wage price spiral might go beyond merely counteracting the effect of devaluation and thus have adverse effects. Sometimes, devaluation leads to a rise in domestic prices in anticipation and the effect of devaluation is rendered nil.

Devaluation requires time to be effective. Consumers take time in reacting to price changes. It needs some time for the consumers to be aware of the cheaper products. Reaction to price changes might require certain changes in the consumption pattern which cannot be affected overnight without much inconvenience. The use of foreign cheaper producer's goods might require certain technological adjustments which might not be profitable in the short run because the loss from the scrapping of existing equipment exceeds the gain from the use of new cheaper goods. Similarly, on the supply side, the supply is more elastic in the long run than in the short run. In the short run, assuming that there exists no excess capacity, the supply can be increased only by overworking the existing plants which will raise the supply price rapidly and thus dampen the effect of devaluation. In the long run, the production can be increased either by increasing the number of plants of the existing size or by enlarging the scale of the existing plants or by a combination of the two. This might lower the long run supply price by bringing in the economies of production and thus strengthen the effect of devaluation. Thus, it is just possible that devaluation might worsen the balance of payments in the short run while improve it in the long run when the supply of and the demand for imports and exports have adjusted to changed relative prices. It, therefore, is not very useful for countries possessing scanty monetary reserves and needing immediate redress of disequilibrium in the balance of payments.

Devaluation is a suitable remedy if the disequilibrium in the balance of payments is due to a disparity in the movement of domestic and foreign price levels. It is not very effective and useful if the deficit is due to certain structural maladjustments: it might even prove harmful and accentuate the problem by increasing the value of imports, creating inflationary trends, and deteriorating the terms of trade. If we analyse the causes of the disequilibrium in the balance of payments of the underdeveloped countries, we find that it is, mainly, due to huge imports of capital goods, technical know-how, and essential raw materials required for the development programmes and the maladjustments in the production structure. Devaluation, therefore, is not a suitable remedy.

Devaluation might be taken as a sign of weakness of the economy and thus lead to a loss of confidence in the future stability of the currency. It will discourage inflow and encourage outflow of capital. It might encourage exporters to postpone the receipt of the export proceeds, in expectation of gains from devaluation and importers to make advance payments to avoid the risk of depreciation. It might lead to anticipatory imports and consequently to a waste of investment in inventories which could have been used better for production purposes.

Devaluation is a general rather than a selective measure. It restricts the import of non-essential goods as well as that of goods essential for development. Selective measures like quotas, exchange control, tariffs etc. are more suitable for the developing economies as they allow the import of goods essential for carrying on the development programmes.

Almost all the advantages of devaluation can be obtained by a suitable system of taxes and subsidies on imports and exports without involving most of its disadvantages. The effect of a general devaluation on the balance of payments will be counteracted to the extent there exist commodities with an clasticity of demand of less than unity. Taxes and subsidies have got the advantage that they can be adjusted according to the elasticities of the demand for and the supply of individual imports and exports.

DEPRECIATION AND THE I.M.F.

The articles of agreement of the I.M.F. provide that "A member shall not propose a change in the par value of its currency except to correct a fundamental disequilibrium."[15] The Fund shall raise no objection to changes in the par value of a currency which do not exceed ten per cent of the initial par value. Any change beyond this can be made only with the approval of the Fund and it will approve "if it is satisfied that the change is necessary to correct a fundamental disequilibrium."[16] The Fund Agreement does not define the term fundamental disequilibrium and leaves it to the discretion of the managers of the Fund to judge whether or not the situation is that of a fundamental disequilibrium.

Continuous loss of gold or foreign exchange due to capital exports cannot be regarded as a situation of fundamental disequilibrium because the articles of agreement of the Fund permit exchange control to prevent capital movements.

Fundamental disequilibrium will exist when there occurs a serious and protracted decline in the reserves of gold and foreign exchange due to a persistent deficit in the current balance of payments. There arises, however, the difficulty of defining the international reserves. The most accepted definition of international reserves is the sum of the gold and equilibrating or accommodating capital movements. How are the 'equilibrating capital movements' to be defined? Often, these have been identified with the short-term capital movements. This, however, is not correct. Some of the short-term capital movements might be of a spontaneous nature. Similarly, some of the long-term capital movements might be induced by a deficit in the balance of payments and may thus be of an equilibrating nature.

The absence of a persistent deficit in the current balance of payments cannot be identified with an absence of a fundamental disequilibrium. There may exist a fundamental disequilibrium under certain circumstances even if there is no deficit in the current balance of payments. Ragnar Nurkse points out a situation in the United Kingdom during the period 1925-30, when the rate of exchange was overvalued without a deficit in the balance of payments or an outflow of gold. During this period, the equilibrium in the balance of payments was achieved with larger mass unemployment and more depressed business conditions at home as compared with the outside world. Ragnar Nurkse points out that an equilibrium in the balance of payments can be achieved at different exchange rates by maintaining income and employment at different levels.[17] Similarly, a fundamental disequilibrium can exist without a deficit in the current balance of payments if the imports are restricted by trade and exchange controls and exports are artificially stimulated by subsidies and other such measures.

Can mass unemployment, particularly in export industries, be identified with the existence of a fundamental disequilibrium? Certainly not. Mass unemployment, for instance, may be owing to structural maladjustments rather than monetary factors. Under such conditions, devaluation of the domestic currency may not be the appropriate remedy for unemployment; it may rather worsen the position. Further, it may lead all countries to put forward their claims for a devaluation in a period of worldwide depression. This problem, however, can be solved by recognising the claim of a country for devaluation only if the unemployment in it is substantially larger than that in the rest of the world. Mass unemployment without a deficit in the balance of payments is not a suitable criterion of fundamental disequilibrium.

> ...if the starting point is an even balance, depreciation will lead to a gold out-flow from other countries which, under the balance of payments criterion would constitute an overvaluation of other currencies. This suggests the conclusion that permission for depreciation should be given only if there is an actual balance of payments deficit.[18]

Haberler concludes that fundamental disequilibrium should be interpreted in terms of an objective, unambiguous, and observable criterion. Such a criterion can only be an actual deficit in the balance of payments. He proposes that it should be left to the judgement of the managers of the Fund to decide as to how large the deficit must be and how long it must last before the disequilibrium can be identified as the fundamental.[19]

Hensen places a special emphasis on the cost-price structure instead of placing it on the deficit in the balance of payments. He maintains that the price elasticity of exports and imports is not sufficiently high to correct a deficit in the balance of payment by depreciation. He states, "An incorrect exchange rate often creates a disequilibrium not so much in the balance of payments as in internal cost-price of the country in question."[20] According to him an equilibrium exchange rate is one "that represents a 'parity' in the cost structure of the different countries."[21]

Robert Triffin defines a fundamental disequilibrium

> as maladjustment in a country's economy so grave and persistent that the restoration or maintenance of satisfactory levels of domestic activity, employment, and incomes would prove incompatible with equilibrium in the balance of payments, if not accompanied by extraordinary measures of external defence, such as a change in the exchange rates, increased tariff or exchange control protection, etc.[22]

Triffin's definition is not precise because the word 'equilibrium' can be interpreted differently by different authors. There is no unambiguous definition of the term equilibrium. The remarks of Robinson are very pertinent in this connection.

> There is no one meaning for 'equilibrium' and, therefore, no clear standard for 'fundamental disequilibrium'. It seems that any country which wishes to alter its exchange rate can find plenty of arguments to show that it is in fundamental disequilibrium, in one sense or another, and equally the managers of the Fund can always find plenty of arguments to show that it is not.[23]

NOTES

1. Bo Sodersten, *International Economics*, p. 318.
2. G. Haberler, *The Theory of International Trade* (London, 1956), p. 37.
3. League of Nations, *International Currency Experience* (Princeton, N.J., 1944), pp. 210-11.
4. International Monetary Fund, *Annual Report,* 1951 (Washington, 1951), p. 38.
5. Fritz Machlup, "Elasticity Pessimism in International Trade", *Economia Internazionale* (February 1950), pp. 122-24.
6. Fritz Machlup, "Elasticity Pessimism in International Trade", *Economia Internazionale* (February 1950), p. 129.
7. *Ibid.*, p. 134.

8. Joan Robinson, "Beggar-My-Neighbour Remedies for Unemployment", *Readings in the Theory of International Trade* (London, 1953), p. 400.

9. United Nations, *A Study of Trade Between Asia and Europe* (Geneva, 1953), p. 10.

10. S.S. Alexander, "Effects of a Devaluation on a Trade Balance", *International Monetary Staff Papers* (April, 1952), pp. 263-78.

11. Fritz Machlup, "Relative Prices and Aggregate Spending in the Analysis of Devaluation", *American Economic Review* (June 1955) reprinted in his *International Monetary Economics* (London, 1964), pp. 191-92.

12. *Ibid.*, p. 193.

13. *Ibid.*, pp. 185-86.

14. S.S. Alexander, "Effects of a Devaluation: A Simplified Synthesis of Elasticities and Absorption Approaches", *American Economic Review* (March 1959).

15. Article IV, Sec. 5 (a).

16. Article IV, Sec. 5 (b).

17. Ragnar Nurkse, *International Currency Experience: Lessons of the Inter-war Period* (Princeton, N.J., 1944), p. 126.

18. G. Haberler, "Currency Depreciation and the International Monetary Fund" in S.E. Harris, ed *Foreign Economic Policy for the United States* (Cambridge, Mass., 1948), p. 389.

19. *Ibid.*, p. 392.

20. Alvin H. Hensen, "Fundamental Disequilibrium" in S.E. Harris ed., *Foreign Economic Policy for the United States* (Cambridge, Massachusetts, 1948), p. 380.

21. *Ibid.*, p. 381.

22. Robert Triffin: "National Central Banking and the International Economy", *International Monetary Policies, Postwar Economic Studies* No. 7 (Washington, 1947), pp. 77-78.

23. Joan Robinson, "Exchange Equilibria", *Economia Internazonale* (May 1950), p. 400.

Exchange Control

10

INTRODUCTION

Broadly speaking, exchange control means government intervention to affect the level of exchange rates. Government intervention affecting exchange rates may take a number of forms viz. regulation of domestic money by the Central Bank, regulation of capital movements, pegging operations of the stabilisation funds, informal support of exchange market, etc. Conventionally, however, the term 'exchange control' is used in a narrow sense. In its narrow sense, it refers to the measures which directly regulate the demand for and supply of foreign exchange. In what follows the term will be used in this sense.

Under the most comprehensive form of exchange control, exporters and others obtaining foreign exchange are not free to dispose of their foreign exchange in any manner they like. They are required to deposit all their foreign exchange receipts with the exchange control agency in exchange for domestic currency. Importers and others having to make foreign payments can obtain foreign exchange only from the exchange control agency which may not be able to supply foreign exchange in amounts required by them at the prevailing exchange rate.

To make exchange control successful, exchange restrictions have often to be supplemented by an effective regulation of commodity trade. Exchange restrictions, therefore, generally, bring in their train trade restrictions.

OBJECTIVES OF EXCHANGE CONTROL

(a) *To Prevent the Flight of Capital:* Large scale movements of capital because of political and psychological factors, distinct from normal capital movements owing to variations in interest rates, have presented a very serious problem. These threaten a breakdown of the financial system and are very harmful for the whole economy. Because of the growing rigidity in the economies of various countries, indirect methods of checking unwanted capital movements have become, ineffective. Exchange control is the best instrument of checking such capital movements promptly and effectively.

(b) *To Correct a Disequilibrium in the Balance of Payments:* The most important factor leading to the institution of exchange control has been a shortage of foreign exchange. Exchange control is used for restricting imports to the level permitted by the available foreign exchange earnings.

(c) *To Stabilise the Exchange Rates:* Violent fluctuations in exchange rates caused by day-to-day events and speculative transactions are a great obstacle to the expansion of world trade. Several countries have instituted exchange control to maintain exchange rates at some arbitrarily fixed level.

(d) *To Ensure the Importation of Essential Goods:* A country suffering from a shortage of foreign exchange cannot permit the importation of each and every commodity. It has to make the best possible use of its limited foreign exchange resources. Before it permits the importation of luxury and non-essential goods it has to see that essential goods are imported in the required quantities. In the absence of exchange control, most of the available foreign exchange will be utilised for the importation of luxury and non-essential goods because such goods are consumed mostly by the rich people who can outbid the poor in the purchase of foreign exchange. Most of the developing economies are applying exchange control to use their limited foreign exchange earnings for the importation of capital goods, technical know-how and essential raw materials required for the execution of the development programmes.

(e) *To Protect Domestic Industries:* Exchange control has been used to protect domestic industries by restricting the import of foreign competitive products.

(f) *To Obtain Revenue:* Some countries have used exchange control to obtain revenue for the public treasury. The wider the margin between the prices at which the exchange control authorities buy and sell the foreign exchange, the larger will be the revenue from this source.

(g) *To Support an Overvalued Currency:* Exchange control has often been resorted to maintain the exchange rate of the domestic currency at a level higher than that dictated by the free play of the forces of demand for and supply of foreign exchange. Free exchange rate in many countries having exchange control will be much lower than the official exchange rate.

(h) *To Lower the Prices of National Securities Held Abroad:* Some countries have employed exchange control to prevent their nationals from buying national securities held abroad. By preventing its nationals from buying securities, the government can force the foreign holders of national securities to surrender their securities at considerably reduced prices.

(i) *To Freeze Debts Owed Abroad:* Sometimes exchange control has been used to prevent the nationals from repaying their foreign debts with a view to utilise the available foreign exchange for importing goods and services.

(j) *To Obtain Payment from Debtor Countries:* Creditor countries have used exchange control to influence the debtor country in allocating its receipts of the creditor country's currency between that used for importing goods and services and that for servicing frozen debts.

(k) *To Provide Exchange for Meeting External Debts of the Government:* One of the factors leading to the institution of exchange control has been the existence of huge government debts to be paid to foreign countries. The inability of the government to honour its debts in time is a very serious matter for a country. Once a government fails to honour its debts in time, it loses its credit-worthiness for the future. Further, it lowers the prestige of the country in the world eyes. Governments, therefore, have sometimes introduced exchange control to obtain foreign exchange needed for meeting their external debts. After keeping foreign exchange for meeting its external debt, the government allocates the remaining foreign exchange receipts among the importers and others having to make foreign payments.

(l) *For Commercial Bargaining:* The allocation of foreign exchange for imports offers substantial scope for discrimination between different countries. The country from which a commodity would be imported depends upon the particular currency supplied by the exchange control agency. Further, the quantity imported depends on the amount of the currency supplied. Through discrimination the exchange control can be used to exchange concessions on reciprocal basis between different countries.

(m) *For Economic Planning:* Domestic plans might be disrupted by unexpected fluctuations in prices or in quantities of exports and imports. Such fluctuations are beyond the control of any national government. Exchange control is an effective instrument of insulating the internal economy from, or mitigating the repercussions of, unanticipated external events of a temporary nature.

TECHNIQUE OF EXCHANGE CONTROL

Exchange rates can be regulated in two different ways. Under the first method, the monetary authorities undertake to buy and sell foreign exchange in unlimited amounts at the declared exchange rates. People are free to buy any amount of foreign exchange for any purpose. There are no restrictions on the purchase or sale of foreign exchange. The difference between the demand for and the supply of foreign exchange at fixed exchange rates at different times is met by variations in the foreign exchange and gold reserves of the monetary authority. Exchange Equalisation Account of the United Kingdom and Exchange Stabilisation Fund in the United States provide examples of this method of exchange control. The second method of exchange control restricts the freedom of the people to buy foreign exchange. Under this method the people can buy foreign exchange only after seeking permission from the state. The available foreign exchange is rationed among the importers and others having to make foreign payments. This method of exchange control is more drastic than the previous one.

(a) *The Exchange Equalisation Account:* The object of the British Exchange Equalization Account established in April 1932 was to reduce fluctuations in the exchange rate caused by the short-term capital movements and short-term fluctuations in the balance of payments position. It was not intended to interfere with the long-term rate of exchange. The rate of exchange was left free to move in response to long-term changes in the demand for and supply of foreign exchange. In case there was an excessive inflow of foreign money or an excessive outflow of domestic money, the authorities of the Exchange Equalisation Account sold Treasury Bills in the money market. These Bills were largely bought by the commercial banks. The money so obtained was used to buy foreign balances on the exchange market. The foreign balances were, generally, immediately converted into gold. Thus, the increased supply of foreign exchange was offset by an increased demand for it from the authorities and it was not permitted to exert any significant influence on the exchange rate. In case of an excessive outflow of foreign money, the authorities sold gold and the proceeds of these sales were used to repurchase the Treasury Bills. This method of stabilising the exchange rates, however, disturbed the internal credit structure. In case of an inflow of foreign money, the purchase of Treasury Bills by the commercial banks increased their deposits. Cash reserves remaining the same, an increase in deposits lowered their cash ratio. Lowering of cash ratio led the banks to contract credit which raised the interest rate. Quite the reverse happened in case of an outflow of foreign money. To avoid this effect of the movements of foreign funds on the domestic credit structure, the authorities followed the practice of transferring a part of gold from the Exchange Equalisation Account to the Bank of England in case of an inflow of foreign funds. The Bank of England provided additional money to the commercial banks which enabled them to increase their deposits without lowering their cash ratio. This prevented a rise in the interest rate. Thus, the operation of the Exchange Equalisation Account completely offset the effect of the short-term capital.

(b) *The American Exchange Stabilisation Fund:* The United States established an Exchange Stabilisation Fund in January 1934 for stabilising the exchange value of dollar. The working of the American Fund was somewhat different from the British Exchange Equalisation Account. Its funds consisted of gold instead of domestic currency. In case of an inflow of gold, the Fund bought gold with the funds obtained from the Federal Reserve Banks in exchange for gold certificates. This, however, resulted into an expansion of the domestic credit. If there was an outflow of funds, the Fund sold gold out of its reserves. This resulted into a contraction of domestic credit. The expansion and contraction of domestic credit was, of course, not in proportion to the inflow and outflow of funds. Part of the inflow or outflow of funds was absorbed merely by changes in the ratio of cash reserves instead of leading to changes in the volume of credit. The effect of the movement of funds on the internal credit structure was further weakened by changes in the minimum reserve requirements. To avoid disturbance to the domestic credit structure from the movement of foreign funds, the United States Treasury followed the policy of 'sterilisation' of gold since December 1936. Under this policy, the funds for purchasing gold were obtained not in exchange for gold certificates from the Federal Reserve Banks but by issuing short-term Treasury obligations on the money market.

Characteristics of Exchange Control

The system of exchange control has the following main characteristics:

(a) The official exchange rate is fixed by the central bank of the country.

(b) All foreign currencies have to be surrendered to the central bank.

(c) Foreign exchange dealing can be undertaken only by specified dealers and licensed dealers.

(d) The central bank charges low exchange rates for the import of essential goods and high exchange rates for that of luxuries.

(e) The government has full control over the foreign exchange market.

IMPORTANT METHODS OF EXCHANGE CONTROL

(a) *Multiple Exchange Rates:* Some countries maintain two or more than two exchange rates for the domestic currency. Different exchange rates are applied to different kinds of transactions. Sometimes the official exchange rate is restricted to some transactions and other transactions are permitted at a free rate of exchange. Exporters, for instance, may be required to surrender their foreign exchange earnings from regular exports at the official rate and permitted to sell their foreign exchange earnings from additional exports at the free market rate which is higher than the official rate. Partial recognition of the unofficial market imparts flexibility in the economic system.

(b) *Premium or Surcharge Over the Official Exchange Rate:* Sometimes a premium over the official exchange rate is permitted to encourage exports of particular commodities or to encourage exports to particular destinations. Specially favourable exchange rates, for instance, may be permitted for exports to countries having convertible currencies. Similarly, the import of particular commodities or imports from particular sources may be discouraged by requiring the importers to pay a surcharge over the official rate.

(c) *Blocked Accounts:* Under this system the domestic debtors were required to deposit their dues to foreign creditors into specially designated banks. This checked the purchase of foreign exchange in the black market for paying their debts. The blocked accounts could be spent by the creditors within the debtor country and according to the specification of the debtor country's government. These were classified into several categories according to their source and the use to which they could be put. The use of certain categories of blocked accounts was more restricted than that of others. Blocked accounts were used by Germany also for stimulating exports at the cost of foreign creditors. Foreign importers were permitted to make payment for goods, for which Germany could not compete in the international market, in blocked accounts up to a certain percentage of the invoice price. Because of severe restrictions on the spending of blocked accounts, these were selling at a considerable discount from the official rate in foreign markets. The availability of blocked accounts at considerable discount rates offered an incentive to importers to import from Germany goods for which part of the payment was accepted in blocked accounts. Thus, Germany succeeded in stimulating exports at the cost of its foreign creditors who had to sell their credits in Germany at a substantial loss.

(d) *Restrictions on the Export of Capital:* To check the export of capital, export of domestic currency, bank notes and precious metals is prohibited. Close watch is kept on the assets the people take with them while going abroad. On return, they are required to make a statement on oath of their expenditure abroad. The rights of foreigners to sell their assets in the country are strictly restricted. Foreigners passing through the country are required to declare the amount of foreign exchange possessed by them and they are not permitted while leaving to take with them foreign currencies in amounts larger than those previously declared by them. During the thirties, export of capital was restricted in several countries through the system of blocked accounts.

(e) *Control and Supervision of all Commercial Transactions:* Strict control and supervision of all commercial transactions is very essential for preventing disguised withdrawal of capital through commodity trade. Capital, for instance, can be exported in a disguised manner by over-invoicing imports and under-invoicing exports. A comprehensive and complicated organisation is required to ensure that the values entered in the invoices are fairly correct. Exchange regulations often provide for heavy penalties for false declarations to check such malpractices.

(f) *Compulsory Surrender by Nationals of Their Foreign Exchange Holdings:* At the time of the introduction of exchange control, the exchange control authorities require the nationals to report their foreign assets in the form of securities, bank balances, general claims, real estate etc. Sale or transfer of these assets is subject to strict regulations. If required, the state compulsorily acquires these assets and pays for them in terms of domestic currency.

(g) *Bilateral Balancing of Trade:* Short of foreign exchange, countries often enter into bilateral agreements for procuring needed foreign goods in exchange for domestic goods.

(h) *Clearing Agreements:* With the breakdown of the normal channels of transferring international payments, the choice was between 'no trade at all' or trade without exchange. Institution of exchange control in almost all countries handicapped the transfer of payments. Often, two countries restricted imports from each other because of a shortage of foreign exchange. Clearing arrangements provided an opportunity for the exchange of commodities between such countries. Clearing arrangements were used more often to facilitate imports than to restrict imports. Under such agreements, the importers make payment for imports to their national central bank in local currency instead of making it direct to foreign exporters in terms of foreign currency. The exporters receive payments for exports from the national central bank instead of receiving it directly from the foreign importers. The central banks of the contracting parties offset their claims on each other without the introduction of foreign exchange. The balance, if any, is credited to the party whose exports exceed imports. Generally, payments are made to exporters, out of the funds available in the clearing account, in the chronological order of payments made by the debtors. Sometimes, to encourage the export of particular commodities, priority is given to the exporters of these commodities. In certain cases, full or part of the payment is made in advance to the exporters of certain commodities to stimulate the export of these commodities. The clearing agreements contain provisions regarding the allocation of funds among different classes of claims, viz. claims arising out of current exports, financial arrears, investors' claims, etc. The rate at which the two currencies are to be exchanged or the method of determining the rate of exchange at a particular time is provided in the clearing agreement. The following bases have generally been used for determining the rate of exchange between the two currencies; (i) legal gold parity; (ii) official rate of exchange; (iii) conventional rates: (iv) market rates; (v) mean rate of the day in a given course; (vi) a stable currency of a third country. The nature, quantities and prices of the goods to be exchanged are determined by the parties concerned with the particular transactions. Sometimes, however, the government influences the nature, quantities and prices of goods exchanged. The clearing agreements provide also for the use to be made of the surplus that may arise in the credit of a party after a certain period of time or at the termination of the agreement. Some agreements provide that the surplus in the credit of the debtor party will be used for paying off the frozen debts. Often clearing agreements have been thrust upon the weak debtor nations by the powerful creditor nations for getting the frozen, claims of their nationals liquidated. Some agreements authorize the surplus country to dispose of the surplus in any manner it likes; some other provide for the disposal of surplus by the mutual consent of the two parties. Regarding the balance at the termination of the agreement it is generally provided that the importers of the surplus country will continue paying in the clearing account till the accounts in the two clearing houses are squared. Balances in clearing agreements bear no rate of interest.

Other things remaining the same, an excess of imports over exports will cause a deflationary pressure because the payments collected by the central monetary authority will exceed the payments disbursed by it. The deflationary effect of an excess of inpayments over outpayments is similar to that of a loss of foreign exchange or gold. Excess of exports over imports will not change the total supply of money in circulation because payments to exporters are generally made out of the funds made available by the importers and the exporters have to wait for payment when the exports exceed imports. Inflationary pressure, however, will result in the surplus country inspite of the amount of money in circulation remaining unchanged. Excess of exports over imports will decrease the total amount of goods to be exchanged for the unchanged supply of money. This will raise the prices of goods and thus cause inflationary pressures. The inflationary pressures in the surplus country will be stronger if the central monetary authority increases the supply of money to make advance payments to the exporters.

Clearing agreements are, generally, bilateral. There are, of course, a few instances of triangular arrangements, too. Under a triangular agreement the deficit (or surplus) in a country's account with another country can be offset with a surplus (or deficit) in its account with a third country. Sometimes, clearing agreements have covered payments arising not only from trade and frozen debts but also those arising from other expenditures, viz. insurance premiums and freight payments, tourists' expenditures, diplomatic expenditures, patent fees, etc. There has been a tendency to enlarge the coverage of the clearing agreements as the officials administering the agreements get more and more experience. Some clearing agreements cover only a few classes of commodities. Trade in other commodities takes place through the normal channels. Clearing agreements have usually been made for short periods, viz. from three months to a year. It is not possible to make long-term agreements because of the unstable nature of the balance of payments between pairs of countries. Instability in the balance of payments necessitates frequent adjustments in the agreement. Agreements have, however, generally been renewed with or without modifications. Often, the formal agreement lays down only the broad principles and details are left to the continuous negotiation and consultation of the contracting parties. Sometimes a permanent commission consisting of the members appointed by each contracting party is established which meets from time to time to review the working of the agreement and to suggest the necessary modifications.

Clearing agreements divert trade into bilateral channels which may not be in consonance with the dictates of the principle of comparative advantage. These divert the trade of the debtor country towards the creditor country and thereby prejudice the interests of the third countries. This may cause friction in the international relations of different countries. Importers in the debtor country have a tendency to buy more and more from the clearing partner because the capacity to import is not limited by the shortage of foreign exchange as is the case with imports from the non-clearing countries. Assurance of payment through the clearing arrangements offers an incentive to the exports in the creditor country to export to the clearing partner instead of exporting to the non-clearing countries payments from which may be withheld because of several reasons. Exchange control is usually resorted to support an overvalued currency. The official exchange rate in the clearing agreement, therefore, is likely to overvalue the currency of the debtor country which maintains exchange control. An overvalued exchange rate encourages imports into and discourages exports from the debtor country. Further, there is an incentive for exporters to export to non-clearing countries from which they obtain free exchange which generally sells at premium prices.

During the thirties, Germany exploited the clearing arrangements to borrow extensively from the poorer countries of southern Europe. Under clearing arrangements, Germany extensively imported raw materials and foodstuffs for war preparation from Yugoslavia, Rumania, Bulgaria, Hungary, etc. These large imports were made possible by the attractive prices offered by Germany, and by lack of demand and consequently lower prices prevailing in the Western Europe because of worldwide depression; during the depression, Germany was the only fully-employed economy. This led to the accumulation of large claims on Germany. These claims could be used for the importation of only those goods which Germany could spare without significantly affecting her rearmament programme and at prices dictated by her. In this way Germany improved her terms of trade *vis-à-vis* the Southern Europe.

(i) *Payments Agreements:* Payments agreements are similar to the clearing agreements to the extent they are arrangements to obtain payment reciprocity. They differ from the clearing agreements in that they do not dispense with the normal channels of making payments. Under payments agreements, the volume of transactions between the two parties is regulated in order to achieve an equilibrium in the balance of payments of the parties concerned over a period of time. The scope of payments agreements is, generally, broader than that of the clearing and compensation agreements. They aim not only at balancing payments and receipts arising from trade but also at liquidating frozen debts. The latter is, often, the principal purpose of the payments agreements. Clearing and compensation agreements are entered into, generally (not invariably), between countries which have instituted exchange control and free-exchange countries. The payments agreements specify the manner in which the exchange-control country is to allocate the foreign exchange obtained from exports to the free-exchange country. Generally, first priority is given to the claims arising out of imports from the free-exchange country. A certain percentage of the rest of the foreign exchange obtained from the free exchange country is reserved for the payment of interest, debts and certain other specified claims owed the free-exchange country. The right of disposing of any foreign exchange that may remain after these payments have been made may be given to the free-exchange country. Although exact balancing of reciprocal claims during every period is not required, the surplus country is required to make efforts to accelerate imports from the deficit partner. Payments agreements specify the rate at which the currencies of the parties to the agreement are to be converted into each other. The agreement may be for a definite period or for an indefinite period, each party having the right to withdraw after giving a reasonable notice. At the time of the termination of the agreement, any balance in favour of one party is paid off in terms of gold or in any other manner provided in the agreement.

Payments agreements have the advantage that the direct relation between the exporters and importers is maintained. Under clearing agreements, the payments for imports and exporters are made to and received from the national central bank; this diminishes the direct contacts between the exporters and importers which are very useful for the expansion of trade and for the smooth working of trade relations. Through personal contacts, sellers acquire knowledge about the financial position of their buyers which is very essential for the completion of the contract. In addition, payments through the clearing office involve a lot of inconvenience and waste of time. Free-exchange countries favour payments agreements because under these the primary responsibility of carrying out the provisions of the agreement rests on the controlled-exchange country. As compared with the clearing agreements, the payments agreements have given rise to lesser friction and complaints. Under payments agreements, the chances of a disequilibrium in the balance of payments of the exchange control country are smaller because imports cannot be obtained without making the payment in terms of foreign currency. Under clearing agreements, imports can be obtained without making payments in terms of foreign currency.

(j) *Compensation Agreements:* Compensation agreements have developed generally out of a shortage of foreign exchange. These are barter arrangements. Goods are exchanged for goods without the intervention of foreign exchange. Compensation agreements may be between private parties with or without government control and supervision or between government or semi-government agencies. A private compensation agreement generally requires the collaboration of four parties. Suppose, for illustration, that Indian cloth is to be exchanged for Pakistani jute. To affect this transaction four parties are required, viz. an importer of jute in India, an exporter of jute in Pakistan, an importer of cloth in Pakistan, and an exporter of cloth in India. The Indian importer will import jute of a value equivalent to that of cloth exported by the Indian exporter. The Indian importer of jute will make the payment to the Indian exporter of cloth in terms of domestic currency instead of making it to the Pakistani exporter of jute in terms of Pakistani currency. Similarly, the Pakistani importer will import cloth of a value equivalent to that of the jute exported by the Pakistani exporter. Pakistani importer of cloth will make the payment to Pakistani exporter of jute in terms of domestic currency instead of making it to the Indian exporter of cloth in terms of Indian currency. Thus, the importers and exporters in the two countries make and receive payments for their imports and exports without the transfer of foreign exchange. In case the agreement is on a governmental level, the government in each country makes payment to the suppliers of goods in terms of domestic currency. Compensation agreements do not specify the conversion rate between the currencies of the contracting parties. The parties to the agreement are free to decide any conversion rate. This imparts flexibility to the trading system. It makes possible the barter exchange of goods whose import or export may not be profitable at the official rate of exchange. Compensation arrangements make possible the importation of goods which cannot be imported otherwise because of a shortage of foreign exchange.

Arrangement of compensation transactions involves several difficulties. It requires the collaboration of four instead of the two parties. Conclusion of an agreement among four parties as to the price, quality and amount of the goods to be exchanged is far more difficult than that between the two parties. This difficulty, however, has been eased to some extent by the development of agencies whose function is to bring together possible importers and exporters for acting as partners to a compensation transaction. In case of seasonal goods, there is the difficulty of balancing imports and exports at a particular time if the seasons of import-commodities and export-commodities occur at different times. Exports of agricultural countries, for instance, are concentrated at certain season while their imports which consist mostly of manufactured goods are spread over the whole year. Compensation agreements diminish the amount of foreign exchange at the disposal of the exchange control authorities. They may lead to the importation of inessential goods in large quantities while it may not be possible to import essential goods in sufficient quantities because of a shortage of foreign exchange.

To ensure that compensation agreements do not go against the interest of the country, the government generally maintains a strict supervision and control over the compensation transactions. Sometimes the export of only those goods is permitted on compensation basis which cannot compete in the world market at the official rate of exchange. Government specifies the goods which can be exported on compensation basis. Some countries permit exports on compensation basis subject to the condition that the exporters furnish evidence to the effect that it is not possible to export these goods through normal channels. Some countries permit the importation of only essential goods on compensation basis.

EXCHANGE CONTROL VS. TARIFFS AND QUOTAS

Some of the invisible items in the balance of payments are more easily amenable to exchange control than to other methods of restriction. Tourist expenditure, for instance, can be taxed only if the exact amount spent abroad is known. This can be known better if there exists strict exchange control and money to be spent abroad is sanctioned by the exchange control authority.

Exchange control being generally administered by the executive is more flexible than the tariffs which requires legislative approval.

It can be adjusted to changing conditions frequently and promptly. This advantage of exchange control over tariffs, of course, does not exist in countries in which the executive is authorised to vary tariffs within broad limits and to levy temporary taxes for taking advantage of the changed circumstances.

Exchange control is superior to tariffs as an instrument of discrimination. Tariffs can discriminate only between broad categories of commodities and countries of origin. Discrimination between countries, categories of commodities, categories of importers and exporters can be much finer under exchange control because foreign exchange for each and every transaction has to be sanctioned by the exchange control authorities. Discrimination through tariffs is further handicapped by the most favoured nation treaties. Under exchange control even if it is evident to all that discrimination is being practiced, there is no unambiguous, clear and rational criteria to prove its existence or otherwise; if a country desires, it can evade the most favoured nation commitments without much difficulty.

Exchange control is more effective than tariffs as an instrument of commercial bargaining. Imports can be regulated more precisely and promptly with the help of exchange control than with that of tariffs. Exchange control agreements can be kept secret. This is not possible in case of tariff agreements because, generally, they require legislative approval. Further, it is essential that trades should know in advance the rates of duty which they will have to pay on their imports and exports; this requires publication of tariff schedules.

The scope of exchange control is much wider than that of quotas or tariffs. Quotas and tariffs, generally, apply only to merchandise trade. In addition to merchandise trade, exchange control can cover all other international transactions which are not easily amenable to control with tariffs and quotas viz. services, tourist expenditure, diplomatic expenditure, capital movements, etc. Because of its comprehensive nature, exchange control is a better instrument of regulating international payments.

Exchange control, of course, suffers from the disadvantage that it is not so easily amenable to selective control as are the tariffs and quotas. Selective exchange control in the form of multiple exchange rates requires a cumbersome administrative machinery to collect foreign exchange proceeds from exporters, to distribute the same among importers, to see that the foreign exchange is spent on the products for which it is sanctioned and there are no arbitrage dealings (i.e. buying foreign exchange in the cheap market in order to sell it in the dear market) etc.

MULTIPLE EXCHANGE RATES

Case for and Use of Multiple Exchange Rates

Multiple exchange rates can be used to cure a deficit in the balance of payments. A lower rate of exchange may be applied to some commodities for stimulating their export. It may be applied to commodities whose domestic price is higher than the world price or whose social cost of production is lower than the private money cost. Export industries might be granted foreign exchange for the import of capital goods, technical know-how and essential raw material at a favourable exchange rate. To induce the exporters to increase exports, they may be allowed to sell a part of their foreign exchange earnings from additional exports in the open market. Multiple exchange rates can be used to encourage exports to and to discourage imports from hard currency areas.

Multiple exchange rates are more effective than an overall depreciation in curing a deficit in the balance of payments. The effect of an overall depreciation is offset to some extent by commodities whose elasticity of home demand for imports or that of foreign demand for exports is less than unity. A selective depreciation can be applied to those commodities only whose elasticity of home demand for imports or that of foreign demand for exports is more than unity. An overvalued exchange rate might be applied to other commodities in order to achieve the best results.

Multiple exchange rates are a very useful method of correcting a disequilibrium in the balance of payments with particular countries. A country might have a deficit with one or two countries and an overall surplus with the world as a whole. The developing countries are likely to have a disequilibrium in their balance of payments only with those particular countries which are an important source of the supply of capital goods, technical know-how and essential raw-materials. In a world in which the currencies are not mutually convertible, it is better for a country having deficit with some countries to lower its rate of exchange only *vis-à-vis* these particular countries rather than lowering the overall exchange rate. Lowering of the overall exchange rate to cure a deficit with particular countries will accentuate the problem of the rest of the world with which this country is having a surplus. Thus, multiple exchange rates can cure a disequilibrium with particular countries by restricting the minimum world trade.

Multiple exchange rates may be used to discourage the outflow of domestic or foreign capital by fixing a lower exchange rate for the outflow of capital. Similarly, the inflow of foreign capital can be encouraged by offering a favourable exchange rate for the inflow of new capital. It will accelerate the rate of investment and mitigate deficits in the balance of payments. This, however, is likely to have adverse effects on the inflow of capital by generating a feeling of uncertainty and risk about the exchange rate at the time of repatriation of capital or income therefrom. Multiple exchange rates might be used to channel foreign capital into desirable lines of production in conformity with the national plans for development.

Multiple exchange rates might be used to stimulate the import of capital goods, technical know-how, essential raw materials etc. and to discourage the import of consumer and luxury goods. Restriction of the import of consumer and luxury goods is an important method of checking the consumption of these goods as most of the luxury goods are imported from abroad.

Multiple exchange rates can be used to protect fading industries or to foster new industries by fixing a favourable exchange rate for the export of the products of these industries. Similarly, by fixing a low rate for the export of processed goods and a high rate for that of raw materials, the export of processed goods can be encouraged and that of raw materials discouraged. This will diversify the economy, create more employment and increase the foreign exchange earnings.

Multiple exchange rates are a rich source of revenue for the government especially when the difference between the buying and selling rates is considerable. These can also be used to decrease the government expenditure by fixing a favourable exchange rate for government imports. Multiple exchange rates affect government revenue indirectly, too. An encouragement of domestic industries, for instance, will increase revenue from excise duties and other domestic taxes levied on these industries.

Multiple exchange rates can be used to keep down the cost of living by allowing the import of essential consumer goods at an exchange rate more favourable than that for the import of luxury goods, which are, generally, consumed by the rich people. By keeping down the prices of goods consumed mostly by the poor strata of society, the cumulative wage price spiral can be avoided. This, however, will have an adverse effect on home production if these essential goods are produced at home, too. This can be well demonstrated with the examples of meat industry in Peru and of wheat flour in Ecuador the production of which declined substantially after the import of these goods was allowed at a favourable rate of exchange.[1] Further, the revenue collected from multiple exchange rates can be used as an anti-inflationary measure.

Multiple exchange rates might be used to mop up the abnormal profits of the exporters arising from a shortage of export goods coupled with a high foreign demand for these. While mopping up export profits, care should be taken, however, that the higher exchange rate does not adversely affect the supply of exports; particularly, if the shortage of export goods is temporary, normal exchange rate should be allowed to have its full impact on supply so that the long run expansion of the export is not affected adversely. Abnormal export profits can better be mopped up by a profit tax than by fixing a low rate of exchange.[2] Similarly, abnormal profits of the importers from the commodities, the import of which has been restricted might be mopped up by fixing a lower exchange rate for the import of these commodities.

Multiple exchange rates might be used to buy imports at the cheapest rates from various sources and to sell exports at the dearest rates to various customers by fixing suitable different exchange rates for different sources of supply of imports and for different customers for exports according to the varied elasticities of demand and supply.

Quantitative restrictions in the form of licensing system encourage corruption, favouritism, and involve demoralisation of business and government administration. Importers expecting fabulous profits from import and export licences are ready to offer substantial bribes to the government officials for getting licences. It involves a lot of red tapism and delay in disposing of applications for licences. All these unpleasant things can be avoided by using multiple exchange rates which work automatically through the price mechanism.

Administrative discretion is required only in categorising the commodities for the application of different exchange rates. Decisions regarding categorisation of various commodities can be taken at the highest levels of administration and all the above mentioned evils avoided.

The effect of multiple exchange rates is quite similar to that of duties and subsidies on imports, exports and capital movements. It is surprising that the International Monetary Fund prohibits the use of multiple exchange rates while permits the use of tariffs and subsidies. It will be better if the Fund permits the use of multiple exchange rates where they can rectify a deficit in the balance of payments with harm to world trade less than that involved in the application, of other methods.

Case against Multiple Exchange Rates

It is not appropriate to divide all exports into a few categories and apply a single exchange rate to each category containing goods of varying nature and importance. If the number of categories, into which the exports and imports are divided, is increased, the simplicity of multiple exchange rates decreases. In the limiting case, where each good forms a separate category, multiple exchange rates system is transformed into a full-fledged exchange control system. Taxes and subsidies have the advantage that these can be adjusted according to the nature and importance of each commodity. The affected countries, Fund and GATT consider fiscal devices (i.e. taxes, subsidies, licence fees etc.) as less objectionable than the multiple exchange rates. Multiple exchange rates require a cumbersome administrative machinery to collect foreign exchange proceeds from exporters, to allocate the same among importers to see that the foreign exchange is spent on the products for which it has been sanctioned and there are no arbitrage dealings (buying foreign exchange in the cheap market in order to sell it in dear market). Fiscal devices do not require so heavy an administrative machinery. Fiscal devices, however, have the disadvantage that it is very difficult to tax some of the invisible items in the balance of payments. Tourists' expenditure, for instance, can be taxed only if the exact amount spent abroad is known. This can be known better if there exists strict exchange control and the money to be spent abroad has got to be sanctioned by the exchange control authority.

Moreover, fiscal devices are, generally, administered by the legislature and are thus inflexible whereas multiple exchange rates, administered by the monetary authority, are more flexible and can be adjusted easily and quickly to changed conditions.

Multiple exchange rates discriminate against particular countries and thus arouse protests and lead to the embitterment of international relations. To rectify a disequilibrium in the balance of payments, for instance, a country might use a favourable exchange rate for some exports and an unfavourable one for some imports; this will adversely affect the countries exporting products similar to its imports and exports to which unfavourable and favourable exchange rates have been applied respectively. If the deficit is cured by a depreciation, the expansion of exports and the contraction of imports will be spread over many commodities and thus over many countries. Even if the spread is not uniform and hits some countries more severely, it will not arouse protest from these countries because the discrimination is not intentional.

Multiple exchange rates lead to arbitration (buying foreign exchange in the cheap market for selling it in the dear market) and thus encourage corruption and blackmarketing. If the favoured import rate for a particular commodity is less than the export rate, re-export of the imported goods either in the original form or after slight processing will be encouraged. Such re-export trade will be carried on a large scale if the difference between the two rates is fairly wide.

Fixation of multiple exchange rates for the import and export of different commodities for achieving certain objectives assumes a knowledge of the elasticities of demand and supply of the import and export of all commodities. In the absence of this knowledge, the penalty rates might be fixed at a level that restricts imports by more or less than that required for the achievement of the particular objectives. Moreover, the desired results might not be achieved immediately (as in case of quotas) because the market takes some time to adjust according to changed circumstances. This method, therefore, might not be useful in the short-run for countries possessing insufficient reserves of gold or of other acceptable currencies.

Multiple exchange rates are not a very sound method of financing economic development. Revenue from this source is likely to be highly volatile in response to changes in the composition and quantity of exports and imports, balance of payments position (which might necessitate changes in various exchange rates), etc. while development requires continuous finance. Further, if revenue is the predominant factor in the determination of exchange rates, a very important instrument of correcting a disequilibrium in the balance of payments (i.e. changes in exchange rates) is lost. Moreover, it brings in all the disadvantages, generally, associated with a wrong exchange rate. Effective protection requires that penalty rates are applied to commodities with a highly elastic demand whereas revenue considerations require application of such rates to commodities with an inelastic demand. Revenue from multiple exchange rates does not satisfy the cannon of equity, which is one of the most important cannons of taxation. It may be mentioned, however, that revenue as a by-product (where it is not the main consideration) of multiple exchange rates when used for other useful purposes is not bad.

Multiple exchange rates as a method of restricting imports and promoting exports are useful only in those cases in which the demand for imports and the supply of exports is fairly elastic. They cannot restrict imports and promote exports if the demand for imports and supply of exports is inelastic. The demand of underdeveloped countries for imports consists mainly of capital goods, 'technical know-how,' foodstuffs and raw materials essential for development and is, therefore, almost inelastic. Similarly, the capacity to export is limited by the lack of excess capacity, non-availability of complementary factors, increased domestic demand for exportable goods for development programmes going on in these countries.

As a method of maximising foreign exchange earnings and minimising foreign exchange expenditure, multiple exchange rates are not very useful for most of the underdeveloped countries. Variations in the supply of their exports and those in the demand for their imports do not affect world prices much in terms of foreign currency; the elasticity of world demand for exports and that of world supply of imports to individual underdeveloped countries is considerably high and any individual country cannot change world prices by varying its imports and exports. This is particularly so in the case of small countries.

Goods placed in the favourable categories might be imported and stockpiled in large quantities in anticipation of a reclassification of imports. This would involve wastage of investment (which could have been used for production purposes) in inventories and accentuate the foreign exchange problem. The fear of a reclassification might necessitate an actual reclassification where it would have not been necessary otherwise.

Multiple exchange rates as a method of changing the composition of imports or restricting these might not be as effective and certain as are quantitative restrictions. An unfavourable exchange rate for the import of a commodity may or may not restrict imports while the quantitative restriction will do the needful without fail. This is particularly likely in case of luxuries which are consumed mostly by the very rich people for whom prices do not make much difference. In underdeveloped countries, because of extremely uneven distribution of income, luxuries account for considerable expenditure. Moreover, the effect of multiple exchange rates might be nullified by the monetary and fiscal policies pursued by the domestic or foreign governments or other changes occurring at home or abroad whereas quantitative restrictions are not susceptible to such changes.

A combination of multiple exchange rates and quantitative restrictions is much better than either alone. If exchange rate differentials are not large enough to limit imports to the desired extent, quantitative restrictions provide the second line of defence and eliminate the chance of leakage and uncertainty pervading the multiple exchange rates system. If exchange rate differentials are ineffective, imports are limited by quantitative restrictions. Multiple exchange rates help in mopping up a part of the abnormal profits resulting from the restriction of imports.[3] Further, restrictions can be used to prevent rich people from acquiring all the foreign exchange sanctioned for a particular category by limiting the amount of foreign exchange that the importers of a particular commodity can buy.

TRIFFIN PLAN

The Triffin Plan proposes that all foreign exchange proceeds earned from exports and other easily controllable sources would be deposited with the central bank at the official rate of exchange. Foreign exchange proceeds from unimportant and practically uncontrollable transactions could be freely sold and bought in the free exchange market. This would avoid giving a premium to illegal evasion where transactions cannot be controlled effectively and would, also, provide an escape valve for the control system. All transactions requiring foreign exchange would be divided into two categories according to their importance for the society. First category will consist of absolute necessaries and the foreign exchange for these would be provided at the lowest rate in order to avoid hardships to the masses from high prices and consequent high cost of living. After meeting the needs of the first category, the remaining foreign exchange would be sold in one or few auction markets for the import of luxuries, tourist expenditure, export of capital, etc. The difference between the fixed multiple exchange rates and the Triffin Plan is that it is the different rates or the quantitative restrictions (when fixed multiple exchange rates are combined with quantitative restrictions) which restrict imports under the former whereas it is the cost restrictions which limit imports under the latter system. The Triffin Plan is preferred to the ordinary licensing system on the following main grounds.

By substituting price mechanism for the administrative discretion, it lessens corruption, favouritism, bribery and demoralisation of business. Administrative discretion is used only in dividing the commodities to be imported into different categories. Decisions regarding this can be taken at high levels where the chances of corruption are not very significant.

The scheme provides revenue for the government which can be used for the general welfare of the society. Under the ordinary licensing system, the margin between the import price and the domestic sale price is appropriated by the importers.

The plan is self-reversing in character. Trade and exchange controls have a tendency to outlive their need because of the inertia of bureaucratic administration and the vested interests created by the controls. Businessmen who make fabulous profits out of control become interested in their continuance and use all fair and foul means to influence the administration for the retention of these.

It will mop up the purchasing power of the rich buying foreign exchange in the auction and thus have a deflationary effect.

In spite of the above mentioned advantages generally claimed for the Plan, it is doubtful if the plan can be of much use, especially when applied to the underdeveloped countries.

The foreign exchange needs of the developing countries for the import of capital goods, technical know-how and essential raw materials for development plans are so large that it is doubtful if these countries can afford to import luxuries and inessential goods. A country which wants to develop at a fairly rapid rate has got to tighten its belt and invest every penny that it can spare after meeting the necessaries. The history of development of Japan, Russia and China well illustrates the degree of austerity required for rapid economic development. If rich people start importing luxuries by outbidding the poor and middle class people in the foreign exchange auction market, the poor and middle class people (which are the main instrument of development) might refuse to undergo the sweat and toil necessary for economic development and start demanding higher wages. Primary producing countries earn most of their foreign exchange by exporting commodities produced with the sweat and toil of the poor classes and these cannot tolerate that the rich people should enjoy luxuries at their cost. And if these countries cannot afford to import luxuries and inessential goods, the question of an auction does not arise.

The efficient functioning of the plan assumes a sufficient degree of competition among the importers. In most of the underdeveloped countries, however, the number of importers is very small. They might combine and defeat the purpose of auction and thus enjoy fabulous profits at the cost of consumers and government revenues.

The government might misuse the plan to collect as much revenue as possible from the auction by transferring goods from the "essential category" to the "auction category." This is particularly likely to be the case in underdeveloped countries in which the governments are not very strong and are in search of methods of collecting revenue involving least resistance from the public. This will lead to a wastage of precious foreign exchange earnings in the import of luxuries which could have better been used for development purposes.

It is not very scientific to divide all imports into two or a few categories, each category containing goods of varying nature and importance. If the number of categories is increased, the simplicity of the Plan decreases. In the limiting case, where each good forms a separate category the Triffin Plan is transformed into a full-fledged exchange control system.

The Plan will destabilise the price level as the foreign exchange rate in the auction market will very from time to time according to the supply of and the demand for foreign exchange. Once the foreign exchange has been auctioned, the importers are free to charge any price as there is no price control afterwards. They will take full advantage or suffer full loss of all Changes (i.e. variations in auction price at subsequent auctions, changes in supply price in the exporting country etc.) that occur after the auction has taken place. It will not only destabilise prices but also expose the importers to risks greater than those necessary under the ordinary licensing system coupled with domestic price control and rationing under which the sale price is fixed at import price plus a reasonable margin for the importers.

Regarding its self-reversing character, it may be mentioned that this is no speciality of the Triffin Plan. Even the ordinary licensing system of exchange control is self-reversing. There is no reason why licensing system should outstay its need. The moment the authorities get enough foreign exchange to meet all the applications and no application is rejected, the exchange control become inoperative and can be removed.

In regard to the revenue argument, the government can appropriate the margin between the domestic demand price and import price by charging licence fees and/or import taxes. Licence fees and import taxes have the additional advantage that these can be varied from commodity to commodity according to its essentiality rather than having two or a few categories with each category containing commodities of varying importance.

Regarding corruption, it is not inherent in the ordinary licensing system. It arises because of defects in the government machinery administering the licensing system. It is a defeatist solution to forego all the advantages of the licensing system simply because the government machinery is defective. The proper way is to improve the government machinery. If sincere and genuine efforts are made by the top leaders, there is no reason why it should not be possible to eradicate corruption. This has been demonstrated by Russia and China. If it has not been possible to eradicate corruption in India so far, it is because the top itself is not above board.

ADVANTAGES AND DISADVANTAGES OF EXCHANGE CONTROLS

Every country whether rich or poor, big or small, capitalist or communist has been exercising and still exercises the system of exchange control in its one form or another. This is because this system has following advantages—

(a) By having strict exchange control policy against a hostill country, a country can prevent the repatriation of its funds.

(b) Foreign loans can be repaid easily.

(c) Exchange Rate stability is maintained.

(d) Erratic outflow of domestic capital is controlled

(e) Easy availability of essential commodities is guaranteed to the domestic consumers.

As known to everybody, anything that has merits, is bound to have demerits. The system of exchange control is no exception to it. Its main disadvantages are as under—

(a) This system leads to complacency, hence inefficiency of domestic producers.

(b) The system in itself has an arbitrary criterion laid down for its various forms. It is the bureaucrats who at the end of the day decide the ones to be enforced. Obviously, it creates vested interests.

(c) Exchange control creates a black market in foreign exchange. No matter how strict an exchange control system is, 'hawala' money is always there in the economy.

NOTES

1. E.M. Bernstein, "Some Economic Aspects of Multiple Exchange Rates", *I.M.F. Staff Papers* (Washington, September 1950), p. 230.
2. *Ibid.*, p. 233.
3. E.R. Schelesinger, *Multiple Exchange Rates and Economic Development* (Princeton University, 1952), p. 17.

Trade Restrictions and Economic Development

11

The traditional case for free trade is based on the doctrine of comparative costs. We have already seen in chapter 2 that this doctrine is not very relevant to the underdeveloped countries. Now we shall briefly examine important arguments for trade restrictions.

INDUSTRIALISATION AND BALANCED GROWTH

In recent years, trade restrictions have been proposed for stimulating industrialisation in the primarily agrarian economies to redress the imbalance caused by the lopsided development in the past. The need for protection for this purpose was recognised long back by Alexander Hamilton in his classic *Report on Manufactures* presented in 1791. Hamilton argued that since the restrictive regulations abroad were making it difficult for the increasing surplus of the American produce to find an outlet in foreign markets, it was necessary to create extensive demand at home for this surplus by developing manufactures. He refuted the contention that agriculture was more productive than manufacturing. He held that manufacturing gave more opportunities for division of labour and use of machinery, made possible a fuller utilisation of the potential productivity of the labour of women and children, offered scope for diversity of talents and dispositions, attracted foreign labour and capital, provided for a more ample and varied field for enterprise, and created a stable demand for the products of domestic agriculture. According to him, countries having both extensive agriculture and well developed manufacturing would be economically more prosperous than those depending solely or primarily on agricultural activities. In support of this contention he gave three principal arguments: (i) the two types of industry provided dependable domestic market for each other's products and diminished the reliance of the nation's business upon undependable foreign market, (ii) the two offered a greater variety of goods to foreign customers and thus stimulated exports; (iii) the development of both agriculture and manufacturing decreased the dependence of the country on one or a few products and thus the injury caused to the country as a consequence of the failure of the market for a particular commodity. He argued that manufacturing on a significant scale would not be established in a country where agriculture was and had long been the predominant industry because of "the strong influence of habit and the spirit of imitation; the fear of want of success in untried enterprises; the intrinsic difficulties incident to first essays towards or competition with those who have previously attained to perfection in the business to be attempted; (and) the bounties, premiums, and other artificial encouragements with which foreign nations secured the exertions of their own citizens, in the branches in which they are to be rivalled".[1] Consequently, he recommended protection and subsidies for the establishment of domestic industry. He, of course, did not plead for indiscriminate protection. He pleaded protection only where the country was sure of the availability of raw materials for the industry, of the availability of market for its products and of the possibility of using machinery to the extent needed because of the shortage of labour in America.

The most eloquent case for protection for the establishment of manufacturing was for the first time presented by Friedrich List. Gaining experience from American protectionist policy, List pleaded for the development of manufacturing in Germany with the aid of protection. In List's analysis, manufacturing was a great dynamic force. It stimulated increase in productivity in agriculture by providing growing demand for its output by the non-farm (manufacturing) population and by the application of more rational and efficient methods of production developed in manufacturing. Establishment of manufacturing led to a fuller utilisation of natural resources. It furthered accumulation of capital. It promoted commerce and navigation. Dynamism of manufacturing was not confined only to the economic field. It extended also to political, social and cultural fields.

> In a country devoted to mere raw agriculture, dullness of mind, awkwardness of body, obstinate adherence to old notions, customs, methods and processes, want of culture, of prosperity, and of liberty, prevail. The spirit of striving

> for a steady increase in mental and bodily requirements, of emulation, and of liberty, characterise, on the contrary, a state devoted to manufacturing and commerce.[2]

A high state of civilization could not be attained without the development of manufacturing. Exclusively agricultural people were necessarily rude and barbarous.

List advocated a balanced and harmonious development of the economy. He emphasized the importance of balance between material and mental occupations, between agriculture, manufacturing and commerce, and between different branches of manufacturing. He fully recognised the connection between development and complementaries both on technical side and on the demand side. He warned against lopsided development arising from specialisation in agriculture and dependence on imported manufactured goods.

List held that a country could introduce manufacturing under free trade if all countries engaged at the time in manufacturing were at the same level of progress and civilisation. In case certain countries were far ahead of others in manufacturing, commerce, and navigation, this could be done only by protecting domestic industry from foreign competition. List, of course, did not advocate indiscriminate protection. Protection was to be afforded temporarily and only if the nation had a natural basis for industry. List believed that countries only in the temperate zone possessed a natural basis for industry. Under no circumstances was agriculture to be afforded protection. Agriculture greatly benefited from the existence of a powerful industry. Industry required cheap food and raw materials. Moreover, differences in soil and climate afforded agriculture a kind of natural protection. In List's analysis, protection was only a transitional measure aimed at bringing all suitable nations up to the level of the most developed nation (which at that time was England) and ultimately was to be replaced by a system of universal free trade.

Recently, the development of industry has been strongly emphasised in the agricultural countries. The slogan "industrialise or perish" has gained much popularity in these countries. The supporters of industrialisation gave a number of arguments in favour of the establishment of industry. The most forceful case for industrialisation rests on the fact that the per capita income is higher in industrial than in agricultural countries. Even in the same country industrial workers are generally more prosperous than the agricultural workers. Industry is considered to be more profitable than agriculture. Jacob Viner, however, does not agree with this view.

> The agriculture is not necessarily associated with poverty becomes obvious when one considers Australia, New Zealand, Denmark, or Iowa and Nebraska. That industrialization is not necessarily associated with prosperity becomes obvious when one considers Italy or Spain.[3]

A similar observation has been made by Dr. Loeb:

> Countries with a lower percentage of economically active population in agriculture and a high percentage of economically active population in industry are generally countries having a high per capita income. But the relationship is not an absolute one. For instance, the proportion of the population of Canada, New Zealand, and Sweden occupied in agriculture is about four times than that of the United Kingdom, yet their real income per head is greater. The United Kingdom has an appreciably larger proportion of its population occupied in industry than the United States, but a considerably lower real income per head. The same applies to Belgium as compared with Switzerland, Australia compared with New Zealand, Sweden compared with Western Germany....[4]

Sometimes it is argued that industrialisation is not the cause of higher per capita income and that both industrialisation and higher incomes are the result of certain common factors like rich natural resources, enterprising, skilled and energetic people, topography and climate favourable to production, a higher land-labour ratio etc. Generally, industry is more capital-intensive than agriculture. The higher per capita income in industry is partly because of a larger amount of capital associated with a worker in industry. If an equivalent amount of capital is associated with a worker in agriculture, productivity in agriculture will rise considerably. In fact, because of lack of adequate and reliable data, it is very difficult to say anything definite as to whether or not the industrialisation is the cause of the higher per capita income.

The case for industrialisation is stronger from a long-term than from a short-term view of economic development. Because the amount of arable land is limited, it is not possible to absorb the whole population in agriculture. Ultimately, a large portion of the population will have to find employment outside agriculture and mining. With the introduction of mechanisation, the number of workers required in agriculture will decline considerably. Industry, on the other hand, requires very little land. If sufficient capital is available, industry can absorb a far larger number of workers. Law of diminishing returns starts operating earlier in agriculture. In contrast, although ultimately subject to diminishing returns, the limits within which the industry operates under increasing returns are very wide. Marginal productivity, distinct from average productivity, is likely to be higher in industry than in agriculture because of the existence of far larger resources in agriculture than in industry. During business cycles, fluctuations in the prices of agricultural products are larger than those in the prices of manufactured goods. Agricultural economies, therefore, are more unstable than the industrial economies. Fertility rates are higher among the rural population than among the urban industrial classes. The possibility of the increase in production being dissipated by an increase in population, therefore, is larger in agriculture than in industry.

Past experience shows that technological progress has been more rapid in manufacturing than in agriculture. Comparatively slower technological progress in agriculture would not make specialisation in agriculture unprofitable if the rapid technological progress in industry is reflected in lower prices and not in higher profits because, under these conditions, terms of trade will move in favour of agricultural countries and thus they would obtain the full benefit of rapid technological progress in industry. Actual experience, however, shows that rapid technological progress in industry has not fully reflected itself into lower prices and, therefore, the benefit obtained by industrial countries has been larger than that obtained by the agricultural countries.

Prof. Hirschman supports the case for industrialisation on the ground that a certain amount of initial investment in industry stimulates a larger amount of secondary investment than that stimulated by the same amount of investment in agriculture.

> The case for inferiority of agriculture to manufacturing has most frequently been argued on grounds of comparative productivity. While this case has been shown not to be entirely convincing, agriculture certainly stands convicted on the count of its lack of direct stimulus to the setting up of new activities through linkage effects; the superiority of manufacturing in this respect is crushing. This may yet be the most important reason militating against any complete specialisation of underdeveloped countries in primary production.[5]

It is held by the supporters of industrialisation that, in the coming years, the terms of trade are likely to move against the primary-producing countries because of a number of factors, viz. rapid increase in the production of foodstuffs and agricultural raw materials in all countries, particularly in developed countries; increased use of synthetic fibres, plastic, aluminium etc. recent inventions drastically decreasing the required amount of raw materials and fuel per unit of manufacturing output; vast increase in the demand for capital goods in exchange for primary products from developing countries; low income-elasticity of demand for foodstuffs. Singer states that:

> It is a matter of historical fact that ever since the seventies the trend of prices has been heavily against sellers of food and raw materials and in favour of the sellers of manufactured articles, 'The statistics are open to doubt and to objection in detail, but the general story which they tell is unmistakable.[6]

A similar view is held by the experts of the Economic Commission for Latin America under the direction of Prebisch. They state "had the rise in income, in the industrial centres and the periphery, been proportionate to the increase in their respective productivity, the price relations between primary and manufactured products would have been the same as if prices had fallen in strict proportion to productivity. Given the higher productivity of industry, the price relation would have moved in favour of the primary products."[7] But because of changes in actual money income, "while the centres kept the whole benefit of the technical development of their industries, the peripheral countries transferred to them a share of the fruits of their own technical progress."[8] On the other hand, there are some who hold that the terms of trade are likely to move in favour of primary-producing countries. A number of reasons are put forward in support of this prediction, viz. increase in population, increase in demand for and decline in supply of primary products owing to the implementation of industrialisation programmes in almost fall underdeveloped countries, production of primary products being subject to the law of increasing costs etc. In fact, it is difficult to say anything definite about the future course of the terms of trade between the primary and manufactured products.

Industrialisation is a pre-requisite for improvements in agriculture. Agricultural reforms, the mechanisation of agriculture or the introduction of co-operative farming, will render considerable manpower surplus in agriculture. Such reforms can be effected without arousing social discontentment only if employment opportunities are created outside agriculture for the manpower rendered surplus by these reforms.

A harmonius development of agriculture and industry is very essential if bottlenecks, shortages and excess capacities are to be avoided. Development in one sector will be checked if the other sector is not correspondingly developed.

> If manufacturing is to continue its expansion it must be accompanied by an expansion of either agriculture or production for export, or by import substitution. In the same way, an expansion of agriculture must be accompanied by an expansion of either manufacturing or production of export goods or by import substitution, although about this case there are no differences of opinion.[9]

INFANT INDUSTRIES

A more specific form of the general industrialisation argument is the infant industries argument. Restrictions are very essential to protect the infant industries of an infant country during the initial stages of their development. Though believing primarily in free trade, the need for protection for infant industries has been recognised even by the classical and neo-classical economists.

> The only case in which, on mere principles of political economy, protecting duties can be defensible, is when they are imposed temporarily (especially in a young and rising

> nation) in hopes of naturalising a foreign industry, in itself perfectly suitable to the circumstances of the country.[10]

It may be admitted that there is some force in the claim that a protective tariff is needed to aid giant business in establishing a complete standardisation on the most advanced modern model.[11]

Even the presently developed countries had to resort to protection during their early stages of development.

> Protection has played a prominent part in relieving the birth-pangs of the modern industrialism. Almost every industrialised country had to protect its industries against foreign competition for a temporary period so as to enable them to consolidate their position. Rationally applied, protection enables the most effective utilisation of the natural resources, human skill and aptitudes.[12]

Enke and Sakra have laid down the following three conditions for labelling industries as infant industries:[13]

(a) are justifiable and self-financing in the long run;

(b) inevitably sustain losses during their early years;

(c) would never be established in the absence of protection.

This industry by industry technique of examining the case for protection is not appropriate in underdeveloped countries. Each industry considered in isolation has no chance of standing on its own feet even in the long run. It is the simultaneous development of several industries combined with fundamental changes in the economic and social environments which is essential for enabling all these industries to stand on their own feet. Each individual industry creates certain external economies which increase the chances of success of other industries. External economies arise from the existence of the relation of complementarity between wants, between factors and between factors and products at various stages of production. Establishment of a new industry enlarges the market for the products of other industries. For illustration, let us suppose that a new industry *X* is established. It will employ labour, capital and land. Increase in the demand for labour, capital and land will increase the remuneration of the owners of labour, capital and land and thereby their demand for the products of other industries. The larger will be the increase in demand for products of other industries, the lower is the income-elasticity of demand for the products of industry *X*. Further, industry *X* will employ not only factors of production but also the products of other industries, viz. machinery, raw materials, semi-manufactured goods etc. Investment in a consumer goods industry directly increases demand for products of producer-goods industries which constitutes the inputs of the consumer-goods industry. If the producer-goods industries are subject to the law of increasing: returns, installation of a consumer-goods industry will lower the cost of production in these industries by increasing the demand for their products. Decline in the cost of production in these industries will benefit all consumer-goods industries. Profitability of those industries will also be increased whose products are consumed in conjunction with the products of the industry in which investment is made. External economies from the establishment of a new industry or from the expansion of an existing industry also arise in the form of improvements in the general facilities, viz. transportation and communications, credit and finance, skilled labour, trade journals etc. Economies arising from the installation of an industry accruing to other industries engaged in production at the same stage are known as horizontal external economies, e.g. economies arising from the installation of a consumer-goods industry and accruing to other consumer-goods industries, or economies arising from the installation of a producer-goods industry and accruing to other producer-goods industries. Economies arising from the installation of a new industry or from the expansion of an existing industry and accruing to other industries engaged in production at a different stage are known as vertical external economies, e.g. economies arising from the installation of a consumer-goods industry and accruing to producer-goods industries, or economies arising from the installation of producer-goods industry and accruing to consumer-goods industries. Industries at different stages of production are more complementary and less competitive than the industries at the same stage of production. Vertical economies, therefore, are likely to be more important than the horizontal economies. Consequently, the simultaneous investment in industries at different stages of the same line of production will give rise to larger external economies than the simultaneous investment in industries at the final stage of different lines. Installation of a new industry or the expansion of an existing industry creates not only external economies but also external diseconomies. Establishment of a new industry increases the demand for the factors of production. Unless the supply 'of the factors of production is perfectly elastic, this will raise their prices and thereby increase the cost of production in all industries. In underdeveloped countries, the elasticity of the supply of skilled labour, capital, arable land and entrepreneurship being very low, an increase in the demand for these factors will considerably raise their prices. Further, the establishment of a new industry will decrease demand for the products which can be directly or indirectly substituted for the products of the newly established industry and thereby decrease the profitability of industries producing these products. Though the establishment of a new industry gives rise to external economies as well as external diseconomies, in actual practice, the economies are likely to be much more powerful than the diseconomies. This is particularly likely in the initial stages of development. The external economies in the form of an expansion of market, training of labour, creation of an industrial atmosphere, development of technology, development of financing institutions, building of means of transportation and communications etc. cannot be considered in the profit and loss accounts of each industry. While deciding the case for protection for an industry, therefore, we should examine the possibility of its standing on its feet not in isolation but in an industrial atmosphere in which all the above mentioned and other external economies are available to it.[14]

It is held by some that protection is not essential for the development of infant industries in the underdeveloped countries. They argue that in advanced countries, too, most of the successful trades commenced with losses. This can best be illustrated with the example of the automobile industry. But private funds were usually forthcoming to incur the early losses in expectation of later higher profits. They hold that private investors will undertake investment if the long-term profits outweigh the early losses discounted at the current rate of interest. This, however, is not likely to hold because the environments of the present underdeveloped countries are different from those of the pre-development period of the advanced countries. The advanced countries developed under conditions of expanding world markets and absence of strong competition. If the pioneers suffered losses, these were not because of cut-throat competition from abroad but because of inefficiency or wrong estimates of demand or costs of production on the part of the producers. The presently underdeveloped countries have to face strong competition from developed countries in procuring raw materials as well as in selling final products. Producers in advanced countries, often, use unfair means for killing the rising industries in underdeveloped countries. The underdeveloped countries have to traverse the path in years which was traversed by the now developed countries in generations. Most of the advanced countries developed at a very slow pace. Capital arid entrepreneurship were available in abundant quantities while the outlets for investment were limited. One or the other entrepreneur, therefore, was ready to undertake the enterprise even if it involved losses in the initial stages. The underdeveloped countries cannot afford to wait for such a long period. They, therefore, have to simultaneously start a number of industries while capital and entrepreneurship are scarce. Opportunities for investment yielding high and quick returns (e.g. consumer-goods industries) are so many that it is not possible to attract private funds for infant industries involving losses in the initial stages. Entrepreneurs in underdeveloped countries are generally, short-sighted and unwilling to undertake enterprises which yield profits after a long period. They believe in get-quick-rich methods. Things were more steady when the advanced countries developed and those who suffered losses in the initial stages were sure of the later fabulous profits. Today, the world has become much more dynamic i.e. technology, tastes, etc. are changing much more rapidly. Those who suffer losses in the early period of infancy are not very sure of later profits because the changes in technology or demand may alter the things in such a way that their investment becomes useless before the period of infancy is over. In the past, patents were respected and the risk-takers were more sure of their early losses being compensated by later fabulous profits. These days patents have lost their value. Any paying product is immediately copied by others, with or without slight changes in the product, by making minor changes in the trade mark. Recently Indian firms have started exploiting the trade marks "Made in England", "Made in U.S.A." etc. by using trade marks like "Made as in England", "Made as in U.S.A." etc. writing as in small type and in such a way that a cursory glance fails to differentiate between the real and the deceptive marks. Similarly, to copy the famous "Sunlight" soap, there has appeared a soap of exactly the same size and wrapped in a cover similar in design and colours with the mark "Sonlight". Such instances can be easily multiplied. Because of shortage of capital, the rate of interest is comparatively higher in underdeveloped countries. If the private investors discount later profits at this high rate of interest, sufficient funds may not be forthcoming for rearing infant industries. If the infant industries are to be developed, therefore, the government must come forward to prevent early losses by protecting these industries from the competition of imported cheaper products.

Graphical Illustration of the Infant-industry Argument

The infant-industry argument can be illustrated by the following figure.

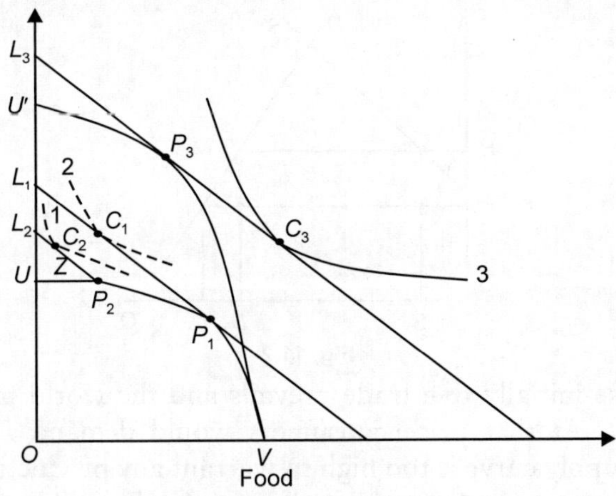

Fig. 11.1

The initial production possibilities frontier is given by curve UV and the international price ratio by the absolute slope of lines L_1P_1, L_2P_2, and L_3P_3. Under laissez-faire, the economy produces at P_1 and consumes at C_1 after a production subsidy is given to the infant clothing industry, however, the production-possibility frontier shifts outward gradually as a result of the continuous improvement in skills and production techniques, until it eventually attains the position shown by curve *U′V*. The above figure illustrates the most favorable case, in which the infant industry (clothing) grows to become a net exporter. Thus, the economy eventually produces at P_3 and consumes at C_3.

One important point to note is that a temporary production subsidy to the infant industry is more efficient than tariff protection. With a production subsidy, there is no consumption loss—the domestic consumers continue to trade at world prices. Immediately after the production subsidy goes into effect, consumption shifts to C_2, where line L_2 P_2 is tangent to the highest possible social indifference curve, as shown by 1. With an equivalent tariff instead, consumption would move to a point such as *Z*, where the marginal rate of substitution is equal to the lower domestic price ratio.

An Analytical Example

Consider the market for a manufactured good such as textiles in a small less developed country. Supply and demand curves can be given by the Fig. 11.2.

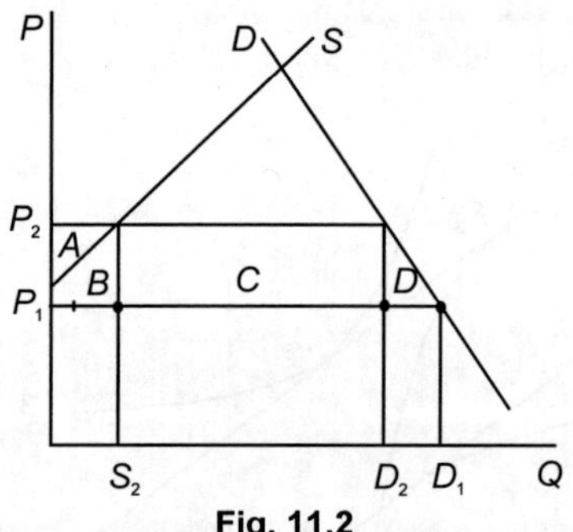

Fig. 11.2

Suppose initially free trade prevails and the world price of the good is P_1. At that price consumers would demand D_1 but the domestic supply curve is too high to warrant any production. This is the case then where domestic producers simply could not produce the product cheaply enough to compete with firms in the rest of the world. Thus the free trade level of imports would be given by the line from P_1 which is equal to domestic demand, D_1.

Suppose that the infant industry argument is used to justify protection for this currently non-existent domestic industry. Let a specific tariff be implemented which rises the domestic price to P_2. In this case the tariff would equal the difference between P_2 and P_1, i.e. $t = P_2 - P_1$. The increase in domestic price is sufficient to stimulate domestic production of S_2. Demand would fall to D_2 and imports would fall to $D_2 - S_2$ (line from P_2).

The static (i.e. one period) welfare effects of the import tariff for importing country is shown as follows.

Consumer surplus = – (A + B + C + D)

Producer surplus = + A

Govt. Revenue = + C

National welfare = – (B + D)

Consumers of textiles are harmed because of the higher domestic price of the good. Producers gain in terms of producer surplus. In addition, employment is created in an industry that did not even exit before the tariff. Finally, the government earns tariff revenue which benefits some other segment of the production.

The net national welfare effect of the import tariff is negative. Although some segments of the population benefit, there remains two deadweight losses to the economy. Area *B* represents a production efficiency loss while area *D* represents a consumption efficiency loss.

Dynamic Effects of Infant-industry Protection

Now we suppose that the infant industry argument is valid and that by stimulating domestic production with a temporary import tariff, the domestic industry improves its own productive efficiency. We can represent this as a downward shift in domestic industry supply curve, illustrated as in fig. 11.3.

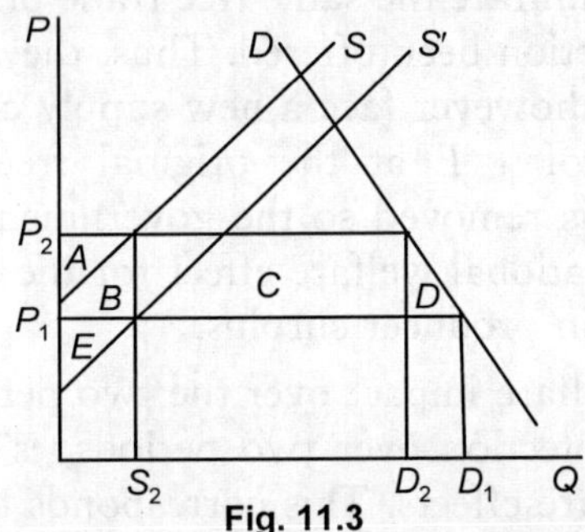

Fig. 11.3

In reality this shift would probably occur gradually over time as the learning effects are incorporated in the production process. For analytical simplicity we will assume that the effect occurs as follows. First imagine that the domestic industry enjoys one period of protection in the form of a tariff. In the second period we will assume that the tariff is removed entirely but that the industry experiences an instantaneous improvement in efficiency such that it can maintain production at its period one level, but, at the original free trade price. This efficiency improvement can be shown as a supply curve shift from *S* to *S′*.

This implies that in the second period free trade again prevails. The domestic price returns to the free trade price of P_1, while domestic demand rises to D_1. Because of the efficiency improvement domestic supply in free trade is given by S_2 and the level of imports is $D_1 - D_2$.

The static (one period) welfare effects of the tariff removal/efficiency improvement for the importing country can be summarized as:

Consumer surplus	=	0
Producer surplus	=	+ E
Government revenue	=	0
National welfare	=	+ E

These effects are calculated relative to the original equilibrium before the original tariff was implemented. This is done because we want to identify the welfare effects in each period relative to what would have occurred had the infant industry protection not been provided.

Consumers again face the same free trade price that they would have had no protection been offered. Thus, they experience no loss or gain. Producers however face a new supply curve that generates producer surplus of + E at the original free trade price. The government tariff is removed so the government receives no tariff revenue. The net national welfare effect for the second period then is simply the gain in producer surplus.

The overall welfare impact over the two periods, relative to no infant industry protection over two periods, is simply the sum of each period's welfare effects. This corresponds to the sum of areas (+ E – B – D) which could be positive or negative. If the second period producer surplus gain exceeds the first period deadweight losses then the protection has a positive two period effect on national welfare.

The efficiency improvement in the domestic industry would remain, if not improve, in all subsequent periods as well. Thus it is not complete to consider the effects only over two periods. Instead, and for simplicity again, suppose that the new supply curve prevails in all subsequent periods. In this case the true dynamic national welfare effects would consist of area *E* times the number of future periods we wish to consider minus the one period deadweight losses. Thus even if the costs of the tariff are not made up in the second period they may well be made up eventually at some point in the future. This would make it even more likely that the temporary protection would be beneficial in the long run.

If in addition to the direct efficiency effects within the industry there are spillover efficiency effects to other industries within the domestic economy then the likelihood that temporary protection is beneficial is enhanced even further. In other words, over time workers and managers from the protected industries may establish firms or take jobs in other sectors of the economy. Since they will bring their newly learned skills with them, it will cause an improvement in productive efficiency in those sectors as well. In this way the supply of many manufacturing industries will be increased allowing these sectors to compete more easily with firms in the rest of the world. Industrialization and GDP growth then is stimulated by the initial protection of domestic industries.

Thus protection of an infant industry may be beneficial for an economy. At the heart of the argument is the assumption that production experience generates efficiency improvements either directly in the protected industry or indirectly in other industries as a learning spillover ensures. The infant industry relies on a dynamic view of the world rather than the static description used in classical trade models. Although protection may be detrimental to national welfare in the short run, it is conceivable that the positive dynamic long run effects will more than outweigh the short run (or static) effects.

The Economic Argument against Infant Industry Protection

The main economic argument against infant industry protection is that protection is likely to be a second-best policy choice rather than a first-best policy. The key element of the infant industry argument is the presence of a positive dynamic production externality. It is assumed that production experience causes learning which improves future productive efficiency. Alternatively it is assumed that these learning effects spill over into other industries and improves those industries' future productive efficiencies as well.

The theory of the second best states that in the presence of a market distortion, such as a production externality, it is possible to conceive of a trade policy that can improve national welfare.

However, in this case the trade policy, namely the import tariff, is not the first-best policy because it does not attack the distortion most directly. In this case the more efficient policy is a production subsidy targeted at the industries that generate the positive learning effects.

To demonstrate this result we will consider the following analytical example. We will use the same supply and demand conditions as in the original example. Let us consider Fig. 11.4.

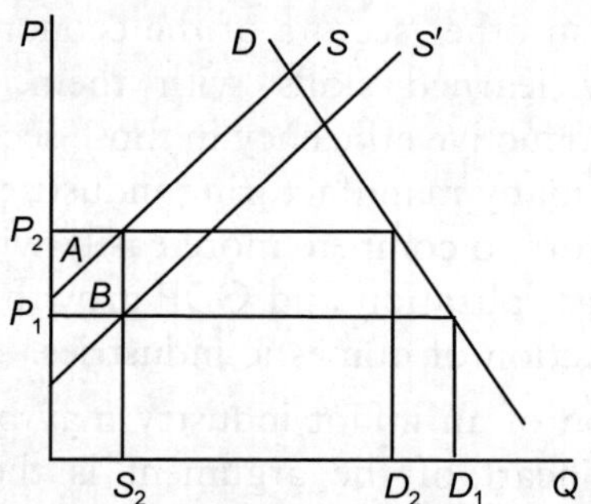

Fig. 11.4

The domestic supply and demand curves are given by *D* and *S* respectively. The initial free trade world price of the good is P_1. At that price consumers would demand D_1 but the domestic supply curve is too high to warrant any production. Thus the level of imports is given by D_1.

Now suppose that the government implements a specific production subsidy equal to the difference in prices $P_2 - P_1$. The subsidy would raise the producer price by the amount of the subsidy to P_2 and hence domestic supply will rise to *S'*. The domestic consumer price would remain at P_1 so demand would remain at D_1. Imports would fall to $D_1 - S'$.

The static welfare effects of the production subsidy of importing country can be described as:

Consumer surplus = 0

Producer surplus = + A

Government revenue = – (A + B)

National welfare = – B

Consumers of textiles are left unaffected by the subsidy since the domestic price remains the same. Producers gain in terms of producer surplus since the subsidy is sufficient to cause production to begin. In addition, employment is created in an industry. The government, however, must pay the subsidy. Thus someone pays higher taxes to fund the subsidy. The net national welfare effect of the production subsidy is negative. Although some segments of the population benefit, there remains a production efficiency loss.

Here one important point to be noted is that relative to an import tariff that generates the same level of domestic production, the subsidy is less costly in the aggregate. The production subsidy causes only a production efficiency loss while the tariff causes an additional consumption efficiency loss. If the positive dynamic gains in efficiency in subsequent periods are the same, then the production subsidy would generate the same positive stream of benefits but at a lower overall cost to the country. For this reason the production subsidy is the first best policy to choose in light of the dynamic production externality. The import tariff remains second best.

For this reason economists sometimes argue that although an import tariff may indeed be beneficial in the case of infant industries, it does not necessarily mean that protection is appropriate.

Other Arguments against Infant Industry Protection

Political economic problem—Political pressure in democratic economies can make it difficult to implement infant industry protection in its most effective manner. In order for protection to work in the long run it is important that protection be temporary. There are two main reasons for this. Firstly, it may be that the one period efficiency improvement is less than the sum of the deadweight costs of protection. Thus if protection is maintained, then the sum of the costs may exceed the efficiency improvements and serve to reduce national welfare in the long run. Secondly, and more critically, if protection were expected to be long-lasting then the protected domestic firms would have less incentive to improve their productive efficiency. If political pressures are brought to bear whenever the tariffs are scheduled to be reduced or removed, industry representatives might convince legislators that more time is needed to guarantee the intended efficiency improvements. In other words firms might begin to claim that they need more time to compete against firms in the rest of the world. As long as legislators provide more time to catch-up to world efficiency standards, protected firms have little incentive to incur the investment and training costs necessary to compete in a free market. After all, the tariff keeps the price high and allows even relatively inefficient production to produce profits for the domestic firms.

Thus one big problem with applying the infant industry protection is that the protection itself may eliminate the need for the firms to grow up. Without the subsequent efficiency improvements, protection would only generate costs for the economy in the aggregate.

Informational problems—In order for infant industry protection to work it is important for governments to have reliable information about industries in their economies. They need to know which industries have strong learning effects associated with production and which industries are most likely to generate learning spillover effects to other industries. It would also be useful to know the size of the effects as well as the timing. But, not only must governments decide which industries to protect, they must also decide how large the protective tariffs should be and over what period of time the tariff should be reduced and eliminated. If the government sets the tariff too low the protection may be insufficient to generate very much domestic production. If the tariff is set too high, the costs of the tariff might outweigh the long term efficiency improvements. If the tariff is imposed for too long a period then firms might not have enough of an incentive to make the changes necessary to improve efficiency. If set for too short a time, then firms may not learn enough to compete with the rest of the world once the tariffs are removed.

Thus in order for infant industry protection to work it is important to set the tariff for the correct industries, at the correct level, and for the correct period of time. Determining the correct industries, tariff level and time period is not a simple matter. Indeed some people argue that it is impossible to answer these questions with a sufficient amount of accuracy to warrant applying these policies.

Failure of import-substitution strategies—One popular development strategy in the 1950s and 1960s was known as import substitution. Essentially this strategy is just an application of the infant industry argument. However, many of the countries who pursued these kinds of inward-looking strategies, most notably countries in Latin America and Africa, performed considerably less well economically than many countries in Asia. The Asian countries such as South Korea Taiwan, Hong Kong and Japan pursued, what have been labeled, export-oriented strategies instead. Since many of these Southeast Asian countries performed so much better economically, it has lent some empirical evidence against the application of infant industry protection.

Balance of Payments

Rapid development generally brings in its train a disequilibrium in the balance of payments. Besides the indirect effects, rapid development affects the balance of payments adversely, mainly speaking, in two ways. Firstly, import of huge quantities of capital goods, technical know-how and essential raw materials is required to carry on the development plans. Newly set-up industries might require continuous imports of spare parts, raw materials etc. Secondly, many goods which were previously available for export may now be consumed by the newly created domestic industries. In addition to the above mentioned direct effects, rapid development affects the balance of payments adversely, mainly speaking, in two indirect ways, i.e. through income effect and price effect. The additional expenditure on development projects results in an increase in income in the hands of the consumer. With the increase in income the demand for imports rises, too, the extent depending on the marginal propensity to import. The marginal propensity to import is, generally, high in underdeveloped countries. With the increase in income, the demand for superior goods and luxuries increases which are not available within the country. Increased incomes in the hands of the consumers affect the balance of payments not only through increased imports but also through decreased exports. Some of the goods which were being exported previously might now be consumed within the country. The expansion of home market which is profitable enough might relax the interest of the industrialists in foreign markets which have recently become highly competitive. Secondly, development at a rate higher than that allowed by the available resources, generally, results in a rise in the price level. This is particularly so in underdeveloped countries in which a high marginal propensity to consume is combined with comparatively inelastic production due to lack of excess capacity, shortage of complementary factors and other bottlenecks. In addition, because of lack of other sources, deficit financing has got to be resorted to step up the rate of economic development. A rise in the comparative price-level encourages imports and discourages exports. Stimulation to imports may not be very strong in controlled economies yet the discouragement to exports works fully (unless the rise in the price of exports is counterbalanced by subsidies or other export promotion measures). No doubt, development has also got favourable effects on the balance of payments. It affects the balance of payments favourably by increasing the capacity to export with the increase in production and by decreasing the necessity to import because many goods which were being imported previously may now be produced by the industries newly established within the country. In the preliminary stages of development, however, the unfavourable effects are more powerful than the favourable ones because the investment undertaken during a certain period increases the money incomes almost simultaneously but starts yielding real goods after the lapse of some time. Whether or not economic development is followed, by a deficit in the balance of payments and its magnitude depends on a number of factors, viz. size of previous surplus, financing policies, magnitude and direction of investment, the extent to which export capacity is correspondingly expanded, the degree to which increased productivity occurs in the existing industries, rapidity with which new consumable products become available from new investment, the degree to which the economy has been and can continue to be self-sufficient in foodstuffs production, the extent to which the domestic raw materials can be utilised in developing industries, the level of consumption presently prevailing, the geographic size of the country, the amount and nature of natural resources which it has available etc.

But the question arises, are there no ways other than the restriction of imports to cure a deficit in the balance of payments? With the emergence of control and planning in almost all countries, automatic forces tending to bring about an equilibrium in the balance of payments have lost their effectiveness. Moreover, these involve a deflation of prices and income which may sabotage the whole process of economic development. Devaluation, generally, is not effective because of the particular elasticities of demand for and supply of the exports and imports of the underdeveloped countries. Even if it can do something to cure the deficit, it may prove too costly, i.e. the terms of trade may move substantially against the devaluing country, the burden of its debts if expressed in foreign currency may increase etc. It might lead to a flight of capital. In addition, the market requires some time to adjust to the changed prices and, therefore, devaluation may not be very useful immediately. Scope for export promotion is limited by the capacity of the underdeveloped countries to export and the same of the developed countries to import. Moreover, it is a long-term solution. Restrictions may be necessary meanwhile if the country does not possess sufficient reserves of gold or other means of payments acceptable to the surplus country.

The IMF and GATT allow countries to impose temporary restrictions to cure a deficit in the balance of payments. The transitional period of development in underdeveloped countries, however, is likely to be spread over, if not decades, at least, several years. Trade restrictions, therefore, will be essential for a fairly long period rather than being temporary. Moreover, import restrictions on inessential goods are essential for underdeveloped countries even when they are having a highly favourable balance of payments. It will be better if these countries conserve foreign exchange resources during periods of surplus balance of payments for future expenditure on the import of capital goods rather than wasting it on the import of consumer goods and luxuries.

Tariff Factories

Imports may be restricted to stimulate the establishment of tariff factories with foreign capital and enterprise to produce the imported goods at home. These may be new enterprises or the subsidiaries of the already established firms operating in foreign countries. Doubts have been expressed regarding the benefits of 'tariff factories' to the country in which they are set up. The capital invested in these industries does not add to the wealth of the country and has got to be repatriated sooner or later.[15] The cost of production of these subsidiaries is likely to be higher than the import price because of the small size of the domestic market and the absence of basic facilities in underdeveloped countries. Foreign investment in the form of 'tariff factories' solves the immediate problem of foreign exchange at the cost of future years when the recurring profits and the original capital have got to be repatriated. The nationals are deprived of several opportunities for investment in industries which are occupied by the foreign investors before they are in a position to undertake these. Had these opportunities remained unutilised, the nationals would have utilised these sooner or later.

So far we have been examining the dark side of the picture. Let us now turn to the bright side. The 'tariff factories' will provide some employment to the domestic factors of production. Though managerial and skilled labour may be imported, unskilled labour and certain raw materials are likely to be used from within the country. These will create an industrial atmosphere, the importance of which cannot be overemphasised for the industrialisation of the primary producing countries. These provide revenue to the government in the form of several taxes, viz. income tax, profit tax, excise duty etc. These create external economies (viz. training of labour, creation of skill and technology, building country's reputation for industrial products etc.) which are very useful for the establishment of other industries and thus facilitate the process of industrialisation. The cost of production of the 'tariff factories' will be lower than the import price to the extent the transfer costs of the imported factors of production required for the production of the product are lower than those of the imported finished product. Other things being equal, the cost of production of the 'tariff factories' will be substantially lower than the import price if most of the factors required for the production of the concerned product are available within the country at equivalent prices. The unskilled labour is available in underdeveloped countries at much lower wage rates. Many imported products contain raw materials exported by the underdeveloped countries. The costs of transfer involved in exporting raw materials and those involved in importing manufactured products containing the same raw materials will be saved if these products are made at home by the subsidiaries. These economies, however, will have to be discounted by the costs of transfer involved in importing equipment, raw materials, managerial and skilled labour required by the subsidiaries. Further, imported managerial and skilled labour might have to be paid higher wages to attract sufficient supplies thereof. The domestic price of the product from subsidiaries may not rise in spite of the unfavourable conditions under which these have to work if the foreign firm had a monopoly and was charging a very exorbitant price; the enhanced cost of production will be met out of monopoly profits rather than by raising the price.[16] Establishment of subsidiaries will be useful during the war because there will be no risk of the stoppage of supplies. It is feared by some people that the factories may interfere in the internal politics of the country and thus threaten its independence. These fears, which had some justification in the past, are, now, absolutely baseless because most of the underdeveloped countries possess governments strong enough to prevent any such interference in their national affairs. Moreover, the establishment of world organisations (like the U.N.O.) has considerably decreased the chances of such happenings. Considering all the above mentioned benefits of 'tariff factories', it is difficult to reconcile with the conclusion reached by Enke and Salera "...in normal course of affairs no valid case can be made in favour of encouraging tariff factories."[17]

The real question is not whether or not these tariff factories are beneficial for the underdeveloped countries but whether or not the import restrictions will lead to the establishment of these factories. As the market in underdeveloped countries for most of the imported goods is small, the chances of the establishment of tariff factories are not very bright.[18] "Tariff protection, if it can help at all, can help the strong—it cannot help the weak."[19] The conditions in underdeveloped countries, however, are not so discouraging as viewed by Prof. Nurkse. There exists sufficient demand for many industries producing consumer goods used by the masses. For other industries, for which market is not sufficient in individual countries, plants can be set up in some countries and all neighbouring countries supplied from these plants. The costs of transfer of these goods from a neighbour country will be lower than those from an advanced country situated at a distance of thousands of miles. Moreover, as noticed earlier, the market in these countries is small not because of small population but because of low per capita income and consequently low per capita expenditure. As the industrialisation process proceeds, per capita income and hence expenditure will increase and the industries for which demand is not sufficient at present will find enough profitable market after some time.

Stability

A little less but stable income is, generally, preferred to a little more but highly unstable one. Human psychology tells that a certain cut in income gives more pain than the pleasure gained from an equivalent increment. Diversification of the economy is essential for its stability. Most of the underdeveloped countries depend for a major part of their foreign exchange earnings on the export of a very limited number of commodities.

> ...rice has recently accounted for about 80 per cent of the value of imports from Burma. Ninety per cent of exports from Pakistan have consisted of jute, cotton, tea, wood, hides and skins. Exports from the Federation of Malaya consisted almost exclusively of rubber and tin. Seventy six per cent of Indonesia's exports have been petroleum, rubber and tin. Over 80 per cent of Philippine exports are covered by sugar, copra and vegetable oils and abaca. Tea, rubber, copra and oil form about 90 per cent of the entire exports of Ceylon, while Thailand's rice, rubber and tin exports account for 80 per cent of total exports.[20]

When a country depends mainly on the export of one or two commodities, any happening lowering the price of these commodities, will endanger the stability of the whole economy. It will affect not only the income of the producers of these commodities, but also the receipts of the government, foreign exchange available for imports and thereby production and employment in industries using imported products and so on and so forth. If a country exports several products, there is every likelihood that the fall in the prices of some of its exports will be offset by a rise in the price of other exports. In addition, a diversified economy is comparatively more flexible. It can shift its resources from the production of commodities whose prices are falling towards those whose prices are rising. Trade restrictions can also be used to prevent or mitigate the transmission of business cycles arising abroad. A bumper crop abroad, for instance, may affect domestic production by temporarily lowering the price of imports. In this case, restriction of imports can help in maintaining the domestic price level and thereby in avoiding undesirable repercussions on domestic production. Even in case of permanent changes in comparative costs position owing to changes in tastes and techniques of discovery of new resources, trade restrictions may be used to provide temporary relief to domestic industries during the transitional period in order to avoid sudden jerks to the economy.

Creation of Market

Lack of market is an important hinderance to the development of an underdeveloped economy.

> .... One of the difficulties of industrial development in underdeveloped countries, and one of the great hinderances to giving real momentum to a development policy, is that internal demand must be built up simultaneously with supply. The unlikelihood or, anyhow, the exasperating slowness of any self-engendered proccss of "natural growth" offers a main explanation why sustained stagnation becomes a sort of natural equilibrium and why policy interventions are called for. Indeed, the entire idea of a policy of economic development is to break away from this low-level equilibrium.[21]

Existence of sufficient effective demand is very essential to induce investment in any industry. The nature of the shortage of effective demand in underdeveloped countries is, of course, widely different from that in developed countries. In developed countries the shortage of demand arises from oversaving. Such a shortage of demand can easily be remedied by monetary expansion. Shortage of demand in underdeveloped countries arises not from over-saving but from low incomes and consequent small purchasing power of the people. In other words, the shortage of demand arises from a shortage of supply to offer in exchange in the market. Mere monetary expansion cannot remedy such a shortage of demand. It will lead simply to inflation. Import restrictions have been pleaded for the creation of market through a simultaneous development of a number of industries.

> A wave of capital investments in a number of different industries can economically succeed while any substantial application of capital by an industrial entrepreneur in any particular industry may be locked or discouraged by the limitations of the pre-existing market.[22]

Say's law of demand applies more to underdeveloped than to developed countries. In underdeveloped countries, because of the very low standard of living, marginal propensity to consume is almost unity. When an overwhelming majority of people are living just on subsistence level, any increase in incomes will be utilised for immediate consumption. Production thus creates its own demand and the size of the market depends upon the volume of production. Say's law will hold only if the increase in production is spread over a number of industries so that the people employed in these industries provide demand for each other's products. "Every increase of production, if distributed without miscalculation among all kinds of produce in the proportion which private interest would dictate creates, or rather constitutes, its own demand."[23] Say's law would not hold true in case the whole increase in production is concentrated in a single industry. Let us illustrate this point by faking Nurkse's example of a shoe industry. Suppose a shoe industry is set up in an underdeveloped country. People employed in this industry would not spend whole of their income on shoes. They require a number of other things, too. If the incomes of the people other than those employed in the newly set up shoe industry remain unchanged, the demand for shoes will be very small. Only a small part of their unchanged incomes will be diverted from other products to shoes. Shortage of demand for shoes may lead to a failure of the shoe industry, in contrast, if a simultaneous investment is made in a number of industries producing mass consumption goods, people employed in these industries will provide demand for each other's products. Thus production will create its own demand if it is spread over a number of industries proportioned in a manner which corresponds to the pattern of consumers' preferences.

Often there exists a misunderstanding that the balanced growth in the above sense is incompatible with international trade. It is argued that the balanced growth requires a simultaneous expansion of mutually supporting industries while the doctrine of comparative advantage states that the available resources should be concentrated on a limited number of industries in which the country possesses a comparative advantage. In fact, balanced growth is compatible with international specialisation and the two are not mutually exclusive. A country having no foreign trade can increase its total output by participating in world trade. Once a country has specialised in accordance with the dictates of the doctrine of comparative costs, is there no way of achieving further development, if the external demand conditions do not induce it? Certainly, there is: the possibilities of economic development are not exhausted with international specialisation according to the dictates of the principle of comparative costs. If certain unemployed productive resources are available, without interfering with foreign trade, a country can develop by expanding home market through a simultaneous expansion of mutually supporting industries. Underdeveloped countries possess vast amounts of unemployed and underemployed labour. It can be used for producing domestic goods without interfering with foreign trade.

> Balanced growth is the best friend that international trade can have. Filling the vacuum in the domestic economy is the best foundation for foreign trade, since it means increasing the level of productivity and real purchasing power. After all, that is why the advanced nations are each other's best customers.[24]

The new industries built with the resources which would have remained unemployed in an open economy cannot compete with their counterpart industries abroad and can continue production only if protected from foreign competition. Additional import restrictions will be required if the additional purchasing power generated by these industries is not to be permitted to cause balance of payments difficulties.

Dumping and State Subsidisation

Vested interests in foreign countries might indulge in temporary dumping to kill the rising industries in underdeveloped countries with a view to reserve these markets for themselves. The immediate danger to the rising industries of the underdeveloped countries, however, is not so much from private dumping as from direct and indirect state subsidisation (viz. remission of taxes, rebate on imports required for export industries, cheap transport rates for exports, liberal expenditure out of public revenue on market exploration schemes etc.) of exports in advanced countries under the guise of export promotion schemes. Trade restrictions are necessary to prevent dumping and state subsidisation.

To Safeguard Wage Standards

In keeping with the spirit of socialism and to prevent communism, many underdeveloped countries have declared 'welfare state' to be their goal. Recent awareness of wage standards in advanced countries has led the labourers in underdeveloped countries to demand wages higher than their marginal productivity at world prices. It is contended by the labour that their low marginal productivity is not due to their own faults. It is mostly due to causes beyond their control, viz. defective organisation of the industry, small amount of capital, and other complementary factors per labourer, lack of education and training facilities, low wages and consequently inferior health etc. and, therefore, they should not be made to suffer for the low productivity. In a democratic country, it is difficult for the government to resist the demands of labourers even if these are unreasonable to some extent; the government is afraid of losing the votes of the labouring classes which constitute a substantial part of the total votes. Restriction of imports, therefore, is necessary to safeguard domestic industries paying wages higher than the marginal productivity of labour at world prices.

To Step up Investment

Trade restrictions promote savings by limiting the importation of inessential goods. It is not unlikely that a part of the money which was being spent on inessential imported commodities may be saved up instead of being spent on domestic goods when the import of these commodities is restricted. Further, restriction of imported goods creates profitable avenues for investment. This coupled with increased savings will accelerate capital formation.

To Safeguard Indigenous Plants from Minor Technological Changes

Import restrictions may be used to safeguard indigenous plants from minor technological advancements abroad, the benefit of which to consumers is far less than the loss to producers from their plants becoming useless. Such restrictions are specially important in underdeveloped countries suffering from a severe shortage of capital particularly in cases where (a) the price difference between imported and indigenous goods is small or the difference is only in design; (b) the average service life of the plant is fairly long; (c) the plants are of a specialised nature and lack mobility.

Tariffs to Offset Domestic Excise Duties

Tariffs may be levied on imported goods to counterbalance excise duties on domestic goods if the imported goods do not bear excise duties in their country of origin or bear at a rate lower than that borne by the domestic goods. Revenue from such duties will be much more productive and stable. If these restrict imports, domestic production will be encouraged and the loss of revenue from tariffs will be compensated by increased revenue from domestic excise duties. Application of such duties in actual practice, however, involves a number of difficulties. Further, while equalising taxes, care should be taken that direct and indirect benefits flowing from government expenditure are also equalised. If the taxes levied and the facilities provided by the state in country *A* are higher than those in country *B,* there is no justification for a compensatory, tariff by country *A* on goods imported from country *B*.

To Achieve Favourable Terms of Trade

Disequilibrium in the balance of payments may be cured with import restrictions instead of rectifying it with devaluation which might deteriorate the terms of trade. This may not be a wise policy if import restrictions cause certain adverse effects which devaluation may not involve. Similarly, the terms of trade might be improved by making foreigners pay whole or part of tariffs. Recognising the possibility of an improvement in a country's terms of trade through the imposition of a tax on imports, and exports, Edgeworth states "...under conceivable circumstances advantage may result to the home country from a tax on exports and imports."[25]

Government Revenue

Tariffs are an important source of revenue for the government in many underdeveloped countries. A very important reason for this is that the administrative apparatus for taxing domestic production, profits and income is not so well developed as that for taxing foreign trade. A substantial portion of the income in these economies is non-monetary. Producers being illiterate cannot keep accounts in the modern form which is very essential for taxation. Restrictions affect revenue indirectly, too. These, for instance, generate inflation. Inflation raises money incomes and thereby broadens the base for income tax. Overall devaluation, also, increases revenue by increasing the value of gold and foreign exchange reserves possessed by the

Government. Revenue from this source, however, differs from that from tariffs. Revenue from devaluation does not affect the income of the private sector and thus has no anti-inflationary effects while tariffs decrease the income in the private sector and thus have anti-inflationary effects. Revenue from devaluation is once for ever and not continuous as that from tariffs and, therefore, less suitable for financing development which requires continuous finance. Abnormal increase in revenue from devaluation might lead to wasteful expenditure in case the government is not enough far sighted. Tariffs are considered to be a superior source of revenue on a number of grounds. Tariffs kill two birds with one stone. These provide revenue as well as protection to domestic industries. It is contended by free traders that the two objectives (i.e. revenue and protection) are inconsistent. Tariffs which provide more revenue will afford less protection and those which afford more protection will yield less revenue. In the limiting case, a prohibitive tariff which provides effective protection by completely preventing imports will yield no revenue. On the other hand, a sufficiently low rate of duty provides substantial revenue but no protection. Similarly, we can go to the other extreme and prove that the two objectives are compatible, i.e. zero rate of tariff yields neither revenue nor protection. The actual cases, however, lie somewhere in the middle and tariffs provide protection as well as revenue. Further, it may be pointed out that the yield of revenue is, generally, a by-product and not the main consideration in imposing tariffs. The amount collected, therefore, does not matter much. Another advantage of tariffs over other methods of raising revenue is that the whole or a part of the tariff is paid by the foreigners. The relative share of the tariff paid by the foreign producer and the domestic consumer depends upon the elasticity of supply of the foreign producer and the elasticity of demand of the domestic consumers. In the limiting case, if the demand of the domestic consumers is infinitely elastic and the supply of the foreign producer perfectly inelastic, whole of the tariff will be paid by the foreign producer. On the other hand, if the supply of the foreign producer is perfectly elastic and the demand of the domestic consumers perfectly inelastic, whole of the tariff will be paid by the domestic consumers. In actual practice, however, most of the tariff is likely to be paid by the domestic consumers as the import of a commodity by a particular single country is so small a part of the total world exports of the commodity as does not affect the world price much. This is particularly so in the case of a small country.[26]

Export Restrictions

So far we were discussing import restrictions. Let us now turn to export restrictions. Export restrictions can be used to encourage domestic industries. Export of raw materials which are in short supply for domestic industries may be prohibited. Export may be prohibited to lower the price of raw materials for domestic industries in order to increase their competitive strength in the world market. Export of raw materials may be restricted to encourage domestic processing industries. Raw materials in short supply should be used for the import of goods which are in short supply through bilateral agreements. Export control may be used to divert exports to hard currency areas. In case of a temporary shortage of certain exportable goods, export control may be used to equitably distribute the limited exportable surplus among the established customers; if some customers are once lost and captured by other exporting countries, it becomes very difficult to recapture them when exportable capacity has recovered. Many underdeveloped countries are exporting exhaustible natural resources at such a speed that by the time these countries are in a position to establish their own industries, the resources might have exhausted and the domestic industries might suffer from a shortage of natural resources. State regulation of the export of such resources is very essential for safeguarding the interests of the coming generations.

Special Case for Restrictions of Underdeveloped Countries

Owing to a number of reasons, the underdeveloped countries have a special claim to institute import restrictions and, therefore, these should not be resented or retaliated by the advanced countries. Firstly, the rate of development in the developing economies is accelerated with the concerted efforts of the state to a level higher than that at which these countries would have developed in an atmosphere of free enterprise with the government performing only the minimum necessary functions. The high rate of development, as discussed above, increases imports and decreases exports to an abnormal level. Control of the abnormal part of the increased imports should not be resented by the advanced countries.[27] Similarly, on the export side, there is a special case for the underdeveloped countries to check the abnormal part of the fall in exports. Export promotion activities of the underdeveloped countries aimed at maintaining the previous share in world exports should not, therefore, be resented and retaliated by other countries.

Secondly, the nature of import restrictions of the underdeveloped countries differs from those of the developed countries. Import restrictions of the underdeveloped countries are of a selective nature and do not restrict total world trade and are thus of a more or less harmless character. Restrictions are imposed mainly to utilise the available foreign exchange earnings for the import of commodities essential for economic development rather than for that of consumer goods and luxuries. The only limitation on their imports is imposed by the amount of exports permitted by other countries, i.e. the availability of foreign exchange earnings. If the advanced countries permit underdeveloped countries to export more, the latter will be very glad to increase their imports from advanced countries. It will enable these countries to import more capital goods, technical know-how and essential raw materials and thereby help in accelerating their rate of development. In case import restrictions lead to a shift of resources from export industries to protected domestic goods industries, these will decrease total foreign exchange earnings and thereby total world trade.[28] Shift of resources from export to domestic goods industries, however, can be checked by suitable investment controls. Underdeveloped countries require huge amounts of foreign exchange for the importation of capitals goods, technical know-how and essential raw materials for executing their development programmes. They cannot afford to permit such a shift of resources. The likelihood of such a shift in actual practice, therefore, is very small. No doubt, selective restrictions of the underdeveloped countries cost developed countries to the extent these necessitate certain structural changes in their pattern of production and, also, might cause some frictional unemployment in the short run. Restrictions, on consumer goods, for instance, will cause some fractional unemployment in consumer goods producing industries till the labourers relieved from these industries get themselves absorbed in capital goods producing industries the demand for which increases as a result of the huge development programmes going on in the developing economies. The transitional difficulties, however, have been exaggerated by the developed countries. In actual practice, the transition is not likely to be very difficult because of the comparatively greater flexibility of these economies. Labour is comparatively more mobile in advanced countries. These countries have better training facilities for labour. Labour relieved from consumer goods industries can be easily trained for producer goods industries and absorbed there. These countries have got enough capital to start new industries the demand for whose products has increased. Thus, the transition is not likely to be very difficult. In contrast, import restrictions of the developed countries with a surplus balance of payments restrict the world trade and are, therefore, responsible for a decrease in the economic welfare of the world as a whole.

Thirdly, restrictions of the developing countries are in the long run interest of the developed countries, too. Their restrictions are just a transition to increased trade. Once the underdeveloped countries have developed, their trade will considerably increase. Foreign trade considerably increases with the increase in income. A major portion of the world trade is carried on among developed countries and not between developed and underdeveloped or within underdeveloped countries themselves. Sixty six per cent of the world trade is shared by advanced countries and only 34 per cent by less developed countries.[29] Further, discriminating restrictions of the underdeveloped countries will rectify the mal-allocation of world resources which is, primarily, due to historical reasons. Many advanced countries have got a strong hold over some industries just because they were the first to undertake these industries and not because they are better fitted for the production of these goods. Once a country gets a hold over an industry, it acquires additional advantages (viz. development of skill specific to that industry, economies of large scale, reputation in world market for the products of the industry etc.) and thus its competitive position grows stronger and stronger. Protection of infant industries, which have got some natural advantages in underdeveloped countries and can deliver goods at comparatively cheaper prices when fully developed, in the initial stages will benefit not only underdeveloped but developed countries, too.

Case against Trade Restrictions

So far we have been examining the bright side of the picture of trade restrictions. It has, also, got its dark side. The appraisal of dark side, however, is not so easy as that of the bright one. "The effects of tariffs resemble those of many other phenomenon in that the favourable aspects are concentrated in one place and can be seen plainly, whereas the other aspects are more diffused over the economy and extended over a longer time."[30] Used injudiciously, trade restrictions might sabotage the whole process of economic development. According to Nicholson, "Free trade, like honesty, still remains the best policy."[31] Edgeworth maintains, "protection might procure economic advantage in certain cases, if there was a government wise enough to discriminate those cases and strong enough to confine itself to them; but this condition is very unlikely to be fulfilled."[32]

An excessive restriction of the import of consumer goods might generate inflationary pressures and thereby endanger the stability of the whole economy. Expenditure diverted from imported goods might turn towards domestic or exportable goods. The first will cause inflation and the second a decrease in foreign exchange earnings. Substitution of exportable goods for imported goods will diminish world economic welfare by eliminating the gain from world trade. In case the supply of domestic and export-goods industries is elastic enough, the inflation and fall in exports may not occur. Further, restriction of import of consumer and luxury goods might lead to a transfer of investment from capital goods producing to consumer and luxury goods producing industries. It would not help development much if the import of capital goods is stimulated at the cost of consumer and luxury goods and these imported capital goods are used to produce consumer and luxury goods. Transfer of investment from capital goods producing industries to consumer and luxury goods producing industries can, however, be avoided by suitable domestic measures, viz. capital issue control, taxes and subsidies, prohibition of the production of undesirable goods etc.

Import restrictions used to cure a deficit in the balance of payments might keep the exchange rate overvalued. An overvalued exchange rate would adversely affect the exports of the country. It would adversely affect particularly the export of the products of new industries and thus discourage investment in these industries.

Restriction of imports will raise the prices of imported goods and thus adversely affect the export industries which extensively use these goods. Similarly, protection of inefficient industries will hinder exports if the export industries use the products of these industries. To avoid such harmful effects, care should be taken that the import of the inputs of the export industries is not unduly restricted.

Protection of genuine infant industries is essential for their development. Experience, however, shows that protection has been afforded indiscriminately to industries which have no possibilities of standing on their own feet even in the long run. Further, it is very difficult to foretell whether or not a particular infant industry will be able to stand on its own feet. Competitive capacity of an industry is determined not only by the prevailing circumstances but also by the future developments. Future changes in the demand for and supply of the commodity (or its close substitutes) might render the industry unprofitable. Similar might be the effect of changes in technology or that of the discovery of new resources abroad. Protection is often sought under the pretext of infant industry to recover losses arising out of the inefficiency and defective organisation. Protection once granted, vested interests are created which arrange to manipulate the lobbies by fair or foul means for the continuation of protection. "History is replete with instances of infants that secured protection, but history is empty of cases that subsequently grew up to admitted manhood."[33] If suitable measures are taken, however, the danger of the springing up of uneconomic industries can be avoided to a large extent. Following are some of the important measures which may be adopted to safeguard against this danger: (a) Impartial and expert tariff boards should be constituted to examine the case for protection for an industry. Protection should be granted only after a thorough examination of the facilities available and the likelihood of the industry's standing on its own feet without protection after a reasonable period. (b) Protection might be gradually lowered after a maximum necessary period to prevent slackness on the part of the industrialists. (c) Progress of the protected industries should be regularly scrutinised.

Tariffs as a method of raising revenue suffer from all the disadvantages generally associated with indirect taxes. These, however, unlike many other indirect taxes, are generally, not regressive in nature. This is because it is the import of luxury goods which is restricted and essential goods consumed by the masses are generally permitted free of duty. Tariffs are levied on essential goods only in those cases in which the industries producing these goods are desired to be established at home with the help of protection. Revenue from tariffs is highly volatile in response to changes in the composition and quantity of exports and imports, balance of payments etc. and, therefore, is not a very sound method of financing economic development. This, however, is not a very serious disadvantage of tariffs because of two main reasons. Firstly, most of the other methods of raising revenue available in underdeveloped countries are no better. Secondly, tariffs are levied primarily for purposes other than revenue and the revenue is just a by-product.

Restrictions often lead to the emergence of domestic monopolies. Present or potential foreign competition is a great check to monopolies. Restrictions might directly encourage monopolies if the import licences are given to a few large firms instead of being distributed widely. In order to maximise their profits, monopolists might restrict imports beyond what is desirable and thus exploit consumers. Protected from foreign competition, domestic producers might become slack, use obsolete machinery and conduct management inefficiently.

Import restrictions, particularly if these are subject to frequent changes, might lead the importers to import huge amounts in anticipation of the restrictions; this involves not only an immediate accentuation of the balance of payments difficulties but also a diversion of investment from productive enterprises to inventories.

Protection alone is not sufficient for development. It provides only opportunities for development. For actual development, these opportunities have got to be utilised by the establishment and efficient running of the industries. Setting up of new industries requires a large amount of capital. It is here that most of the underdeveloped countries have failed and, therefore, protection did more harm to the country employing it and to the outside world than good to any party.[34] "Infant creation must take precedence over infant protection."[35]

Restrictions as a method of increasing employment are not very successful. The exports of a country to a large extent depend on its imports. The capacity of other countries to import from India, for instance, depends upon the availability of Indian currency to these countries, i.e. the amount of imports permitted by India from these countries (assuming away capital and gold movements). Cutting of imports, therefore, will reduce exports and thereby offset the increase in employment in import-substitute industries. This method of increasing employment will be useful only if export industries employ little labour and more capital which can be diverted to other sectors of production or employ labour which can be used for domestic production whereas the labour employed in the production of import substitutes cannot be used elsewhere and will remain unemployed. These, however, are exceptional cases and generally an increase in employment in import substitute industries is very likely to be counterbalanced by a decrease in employment in export industries involving the loss of gains arising from international trade.

Restriction of imports from developed countries will decrease the surpluses in their balance of payments and thereby their capacity to invest in underdeveloped countries.

All the earlier mentioned benefits of trade restrictions for a particular country depend upon the unrealistic assumptions that the trade restrictions of all other countries remain unchanged and these countries do not retaliate. If other countries retaliate, the world trade might precipitately dwindle. The harmful effects of any such shrinkage of world trade for both developed and underdeveloped countries, particularly for the latter countries, cannot be overemphasised. As mentioned earlier, however, the underdeveloped countries have got special justifications for imposing trade restrictions and these should not be retaliated by the advanced countries.

TRADE RESTRICTIONS VERSUS FOREIGN AID

Free trade policies will lead to efficient world allocation of resources and a Pareto-optimal distribution of goods an services among countries, but they tend to have deleterious effects on the global distribution of welfare; rich countries get richer and poor countries poorer. The doctrine is usually expressed in context of technological change and economic growth; it is maintained that the engines of growth are a few industrial countries (such as Great Britain in the nineteenth century and the United States in the 1950s) whose technical progress brings about a deterioration of terms of trade of the "peripheral" countries and results in chronic "dollar shortage." These countries thus fail to share in the increasing prosperity unless they take remedial measures. Such measures usually take the form of (a) borrowing or procuring aid from abroad, or (b) protectionist policies of various kinds.

In the 1980s these doctrines have been revived, with Japan as the new culprit replacing the United States, and the latter as the new victim replacing the periphery. The situation is described as "declining international competitiveness," and while the remedies proposed include policies to encourage saving and growth of productivity, most of the ones actually resorted to again come under the heading of (a) foreign borrowing to finance massive budget deficits or (b) protectionist policies.

In all these accounts one finds two interrelated analytic problems: (a) If a country experiences unfavourable circumstances which lead to either a loss of welfare or a failure of welfare to achieve expected or target levels, is there a convenient and accurate way to measure this welfare loss as a monetary magnitude? (b) Can this welfare measure usefully provide a ranking of alternative policies to mitigate the welfare losses? In particular, can it evaluate the relative merits of protectionism and foreign financing as means to alleviate a welfare loss?

Suppose that a country experiences a deterioration in its terms of trade. This is analogous to the situation of an individual who experiences a rise in the market price of a commodity he consumes. In the latter case, we may consider (a) a hypothetical rise in income which, following the price increase would exactly compensate the individual for the rise in price; or (b) a hypothetical fall in income which, at the original prices, would have led to the same welfare loss as was brought about by the price increase with constant income. The first of these (with opposite sign) is Hick's compensating variation, and the second is his equivalent variation. In the case of a country that is assumed to behave as a rational unit, an analogous procedure is possible provided that on the basis of some ethical postulates we can interpret the utility the country acts as if it maximizes as a measure of the country's "welfare." In place of a consumer's utility function that has amounts consumed as arguments, we may substitute, following Meade (1952), a trade-utility function whose arguments are the amounts traded—specifically the net imports—of the tradable commodities.

Analogously to the Marshallian demand function, whose values are amounts consumed and whose arguments are prices and income, the trade-demand function has as its values the country's net imports of tradable commodities (imports and negatives of exports) and as its arguments the prices of tradables and the deficit in the country's balance of payments on goods and services. Thus, if a country faces a deterioration in its terms of trade, say a rise in the nominal prices of its imports, we may consider (a) the amount of foreign aid it would have to receive (i.e. the necessary increase it would have to experience in its payments deficit) to compensate for the worsened terms of trade; or (b) the hypothetical reduction in foreign aid it would have had to undergo—or increase in aid it would have had to provide to other countries (i.e. the necessary fall in its payments deficit or rise in its payments surplus)—at the original external prices, in order to suffer exactly the same loss of welfare as caused by the rise in import prices. The first of these (with opposite sign) we might provisionally take as our measure of Compensating Trade Variation and the second as the measure of Equivalent Trade Variation. The negatives of either of these could be taken as a measure of "dollar shortage," or more generally, "shortage of foreign exchange."

However, an important difference between the case of an individual and that of a country makes the above analogies unnatural. If a transfer of income is made to an individual, it is quite reasonable to assume that the prices faced by this individual remain constant; in the case of a country, however, it is in the nature of the case that a transfer generally changes its terms of trade. Of course, there are special assumptions under which a unilateral transfer from one country to another will leave the terms of trade unaffected; but it would be quite limiting to have to restrict one to these assumptions. One could argue that, as in the case of an individual, if a country is very small compared to the rest of the world, a transfer will have a negligible effect on its terms of trade; the analysis would then be of interest in the case of "small countries." However, the literature on dollar shortage is replete with illustrations of tradeoffs between foreign aid and import restrictions, it being assumed that by restricting its imports a country can improve its terms of trade. To find a precise concept of "dollar shortage" that can be usefully employed to analyze the issues dealt with in the literature, it is therefore better to take explicit account of the transfer problem.

From a global point of view a unilateral lump-sum costless transfer from a rich to a poor country is preferable to restrictive measures imposed by the poor country; for, it follows immediately from the so called Fundamental Theorem of Welfare Economics that there exists a transfer from the rich country to the poor one that would make both of them better off than if a tariff were imposed by the poor one. Likewise, if the poor country imposes a tariff we know that there is some transfer from the poor country to the rich one that would make both countries worse off than under free trade. However, it is not obvious that a country imposing a tariff is worse off than it would be if it instead received an amount of foreign aid equal to the previous tariff revenues.

MONETARY MEASUREMENT OF CHANGE IN A COUNTRY'S WELFARE

The simplest conceptual tool to use in evaluating different circumstances a country may face is that of the trade-demand function, which expresses the dependence of a country's trade in a commodity on the prices (on domestic markets) of the traded commodities and the deficit in the country's balance of payments on goods and services (or "trade balance" for short). For analytic simplicity we consider the case of two tradable goods; the derivation of a country's trade-demand function from its aggregate demand function and production relations is carried out considering the cases in which (a) each country produces both commodities (but no nontradables) with the aid of two factors of production, and (b) each country produces an export goods and a nontradable goods (but no import-competing goods) with two factors of production.

Let us denote country *k*'s trade-demand for commodity *j* by

$$z_j^k = h_j^k(p_1^k, p_2^k, D^k; l^k),$$

where $z_j^k = x_j^k - y_j^k$ denotes the net import of commodity *j* and

x_j^k and y_j^k denote consumption and production of this commodity;

p_j^k denotes the price of commodity *j* on country *k*'s markets;

D^k denotes the deficit in country *k*'s trade balance;

l^k denotes the vector of country *k*'s factor endowments.

For $j = 1, 2$ these maximize country k's trade-utility function $U^k = (z_1^k, z_2^k; l^k)$ subject to the balance of payments constraint $p_1^k z_1^k + p_2^k z_2^k \le D^k$. Country k's indirect trade-utility function may be defined as

$$\hat{V}^k(p_1^k, p_2^k, D^k; l^k) = \hat{U}^k\left(\hat{h}_1^k(p_1^k, p_2^k, D^k; l^k), \hat{h}_2^k(p_1^k, p_2^k, D^k; l^k); l^k\right) \tag{1}$$

This function satisfies the Antonelli-Allen-Roy partial differential equation

$$\frac{\partial \hat{V}^k}{\partial p_j^k} = -\hat{h}_j^k(p_1^k, p_2^k, D^k; l^k)\frac{\partial \hat{V}^k}{\partial D^k} \quad (j=1, 2) \tag{2}$$

Since by convention we assume that country k exports commodity k, it follows (assuming local nonsatiation of trade-preferences, implying that $\partial \hat{V}^k / \partial D^k > 0$) that for country 1, $\partial \hat{V}^1 / \partial p_2^1 < 0$ (since $\hat{h}_2^1 > 0$), whereas for country 2, $\partial \hat{V}^2 / \partial p_2^2 > 0$ (since $\hat{h}_2^1 > 0$). In words, country 1 gains, *ceteris paribus*, from a fall in the domestic price of its import goods, while country 2 gains from a rise in the price of its export goods (its terms of trade). This is illustrated for $k = 1$ in the three panels (a), (b) and (c) of the following figure, where $D^1 = 0$, $D^1 < 0$ and $D^1 > 0$ respectively, it being assumed that country 1 initially exports commodity 1 and imports commodity 2.

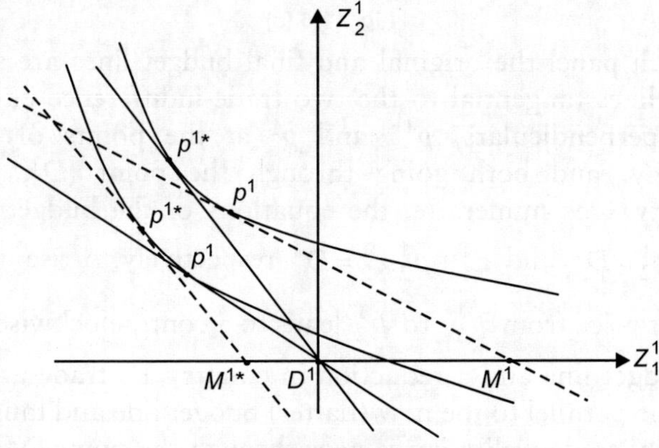

Fig. 11.5 (a)

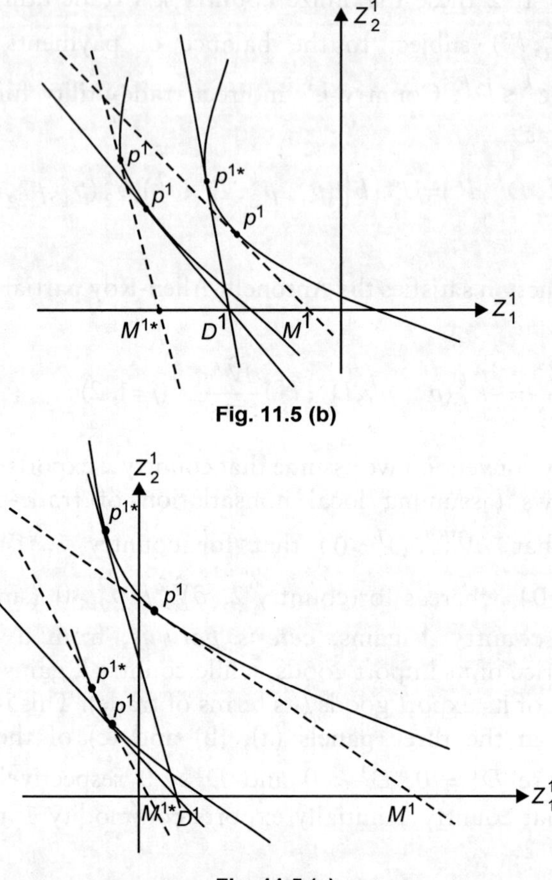

Fig. 11.5 (b)

Fig. 11.5 (c)

In each panel the original and final budget lines are shown as the solid lines tangential to the two trade-indifference curves with normal (perpendiculars) p^{1*} and p^1 at the points of tangency respectively, and both going through the point (D^1, 0). With commodity 1 as numeraire, the equations of the budget lines are $z_1^1 + p_2^{1*} z_2^1 = D^1$ and $z_1^1 + p_2^1 z_2^1 = D^1$ respectively. A rise in country 1's import price from p_2^{1*} to p_2^1 leads to a contraclockwise rotation of the budget line and a reduction in country 1's trade-utility. The dashed line parallel to the new (flatter) budget line and tangential to the original trade-utility curve goes through the point (M^1, 0); this corresponds to the maximum balance of trade (i.e. the minimum trade deficit) at the new prices subject to the old welfare level. The segment M^1D^1 measures (in absolute value) the compensating trade-variation in units of commodity 1. Likewise, the dashed line parallel to the old (steeper) budget line and tangential to the new trade-indifference curve goes through the point $(M^{1*}, 0)$; this corresponds to the maximum balance of trade at the old prices subject to the new welfare level. The segment D^1M^{1*} measures (in absolute value) the equivalent trade-variation in units of commodity 1.

It is of some interest to note that in panel (*c*), the point of maximum trade balance subject to the old welfare level is one in which country 1 imports both commodities.

Analogously to McKenzie's (1957) minimum-income function and Hurwicz and Uzawa's (1971) income-consumption function, we may define country *k*'s minimum-deficit function as

$$\hat{\mu}^k(p_1^k, p_2^k, p_1^{k*}, p_2^{k*}, D^{k*}, l^{k*}) = \min\{D^k : \hat{V}^k(p_1^k, p_2^k, D^k; l^{k*}) \geq \hat{V}^k(p_1^{k*}, p_2^{k*}, D^{k*}; l^{k*}\} \qquad (3)$$

where p_1^k, p_2^k, D^k are the current prices of the tradables (on country *k*'s home markets) and country *k*'s trade deficit, and $p_1^{k*}, p_2^{k*}, D^{k*}$ are the same variables in some base period; l^{k*} is country *k*'s factor endowment vector in the base period. Finally, by analogy with the definitions in Chipman and Moore (1980) we may define the compensating trade variation in going from $(p_1^{k*}, p_2^{k*}, D^{k*}, l^{k*})$ to $(p_1^k, p_2^k, D^k, l^{k*})$ by

$$\hat{C}^k(p_1^k, p_2^k, D^k; p_1^{k*}, p_2^{k*}, D^{k*}, l^{k*}) = D^k - \hat{\mu}^k(p_1^k, p_2^k; p_1^{k*}, p_2^{k*}, D^{k*}, l^{k*}) \qquad (4)$$

and the equivalent trade-variation in going from $(p_1^{k*}, p_2^{k*}, D^{k*}, l^{k*})$ to $(p_1^k, p_2^k, D^k, l^{k*})$ by

$$\hat{E}^k(p_1^k, p_2^k, D^k; p_1^{k*}, p_2^{k*}, D^{k*}, l^{k*}) = \hat{\mu}^k(p_1^{k*}, p_2^{k*}; p_1^k, p_2^k, D^k, l^{k*}) - D^{k*} \qquad (5)$$

Assuming $p_1^1 = p_1^{1*} = 1$ and $D^1 = D^{1*}$ to be constant and $p_2^1 > p_2^{1*}$ (country 1's terms of trade to worsen), the three panels of the above figure show for $k = 1$ the compensating and equivalent trade-variations corresponding to the three cases, where $M^1 = \hat{\mu}^1(1, p_2^1; 1, p_2^{1*}, D^1, l^{1*})$ is the minimum trade deficit (hence $M^1$is the maximum trade balance) at the new prices and old welfare level, and $M^{1*} = \hat{\mu}^1(1, p_2^{1*}; 1, p_2^1, D^1, l^{1*})$ is the minimum trade deficit (hence M^{1*} is the maximum trade balance) at the old prices and new welfare level.

Either one of these concepts would provide a reasonable measure of shortage of foreign exchange in the sense not of "shortage" that might result from foreign exchange control but in the programming sense indicating the amount of foreign aid required to compensate for a terms-of-trade deterioration—or the loss of foreign aid that would be equivalent to a terms-of-trade deterioration—provided these compensating or equivalent transfers did not themselves affect the terms of trade. With this qualification it would be reasonable to use either one of them as an indicator of what Machlup (1950) called "a programme balance, i.e. a balance of hopes and desires," as opposed to the more usual accounting definitions of the balance of payments. However, it seems worth while to examine how the concept should best be altered when the qualification is removed. Suppose we consider a case in which there is technical change in country 2 that worsens country 1's terms of trade. In terms of the traditional model in which there are no nontradable goods, as first pointed out by Haberler (1948) and later by Hicks (1953), this would require that technical change in country 2 be import-biased, that is, concentrated in its import-competing industry. In particular the result would follow if there were factor-augmenting technical improvement in the factor used relatively intensively in country 2's import-competing industry (normally this would be its relatively scarce factor). In this case, at the existing prices country 2, by virtue of the Rybczynski theorem, would shift its resources from exportables to importables. This would reduce the supply of country 2's export good (commodity 2) and increase its supply of its import goods (commodity 1). The net result would be an improvement in country 2's terms of trade and a worsening of country 1's. By a similar argument, a technical improvement in country 2 taking the form of increasing efficiency of the factor used relatively intensively in its export industry would worsen its terms of trade and improve country 1's.

Under these same circumstances, with identical and homothetic preferences between as well as within countries (hence identical marginal trade-propensities to spend as between countries on either of the two tradable commodities), a transfer from one country to the other will, according to Samuelson's (1952) criterion, have no effect on the terms of trade. The above concepts of foreign-exchange shortage would then provide reasonable measures of the actual amount of foreign aid needed to compensate for (or the reduction in foreign aid equivalent to) the worsened terms of trade. Suppose we consider, on the other hand, the kind of model that would lead to what Samuelson (1952) called the "orthodox presumption" that a transfer would improve the receiving country's terms of trade. An example of such a model would be one in which each country produces an export goods and a nontradable goods, but does not produce any import-competing goods; this would be a likely result of its having fewer than three factors of production–for definiteness we shall assume that each country has two factors. In these circumstances, assuming all goods to be superior goods in consumers' preferences, a transfer from country 2 to country 1 would reduce purchasing power in country 2 and increase it in country 1; the increased demand for the nontradable in country 1 would require its resources to move into the nontradables sector out of its export industry (since it does not produce import-competing goods), and likewise the reduced demand for nontradables in country 2 would require its resources to move out of the nontradables sector into its export industry. The net result would be a rise in the world output (equal to country 2's output) of commodity 2 and a fall in the world output (equal to country 1's output) of commodity 1. If the three goods are Hicksian substitutes this must result in an improvement in country 1's terms of trade.

Now suppose a technical change in country 2 is concentrated largely in its non-tradables sector. In particular, suppose there is factor augmenting technical improvement in the factor used relatively intensively in its nontradables sector. In this case, at unchanged prices there would be an increased demand for imports; since, however, at unchanged prices of tradables the prices of nontradables would fall, there would–assuming the three goods to be Hicksian substitutes—be a diversion of demand towards nontradables away from imports which might be strong enough to counteract the original income effect.

Thus, there could be, but need not be, a fall in demand for imports and thus an improvement in country 2's, and thus worsening of country 1's, terms of trade. An unambiguous result can be obtained, however, in the case in which the technical improvement increases the efficiency of the factor employed relatively intensively in the export industry. As before, at unchanged prices there is an increased demand for imports; but at unchanged prices of tradables the technical change will increase the price of nontradables and—again assuming the goods to be Hicksian substitutes—cause a diversion of consumer demand from nontaxable to importable. Since both effects go in the same direction, there is an increased demand for imports and a worsened terms of trade for country 2.

It is worth noting that if both countries produced import-competing goods as well as export and nontradable goods (which would be more likely if they had a third factor of production), there would be no strong presumption that either a technical improvement in country 2's non-tradables sector or a transfer of funds from country 1 to country 2 would draw more resources out of country 2's export industry than out of its import-competing industry. Thus, there is no strong presumption that either the technical improvement or the transfer would affect the terms of trade. It follows that if country 2's technical change takes the form of factor-augmenting improvement in the factor used relatively intensively in its nontradables sector, the circumstances that make it likely that this technical improvement will worsen country 1's terms of trade also make it probable that a compensating transfer from country 2 to country 1 will result in an offsetting improvement in country 1's terms of trade. Thus there is a general presumption that the above measures of foreign-exchange shortage will overestimate the magnitude of the compensating or equivalent transfers needed to alleviate a worsening of a country's terms of trade.

TECHNICAL IMPROVEMENT AND THE TERMS OF TRADE

This section will be devoted to deriving explicit conditions for factor augmenting technical change to improve or worsen a country's terms of trade in a model of two countries endowed with two factors of production and trading in two commodities. Two cases will be considered:

(a) the standard model in which these two commodities and no others are produced by both countries, and

(b) a model in which each country specializes in an export good and a nontradable good.

For the standard model a fairly general taxonomy has been developed in the literature using traditional geometrical techniques. The theoretical analysis of the second model is less well developed, though there have been pertinent contributions by Balassa (1964), Aukrust (1970), McKinnon (1971), Haberler (1973), Edgren, Faxen, and Odhner (1973), and Corden and Neary (1982), all of which have stressed that technical change tends to be more rapid in the tradables sector (both export and import-competing) than in the nontradables sector. In general this carries important implications for the "real exchange rate" (considered as the ratio of prices of non-tradables to those of tradables) rather than the terms of trade, but in the special case in which no import-competing goods are produced it implies that one could generally expect technical improvement to worsen the progressive country's terms of trade.

In this section a uniform analytic treatment will be applied to both models. Assuming factors of production to be measured in efficiency units, increases in endowments will be interpreted as increases in their efficiency. We will consider technical improvements in each factor separately as well as a uniform proportionate improvement in both. In the case of uniform improvement it is shown under fairly mild theoretical assumptions (basically, identical homothetic preferences) that in both models technical improvement will worsen the terms of trade of the progressive country. An improvement that takes the form of increased efficiency of the factor used relatively intensively in the export industry will have an even greater tendency to worsen the terms of trade of the expanding country. In the case of the first model, technical improvement in the form of increased efficiency of the factor used relatively intensively in the import-competing industry unambiguously improves the terms of trade of the expanding country.

In the case of the second model the results of increased efficiency of the factor employed relatively intensively in the non-tradables sector are less clear-cut. The income effect of the technical improvement will lead to increased demand for imports, tending to a worsening of the progressive country's terms of trade; but the substitution effect of the fall in the price of the nontradable relative to that of the export goods will lead consumers (at unchanged terms of trade) to switch from importables to non-tradables; only if this outweighs the income effect will there be a net fall in the demand for imports and therefore an improvement in the progressive country's terms of trade.

World equation is defined by the equation:

$$\hat{h}_2^1(p_1, p_2, A^1; l_1^1, l_2^1)+\hat{h}_2^2(p_1, p_2, -A^1; l_1^2, l_2^2)=0 \qquad (6)$$

where the $\hat{h}_2^k$ are the countries' trade-demand functions for commodity 2, A^1 is the amount of foreign aid country 1 is getting from country 2, and l_i^k is country k's endowment in factor i. Since the l_i^k are measured in efficiency units, a rise in l_i^k will be interpreted as a factor—i—augmenting technical improvement in country k. Fixing the price of commodity 1 as numeraire, i.e. setting $p_1=\bar{p}_1$, equation (6) implicitly defines the function

$$p_2=\bar{p}_2(A^1, l_1^1, l_2^1, l_1^2, l_2^2) \qquad (7)$$

Differentiating equation (7) with respect to l_i^2 we have from (6)

$$\frac{\partial\bar{p}_2}{\partial l_i^2}=-\frac{\partial\hat{h}_2^2/\partial l_i^2}{\partial\hat{h}_2^1/\partial p_2+\partial\hat{h}_2^2/\partial p_2} \qquad (8)$$

The denominator of (8) is negatively by the usual dynamic stability condition, hence

$$\frac{\partial\bar{p}_2}{\partial l_i^2}>0 \Leftrightarrow \frac{\partial\hat{h}_2^2}{\partial l_i^2}>0 \qquad (9)$$

A rise in country 2's endowment in factor i will improve its terms of trade if and only if, at unchanged world prices, it raises its trade-demand for its export goods (commodity 2). Since h_2^2 is negative, what this means is that country 2's terms of trade will improve if and only if the increased endowment of factor i lowers country 2's supply of exports. It is in conformity with intuition that the increased world scarcity of commodity 2 will cause its price (country 2's terms of trade) to rise.

For the case of uniform technical improvement we may define the composed function as

$$\hat{\hat{h}}_2^2(p_1, p_2, D^2; l_1^2, l_2^2, \lambda) = \hat{h}_2^2(p_1, p_2, D^2; \lambda l_1^2, \lambda l_2^2) \tag{10}$$

Likewise, defining

$$\hat{\bar{p}}_2(A^1, l_1^1, l_2^1, l_1^2, l_2^2, \lambda) = \bar{p}_2(A^1, l_1^1, l_2^1, \lambda l_1^2, \lambda l_2^2),$$

formula (8) is replaced by

$$\frac{\partial \hat{\bar{p}}_2}{\partial \lambda} = -\frac{\partial \hat{\hat{h}}_2^2 / \partial \lambda}{\partial \hat{\hat{h}}_2^1 / \partial p_2 + \partial \hat{\hat{h}}_2^2 / \partial p_2} = -\frac{\dfrac{\partial \hat{h}_2^2}{\partial l_1^2} l_1^2 + \dfrac{\partial \hat{h}_2^2}{\partial l_2^2} l_2^2}{\dfrac{\partial \hat{h}_2^1}{\partial p_2} + \dfrac{\partial \hat{h}_2^2}{\partial p_2}} \tag{11}$$

The standard two-commodity two-factor case:

Let us first consider the standard case in which each country produces and trades two commodities with two factors of production, factor i being used relatively intensively in the production of commodity i for $i = 1, 2$. Country 2's trade demand function is given by

$$\hat{h}_2^2(p_1, p_2, D^2; l_1^2, l_2^2) = h_2^2(p_1, p_2, \Pi^2(p_1, p_2, l_1^2, l_2^2) + D^2) - \hat{y}_2^2(p_1, p_2, l_1^2, l_2^2) \tag{12}$$

where Π^2 is country 2's national product function and $\hat{y}_j^2 = \partial \Pi^2 / \partial p_j$ is its Rybczynski (supply) function for commodity j. Then

$$\frac{\partial \hat{h}_2^2}{\partial l_i^2} = \frac{\partial h_2^2}{\partial y^2}\frac{\partial \Pi^2}{\partial l_i^2} - \frac{\partial \hat{y}_2^2}{\partial l_i^2} = c_2^2 w_i^2 - \frac{\partial \hat{w}_i^2}{\partial p_2} = \frac{w_i^2}{p_2}\left[p_2 c_2^2 - \frac{p_2}{w_i^2}\frac{\partial \hat{w}_i^2}{\partial p_2}\right] \tag{13}$$

where $c_j^2 = \partial h_j^2 / \partial Y^2$ and use is made of Samuelson's (1953) reciprocity condition $\partial \hat{y}_j^2 / \partial l_i^2 = \partial \hat{w}_i^2 / \partial p_j$, the $\hat{w}_i^2(p_1, p_2)$ being the Stolper-Samuelson functions. Since by the factor-intensity assumption the Stolper-Samuelson theorem gives

$$\frac{p_2}{w_1^2}\frac{\partial \hat{w}_1^2}{\partial p_2} < 0 \text{ and } \frac{p_2}{w_2^2}\frac{\partial \hat{w}_2^2}{\partial p_2} > 1,$$

it follows immediately-assuming both goods to be superior, i.e. $c_j^2 > 0$, that $\partial \hat{h}_2^2 / \partial l_1^2 > 0$ and $\partial \hat{h}_2^2 / \partial l_2^2 < 0$, hence from (9), $\partial \bar{p}_2 / \partial l_1^2 > 0$ and $\partial \bar{p}_2 / \partial l_1^2 > 0$. Thus a rise in the efficiency of the factor used relatively intensively in country 2's import-competing industry will improve country 2's terms of trade, while a rise in the efficiency of the factor used relatively intensively in country 2's export industry will worsen country 2's terms of trade.

Now consider the case of uniform factor-augmenting technical change. For this case we will need to assume homotheticity of preferences, implying that $\partial \hat{h}_j^2 / \partial Y^2 = \hat{h}_j^2 / Y^2$, where Y^2 is country 2's disposable national income (absorption) $\Pi^2 + D^2$. Differentiating (10) with respect to λ and using the homogeneity of degree 1 of Π^2 and $\hat{y}_2^2 = \partial \Pi^2 / \partial p_2$ in l_1^2, l_2^2 and the budget equation $p_1 x_1^2 + p_2 x_2^2 = Y^2$, we obtain from (12)

$$\begin{aligned}\frac{\partial \hat{h}_2^2}{\partial \lambda} &= \frac{\partial h_2^2}{\partial Y^2}\Pi^2 - y_2^2 = \frac{\Pi^2}{Y^2}x_2^2 - y_2^2 \\ &= \frac{x_2^2}{Y^2}(p_1 y_1^2 + p_2 y_2^2) - y_2^2 \\ &= \frac{p_1 x_1^2 y_1^2}{Y^2}\left[\frac{x_2^2}{x_1^2} - \frac{y_2^2}{y_1^2}\right] < 0 \end{aligned} \tag{14}$$

the inequality following from the fact that country 2 by assumption exports commodity 2 and imports commodity 1, hence $x_1^2 > y_1^2$ and $x_2^2 < y_2^2$, so that

$$\frac{x_2^2}{y_2^2} < 1 < \frac{x_1^2}{y_1^2}.$$

Thus, a uniform technical improvement in both factors will worsen country 2's terms of trade. These results are valid even if country 2's trade is unbalanced ($D^2 \neq 0$), but not so unbalanced as to prevent commodity 1 from being imported and commodity 2 from being exported.

THE CASE OF SPECIALIZATION ON EXPORTS AND NON-TRADABLES

Now let us consider a model of two countries specializing in exports and non-tradables with two factors of production. Let country 1 produce commodities 1 and 3 and country 2 produce commodities 2 and 3, the third commodity being non-tradable; let each country have two factors of production. We will assume that in country 2 factor 2 is used relatively intensively in the export sector (industry 2), and thus factor 1 is used relatively intensively in the nontradables sector (industry 3).

To obtain the expression for $\partial \hat{h}_2^2 / \partial l_2^2$ we need to derive country 2's trade demand function. Let $\Pi^2(p_2, p_3^2, l_1^2, l_2^2)$ denote country 2's national product function, equal to the maximum national product at prices p_2, p_3^2 and factor endowments l_1^2, l_2^2 and let

$$y_j^2 = \hat{y}_j^2(p_2, p_3^2, l_1^2, l_2^2) = \frac{\partial}{\partial p_j^2} \Pi^2(p_2, p_3^2, l_1^2, l_2^2)$$

$$(p_2^2 = p_2) \tag{15}$$

denote country 2's Rybczynski function (supply function) for commodity j = 2, 3. Let the aggregate consumer demand function for commodity j in country 2 be denoted $x_j^2 = h_j^2(p_1, p_2, p_3^2, Y^2)$, where Y^2 is disposable national income. Equating the aggregate demand and supply of the nontradable goods implicitly defines the price of the nontradable as a function of the remaining variables, i.e.

$$h_3^2\left(p_1, p_2, \tilde{p}_3^2(.), \Pi^2\left(p_2, \tilde{p}_3^2(.), l_1^2, l_2^2\right)+D^2\right)=\hat{y}_3^2\left(p_2, \tilde{p}_3^2(.), l_1^2, l_2^2\right) \tag{16}$$

where

$$p_3^2=\tilde{p}_3^2(p_1, p_2, l_1^2, l_2^2, D^2) \tag{17}$$

Country 2's trade demand for its export goods (commodity 2) is then defined by

$$\hat{h}_2^2(p_1, p_2, D^2; l_1^2, l_2^2)= h_2^2\begin{pmatrix} p_1, p_2, \tilde{p}_3^2(p_1, p_2, l_1^2, l_2^2), \\ \Pi^2(p_2, \tilde{p}_3^2(p_1, p_2, l_1^2, l_2^2), l_1^2, l_2^2)+ D^2 \end{pmatrix}$$

$$-\hat{y}_2^2\left(p_2, \tilde{p}_3^2(p_1, p_2, l_1^2, l_2^2), l_1^2, l_2^2\right) \tag{18}$$

Differentiating (17) implicitly in (16) we obtain, using the usual duality relationship the following

$$\frac{\partial \tilde{p}_3^2}{\partial l_i^2}=\frac{-1}{s_{33}^2-t_{33}^2}\left[\frac{\partial h_3^2}{\partial Y^2}w_i^2-\frac{\partial \hat{y}_3^2}{\partial l_i^2}\right] \tag{19}$$

where w_i^2 is the rental of factor i in country 2 and

$$s_{ij}^2=\frac{\partial h_i^2}{\partial p_j^2}+\frac{\partial h_i^2}{\partial Y^2}h_j^2 \text{ and } t_{ij}^2=\frac{\partial \hat{y}_i^2}{\partial p_j^2} \tag{20}$$

define country 2's Slutsky and transformation terms. Defining also $c_j^2=\partial h_j^2/\partial Y^2$, these terms satisfy

$$\begin{aligned} &p_1 c_1^2+p_2 c_2^2+p_3^2 c_3^2=1 \\ &p_1 s_{13}^2+p_2 s_{23}^2+p_3^2 s_{33}^2=0 \\ &p_2 t_{23}^2+p_3^2 t_{33}^2=0 \end{aligned} \tag{21}$$

From (18), (19) and the fact that $\partial\Pi^2/\partial p_3^2 = y_3^2 = x_3^2$ we have

$$\frac{\partial \hat{h}_2^2}{\partial l_i^2} = \left[\frac{\partial h_2^2}{\partial Y^2} w_i^2 - \frac{\partial \hat{y}_2^2}{\partial l_i^2}\right] - \frac{s_{23}^2 - t_{23}^2}{s_{33}^2 - t_{33}^2}\left[\frac{\partial h_3^2}{\partial Y^2} w_i^2 - \frac{\partial \hat{y}_3^2}{\partial l_i^2}\right] \tag{22}$$

Using Samuelson's (1953) reciprocity conditions, the bracketed terms in (22) may be written as

$$\frac{\partial h_j^2}{\partial Y^2} w_i^2 - \frac{\partial \hat{y}_j^2}{\partial l_i^2} = \frac{w_i^2}{p_j^2}\left[p_j^2 c_j^2 - \frac{p_j^2}{w_i^2} \cdot \frac{\partial \hat{w}_i^2}{\partial p_j^2}\right] \tag{23}$$

Thus, (22) becomes

$$\frac{\partial \hat{h}_2^2}{\partial l_i^2} = \frac{w_i^2}{p^2}$$

$$\left\{\left[p_2 c_2^2 - \frac{p_2}{w_i^2}\frac{\partial \hat{w}_i^2}{\partial p_2}\right] - \frac{p_2(s_{23}^2 - t_{23}^2)}{p_3^2(s_{33}^2 - t_{33}^2)}\left[p_3^2 c_3^2 - \frac{p_3^2}{w_i^2} \cdot \frac{\partial \hat{w}_i^2}{\partial p_3^2}\right]\right\} \tag{24}$$

The first bracketed term in (24) gives the effect the technical change would have if the price of the nontradable goods were fixed. This is the same as the bracketed term in (13). The second term gives the effect of change in the price of the nontradable. From (19) and (23) we have

$$\frac{\partial \tilde{p}_3^2}{\partial l_i^2} = \frac{-1}{s_{33}^2 - t_{33}^2}\frac{w_i^2}{p_3^2}\left[p_3^2 c_3^2 - \frac{p_3^2}{w_i^2} \cdot \frac{\partial \hat{w}_i^2}{\partial p_3^2}\right] \tag{25}$$

where from the Stolper-Samuelson theorem and the assumption that all goods are superior,

$$p_3^2 c_3^2 - \frac{p_3^2}{w_1^2} \cdot \frac{\partial \hat{w}_1^2}{\partial p_3^2} < p_3^2 c_3^2 - 1 < 0 \text{ and}$$

$$p_3^2 c_3^2 - \frac{p_3^2}{w_2^2} \cdot \frac{\partial \hat{w}_2^2}{\partial p_3^2} > p_3^2 c_3^2 > 0 .$$

Thus, as is to be expected, $\partial \tilde{p}_3^2/\partial l_1^2 < 0$ and $\partial \tilde{p}_3^2/\partial l_2^2 > 0$, i.e. the price of the non-tradable falls when the factor used relatively intensively in the nontradables sector becomes more efficient and rises when the factor used relatively intensively in the export sector becomes more efficient. Owing to the factor-intensity situation, the bracked terms in (24) necessarily have opposite sign; hence if goods 2 and 3 are substitutes in the sense that $s_{23}^2 - t_{23}^2 > 0$, since necessarily $s_{33}^2 - t_{33}^2 < 0$, formula (24) does not allow for an unambiguous sign.

The solution to this problem is to study country 2's demand for imports rather than its supply of exports. Since

$$p_1 \frac{\partial \hat{h}_1^2}{\partial l_i^2} + p_2 \frac{\partial \hat{h}_2^2}{\partial l_i^2} = 0,$$

these derivatives of course have opposite sign; further, since $y_1^2 = 0$ we have $\partial \hat{y}_1^2 / \partial l_i^2 = \partial \hat{w}_i^2 / \partial p_1 = 0$. Thus,

$$\frac{\partial \hat{h}_1^2}{\partial l_i^2} = \frac{w_i^2}{p_1} \left\{ p_1 c_1^2 - \frac{p_1 s_{13}^2}{p_3^2 (s_{33}^2 - t_{33}^2)} \left[p_3^2 c_3^2 - \frac{p_3^2}{w_i^2} \cdot \frac{\partial \hat{w}_i^2}{\partial p_3^2} \right] \right\} \tag{26}$$

In the case $i = 2$ the bracketed term in (26) is unambiguously positive, by virtue of the Stolper-Samuelson theorem and the assumption that all goods are superior. Assuming commodities 1 and 3 to be Hicksian substitutes (i.e. $s_{13}^2 > 0$), the term preceding the bracketed expression in (26) is negative; consequently we can conclude that $\partial \hat{h}_1^2 / \partial l_2^2 > 0$ and hence $\partial \hat{h}_2^2 / \partial l_2^2 < 0$. The intuitive explanation is straightforward: the term $p_1 c_1^2$ corresponds to the increased demand for imports at unchanged prices—there being of course no change in the (zero) supply of importables. Now an increase in the efficiency of the factor used relatively intensively in the export industry causes the price of the nontradable to rise; the import good by hypothesis being a Hicksian substitute of the nontradable, this price rise causes consumers to switch from nontradables to imports. Therefore, both effects lead to an increase in the demand for imports, resulting in a worsening of country 2's terms of trade. This is fully in accord with the results of the standard model with no nontradables, except that the negative effect on country 2's terms of trade is stronger in this case.

In the case $i = 1$ the bracketed term in (26) is negative, as is the term preceding it (assuming substitutability between commodities 1 and 3); thus the term within braces is the difference between two positive terms, an income effect and a substitution effect. Thus, while the technical change with unchanged relative prices will as before lead to an increase in the demand for imports, it will cause the price of the nontradable to drop, causing consumers to switch from importables to nontradables. If this substitution effect is sufficiently strong, it will outweigh the income effect and the demand for imports will fall. Thus it is possible but by no means certain that the technical change will improve country 2's terms of trade.

Now we consider the case of uniform factor augmenting technical progress. Assuming preferences to be homothetic we find readily that

$$\frac{\partial \hat{\hat{h}}_2^2}{\partial \lambda} = \left[\frac{\Pi^2}{Y^2} x_2^2 - y_2^2\right] - \frac{s_{23}^2 - t_{23}^2}{s_{33}^2 - t_{33}^2} \left[\frac{\Pi^2}{Y^2} x_3^2 - y_3^2\right] \tag{27}$$

If trade is balanced, $\Pi^2 = Y^2$ (national product equals absorption) and the second term vanishes; the whole expression reduces to country 2's export, z_2^2, of commodity 2 (a negative quantity). Thus, under these circumstances a uniform factor-augmenting technical improvement in country 2 must worsen country 2's terms of trade. If trade is unbalanced a small amount either way, then by continuity the qualitative result still holds.

To summarize, as in the case of the standard model either a uniform improvement in factor efficiency or an improvement in efficiency of the factor employed relatively intensively in country 2's export industry will worsen country 2's terms of trade. In the standard model an improvement in efficiency of the factor used relatively intensively in country 2's import-competing industry will improve its terms of trade, while in the model in which country 2 produces only export and nontradable goods an improvement in efficiency of the factor used relatively intensively in the nontradables sector may, but need not, improve country 2's terms of trade. Thus, in the second model it is less likely for technical progress in country 2 to worsen country 1's terms of trade; and even if it does have this effect, a smaller transfer payment from country 2 to country 1 will be needed than in the first model to compensate country 1 for its welfare loss.

IMPORTS RESTRICTIONS VERSUS FOREIGN AID

Suppose that country 1 is in the process of receiving a certain amount A^1 of foreign aid from country 2, and/or tariff revenues from country 2 resulting from its imposition of a tariff of $100\tau_2^1\%$ on its imports of commodity 2 from country 2. For simplicity we will consider the tariff factor $T_2^1=1+\tau_2^1$ in place of the tariff rate τ_2^1. As is customary, the price of country 1's export good (commodity 1), which will be the same in both countries (i.e. $p_1^1=p_1^2=\bar{p}_1^2$), will be taken as numeraire.

Country 1's excess demand for its own import good (commodity 2), expressed as a function of the external (country 2) prices of the two tradable goods, is defined as the solution of the functional equation

$$\hat{z}_2^1(p_1^2, p_2^2, A^1, T_2^1, l^1)$$
$$=\hat{h}_2^1\left(p_1^2, T_2^1 p_2^2, A^1+(T_2^1-1)p_2^2\hat{z}_2^1(p_1^2, p_2^2, A^1, T_2^1, l^1); l^1\right) \quad (28)$$

Country 2's excess demand for commodity 2 (its export goods) is defined simply by

$$\hat{z}_2^2(p_1^2, p_2^2, A^1, T_2^1, l^2)=\hat{h}_2^2(p_1^2, p_2^2, -A^1; l^2) \quad (29)$$

World equilibrium is then defined by the equation

$$\hat{z}_2^1(p_1^2, p_2^2, A^1, T_2^1, l^1)+\hat{z}_2^2(p_1^2, p_2^2, A^1, T_2^1, l^2)=0 \quad (30)$$

Recalling that $p_1^2=\bar{p}_1^2=$ constant, and assuming the countries' factor endowments l^1, l^2 also to be constant, equation (30) which holds for all values of the parameters A^1, T_2^1—implicitly defines the functions

$$p_2^2=\bar{p}_2^2(A^1, T_2^1)$$

$$p_2^1=\bar{p}_2^1(A^1, T_2^1)\equiv T_2^1\bar{p}_2^2(A^1, T_2^1) \text{ and}$$

$$z_2^1=\bar{z}_2^1(A^1, T_2^1)\equiv\hat{z}_2^1\left(\bar{p}_1^2, \bar{p}_2^2(A^1, T_2^1), A^1, T_2^1, l^1\right) \quad (31)$$

Now suppose country 1 initially receives no foreign aid but imposes a tariff of $\tau_2^1 = T_2^1 - 1 > 0$ on its imports of commodity 2 from country 2. Its tariff revenues, which are equal to its trade deficit (denominated in its own prices), are then equal to

$$R^1(T_2^1) = (T_2^1 - 1)\bar{p}_2^2(0, T_2^1)\bar{z}_2^1(0, T_2^1) \tag{32}$$

Now, suppose country 1 is offered an amount A^1 of foreign aid by country 2 equal to these tariff revenues (32), on condition that it removes its tariff; then its trade deficit (denominated in its own prices) remains equal to the quantity (32). Is country 1 better or worse off than before? The question can also be put in the converse form. Suppose country 1 was initially receiving an amount A^1 of foreign aid from country 2, and imposed no tariffs. Now country 2 withdraws the foreign aid; if country 1 in these circumstances imposes a tariff at a level such as to yield tariff revenues equal to the previous level of foreign aid (i.e. T_2^1 satisfying $R^1(T_2^1) = A^1$), will it be better or worse off?

This question may be answered by considering each country's indirect trade utility function. For example, we may take this to be the equivalent trade variation (5) for some fixed base prices of tradables and factor endowments.

With the tariff, country 1's potential welfare is

$$u_T^1 = \hat{V}^1\left(\bar{p}_1^2, T_2^1\bar{p}_2^2(0, T_2^1), (T_2^1 - 1)\bar{p}_2^2(0, T_2^1)\bar{z}_2^1(0, T_2^1); l^1\right) \tag{33}$$

whereas with foreign aid it is equal to

$$u_A^1 = \hat{V}^1\left(\bar{p}_1^2, \bar{p}_2^2(A^1, 1), A^1; l^1\right) \tag{34}$$

where

$$A^1 = (T_2^1 - 1)\bar{p}_2^2(0, T_2^1)\bar{z}_2^1(0, T_2^1)$$

Since (33) and (34) have identical first and third (as well as fourth) arguments, and country 1 must be better off, ceteris paribus, with a lower domestic price of its import goods, we have the simple criterion

$$u_A^1 \gtreqless u_T^1 \tag{35}$$

according as $\bar{p}_2^1(A^1, 1) = \bar{p}_2^2(A^1, 1) \lesseqgtr T_2^1\bar{p}_2^2(0, T_2^1) = \bar{p}_2^1(0, T_2^1)$.

Thus, in order for country 1 to be better off with foreign aid than with a tariff that will yield the same revenue as the foreign aid, it is necessary and sufficient that the internal price of its import goods be lower (relative to the price of its export goods) with the foreign aid than with the tariff.

A sufficient condition for this result is readily established. Suppose that the following two conditions hold:

(a) A transfer from country 2 to country 1 has the "orthodox" effect of improving (or at least not worsening) country 1's terms of trade in the absence of tariffs, i.e.

$$\bar{p}_2^2(A^1, 1) \leqq \bar{p}_2^2(0, 1).$$

(b) A tariff imposed by country 1 does not lead to the "Metzler paradox", i.e. does not lower the domestic price of its import good.

$$\bar{p}_2^1(0, T_2^1) \geqq \bar{p}_2^1(0, 1)$$

Then

$$\bar{p}_2^2(A^1, 1) \leqq \bar{p}_2^2(0, 1) = \bar{p}_2^1(0, 1) \leqq \bar{p}_2^1(0, T_2^1) = T_2^1 \bar{p}_2^2(0, T_2^1) \qquad (36)$$

From (35) and (36) we may conclude that $u_T^1 \leqq u_A^1$, with strictly inequality holding if either of the inequalities (a) or (b) is strict. Thus under conditions (a) and (b) country 1 can never be better off with a tariff than it would be with an amount of foreign aid equal to the tariff revenues; and if either (a) a transfer to country 1 strictly improves the latter's terms of trade or (b) a tariff imposed by country 1 strictly raises the domestic price of its import good, then country 1 must be better off with foreign aid than with a tariff yielding the same amount of revenues.

A simple alternative sufficient condition can be stated for this result as follows. Suppose that

$$\bar{p}_2^2(0, T_2^1) \geqq \bar{p}_2^2(A^1, 1) \qquad (37)$$

where

$$A^1 = (T_2^1 - 1)\bar{p}_2^2(0, T_2^1) \text{ and } T_2^1 > 1$$

Then

$$\bar{p}_2^1(0, T_2^1) = T_2^1 \bar{p}_2^2(0, T_2^1) > \bar{p}_2^2(A^1, 1) = \bar{p}_2^1(A^1, 1), \tag{38}$$

hence $u_T^1 < u_A^1$ by (35). Thus if foreign aid leads to at least as great an improvement in country 1's terms of trade as a tariff that yields the same amount in revenues, then the domestic price of imports is greater under the tariff and consequently country 1 is better off with the foreign aid than with the tariff.

It might be thought that by reversing the two inequalities in (a) and (b) one could reverse the conclusion; i.e. that by assuming (a) that a transfer has the "anti-orthodox" effect of worsening the receiving country's terms of trade and (b) that the Metzler paradox holds, one could conclude that country 1 would be better off under a tariff than with an equal amount of foreign aid. However, it has been shown in Chipman (1990) that the Metzler paradox can occur only if the orthodox presumption of the transfer problem holds. Thus, (a) and (b) cannot both be true and we cannot therefore obtain the converse result.

To understand the situation it is instructive also to investigate necessary conditions. Suppose we assume that country 1 will be better off with the tariff and that the Metzler paradox does not hold. Then, using the corresponding two inequalities (35) and (b) in succession we obtain

$$\bar{p}_2^2(A^1, 1) > T_2^1 \bar{p}_2^2(0, T_2^1) = \bar{p}_2^1(0, T_2^1) \geqq \bar{p}_2^1(0, 1) = \bar{p}_2^2(0, 1)$$

This shows that a transfer must have the anti-orthodox effect of worsening the receiving country's terms of trade. Likewise, suppose that country 1 will be better off under the tariff and that the orthodox presumption holds that foreign aid will improve or at least not worsen its terms of trade. Then using the corresponding inequalities (35) and (a) in succession we obtain

$$\bar{p}_2^1(0, T_2^1) = T_2^1 \bar{p}_2^2(0, T_2^1) < \bar{p}_2^2(A^1, 1) \leqq \bar{p}_2^2(0, 1) = \bar{p}_2^1(0, 1)$$

This implies that the Metzler paradox must hold. Thus we may conclude that in order for country 1 to be better off under a tariff than with foreign aid equal to the amount of the tariff revenues, it is necessary either that the tariff give rise to the Metzler paradox, i.e.

cause a lowering of the post-tariff internal import price, or that the foreign aid have the anti-orthodox effect of worsening its terms of trade. Thus, one of two anomalies must hold if it is to be the case that country 1 is better off with the tariff. As pointed out above, it is logically impossible for both these anomalies to hold simultaneously.

POSITIVE CASE FOR TRADE

> My overall conclusion is that international trade has made a tremendous contribution to the development of less developed countries in the nineteenth and twentieth centuries and can be expected to make an equally big contribution in the future, if it is allowed to proceed freely. It does not necessarily follow that a 100 per cent free trade policy is always most conducive to most rapid development. Marginal interferences with the tree flow of trade, if properly selected, may speed up development. But I do not want to leave any doubt that my conclusion is that substantially free trade with marginal insubstantial corrections and deviations, is the best policy from the point of view of economic development.[36]

Though the present author does not agree with the above conclusion and holds that not marginal but substantial deviations are required from the free trade position, yet does not depreciate the importance of trade. Haberler mentions four main ways in which trade helps the underdeveloped countries in accelerating their rate of economic development.[37]

Firstly, it enables the underdeveloped countries to obtain capital goods, machinery, essential raw materials etc. required for executing the development programme.

Secondly, trade enables the underdeveloped countries to import technical know-how, skills, managerial talents and entrepreneurship, which are even more important than the material means.

Thirdly, trade serves as the vehicle for the-international movements of capital. No doubt, capital movements can take place even in the absence of trade, but it cannot be denied that trade facilitates international movements of capital. The larger the volume of trade, the easier is likely to be the transfer of capital and the retransfer of capital and the interest thereupon.

Fourthly, free trade promotes healthy competition and checks inefficient monopolies.

In underdeveloped countries, the incentives for investment are weak because of the small size of the market for most of the industries. Size of the market is limited even in countries of geographically large size because of low per capita income and hence low purchasing power. International trade widens the market and thus increases the incentives for investment. The expansion of the market gives rise to a number of internal and external economies and thereby lowers the cost of production.[38]

CONCLUSION

The above analysis leads to the conclusion that what is appropriate for developing countries is neither completely free trade nor a completely closed economy but *controlled, regulated and selective trade.* Following may be mentioned among the guidelines which should be kept in view while determining the pattern of trade for the developing countries.

(a) The import of inessential and luxury goods should be restricted.

(b) The import of goods which the countries plan to produce at home should be restricted.

(c) The import of goods, the restriction of whose imports will lead to the establishment of tariff factories, should be restricted. Care should be taken that the cost of production of the tariff factories is not higher than the import price to such an extent as will offset the whole benefit accruing to domestic economy from the establishment of such factories.

(d) The import of goods which can be produced at home with the help of unemployed factors of production should be restricted even if their private domestic cost of production is much higher than the import price.

(e) The available foreign exchange should be used for the importation of capital goods, technical know-how, essential raw materials and foodstuffs.

(f) On the export side, the underdeveloped countries should restrict the export of exhaustible precious minerals which will be required by the domestic industries when established.

(g) The export of raw materials which can be exported in processed form should be restricted.

(h) The export of the products of cottage industries should be promoted as far as possible.

(i) Attempt should be made, as far as possible, to earn the needed foreign exchange from the export of non-exhaustible raw materials, manufactured consumer goods and, wherever possible, producer goods. In case it is not possible to earn enough foreign exchange from these products, there is no alternative but to export exhaustible raw materials. But the export of exhaustible raw materials should be the last resort.

NOTES

1. Henry Cabot Lodge (ed.) *The Works of Alexander Hamilton* (New York 1944), IV, p. 124.
2. Friederich List, *National System of Political Economy,* translated by G.A. Mantle, Stephen Colwell, ed. (Philadelphia, 1856), p. 159.
3. Jacob Viner, *International Trade and Economic Development* (Oxford, 1953), p. 45.
4. G.F. Loeb, *Industrialisation and Balanced Growth* (Netherlands. 1957), p. 15.
5. Albert O. Hirschman, *The Strategy of Economic Development* (New Haven, 1960), pp. 109-10.
6. H.W. Signer, "The Distribution of Gains between Investing and Borrowing Countries," *American Economic Review, Papers and Proceedings,* 40 (May, 1950), p. 477.
7. United Nations Economic Commission for Latin America; *The Economic Development of Latin America and Its Principal Problems* (New York, 1950), p. 10.
8. *Ibid.*
9. O.F. Loeb, *Industrialisation and Balanced Growth* (Netherlands, 1937), p. 57.
10. J.S. Mill, *Principles of Political Economy,* ed W.J. Ashley (London, 1940), p. 122.
11. Alfred Marshall, *Money, Credit and Commerce* (London, 1929), p. 218.

12. R.L. Varshney, *India's Foreign Trade* (Allahabad, 1954), p. 229.
13. Enke and V. Salera, *International Economics* (London 1950), p. 288.
14. D.T. Lakdawala, *International Aspects of Indian Economic Development* (Bombay, 1951), p. 138.
15. Enke and V. Salera, *International Economics* (London, 1950), p. 290.
16. *Ibid.*, pp. 290-91.
17. *Ibid.*, p. 291.
18. Ragnar Nurkse, *Problems of Capital Formation in Underdeveloped Countries* (Oxford, 1955), p. 106.
19. *Ibid.*
20. United Nations, *A Study of Trade Between Asia and Europe* (Geneva, 1958), p. 10.
21. Gunnar Myrdal, *An International Economy* (New York, 1956), p. 276.
22. Ragnar Nurkse, *Problems of Capital Formation in Underdeveloped Countries* (Oxford, 1955), p. 9.
23. J.S Mill, *Essays on Some Unsettled Questions of Political Economy,* (London School of Economics Reprint, 1948), p. 73, *cf.* Ragnar Nurkse, *Problems of Capital Formation in Underdeveloped Countries* (Great Britain, 1955), p. 9.
24. Ragnar Nurkse, "The Conflict Between 'Balanced Growth' and International Specialisation" in *Lectures in Economic Development* (Istanbul, 1958), pp. 172-73.
25. F.Y. Edgeworth, *Papers Relating to Political Economy* (London, 1925), II, pp. 16-17.
26. G. Haberler, *The Theory of International Trade* (New York, 1956), p. 293.
27. D.R. Khatkhate, *Problems of Monetary Policy in a Developing Economy* (Bombay, 1954), pp. 134-35.
28. G. Haberler, *International Trade and Economic Development* (Cairo, 1959), p. 27.
29. GATT, *International Trade, 1956* (Geneva, 1957), p. 7.
30. G. Haberler, *Theory of International Trade* (New York, 1965), p. 277.
31. *Cf.* F.Y. Edgeworth, *Papers Relating to Political Economy* (London, 1925), II, p. 17.
32. *Ibid.*, p. 18.
33. G. Haberler, *The Theory of International Trade* (New York), 1956, p. 270.

34. Ragnar Nurkse, *Problems of Capital Formation in Underdeveloped Countries* (Oxford, 1955), p. 105.
35. *Ibid.*
36. G. Haberler, *International Trade and Economic Development* (Cairo, 1959), p. 5.
37. *Ibid.* pp. 4-10.
38. J.R. Hicks, *Essays in World Economics* (Oxford, 1959), pp. 183-84.

Tariffs

12

It is a well-known fact that the free trade benefits each and every nation of the world and in the best way out to maximize the total world output. Yet, practically every nation imposes some trade restrictions to prevent the free flow of the goods from and into its territories due to one or another reason. The most common type of trade restriction is "tariff".

A tariff is a duty on a tax which is imposed on a commodity when it crosses the national borders. Tariffs can be classified into different classes on account of different bases.

CLASSIFICATION OF TARIFFS

On the Basis of Origin and Destination of the Goods

On the basis of the origin and destination of the goods crossing the national boundary, tariffs can be classified into three general classes viz. "import duty", "export duty" and "transit duty".

(a) *Import Duties*: Imposed on goods originating abroad destined for the duty-levying country.

(b) *Export Duties*: Imposed on goods originating from the duty-levying country destined for some other country.

(c) *Transit Duties*: Levied on goods crossing the national frontier originating from and destined for other countries.

On the Basis of Quantity and Quality

The duty may be levied either according to the value of the commodity or according to its weight or quantity. Thus, on the basis of the quantity and quality, the tariffs can be—"specific duty", "*ad valorem*" or "compound duty".

(a) *Ad valorem* Duty—*Ad valorem* is a latin word that means "on the value." *Ad valorem* duty is hence levied on the value of the traded commodity and is expressed as a fixed percentage of this value. *Ad valorem* tariff is imposed on goods like paintings diamonds, television sets, etc. on which the duties can not be estimated by weighing them physically.

(b) *Specific Duty*: Specific duty is a fixed sum of money charged upon each unit of the commodity imported.

(c) *Compound Duty*: A duty on which both the above written forms (*ad valorem* and specific) of duties are combined is known as a compound duty.

On the Basis of Objective

There can be two types of tariffs on the basis of the objective they serve. They are "revenue tariff" and "protective tariff".

(a) *Revenue Tariff*: The main object of the revenue tariff is to obtain revenue for the public treasury. Such tariffs are generally kept low so as not to restrict imports appreciably. In order to place the foreign and domestic producers at the same level, revenue duties on imported articles are generally combined with equivalent excise duties on domestic production. In case the revenue duty on imported commodity is not supplemented by an equivalent excise duty on the production of similar domestic article, the duty even if levied solely for the purpose of revenue will afford some protection to the home production of the commodity on which the duty is levied or of the commodities which can be directly or indirectly substituted for it.

(b) *Protective Tariff*: The primary object of a protective duty is to protect domestic producers of a commodity from foreign competition by limiting the imports of similar commodities from abroad. A completely protective duty stops imports altogether and yields no revenue. Generally, however, protective duties are not so high as to prevent imports altogether and, therefore, in addition to protecting domestic producers, yield some revenue. Sometimes, the duty is levied with the dual purpose of collecting revenue for the public treasury and for protecting domestic producers from foreign competition.

On the Basis of Application between Different Countries

The tariff system can be classified into three main types regarding its application between different countries, viz. (a) single-column tariff; (b) double-column tariff and (c) triple-column tariff.

(a) *Single-Column:* It provides a single rate of duty for each commodity without any regard as to the country of origin. The rates of duty are, generally, determined autonomously. Even if the rates of duty on some articles result from the conclusion of treaties with particular countries, these are generalised to all other countries. It does not discriminate between different countries. Because of its simplicity, it is easier to construct and administer. It, however, cannot be used as an instrument of commercial bargaining because the country having this form of tariff has nothing to offer in exchange for negotiating a reciprocal concession.

(b) *Double-Column Tariff:* This system of tariff provides two rates of duty for some or for all commodities. Both the rates may be fixed by the legislature from the very beginning, or one rate may be fixed by the legislature at the very start and the other result from the conclusion of commercial treaties with other countries. Double-line tariffs are difficult to construct and administer. Under this form of tariff, imports from some sources are permitted at one rate and those from other sources at another rate. This makes it difficult to predict the extent of protection which the domestic producers would obtain or the amount of revenue which the public treasury would obtain from a particular set of rates. The double-column tariff can be broadly classified into two systems, viz. (i) "General and Conventional" tariff and (ii) "Maximum-and-Minimum" tariff.

General and Conventional Tariff: This system consists of two schedules of tariffs. One (the general) is fixed by the legislature at the very start and the other (the conventional) results from the conclusion of commercial treaties with other countries. This form of tariff is an important instrument of commercial bargaining. This system imparts stability into the tariff system because the contracted rates of duty cannot be changed autonomously without denouncing the treaties. Stability of tariffs helps the expansion of world trade and production. This system has also got some disadvantages. The fixing of conventional rates requires long and protracted negotiations. Meanwhile the general higher rates are applied which may be injurious not only to the interests of foreign countries but also to those of the domestic economy because these are generally set at a level higher than that required by the needs of the domestic economy so as to provide enough scope for bargaining. If the negotiations are not successful, the general rates may have to be maintained permanently even if these are harmful for the domestic economy; because if these are unilaterally lowered after the failure of negotiations, the future bargaining strength of the country will be considerably weakened. In case the treaty-making power is in the hands of the executive, the replacement of the general rates by the negotiated conventional rates will tantamount to a usurpation by executive of the legislative powers which may be against the spirit of a true democracy. Conventional tariffs tie the hands of the country. The country is not free to fix the rates of duty according to the needs of the domestic economy. Further, it cannot adjust tariffs according to the changed requirements of the domestic economy. Under the autonomous system, tariffs are adjusted regularly and gradually according to the changed conditions. Under the conventional system, changes in tariffs are sudden and violent because the expiration or termination of treaties involves a substantial revision of the tariff system. Desired changes cannot be affected without renegotiating a number of treaties. Renegotiation of treaties is a very long, protracted, complicated and difficult process. A number of vested interests grow up during the period of the treaty which make the renegotiation of treaties extremely difficult. The uncertainty that prevails during the long protracted period of negotiation of treaties is highly injurious to world trade and production.

'Maximum-and-Minimum' Tariff: This system contains two autonomously determined schedules of tariffs, viz. the maximum schedule and the minimum schedule. The minimum schedule applies to the imports from those countries who have obtained the concession as a result of the treaty or through the most-favoured nation pledge. The maximum schedule applies to all other countries. The 'Maximum-and-Minimum' tariff differs from the 'general-and-conventional tariff in two respects. Firstly, it contains two rates for every commodity subject to duty while the latter contains two rates only for those commodities in respect of which treaties have been concluded with other countries. Secondly, both the rates under it are fixed autonomously whereas the conventional rates under the latter form are fixed by agreement with the foreign countries. As both the rates are fixed autonomously, these can be changed according to changed conditions without the consent of any other country. This system is introduced generally to restrain the powers of the treaty-making authority. Under the 'general-and-conventional'

tariff system, the treaty making authority is free to accord any amount of concession in the rate of duty. Under the 'maximum-and-minimum' tariff system, both the sets of rates are fixed by the legislature and the treaty-making authority cannot offer concessions which require the fixation of rates lower than those provided in the minimum schedule. The minimum schedule represents the minimum requirements of the economy for tariffs. The treaty-making authority can accord either the minimum rate or no concession at all. It cannot accord any rate between the maximum-and-the minimum rates. This impairs the bargaining power of the country because the amount of concession which it can accord is known to the other party before hand. Sometimes, a much larger concession might have to be given in exchange for a certain concession because treaty-making body is authorised to accord only the minimum rate and no other rate in between the maximum-and-the minimum rate in exchange for which the other party would have agreed to accord the same concession. Under the 'maximum-and-minimum' tariff the domestic producers are sure of at least the protection afforded by minimum rates. There prevails uncertainty, however, to the extent that both the rates are determined autonomously and can be changed at any time without seeking the consent of any other party.

(c) Triple-Column Tariff: It consists of three autonomously determined sets of rates, viz. (i) a general rate, (ii) an intermediate rate and (iii) a preferential rate. The general and the intermediate rates are similar to the maximum-and-minimum rates discussed above. The preferential rate is generally applied to imports from the mother country or from the colonies. Triple-column tariff makes possible a higher degree of discrimination and, therefore, is a better instrument of commercial bargaining than the double-column tariff. It is comparatively difficult to construct and administer. Application of different rates to the same commodity originating from different sources gives rise to the botheration of ascertaining the origin of the imported commodities. Preferential rate often leads to the embitterment of international relations.

On the Basis of Retaliation

There are two types of tariffs based on retaliation namely "retaliatory tariffs" and "countervailing tariffs".

(a) *Retaliatory Tariff*: The tariff duty imposed by one country on the imports of another country to punish the latter for its trade policy that harms its balance of payment position is termed as the retaliatory tariff.

(b) *Countervailing Tariff*: This is an additional duty which is imposed on a commodity whose export price is reduced through an export subsidy. It is done to raise the price of the commodity and prevent its producers in the importing country from the cheap foreign lot.

EFFECTS OF TARIFFS

A tariff "is likely to alter trade, prices, output and consumption and to reallocate resources change factor proportions redistribute income, change employment and alter the balance of payments". Thus a tariff costs its impact on vast ranging fields of an economy.

The effects of a tariff may be examined in terms of the economy as a whole, or in terms of the market for a particular goods. Considerable insight into the effects can be obtained by confining our attention previously to the analysis of a single goods. Such analysis is known as "partial equilibrium analysis". Later on, we shall extend our study to the analysis of the whole economy and this analysis is known as "general equilibrium analysis".

Partial Equilibrium Analysis

To do the partial equilibrium analysis we assume that demand and supply relationships of the chosen commodity are given and remain constant. On the demand side, tastes, other prices, and consumer's money income all remain fixed. On the supply side, technological change, externalities, and other changes in cost conditions are ruled out. In particular, any tariff on the raw material or any other input used in the production of the commodity.

Given these assumptions, the tariff can have following effects under partial equilibrium analysis—

(a) Price Effect

(b) Consumption Effect

(c) Production Effect

(d) Fiscal Revenue Effect

(e) Redistribution Effect

(f) Balance of Payments Effect

(g) Income and Employment Effect.

(a) *Price Effect*: While studying the price-effect of a tariff imposed on the import of the commodity, we can take two cases. Number one is the case of a small country and number two is the case of a large country.

In the case of a small country, it is assumed that the world price of the commodity remains unchanged when the importing country imposes tariff. This is because the importing country is a small country and its actions do not affect the world market. The analysis of such a country can be had from Fig. 12.1 where the prices of the commodity are measured on Y axis and the quality supplied and demanded is measured on X axis. D and S are the domestic demand and supply curve respectively. OP_W is the world price (which is constant since it remains unchanged) at which the commodity can be imported under free trade. At this price OQ_1 quantity is produced domestically and Q_1Q_4 quantity is imported so as to make the total supply equal to the total demand. Note that there is no demand for imports at a price higher than the autarky price, P_A. At a price lower than P_M where the domestic supply curve cuts the vertical axis and the quantity supplied equals zero, the import demand curve becomes same as the market demand curve. At prices between P_A and P_M, the quantity of imports demanded is the difference between the quantity demanded and the quantity supplied domestically.

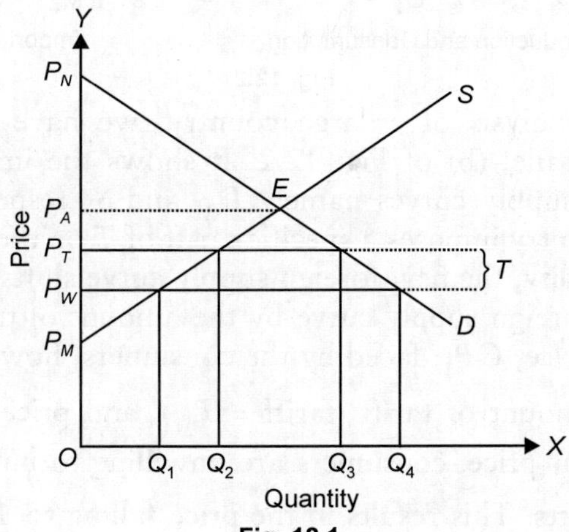

Fig. 12.1

Now suppose the importing country imposes a tariff (equal to T) on the import of the commodity. As a result, the price of the commodity will rise by the amount of tariff and become OP_T.

Under the assumption of constant costs abroad, the foreign price remains unchanged, but the price in domestic market has increased. However, if some or all of the tariff is redundant, the domestic price will not rise by the full amount of the tariff. For example, a tariff of $P_W P_N$ would raise the domestic price only to OP_A, the domestic no-trade price.

In the case of a large country, it is assumed that it influences the world price when changes the amount of a given commodity it imports, by imposing a tariff on the import. Here also, we continue to ignore the effects of any change outside the industry of the commodity which we are studying.

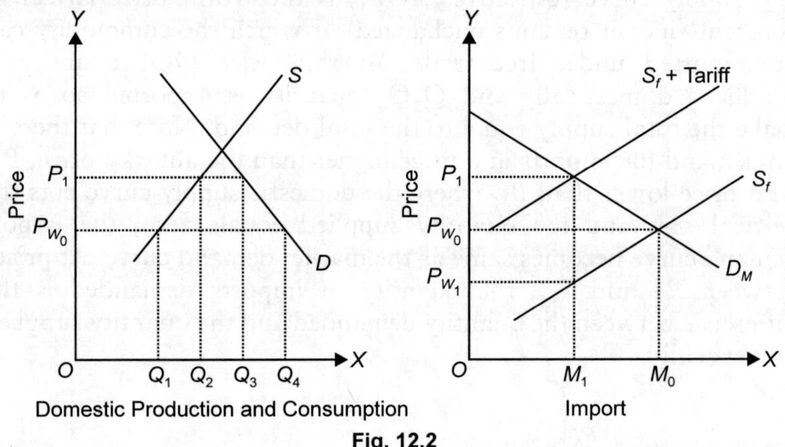

Fig. 12.2

For the analysis of a large country, we have extended our Fig. 12.1 to panel (b) of Fig. 12.2. It shows the import market's demand and supply curves namely D_M and S_F respectively. If the importing country imposes a specific tariff of T on the import of the given commodity, the new foreign supply curve shifts up parallel to the original foreign supply curve by the amount of tariff. The new equilibrium price, OP_1, faced by the consumers, however, does not rise by the amount of tariff (tariff = $P_{W_1} P_1$ and price rise = $P_{W_0} P_1$), because at that price, consumers are unwilling to buy the quantity OM_0 of imports. This results in the price falling to P_{W_1}. Because of this fall, the foreigners supply a smaller quantity of imports. Because the price consumer faces rises from P_{W_0} to P_1, they only wish to demand this smaller quantity of imports.

(b) *Consumption Effect*: As the effect on consumptions a tariff not only reduces the consumption of the commodity on which the tariff is imposed, but also decreases the consumer's satisfaction. In Fig. 12.3, OP_W is the free trade price and OP_T is the price after the imposition of tariff. At price OP_W, the quantity being domestically was OQ_1 and demanded domestically was OQ_4 but after the imposition of tariff, at price OP_T, the domestic supply has rised to OQ_2 but the demand has decreased to OQ_3. Thus, Q_3Q_4 ($OQ_4 - OQ_3 = Q_3Q_4$) represents the decrease in consumption and is the consumption effect. Also, the consumer's satisfaction loses upto the area P_TP_Wbd (shaded part).

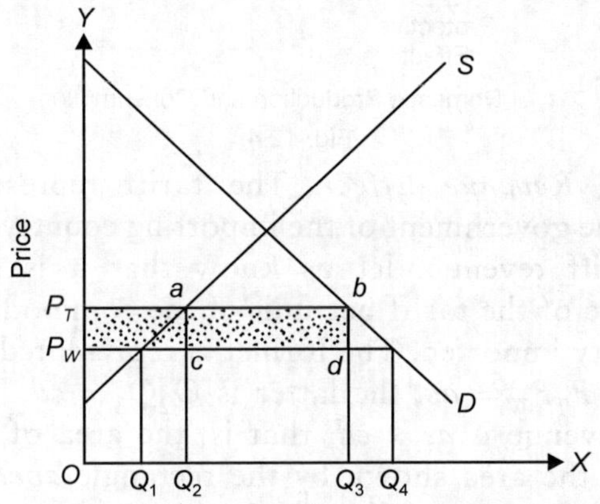

Fig. 12.3

(c) *Production Effect*: This effect is also known as the protective effect of tariff because more often than not the clause or the reason presented in front of the world by the importing country is that it wants to protect its industry from the stiff competition which can be posed by the easy availability of imports. Hence, tariff imposition is justified. In Fig. 12.4, at free trade world price OP_W, the domestic supply (Production) was QQ_1 but after the imposition of tariff and increase in price to OP_T the domestic production increases to OQ_2. Thus, the difference ($OQ_2 - OQ_1$) Q_1Q_2 is the production or the protective effect of tariff.

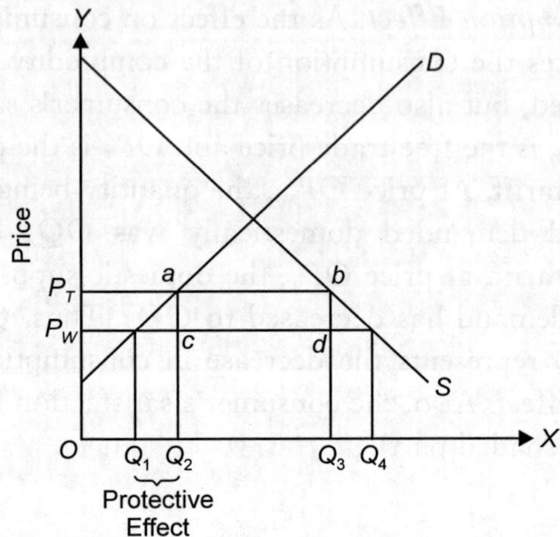

Domestic Production and Consumption

Fig. 12.4

(d) *Fiscal Revenue Effect*: The tariff represents a fiscal revenue for the government of the importing country. To calculate the total tariff revenue, let us know that it is given by the absolute value of the tariff per unit of the commodity multiplied by the quantity imported. The former is represented by $P\ (1 + d_1) - P = d_1\ P = P_T P_W = ac$, the latter is $Q_2Q_3 = cd$. Therefore the total tariff revenue is $ac \times cd$, that is, the area of the rectangle abcd. Hence, the area shown by the rectangle *abcd* in Fig. 12.5 shows the fiscal revenue effect of the tariff.

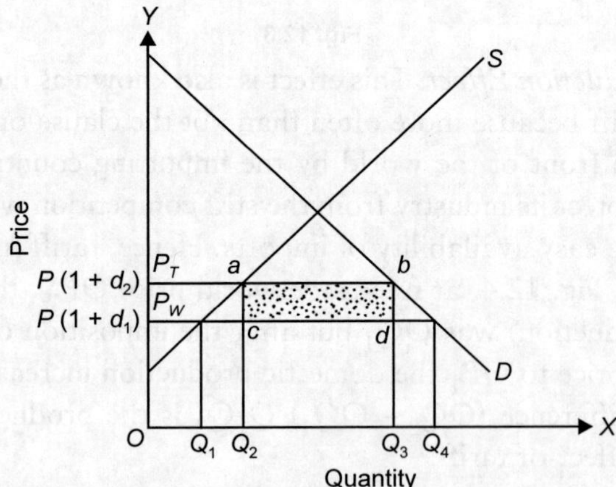

Fig. 12.5

(e) *Redistribution Effect*: Redistribution effect of tariff is also known as the transfer effect of tariff. Since the price of the commodity increase due to the imposition of tariff, there happens to be a redistribution of income from consumers to producers. Now the producers receive a higher price for the commodity. This amount is a surplus over production costs. To understand the redistribution effect further, let us go through the following explanation which is illustrated through Fig. 12.6.

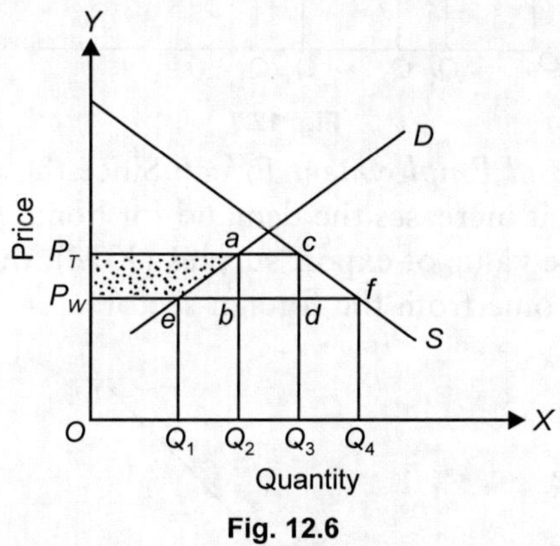

Fig. 12.6

After the imposition of tariff, net consumer satisfaction loss = P_TP_Wcd. Government charges its revenue equal to the amount *abcd*. Now out of the total amount, the residual P_TP_Wae (shaded portion) goes to the producers and is the redistribution effect.

(f) *Balance of Payments Effect*: If the imports in a country are reduced, it leads to a favourable balance of payment for that country and *vice versa*. Imposition of tariff beings for sure, a favourability in the balance of payments of the importing country. The balance of payments effect of tariff can be illustrated through Fig. 12.7 in which OQ_4 commodity is imported at OP_W price under free trade. But after the imposition of tariff, the price increases to OP_T and the total imports become Q_2Q_3 ($Q_2Q_3 < Q_1Q_4$). Now before the tariff imposition, the total revenue going to the foreign country was a Q_1Q_4 while now it has reduced to bQ_2Q_3C. Hence, it is the balance of payments effect of tariff.

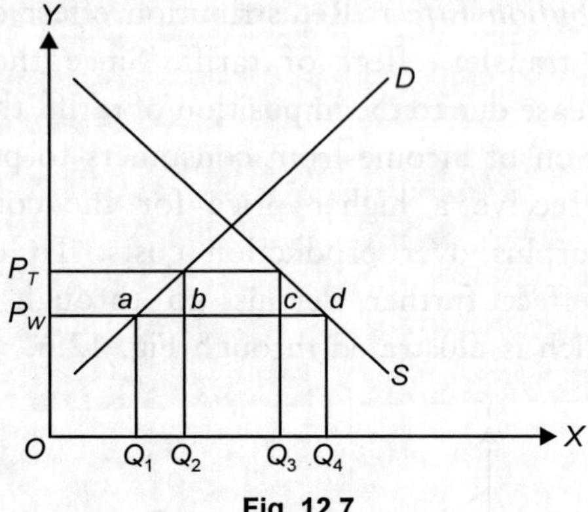

Fig. 12.7

(g) *Income and Employment Effect*: Since the tariff imposition reduces imports, it increases the demand for home produced goods. This increases the value of export surplus (*X-M*), thereby increasing the inflow of income from the foreign sector.

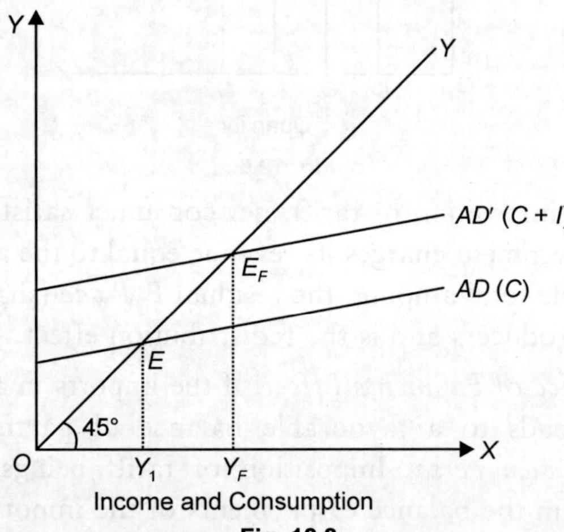

Fig. 12.8

In Fig. 12.8, *AD* represents the total expenditure (consumption) or aggregate demand of the economy which intersects the income curve, *Y*, at point *E*. This is the unemployment equilibrium of this economy.

When a tariff is imposed, the imports decrease by an amount *DM* due to which the demand hence investment for local good increases. This shifts *AD* curve upward to *AD*. *AD* intersects *Y* at *E* which is the full employment equilibrium. At this point national income is OY_F which is higher than previous OY_1. Hence, as an effect of tariff imposition the income and employment level of the importing country improve.

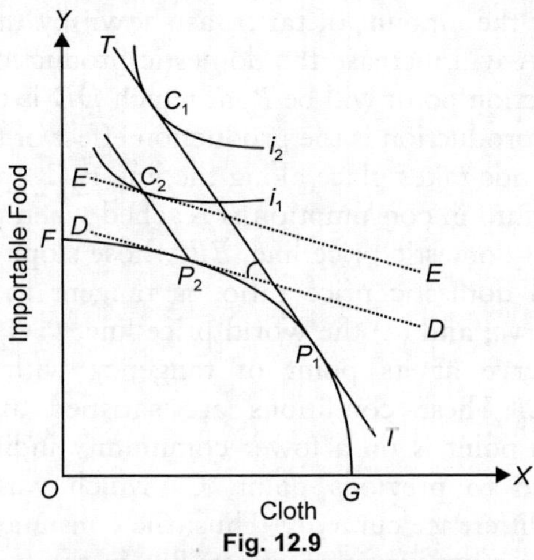

Fig. 12.9

GENERAL EQUILIBRIUM ANALYSIS

The partial equilibrium analysis, as concluded above, in general believes that tariff imposition brings loss to the consumers of the importing country. In general equilibrium analysis, when tariffs are imposed by a country on its imports, import substitution takes place in the importing country, leading to a contraction in output of other production sectors in the economy. This analysis also studies the cases of the small country and large country.

(a) *Case of Small Country:* To make our analysis simple, we assume that there are two countries namely country A and the rest of the world between whom the trade is taking place. Also country is a small country and any charge brought by it in the prices of the commodity it imports, i.e. food does not affect the rest of the world. It specializes in production of cloth.

The analysis can be illustrated by Fig. 12.9. The production possibility curve country A between the two goods in *FG*. Under free trade equilibrium the production will take place at point P_1 where *FG* is tangent to the world price ratio shown by the slope of *TT* and the consumption will be at point C_1 where *TT* is tangent to the indifference curve i_2.

Assuming that the world price ratio between the two commodities remains unchanged, an imposition of a tariff on the import of food results in raising the food price in the domestic market as compared to the cloth by the amount of tariff, as shown by the slope of line *DD*. Country A will increase the domestic production of food and the new production point will be P_2 at which *DD* is tangent on *FG*. This increased production is the production effect of tariff. How the international trade takes place along the line P_2C_2 (parallel to *TT*). A new equilibrium in consumption is reached when two conditions are satisfied (1) domestic price line, *EE* whose slope is equal to the tariff distorted domestic price ratio, is tangent to a community indifference curve; and (2) the world price line, P_2C_2 intersects this indifference curve at its point of tangency with the domestic price line, *EE*. These conditions are satisfied at point C_2 in Fig. 12.9. This point is on a lower community indifference curve, i_1, as compared to previous point, C_1 which was on a higher community indifference curve, i_2. Thus, the consumer's satisfaction is decreasing as a consumption effect. But in the midst of it all; it must also be noted that the production of cloth has decreased as a result of tariff imposition. Thus in all there is a loss in country's welfare.

(b) *Case of a Large Country*: In this analysis, we keep all our assumptions as same to our small country analysis except for the one which said that the world prices are not affected. Here, since our country A is large enough, it will influence the world price of what it buys. To continue the same example, when country A levies a tariff on food, the result may be that the world price of food falls relative to the price of cloth. The case may be illustrated through Fig. 12.10 where conditions are the same as in the case described under small country except that the tariff now causes the world price ratio to change from the slope of the line *TT* to the slope of the line P_3C_3. After the imposition of tariff the production takes place at P_3 and consumption takes place at point C_3. Thus, we see that the domestic production of food increases (P_3 is higher than P_1) and that of cloth decreases as a production effect of tariff. As far as the consumption effect is concerned, now the consumers are at a higher community indifference curve hence the consumer satisfaction increases (C_3 is higher than *G*). Thus, it can be said that there is a welfare of the tariff-imposing country.

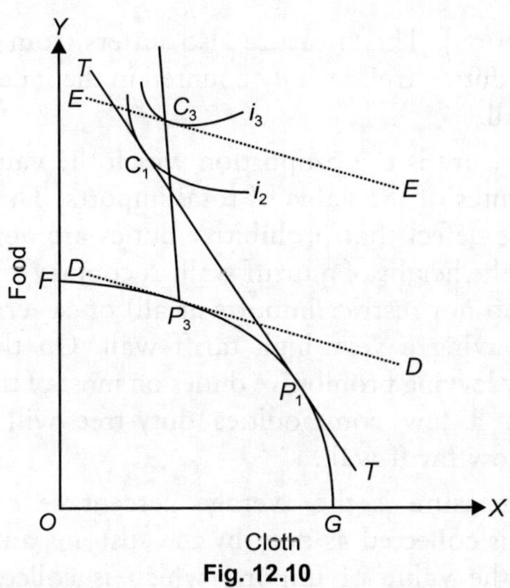

Fig. 12.10

Measuring the Height of a Tariff

Some measurement of the height of a tariff is very essential if the tariff systems of different countries of those of the same country at different times are to be compared. Measuring the height of a tariff, however, involves highly complicated problems. There exists no formula which can measure the height of a tariff precisely and unambiguously. Statistical difficulties aside, even the concept of the height of a tariff is not very clear and unambiguous.

A crude measure of the height of a tariff wall is given by the percentage which the value of dutiable imports forms of the total value of all imports, i.e. dutiable imports and free imports. This measure suffers from the defect that the more prohibitive a duty becomes, the less it is counted in the measure. To illustrate this, let us take a hypothetical example. Suppose a country was importing one hundred commodities before the tariff system was instituted. It levies so high tariffs on the import of ninety-nine commodities as stop the import of these altogether. The import of the hundredth commodity is permitted free of any duty. According to the above formula the height of tariff wall in this case is nil. But actually the tariff wall is so high as stops imports almost completely.

A second measure is the average burden of import duties. The average burden is the percentage which the sum of import duties collected forms of the total value of all imports, (or the total value of dutiable imports). This measure also suffers from the defect that the prohibitive duties are not fully counted in the index of the height of the tariff wall.

A third measure is the proportion which the value of duty-free imports constitutes of the value of total imports. This measure also suffers from the defect that prohibitive duties are not fully counted in the index of the height of a tariff wall. A country levying very low duties (which do not restrict imports at all) on several articles, will be shown as having a very high tariff wall. On the other hand, another country levying prohibitive duties on most of the commodities and permitting a few commodities duty-free will be shown as having a very low tariff wall.

A fourth measure is the average percentage of the value of imports which is collected as duty by the customs authorities. First, percentage of the value of imports which is collected as duty is calculated for each individual commodity subject to duty. This is very simple in case of *ad valorem* duties. Calculation of the percentage in case of specific duties requires conversion of specific duties into *ad valorem* duties. After calculating the percentage for each individual commodity, an average is taken which shows the average percentage of the value of imports collected as duty. Calculation of this index of the height of a tariff wall of a country involves a number of difficulties, complications and choices.[1]

Firstly, there is the problem of converting the specific duties into *ad valorem* duties. It may be difficult to obtain the value of certain goods. There may be no uniform market price of the commodity. There may be several varieties of the commodity, each variety having a different price.

Secondly, there arises the problem of determining suitable weights to be attached to different duties. All duties are not equally important. A duty on the importation of cloth is much more important than a duty on the importation of gramophone needles. Weights can be determined on a number of basis, viz. share of the commodity in total imports, share in total exports, share in total world trade, share in total production in the country concerned, share in total world production etc. Further, whichever basis is selected the magnitude of the share will be affected by the level of duty.

Thirdly, it is not possible to take into account all the commodities. The number of commodities entering into international trade is very large. The number is further increased by the greater specialisation of the modern tariff schedules. A limited number of commodities have to be selected to be included into the index. There are a number of alternative ways of selecting these commodities. Commodities may be selected out of only those which are imported by the country concerned. Under this method, a duty will stop affecting the index as soon as it 'reaches so high as to prohibit imports altogether. A second alternative is to select goods out of those exported by another country. A third alternative is to select those goods which are most important in the world trade.

Fourthly, the tariff walls of equal height will restrict imports by different degrees in different countries because of variations in the demand and supply conditions. Thus, to compare the restrictive effect of tariff walls, of different countries, it is not sufficient to compare only their heights; several other things have got to be taken into account.

Fifthly, the same rate of duty may differently affect imports from different countries. This will require the construction of a series of tariff-indices for any country, one for each exporting country instead of a single index.

The solution of the problems, and the selection out of possible alternatives, mentioned above will depend upon the purpose for which the index is to be constructed.

TARIFF REFORM

By post-Paretian convention the well-being of a single country is said to increase as the result of an agreement if and only if no resident of that country is left worse off and at least one resident is left better off. In this section, our focus is on the characteristics of tariff reforms that accommodate this informal constraint, interpreted in the sense of Pareto and, for that reason, referred to as Pareto-improving. We will require that tariff reforms leave the world on its contract locus, in a Pareto-optimal position. Thus in this section our focus is on reforms that satisfy a two-edge Paretian rule which restricts the set of feasible reforms, and in unexpected directions. For this purpose we will focus on the familiar case of two commodities and two countries, in which case the most-favoured-nation (MFN) clause plays no role. Here we will show that the set of tariff reforms that satisfy the Paretian rule:

(a) is always non-empty;
(b) might include no reforms that end in worldwide free trade;
(c) always includes reforms that are incompatible with free trade and, in particular, always includes reforms that impose negative import duties and/or positive export duties;
(d) might include reforms that support a Pareto-optimal and Pareto-improving allocation but that also support other allocations without either of those characteristics.

Out of above four conclusions, (a) is the basic existence proposition for two-by-two economies and (b) affirms that there are circumstances in which free trade is ruled out by the two-edged Paretian rule. Conclusion (c) states that, whether or not free trade is attainable, there are always available reforms that impose negative import duties and/or positive export duties and finally (d) describes a fundamental obstacle to the attainability of particular allocations associated with tariff reform. These findings establish a sharp contrast between redistribution attainable by means of distorting tariffs and redistribution attainable by non-distorting lump-sum Grandmont-McFadden-Grinols (GMG) compensation. Moreover, they carry the possibility disturbing implication that an import subsidy and/or an export tax may be necessary elements of a pure tariff reform, that is, a tariff reform unaccompanied by international transfers. Finally, they generalize the classical gains from trade proposition, in which the initial tariffs are jointly prohibitive and in which all new tariffs are zero.

Let us consider two pure-exchange economies, the home and the foreign, each with a single representative agent. The two commodities differ only in the point in time at which they become available; thus international borrowing and lending are permitted. The home country has an endowment of one unit of commodity 1 and the foreign country has an endowment of one unit of commodity 2. The two agents share a symmetrical, increasing and strictly quasi-concave utility function of the form

$$u = x + y + \alpha x y, \quad \alpha > 0$$

where x and y denote the amounts consumed.

Now let us draw the unit Edgeworth box diagram.

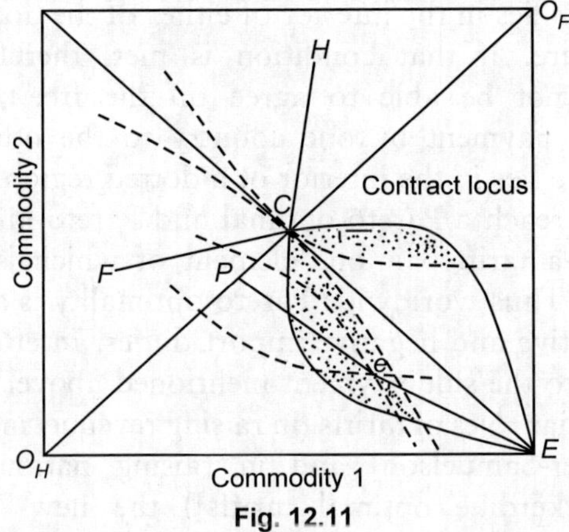

Fig. 12.11

In the above Edgeworth box diagram *E* is the initial endowment point and the contract locus coincides with the diagonal joining the home and foreign origins, O_H and O_F. At all points on the contract locus, the two marginal rates of substitution are equal to one.

The unique free-trade equilibrium is represented by point *C*, where the two offer curves, *EH* and *EF*, intersects and where two dashed indifference curve, one for each country, are tangential. The equilibrium world price ratio is equal to one, and each country exports half of its endowment. Now suppose that each country imposes a non-negative tariff on its imports. Possibly but not necessarily they forms a Nash solution to a tariff war; possibly one is optimal, the other zero; possibly they are jointly prohibitive. The tariff-distorted curves intersect at a point *e* in the 'lens' *CE* formed by the free-trade offer curves.

If exceptionally, each tariff is initially imposed at the same rate, *e* must lie in the open segment *EC*. In that case both countries benefit from any equi-proportional reduction of the two tariffs; in particular, this is so if the tariffs are eliminated in favour of free trade. Moreover, any Pareto-optimal and Pareto-improving point other than C can be reached by negotiating a tariff pair one element of which is positive, the other negative. On the other hand if the two tariffs are initially imposed at different rates, then it is possible that one country will be harmed by a retreat to free trade.

Indeed this outcome will emerge if and only if the tariff-distorted point *e* lies in the interior of either of the dotted regions in the above figure. If that condition is met, therefore, the two countries will not be able to agree on the free-trade outcome without a side payment by one country to the other. However, whether or not *e* lies in the interior of a dotted region, the countries will be able to reach a Pareto-optimal and Pareto-improving point by negotiating a tariff pair one element of which is positive, the other negative. Thus worldwide Pareto-optimality is attainable in a context of positive and negative import duties. In effect, the tariffs are equivalent to the side payment mentioned above. Thus we may add to the familiar roles of tariffs (in raising revenue, in redistribution income [Stolper-Samuelson] and in raising national well-being [Edgeworth-Bickerdike optimal tariffs]) the new fiscal role of extending foreign aid. It suggests that negotiating countries should not constrain their negotiations by imposing equi-proportionality, thus ruling out import subsidies. Without recourse to import subsidies it is generally impossible to achieve a world allocation that is both Pareto-optimal and Pareto-improving; in particular, it is generally impossible to reach the free-trade point *C* without harming one country. This can be proved straightforwardly as follows.

Let us consider a point e in the dotted region of the above figure and any Pareto-optimal and Pareto-improving point *P*. At *P* there is a shared marginal rate of substitution (MRS = 1), which differs from the terms of trade ($p_2/p_1 \neq 1$). Suppose that *P* can be attained by means of an ordered semi-positive (non-negative and non-zero) pair of specific tariffs (t^H, t^F). Then

$$(p_1 + t^F)/P_2 = p_1/(p_2 + t^H).$$

Since the pair of tariffs is semi-positive, however,

$$(p_1 + t^F)/p_2 > p_1/(p_2 + t^H)$$

a contradiction.

The above analysis has been based on several simplifying assumptions. Now we will relax these assumptions. In our analysis we have assumed that the two agents share the same symmetrical utility function, ensuring that the contract locus coincides with the positively sloped diagonal of the Fig. 12.11. This assumption is not necessary and if we abandoned this assumption we get the following figure but our conclusion remains intact.

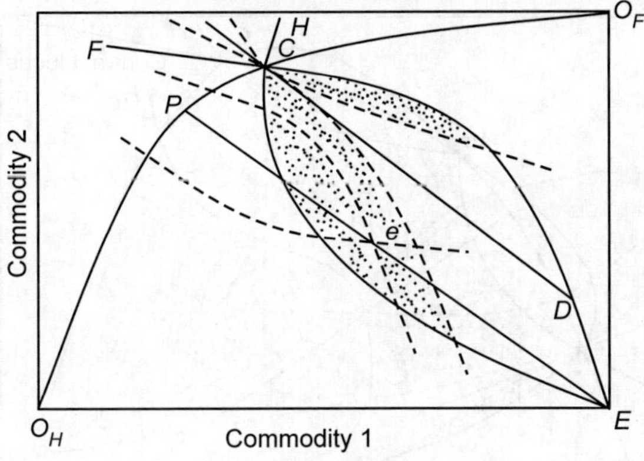

Fig. 12.12

In particular, from any point *e*, whether it is in the doted or undotted region of the lens *EC*, it is possible by adopting new tariffs to move to any point *P* that is Pareto-optimal and Pareto-preferred to *e*. If *e* lies in the straight segment *CD* and *P* coincides with *C*, then the new tariffs will be zero; hat is, free trade will obtain. Otherwise, one of the new tariffs must be positive, the other negative. But we will now assume that there is a single agent in each country. The indifference contours of Figs. 12.11 and 12.12 can be interpreted as Scitovsky community indifference contours based on the individual contours of any number of heterogeneous agents, with a GMG scheme of lump-sum compensation ensuring that, in the general context of tariff-cum-subsidy reforms as in the traditional special context in which free trade replaces autarky, the economies move to ever-higher Scitovsky contours. Thus point *P* in Fig. 12.11 or Fig. 12.12 is not only Pareto-optimal and Pareto-improving in relation to point e but readily implementable by means of GMG compensation.

Till now we have focused on a particular endowment point. However, it is possible to accommodate any initial endowment point compatible with autarkic subsistence and by reinterpreting the indifference curves as trade indifference curves, to accommodate production. It is also possible to accommodate initial tariffs that are jointly prohibitive. We need only recall that the free-trade allocation is Pareto-optimal and Pareto-preferred to E which, if the tariffs are prohibitive, coincides with e.

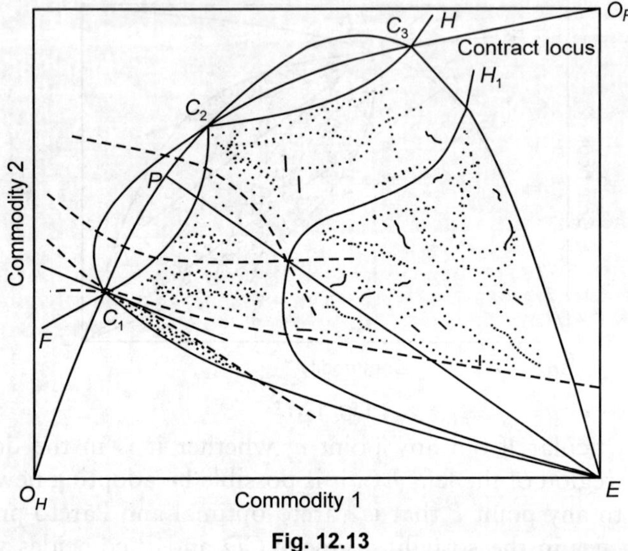

Fig. 12.13

Earlier we have considered that the free trade and tariff-distorted world equilibria are unique. Suppose that this is not so and thee are three free trade equilibria, as shown in the above figure.

If the home country imposes a positive import duty, its offer at each terms of trade contracts (perhaps to zero), so that its new tariff-distorted offer curve EH_1 lies uniformly 'inside' its free-trade offer curve EH; similarly for the foreign country. Thus, corresponding to each pair of positive tariffs there is a pair of tariff-distorted offer curves. The curves may or may not intersect in the interior of the region inside both EH and EF; and, if the curves do intersect, they may intersect less than or more than three times now consider any point e which is an interior equilibrium for some pair of positive tariffs. The dotted region of the Fig. 12.13 is associated with the free trade equilibrium C_1, the dotted region of the following figure (Fig. 12.14) is associated with the free trade equilibrium C_2, and the dotted region of the Fig. 12.15 is associated with the free trade equilibrium C_3.

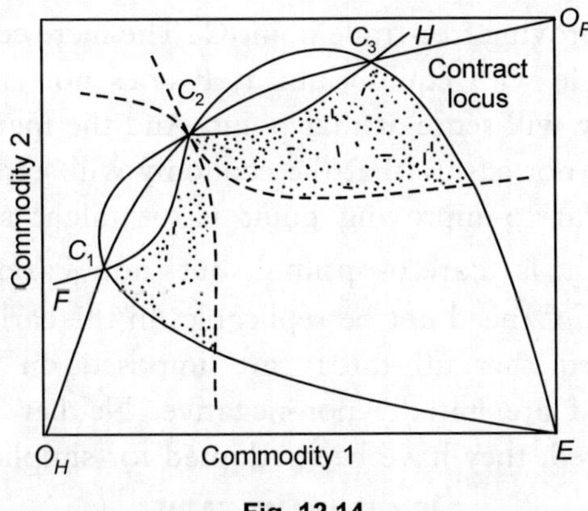

Fig. 12.14

Evidently, the three dotted regions are not disjoint; they overlap, so that point *e* might lie in as many as threc shaded regions. But, however that may be, our proposition survives. Given *e* in a dotted region and any Pareto-optimal and Pareto-improving point *P*, there exists a new tariff pair, with one member positive, the other negative, that is compatible with the world equilibrium at *P*; given *e* in a non-shaded region, there exists a Pareto-optimal

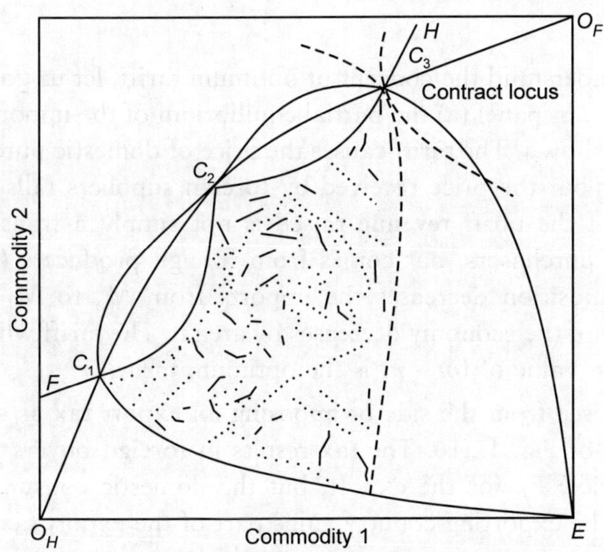

Fig. 12.15

and Pareto-improving free-trade point C_j. The mere considering of a tariff compatible with equilibrium at P does not ensure that the world economy will settle at that point. And the mere adoption of free trade does not ensure that the economy will settle at a Pareto-optimal and Pareto-improving point C_i; it might settle at point C_j $(j \neq i)$, which is Pareto-optimal but not Pareto-improving. In other words, C_i need not be replicable. In the earlier section we have considered that all tariffs are imposed on the imported commodity and are initially non-negative. Neither assumption is logically required, they have been adopted for simplicity only.

THE OPTIMUM TARIFF

The effect of a tariff, let us remember, is to restrict the trade by decreasing the volume of imports and exports. It also aims at improving the imposing country's terms of trade. If a country is in a situation of free trade, it can always improve its welfare by applying the right tariff. This tariff, that maximises a country's welfare, is called the optimum tariff. It must be noted that the optimum tariff is optimal only for the country imposing the tariff and not for the world.

Concept

To understand the concept of optimum tariff, let us go through Fig. 12.16. In panel (a) the partial equilibrium of the import market has been shown. The tariff causes the price of domestic purchases to rise to P_c but the price received by foreign suppliers falls to P_f. A portion of the tariff revenue raised is not simply a transfer from domestic purchasers, but comes from foreign producers (area m). Tariff imposition decreases the imports from M_0 to M_1 and the efficiency of the economy decreases by area n. The tariff which gives the largest value of $(m - n)$ is the optimum tariff.

If we see from the side of imposing an export tax as shown in panel (b) of Fig. 12.16. The tax results in foreign buyers paying a higher price, P_f, for the export, but the domestic consumers now pay P_d. The exporting country gains part of the export tax revenue at the expense of foreign buyers, which is shown by area m. Efficiency less may be offset by the gain, shown by area n. The optimal tax here again would be the one that maximises the difference between m and n.

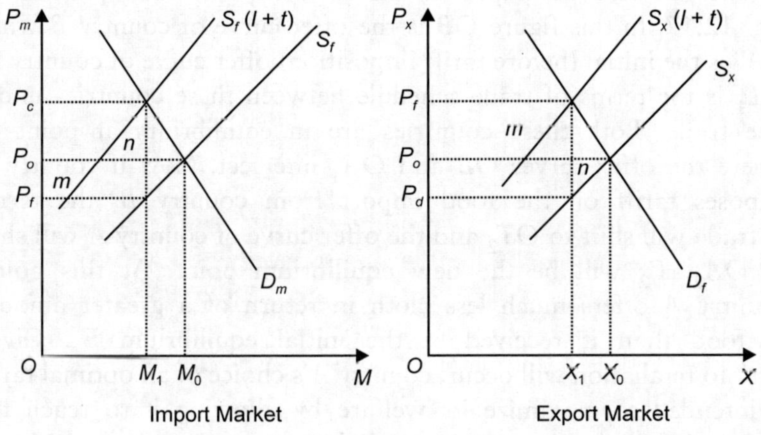

Fig. 12.16

Regardless of whether there is import tax or export tax, the optimum tariff brings benefits to the levying country at the expense of the rest of the world. It is because the tariff reduces the degree of specialisation in the world economy. So what is the reason behind optimal tariff when it reduces the world welfare? Actually, it is justified by the terms of trade argument which states that a nation may be able to use a tariff to take for itself a larger share of the gains from trade, thereby improving its welfare. The optimum tariff is expected to decline over time in the whole world.

But as of now, we have a different way also to show optimum tariff. The opportunity for a country to improve its terms of trade by levying the optimum tariff can also be analysed by the use of offer curves. Such an analysis based on the following assumptions—

(a) There are two countries, *A* and *B*.

(b) There are two commodities, cloth and food.

(c) Country *A* exports cloth and country *B* exports food.

(d) Country *A* imposes tariff on the import of country B's food.

(e) Country *B* does not retaliate to the tariff imposition on its exports in country *A*.

Given these assumptions, the analysis can be explained by Fig. 12.17. In this figure *OB* is the offer curve of country *B* while OA_1 is the initial (before tariff imposition) offer curve of country *A*. OT_1 is the terms of trade schedule between these countries under free trade. Both these countries are in equilibrium at point *E*, where the offer curves *OB* and OA_1 intersect. Now if country *A* imposes tariff on the food import from country *B*, the terms of trade will shift to OT_2 and the offer curve of country *A* will shift to OA_2. E_2 will be the new equilibrium point. At this point, country *A* offers much less cloth in return of a greater amount of food than it received at the initial equilibrium E_1. Given that no retaliation will occur, country *A*'s choice of an optimal tariff is intended to maximize its welfare by allowing it to reach the highest possible community indifference curve. James Meade developed the concept of trade indifference curve (shown as *TT* in the figure) and demonstrated that country *A* should set the tariff (as its optimum tariff) that allows it to reach the point where the highest possible trade indifference curve is tangent to country *B*'s offer curve.

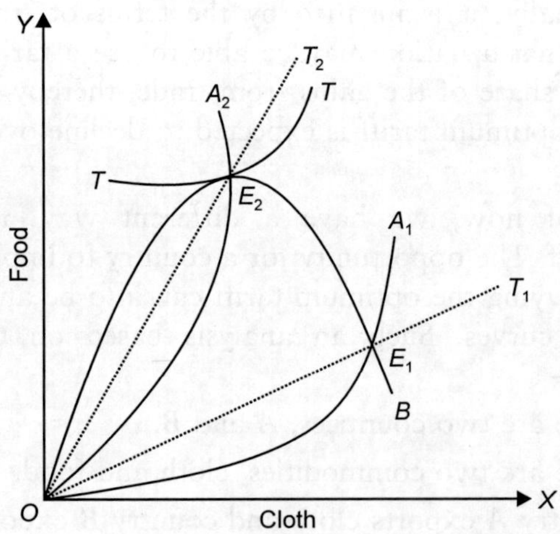

Fig. 12.17

But it has to be kept in mind that a country would have an advantageous tariff if and only if the offer curve of the other country is less than perfectly elastic. If the offer curve of the other country is perfectly elastic, tariff imposition would not lead to any welfare. Figure 12.18 shows such a situation. Here OA_1, is the free trade offer curve of country A and OB is the perfectly elastic offer curve of country B. T_1 is the initial equilibrium when country A imposes the tariff, its offer curve shifts to QA_2. The offer curve of country B remaining unchanged the new equilibrium now set at point T_2. Hence, we see that the terms of trade remain unchanged. Hence, no tariff will be the optimum tariff in this condition.

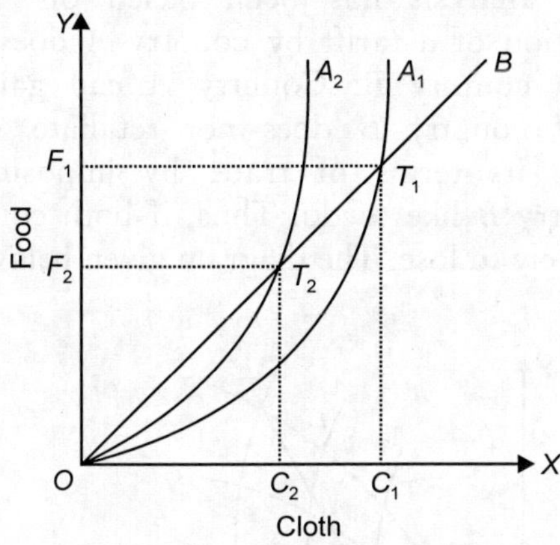

Fig. 12.18

Formula

The formula to measure the optimum tariff rate has been very simply given by Kindleberger. This formula can be stated as—

$$t = \frac{1}{e - 1}$$

where t = optimum tariff rate

e = point elasticity of the offer curve of the opposite country.

Hence, if the offer curve of the other country has perfect elasticity, the optimum tariff is—

$$\frac{1}{\alpha - 1} = 0$$

This tells that no tariff can improve the terms of trade in this condition. Thus, to reach a higher welfare a tariff imposition is successful, only when the elasticity of the offer curve of the country facing tariff is less than perfectly elastic (i.e. $e < \alpha$).

RETALIATION

So far the analysis has been based on the assumption that the imposition of a tariff by country *A* does not invite any retaliation from country *B*. Country *A* can gain by imposing a tariff only if country *B* does not retaliate. But if country *A* can improve its terms of trade by imposing a tariff, so would the country *B* like to do. Thus, if both countries retaliate, both are very likely to lose. The diagram given below depicts such a case.

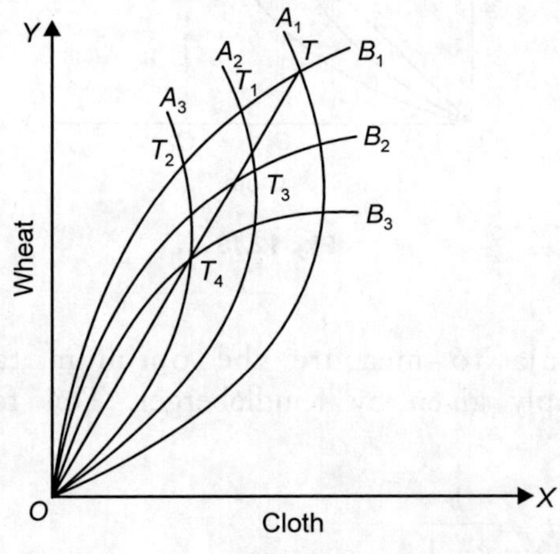

Fig. 12.19

Let us suppose that country *A* imposes an optimum tariff which shifts its original trade offer curve OA_1 to OA_2. This improves her terms of trade from *OT* to OT_1. Now country *B* retaliates by imposing an optimum tariff which shifts its original trade offer curve OB_1 to OB_2. Another similar round of increase in tariffs of both the countries shifts country A's trade offer curve to OA_3 and that of country B to OB_3. At the new equilibrium point T_4, the terms of trade between the two countries, represented by OT_4, are the same as the free trade terms of trade, indicated by OT. At the new equilibrium point T_4, while the terms of trade remain unchanged, the volume of trade is much smaller than that at the free trade equilibrium point T. Each country would have been prepared to buy and sell much larger quantities at these terms of trade if the price relationship in domestic trade were same. But the successive increases in country A's tariff on food and the country B's tariff on cloth have raised the price of the imported commodity after payment of duty in each country and necessitated a restriction of consumption at these prices. Thus, the imposition of tariffs to improve the terms of trade, followed by retaliatory action, result in a loss for both the countries. Landed in such a situation, both the countries can gain by a reciprocal removal of tariffs. This provides the rationale behind the efforts of the General Agreement on Tariffs and Trade for bringing about a mutual reduction in the tariffs of the different countries.

We have seen that the retaliatory tariff increases, and that each one, as an optimum countermove to the other country's tariff policy, results in a smaller and smaller volume of international trade between the countries. The question arises whether retaliation will continue till finally the volume of trade declines to zero. In order to answer this question, we recall that it is the position of one country's trade indifference curve in relation to the other country's trade offer curve which is decisive so far as the height of the optimum tariff is concerned. If one country's trade indifference curve is tangent to the other country's trade offer curve at a point which already lies on the first country's trade offer curve, no further tariff could allow the first country to reach a higher trade indifference curve. In the figure we see that country A's counter-retaliatory move reduces the volume of trade to point T_3. Now if country B's trade indifference curve is already tangent to the country A's trade offer curve at this point, no further tariff imposed by country B will allow it to reach a higher trade indifference curve and country B, therefore, will have no incentive to modify its trade offer curve OB_2 any further. If country B does not change its existing tariff structure, country *A* has no incentive to modify its tariff either. Point T_3, therefore, will become the final point of equilibrium, and no further retaliatory tariffs are to be expected.

NOTE

1. G. Hakerler, *Theory of International Trade* (London, 1956), pp. 56-59.